Henry Tibbats Stainton

The Tineina of Southern Europe

Henry Tibbats Stainton

The Tineina of Southern Europe

ISBN/EAN: 9783337003371

Printed in Europe, USA, Canada, Australia, Japan

Cover: Foto ©ninafisch / pixelio.de

More available books at **www.hansebooks.com**

THE TINEINA

OF

SOUTHERN EUROPE.

BY

H. T. STAINTON, F.R.S., Sec. L.S.

LONDON:
JOHN VAN VOORST, PATERNOSTER ROW.
MDCCCLXIX.

PRINTED BY TAYLOR AND FRANCIS,
RED LION COURT, FLEET STREET.

PREFACE.

THE object of the present volume is to supply the Entomologist who visits Southern Europe with one portable volume comprising all that has been written on the Tineina of that portion of the globe.

The aim has been to reproduce accurately the records of each observer, but at the same time to place them, if possible, more clearly and distinctly before the reader than they appeared when originally published.

The descriptions are reproduced in the actual words of the respective authors, it being thought that he who is trying to make out a species will always prefer to refer to the original than to any translation however perfect. A translator, indeed, who has not the actual insect before him is always liable to make errors which may altogether vitiate the description; for, though correctly translating the *words*, he may, from misapprehending their *meaning*, give a very different signification to the passage.

The new matter in the volume is really extremely limited, less than a tenth being devoted to the chapter which treats of the author's doings in Southern Europe.

But it is thought that the synthetic arrangement of all that has been done in the last twenty-five years, and the addition to that of all that had been written by previous authors, even going back to the year 1750, on the Tineina of Southern Europe, will much facilitate the further study of these insects.

I would gladly have added another chapter as an epitome of the more interesting Southern forms included in this volume; but the extent to which the subject had already swollen, and a lurking doubt whether the proposed epitome might not itself grow to rather unreasonable dimensions, induced me to leave that chapter unwritten.

My best thanks are due to all those who have so liberally assisted me with specimens or information during the progress of this volume.

And I have also to thank the subscribers to the 'Natural History of the Tineina' for the patience with which they have waited for the appearance of vol. xi. (the first of the new series); the printing of that volume is nearly completed, and, but for the probability of delay in the colouring of the plates, would most likely be issued simultaneously with this—which has an advantage in that respect, not having any colourer to wait for.

The single Plate which accompanies this volume is nearly a facsimile reproduction of the original plate in the first volume of the 'Mémoires de Mathématique et de Physique présentés à l'Académie Royale des Sciences,' one or two details only being omitted so as to enable the original quarto to be reproduced in an octavo form.

I shall hope now soon to be able to turn my attention to the promised volume on the Tineina of Scandinavia; but I hope next summer to have more breathing-time for outdoor entomology; for I must confess that this summer, with the two volumes going through the press, I have found very little spare time, and, not having set an insect for the last two months, the *Psoci* on my setting-boards are nearly starved.

When Professor Zeller started from Glogau one cold January morning twenty-five years ago, little did he foresee that one of the results of his then journey would be the appearance of the present volume; I have endeavoured here and there to give it some flavour of the sunny south, recognizable, perhaps, by those who have visited the Mediterranean region; and if I succeed in inducing one British entomologist to make his first Southern trip, I shall feel that my labour has not been thrown away.

H. T. STAINTON.

Mountsfield, Lewisham, near London,
October 4th, 1869.

CONTENTS.

CHAPTER I.

PROFESSOR ZELLER.

Sect.   Page
Professor Zeller's visit to Italy and Sicily in 1844............ 1

CHAPTER II.

HERR JOSEPH MANN 53

I. Tineina collected in Tuscany in 1846 54
II.   ,,   ,,   near Fiume in 1853...................... 90
III. ,,   ,,   in Upper Carniola in 1854 105
IV. ,,   ,,   in Corsica in 1855 116
V.   ,,   ,,   in Sicily in 1858 126
VI. ,,   ,,   in Croatia in 1866 132
VII. ,,   ,,   in Dalmatia in 1850, 1862, and 1806 132

CHAPTER III.

DR. STAUDINGER.................... 135

I. Letters from Dr. Staudinger 136
II. New Tineina collected in Spain in 1857 and 1858 140
III. ,,   ,,   ,,   ,,   in 1862................... 163

CHAPTER IV.

MONSIEUR PIERRE MILLIÈRE.

New Tineina from the South of France 166

CHAPTER V.

Rev. Henry Burney and others.

I. Tineina collected by the Rev. Henry Burney at Mentone, 1864–65 196
II. Tineina collected by Professor Rosenhauer in Andalusia in 1849.. 199
III. Tineina collected by Count v. Hoffmannsegg in Andalusia in 1865.. 199
IV. New Tineina collected by Herr Erber in Dalmatia and the Island of Syra in 1867 202
V. Tineina received by Dr. J. Delaharpe from Sicily in 1858 204

CHAPTER VI.

The Author.

I. Tineina observed in Italy in February and March 1863 206
II. „ „ at Cannes and Mentone in March 1866 207
III. „ „ „ „ in February and March 1867 216
IV. Larvæ of Tineina received from Southern Europe in 1868 233
V. Tineina observed in Southern Europe in the winter of 1868–69 234

CHAPTER VII.

German Authors.

I. South-European Tineina noticed by Herrich-Schäffer in his 'Schmetterlinge von Europa' 238
II. South-European Tineina noticed in Herrich-Schäffer's 'Neue Schmetterlinge aus Europa und den angrenzenden Ländern' 246
III. Species of *Butalis* from Southern Europe described by Professor Zeller in the 10th volume of the 'Linnæa Entomologica' .. 250

CHAPTER VIII.

French Authors.

Tineina from the South of France noticed by Godart and Duponchel 258

CHAPTER IX.

ITALIAN AUTHORS.

Sect. | Page
I. Tineina noticed by Costa in the Fauna del Regno di Napoli .. 266
II. „ enumerated by Ghiliani in the 'Lepidoptera of the Sardinian states' 277

CHAPTER X.

AUTHORS OF THE LAST CENTURY.

I. South-European Tineina described by Linné 295
II. „ „ „ „ by Fabricius............. 296
III. Tineina described by Scopoli in his 'Entomologia Carniolica'.. 298

CHAPTER XI.

THE LOST PLEIAD 309

Antispila Rivillei..................................... 310

CHAPTER XII.

GEOGRAPHICAL SUMMARY ...., 320

CHAPTER XIII.

BOTANICAL SUMMARY 356

Index of the new Species described in this volume 370

Explanation of the Plate, see page 319.

ERRATA.

Page line
61,   7, *for* Legorn *read* Leghorn.
98,   15 from bottom, for *drymidis* read *drypidis*.
98,   14 from bottom, for *Drymis* read *Drypis*.
108,   6, for *turbidella* read *tabidella*.
111,   7, *for* town *read* castle.
141,   15 from bottom, for *alba* read *albidus*.
152,   15, for *alba* read *albidus*.
169,   6 from bottom, for *Godartella* read *Goedartella*.
226,   13 from bottom, for *Urodela* read *Urodeta*.

THE TINEINA

OF

SOUTHERN EUROPE.

CHAPTER I.

PROFESSOR ZELLER.

PROFESSOR ZELLER'S VISIT TO ITALY AND SICILY IN 1844.

A MOST important event in the history of the Tineina of Southern Europe (that which, in fact, has gradually led to the dissemination of a knowledge of these small insects amongst Western, Central, and Northern Europe) was Professor Zeller's visit a quarter of a century ago to the Italian peninsula. Exchanging in midwinter the sandy fir-forests of Glogau, on the banks of the Oder, for the rocky hills of the South, terraced with vineyards and olive-plantations, he brought to bear on the new phase of insect-life he saw around him his highly concentrated powers of observation.

Much which to a native of Italy, even though he had attained some proficiency as an entomologist, would have appeared ordinary and commonplace (for that which we see constantly can seldom strike us), must to one coming from Northern Germany have produced a very different impression; and hence we find, in the pages of the 'Isis' for 1847, in which are recorded the observations made by Professor Zeller on the Lepidoptera noticed on this journey, many an interesting remark, which may even now prove of value to the philosophical reader in opening out new trains of thought as to the habits and customs of species, &c.

In the 'Bulletin de la Société Impériale des Naturalistes de Moscou,' 1854, pp. 3–52, Professor Zeller has given a detailed account of the Sicilian localities which he visited—Messina, Syracuse, and Catania. He arrived at Messina on the 26th January, 1844, and remained there till after the middle of April. On the 21st of April he took up his residence at Syracuse, which he left on the 24th of June for Catania, whence, on the 29th–30th June, he made an excursion to the summit of Mount Etna. Leaving Sicily on the 6th August, he spent fourteen days at Naples, whence on the 22nd August he proceeded by Terracina to Rome, where he remained only nine days.

B

Species collected by Professor Zeller in Italy and Sicily in 1844, enumerated in the 'Isis' for 1847, pp. 801-859, 881-898.

Talæporia ——? One case on an oak tree near Trieste.

T. lapidicella, Z. Two cases on the walls of the dome of St. Peter's at Rome on the 2nd of September.

Tinea imella, Hb. [a variety noticed p. 15]. Two males taken in dull weather at sunset on the 29th of April on a grassy place of the ancient Neapolis near Syracuse.

T. granella, L. One male taken on the 14th of August in the wood of Camaldoli, near Naples, far removed from human dwellings.

T. pellionella, L. Occurred but rarely; a pair were taken on the 4th and 8th of May near Syracuse which differed slightly.

T. crassicornella, n. sp. [Described, see p. 15.] Two males on the 19th of May and two on the 7th of June towards evening amongst grass and flowers on a grassy footpath near the Temple of Jupiter at Syracuse near the Anapo.

Calantica dealbatella, n. sp. [Described, see p. 16.] I found this species in great plenty in the oak-woods to the south of the Lake of Agnano near Naples. I beat it from the leaves of low oaks (*Quercus robur fructu sessili*) on the 15th and 19th of August, most freely towards sunset. It flies rather restlessly, first downwards and then again gradually upwards to reach an oak-leaf or a chestnut-leaf, along which it runs quickly, seeks the underside and there settles to repose. Sometimes it settles at once on the underside of a leaf. I also saw them sit on the upperside of leaves, which had a slanting position. Sometimes, from the force of the wind, they were obliged to seek shelter on the trunk of a tree; and in the evening, when beaten out, many settled on my clothes. When at rest it seemed to me to have some resemblance to *Argyresthia Goedartella*. Its anterior legs are stretched out obliquely in front, and from its tibiæ being so thick it has a peculiar appearence; the middle legs are directed obliquely backwards under the wings; the hind legs are not visible. The wings are roof-shaped and raised posteriorly; the head is kept low down. I also beat out two pair *in copulâ*; they flew obliquely to the ground: the wings of the male were half covered by those of the female.

Eriocottis fuscanella, n. sp. [Described, see p. 18.] This flies in April at Messina and Syracuse. I took the first specimens on the 2nd of April on the eastern slope of a mountain by the Palermitane Strasse at Messina; on the subsequent days it was very plentiful amongst Arbutus and heath higher up the hill. It flew principally in the morning, was easily started, and settled, after a comparatively short flight, on all sorts of bushes and grass. In repose the wings form a steep roof, and the cilia of the hind margin stick up.

On the 5th of April I took it high up the Peloro Mountains, on a sunny, dry, grassy place, amongst *Erica arborea*, from which I frequently beat it out late in the afternoon. Amongst the numerous specimens, I only took two females; hence they must rest much more concealed and be reluctant to fly. I saw a few specimens at Syracuse at the end of April.

Micropteryx calthella, L. Abundant near Syracuse on the 23rd of April in a moist meadow, on the flowers of *Ranunculus* (*acris* ?).

M. sicanella, n. sp. [Described, see p. 19; afterwards recognized as *Paykullella*, Fabricius, see ' Linnæa Entomologica,' vol. v. p. 329.] This species is not scarce all around Messina in the latter half of March and beginning of April, in some places abundant. I first found it on the 18th of March in the Peloro Mountains in the deep valley above Cascatelli; it was swarming in the sunshine on *Euphorbia characias*, then in blossom; it sat generally on the leaves, more rarely in the flowers, where, on account of the large involucre, it was not easy to catch it. When I had ascended some hundreds of feet higher, I found it on a sunny slope not scarce on the flowers of *Erica arborea*, and in one luxuriantly weedy place it was swarming in the grass. It has quite the habit of *aruncella*. In dull weather I beat it rather freely at this place from the heath-blossoms into my net, and then secured it in the forceps. At another spot it was flying amongst *Coronilla emerus* and bramble bushes.

M. fastuosella, Z. A single male beaten from an oak bush on the slope of a mountain near Messina, on the 2nd of April. It is a small specimen, but certainly referable to this species. There were no sloe-bushes near. As this species also occurs in Livonia, it has a very wide range.

Nematopogon sericinellus, n. sp. [Described, see p. 20.] In April around Messina; scarce on the mountains by the Palermitane Strasse in the thickets of oaks mixed with *Cytisus* and *Cistus*.

Adela viridella, Scop. Scarce near Messina on the eastern slope of the Peloro Mountains along the Palermitane Strasse in mixed thickets of *Quercus pubescens* at the end of March and in April. In one mountain-ravine Herr Nymann, a Swedish botanist, observed a whole swarm hovering round and settling on blooming *Euphorbia characias*. I have never found *Adela viridella* on flowers; it always swarmed in fine weather rather high up on the twigs of oaks. But that it was this species that Nymann saw is certain, as he brought back a specimen.

Nemotois Latreillellus, F. This pretty species is already on the wing at Syracuse at the end of April (I even took a female on the 30th April), but principally in May. Its favourite localities are grassy and flowery sheltered meadows and mountain-slopes, whether on dry or moist ground. It lives gregariously. In bright weather it swarms on different flowers in the sunshine, being most partial to those of *Scabiosa columbaria* ; in dull weather it sits on the flowers, and is then very easily captured. As it does not conceal itself, its beauty is soon damaged by the rain, and by the end of the month its period of flight is over for the year. It occurs also near Messina, probably first in May.

N. mollellus, Tr. I took a single female near Syracuse on the 30th April on a flower in the road towards the peninsula Magnisi.

Plutella cruciferarum, Z. Everywhere round Messina and Syracuse throughout the entire spring and summer in fields and grassy places. At Messina, on the sunny slope of the Castellaccio, I took a this year's specimen as early as the 9th of February, at a spot where much *Clypeola maritima* was growing.

At Naples I took a specimen on the 18th of August.

Ypsolophus verbascellus, S. V. I found the larvæ in the spring at Messina high up the mountains, abundant on a species of *Verbascum* which is common there. In habits they were quite similar to those we find in Germany. At Syracuse I took the imago singly and scarce in May and June. At Messina a small male, which had not flown, on the 25th July. Hence this species is there, as with us, double-brooded.

Y. exustellus, n. sp. [Described, see p. 21.] I took a pair of this species at Syracuse on dry limestone near the Capuchin Monastery on the 17th and 21st of June; three specimens, which all appear to be females, I took in the Campagna to the south of Rome in dry grass on the 28th of August. Its habit was similar to that of *Y. humerellus.*

Y. striatellus, S. V. Not scarce near Syracuse on the western slope of the ancient Neapolis, which is clothed with small weeds of all sorts, in places where *Rumex bucephalophorus* grew abundantly, in May and the beginning of June. I took a pale specimen on the 24th of April. [The dark variety is described, see p. 22.]

At Glogau I once met with the species in plenty at the end of May in a sandy field covered with *Rumex acetosella*; but it is most plentiful, as already mentioned in the 'Isis,' on the flowers of *Tanacetum vulgare.*

Anchinia brevispinella, n. sp. [Described, see p. 22.] This flies near Syracuse on the slopes and meadows of the ancient Neapolis, not very scarce in grass at the end of April and throughout May; it has the habits of *Anchinia bicostella.*

Œcophora Lewenhoekella, S. V. A fine female taken on the 15th of April near Messina in the grass of a mountain-field. It is of the usual size and markings; the cilia of the hind margin are at basal half purple-coloured, those of the costa violet.

Œcophora Knochella, Tr.; *Œ. punctivittella,* Costa, p. 14, tab. 5. f. 1. I took two males and one female on the 26th of June at the foot of Mount Etna above Catania at Trecastagne in an oak bush on lava-ashes; I found a small female together with a male at Camaldoli near Naples on the 16th of August on the blossom of yarrow, and took two other small males in the pass of Itri on the 23rd of August, and in the Campagna to the north of Rome on the 3rd of September. Hence it appears to be double-brooded.

Œ. chenopodiella, Hb. One male and two females on the 9th, 10th, and 17th of May near Syracuse, on cultivated parts of Acradina and Neapolis. They belong to a very dark variety.

Œ. gravatella, n. sp. [Described, see p. 23.] I took five specimens (4 ♂, 1 ♀) near Messina on the north side of Castellaccio, starting them out of dry grass on the 23rd and 25th of July.

One male (rather different) was taken on the 14th of September on the Karst at Trieste.

Œ. dissitella, n. sp. [Described, see p. 24.] A pair taken on the 25th and 26th of April near Syracuse on meadows round the Syraca.

Œ. tributella, n. sp. [Described, see p. 25.] I took a fine pair of this plainly marked species on the 4th of May near Syracuse in grass on the woody slopes of the ancient Neapolis.

Œ. terrenella, n. sp. [Described, see p. 25.] I collected six specimens (one of which is a female) in dry grass on the Castellaccio near Messina on the 22nd, 23rd, and 26th of July. On the 28th of August I took a male near Rome, in the Campagna towards Albano, likewise in a dry grassy place; it has the anterior wings brighter and more shining, and the posterior wings of a more violet-grey; but, from its other characters, I cannot look upon it as a distinct species.

Œ. roscidella, n. sp. [Described, see p. 26.] I beat several specimens from young oak trees on the 15th and 19th of August near Naples above the Lake of Agnano and at Camaldoli.

[*Œ. oleella*, Boyer, which is not enumerated in the 'Isis' of 1847, is thus mentioned in the Ent. Zeit. 1850, p. 148:—"I have myself taken a fine male at Syracuse, on the 21st of June."]

Hyponomeuta malinellus, Z. A bad specimen, with no cilia, taken on the 16th of August in the vicinity of Camaldoli near Naples; it flew beneath a large apple-tree. The wings appear narrower than in the ordinary *malinellus*.

H. Evonymi, Z. On the same day I beat a specimen from a spindle bush on the hill at Antignano near Naples. It is smaller than the specimen of *malinellus* and less worn; on the underside of the anterior wings is a very fine white line on the costa before the apex.

Psecadia sexpunctella, Hb. On the 25th of April I found a male which was drowned in a cattle-trough near the Temple of Jupiter at Syracuse.

P. echiella, S. V. On a species of *Echium* I found a small larva near Syracuse on the 12th of May, but did not breed it.

Depressaria assimilella, Tr. I caught a specimen on the 15th of August to the south of the Lake of Agnano in the chestnut-wood, on the borders of which the food of the larva (*Spartium scoparium*) grows abundantly.

It is a rather large male, with very pale anterior wings, on which the two black spots are quite distinct; but the dark blotch beyond them is wanting; the last joint of the palpi has only a few dark scales in the middle. In other respects it is an ordinary *assimilella*.

D. peloritanella, n. sp. [Described, see p. 27.] This species is very abundant in the mountains around Messina. After hybernation I met with it several times in thickets on the mountains by the Palermitane Strasse, at the end of February and in March, for the most part much wasted. On one of those scarce, calm, mild April evenings it flew up there rather abundantly, but the specimens were quite unserviceable. In a similar locality I took a perfectly fresh specimen on the 10th of July on the north side of a high mountain; it was first started as I trod down the fern with which the slope is there covered. The larva probably feeds there on *Spartium junceum* or *Erica arborea*; the earliest time of appearance is July. Doubtless it is only single-brooded; but the development is very irregular, as in several of our commonest *Depressariæ*, such as *laterella*, some of which also hybernate.

Depressaria thapsiella, n. sp. [Described, see p. 28.] This probably occurs in all localities where *Thapsia garganica* grows. At Messina this plant occurs both on the sea-coast and on the slopes and in the ravines of the Peloro Mountain; and I found this larva on it everywhere, most freely in the higher places, of very different sizes after the middle of March. The young larvæ not unfrequently live in multitudes, not in a common web, but yet so close to one another that one might easily fancy they had a common web; they especially inhabit the youngest, innermost leaves, which they eat, and hence come constantly nearer together. By degrees they commence operating on the older leaves; and as they spin webs on them and devour the margins they form a large compressed knob, which is readily perceived from a distance. The more adult larvæ, often mixed with the younger ones, live more scattered on the ends and margins of the largest leaves, in a white silken tube which they have placed between two leaf-tips. From time to time they seek out other dwellings. They generally sit with the head directed downwards. They are extremely lively, like all the other *Depressariæ*. One plant is sometimes frequented by from 50 to 60 larvæ. [Description of the larva, see p. 29.]

By the 3rd of April great numbers had already changed to the pupa state, whilst larvæ which were very young were still occurring. For pupation they form a light silken cocoon on the floor of the cage, and cover it externally with dirt. The larva-skin comes off in three or four days. [Pupa described, see p. 30.]

The first imago was hatched in Syracuse on the 30th of April; the others followed up to the 4th of June: hence the period of pupation lasts from three and a half to four weeks. At Syracuse I also found traces of the abodes of the larvæ on the leaves of the *Thapsia*. At large I never saw any symptoms of the imago.

D. ferulæ, n. sp. [Described, see p. 30.] I collected a few larvæ of this insect on the 15th of April on the mountains near Messina, on some plants of *Ferula communis*, on the leaves of which they lived. I have not noted what they were like in my journal, and cannot now remember it. They changed to the pupa state along with *D. thapsiella*; and my five specimens of the perfect insect emerged at Syracuse on the 15th, 16th, 18th, and 19th of May. The species does not seem to be at all abundant, since I only found the larvæ in a single locality.

Depressaria veneficella, n. sp. [Described, see p. 31.] This occurs at Syracuse on *Thapsia garganica*, where the larvæ are abundant in the unexpanded umbels still enclosed within their sheaths: it devours the flowers and the tender stems; in the latter it bores holes, so that not unfrequently the stems become black and die off. It eats out the inner pith of the stem, into which it bores at intervals. When the blossoms have unfolded, it spins them together and remains amongst them. In company with these larvæ I also found those of *Penthina thapsiana*. On the 30th of April I found larvæ of the most different ages, even on one plant, where they probably all came from one mother.

Till nearly June I still met with the larvæ around Syracuse. On Mount Etna I found larvæ on the 30th of June, on the *Thapsia*-plants which are here and there abundant on the lower margin of the wooded region, on which I likewise perceived distinct signs that they had also nourished the larvæ of *thapsiella*, which had already disappeared. The pupation takes place, as in *thapsiella*, under decayed remains of plants in a slight cocoon after two to three days. [Description of the pupa, see p. 32.] The perfect insects made their appearance from the 20th of May to the 5th of June, thus after remaining in the pupa-state from twenty to twenty-four days. I obtained a few in June by treading down the then quite dried *Thapsia*-plants, whereby I caused them to fly. From my larvæ I obtained altogether few moths, and most of these have become very greasy; indeed grease seems to form more on this species than on other *Depressariæ*.

The origin of the name of this species was as follows:—Already, when collecting the larvæ of *thapsiella*, suspecting no evil, after carelessly plucking the leaves of the *Thapsia*, I had remarked a long-continued itching about the eyes, the ears, and the neck. Being suspicious of the *Thapsia*, I made inquiry whether the plant were poisonous, and was assured it was not so. Besides this I had noticed a goatherd who cut down a whole armful of these leaves and threw them to his goats, which devoured them with great relish. But as the itching occurred every time I collected *Thapsia*-leaves wherewith to feed my larvæ I mistrusted the plant. At Syracuse on the 30th of April, on the road which goes over the ancient Acradina towards Priolo, I collected from the *Thapsia*-plants which are there a whole pocketful of undeveloped umbels infested with larvæ of *veneficella*. These being enclosed in the sheath have a club-like appearance and are covered with a slight rime. When I returned to the house I pulled the plants to pieces, collected the larvæ together and put them into a box. Then I washed my hands carefully with soap, having taken care as I walked home not to touch my face with them. I thought now, therefore, I should be secure from the above-named itching. But in the night my face swelled, and the swelling increased rapidly the following day; the lids of the left eye swelled to large balls, which more and more impeded my sight. Around the inner corner of the eye the skin was thickly covered with small pustules. The right eye was less affected. About the eyes and the upper part of the nose I felt an unpleasant burning sensation, and had a violent itching in the ears and about the mouth and chin; I was obliged therefore, on the 1st of May, to keep my room. On the 2nd of May the swelling of the left eye had so much increased that I could hardly see out of it; the right eye was also much swollen, but was more serviceable. The eyelids were like balls; and the whole shapeless, swollen face was covered with small pustules, which on the chin and on the inner corner of the left eye had united in masses. On the neck and wrist the itching was most disagreeable. My landlord was much horrified when he saw my dreadful face, and wished to fetch the physician; but as I now knew precisely the cause of the evil, I preferred leaving nature to effect her cure. Towards noon the evil appeared to be stationary: in the evening I could already see better with the left eye; the burning sensation had ceased, but the itching still continued to be most unpleasant. I could not think of going out. On the 3rd of May the eyes had very much improved, and I could now see quite well with the left eye; but on the lower lip and around the eye was all like a scab. It was not till the 4th of May that, except about the eyes, the swelling had subsided; but from the whole face, excepting the forehead, the skin came off. I was now able to go out, but with my disfigured countenance attracted more than usually the notice of those I met.

Henceforth I always treated the *Thapsia* with the greatest respect: I did not pluck it, but cut it with a knife; nor even ventured to do that with my bare hands, but always in gloves, and afterwards washed knife, gloves, and hands most carefully.

Carcina fagana, S. V. Three specimens on the 19th of August beat from oaks on the southern side of the Lake of Agnano, and a single beautiful male on the 5th of September from garden-hedges (in which, as far as I remember, were neither beeches nor oaks) behind Fuligno. They differ in nothing from German specimens.

Gelechia vilella, n. sp. [Described, see p. 33.] I took two specimens in a ravine on the slopes of the ancient Neapolis near Syracuse, on thorny bushes, on the 12th of May. A smaller female, already much worn but yet recognizable, was taken in Asia Minor by Loew at Mermeriza on the 20th April.

G. detersella, n. sp. [Described, see p. 33.] Three males and two females from Syracuse, taken singly in the latter half of June on the dry chalk-hills at Acradina and Tyche. Some, if I am not mistaken, were beaten, along with *Gel. Kollarella*, from *Poterium*.

G. segetella, n. sp. [Described, see p. 34.] This species occurs near Syracuse in the neighbourhood of the ancient Neapolis, and on the further side of the Anapo towards the temple of Jupiter, in wheat-fields, from the borders of which I started it in May after sunset along with *Sciaphila segetana*. I also took some on the yellow flowers of a plant like a *Chrysanthemum*.

G. flammella, Hb. This was abundant here and there round Syracuse at the end of April and in May; it frequented not only grassy and weedy dry slopes of the ancient Neapolis and the adjoining fallow fields of the low ground, but also the higher flowery borders of the moist meadows on the further side of the Anapo, where it haunted the blossoms of the *Compositæ*. Towards evening it flew briskly in zigzag, and was hence distinguished from *Cosmopteryx argyrogrammos*, which occurred along with it in fallow fields.

G. Kollarella, Costa. This species was scarce at Syracuse, occurring on the chalk-hills of Tyche in the middle of June and only on *Poterium spinosum*; when disturbed it settled again on this thorny shrub and generally concealed itself. Costa found it at Camaldoli near Naples, where I have not observed any of this *Poterium*. Duponchel obtained it from Montpellier, Fischer von Röslerstamm from Hungary.

G. terrella, Hb. I took a female on the 15th of August in the woods above the Lake of Agnano. I can, on the closest examination, perceive no difference from the species so common with us. It is a specimen of medium size, of the colour of the pale variety figured by Fischer v. R. pl. 80. fig. 1 *a*. The upper discoidal spot is somewhat prolonged lengthwise, and larger than that on the fold. The third spot, posteriorly placed, is very small; the pale angulated fascia is very faint; along the hind margin are some indistinct streak-like brown spots. The second joint of the palpi is not darkened externally.

G. plebejella, n. sp. [Described, see p. 36.] I took a single fine specimen at Syracuse on the 5th of May; it was raining at the time and I was poking about some plants at the edge of a wheat-field, which made it fly out.

G. lamprostoma, n. sp. [Described, see p. 36.] I took a single male at Syracuse near the Capuchin Monastery, on a part of the chalk-rock covered with short grass, towards evening.

G. humeralis, Z. At Glogau and Frankfort on the Oder this species occurs on oaks; at Reichstadt in Bohemia, Fischer v. Röslerstamm states that three specimens were taken on *Pinus picea*. With us it must certainly feed on oak. I took two fine specimens on the 17th of July, and it also occurs again in October. It lives through the winter, and is beaten out in March and April. It does not seem to be scarce, but can only be induced to fly by beating the stems when the weather is quite bright and calm. Thus on the 22nd of April, 1837, I obtained seventeen specimens in a short time from the trunks of a few oak trees close together; most of them, however, were already much wasted.

I took my two Sicilian specimens at Messina on the 26th and 27th of February in two different places, beating them from the dry leaves of oak bushes (*Quercus pubescens*); they had evidently hybernated. No doubt the species is there double-brooded.

G. salinella, n. sp. [Described, see p. 37.] This species is very plentiful near Syracuse in the salt parts of the marsh near the great Harbour, amongst the *Salicornia*, which grows there in large patches.

It flies readily, especially on cloudy days or towards evening, but is very nimble, and when it settles again immediately runs down the plant to the ground, where it generally escapes observation till it again takes wing. It appears at the end of April and in May. In windy weather or during sunshine, I usually only saw it as it flew out and then vanished. Already by the middle of May the specimens were mostly in bad condition.

G. remissella, n. sp. [Described, see p. 39.] I took one specimen at Syracuse on the 9th of May in a grassy ravine of the slope of Neapolis; on the 11th of July I took a second at Messina in grass on a hill along the Palermitane Strasse. Hence, in all probability, the species is double-brooded.

G. diminutella, n. sp. [Described, see p. 40.] This little moth flew on the Castellaccio hill at Messina on the 23rd, 26th, and 27th of July, in company with *Œcophora terrenella*, *gravatella*, *Elachista Dohrnii*, and *Phycis cantenerella*; it was scarce.

[Of a species allied to *diminutella*, which Staudinger described in the 'Stettin. ent. Zeitung' for 1859, p. 241, as *Gelechia promptella*, Professor Zeller took a specimen near Syracuse on the 23rd of May.]

G. nigrinotella, n. sp. [Described, see p. 40.] I took a single specimen on the 26th of July from oak-leaves on a lava-waste at Vieranni, above Catania, at the foot of Etna.

G. nigritella, n. sp. [Described, see p. 41.] I took a single male on the 3rd of April, high up the mountains near Messina, on the southern slope of a hill, amongst wild lupin.

G. anthyllidella, Hb. I took two males on the 12th of May, near Syracuse, on the slopes of the ancient Neapolis, in the grass. They differ slightly from our German specimens, but not sufficiently so to allow me to repute them a different species. They are not larger than our smallest specimens. In the best specimen the costal spot of the anterior wings is almost pure white. In both, the face and palpi are whiter; on the terminal joint of the palpi the edge and the longitudinal line on the inner side are still finer and of a paler blackish. The length of the palpi and form of the hind wings are quite the same as in our specimens.

G. paupella, n. sp. [Described, see p. 42.] I took a single male near Syracuse, on a flowery path through the moist meadow between the Anapo and the pillars of the Temple of Jupiter on the 19th of May.

G. Hermannella, F. One male, taken near Naples on the 20th of August. This species therefore is, as far as we know, distributed all over Europe, from Riga to Naples.

The specimen is small; on the anterior wings the shining line which runs out from the costa at the fascia and goes towards the apex of the wing is interrupted in the middle.

NOTE.—I still possess several Sicilian species of *Gelechia*, mostly single specimens, and not always in fine condition; as they are probably all new, I omit them here. Herr Mann will probably meet with them in Central Italy, and I shall then hasten to notice the species now omitted.

Röslerstammia granitella, Tr. Near Messina. A worn, pale female, with protruding ovipositor on the 14th of February, together with one specimen quite wasted; a very fine specimen, which also appears to be a female, but has no protruding ovipositor, I took on the 17th of February: all on the hills near the Palermitane Strasse.

This species has on the middle of the costa of the anterior wings two spots, which, though faint, are larger and darker than those which follow nearer to the apex: in Fischer von Röslerstamm's figure these are not more distinctly expressed than the other markings, and the wings are represented too broad.

The fine specimen obtained on the 19th of February has the entire surface of the anterior wings darker, whence the costal spots seem less distinct; the white triangular spot on the middle of the inner margin is very small, and only reaches to the fold of the wing; the brown marginal spots before and beyond it, on the other hand, are larger, and the darkest, which precedes the white triangle, is considerably broader than in Fischer's figure L. Before the anal angle there is on the inner margin a sharply defined white spot. That these differences only refer to the individual is shown by the second specimen, the markings on which offer no peculiarities.

This species is hence double-brooded.

Æchmia metallicella, F. v. R. In the beginning of April I took several specimens near Messina, in mixed bushes on the eastern slope of a mountain, principally near oak bushes. They differ in no respect from our Glogau specimens, and I was much surprised, a few hundred miles further south than Glogau, on a morning most favourable for the capture of insects, to meet with hardly anything but ordinary North-German forms, such as *Lycæna Argiolus*, *Thecla rubi*, *Hipparchia Megæra* and *Pamphilus*, *Argynnis Lathonia*, *Micropteryx fastuosella*, &c.; and even these were very scarce.

Coleophora Mayrella, Hb. Only one male taken on the 29th of April at Syracuse.

C. argentipennella, Dup. I took three males and one female, all in good condition, on the 6th of September in the States of the Church, at Tolentino, on a weedy dry hill where there was no heather; the weather being cloudy, they flew rather readily.

C. crepidinella, n. sp. [Described, see p. 43.] I took two males and one female (the latter rather smaller) near Syracuse on the 19th of May, towards evening, on a grassy flowery footpath between the Anapo and the columns of the temple of Jupiter.

C. præcursella, n. sp. [Described, see p. 44.] This species appears earlier in the season than any other *Coleophora* I know. It occurs in the neighbourhood of Messina. On the 17th of February, late in the afternoon, I beat a pair from the flower of a rigid grass (named, if I am not mistaken, *Arundo mauritanica*); and on the 26th of February I obtained a female by the sweeping-net. In another part of the mountains I obtained a pair on the 5th of March. Since this grass also grows in other mountainous parts of Italy, the insect probably occurs in other localities.

C. fretella, n. sp. [Described, see p. 45.] I took a single male specimen in fine condition on the 16th of April amongst short grass on the sandy peninsula of the lighthouse at Messina.

C. pabulella, n. sp. [Described, see p. 45.] I took a single male at Messina on the 2nd of April in the grass of a vineyard.

C. deviella, n. sp. [Described, see p. 46.] Three male specimens were taken flying in the forenoon of the 4th of May amongst *Juncus acutus* in the marshes at Syracuse.

C. alcyonipennella, Kollar. A beautiful male taken on the 17th of August, near Naples, in the fertile plain to the south of the town amongst *Atriplex*; a second specimen, which I saw at the same time, escaped. That captured has the brilliant colouring of our Glogau female specimens. Here we have only found the species in May and June; hence there is a second brood, at least in the south.

In this genus there are assuredly a multitude of species in Italy, of which only a minority occur likewise in Germany, if I may judge from my own experience; of eleven species which I captured, only three occur in Germany. I have only enumerated the foregoing, as it is not advisable to found obscure species in this genus on single or defective specimens.

Gracilaria lacertella, Fischer v. R. I took two specimens, which do not at all differ from those of Germany, near Messina, on the 13th of March and 3rd of April, in the mountains, accidentally, amongst bushes; it would seem that its true period of flight there is the end of March.

Cosmopteryx argyrogrammos, Z. This species was not scarce about Syracuse, flying in fallow fields in the evening, in the middle of

May, around thistles and in the grass along with *Gelechia flammella*. From that species, which flies briskly in a zigzag way, *argyrogrammos* was readily distinguished by its weaker, more hovering flight, more like that of a *Gracilaria*. Unfortunately I have not observed its position in repose. Single specimens still occurred in June. I also took a few specimens at Rome at the end of August; hence it is double-brooded. The eyes, when alive, are of a glowing blood-red; in dried specimens they are brown.

[Supplementary description already given in the 'Tineina of Syria and Asia Minor,' p. 9.]

Elachista testaceella, Hb. One male taken on the 6th of June near Syracuse on the far side of the Anapo, amongst moist meadows. It is smaller than usual, and has the ground-colour of the thorax and the anterior wings more yellowish; in other respects it possesses all the characters of the species.

E. Dohrnii, n. sp. [Described, see p. 46.] I took several specimens in the latter half of July, late in the afternoon, amongst dry grass on the Castellaccio hill, near Messina. When started out they flew for a short distance and then settled again on the ground amongst the grass, and turned themselves round like *Elachista pomposella*, only not so briskly.

E. magnificella, Fischer v. R. [*Brunnichella*, L.]. I took by chance a single male at Messina on the 20th of March on the hill of the Castello Gonzaga in the grass, in a spot where many *Papilionaceæ* were growing.

E. nigrella, Hb. Three males taken on the mountains near Messina on the 18th of March; they were flying on a weedy slope late in the afternoon quite in the style of our German *nigrella*. [Some minute points of difference are then given, see p. 47.]

E. contaminatella, n. sp. [Described, see p. 48.] I took three specimens in the evening of the 23rd of April near Syracuse; they were flying in a moist meadow near the Great Harbour. This species has probably, like *cerussella*, the habit of flying in the evening.

E. disemiella, n. sp. [Described, see p. 48.] I found this species near Messina at the end of February, in March and in April in the mountains on *Erica arborea*, but only obtained a few specimens.

On the 17th of February I beat three specimens, one of which was a female, from bushes. In the same locality, on the 15th of July, I obtained a remarkably small specimen, which evidently belongs to the second brood.

E. cygnipennella, Hb. A solitary male taken near Syracuse on the 19th of May in the fertile plain between the Anapo and the pillars of the Temple of Jupiter. It is one of the largest specimens; the white has a more yellowish tinge than in German specimens; the anterior wings are a trifle narrower; the palpi rather longer. Since it has on the whole the general appearance of our well-known species, I look upon these aberrations as only individual peculiarities. Hence it would appear as though *cygnipennella* were distributed over the whole of Middle and Southern Europe, even to the coast of Asia; for the female taken at Carajasu shows no difference.

Opostega, n. sp. [*Cemiostoma*, noticed at p. 49.] I beat a specimen of this species, closely allied to *spartifoliella*, on the 8th of April near Messina, from bushes on a slope clothed with *Cytisus triflorus* and *Arbutus*, having already met with one specimen several weeks earlier.

Opostega suffusella, n. sp. [*Phyllocnistis suffusella*, Z., now too well-known to require re-describing.] I took a single female on the 19th of August in the neighbourhood of the Lake of Agnano, near Naples; the larva there probably feeds on poplar-leaves.

Lyonetia, sp.? [*Nepticula*, sp.? The description is too brief to be worth quoting.] I took a single specimen near Naples in the woods above the Lake of Agnano on the 15th of August.

L. somnulentella, n. sp. [*Bedellia somnulentella*, Z., the now well-known and widely distributed species.] I took a female near Messina on the mountains on the 3rd of April, and two males near Syracuse on the 12th of May and 7th of June in fields near the Syraca.

Lithocolletis Messaniella, Z. Around Messina (Linn. Ent. i. p. 222) from the middle of February to the end of March, on the hills on both sides of the road towards Palermo, at Buonretiro, Tremmonti, and San Michele. It frequented the dry leaves of the bushes of *Quercus pubescens*. Probably it is not scarce there: as at that time the weather was windy and bad, they flew out but rarely on my beating the bushes; and as I thought it was only our common *L. quercifoliella*, I gave myself less trouble about them than I should otherwise have done. Probably it occurs in other parts of Southern Europe on the same species of oak.

Tischeria Emyella, Dup. [*T. marginea*, Haw.] Two males, among gardens near Syracuse on the 23rd of April and 17th of May. At Glogau I took a female from a hedge on the 8th of May. Duponchel's specimen seems to have come from Livonia; so that the species is widely distributed.

Pterolonche albescens, n. sp. [Described, see p. 50.] I took a beautiful pair near Messina on the Castellaccio hill, after sunset on the 22nd and 25th of July, amongst dry grass.

P. pulverulenta, n. sp. [Described, see p. 51.] I took three pairs, by degrees, during the month of May near Syracuse, from a dry pasture-ground near the Capuchin Monastery, where I started them with difficulty from the stunted shrubs on which the goats had browsed. I obtained one pair on the 31st of May on the far side of the Anapo, in dry grass in a ravine.

'Isis,' 1847, p. 809.

TINEA IMELLA, Hüb.

Var. b. *Alis anterioribus fuscis violaceo-nitidulis, puncto medio hyalino, costa tenuiter, dorso late flavidis, capite thoraceque luteolis* (♂). Grösse der kleinsten Exemplare. Kopf und Rückenschild weniger lebhaft rostgelb, vielleicht, wegen des etwas verflogenen Zustandes. Taster wie dort am Ende des zweiten Gliedes obenauf mit 3 aufgerichteten Borsten. An den braunen, violettlich schimmernden Vorderflügeln ist der Vorderrand schmal hellgelb vom Anfange des zweiten Längsviertels an, und die dadurch gebildete gelbe Linie erweitert sich gegen die Spitze mehr als bei der gewöhnlichen *imella*. Der ganze Innenrand ist bis zur Flügelfalte hell rostgelb, ähnlich der *ferruginella*; diese Innenrandstrieme fehlt der *imella* gewöhnlich; doch ist der Innenrand bisweilen gelblich bestäubt, und an einem unversehrten Männchen meiner Sammlung sind die gelblichen Stäubchen sehr reichlich und geben dem Innenrande eine unreine gelbliche Strieme. Der durchsichtige Fleck in der Mitte scheint eine längliche runde Gestalt zu haben, statt wie gewöhnlich, die eines länglichen Dreiecks.

Am 29. April fing ich bei trübem Wetter bei Sonnenuntergang zwei Männchen bei Syracus auf einer begrasten Stelle der ehemaligen Neapolis.

'Isis,' 1847, p. 810.

TINEA CRASSICORNELLA, n. sp.

Antennis crassiusculis, longioribus, griseis, capillis rufescentibus, thorace alisque anterioribus flavescenti-cinereis, sericeo-nitentibus unicoloribus (♂).

Eine ächte *Tinea*, aus der nächsten Verwandtschaft der *pellionella*. Grösse der allerkleinsten *pellionella* (Vorderflügel 2¼'''). Kopf lichthell rostgelb behaart. Fühler fast so lang wie die Vorderflügel, also von beträchtlicher Länge, auffallend dick, gegen die Spitze etwas dünner, mit gedrängten Gliedern, unbehaart, glänzend staubgrau. Lippentaster hängend, von Kopfeslänge, spitz, glänzend staubgrau; das zweite Glied am Ende ohne Borsten, unterwärts mit einer Spitze aus wenig verlängerten Haarschuppen. Rüssel verkümmert. Beine von der Farbe der Taster. Rückenschild seidenglänzend graugelblich; Hinterleib grau mit gelblichem Afterbusch.

Vorderflügel wenig gestreckt, kürzer als bei *pellionella*, einfarbig bleigrau mit gegen die Basis zunehmender gelblicher Beimischung, überall lebhaft seidenglänzend. Ein Exemplar hat die gelbliche Mischung über die ganze Fläche verbreitet. Die Franzen bleiben hellgrau, wie die gleichfalls stark glänzenden Hinterflügel. Auf der Unterseite sind die Vorderflügel dunkelgrau mit gelblichem Schimmer und gegen die Spitze stärker hervortretenden Adern.

Weibchen unbekannt, wahrscheinlich viel grösser, und mit langem Legestachel.

Vaterland Syracus beim Anapo. Auf einem grasreichen Fusssteige zwischen den Feldern in der Gegend des Jupiter-Tempels fing ich 2 Männchen am 19. Mai, und 2 am 7. Juni gegen Abend zwischen Gras und Blumen.

'Isis,' 1847, p. 811.

CALANTICA, Heyden in lit., nov. gen.

Caput longe crinitum, epistomio lævigato.
Oculi hemisphærici valde distantes. Ocelli nulli.
Antennæ mediocriter longæ, articulo basali squamis in conchulam dilatato.
Palporum maxillarium vix rudimentum adest ; palpi labiales breves, penduli, acuti.
Haustellum brevissimum.
Pedes breviusculi, TIBIÆ ANTICÆ SQUAMIS INCRASSATÆ IN QUIETE PROTENSÆ ; *tibiæ posticæ pilosæ bis bicalcaratæ, pari calcarium superiore e medio prodeunte.*
Alæ latæ ; anteriorum cellula mediana postice truncata venas tres in marginem costalem, sex in posticum emittente ; vena subdorsalis in basi furcata. Cilia haud ita longa.

Genus habitu *Tineis* ex familia *Swammerdamiarum* simile, antennarum structura ad *Lyonetiam* et *Opostegam* accedit, alis latis, venarum in iis copia et tibiis anticis *Liparidis* modo per quietem porrectis insignitur.

Nomen generis ornatum capitis mulierum exprimit.

C. DEALBATELLA, n. sp.

Nivea ; alæ anteriores squamis brunnescentibus hic illic congestis nebulosæ, subtus in femina niveæ ; posteriorum apex vix fuscescit.

Grösse wie *Tinea cerasiella*, Körperbau aber kräftiger und die Flügel breiter. Kopf breit und ziemlich flach (nach Abreibung der Schuppen) und die halbkugelichten Augen durch einen sehr breiten Raum getrennt. Die Schuppenhaare sind nach allen Seiten hin geneigt, also nicht schopfig ; das Obergesicht ziemlich glatt. Fühler von ⅔ Vorderflügellänge, weiss, mit deutlichen Gliedern und dadurch schwach dunkler geringelt, faserspitzig gezähnelt, am stärksten beim Männchen ; das Wurzelglied lang, reichlich mit ausgebreiteten Haarschuppen besetzt, die so einen Augendeckel bilden. Lippentaster kurz, etwas dick, hängend, spitz, weiss behaart, das Endglied von der Länge des zweiten Gliedes. Vorderschiene und -fuss kurz ; jene durch reichliche Schuppenhaare verdickt, welche einen Theil des Fusses verhüllen und diesen dadurch noch kürzer erscheinen lassen. Hinterschiene nach hinten zunehmend behaart und dadurch zusammengedrückt keulenförmig ; die obern Dornen sitzen an der Mitte und sind ungleich und nicht lang. Der ganze Körper mit seinen Theilen ist schneeweiss, der Hinterleib grau ; Vorderschenkel und -schiene sind vorn gelbbraun bestäubt ; die 3 letzten Vorderfussglieder und die Spitze des Mittel- und Hinterfusses,

dessgleichen die Spitzen der untersten Hinterschienenhaare auf der Lichtseite sind braun.
Vorderflügel ziemlich breit und spitz mit ziemlich kurzen Franzen. Die Basis des Vorderrandes braun. An der Mitte des Innenrandes und am Hinterwinkel ist ein gelbbrauner Schuppenfleck. Einzelne braune Schuppen zeigen sich im Mittelraum gegen die Basis. Der hintere Flügelraum ist mit einem aus gehäuften, zarten, braungelben Schuppen gebildeten Gewölk gefüllt, welches an 2 Stellen den Vorderrand berührt. Die Spitze und der Hinterrand ist auf den Franzen in ziemlicher Breite von ähnlichen Schuppen umzogen. An den Enden sind die Franzen hellgoldbräunlich, am lebhaftesten um die Flügelspitze.
Die gleichfalls spitzen Hinterflügel sind an der Flügelspitze spärlich bräunlich beschuppt, sonst wie die Franzen einfarbig weiss. Die ganze Unterseite ist glänzend weiss, und beim Weibchen sind nur die Franzen der Vorderflügel an der Spitze bräunlich; beim Männchen ist der Vorderrand von der Basis aus in einem zugespitzten Fleck weiss; der Hinterraum des Flügelraumes aber gelbbräunlich beschuppt.
Das Weibchen ist etwas grösser und leicht an den Fühlern, dem Hinterleibe und der weissen Farbe der Unterseite der Vorderflügel zu erkennen.
Die befruchteten (vielleicht auch die unbefruchteten) Weibchen haben einen grünlichen Hinterleib, und diese Farbe vergeht an den getrockneten Exemplaren nicht immer gänzlich.
Die Schabe, nach welcher Herr von Heyden das Genus gründete, scheint mir von der italienischen specifisch verschieden. Sie ist in beiden Geschlechtern grösser und noch etwas breitflügliger. Einen Unterschied in der Vorderflügelzeichnung wage ich nicht aufzustellen, da das eine Weibchen und die zwei Männchen, die ich von Herrn von Heyden erhielt etwas verwischt sind. Das Weibchen hat aber auf der Unterseite der Vorderflügel im Mittelfelde einen starken, braunen Wisch und am Vorderrande gegen die Basis braune Stäubchen. Beim Männchen ist fast die ganze hintere Hälfte der Hinterflügel bräunlich bestäubt; auch ist die Unterseite der Vorderflügel reichlicher verdunkelt. Diese Art, welche Herr von Heyden im Juli an Eichen im Taunusgebirge gefangen hat, heisst *albella*, Hdn., welcher Name wenn sich die specifische Verschiedenheit nicht bestätigt, billigerweise auf die ganze Art übertragen werden sollte, da ich mich zur Bildung des Wortes *Dealbatella* erst bei der jetzigen Untersuchung veranlasst gefunden habe.

'Isis,' 1847, p. 812.

ERIOCOTTIS, nov. gen.

Caput superne et in facie lanatum.
Oculi mediocres; ocelli magni supra oculos pone antennas positi.
Antennæ mediocres, tenues, pubescentes, setaceæ.
Palpi maxillares longiusculi, filiformes.

Palpi labiales mediocres, porrecti, acuti, articulo secundo infra setis dispersis instructo.
Haustellum brevissimum.
Oviductus feminæ longe exsertus.
Alæ anteriores oblongæ; cellulæ medianæ pars superior areolam format: ambitus decem venas emittit, quarum quatuor in marginem costalem, reliquæ in postioum; vena subdorsalis basis furcata.
Alæ posteriores ovatæ, mediocriter ciliatæ; e cellulæ medianæ ambitu venæ sex prodeunt.
Genus differt a *Tineis* propriis : ocellis, alarum anteriorum cellula mediana areolam separatam continente et venas quatuor, non quinque in marginem costalem emittente.

E. FUSCANELLA, n. sp.

Alæ anteriores maris lutescenti-griseæ, postice fuscescenti rarius conspersæ, puncto distinctiore dorsali ante angulum internum; feminæ fusco creberrime conspersæ, puncto post medium obscuriore. Caput griseo-lutescens.

Var. b. litura fusca ex costa ante apicem alarum ant. descendenti (♂).

Grösse des Männchens wie von einer kleinern *Masculella*, des Weibchens etwas beträchtlicher. Kopf, Rückenschild und Vorderflügel ein helles, reichlich mit Grau gemischtes Lehmgelb. Kopf auf Scheitel und Gesicht dichtstruppig behaart. Die Ocellen, etwas vom obern Augenrande entfernt, bisweilen durch die Haare verdeckt. Fühler borstenförmig, hell und dunkel geringelt, microscopisch pubescirend, nicht gefranzt. Lippentaster hell, horizontal oder etwas abwärts geneigt, wenig über die Stirnhaare hinausreichend, ziemlich dünn; das zweite Glied ist an der ganzen Unterseite mit zerstreuten Borsten besetzt, und obenauf trägt es an der Spitze ein Paar aufgerichtete Borsten; das Endglied unten etwas dunkler, kürzer als das zweite Glied. Beine fahlgelblich, auf der Lichtseite bräunlich grau ausser an den Enden der Glieder. Hinterschienen mit ziemlich langen Schuppenhaaren bekleidet, und mit 2 Paaren ungleicher Dornen. Hinterleib grau, an den Segmenträndern hellschuppig; männliche Afterklappe gross, durch lange Haarschuppen verdeckt.

Vorderflügel länglich, ziemlich breit mit deutlichem Vorderwinkel, gelblichschmutziggrau, etwas glänzend; besonders gegen die Spitze sind gelbbraune Stäubchen gestreut, aus denen sich bisweilen ein Punkt hinter der Mitte bildet. Gewöhnlicher zeigt sich ein deutlicher, brauner Punkt am Innenrande vor dem Innenwinkel. Franzen heller, auswärts dunkler, besonders am Innenwinkel. Hinterflügel grau, gegen die Spitze dunkler. Franzen von mittelmässiger Länge, am Schwanzwinkel am längsten und hellsten.

Unterseite glänzend, einfarbig; die der Vorderflügel bräunlichgrau, die der Hinterflügel sehr hell grau.

Var. *b*, ein Männchen, hat die beiden Punkte—im Mittelraum hinter der Mitte am Innenrande vor dem Innenwinkel—fleckartig; ausserdem hängt ein Fleck am Vorderrande vor der Spitze, der sich verdünnt, dem Hinterrande parallel, bis zum Innenrandfleck fortsetzt. Am Hinterrande sind sehr verloschene braune Pünktchen. Das grössere Weibchen ist überall viel dunkler als das Männchen, mit Ausnahme der Hinterflügel. Auf den Vorderflügeln ist die ganze Fläche sehr dicht braun besprengt, fast einfarbig, mit violettlichem Schimmer und einem braunen Punkt hinter der Mitte. Der lange Legestachel horngelblich, am Ende spärlich behaart.

Da diese *Eriocottis* nicht in Oliven leben kann, indem an der Stelle, wo ich sie am 5. April fand, weit und breit, kein Oelbaum wächst, so kann sie nicht mit des Fabr. *Tin. oleella*, Ent. Syst. iii. 2. 308, zusammengehören, deren sehr ungenaue Beschreibung ziemlich zutrifft.

'Isis,' 1847, p. 814.

MICROPTERYX SICANELLA, n. sp.

Capillis dilute vitellinis; alis anterioribus basi aureola, postice purpureis, fascia media maculaque postica magna costæ adhærente aureis.

Var. b. *fascia supra medium interrupta.*
Var. c. *ut a. sed puncto costali inter fasciam ac maculam.*

Sie hat einige Aehnlichkeit mit *Micropteryx Allionella*, ist aber viel kleiner und entbehrt der ersten Binde auf den Vorderflügeln, wofür diese hier hellgoldgelb sind; auch ist die Farbe und Gestalt der Flecke eine andre.

Grösse der *Calthella* oder wenig darüber. Behaarung des Kopfes hell dottergelb. Fühler fadenförmig, braun mit sehr gedrängten Gliedern. Taster hellgelblich. Rückenschild vorn goldgelblich. Beine seidenglänzend, gelblich und grau schimmernd. Hinterleib schwärzlich, spärlich mit langen grauen Haaren bekleidet; der After unterwärts mit 2 längern, gegen einander gekrümmten Zangen. Beim Weibchen ist der After abgestutzt und mit längern, gerade ausstehenden Haaren besetzt.

Vorderflügel mit mehrern tiefen Längsfurchen, an der Basis hell goldgelb, darauf an Lebhaftigkeit gegen die Spitze zunehmend purpurfarben, in der Spitze violett. Auf der Basis der Medianader ist manchmal ein purpurfarbener Punkt. In der Mitte des Vorderrandes fängt eine goldgelbe Binde an, die schief hinüber bis an den Innenwinkel zieht und bisweilen in der Mitte einen Winkel bildet. Noch öfter ist sie über der Mitte breit durchbrochen und besteht so aus zwei Gegenflecken (*var.* b), deren Spitzen nicht immer gegen einander gerichtet sind. Schon vor ihr nimmt die gelbliche Grundfarbe einen purpurröthlichen Anstrich an. Vor der Spitze hängt am Vorderrande ein grosser, goldgelber Fleck, der sich unterwärts erweitert und einwärts eine Ecke bildet; er reicht nicht selten bis nahe an den Hinterrand. Die Flügelspitze ist sehr schön violettglänzend. Bei *var.* c hat der Vorderrand zwischen der Binde und dem grossen Fleck, näher dem letztern, einen goldgelben Punkt von verschiedener Grösse. Franzen violettschimmernd, um die Spitze etwas gelblich.

Hinterflügel grau, gegen die Spitze in Gelb und zuletzt in Purpurfarbe übergehend.

Unterseite grau, etwas gelblich schimmernd, in der Spitze violettlich.

[Afterwards recognized as *Paykullella*, Fab. See 'Linnæa Entomologica,' vol. v. p. 329.]

'Isis,' 1847, p. 816.

NEMATOPOGON SERICINELLUS, n. sp.

Alis anterioribus elongatis, apice minus acuto sericeis, flavidis, vix reticulatis, ciliis externe fuscescentibus; posterioribus cinerascentibus, ciliis dilutioribus; palpis griseis.

Eine Mittelart zwischen *Nem. Swammerdammellus* und *Schwarziellus*, subtil, aber sicher von beiden verschieden. Sie hat nur die Grösse der letztern, ist also viel kleiner als *Swammerdammellus*. Vorderflügelgestalt die des letztern, aber der Hinterrand geht weniger schräg und lässt demnach den Vorderwinkel beträchtlich weniger spitz erscheinen; die Farbe der Fläche ist viel heller, und wenn auch hier und da ein verloschenes Querfleckchen sichtbar wird, so fehlt doch ein Gitter, wie es *Swammerdammellus* so deutlich hat, völlig. Ein verloschener Querstrich zeigt sich immer hinter der Mitte, und die Franzen sind auf den äussern ⅔ bräunlich, an Dunkelheit gegen den Innenwinkel zunehmend, während bei *Swammerdammellus* nur die Franzenspitzen eine bräunliche Farbe haben. Hinterflügel sehr licht grau; die Franzen—bei *Swammerdammellus* einfarbig gelblich—sind gelblich, nach aussen grau. Auf der Unterseite zeigt sich derselbe Unterschied an den Franzen. Einen sehr sichern Unterschied giebt aber die Färbung des Gesichts und der Taster. Bei *Swammerdammellus* werden die Haare, die bei den Fühlern hell rostgelb sind, nach unten immer heller und gehen zuletzt in die weissliche Farbe der Fresswerkzeuge über; bei *Sericinellus* sind sie auf der Stirn nur blassgelb, nach dem Munde zu werden sie immer schmutziger, und über den staubgrauen Tastern sind sie bräunlich.

Letzterer Unterschied gilt auch für *Schwarziellus*, wo die Taster weisslich sind. Die Vorderflügel dieser Art sind gestreckter und noch spitzer als bei *Swammerdammellus*, daher sehr verschieden von denen des *sericinellus*; sie sind etwas dunkler und etwas deutlicher gegittert; ihre Franzen werden nur auswärts grau. Die Franzen der Hinterflügel sind einfarbig grau ohne die gelbliche Basallinie des *sericinellus*.

Die übrigen *Nematopogon*-Arten sind entweder durch ihre Farbe oder ihre nach hinten sehr erweiterten Vorderflügel so verschieden, dass sie nicht weiter berücksichtigt werden dürfen.

Um Messina im April, selten in den Bergen an der Palermitaner Strasse in den mit Eichen, *Cytisus* und *Cistus* gemischten, dichten Gesträuchen.

'Isis,' 1847, p. 820.

YPSOLOPHUS EXUSTELLUS, n. sp.

Thorace, capite palpisque albis ; alis anterioribus brunnescentibus, vitta costali nivea, ciliis niveis nigro-strigatis ad apicem nigro exustis (♂, ♀).
Nächst verwandt mit *Yps. humerellus*, dessen Vorderflügelfranzen auch kein Schwänzchen bilden, leicht von ihm zu unterscheiden durch die weisse Farbe des Kopfes und der Taster. *Sicariellus* und *chilonellus* haben in den Franzen ein Schwänzchen.
Grösse des *Ypsolophus humerellus*. Schulterdecken, Vordertheil des Rückenschildes und Kopf weiss. Taster schneeweiss, auf der Unterseite des zweiten Gliedes weniger dicht bürstenhaarig als bei *humerellus*. Fühler anfangs auf dem Rücken weisslich dann bräunlich und verloschen weisslich geringelt. Beine schmutzig gelbgrau, glänzend; alle Füsse auf der Lichtseite mit weissen Gliederspitzen; Hinterschienen einwärts weisslich mit eben solchen Haaren. Hinterleib gelblichgrau, am After mit gelblichen Haaren, aus denen der Legestachel ein wenig hervorragt.
Vorderflügel etwas kurz, gelbbräunlich; am Vorderrande mit einer sehr breiten Strieme, die vor der Mitte sich mit ihrem obern Rande von ihm entfernt, indem sie von da ab schmäler wird; sie vereinigt sich an ihrer Spitze mit einem sehr schief vom Vorderrand aus nach hinten gehenden Strich, der von ihr nur durch die bräunliche Farbe getrennt wird, welche den schmalen Raum zwischen ihr und dem Vorderrande ausfüllt. Einwärts wird sie durch die verdunkelte Grundfarbe sehr scharf begrenzt; diese bildet hier einen nach hinten erweiterten und dann schief abgeschnittenen Längsstreif, unter welchem der Grund bis zum Innenrande heller ist; hinter ihm sind ein Paar verwischte, weissliche Längsstrichelchen, die mit der weissen Strieme zusammenhängen. Hinter dem weissen, schiefen Vorderrandstrich ist der Grund bis an eine ihm fast parallel laufende Grenzlinie bräunlich und grau zart gepünctelt; es folgt dann auf den Franzen ein weisser Raum, von einer feinen Querlinie durchzogen; diese geht in einem Bogen um die Flügelspitze herum durch die gleichfalls weisse untere Franzenfläche. Aus der Flügelspitze reicht ein brandigschwarzer, kurzer Strich durch den doppelten gelbbräunlichen Franzensaum. Die untere Franzenfläche ist breiter als die obere, und ihr schliesst sich am Innenwinkel ein weisslicher Haken an, der sich schief auswärts biegt, um dem Vorderrandstrich zu begegnen, was bei einem Exemplar auch ganz deutlich geschieht.
Hinterflügel hellgrau mit dunkler Spitze des Vorderwinkels; ihm gegenüber sind die blassen Franzen etwas gebräunt.
Unterseite der Vorderflügel gelbbräunlich grau ohne Vorderrandstrieme; die schneeweissen Franzen sind fast so lebhaft gezeichnet wie auf der Oberseite; am Innenwinkel und Vorderrande sind sie bräunlich, ausserdem ganz weiss; zwei schwarze, feine Linien ziehen quer hindurch, und der schwarze Saum bildet die dritte; durch alle drei geht der Brandfleck der Flügelspitze. Die Hinterflügel sind etwas dunkler als auf der Oberseite.

'Isis,' 1847, p. 821.

YPSOLOPHUS STRIATELLUS.

Var. b. *Alis anterioribus cinereo-brunnescentibus, striga costali postica abbreviata.*

Es ist diess dieselbe Varietät, die ich in der Aufzählung der kleinasiatischen Schmetterlinge besprochen habe. Sie waren unter den hellen Exemplaren nicht selten, und da ich mir ihre Auswahl vorzüglich angelegen sein liess, so habe ich von der hellen Stammart nur ein Exemplar mitgebracht. Meine 10 dunkeln syracusischen Exemplare entbehren auf den Vorderflügeln die feine aus der Basis entspringende Mittellinie völlig; bei einem bemerke ich in der Flügelfalte einige weisse, der Länge nach liegende Schuppen. Der längliche braune Punkt in der Falte vor der Flügelmitte ist vorhanden, gewöhnlich aber durch weissliche Schuppen verkleinert. Dasselbe gilt von dem Punkt im hintern Raum vor der weissen Querlinie; sie erreicht nie, wie bei dem gewöhnlichen *Striatellus*, den entsprechenden Strich in den Hinterrandfranzen, sondern wird vorher durch die Grundfarbe verfinstert, und, was mir jetzt sehr auffällt, sie nimmt nicht die Richtung auf den der Flügelspitze nächsten, sondern auf den zweiten (bei den kleinasiatischen sehe ich beide Richtungen), bei einigen ist nur ihr Anfang auf dem Vorderrande und zwar sehr deutlich ausgedrückt. Hinter ihr sind 2, seltner 3 weissliche Vorderrandhäkchen.

'Isis,' 1847, p. 822.

ANCHINIA BREVISPINELLA, n. sp.

Alis anterioribus dilutissime ochraceis, vitta juxta costam albidam brunnea, palporum articulo terminali brevi.

Var. b. *Major, vitta alarum anteriorum obsoleta.*

Nächst verwandt mit *A. pyropella*, für welche ich sie bisher ansah und daher nur in wenigen Exemplaren einsammelte. Gewöhnlich von der Grösse der allerkleinsten *pyropella*, hat sie deren ganze Gestalt, und gleichfalls etwas Veränderlichkeit in der Länge der Vorderflügel. Diese glänzen etwas weniger und haben blass ochergelbe Grundfarbe, also einen ganz von dem der *pyropella* verschiedenen Ton des Gelben. Die an den kleinen Exemplaren gewöhnlich recht dunkle Strieme, die längs des hellen Vorderrandes bis in die Flügelspitze zieht, ist bei den 4 grössern Männchen mehr oder weniger verloschen. Bei wenigen kleinen Exemplaren zeigt sich dicht an ihr in der Flügelmitte ein feines braunes Pünktchen. Rückenschild, Kopf und Taster nehmen an der Färbung der Vorderflügel Theil; letztere sind auswärts an der untern Hälfte und einwärts gegen die Spitze braun. Den specifischen Unterschied giebt die Länge des Endgliedes der Taster; dieses ragt kaum um die Hälfte seiner Länge über die Haarschuppen des vorletzten Gliedes hinweg, ohne dass es weiter von dem Ende derselben zu entspringen scheint. Bei *A. pyropella*, wo das vorletzte Glied nur auf dem Rücken gelbliche

Haare hat, ist das Endglied viel länger und steht um ⅔ über das vorletzte Glied hervor.

'Isis,' 1847, p. 831.

ŒCOPHORA GRAVATELLA, n. sp.

Parva, palpis longiusculis; alis anterioribus virescenti-griseis, posterioribus ovato-lanceolatis fuliginosis violaceo-nitidulis; ventre pallido, tibiis posticis externe albidis.

Grösse und nahe Verwandtschaft der *Œc. laminella*, Tr. (worunter ich Exemplare verstehe, die ich von Fischer von Röslerstamm als die Treitschkische Art erhielt, deren Vorderflügel aber nicht dunkelgrün oder flaschengrün sind, sondern in einem reichlich mit Braungrau gemischten Grün viel blässer und grauer als bei *Esperella* und *cuspidella*, wie es durch Treitschke's *viridi-griseus* der Diagnose gut ausgedrückt ist), aber sehr verschieden durch viel längere, aufgekrümmte, helle Taster (dort sind sie von Kopfeslänge, fast gerade und dunkel), länger zugespitzte Hinterflügel und dicht gelblich beschuppten Bauch (dort hat er gar nichts Gelbliches, wenigstens beim männlichen Geschlechte, welches ich von *laminella* bloss kenne) in beiden Geschlechtern. Von der grössern *Œcoph. apicalis* (im Verhältniss der kleinasiatischen Falter) unterscheidet sie geringere Grösse, viel hellere Färbung, Mangel des violetten Glanzes an Flügeln und Hinterleib und ganz besonders die Färbung des weiblichen Bauches. Durch einfarbigen, dunkeln Bauch im männlichen Geschlecht und dunklere Färbung ist auch *Œc. parvella*, F. v R. *in litt.* verschieden. Eine hier bei Glogau von mir aufgefundene neue Art, *potentillana*, m., hat ausser andern Verschiedenheiten nur im weiblichen Geschlechte auf dem Bauche getrennte, gelbliche Haarschuppen, kürzer zugespitzte Hinterflügel und auf diesen eine hellere Farbe ohne Violettschimmer.

Rückenschild und Kopf haben wie die Vorderflügel ein gelbliches Braungrau, mit sehr wenig grünlicher Beimischung und etwas Glanz.

Taster von Rückenschildslänge, aufgekrümmt, fadenförmig, auf der Rückseite hellgelblich, unten dunkel bräunlich, das zweite Glied gegen die Spitze etwas verdickt, das Endglied von ⅔ Länge des zweiten Gliedes, dünn zugespitzt. Fühler fein, fadenförmig, microscopisch gefranzt. Hinterleib dunkler als das Rückenschild, etwas metallglänzend, ohne Violett. Bauch ausser am Rande gelblich bis auf die Afterklappen; beim Weibchen verbindet sich die dunkle Seitenfarbe an dem Aftergliede durch einen schmalen Rand. Beine schmutziggrau, auswärts hell und gelblich schimmernd, besonders an den durch längere helle Haare verdickten Hinterschienen.

Vorderflügel ziemlich gestreckt, mit Haarschuppen bekleidet, von denen die in der Flügelfalte verloschen gelblich gefärbt sind, eben solche lassen sich auch einzeln gegen die Spitze wahrnehmen. Doch findet darin bei verschiedenen Exemplaren ein Mehr und Minder Statt. Hinterflügel viel schmäler als die Vorderflügel, eiförmig lanzettlich mit ziemlich langer Spitze; dunkel braungrau

mit, besonders unter der Loupe recht merklichem violettem Schimmer. Franzen braun, gegen die Spitze gelblich.
Unterseite aller Flügel einfarbig, wie die Oberseite der Hinterflügel. Ein Männchen, am 14. September bei Triest am Karst gefangen, weicht etwas ab; bei gleichem Fühlerbau und gleicher Färbung des Bauches hat es in der Flügelfalte auf den Vorderflügeln keine von der Grundfarbe abweichende Färbung, und auf der ganzen Unterseite der Flügel nichts Violettliches; das Wurzelglied der Taster verdickt durch auffallend weissliche Haarschuppen, das zweite Glied ohne Verdickung gegen die Spitze, das Endglied länger. Wegen dieser Verschiedenheit in den Tastern kann es wohl eine verschiedene Art seyn. Ich lasse es als *Var.* b, *palporum articulo secundo non incrassato, alis subtus non violaceo-nitidulis* gelten.

'Isis,' 1847, p. 833.

ŒCOPHORA DISSITELLA, n. sp.

Parva, palpis longiusculis; alis anterioribus olivaceis, parum violaceo-nitidulis; posterioribus ovato-lanceolatis, fuliginosis, margine œnescente; tibiis posticis obscuris; ventre feminæ ante apicem maculam obsoletam flavescentem gerente.

Sehr nahe der *Parvella*, F. R. in *lit.*, von der ich nur ein Männchen besitze und von dieser durch beträchtlich längere Taster und gestrecktere Vorderflügel, sowie durch den erzglänzenden Rand der Hinterflügel unterschieden. *Œcophora apicalis* und *seliniella* sind grösser und breitflügliger, haben zwar im männlichen Geschlecht den metallschimmernden Hinterflügelrand; aber erstere hat auf den Vorderflügeln ein gelbliches Grün; letztere ein dunkleres, gegen die Spitze violettliches; erstere hat im weiblichen Geschlechte am Bauche hinten einen grossen, hellgelben, scharfumgrenzten Fleck; bei letzterer ist er schneeweiss und bändformig; *dissitella* hat ihn sehr verloschen, bräunlich gelb und in einer Spitze auf das Aftersegment auslaufend. Bei der folgenden viel kleinern *tributella* sind die Taster kürzer und fast gerade und die Hinterflügel viel schmäler.

So klein wie die vorige, mit ein wenig kürzern Vorderflügeln. Diese sind so wie die ganze Körper dunkel olivengrün mit schwachem, gelblichem Schimmer gegen die Spitze und noch schwächerm, violettlichem gegen die Basis. Männliche Fühler unter der Loupe merklicher gefranzt als bei *gravatella*, weibliche mit sehr zartem Flaum. Taster von Rückenschildslänge, aufgekrümmt, das zweite Glied nur an der Basis etwas verdünnt; das Endglied von ¾ der Länge des zweiten Gliedes, dünner, sehr fein zugespitzt. Beine und Hinterleib ganz einfarbig, dunkel, etwas metallglänzend. Der Bauch des Weibchens hat vor der Spitze einen schmutzig gelblichen, unter dem Schimmer in gewisser Richtung fast verschwindenden Fleck von rundlicher Gestalt, mit einer auf die Mitte des Aftergliedes auslaufenden Spitze.

Die Hinterflügel sind messerförmig, ohne ausgezogene Spitze, bloss scharf zugespitzt rauchgrau, an Vorder- und Hinterrand mit gelblich schimmernden Schuppen, beim Männchen lebhafter als beim Weibchen. Franzen dunkel, kaum mit einer violettlichen Beimischung.

Unterseite aller Flügel braungrau, etwas glänzend.
Ein Pärchen bei Syracus auf Aeckern um die Syraca am 25. und
26. April.

'Isis,' 1847, p. 833.

ŒCOPHORA TRIBUTELLA, n. sp.

*Parva, palpis brevioribus, vix curvis; alis anterioribus olivaceis
nitidulis, posterioribus ovato-lanceolatis fuliginosis; abdomine feminæ
ante apicem maculam lutescentem gerente.*

Kleiner als die vorige; Vorderflügellänge 2'''. Von der vorigen
unterscheiden sie ausser der Kleinheit die kürzern, fast geraden
Taster und die schmälern Hinterflügel.

Der ganze Körper mit seinen Theilen olivengrünlich, in der Farbe
meiner Stammform von *Laminella*, etwas glänzend. Taster von
mehr als Kopfeslänge, wenig gekrümmt; das zweite Glied nach oben
etwas verdickt; das Endglied dünner, von ¾ Länge desselben,
zugespitzt. Der Bauch hat beim Weibchen die 2 Glieder vor dem
Aftergliede mit Ausnahme des Seitenrandes hell lehmgelblich, jedoch
unter dem Schimmer in gewisser Richtung kaum bemerkbar. Beim
Männchen ist alles einfarbig dunkel, auch die Afterhaare.

Vorderflügel in der Gestalt wie bei der vorigen, kaum etwas dunkler
als der Rückenschild, mit äusserst schwachem, röthlichem Schimmer
gegen den Vorderrand. Hinterflügel halb so breit wie die Vorderflügel, in eine lange Spitze verdünnt, bräunlich grau, ebenso ohne
röthlichem Schimmer wie die ganze gleichfarbige Unterseite.

Diese sehr einfach gezeichnete Art fing ich im einem guten
Pärchen am 4. Mai bei Syracus an dem kräuterreichen Abhange der
ehemaligen Neapolis im Grase.

'Isis,' 1847, p. 834.

ŒCOPHORA TERRENELLA, n. sp.

*Parva, palpis brevioribus parum arcuatis; alis anterioribus lutescenti-
griseis nitidulis; posterioribus ovato-lanceolatis cinereis; ano pilis
lutescentibus marginato (♂, ♀).*

So gross und gestaltet wie die vorige Art, leicht durch die sehr
helle, graugelbliche, etwas erzglänzende Grundfarbe zu erkennen.

Rückenschild und Kopf in der Farbe der Vorderflügel, Fühler
beider Geschlechter microscopisch sehr fein pubescirend gefranzt.
Taster etwas länger als der Kopf, heller als das Rückenschild, etwas
aufgekrümmt, borstenförmig, fein zugespitzt, Endglied von ¾ Länge des
zweiten Gliedes. Beine und Bauch in der fahlen, graugelblichen Farbe
der Taster, schwach schimmernd, und diese Farbe tragen auch die
das Afterglied kränzenden Haare. Obenauf ist der Hinterleib grau.

Auf den Vorderflügeln zeigt sich über der Flügelfalte die Subcostalader als eine etwas erhabene, bis zur Längshälfte reichende
Linie, und der Raum dazwischen ist mit mehr oder weniger hellgelb-
lichen Haarschuppen bekleidet, die bei einem Exemplar eine ganz
deutliche am Innenwinkel aufhörende Längslinie bilden.

Hinterflügel grau; nur so schmal wie der Innenrandtheil der

Vorderflügel bis zur Flügelfalte, aber länger, in eine dünne Spitze verlängert; Franzen mehr gelblich gemischt. Ganze Unterseite wie die Hinterflügel oben.

'Isis,' 1847, p. 834.

ŒCOPHORA ROSCIDELLA, n. sp.

Palpis adscendentibus acutis ; alis anterioribus griseis, parte basali obscuriore, fascia cana ante, striga fuscescente post medium obsoletis (♂).

Nächst verwandt mit *Œcoph. phycidella*, 'Isis,' 1839, S. 196, 35, verschieden durch geringere Grösse, die vor und hinter der hellen Binde sehr verdunkelten Vorderflügel, die grössere Annäherung der Binde an die Basis und die stumpfere Gestalt der Vorderflügel.

Grösse etwas über *Œc. siccella*; Vorderflügellänge $2\frac{1}{2}'''$. Rückenschild und Kopf dunkelgrau, schimmernd und daher bei veränderter Haltung heller oder dunkler erscheinend. Fühler etwas dick, oben und unten schwach gezähnt, unten microscopisch gefranzt; das Wurzelglied durch Beschuppung erweitert, auf der untern Seite der Länge nach seicht ausgehöhlt erscheinend, auf dem vorderen Seitenrande mit abstehenden Haarschuppen; dieses Glied ist auf dem Rücken heller als der Kopf. Taster, wie es scheint, so lang und gestaltet wie bei *Œcoph. phycidella*, aufgekrümmt, fadenförmig, sehr schwach zusammengedrückt; das Endglied von $\frac{2}{3}$ Länge des zweiten Gliedes, dünner und fein zugespitzt; auswärts ist die Farbe bräunlich besprengt, an den Enden des zweiten und dritten Gliedes hell, gelblich, wie auf der Innenseite. Beine staubig gelbbräunlich, an den Gliederenden sowie auf der dem Leibe zugewendeten Seite gelblich; Hinterschienen auf der gelbliche Seite gelblich langhaarig. Hinterflügel schimmernd dunkelgrau; der Afterring mit einem Kranze langer fahlgelblicher Schuppen.

Vorderflügel etwas stumpf—auf der Unterseite, wo sich ihr Rand von den Franzen gut unterscheiden lässt, zeigt ihre Spitze sich merklich abgerundet, im Vergleich mit *Œcoph. phycidella*—staubgrau, gegen die Basis dunkler. Unter der Loupe zeigen sich die Schuppen an ihren Enden dunkel mit feinem, hellem Rande, wodurch sie auf viel dunklerem Grunde weisslichgrau punctirt aussehen. Von den Franzen sind nur die dem Innenwinkel nähern zum grössern Theil unverdeckt von solchen Schuppen. Auf dem Anfange des zweiten Längsdrittels steht eine helle, weisslichgraue, ziemlich gerade, schmale Binde, auswärts dunkler eingefasst als einwärts, aber nicht scharf gerandet. (Bei *Œcoph. phycidella* ist sie, wenn man den hellen Raum als Binde annehmen will, nach aussen convex, viel breiter und einwärts ganz in die Grundfarbe übergehend; auswärts wird sie von zwei stärkern, schwärzlichen Gegenflecken begrenzt, die in der Mitte durch ein verloschenes Fleckchen verbunden werden, oder auch ganz in einen bindenförmigen, krummen Querstreif zusammenfliessen). Auf dem Anfange des letzten Drittels steht auf dem Innenrande ein wenig merklicher, dünner, dunkler Querstrich, der den Vorderrand nicht erreicht.

Hinterflügel am Hinterwinkel fast so breit wie die Vorderflügel, von da aus sich messerförmig verdünnend und ziemlich lang zuspitzend; Hinterrand wenig convex; Grundfarbe grau, gegen den Vorderwinkel dunkler. Franzen lang, an der Basis gelblich, übrigens grau.

Unterseite glänzend grau, auf den Vorderflügeln mehr staubig grau. Ich klopfte von dieser Art einige Exemplare am 15. und 19. August bei Neapel oberhalb des Agnanosees und bei Camaldoli von jungen Eichenstämmen.

'Isis,' 1847, p. 837.

DEPRESSARIA PELORITANELLA, n. sp.

Parva, alis anterioribus dilutissime griseis, punctulo altero nigro ante, altero post medium; palporum articulo secundo apice squamis incrassato, tertio non annulato; ventre fusco-bivittato.

Eine der kleinsten und unscheinbarsten Arten des Genus, etwas grösser als *D. vaccinella*, so gross wie meine *Capreolella*, der sie ziemlich nahe steht. Sie unterscheidet sich aber leicht von ihr durch den Mangel des kurzen, hellern Wurzelfeldes der Vorderflügel, die viel hellere, mehr fahlgelbliche Grundfarbe derselben, die etwas grauer ist als bei *Hypsolophus verbascellus*, und durch die hellen, ungeringelten Taster. Rückenschild und Kopf den Vorderflügel gleich gefärbt, verschossen lederfarbig mit Staubgrau gemischt. Hinterkopfhaare nach vorn aufgerichtet. Wurzelglied der Fühler auswärts an der Seite mit einigen abstehenden Schuppenhaaren. Taster ziemlich lang, aufgekrümmt; das zweite Glied ist an der Endhälfte stark verdickt; die Schuppen gross und breit und nach beiden Seiten hin gelegt, so dass sie in der Mitte eine lange Rinne zwischen sich lassen, an deren Ende das dritte Glied hervorkommt; dieses ist krumm, feinspitzig. Die äussere Seite der Taster ist etwas heller als der Rückenschild, das zweite Glied unterwärts dunkel. Rüssel obenauf beschuppt. Vorder- und Mittelbeine auf der Vorderseite schwärzlich grau, die letztern an den Füssen hell; Hinterbeine hell ledergelblich, nur an den Schenkeln auf der Vorderseite grau. Hinterleib grau, gerandet mit graugelblichem Afterbusch; Bauch ledergelblich, zu jeder Seite mit einer braunen, nach hinten verdünnten Strieme.

Vorderflügel an der Spitze abgerundet, einfarbig, hinterwärts kaum ein wenig dunkler. Weit vor der Mitte liegt auf der Subcostalader ein schwarzes Pünctchen, und ein zweites, stärkeres folgt hinter der Mitte, etwas näher dem Vorder- als dem Innenrande. Den Hinterrand bezeichnet eine meist ganz verloschene oder fehlende Reihe brauner, zerflossener Puncte. Auf der Fläche sind bei guten Exemplaren sehr zerstreute, bräunliche Atome sichtbar. Hinterflügel glänzender hellgrau, gegen die Basis heller; der Hinterrand ist wie gewöhnlich eingebogen.

Unterseite glänzend, auf den Vorderflügeln braungrau, den Hinterflügeln hellgelblich grau, gegen die Spitze dunkler; die Franzen sind an ihrer Basis mit einer feinen gelblichen Linie umzogen.

' Isis,' 1847, p. 838.

DEPRESSARIA THAPSIELLA, n. sp.

Major, alis anterioribus obtusiusculis carneo-griseis fusco-conspersis, costa fusco-maculata, punctis duobus ante, puncto ocellari post medium nigris; palporum articuli terminalis annulo medio et apice fuscis.
Var. b. macula diffusa fuscescenti supra punctum ocellare.
Var. c. puncto inferiore primi paris deficiente.

Sie gehört zu den Arten, bei welchen die Basis der Vorderflügel bis zu einem nicht weit entfernten Querstrich heller ist, und unter diesen steht sie der *characterella* darin nahe, dass sie wie diese (und wie *arenella*) die äusserste Spitze der Taster braun gefärbt hat; sie unterscheidet sich von ihr aber ausser durch eine ganz andre Grundfarbe auch dadurch, dass sie nicht einen rothen, sondern einen schwarzen, weissausgefüllten Ring auf den Vorderflügeln und die beiden Punkte vor der Mitte nie strichförmig und zusammenfliessend zeigt; auch fehlt ihr der braune Fleck in der Mitte zwischen dem Doppelpunkt und dem Augenpunkt; bei *var. b.* ist zwar ein grösser Fleck da, aber verflossen und mit dem Vorderrande zusammenhängend.

Grösse nach der Reichlichkeit der Nahrung sehr verschieden (Vorderflügellänge $5\frac{3}{4}$–$4\frac{1}{4}'''$). Rückenschild, Kopf und Vorderflügel ein bleiches, mit Fleischfarbe mehr oder weniger stark gemischtes Staubgrau. Schulterdecken mit einigen bräunlichen Stäubchen. Fühler: Wurzelglied braun, nur auf der Unterseite mit einem hellen Längsstrich, an der Seite auswärts mit einigen abstehenden Haarschuppen; die Peitsche wird gegen die Spitze allmählich etwas heller braun und zuletzt nimmt sie bei verschiedener Haltung die glänzende bleiche Farbe bes Rückenschildes an; gegen das verdünnte Ende ist sie viel deutlicher gezähnelt als am Anfange. Stirn viel heller als der Oberkopf und glattschuppig. Taster ziemlich lang, zurückgekrümmt, von der Farbe der Stirn, auswendig bräunlich besprengt; das zweite Glied ist an den obern $\frac{2}{3}$ durch breite Schuppen stark verdickt, auf der Bauchseite mit einer tiefen Längsfurche, und in dieser röthlichgrau wie die Vorderflügel oder dunkler. Das helle Endglied ist fast so lang wie das zweite Glied, an der Basis so dunkel wie das zweite Glied unten, an der Mitte mit einem breiten, schwärzlichen Gürtel; die äusserste sehr feine Spitze gleichfalls schwärzlich. Rüssel obenauf dicht bleich beschuppt; an seiner Basis zeigen sich die sehr kurzen, durch Beschuppung oval scheinenden Maxillartaster gegen einander geneigt. Beine bleich gelblich; die vordern an der ganzen Vorderseite graubräunlich, nur an den Fussgliederspitzen bleich; die mittlern eben da blässer grau, am dunkelsten an den Schienen; die hintern sind nur etwas dunkler und spärlich bestäubt. Hinterleib flach, obenauf grau, mit deutlichem, bleichgelblichem Seitenrande und eben solchem Afterbusch und Bauch; letzterer hat zwei weitgetrennte Reihen schwärzlicher, nicht sehr scharf umschriebener, eckiger Flecke, von denen die vordersten bisweilen zusammenfliessen.

Vorderflügel stumpf und am Vorderwinkel noch ein wenig mehr abgerundet als bei *characterella*. Die Basis bildet ein sehr helles, durch einen braunen, auf dem Innenrande senkrecht stehenden und bis zur Subcostalader reichenden Strich abgegrenztes Feld. Der Vorderrand hat ganz am Anfang ein braunes Fleckchen; hierauf kommen in ziemlich gleichen Abständen 3–4 braune Vorderrandflecke, die etwas verwischt sind, und deren letzter und grösster über der Querader liegt; es folgen noch ein Paar mehr verwischte und kleinere Vorderrandflecke, deren letzter sich an die braune, nicht sehr scharfe Punktreihe des Hinterrandes in Grösse und Deutlichkeit anschliesst. Die Flügelfläche ist grau bestäubt, gegen den Hinterrand am meisten; es lässt sich gewöhnlich auch die helle winklige Binde, wenn auch sehr verloschen, wiedererkennen, in der Gestalt wie bei *arenella, albipunctella*, nicht wie bei *daucella* und *Heracleana*. Vor der Mitte stehen im Mittelfelde an der gewöhnlichen Stelle die 2 schwarzen, gerundeten Punkte schräg untereinander; der obere grösser als der untere, beide ziemlich weit getrennt; fast in gleicher Höhe mit dem untern befindet sich auf der Querader ein kleiner, schwärzlicher, weiss ausgefüllter Ring in der Grösse des grössern Punktes, nicht scharf umschrieben. Bei var. b reicht bis an ihn ein bräunlicher Wisch, der sich oben an den dritten Vorderrandfleckchen anschliesst und den hinter ihm folgenden hellen Winkelstreifen besser hervortreten lässt. Franzen röthlicher und glänzender als die Flächen.

Hinterflügel glänzend bleich gelblichgrau, sehr hell, gegen den Vorderrand wenig dunkler; der weniger als bei *Arenella* abgestumpfte Vorderwinkel hat eine fast deutliche, bräunliche Randlinie. Die Franzen werden an der Basis von einer bleichgelben, dünnen Linie umzogen.

Unterseite glänzend mit gelblichem, bräunlich geflecktem Vorderrande; die Vorderflügel bräunlichgrau mit etwas hellen Franzen; die Randlinie hellgelb mit kurzen, schwärzlichem Strichen. Auch die viel hellern Hinterflügel haben eine hellgelbe, sehr feine Randlinie; diese ist aber nur gegen die Spitze mit schwärzlichen Strichen besetzt. Bei manchen Exemplaren sind die schwärzlichen Striche ganz verblasst, dass sie sehr wenig oder nicht bemerkt werden.

Var. b, mit dem grossen dunklen Wischfleck ist selten; sie wird aber durch häufige Uebergänge, wo ein kleiner, schattiger Fleck zu sehen ist mit *var.* a verbunden. *Var.* c ist ein einzelnes Weibchen, bei dem der obere der beiden schwarzen Punkte klein ist, der untere aber ganz fehlt; dafür sind die 4 ersten Vorderrandflecke sehr deutlich und dunkel.

Beschreibung der Raupe.

Die junge Raupe ist schmutziggrün mit schwarzem Kopf und Nackenschilde; After und Hinterbeine gelb. Fast erwachsen ist sie dunkel braungrün mit grossen, weisslichen, sehr deutlichen Warzen und klaren Borsten auf denselben. Kopf glänzend schwarz. Nackenschild ebenso, in der Mitte mit feiner Längslinie, am Vorder- und Seitenrande schmal röthlich. Vorderbeine gelblich, braunfleckig; Bauchfüsse gelblich mit vollständigen, braunrothen Hakenkränzen; Hinterbeine und Afterschild hellgelb. Erwachsen ist sie viel heller und hat blässere Wärzchen. Kopf und Nackenschild sind bisweilen kastanienbraun.

Beschreibung der Puppe.

Die Puppe ist gelbbraun; das Aftersegment ohne Spitze, mit längerer, abgerundeter, der Länge nach gefurchter Bauchseite; am obern Ende steht eine ziemlich gedrängte Querreihe von 6–8 Widerhäkchen, von denen gewöhnlich einige beim Befreien der Puppe aus dem Gespinnste abbrechen. Der Rücken der drei letzten Ringe ist mit äusserst kurzen, microscopischen Borstenhärchen dicht besetzt.

'Isis,' 1847, p. 840.

DEPRESSARIA FERULÆ, n. sp.

Major, fronte patagiisque flavidis, alis anterioribus obtusis brunneis, basi abrupte flavida, puncto nigro ante, albo post medium; palpis flavidis externe fuscescentibus, articuli terminalis basi annuloque fuscis (♂, ♀).

Sie steht den *Depr. parilella* und *furvella* am nächsten, und zwar jener mehr, als dieser, durch die Aehnlichkeit der Flügelbildung; *parilella* ist aber viel kleiner; ihr Roth auf den Vorderflügeln ist hell, ziegelfarbig; die Hinterflügel sind viel heller mit graugelblichen Franzen; endlich ist das Endglied der Taster nur an der Spitze und bisweilen auch da nicht braun, ohne dunkle Stellen.

Furvella hat breitere Flügel; namentlich sind die hintern in der Gegend des Hinterwinkels auffallend breiter, und ihr Hinterrand entbehrt der bei den *Depressarien* gewöhnlichen Ausbiegung. Die helleren röthlichen Vorderflügel haben statt des weissen Punktes ein kleines, rundes Fleckchen; die Taster sind ganz einfarbig hellgelb, ohne braune Gürtel.

Grösse wie *Depr. furvella* (Vorderflügellänge 5'''). Rückenschild hellgelb, am Vorderrande braun; ebenso, aber schmäler der Anfang der Schulterdecken. Kopf auf der Stirn heller gelb; die aufgerichteten Hinterkopfschuppen sind hellbraun mit gelblichen Spitzen. Fühler braun, schwach gezähnt; das Wurzelglied auswärts mit einigen abstehenden, an der Basis verdünnten Haarschuppen. Die kurzen, dünnen, gelblichen Maxillartaster neigen sich über dem gelbschuppigen Rüssel gegen einander. Die Lippentaster lang, aufgekrümmt, im Grunde hellgelblich wie die Stirn; das zweite Glied an den äusseren $\frac{2}{3}$ stark verdickt durch bräunliche, gerundete Schuppen, die sich zweizeilig auseinander legen; auswärts ist es gelblich und bräunlich besprengt. Das Endglied, von $\frac{2}{3}$ Länge des zweiten Gliedes, ist an der Basis, ferner in einem breiten Gürtel und an der Spitze braun, doch nirgends in scharfen und regelmässigen Grenzen. Beine auf der Lichtseite bräunlich mit gelblichen Gliederspitzen, am dunkelsten die vordern; auf der Schattenseite bleichgelb, ausser an den Füssen, die nur etwas blässer als auf der

Lichtseite gefärbt sind. Hinterleib braungrau mit eben solchem Afterbusch; der graugelbliche Bauch hat zwei sehr breit anfangende braune Längsstriemen, die in verjüngte, getrennte Flecke übergehen.

Vorderflügel am Vorderwinkel fast noch stumpfer als bei *parilella*, gelblich braun, dunkler und brauner als bei *cnicella*, nach hinten etwas gelichtet; die Basis ist schmal hellgelb, hinterwärts scharf abgegrenzt; auf der Subcostalader bildet der Rand einen stumpfen Winkel. Der Raum hinter diesem Felde ist der dunkelste des Flügels; dunklere Flecke zeigen sich nur sehr verloschen auf dem Vorderrande und hier und dort im Mittelraum.

Vor der Mitte liegt in diesem ein schwarzes Pünktchen, an dessen Rande ein Paar weissliche Schüppchen hängen. Bei 2 Exemplaren liegen bis zum nächsten Punkt noch zwei weisse Schüppchen. Etwas hinter der Flügelmitte liegt auf einer kleinen dunklern Stelle ein sehr deutlicher, weissen Punkt, unter der Loupe etwas eckig aussehend. Braune Hinterrandpunkte sind kaum wahrzunehmen. Die Franzen sind etwas heller und glänzen.

Hinterflügel hell braungrau, gegen die Basis heller; die gleichfarbigen Franzen sind an ihrer Wurzel mit einer sehr feinen helleren Linie umzogen.

Unterseite glänzend braungrau, auf den Vorderflügeln bräunlicher; der halbe Vorder- und der ganze Hinterrand ist mit einer gelblichen, braunfleckig unterbrochenen Linie eingefasst.

'Isis,' 1847, p. 842.

DEPRESSARIA VENEFICELLA, n. sp.

Major, alis anterioribus elongatis rotundatis brunneo-griseis, linea disci fusca longitudinali partim pallido-squamata, lineolis ante apicem fuscis; abdomine ciliato, palporum articuli terminalis basi annuloque fuscis.

Grösse und Gestalt wie von der nächstverwandten *Depr. Heracleana*; die Vorderflügel noch etwas gestreckter. Ihre hellröthlichbraune Farbe und ihr längeres, spitzeres Endglied der Taster unterscheiden sie leicht.

Rückenschild und Oberseite des Kopfes heller als die Vorderflügel; ersteres mit verdunkeltem Vorderrande. Stirn fahlgelb. Fühler röthlichbraun, mit helleren Anfängen der Glieder und dadurch geringelt, gegen die Spitze deutlicher gezähnelt als gegen die Basis; das Wurzelglied an der Aussenseite mit kammförmig gestellten Schuppenhaaren, Maxillartaster kurz, dünn, gegen einander geneigt auf der Basis des gelblich beschuppten Rüssels. Lippentaster lang, aufgebogen; das zweite Glied einwärts bräunlich besprengt, fast von seiner Basis aus durch reichliche, dunkelrothbräunliche Schuppen verdeckt, welche sich zweizeilig auseinanderlegen, so dass sie eine tiefe Mittelfurche zwischen sich lassen; das Endglied von $\frac{2}{3}$ Länge des zweiten Gliedes ist fahlgelb, an der Basis und in einem breiten, schiefen Gürtel braun, wodurch die Spitze in um so hellerer Färbung hervortritt. Beine bleichgelb, auf der Lichtseite bräunlich mit hellen Gliederspitzen; die Vorderschienen sind auf dieser Seite blassröthlich und braun punktirt. Hinterbeine am hellsten. Hinterleib obenauf grau, an der Seite mit langen, bleichen Haarbüscheln gefranzt; Afterbusch etwas grauer. Bauch graugelblich, zu jeder Seite ist ein breiter, aus dunkelgrauen, wenig gedrängten Stäubchen zusammengesetzter Längsstreif, der nach hinten heller und schmäler wird.

Vorderflügel gestreckt mit abgerundetem Vorderwinkel, hell röthlichbraun, mit Staubfarbe gemischt, dunkler und weniger röthlich als bei *Depr. daucella*, hier und da mit fahlgelblichen Staubhäufchen und bräunlichen Schmutzflecken bestreut. Die gelblichen Stäubchen bilden eine zusammenhängende, doch ganz deutliche, unter einem spitzen Winkel gebrochene Binde in der Gestalt wie bei *D. Heracleana*; zwischen ihr und der Reihe nicht sehr scharfer, brauner Hinterrandpunkte liegen braune Längslinien, nach der Richtung der Flügeladern; die mittelsten Linien sind die deutlichsten, und jede entspricht einem Randpunkte. Der Innenrand ist von der Basis aus in einer kurzen, dünnen Linie fahlgelblich, einwärts durch einen braunen Schattenfleck gerandet. In der Mittelzelle liegt eine braune, gegen den Vorderrand divergirende Linie, die aber grösstentheils mit fahlgelblichen Schuppen verdeckt wird; nur ihr hinteres Ende, das bis an die helle Querbinde reicht, ist als ein kurzer brauner Strich frei und an seinem Anfange etwas verdickt; unter ihm und parallel damit liegen noch ein Paar kürzere, ungleich lange Längsstriche, und über ihm oft noch einer. Das Strahlige an diesen Linien ist durchaus nicht so auffallend, wie bei *Heracleana*, da sie kürzer und dicker sind. Franzen auswärts heller als die Grundfarbe der Flügel.

Hinterflügel glänzend hellgrau, gegen den Vorderwinkel dunkler; die helleren staubgrauen Franzen haben nächst der Basis eine verloschene, graue Querlinie.

Unterseite glänzend grau. Vorderflügel braungrau, am Vorderrande ziemlich breit, am Hinterrande in einer dünnen Linie staubig gelblich; Franzen röthlich grau. Die viel hellern Hinterflügel haben einen gelblichen Vorderrand, eine gelbliche, dunkelgrau bestäubte Spitze und um dieselbe auf der gelbliche Randlinie braune Fleckchen. Franzen gelblich grau.

Beim Weibchen sind die Flügel etwas kürzer und abgerundeter.

Die Raupe ist erwachsen und zur Verpuppung reif, so gross wie die von *Depressaria thapsiella*, blassgrün, am Rücken röthlich, mit drei dunkleren verloschenen Längslinien, von denen die mittelste, die Rückenlinie, am deutlichsten ist. Nacken und Afterschild nicht von der Grundfarbe verschieden, bloss etwas glänzend; Kopf gelbbraun, obenauf schwarzbraun.

Ganz klein, in der Grösse von $2'''$ ist sie gelblich grau; Kopf schwarz, glänzend, Nackenschild braun, an den Seiten scharf abgesetzt, Krallen schwarz; die Borstenwärzchen schwarz und klein; Afterschild und Beine gelblicher als die Grundfarbe.

'Isis,' 1847, p. 845.

GELECHIA VILELLA, n. sp.

Alis anterioribus griseis, obscurius pulvereis, puncto basali prope marginem dorsalem fusco; posterioribus canis, sericeis (♂, ♀).

Anscheinend aus der Verwandtschaft der *Terrella*, aber dadurch ausgezeichnet, dass ihr letztes Tastergliod länger als ihr vorletztes und ihr Rüssel so kurz und dünn ist. Ihr Aussehen ist, wenn man den starken Seidenglanz ausnimmt, sehr unscheinbar; an dem schwarzbraunen Punkt an der Basis der Vorderflügel, und zwar nahe am Innenrande hat sie ein leichtes und sicheres Merkmal.

Grösse wie *Gel. cinerella*; Vorderflügellänge etwas über 4‴. Kopf und Rückenschild wie die Vorderflügel gelblich staubgrau, aber ohne die dunklern Stäubchen der letztern. Am Hinterkopf sträuben sich bloss die seitlichen Schuppenhaare etwas; die andern Schuppen sind gross, abgerundet und glatt anliegend. Fühler bräunlich, schwach geringelt, microscopisch pubescirend gefranzt. Maxillartaster klein, spitzig, auf dem beschuppten Rüssel liegend. Lippentaster lang, aufgekrümmt; das zweite Glied bleich gelblich, an den letzten ⅔ durch Schuppen stark verdickt, auf der Unterseite mit tiefer Mittelfurche: das Endglied länger, dünn zugespitzt, auf der Bauchseite mit fast anliegenden Haarspitzchen, vor der Spitze beim Männchen mit einem braunen Ringe. Beine bleich; die vier vordern auf der Lichtseite ausser an den Gliederspitzen bräunlich. Hinterschienen langhaarig; der längere obere Dorn hat die halbe Schienenlänge. Hinterleib grau, mit aufgeworfenem Seitenrande und ziemlich langem, etwas gelblichem Afterbusch; der Bauch hat zwei verloschene helle Mittelstriemen dicht neben einander.

Vorderflügel schmal, graustaubig, am Innenrande am hellsten. In der Mitte ist die Spur einer braunen Längslinie, an deren Anfang und Ende ein hell eingefasstes, kaum merkliches Pünktchen. Gegen die Spitze verdunkelt sich der Grund etwas. Nahe der Basis und dem Innenrande liegt ein deutlicher, schwarzbrauner Punkt, und auf der Basis der Medianader selbst ein sehr feines Pünktchen; der Vorderrand ist nur etwas verdunkelt.

Hinterflügel viel breiter als die Vorderflügel, spitz, ohne Auswendung vor der Spitze, mit starker Convexität des Hinterrandes an der gewöhnlichen Stelle, lebhaft seidenglänzend, weissgrau, etwas durchscheinend. Franzen mehr staubig grau, weniger glänzend.

Unterseite einfarbig, glänzend; die Vorderflügel grau, hinten mit einer sehr feinen gelblichen Linie eingefasst. Hinterflügel am Vorderrande staubgrau, sonst wie auf der Oberseite.

'Isis,' 1847, p. 846.

GELECHIA DETERSELLA, n. sp.

Alis anterioribus exalbidis, obsolete lutescenti-subvenosis, puncto disci post medium fusco, lineola obliqua baseos cinnamomea, antennis fusco alboque annulatis (♂, ♀).

Grösse der *Cinerella*, aber die Flügelbildung eine ganz andre;

nehmlich die Hinterflügel fast so schmal, wie die Vorderflügel und vor der stark vorgezogenen Spitze tief ausgerandet; unter allen mir bekannten *Gelechien* zeichnet sich *detersella* durch den zimmetbraunen Strich auf den bleichen Vorderflügeln aus, der von der Schulter herabgeht und sehr schräg bis zur Flügelfalte reicht. Ihren Tastern nach gehört sie zur ersten Abtheilung der *Gelechien*. Kopf, Rückenschild und Vorderflügel gelblichweiss; der obere Augenrand hinter den Fühlern, der Rückenschildrand unter den Schulterdecken und diese selbst an ihrem Innenrande hell zimmetbraun.

Wurzelglied der Fühler lang, nach oben verdickt, gelbbraun auf der Unterseite, desgleichen in einer Längslinie auf der Vorderseite und am obern Rande weiss; die Peitsche zierlich weiss und braun geringelt, auf der Unterseite mit sehr getrennten kurzen Sägezähnen, die gegen die Spitze deutlicher werden. Maxillartaster dünn fadenförmig, auf der Basis des kurzen beschuppten Rüssels gegen einander geneigt. Lippentaster lang, sehr gekrümmt, zusammengedrückt, weisslich; das zweite Glied gelblich beschmutzt, gegen die Spitze nicht erweitert; das dritte Glied dünner, ein wenig länger als das zweite, zugespitzt, gegen die Spitze verdunkelt bräunlichgelb, auf der Schneide mit weisser Längslinie.

Beine schmutzig gelblich weiss; die 4 vordern auf der Vorderseite ausser der Vorderhüfte und den Gliederspitzen gebräunt. Hinterschienen auf der Rückenschneide reichlicher und länger behaart als auf den entgegengesetzten. Hinterleib mehr mit Grau gemischt als der Rückenschild, mit ziemlich langem Afterbusch.

Vorderflügel schmutzig weiss, auf den Adern verloschen lehmgelblich; diese Färbung tritt am meisten hervor vor der Mitte, wo in der Flügelfalte ein kurzes, bräunliches Längsstrichelchen liegt, ferner auf den Adern hinter dem Queräderchen, auf welchem ein länglicher, brauner Punkt liegt, und zuletzt in der Flügelspitze. Einzelne lehmgelbe Schuppenspitzen reichen bis auf die Mitte der Franzen. Von den Schultern geht ein sehr schiefer, hell zimmetbrauner Strich verjüngt bis zur Flügelfalte.

Hinterflügel sehr hellgrau, unter der langen Spitze stumpfwinklig tief ausgerandet; die bleichgelblichen Franzen sind sehr lang.

Unterseite bleichgelb, die Vorderflügel beim Männchen im Mittelraum bräunlichgrau staubig, mit matt durchschimmerndem bräunlichem Mittelpunkte. Das Weibchen hat etwas kürzere Flügel und einen spitzern, breitern Hinterleib; die Vorderflügel sind unten im Mittelraum nicht verdunkelt.

'Isis,' 1847, p. 847.

GELECHIA SEGETELLA, n. sp.

Alis anterioribus vitellinis, lituris tribus dilute cinnamomeis (prima subfasciata obliqua, secunda annulata, tertia apicali); posteriorum ciliis cinereo-flavescentibus (♂, ♀).

Sehr ähnlich der *Gelechia ferrugella*, aber sicher verschieden; grösser; der zweite Wisch der Vorderflügel hat eine gegen die Basis gerichtete, scharfe Ecke; die Hinterflügel haben einen vor der Spitze convexeren Hinterrand und die Spitze selbst schärfer, die Hinterflügelfranzen sind gelbgrau oder ganz gelb. Auch der folgenden *flammella* ist sie ähnlich und verwandt; aber diese ist kleiner und hat einen blassgelben Thorax mit rostgelben Schulterdecken; die Spitze der Vorderflügel ist rostroth, die der Hinterflügel spitzer, etc.

Kopf, Rückenschild und Vorderflügel dottergelb; die Hinterkopfschuppen aufwärts und etwas gegen einander gekämmt. Wurzelglied der Fühler lang, gelb; Peitsche auf dem Rücken kurzborstig, gegen die Spitze immer deutlicher gezähnet; auf der Bauchseite sehr zart gefranzt; ihre Farbe ist grau, nach oben etwas geringelt. Maxillartaster gelb, kurz und dünn, auf der Basis des gelbschuppigen, aufgerollten Rüssels ruhend. Lippentaster lang, aufgekrümmt, schlank, dottergelb. Das zweite Glied zusammengedrückt, überall gleich breit, oben abgeschnitten; das dritte Glied von $\frac{2}{3}$ Länge des zweiten, dünn, feinzugespitzt.

Beine helldottergelb; die Vorderbeine mehr als die Mittelbeine auswärts grau bestäubt, gegen die Füsse lichter. Hinterschienen verdickt, langhaarig, besonders obenauf; von den 4 Dornen ist der eine des obern Paares der längste; er reicht fast bis zur Spitze des Schienbeins. Hinterleib hellgelb, auf dem Rücken in der Mitte der Ringe grau; der Bauch ist in der Mitte gekielt und zu beiden Seiten der Schneide in einem nach hinten verdünnten Streifen zimmetfarbig angeflogen. Afterbusch mässig lang; beim Weibchen steht der Legestachel aus demselben hervor.

Vorderflügel schmal, mit zugespitztem, doch nicht scharfem Vorderwinkel, am Hinterwinkel abgerundet, 4''' lang, dottergelb, an der Basis des Vorderrandes etwas verdunkelt. Vor der Mitte geht ein schräger, bindenförmiger Wisch gewöhnlich vom Vorderrande aus und erreicht selten, und nur verloschen und verdünnt den Innenrand. Der zweite Wischfleck liegt weit hinter der Flügelhälfte; er fängt auf dem Vorderrande mit einem dunklen Flecke an; sein Innenrand bildet über der Mitte einen spitzen, gegen die Basis gerichteten Winkel, dessen viel längerer, unterer Schenkel schief in den Innenwinkel läuft; nach aussen ist dieser Flecken nicht abgegränzt, indem er hier mehr in die Grundfarbe verschmilzt; er wechselt sehr in der Breite bei den verschiedenen Exemplaren. Der dritte Wisch kommt schief aus der Flügelspitze und geht nicht selten mit dem vorhergehenden Fleck über dessen Mitte zusammen. Zwischen beiden bleibt ein auffallender, heller Vorderrandfleck, der schief einwärts gerichtet ist, und dem über dem Innenwinkel eine lichte Stelle als Gegenfleck entspricht. Auch der Hinterrand ist verdunkelt. Alle diese Zeichnungen haben eine helle zimmetbraune Farbe. Die Franzen sind lichter als die Wische, am dunkelsten über der Flügelspitze.

Hinterflügel bleigrau, etwas glänzend; die Franzen graugelblich, am hellsten gegen die Spitze.

Unterseite etwas glänzend; die dunkelgrauen Vorderflügel haben an der Mitte und vor der Spitze des Vorderrandes und ausserdem am Hinterrande einen hellgelben Wisch, welche Zeichnungen oft sehr verwischt und unkenntlich sind; ebenso sind die Vorderflügel. Die hellgrauen Hinterflügel sind an der Spitze etwas strichig gelb; die Franzen wie auf der Oberseite; nur durch eine deutlichere gelbe Linie von der Flügelfläche getrennt.

'Isis,' 1847, p. 850.

GELECHIA PLEBEJELLA, n. sp.

Alis anterioribus nitidulis lutescenti-griseis, punctis ad basim duobus, quatuor in disco (1, 2, 1) *longitudinaliter dispositis fuscis, posterioribus apice abrupte producto; palporum articulo ultimo fuscopunctato* (♂).

In der Mitte stehend zwischen *Gelechia terrella* und *senectella*; in der Grösse noch unter den kleinsten Exemplaren der ersteren, dagegen ansehnlich über der *senectella*. Von ersterer unterscheidet sie sich sehr leicht durch die längere, durch eine tiefere Ausrandung mehr hervortretende Spitze der Hinterflügel,—*senectella* hat sie ebenso,—von beiden durch das ein wenig kürzere Endglied der Taster und die Zeichnung der Vorderflügel. Auf dem, wie bei der hellen var. von *terrella* gefärbten, nur reinerem Grunde liegt auf dem Vorderrande nicht ganz an der Basis ein scharfer, schwarzbrauner Punkt; unter ihm ein weniger gut abgegrenzter dicht am Innenrande; diese beiden Punkte fehlen bei den genannten beiden Arten, und der dritte ist, wenn er vorkommt, verwischt; er liegt nicht sehr weit von ihnen auf der Flügelfalte und ist länglich. Das Mittelpaar ist so deutlich wie der einzelne hintere. Die helle Querbinde ist kaum als solche kenntlich; an der Spitze ihres nach aussen gerichteten Winkels ist ein ziemlich deutlicher Punkt, der Raum dahinter aber staubig verdunkelt.

Die Hinterflügel sind glänzender und heller grau; die Franzen an der Basis gelblich.

Auf der Unterseite sind die Vorderflügel von den Franzen durch eine feine, gelbliche Linie geschieden.

Kopf und Rückenschild sind fahlgelblich, heller als die Vorderflügel, vorzüglich das Obergesicht. An den braun und gelbgrau geringelten Fühlern ist das Wurzelglied obenauf schwarzbraun. An den Tastern ist das zweite Glied auswärts nicht verdunkelt, und das Endglied auf der Bauchseite (bei *terrella* weniger deutlich) mit 5–6 braunen Punkten der Länge nach gezeichnet. Die Beine sind gelblicher als bei den zwei verwandten Arten.

Das einzelne schöne Exemplar fing ich bei Syracus am 5. Mai, als ich bei Regenwetter am Rande eines Weizenfeldes einige Pflanzen ausrupfte, wodurch es zum Auffliegen gebracht wurde.

'Isis,' 1847, p. 851.

GELECHIA LAMPROSTOMA, n. sp.

Alis anterioribus fuscis, vitta dorsali flavescente, striga media maculaque costæ postica niveis; palpis albis nitidis (♂).

Keiner mir bekannten Art ähnlich und sehr schön. Grösse der

Gelechia flammella, aber mit stumpferen Vorderflügeln. Kopf und Rückenschild hell lehmgelb, Schulterdecken weisslich. Fühler bräunlich, schwach geringelt; Wurzelglied lang, nach oben verdickt, obenauf braun, unten weisslich; Peitsche auf der Unterseite sehr weitläufig und ziemlich stark sägezähnig (mit etwa 32 Zähnen) und dazwischen gefranzt. Maxillartaster dünn, fadenförmig, auf dem schmalen Rollrüssel liegend. Lippentaster lang, aufgekrümmt, seidenglänzend weisslich, das zweite Glied, zusammengedrückt, schneidig, an der Spitze grau; Endglied von $\frac{2}{3}$ Länge desselben, dünn, zugespitzt, auf dem Rücken der Länge nach weiss, übrigens grau.

Beine schmutzig hellgelb grau, glänzend, die vier vordern auf der Lichtseite bräunlich. Hinterschienen obenauf spärlich mit längern, braunen Haaren bekleidet. Hinterleib braungrau, an Bauch und Afterspitze seidenglänzend weissgrau.

Vorderflügel fast 3''' lang, nach hinten wenig erweitert, etwas stumpf mit schrägem Hinterrande, tief gelbbraun, auf der Hinterhälfte heller. Den Innenrand bildet eine nicht sehr breite, hellgelbliche Strieme, die von der Mitte einwärts eine kleine Ecke hat. Der Vorderrand ist von der Basis auf $\frac{1}{4}$ der Flügellänge glänzend dunkelgrau. Auf der Mitte kommt ein vom Vorderrand schräg auswärts herabgehendes, anfangs breites, dann allmählich verdünntes, schneeweisses Querband, welches gegen die Basis zu sehr scharf begrenzt ist, hinterwärts aber in glänzende, silbergraue Färbung übergeht. Dahinter folgt ein schwarzer Mittelpunkt. Vor der Flügelspitze ist ein grosser, schneeweisser Vorderrandfleck, aus dessen Spitze bis zum Hinterrande eine gebogene, silbergraue Linie herabgeht. Den Hinterrand fassen schwarze Schuppenstriche ein, die um die Flügelspitze mit weissen, einzelnen Schuppen gemischt sind. Franzen grau einwärts perlartig schillernd.

Hinterflügel hellgrau, nach hinten erweitert, vor der etwas vorgezogenen Spitze mit einer stumpfen Ausrandung. Franzen dunkler grau, an der Basis gelblich.

Unterseite glänzend grau, auf den Vorderflügel scheinen die Querlinien, der schwarze Punkt dahinter und der weisse Flecken vor der Spitze sehr verloschen durch; der Innenrand ist gelblich.

Das einzelne Männchen fing ich bei Syracus in der Gegend des Capucinerklosters auf einer kurzbegrasten Stelle des Kalkfelsens gegend Abend.

'Isis,' 1847, p. 853.

GELECHIA SALINELLA, n. sp.

Alis anterioribus dilute griseis, fusco pulvereis, punctis duobus ante, uno post medium fuscis ferrugineo cinctis; posterioribus paulo latioribus canescentibus; palpis mediocribus, articuli ultimi basi annuloque fuscis (♂, ♀).

Var. b. *alarum anteriorum punctis tantum luteis.*

Sehr nahe der *Gelechia inustella*, Z., die ich Isis, 1839, S. 201, 70, als Varietät der *Gelechia Artemisiella* aufgeführt habe, und die doch wohl eigene Art ist; ausserdem, dass die ganze Färbung von *salinella* viel heller ist, unterscheidet diese sich wesentlich durch die Hinterflügel, welche bei ihr breiter sind als die Vorderflügel, während bei *inustella* das Umgekehrte Statt findet.

In der Grösse ist *salinella* gewöhnlich etwas über *G. Artemisiella*. Kopf, Rückenschild und Vorderflügel sehr hell gelblich grau, letztere am meisten braunstaubig, der Kopf am reinsten und daher am hellsten. Oft sind die Schulterdecken lehmgelblich, wenn nehmlich die Vorderflügel an der Basis ebenso streifig gezeichnet sind. Fühler deutlich braun und weisslich geringelt, am Wurzelgliede auf der Schattenseite gelblich. Lippentaster nur von mittelmässiger Länge, noch heller bleichgelb als die Stirn; das zweite Glied auswärts und am Bauche oft bräunlich bestäubt; es ist zusammengedrängt, aufgekrümmt, an der Basis dünner, dann durch Schuppen stark erweitert, am Bauche (bei seitlicher Betrachtung) gleichsam gekerbt, in der Mitte mit tiefer Längsfurche; das Endglied dünn, zugespitzt, an der Basis braun und vor der Spitze mit einem braunen Ringe, der auf der Bauchseite sich sehr erweitert. Beine bleich, auf der Lichtseite ausser an den Gliederspitzen reichlich bräunlich bestäubt. Hinterleib grau, am Bauche und dem Afterbusch sehr hell schmutzig gelblich. Der weibliche Legestachel steht hervor.

Die Vorderflügel sind am Vorderrande und gegen die Spitze am reichlichsten braunstaubig, und dieser Staub reicht um die Spitze weit in die Franzen hinein, ohne auf denselben deutliche Querlinien zu bilden. Die braunen Stäubchen sind nichts als die braunen Spitzen der langen Schuppen, die an Länge gegen die Spitze zunehmen. Die meisten Exemplare sind auf der Subcostalader und in der Flügelfalte und auf den Adern in der Gegend der Querader hell rost- oder lehmgelblich. Unter den Verdunklungen des Vorderrandes nimmt sich nur eine nicht sehr fern von der Basis als ein Punktfleckchen aus; doch fehlt dieses auch bisweilen. Vor der Flügelmitte stehen auf lichterem Grunde auf rostgelber Unterlage zwei braune Punkte schräg unter einander, der untere näher gegen die Basis in der Flügelfalte (ganz wie bei *inustella*); hinter der Flügelmitte ist fast in gleicher Höhe mit dem obern Punkte des beschriebenen Paares ein strichförmiger, ähnlich beschaffener Punkt, der sich gewöhnlich in zwei auflöst; diese zwei stehen schräg hinter einander, nicht wie bei *inustella* unter einander, und der obere ist der grössere (bei *inustella*, wo sie getrennt sind, ist der untere grösser). Das helle, winklig gebrochene Band zeigt sich bisweilen ganz deutlich. Selten ist die Flügelspitze selbst verdunkelt.

Die Hinterflügel etwas breiter als die Vorderflügel, haben eine ziemlich lange Spitze, aber eine seichtere Ausrandung vor derselben als bei *inustella*; sie sind etwas glänzend, sehr hellgrau mit langen, an der Basis am meisten gelblichen Haaren.

Unterseite bleich gelblich grau, glänzend; alle Flügelspitzen sind mehr oder weniger deutlich punktartig verdunkelt.

Bei *var.* b fehlen auf den Vorderflügeln die dunkelbraunen Punkte und ihre Stelle ist durch Rostfarbe eingenommen.

'Isis,' 1847, p. 854.

GELECHIA REMISSELLA, n. sp.

Capite ac thorace lutescentibus; alis anterioribus griseis, basi lutescentibus, punctis disci fuscis, lineola ciliorum circa apicem fusca; palpis intus nitidis, articuli ultimi lineis duabus longitudinalibus niveis (♂).

Sie gehören zu den Arten, wo die Hinterflügel schmäler sind als die Vorderflügel, und kann bei *Artemisiella* stehen. Die zwei schneeweissen Längslinien an dem braunen Endgliede der Taster und der schwarze Bogen auf den Franzen um die Spitze der Vorderflügel zeichnen sie vor allen Arten aus.

Grösse der *Artemisiella*; Rückenschild und Kopf graugelblich, Stirn heller. Fühler schwarz und weiss geringelt, das lange Wurzelglied auf der Vorderseite mit einer dünnen, weissen Längslinie. Rüssel zusammengerollt, beschuppt. Lippentaster ziemlich lang, aufgekrümmt; das zweite Glied inwendig lebhaft glänzend, gelblich grau; auf dem Rücken und an der Spitze weisslich, auswendig dunkler, zusammengedrückt, allmählich erweitert, an der Spitze abgeschnitten; das Endglied etwas länger als das zweite Glied, dünn, feinspitzig, bräunlich, etwas glänzend, auf dem Rücken und der Schneide der Länge nach in zwei Linien weiss, die auf der Innenseite des Tasters durch eine bräunliche, dünne Linie getrennt werden. Beine schmutzig gelbgrau, auf der Schattenseite und an der Gliederspitzen weisslicher; Füsse am dunkelsten mit glänzend weissen Enden der Glieder. Hinterleib grau, am Bauch und Afterbusch gelblich.

Vorderflügel an der Basis, vorzüglich in der Flügelfalte hell lehmgelblich, übrigens hell staubgrau, bräunlich bestäubt. Etwa in halber Länge der Flügelfalte liegt ein schwarzbrauner Punkt, am Ende der gelblicher Farbe in derselben. Schräg darüber, gegen die Mitte zu, liegt ein verloschenes Pünktchen. Hinter der Flügelmitte in gleicher Entfernung zwischen Vorder- und Innenrand, ist ein deutlicherer, brauner Punkt, hinter welchem die helle Querbinde; diese ist nur bei dem einen Exemplar vollständig, bei dem andern nur in den Enden vorhanden; sie macht einen sehr spitzen Winkel in der Mitte. Die Franzen um die Spitze sind bräunlich bestäubt; sie enthalten vor ihrem Ende einen schwarzbraunen, gegen die Flügelspitze hohlen Bogen; die schwarzbraunen Punkte, woraus dieser besteht, sind die dunklen Enden weissgrauer, schmaler Schuppen.

Hinterflügel merklich schmäler als die Vorderflügel mit parallelen Gegenrändern, glänzend hell bleifarbig; vor der langen dünnen Spitze ist der Hinterrand unter einem stumpfen, fast geradlinigen Winkel tief ausgerandet. Franzen viel breiter als die Fläche, grau mit gelblicher Basis.

Unterseite glänzend grau, matt gelblich umzogen; die Franzen der Vorderflügel zeigen den braunen Bogen um die Spitze verloschen.

'Isis,' 1847, p. 855.

GELECHIA DIMINUTELLA, n. sp.

Minuta, alis anterioribus griseis fusco-pulverulentis, punctis fuscis ferrugineo cinctis; palpis mediocribus intus albis, articuli terminalis annulo fusco.

Noch kleiner als *Gel. inopella* (Isis, 1839, S. 201. 67), also die kleinste bis jetzt bekannte *Gelechia*, verwandt mit *Gel. Artemisiella*, verschieden aber, ausser durch die Kleinheit vorzüglich durch die kürzeren anders gefärbten Taster.

Rückenschild staubiggrau, Kopf weisslicher, um die Augen etwas bestäubt. Fühler braun und weiss geringelt. Lippentaster nur von sehr mässiger Länge und wenig aufwärts gekrümmt, weiss, aussen grau bestäubt; das zweite Glied ist zusammengedrückt und durch die reichlichen Schuppen auf der Unterseite ziemlich dick; das Endglied von wenig mehr als halber Länge des zweiten Gliedes, wenig gekrümmt, dünn, zugespitzt, über der Mitte mit einem breiten, braunen Gürtel. Rüssel aufgerollt, beschuppt; auf der Basis ruhen die weissen Maxillartaster. Beine hellgrau, auf der Lichtseite ausser an den Gliederspitzen bräunlich bestäubt. Hinterleib grau, flach, mit weissgrauem Seitenrande und Bauch und gelblichem Afterbusch.

Vorderflügel 1½–1¾''' lang, hell staubgrau, reichlich bräunlich bestäubt, die Stäubchen sind gegen die Spitze und auf den Franzen um dieselbe gröber. Braune, etwas eckige Punkte zeigen sich in der Flügelfalte, einer nicht sehr fern der Basis, der zweite auf der Mitte der Falte, der dritte schräg darüber mehr nach aussen gerückt, der vierte über den Innenwinkel ziemlich nahe der Flügelfalte, ein fünfter, strichförmiger, verwischter gegen die Flügelspitze. Alle liegen auf mehr oder weniger ausgebreitetem, blass rostgelblichem Grunde.

Hinterflügel merklich schmäler als die Vorderflügel, etwas glänzend, licht bleigrau mit tiefer, sehr stumpfer Ausrandung des Hinterrandes vor der langen dünnen Spitze. Franzen sehr lang, grau, an der Basis gelblich.

Die ganze Unterseite ist weissgrau, mit einer sehr verloschenen, gelblichen Linie umzogen.

'Isis,' 1847, p. 856.

GELECHIA NIGRINOTELLA, n. sp.

Alis anterioribus albis; puncto humerali, maculis 4 disci (prima majore obliqua) e squamis congestis nigris; palporum articuli secundi basi, apicali annulis duobus nigris (♀).

In der Grösse einer ganz kleinen *G. aleella*, F. (*bicolorella*, Tr.), aber sehr verschieden durch die Stellung und Schwäche der Flecke der Vorderflügel; vorzüglich aber durch die Schmalheit der Hinterflügel. Hiernach gehört sie näher zu der kleinern *Gel. lepidella*, F. R. (Isis, 1839, S. 202. 73), deren Zeichnung auch schwarz auf Weiss ist, jedoch auf eine ganz andere Weise; der *nigrinotella* fehlt die schräge Fleckenbinde der Vorderflügel, und ihre Flecke sind viel kleiner; auch sind die Vorderflügel selbst breiter. Rückenschild und Kopf etwas gelblich weiss mit wenigen, sehr feinen, braunen Stäubchen. Fühler schwarz und weiss geringelt. Rüssel breit, aufgerollt, weissschuppig. Taster mässig lang, zusammengedrückt, weiss; das zweite Glied an der untern Hälfte grauschwarz, gegen die Spitze unten beschuppt und erweitert; das Endglied von $\frac{3}{4}$ Länge des zweiten Gliedes, dünn, spitz, aufgekrümmt, unter der Mitte und vor der Spitze mit einem schwarzen Ringe. Beine weiss, auf der Lichtseite, am schwächsten die Hinterschienen, schwarz gescheckt. Hinterleib grau mit zugespitztem After ohne hervorstehenden Legestachel, am Bauche weisslich.

Vorderflügel ziemlich breit, weiss, im Mittelfelde und gegen die Spitze sehr bleich ochergelbfleckig. Der Vorderrand hat ein schwarzes Pünktchen an der Schulter, nicht weit davon einen Fleck und dann in ziemlich gleichen Abständen noch drei; der letzte liegt in der Spitze und auf den Franzen und löst sich mehr noch als die drei andern in Stäubchen auf. Schief unter und hinter dem ersten liegt, mit ihm ein unterbrochenen Schrägstrich bildend, in der Flügelfalte ein grösserer, eckiger Fleck. Zwischen dem zweiten und dritten Vorderrandfleck ist ein Fleckchen im Mittelraum; ein kurzer Staubstrich gegen die Spitze und ein Schuppenhäufchen am Innenwinkel. Die Franzen sind von einer doppelten, schwarzen Staublinie durchzogen, die an der Flügelspitze und mit dem letzten Schuppenfleck sich vereinigt.

Hinterflügel grau, viel schmäler als die Vorderflügel mit parallelem Vorder- und Hinterrande; letzterer ist vor der kurzen, scharfen Spitze sehr stumpf ausgerandet. Franzen sehr lang, an der Basis gelblich.

Unterseite bräunlich grau, die Hinterflügel wie oben. Die Vorderflügel sind dunkler, und die Franzen um die Spitze herum weiss, die des Vorderrandes bräunlich beschmutzt.

Das einzelne Exemplar klopfte ich am 26. Juni aus Eichenlaub in einer Lavawüste bei Vieranni oberhalb Catania am Fusse des Aetna.

'Isis,' 1847, p. 857.

Gelechia nigritella, n. sp.

Alis anterioribus fusco-nigris, guttulis duabus posticis oppositis pallidis obsoletis; posteriorum apice valde producto, palporum articulo terminali longo; antennis fuscis (♂).

Sehr nahe der *Gel. coronillella*, und von ihr nur durch die gestrecktern Vorderflügel und einfarbig braunen, nicht hell geringelten Fühler sicher zu unterscheiden.

Ein wenig grösser als ein gewöhnliches Männchen der *coronillella*. Die Vorderflügel sind schmäler und zugespitzter; dunklere Punkte lassen sich im Mittelraum nicht wahrnehmen, ausser einem schwer bemerklichen in der Flügelfalte zu Anfange des letzten Drittels. Die beiden hellen Gegenpunkte sind sehr klein und verloschen, zumal der untere; dieser steht mehr einwärts gerückt, statt wie bei *coronillella* senkrecht unter dem andern.

Die heller grauen Hinterflügel haben im männlichen Geschlecht eine stärker verlängerte Spitze; die Ausrandung darunter ist viel stumpfer, und der hervortretende Theil des Hinterrandes vor derselben ist flacher abgerundet.

Die ganze Unterseite ist etwas heller als bei *coronillella.*

Die Fühler sind bei dieser recht deutlich braun und weiss geringelt und haben am Wurzelglied an der Unterseite einen weissen Längsstrich; bei *nigritella* sind sie ganz einfarbig braun, auf der Unterseite des Wurzelgliedes weisslich. An den Tastern beider Arten ist das letzte Glied das längste; bei *coronillella* hat es aber auf der äussern und innern Seite eine weisse Längslinie; bei *nigritella* schimmert es auf der ganzen Innenseite wie das zweite Glied, und ebenso auf dem Rücken weisslich, keinesweges in einer feinen Linie. Hinterschiene und Fuss sind bei *nigritella* schlanker.

Das einzelne Männchen fing ich am 3. April hoch im Gebirge bei Messina am Südabhange eines Berges zwischen wilden Lupinen.

'Isis,' 1847, p. 858.

GELECHIA PAUPELLA, n. sp.

Alis anterioribus albidis, lineis longitudinalibus flavidis fusco marginatis; striga marginis postici latiore utrimque attenuata (♂).

Die nächste Verwandte der *Gelechia Inopella* (Isis, 1839, S. 201. 67), und fast scheint sie bloss eine vergrösserte, schärfer und gelblicher gefärbte Form des Südens zu sein; allein ihre Taster sind verhältnissmässig länger und ihr Rüssel ist kürzer.

Beträchtlich grösser, nehmlich Vorderflügellänge 2¾''' (bei *inopella* 2¼'''); im Ganzen wie *inopella* an die *Coleophoren* erinnernd durch die schmalen, langfranzigen Flügel und die längsstreifig Zeichnung der Vorderflügel.

Kopf und Rückenschild weiss; Fühler weisslich, gegen die Spitze deutlicher, dunkelgrau geringelt. Rüssel nur von der Länge der Lippentaster (zufällig aufgerollt). Lippentaster gekrümmt, von dreimaliger Kopfeslänge, dünn, etwas zusammengedrückt, weisslich; das letzte Glied ein wenig dünner als das zweite, kürzer als dieses, zugespitzt. Beine weiss: die 4 vordern auf der Vorderseite braun, an den Gliederspitzen weiss. Alle Schienen sind langhaarig und zwar die langen Hinterschienen zweizeilig. Der hellgraue Hinterleib hat einen langen, weissgelblichen Afterbusch.

Vorderflügel weiss. Von der Basis geht dicht am weissen scharf begrenzten Vorderrande eine nach hinten gespitzte, gelbliche Strieme, vor der Mitte aufhörend (bei *inopella* ist der weisse Vorderrand breiter); unter der Flügelmitte kommt aus der Basis eine zweite, weiter reichende, länger verdünnte Strieme. Zwischen beiden geht eine dritte am zweiten Längsviertel anfangende, dünnere, am Anfange des dritten Drittels aufhörende. Unter der Spitze der zweiten ist nahe am Innenrande eine vierte und über der dritten unter dem Vorderrande eine kurze fünfte. Eine sechste endlich zieht auf dem Hinterrande; sie ist breit, verdünnt sich auf beiden Seiten und erreicht nicht die Gegenränder. Hinter ihr sind die Franzen noch weiss, geben dadurch das Ansehen, als ob der Hinterrand weiter ab sey, und lassen dadurch die Strieme getrennt von demselben erscheinen. Um die Spitze sind die Franzen mit zwei dem Hinterrande ziemlich gleich laufenden braunen Schuppenreihen bezeichnet; zwischen denen der Grund gelblich ist. Der Vorderrand hat an der Basis der Franzen 5 braune, weit getrennte Fleckchen. Alle Striemen sind mit zerstreuten, brauner Schüppchen auf den Rändern eingefasst.

Hinterflügel sehr schmal, etwas glänzend hellgrau mit ziemlich langer Spitze, von welcher der Hinterrand tief und stumpf ausgerandet ist. Franzen sehr lang und gelblichgrau.

Unterseite glänzend hellgrau, auf den Vorderflügeln dunkler; alle Franzen weisslicher als die Fläche.

Das einzelne Männchen fing ich bei Syracus an einem blumigen Wege durch die feuchten Aecker zwischen dem Anapo und den Säulen des Jupitertempels am 19. Mai.

'Isis,' 1847, p. 885.

COLEOPHORA CREPIDINELLA, n. sp.

Antennis albo fuscoque annulatis, articulis 3 basalibus squamatis, palpis mediocribus tenuibus, arcuatis; capite thorace alisque anterioribus nitidulis fusco-cinereis, harum costa anguste alba.

Nahe der *Coleophora niveicostella* und *albicostella*, F. R., in litt., aber ausser durch geringere Grösse, dunklere Farbe und schmäleren weissen Vorderrand der Vorderflügel besonders durch die Taster verschieden, die bei den genannten 2 Arten am zweiten Gliede in einen ziemlich langen Haarbusch auslaufen.

Grösse der gemeinen, im Mai fliegenden *otidipennella*. Kopf, Rückenschild und Vorderflügel sind glänzend dunkelbraungrau. Oberer Augenrand mit einer hinten erweiterten, schneeweissen Linie, die am ersten Fühlergliede hinaufsteigt. Dieses ist verdickt, schimmernd, ohne Haarbusch; die Oberseite der 2 nächsten Glieder ist mit Schuppen bedeckt, aber nur beim Weibchen etwas merkbar verdickt; der übrige Fühlertheil sehr deutlich weiss und braun geringelt. Das Gesicht ist unten fast weiss. Die Taster, beim Männchen etwas länger als beim Weibchen, sind aufgekrümmt, von doppelter Kopflänge, ziemlich dünn und weniger zugespitzt, aussen grau, innen weiss; das zweite Glied ist gegen die Spitze ein wenig verdickt und unterwärts mit etlichen verlängerten Haaren versehen. Rüssel dünn und klein. Beine glänzend grau. Hinterschienen wenig verdickt, spärlich langhaarig. Hinterleib dunkelgrau, auf der Wurzelhälfte obenauf reichlich gelb gemischt, und zwar so auffallend, dass es unnatürlich scheint; doch besitzen meine 3 Exemplare diese eigenthümliche Färbung. Der weibliche Legestachel steht aus dem kurzen, grauen Afterbusch hervor.

Vorderflügel einfarbig glänzend in der angegebenen Farbe, die nur in den Längsfalten bei gewisser Haltung hell streifig aussehen. Der Vorderrand ist von der Basis aus, sich nach und nach etwas erweiternd, fast schneeweiss, was auf dem hintersten Längsdrittel auf den Vorderfranzen allmählich in Grau übergeht.

Hinterflügel lang und dünn zugespitzt, oben sowie alle Flügel auf der Unterseite grau; die vordern an den Vorderrandfranzen heller.

'Isis,' 1847, p. 886.

COLEOPHORA PRÆCURSELLA, n. sp.

Antennis annulatis, basi non fasciculata, palpis apice furcatis; alis anterioribus dilute fuscis, costa lineisque disci longis usque in apicem perductis albis (♂, ♀).

Aus der Verwandtschaft der *otidipennella*, unter allen mir bekannten Arten durch die Zeichnung der langgespitzten Vorderflügel sehr ausgezeichnet; nur im Mittelraum laufen gerade, weisse Linien von der Basis aus zur Spitze, wovon nur die letzte die Spitze erreicht, indem die andern in ungleichen Abständen von denselben aufhören, wie sie auch ungleich anfangen.

Grösse der *lusciniæpennella*, die Flügelgestalt ist aber ganz anders. Rückenschild und Kopf graubraun. Schulterdecken und der obere Augenrand hinten weiss. Fühler bräunlich und weiss geringelt; das Wurzelglied bräunlich, auf dem Rücken mit einer weissen Längslinie, ohne Schuppenbusch; die 2 nächsten Glieder sind durch schwache Beschuppung kaum kennbar verdickt. Rüssel aufgerollt, schwach; Taster von Rückenschildslänge, horizontal, bräunlich; das zweite Glied haarschuppig, nicht sehr dick, an der Spitze mit einem Haarbusch; das Endglied dünn, ein wenig länger als dieser Busch, etwas aufgerichtet und mit ihm eine Gabel bildend. Beine schimmernd, hellbraun, auf der Schattenseite weisslich; Hinterschenkel und Schiene auf der Lichtseite mit weisser Längslinie; Hinterschiene mässig behaart. Hinterleib braungrau.

Vorderflügel in eine lange, dünne Spitze auslaufend, glänzend gelbbraun. Der Vorderrand ist auf $\frac{2}{3}$ seiner Länge von der Basis aus in einer ziemlich breiten, nach hinten verdünnten Linie weiss. Die weissen Linien des Mittelraumes lassen sich zusammengenommen als eine hinten verdünnter Strieme betrachten, welche sehr schräg von Linien der Grundfarbe durchzogen wird. Die erste dieser weissen Linien kommt aus der Mitte der Basis, läuft unter der Flügelfalte und hört verdünnt am Anfange des zweiten Drittels desselben auf; die zweite Linie, über der ersten nahe der Basis verdünnt anfangend, läuft in der Flügelfalte bis ans Ende desselben fort, wo sie abgebrochen aufhört; die dritte beginnt dünn über der zweiten, viel entfernter von der Basis, ist weit dünner und hört entweder vor dem Ende desselben auf oder vereinigt sich über demselben mit der vierten Linie. Diese entspringt fast über der Mitte der dritten und läuft bis zum Hinterrande; vor demselben geht aber ein Ast ab, der sich bis in die äusserste Flügelspitze hin fortsetzt. Der Innenrand hat nichts Weisses. Bei einem Männchen zeigt sich noch in der Nähe des Vorderrandes über der Vereinigung der dritten und vierten Linie eine kurze weisse Längslinie.

Hinterflügel in eine lange, feine Spitze ausgezogen, braungrau. Ebenso die ganze Unterseite, wo aber die 4 Flügelspitzen einen weissen Längsstrich, am deutlichsten auf den Vorderflügeln zeigen.

'Isis,' 1847, p. 887.

COLEOPHORA FRETELLA, n. sp.

Antennis albis obsolete annulatis, articulo basali ochraceo non fasciculato, capite ochraceo, palpis apice furcatis; alis anterioribus ochraceis, subopacis, costa, linea disci longitudinali lineaque plicæ albis (1 ♂).

Verwandt mit *fringillella*, Isis, 1839, S. 208. 21,—viel kleiner; die Vorderflügel fast von der Basis aus verdünnt, statt bis zum Hinterwinkel gleich breit zu bleiben; die weissen Linien nicht scharf; die mittlere kaum den Hinterrand erreichend, statt sich zu biegen und bis in die Nähe der Spitze zu gelangen. Viel ähnlicher ist sie der folgenden Art, und den Unterschied giebt vorzüglich die Farbe des Kopfes und die längere Tastergabel.

Grösse unserer Frühlings-*otidipennella*. Kopf, Rückenschild und Vorderflügel angenehm hell ochergelblich. Fühler etwas dick, weiss, blassgrau geringelt; das Wurzelglied beschuppt, von der Farbe des Kopfes, ohne Haarbusch. Taster von Rückenschildslänge, von der Basis aus verdickt, aussen ochergelb, innen weiss, das zweite Glied endigt in einen, oben der Länge nach ausgehöhlten Haarbusch, der etwa die halbe Länge des zweiten Gliedes hat; das Endglied dünn, etwas aufgerichtet, von der Länge des Haarbusches. Beine schmutziggelb, auf der Schattenseite weisslich; Hinterschiene wenig verdickt mit mässig langen, spärlichen Haaren. Hinterleib dunkelgrau mit weisslichem Afterbusch.

Vorderflügel gegen die Spitze angenehmer gelb, als gegen die Basis; fast ohne allen Glanz. Auf dem Vorderrande zieht eine weisse, an der Basis dünne, allmählich verdickte Linie, die sich auf den Franzen bis in die Spitze fortsetzt; hinterwärts wird sie mehr gelblich. In der Flügelfalte geht von der Basis bis zum Hinterrande eine dünne, weisse Linie. Zwischen ihr und der Vorderrandlinie, doch ihr etwas näher, ist eine weisse, dünne Längslinie, weit vor der Basis und fein anfangend und (doch kaum konntlich) in den Hinterrand mündend. Der ganze Innen- und Hinterrand ist sehr fein weiss eingefasst. Franzen hellgelblich.

Hinterflügel glänzend grau, hellgelblich gefranzt, sanft* zugespitzt.

Unterseite grau, blassgelbfranzig; die Vorderflügel am Vorderrande, die Hinterflügel auf der Hinterhälfte weisslichgelb.

'Isis,' 1847, p. 887.

COLEOPHORA PABULELLA, n. sp.

Antennis albis, obsolete annulatis, articulo basali albido, non fasciculato; capite cinereo; palpis apice brevius furcatis; alis anterioribus ochraceis, subopacis, costa, linea disci longitudinali lineaque plicæ albis (1 ♂).

Der vorigen in der Flügelzeichnung und Färbung so ganz gleich, dass ich sie bisher für dieselbe Art hielt. Die Verschiedenheit in den Tastern scheint aber eine specifische zu sein. Sie sind bei ver-

* See Linnæa Ent. iv. p. 313.

hältnissmässig gleicher Länge dicker; der Busch des zweiten Gliedes ist kürzer, und das dritte Glied ist gleichfalls verhältnissmässig dicker und plötzlicher zugespitzt und, wenn es die Länge des Busches hat, um ein merkliches kürzer als die halbe Länge des zweiten Gliedes. Zu dieser Verschiedenheit kommen weniger bedeutende: der Kopf gelblichgrau, am obern Augenrand, sowie der Aussenrand der Schulterdecken weisslich; das Wurzelglied der Fühler unten grau, obenauf der Länge nach weisslich. In der Körpergrösse steht *pabulella* hinter *fretella* zurück. Die Hinterschienen sind reichlicher behaart. Auf der Unterseite sind die Hinterflügel bloss in der Spitze weisslich beschuppt.

[In the fourth volume of the 'Linnæa Entomologica,' p. 312, Zeller refers this to *O. fretella* as var. *b*, and remarks, " zu den zwei in der Isis als verschiedene Arten beschriebenen Exemplaren fand sich noch ein drittes unter meinen Vorräthen, welches den Uebergang zwischen beiden bildet."]

'Isis,' 1847, p. 888.

COLEOPHORA DEVIELLA, n. sp.

Antennis albis, cinereo annulatis, articulo basali albo, non fasciculato; palpis rectis filiformibus, superne albis; alis anterioribus lutescenti-griseis unicoloribus (3 ♂).

Zu den einfarbigen Arten der Gruppe von *lusciniæpennella, coracipennella* gehörig; in dieser kenntlich durch sehr helle, fast staubgraue Grundfarbe der Vorderflügel.

Grösse unserer Frühlings-*otidipennella*. Rückenschild und Vorderflügel von gleicher Farbe; der Kopf gegen die Taster hin weisslicher. Fühler ziemlich dick, weiss hellgrau geringelt; das Wurzelglied ziemlich kurz, weisslich beschuppt, ohne Haarbusch. Rüssel dünn, aufgerollt, auf dem Rücken beschuppt. Taster kürzer als das Rückenschild, gerade fadenförmig, zugespitzt; aussen schmutzig gelblichweissgrau, innen weiss; das zweite Glied erweitert sich ein wenig gegen die Spitze, das Endglied ist halb so lang, spitz und wie das zweite etwas zusammengedrückt. Beine weisslich, auf der Lichtseite grau mit weisslichen Gliederspitzen, besonders an den Füssen. Hinterschienen nicht so stark zusammengedrückt, mässig behaart. Hinterleib grau mit gelblichem Afterbusch.

Vorderflügel einfarbig hell lehmgelb mit Grau gemischt, also licht gelblichgrau, am Vorderrande ein wenig heller. Franzen mehr grau. Hinterflügel glänzend grau, mit staubgrauen Franzen.

Unterseite wie die Hinterflügel; der Vorderrand der Vorderflügel ist an der Aussenhälfte schmal hell und gelblich; ebenso sind die Franzen und die Spitze.

'Isis,' 1847, p. 890.

ELACHISTA DOURNII, n. sp.

Alis anterioribus dilute vitellinis, basi apiceque albis, maculis disci quinque convexis auratis (♂).

Verwandt mit *Elachista pomposella*, sehr leicht an den in der Diagnose angegebenen Merkmalen kenntlich. Grösse wie *Gracilaria stigmatella*, doch veränderlich; ein Exemplar ist wie *Opostega spartifoliella*.

Kopf und Rückenschild weiss. Fühler kürzer als die Vorderflügel, bräunlich, heller fein geringelt; das Wurzelglied lang gestreckt, unten weiss, obenauf bräunlichgelb ausser an der Spitze. Maxillartaster fehlend. Rüssel sehr kurz, aufgerollt. Lippentaster lang, stark aufgekrümmt; das zweite Glied zusammengedrückt, unten etwas behaart; das Endglied dünn, spitz, kürzer als das zweite Glied, vor der Spitze mit einem grauen oder braunen Ringe. Beine weisslich, die vordern gelbbräunlich und weiss geringelt; die Hinterschiene langhaarig, weisslich und bleichgelb fleckig. Hinterleib gelblichgrau, hinten und am Bauch weisslich.

Vorderflügel am Wurzelviertel weiss mit einem blassdottergelben, schrägen Vorderrandfleck; darauf ist der Grund etwas dunkler gelb, gegen die Spitze aber ganz blass. An der Mitte des Vorderrandes ist ein kleiner weisser Fleck, ein andrer in den Franzen vor der Spitze. Im Mittelraum liegen 5 runde convexe Goldflecke, die zwei ersten vor, die zwei folgenden etwas hinter der Mitte; beide paarweis, jedes Paar schräg gestellt; der fünfte nahe am Hinterrande. Diese Flecke haben sehr grosse Schuppen; die starken Schatten lassen sie braun eingefasst erscheinen. Die Franzen um die Spitze sind weiss, am Hinterwinkel graubräunlich.

Hinterflügel lang zugespitzt, glänzend grau, mit gelblichgrauen Franzen.

Unterseite der Vorderflügel gelblichgrau, am Vorderrande weisslich mit etwas durchscheinenden, weissen Flecken; Hinterflügel weissgrau.

Die Franzen sind wie an der Oberseite.

Das Weibchen kenne ich nicht.

Dieses schöne Thierchen habe ich zu Ehren meines Freundes C. A. Dohrn, Präsidenten des Stettiner entomologischen Vereins, benannt.

'Isis,' 1847, p. 892.

ELACHISTA NIGRELLA, Hübner.

Drei Männchen am 18. März im Gebirge bei Messina gefangen, als sie an einem kräuterreichen Abhange am späten Nachmittag ganz nach der Weise der deutschen *nigrella* flogen.

Sie unterscheiden sich von dieser bei der genauesten Vergleichung in folgendem: Das Grau ihrer Vorderflügel ist heller als gewöhnlich. Bei zweien sehe ich in der Flügelfalte dicht an der weisslichen Binde einen braunen Längsstrich sehr deutlich; kaum merklich ist er beim dritten, kleinsten Exemplar; da er etwas in die Binde hineinragt, so erscheint diese dadurch nicht ganzrandig, sondern an der Mitte eckig. An denselben Stellen haben aber nicht selten hiesige Exemplare einen dunklen Fleck, der nur nicht so sehr hervortritt, weil der Grund dunkler ist, und dann zeigt sich auch der Hinterrand der Binde mehr oder weniger eckig. Eine specifische Verschiedenheit kann ich also um so weniger herausfinden, als Bau und Färbung der Kopftheile ganz einerlei sind.

'Isis,' 1847, p. 892.

ELACHISTA CONTAMINATELLA, n. sp.

Alis anterioribus albis, postice sordidis, costa grisea, lineola plicæ striolaque disci postica pone strigulam costalem fuscescentem nigris (3 ♂).

Nahe verwandt mit *cerussella*, Hb. 183, aber kleiner, mit weniger Gelb auf den Vorderflügeln und mit braunen Zeichnungen gegen die Spitze, die dieser fehlen.

Rückenschild und Kopf weiss. Fühler bräunlich grau, schwach gezähnelt, am verdickten Wurzelgliede weisslich. Maxillartaster von Rückenschildslänge, dünn, schwach gekrümmt, weiss, auch auf der Aussenseite. Beine schmutzig gelblichgrau, nach unten weisslich. Hinterschienen behaart und bedornt wie bei *cerussella*. Hinterleib grau, nach hinten weisslich, mit längeren Haaren an den Genitalien.

Vorderflügel weiss, hinten, sowie am Vorderrande und in der Falte unrein gelblich; der Vorderrand selbst braungrau. In der Flügelfalte liegt nicht weit vom Hinterwinkel ein dicker, schwarzer Längsstrich. Vor dem Anfang des letzten Längsdrittels kommt vom Vorderrande ein bräunlicher schiefer Strich herab, unter dessen Ende, dem Hinterrande etwas näher als dem Vorderrande, ein kleinerer und dünnerer, schwarzer Längsstrich liegt. Hinter ihm sind hier und da bräunlichgelbe Schüppchen zerstreut. Um die Spitze zieht auf der Aussenhälfte der Franzen eine Reihe bräunlicher Schüppchen.

Hinterflügel schmäler und gespitzter als bei *cerussella*, etwas glänzendgrau.

Unterseite grau, auf den Vorderflügeln dunkler; diese sind von einer feinen, blassgelblichen Linie umzogen und dadurch von den Franzen getrennt, welche um die Spitze besonders hell und weissgelblich sind und auch die bräunliche Schuppenreihe, wie auf der Oberseite besitzen.

Das Weibchen ist mir nicht bekannt.

'Isis,' 1847, p. 893.

ELACHISTA DISEMIELLA, n. sp.

Alis anterioribus albis, in ciliis rare fusco-squamulatis, punctis duobus disci distantibus fuscis, in mare costa alarum anteriorum fuscescente, posterioribus obscurius cinereis (♂, ♀).

Sehr ähnlich meiner *Elachista dispilella*, die aber weder braune Schüppchen, noch einen dunklen Vorderrand an den Vorderflügeln besitzt. Noch ähnlicher ist aber eine bei Wien aufgefundene Art, *dispunctella*, F. R. in litt., die irrig für die wahre Treitschkische

Elach. bipunctella angesehen wird; diese hat braune Schüppchen auf der Fläche der Vorderflügel umhergestreut; allein das Männchen (das ich bis jetzt bloss kenne) hat keinen bräunlichen Vorderrand der Vorderflügel, weissliche, nicht graue Hinterflügel und eine sehr helle Unterseite.

Kopf und Rückenschild weiss. Fühler blass gelbbräunlich, an der Vorderseite des weisslichen Wurzelgliedes mit einigen krausen Härchen. Taster hängend, spitz, dünn, weiss, auf der Unterseite etwas braungelblich, wie bei *dispunctella*. Vorder- und Mittelbeine bräunlichgrau; Hinterbeine viel heller, an den Schienen mit langen Dornen und Haaren. Hinterleib grau, nach hinten weisslich.

Vorderflügel weisslich mit einzelnen braunen Schüppchen, vorzüglich auf den Franzen um die Spitze. In der Flügelfalte, nicht weit von ihrem Ende, liegt ein brauner, länglicher Punkt; ein andrer fast auf der Mitte zwischen ihm und der Flügelspitze im Mittelraume. Der Vorderrand ist braun, beim Weibchen jedoch entweder gar nicht oder nur nahe der Basis. Die Franzen sind etwas schmutzig.

Hinterflügel glänzend dunkelgrau, beim Weibchen viel heller; die Franzen hell, besonders um die Spitze der Vorderflügel.

'Isis,' 1847, p. 893.

OPOSTEGA [CEMIOSTOMA], nov. sp.

Eine der *spartifoliella* nächst verwandte Art klopfte ich bei Messina am 8. April an einer mit *Cytisus triflorus* und *Arbutus* bewachsenen Anhöhe aus dem Gesträuch, nachdem ich schon mehrere Wochen früher ein Exemplar gefangen hatte.

Von beiden besitze ich nur einen einzigen Vorderflügel.

Die erste gelbe, braun eingefasste Halsbinde der *spartifoliella* fehlt ganz. Darauf befindet sich bei dieser über oder etwas hinter dem metallglänzenden Fleck eine zweite; bei der sicilischen *Opostega* steht sie dagegen um ein Beträchtliches vor dem Metallflecke. Auch scheint die folgende Zeichnung abzuweichen, was ich jedoch nicht weiter erörtern will, da die gegebenen Merkmale zur Unterscheidung hinreichen. Nur das bemerke ich noch, dass *spartifoliella* weisse, die sicilische Art auswärts braune Franzen hat*.

* This insect was subsequently described by Zeller in the 'Linnæa Entomologica,' vol. iii. p. 277, under the name of

CEMIOSTOMA ZANCLÆELLA, n. sp.

Alis anterioribus niveis, macula costali pone medium nulla, apice luteolo, striolis costalibus notato, macula marginis postici atra argyreo-pupillata.

Diese Art ist beträchtlich kleiner als *spartifoliella* und sogleich durch den Mangel des gelben Vorderrandstrichs hinter der Mitte der Vorderflügel kenntlich. Ich besitze von ihr nur den rechten Vorderflügel. Er ist silberweiss. Sein glänzender Hinterrandfleck hat eine breitere schwarze Einfassung vorn und hinten, als der von *spartifoliella*, und er liegt der Länge nach, statt wie bei dieser, querüber. Das Hellehmgelbe darüber reicht weiter in die Flügelfläche hinein; es ist am Vorderrande einwärts braun gesäumt und enthält einen weissen braungerandeten Vorderrandfleck. Die schwärzlichen Strahlen sind undeut

'Isis,' 1847, p. 896.

PTEROLONCHE, nov. gen.

Capilli decumbentes, epistomium obumbrantes.
Oculi hemisphærici; ocelli nulli.
Antennæ supra oculos antice insertæ, longæ; articuli basalis latus anterius pilis conchulæ instar cristatum est.
Palpi maxillares nulli.
Palpi labiales mediocres, porrecti, compressi, pilosi, articulo terminali declinato, breviore, acuto.
Haustellum nullum.
Pedes longiusculi, tibiæ posticæ compressæ, pilosæ, bis bicalcaratæ, pari calcarium priore ante apicem inserto.
Alæ lanceolatæ, acutæ, longius ciliatæ.
anteriorum cellula mediana simplex, postice 3 venas in marginem costalem, 5 in posticum emittit; venæ subdorsalis basis furcata; pterostigma nullum.
posteriorum cellula mediana postice emarginata unam venam in marginem costalem, 5 in posticum mittit.
Oviductus feminæ non exsertus.
Genus habitu simile *Scirpophago, Anchiniæ*, et *Plutellæ cultrellæ*; ab his generibus venarum et antennarum structura distinguitur, antennarum conchula insignitur. Larva, ut habitus et alarum color prodere videtur, in culmis vel graminum radicibus vivit. Locus generis incertus.

Nomen a πτέρον, ala, et λόγχη, lancea, ex alarum forma desumptum.

Den richtigen Platz für dieses Genus weiss ich noch nicht, und daher führe ich es hier auf. Zu den *Crambiden* gehört es nicht, da es lanzettförmige Hinterflügel hat und die Fühler vor, nicht auf dem senkrechten Durchmesser der Augen eingefügt sind. Eine Stelle bei *Anchinia* scheint zwar der Flügelgestalt und dem Aderverlauf nach vorläufig die passendste; Fühler- und Tasterbildung werden sie aber wohl später als irrig ausweisen.

'Isis,'.1847, p. 896.

PTEROLONCHE ALBESCENS, n. sp.

Major; alis anterioribus latiusculis albis fusco-cinereo-venosis.
Von der folgenden durch beträchtlichere Grösse, breitere Vorder-

---

licher als dort, weil die Franzen nur in der Nähe des glänzenden Hinterrandflecks weisslich, auswärts aber grau sind.
Die Unterseite grau, die Franzen weiss, an der Spitze grau; auch zeigen sich auf den Vorderrandfranzen zwei braune Querstriche.
Of *Zanclæella*, which I have introduced in my descriptions of Italian Lepidoptera as an *Opostega* without a specific name, I took two specimens near Messina in March and April, thinking they were our *spartifoliella*.
The slope on which I started them, from bushes of *Arbutus unedo* and *Cytisus triflorus*, produces, as far as I recollect, no *Spartium junceum*. Probably the *Cytisus* is the food-plant of this scarce species.

flügel, weisse Farbe derselben ohne Bestäubung und die durch dunkle Färbung stark hervorstehenden Adern verschieden.

Grösse wie *Anchinia rostrella* (Vorderflügellänge ♂ 6''', ♀ 7'''). Der ganze Körper ist weiss beschuppt; nur am langen Hinterleibe scheint auf der Oberseite die dunkle Farbe, ausser an den dicht beschuppten Ringrändern durch die weissen Schuppen grau hervor. Die schmutziggelblichen Fühler haben eine auffallende Länge, nehmlich etwas mehr als die Vorderflügellänge, mit kurzen, deutlichen Gliedern und sind schwach sägicht gezähnelt in beiden Geschlechtern; das Wurzelglied ist auf der Unterseite schwach ausgehöhlt und auf der Aussenseite mit einem sehr reichlichen Haarkamm versehen, der, wenn die Fühler anliegen, die Augen von oben her verdeckt; unter den Augen sitzt ein aufwärts gesträubter Haarbush, der sie von unten schützt. Taster und Vorderbeine auswärts gelbbräunlich angeflogen, jene kürzer als der Rückenschild. Hinterschienen mit 2 Paar dünner, ziemlich kurzer Dornen.

Vorderflügel weiss, alle Adern verloschen braungrau. Die Längsfalte unter der Medianader und die die Mittelzelle durchschneidende sind ebenso gefärbt; desgleichen eine Linie in der Mittelzelle, welche den äussersten obern Theil derselben als eine Nebenzelle abgrenzt.

Hinterflügel etwas glänzend, weisslich, nach aussen staubiggrau. Franzen ganz weiss, beim Männchen weniger rein und an der Basis von einer gelblichen, verloschenen Linie durchzogen.

Unterseite grau, die Vorderflügel dunkler, aber am Innenrande bis zur Falte weisslich, wie beim Weibchen alle Franzen. Alle Adern verdunkelt.

Ein schönes Pärchen fing ich bei Messina am Castellaccioberge nach Sonnenuntergang am 22. und 25. Juli im dürren Grase.

'Isis,' 1847, p. 897.

PTEROLONCHE PULVERULENTA, n. sp.

Minor; alis anterioribus angustulis exalbidis, antice griseo-pulverulentis, venis obscurioribus obsoletis.

Kleiner als die vorige Art (Vorderflügellänge 5''') und mit gestrecktorem Flügelbau. Grundfarbe des Körpers schmutzig gelbweisslich. Am Hinterleibe auf den ersten Ringen ausser an den reichlich beschuppten Hinterrändern durchscheinend grau. Taster länger und schlanker als bei *Pt. albescens*, auswärts grau angeflogen. Die den Ober- und Unterwimpern ähnliche Einrichtung der Beharung um die Augen ist beiden Arten gemeinschaftlich. Hinterschienen der *Pt. pulverulenta* schwächer behaart.

Die gelblichweissen Vorderflügel sind gelblich staubgrau angeflogen, am meisten vorn, und zunehmend gegen die Flügelspitze. In dieser Bestäubung treten auch die Adern auf der oberne Flügelhälfte, wenn auch ziemlich verloschen hervor, am deutlichsten die in den Vorderrand auslaufenden.

Hinterflügel glänzend gelblichweiss, an der Spitze ins Grauliche. Alle Franzen haben, sowie die Beharung der Beine einen auffallend gelben Ton gegen *Pt. albescens*.

Unterseite graugelblich glänzend, auf den Hinterflügeln heller, auf den Vorderflügeln mit etwas hervortretenden Adern.

Das Weibchen ist wie bei der vorigen Art an seinem zugespitzten Hinterleibe zu erkennen, der einen kürzern und dünnern Afterbusch hat als beim Männchen.

Ich fing 3 Paar nach und nach im Laufe des Mai bei Syracus auf einem dürren Anger in der Nähe des Kapuzinerklosters, wo ich sie aus verbissenem Gestrüpp schwer aufscheuchte. Ein Pärchen erhielt ich am 31. Mai jenseits des Anapo in einem trocknen Hohlwege im dürren Grase.

CHAPTER II.

HERR JOSEPH MANN.

INCITED, no doubt, by the result of Professor Zeller's visit to Sicily and Southern Italy in 1844, Herr Joseph Mann proceeded in the spring of 1846 to Tuscany, and collected there assiduously till the hot weather set in in July. The record of his then doings was published, with descriptions of the new species by Professor Zeller, in the 'Stettiner entomologische Zeitung' for 1849 and 1850.

It was anticipated that a similar excursion to some other portion of the Italian peninsula would soon have taken place; but Herr Mann's next visit to the south appears to have been in 1849, to Fiume, Istria, and Croatia. Of this excursion, however, we have unfortunately no distinct account, and only find accidental allusions to it in other notices. (Thus we read, ' Wiener entomol. Monatschrift,' 1857, p. 139, " Nachdem ich bereits im Jahre 1849 in der Gegend von Fiume gesammelt hatte.")

In 1850 Herr Mann, in company with Colonel Macchio, visited Dalmatia, and collected there for four months; they first went to the islands of Lesina and Lissa, then to Spalatro, whence they made numerous excursions, and ascended to the summit of Monte Bioccovo in July. (See note at foot of p. 54.)

In 1853 Herr Mann again visited Fiume, and collected in that neighbourhood from April to the middle of July; the account of this excursion appears in the first volume of the ' Wiener entomologische Monatschrift,' in 1857.

In 1854 Herr Mann visited in May and June a portion of Upper Carniola, making Wippach his headquarters, exploring the valley in all directions, and going sometimes over the pass to Görz; the result of this journey appeared in the ' Verhandlungen des zoologisch-botanischen Vereins in Wien ' of the same year.

In 1855 Herr Mann visited Corsica, where he remained from the 19th of April to the middle of July, and he published a notice of his Corsican captures in the ' Verhandlungen des zoologisch-botanischen Vereins in Wien ' for 1855.

In 1856 a journey to Sicily had been projected; but Herr Mann was taken ill *en route*, and obliged to return home. In 1858 he was more successful, and arrived at Palermo on the 10th of April, and remained collecting in that neighbourhood (having taken up his quarters at Morreale) till the beginning of July; the notice of this journey occurs in the ' Wiener entomologische Monatschrift ' for 1859.

In 1862 Herr Mann again visited Dalmatia, and collected at Zara and Spalatro, and also explored the islands of Brazza, Stolta, and Bua*.

The summers of 1860 and 1863 were spent in Asia Minor, and in 1865 Herr Mann visited the Dobrudscha; but in 1866 he returned to Southern Europe, and revisited Croatia, residing at Josefsthal during May and June and the beginning of July; the notice of his captures there occurs in the 'Verhandlungen des zoologisch-botanischen Vereins in Wien' for 1867.

In 1868 Herr Mann paid a third visit to Dalmatia, and collected at Ragusa and Gravosa, whence at the end of May he proceeded for a week to Cattaro, and then returned to Gravosa, which he left in the middle of June for Spalatro, where he remained three weeks*.

(I am aware that in 1867 Herr Mann visited the Tyrol, and collected at Botzen from May 4th to July 8th; but, though some few species collected there, such as *Stathmopoda Guerinii* and *Pyroderces argyrogrammos*, indicate a southern fauna, Botzen, from its geographical position, must rather be regarded as belonging to the Alpine district.)

SECTION I.

Tineina collected by Herr Joseph Mann in Tuscany in 1846, recorded by Professor Zeller in the 'Stettiner entomologische Zeitung,' 1850, pp. 59-64, 134-136, 139-162, 195-209, entitled "Verzeichniss der von Herrn Jos. Mann beobachteten Toscanishen Micro-Lepidoptera."

The opening paper of the series (Ent. Zeit. 1849, p. 200) begins with the following introduction:—

Herr Mann, who has a great reputation amongst entomologists as a dealer in insects, made a journey to Tuscany in the year 1846 principally with the view of capturing Micro-Lepidoptera, and collected there from March till the heats of July compelled him to return. With most indefatigable zeal he explored in turn the neighbourhoods of Pisa and Leghorn, of Florence and of Poppi and Pratovecchio. He found the neighbourhood of Florence much too cultivated, so that he did not obtain a satisfactory amount of captures; even Pratolino with its famed park proved comparatively barren in insects, since the trees and bushes are mostly evergreen, and nourish too few larvæ. Although at Leghorn the ground is also assiduously cultivated, yet he had here a most favourable hunting-ground, on the hills clothed with the most different kinds of trees, from the thick-growing fences of the various properties (poderi), amongst the tamarisk-bushes of the sea-coast, and the marshy meadows which alternated with woods of leaf-trees towards Pisa, in the pasture-fields so full of plants at Ardenza (three miles from Leghorn), and on the heath-clad mountains between Antignano

* Notices of the three Dalmatian journeys appear in the 'Verhandlungen der zoologisch-botanischen Gesellschaft in Wien' for 1869, pp. 371-388.

and Posignano, Montenero and Riparbella. The Apennines also about Pratovecchio and Poppi to near Arezzo, where the valley of Cassentino intersects, furnished a multitude of species of Micro-Lepidoptera. The repayment for trouble and cost was quite satisfactory, and Herr Mann would have already repeated the journey had not the political troubles of Italy commenced........

As I possess a considerable number of the enumerated species from Herr Mann, and have already published a considerable treatise on the Lepidoptera of Southern Italy, I seem to have a special vocation to edit Mann's observations. I give them entire, omitting only the new species which I have not before me for description and on which Mann himself gives no sufficient notice. My own observations are usually introduced between parentheses. The species which were observed in Italy by myself are indicated by an †, those communicated to me by Mann by an *.

1. *Exapate salicella*, Hb. On the 25th of March at Pratovecchio, on the trunks of alders by the Arno; scarce.
2. *Chimabacche fagella*, S. V. On the 9th of March at Florence; at the end of March at Pratovecchio, on the trunks of oaks; abundant.
3. *Talæporia pseudobombycella*, Hb. On the 19th May, several males taken in the marshes near Pisa.
4. **T. conspurcatella*, Kollar in lit. [Described by Zeller, see p. 70.] In March at Pratolino and Pratovecchio on an overhanging rock-face near the Arno; here during dull weather I took in the morning about twenty males.
5. *†*Eriocottis fuscanella*, Z. (*Tinea heterogenella*, Koll. in lit.). From the 21st April to the end of May at Salviano. In a deep grassy ditch both sexes were flying early in the morning and in the evening, but rather sparingly.
6. *Tinea masculella, Hb. At the end of March and beginning of April at Pratovecchio and Stia, not at all scarce, on hedges of wild roses.
7. *T. Zinckenii*, Z. At the beginning of April at Pratovecchio, not scarce among oak bushes.
8. *T. angusticostella*, F. v. R. [Briefly described by Zeller, see p. 71.] At the beginning of May at Ardenza and Montenero this flew singly near hedges, around excrement, late in the afternoon.
9. †*T. imella*, Hb. In the middle of May at Salviano and Leghorn, flying singly in ditches in the evening.
10. *T. rusticella*, Hb. At the end of May at Leghorn and Antignano, scarce in the evening near elder-hedges.
11. *T. ferruginella*, Hb. At the beginning of May in the marshes at Pisa; scarce.
12. *T. fulvimitrella*, Sod. In the middle of May near Leghorn, two specimens from a hedge between 5 and 6 A.M.

13. *T. tapetiella*, L. At the beginning of June at Pratolino, three specimens in a house.

14. *T. clematella*, F. At the end of May at Antignano, several specimens on maple hedges.

15. †*T. granella*, L. In May, near Leghorn; not scarce.

16. *†*T. pellionella*, var. *fuscipunctella*, Haw. In April on the walls of the sitting-room at Leghorn, several specimens every day. [Zeller, in the 6th vol. of the 'Linnæa Entomologica,' p. 158, refers this to *pellionella*, not to *spretella*.]

17. *T. ganomella*, Tr. In May at Antignano, on maple-hedges; scarce.

18. *T. comptella*, Hb. At the end of April and beginning of May at Leghorn, Salviano, Antignano, and Riparbella on growing hedges, especially where there is maple, not very scarce; it flies shortly before sunset, and is much larger than our Viennese *comptella*. (The male specimen sent is smaller than mine taken at Frankfort-on-the-Oder.)

19. *T. cæsiella*, Hb. In June at Pratovecchio, several times on sloe-hedges.

20. *T. cerasiella*, Hb. At the beginning of April at Pratovecchio and Leghorn, not scarce on sloe- and apple-trees.

21. *T. cratægella*, L. In May at Pisa, singly on sloe-bushes.

22. *Calantica dealbatella*, Z. Singly. (With no further notice.)

23. *Ochsenheimeria taurella*, S. V. In May at Leghorn, only twice, under dry leaves.

24. †*Micropteryx calthella*, S. In April at Pisa, singly on rushes.

25. *M. eximiella*, Koll., n. sp. [Described by Zeller, see p. 71.] On the 24th April at Montenero, where it swarmed on myrtle bushes in the midday sunshine.

26. *M. myrtetella*, n. sp. (*Zelleriella*, Mann in lit.). [Described by Zeller, see p. 72.] On the 5th of May at Montenero, not scarce, swarming amongst myrtle bushes and the tall heath in the sunshine before noon.

27. *M. Allionella*, F. At the beginning of June at Pratovecchio, in vineyards in the afternoon. (A male which I received from Mann I cannot distinguish specifically from our German species. It is smaller than usual, and, except in size, comes uncommonly near to *myrtetella*, and like that has no yellow scales on the hind margin of the anterior wings. The first fascia is not connected with the base by yellow scales; and its hind margin is not hollowed, and is sharply defined. The central fascia has the position usual in *Allionella*, but is much thickened, especially on the inner margin. The costal spot reaches almost beyond the middle of the wing; and there is a yellow dot on the costa, nearer to it than to the central fascia. But all these differences occur more or less united in varieties of the ordinary *Allionella*.)

28. *†*M. sicanella*, Z. Was also taken in Tuscany.
29. *M. amentella*, Z. (*violacella*, F. v. R. in lit.). [Described by Zeller, see p. 72.] At the end of March among young oaks on the hill of the castle Romeo.
30. **Nematopogon Swammerdammellus*, L. At the beginning of April at Pratovecchio, singly; in the middle of April near Leghorn, very abundant.
31. *N. Schwarziellus*, Z. In May at Salviano, only twice.
32. **N. Panzerellus*, Hb. [Described briefly by Zeller, see p. 73.] In the middle of April at Florence, Leghorn, and Pisa, on evergreen hedges; scarce.
33. **Adela fibulella*, S. V. In May at Pisa on flowers on the dry grassy places in the marshes; not scarce.
34. **A. cyanella*, Mann, n. sp. [Described by Zeller, see p. 73.] From the 18th of April to the 3rd of May at Leghorn; by a long hedge, in which there was much maple and *Tamarix*, it swarmed in the afternoon sunshine.
35. **A. Frischella*, Hb. In April at Pisa, in the marshes on the flowers of Umbelliferæ; scarce.
36. **A. laqueatella*, Z., n. sp. [Described by Zeller, see p. 74.] In May at Salviano, hovering abundantly over a bramble hedge before noon; it is much darker than our Viennese *Sulzeriella*, and the fascia of the anterior wings is of a more fiery yellow.
37. *A. associatella*, Z. In May at Antignano, three specimens taken on maple.
38. *A. DeGeerella*, L. At the beginning of May, abundant everywhere around Leghorn.
39. *A. paludicolella*, Mann, n. sp. [Described by Zeller, see p. 75.] On the 19th and 20th of May at Pisa in the marshes, on the flowers of a bushy *Erica*.
40. **A. viridella*, Scop. In the middle of April at Leghorn and Pisa, abundant amongst leaf-trees.
41. *A. cuprella*, S. V. At the beginning of April at Pratovecchio, only once, on willows by the Arno.
42. **Nemotois scabiosellus*, Scop. At the end of June at Pratolino; not scarce on scabious.
43. **N. ærosellus*, F. v. R. In the middle of June on the slopes of the Apennines; scarce. [Zeller reputes this not a distinct species, but merely a form of *scabiosellus*.]
44. **N. barbatellus*, Z. In the middle of May at Ardenza and Pisa in pasture-fields; only found a few times. (I received two worn males as *N. minimellus*?: their anterior wings have a less brilliant colouring than in *barbatellus*; and the posterior wings towards the base are of rather a paler grey. The less thickly haired palpi do not make me hesitate in referring them to *barbatellus*; some may have got worn off in flight.)

45. *Euplocamus Fueslinellus*, Sulz. Twice in the middle of May, at Pisa.
46. *Plutella cruciferarum*, Z. At the beginning of April on the Apennines and on the sea-coast, abundantly in several varieties.
47. *P. sequella*, Cl. At the beginning of May at Ardenza, on the trunks of elm trees; scarce.
48. *P. vittella*, L. At the end of May at Pisa, on the trunks of elm trees; not scarce.
49. **P. fissella*, Hb. At the beginning of May at Leghorn in oak woods; not scarce.
50. *P. sylvella*, L. In the middle of May at Leghorn, Antignano, and Montenero, in oak hedges, by no means scarce; also at Florence and Pratovecchio, on oaks.
51. *Plutella nemorella*, L. In May at Leghorn, Pisa, and Florence; in young bushes, singly.
52. *P. harpella*, S. V. In the middle of June at Pratovecchio, on the Apennines, sometimes.
53. *P. scabrella*, L. At the same place and time on the trunks of mulberry-trees; scarce.
54. *P. asperella*, L. At the end of April at Pratovecchio, beaten from oak trees, rarely.
55. *†*Ypsolophus exustellus*, Z. (*leucocephalellus*, Koll. in lit.). At the end of May at Pisa and Orciano, late in the evening on grassy places; scarce.
56. *Y. marginellus*, F. In June at Poppi, Bibbiena, and Pratovecchio in the morning, beat, not at all rarely, from juniper bushes.
57. *Y. juniperellus*, L. In the middle of June at Poppi, on juniper; three specimens.
58. †*Y. verbascellus*, S. V. In May at Leghorn, not scarce; rather greyer than those taken near Vienna.
59. *Y. silacellus*, Hb. At the beginning of May at Leghorn and Pisa, in dry grassy places towards evening; not very scarce.
60. *Y. fasciellus*, Hb. At the end of April and in May at Leghorn, Antignano, and Pisa, and in the beginning of June on the Apennines, in thorn hedges; not scarce.
61. **Y. lineatellus*, Kollar in lit. [Described by Zeller, see p. 75.] On the 20th of May at Pisa and Ardenza, in dry grassy places and pasture-fields. *In copulâ* at sunset.
62. **Y. striatellus*, S. V. Throughout May, everywhere around Leghorn, on the flowers of *Umbelliferæ*, in the sunshine; not scarce.
63. **Y. Kefersteiniellus*, Mann. Throughout May at Pisa and Ardenza, and on the 3rd of June at Pratolino, in the evening singly in pasture-fields and scarcer than *lineatellus*. (Mann considers my *striatellus*, var. *b*, a distinct species, in which view,

however, I still hesitate greatly to follow him. The transition from the markings of *striatellus* to those of *Kefersteiniellus* is very easily shown, and then the only remaining difference is the darker ground-colour of the latter.)

64. *Y. dolosellus*, F. v. R. At the end of May at Ardenza, in pasture-fields late in the evening, singly.

65. **Y. lanceolellus*, Kollar, n. sp. [Described by Zeller, see p. 76.] In the latter half of May at Ardenza and Salviano, in pasture-fields at sunset; very scarce.

66. *Y. imparellus*, F. v. R. On the 19th of May at Pisa, on grass, singly, during the midday heat.

67. *Holoscolia forficella*, Hb. At the end of May and beginning of June at Pisa and Pratolino, in dry grassy places, towards evening not very scarce.

68. *Anarsia spartiella*, Schr. At the beginning of May, at Antignano, in hedges; scarce.

69. **Anchinia punctella*, Costa (*monostictella*, Koll. in lit.). [Described briefly by Zeller, see p. 77.] Throughout May at Leghorn, Montenero, Antignano, Posignano, Riparbella, and Pisa, at the beginning of June at Florence and Pratovecchio, on grassy places and pasture-fields in the evening; not scarce.

70. **A. pyropella*, S. V. In May at Ardenza, on the Bagnio-heath; not at all scarce. Much paler than the Vienna specimens, indeed often of a greenish grey-yellow. (Of two Tuscan males one is indeed of a brighter yellow than my Vienna specimens, but the other scarcely paler; hence the pale colouring cannot be accepted as an inflexible rule for the Tuscan specimens.)

71. *A. rostrella*, Hb. At the end of May at Ardenza, in pasture-fields; much scarcer than near Vienna.

72. *A. bicostella*, L. At the beginning of June at Poppi, singly amongst heather.

73. *Harpella proboscidella*, Sulzer. At the end of May at Antignano and Montenero, among bramble hedges.

74. **H. Geoffrella*, L. (*Gruneriella*, Mann in lit.) From the 26th of April to the middle of May, at Salviano, Montenero, and Ardenza, this flew by thousands amongst evergreen hedges in the sunshine before noon. On account of its resemblance to Treitschke's *Geoffroyella* [for which Zeller has proposed the name *Staintoniella*] I collected but few, and did not discover the difference till I returned home to Vienna. I never saw any moth so abundant as this was.

75. *H. bracteella*, L. At the beginning of June at Pratolino, on young oaks, two specimens.

76. *Hypercallia Christiernini*, Z. From the middle to the end of June in the marshes of Pisa, in grassy places, in company with *Tortrix strigana*; very abundant. It did not occur near Leghorn.

77. *Dasycera Oliviella*, F. In June at Pratolino and Pratovecchio on young oaks, scarce ; its flight is, like that of the *Adelæ*, very jerking, but not of long continuance.

78. *Stenoptera orbonella*, Hb. On the 13th of April this swarmed by the sea-gate at Leghorn in the afternoon amongst vines and *Tamarix* ; on the 4th of May, two specimens at Antignano, likewise on *Tamarix*.

79. *Œcophora maurella*, S. V. In the middle of May at Salviano, on maple hedges, sometimes.

80. *Œ. minutella*, L. At the end of May at Leghorn and Ardenza in hedges under elms ; several specimens.

81. *Œ. trisignella*, Z. (*tripuncta*, Haw.). At the beginning of June at Pratolino, on sunny mountain-slopes, beaten from oaks, only three times.

82. *Œ. sulphurella*, H. At the end of May at Montenero, amongst fir trees before noon.

83. *Œ. albilabris*, Z., n. sp.? [Described by Zeller, see p. 77.] On the 10th of May at Salviano, on the trunks of elms, singly.

84. †*Œ. Lewenhoekella*, L. On the 7th of June [near Pratovecchio] on Monte Falterone, at a height of 7000 feet. [These were afterwards recognized as *Œcophora nodosella*: see captures in Upper Carniola in 1854].

85. *Œ. procerella*, S. V. At the end of May, two specimens at Leghorn on a fig-tree.

86. *Œ. Metznerella*, Tr. At the beginning of May at Antignano and Posignano, in hedges in which grew much barberry, before noon ; scarce.

87. *Œ. tinctella*, Tr. In May at Pisa, in June at Pratovecchio, on oaks.

88. *Œ. flavifrontella*, S. V. In June at Poppi, on oaks.

89. *Œ. lacteella*, S. V. In May at Leghorn in houses and on walls ; not scarce.

90. *Œ. aurifrontella*, H. At the end of May at Antignano, on hedges ; scarce.

91. *Œ. cuspidella*, S. V. At the beginning of June at Poppi, in mountain-meadows ; not scarce.

92. *Œ. gravatella*, Z. Three specimens taken in Tuscany ; Mann also took this species at Fiume, in June, in the evening, on *Salvia*.

93. *Œ. siccella*, Z. In May at Antignano, on the borders of fields, in the afternoon, singly.

94. *Œ. fulviguttella*, Z. In May at Riparbella on hedges ; two specimens.

95. *Œ. phycidella*, Z. Throughout May at Leghorn, Antignano, and Posignano, beaten out from dry thorn hedges, but not abundant.

96. *Œ. oleella*, Boyer de Fonscolombe (*Œ. adspersella*, Koll. in lit.).

[Described by Zeller, see p. 78.] From the 20th to the 30th of April at Salviano, after sunset, on an evergreen hedge; scarce.

97. *Hyponomeuta plumbellus*, S. V. In the middle of June at Pratovecchio, on *Euonymus*; common.

98. *H. irrorellus*, Hb. Along with the preceding, sometimes, on the trunks of trees.

99. †*H. Evonymi*, Z. In May around Legorn; not scarce.

100. *H. variabilis*, Z. In May at Pisa, on wild cherry-trees, several times.

101. †*Psecadia sexpunctella*, Hb. At Montenero, in the middle of May, three times.

102. †*P. echiella*, S. V. In the beginning of May at Leghorn, on a wall.

103. *P. funerella*, F. At the end of April at Montenero, in the evening, in leaf-woods; scarce.

104. **P. aurifluella*, Hb. From the 21st to the 29th of May I took at Ardenza and on the highest mountains of Montenero nearly 60 specimens; it sits on the large thistle-heads in pasture-fields, flies slowly in the noonday heat, and also copulates about the same time.

105. *Depressaria depunctella*, Hb. In June at Pratovecchio and Poppi, beaten from young oaks.

106. **D. liturella*, S. V. In June at Badia, on young oaks; not scarce.

107. *D. pallorella*, Z. In the middle of May at Leghorn, beaten from hedges in the evening; very scarce.

108. *†*D. assimilella*, Tr. In the middle of May at Leghorn, in hedges; not scarce; of a yellower grey than near Vienna. (The specimen sent me is rather small, but in colour resembles most of those of this country, and is thus much darker than my Neapolitan specimen).

109. *D. atomella*, S. V. In the middle of May at Ardenza, in pasture-fields in the evening; scarce.

110. *D. retiferella*, Koll. in lit. On the 26th of May I beat two specimens from *Tamarix* at the sea-gate of Leghorn; it differs from all other *Depressariæ* by the whitish reticulation of the brownish anterior wings. [Zeller in 1850 did not recognize this as a species distinct from *atomella*, but in 1854, in the 9th volume of the ' Linnæa Entomologica,' he admits its claim to specific rank. Zeller was in possession of a specimen from Sicily, not, however, captured by himself. This insect is the now well-known *Rutana* of Fabricius.]

111. *D. arenella*, S. V. At the end of March at Pratovecchio, beaten from oaks.

112. *D. vaccinella*, Hb. At the end of March at Pratovecchio, on bramble bushes, not very scarce; in April and May individual fresh specimens at Leghorn.

[113 is omitted].

114. †*D. rotundella*, Douglas (*peloritanella*, Z., *dilucidella*, Koll. in lit.). Four specimens taken along with *vaccinella*.

115. **D. laterella*, S. V. In the middle of June at Poppí, beaten from young oaks.

116. *D. depressella*, Hb. In the middle of June at Pratovecchio, likewise from oaks.

117. **D. badiella*, Hb. Sometimes taken along with *D. laterella*.

118. **Phibalocera fagana*, S. V. In May at Antignano and Posignano; abundant in oak plantations.

119. **Gelechia populella*, L. At the end of June, at Florence, on the trunks of poplar trees; not scarce.

120. *G. Denisella*, S. V. In the middle of May at Pisa, in the grass, several very small specimens.

121. *G. lobella*, S. V. At the end of April at Leghorn and Salviano, on thorn hedges; scarce.

122. *G. ferrugella*, S. V. In the middle of May at Ardenza, in hedges.

123. †*G. flavella*, Dup. (*segetella*, Z.; *ochrella*, Koll. in lit.). At the end of June at Ardenza, eight specimens taken in the afternoon and evening.

124. †*G. flammella*, Tr. At the end of April and throughout May at Leghorn, Antignano, Posignano, and Pisa, in pasture-fields, in the evening; not at all scarce.

125. **G. isabella*, F. v. R. in lit. [Briefly described by Zeller; this is the now well-known *G. rufescens*, Haworth.] In the middle of May at Leghorn and Antignano in the evening, singly on hedges.

126. **G. cinerella*, L. In May, everywhere around Leghorn; not scarce.

127. **G. velocella*, Dup. On the 19th of May at Pisa, in dry grassy places, in the marshes.

128. **G. gallinella*, Tr. In May at Pisa, on *Erica*; but not abundant.

129. **G. dryadella*, Koll. nov. sp. [Described by Zeller, see p. 79.] At the beginning of June at Poppi and Bibbiena, on very young oaks; very scarce.

130. **G. tamariciella*, Mann, n. sp. [Described by Zeller, see p. 80.] In May at Léghorn and Antignano, not plentiful, on *Tamarix* bushes, on which it flew before and after sunset, and also copulated.

131. *G. alacella*, Dup. At the end of May at Leghorn, sometimes on sloe-bushes.

132. *G. leucatella*, L. In the middle of June at Florence and at Pratovecchio, singly on sloe-bushes.

133. †**G. terrella*, S. V. From the middle of April to the end of May in the marshes at Pisa; very abundant.

134. *G. distinctella*, Z. In the middle of June, at Pratovecchio, beaten singly from oaks.
135. *G. zebrella*, Tr. At the beginning of June on the Apennines; scarce and dark-coloured.
136. *G. solutella*, Z. At the beginning of May at Montenero, singly on sunny slopes.
137. †*G. humeralis*, Z. In the middle of May at Pisa, singly on ash trees.
138. *G. pinguinella*, Tr. At the beginning of June at Pratovecchio, abundant on the trunks of poplar trees.
139. *G. proximella*, Hb. In the middle of May, two specimens at Antignano.
140. *G. triparella*, Z. In the middle of June at Poppi and Bibbiena, scarce, on oak trees.
141. *G. scriptella*, Hb. In the latter half of April at Pisa, on a growing hedge, very abundant; also at Salviano and Montenero.
142. *G. nigrinotella*, Z. (*nyctemerella*, Koll. in lit.). Only one specimen at the beginning of June, at Pratovecchio, beaten from an oak.
143. *G. aleella*, F. In June at Pratolino, Florence, Pratovecchio, Stia, and Poppi, on young oaks; not at all scarce.
144. *G. ligulella*, S. V. In May at Leghorn and Pisa, taken in hedges and on grass.
145. *G. tæniolella*, Z. In the middle of May in the marshes at Pisa, beaten from ash-trees.
146. *G. coronillella*, Tr. In June at Pratovecchio on the borders of woods.
147. *G. umbrosella*, Z. In June at Florence, five specimens taken amongst oak bushes.
148. †*G. anthyllidella*, Hb. In May at Ardenza, in pasture-fields in the evening; not scarce.
149. *G. gerronella*, Z. in lit. [Described by Zeller; this species is now well known.] On the 19th of May at Pisa after sunset, on the dry margins of fields; scarce.
150. *G. tenebrella*, Hb. At the beginning of June at Pratolino, sometimes on sunny mountain-slopes.
151. †*G. paupella*, Z. In the middle of May at Leghorn, Ardenza, and Antignano, on *Tamarix*-bushes, amongst which it flew in the morning, but was scarce.
152. *G. artemisiella*, Tr. At the end of May and in June at Pratovecchio, and everywhere around Leghorn, in pasture-fields; very abundant.
153. *G. nanella*, S. V. In the middle of June at Pratovecchio, on orchard-trees; scarce.
154. †*G. Hermannella*, F. In the middle of May at Leghorn and Antignano, singly on hedges.

155. *G. paucipunctella*, Z. At the beginning of June at Pratolino, on grassy mountain-slopes; scarce.

156. *G. lappella*, L. (*æstivella*, Mtzn.). In May at Ardenza, once taken.

157. †*Röslerstammia granitella*, Tr. In May in gardens at Leghorn, eight specimens.

158. *R. vesperella*, Kollar, n. sp. [Described by Zeller, see p. 81.] From the 12th to 30th April around Leghorn and as far as the river Cecina, on evergreen hedges, late in the evening; not scarce.

159. *R. cariosella*, Z. In the middle of June at Pratovecchio, on the margins of woods, sometimes.

160. *Æchmia thrasonella*, Scop. Throughout May in the marshes at Pisa; very abundant.

161. *Æ. oculatella*, Z., n. sp. [Described briefly by Zeller, see p. 82.]

162. *Æ. Fischeriella*, Z. (*desiderella*, F. v. R. Beitr. Taf. 82. f. 83; *Röslerstammella*, Mann (non Z.), F. v. R. Beitr. p. 242 and 268). In May at Pisa, in the marshes among hedges and in high grass; not scarce. (My Tuscan specimen has, like many of those near Glogau, a white tip to the third joint of the posterior tarsi.)

163. *Tinagma perdicellum*, Z. In May at Montenero, on strawberry-blossom in the sunshine.

164. *T. balteolellum*, F. v. R. In May at Antignano, taken amongst hedges, sometimes.

165. *T. lithargyrellum*, Koll., n. sp. [Described briefly by Zeller, see p. 82.] On the 24th of April, at Montenero, swarmed amongst laurels (? — arbutus?) and myrtle bushes.

166. *Argyresthia pruniella*, Hb. At the end of May at Leghorn, on sloe-hedges; abundant.

167. *A. nitidella*, F. At the end of May at Salviano and Ardenza, on maple trees.

168. *A. fagetella*, Z. (I received as Tuscan a small female, but with no further information.)

169. *A. conjugella*, Z. Only twice, at the beginning of June at Pratolino, on bramble bushes.

170. *A. tetrapodella*, Z. In the middle of May at Antignano, common on sloe-bushes.

171. *A. abdominalis*, Z. In the middle of June at Poppi, very abundant on juniper hedges.

172. *A. sorbiella*, Tr. At the end of May at Pisa, three specimens taken.

173. *A. arceuthina*, Z. In the middle of June at Bibbiena, sometimes on juniper bushes. (With us good specimens of this species are scarce by the middle of June, as its regular time of appearance is the end of May and the beginning of June; Mann's notice on the period of its occurrence in Tuscany seems the more extraordinary

as the other species there appear so unusually early, especially *A. conjugella* and *A. sorbiella*.)

174. *A. Gysseleniella*, Dup. In the middle of June at Pratovecchio, sometimes on young fir trees.

175. *Coleophora albifuscella*, Z. In the middle of May, at Ardenza, some specimens taken in pasture-fields at sunset.

176. †**C*. *mayrella*, Z. At the end of May at Pisa and Orciano, in dry grassy places at sunset; copulation takes place a little later.

177. *C. ochrea*, var. *aridatella*, Goldegg. In the middle of June at Pratovecchio, once taken in the evening.

178. *C. vicinella*, F. v. R. in lit. In the middle of May at Leghorn, several times taken in pasture-fields.

179. *C. fuscociliella*, F. v. R. in lit. At the end of May at Montenero, twice.

180. *C. serenella*, Tischer. At the end of May at Riparbella, several specimens.

181. *C. palliatella*, Zck. At the end of May at Leghorn, sparingly on sloe-hedges.

182. *C. currucipennella*, Z. At Pratovecchio, on oaks.

183. *C. virgatella*, Z. At the end of May at Pisa, in grassy places at sunset; scarce.

184. **C. albicostella*, F. v. R. At the beginning of June at Pratolino, in dry grassy places in the evening; scarce.

185. *C. otitæ*, Z. In the middle of June at Pratovecchio, on mountain-slopes; abundant.

186. *C. cæspititiella*, Z. On the 7th of June at Poppi, by a marshy pool, where it flew amongst rushes in the morning. I also found cases on the rushes, from which in a few days specimens of the imago were produced.

187. *C. lineariella*, Z. At the end of April amongst young fir trees and grass, in the afternoon; scarce.

188. *C. onosmella*, Brahm. At the beginning of June at Pratolino, in the rather boggy parts of the mountains; not scarce. I also found the cases there.

189. *C. hemerobiella*, Scop. In the middle of May at Pratovecchio, beaten from sloe-bushes.

190. **C. badiipennella*, F. v. R. At the end of May at Leghorn, amongst maple trees, but scarce.

191. *C. limosipennella*, F. v. R. At the end of May at Salviano and Ardenza, on elms, singly.

192. *C. coracipennella*, Z. In the middle of June at Pratovecchio, on sloe-bushes; very abundant.

193. *C. paripennella*, Z. In the middle of May at Antignano, in oak hedges, singly.

194. †*C. alcyonipennella*, Kollar. At the beginning of May at Montenero, in grassy places; scarce.

F

195. *Gracilaria Franckella*, Hb. In April and May around Leghorn; not at all scarce.
196. *G. stigmatella*, F. In March at Pratovecchio, in April at Leghorn, amongst oaks; common.
197. *G. hemidactylella*, S. V. In May at Antignano, on maple trees; scarce.
198. *G. rufipennella*, Hb. At the end of May at Antignano, on maple; only three specimens.
199. *G. elongella*, L. In March and April at Pratovecchio and everywhere round Leghorn.
200. *G. roseipennella*, Hb. At the beginning of May at Salviano, two specimens on an evergreen hedge.
201. *G. tringipennella*, Z. In May at Pisa, late in the evening, in the grass.
202. *G. limosella*, Dup. April and May at Leghorn and Antignano, in pasture-fields; in June at Pratolino.
203. **G. syringella*, F. In May around Leghorn; very abundant.
204. †*G. lacertella*, Z. In April and May at Montenero, Antignano, and Pisa, flying in pasture-fields towards sunset.
205. *G. quadruplella*, Z. At the beginning of May at Montenero, three specimens taken on rose-hedges.
206. †*G. quadrisignella*, Z. In the middle of May at Leghorn, on the stems of maple; two specimens.
207. *G. ononidis*, Z. At the beginning of May at Antignano, on sloe-bushes, singly, about sunset.
208. **G. scalariella*, Z., n. sp. [Described by Zeller, see p. 82.] At the end of April at Montenero, at the beginning of May at Ardenza, in pasture-fields, in the evening; very scarce.
209. **G. Kollariella*, Z. At the beginning of May, in the marshes at Pisa, amongst ash trees; singly.
210. *Coriscium quercetellum*, Z. In the middle of March at Pratovecchio, very abundant on oaks; at the end of May at Pisa, newly developed specimens, likewise on oaks; not scarce.
211. **C. alaudellum*, Dup. At Salviano and Antignano in April, on evergreen hedges; very different varieties: there was no privet anywhere near.
212. **C. citrinellum*, F. v. R. In the middle of March at Pratolino and Pratovecchio; in April at Montenero; beaten from young oaks.
213. **Ornix torquillella*, Z., n. sp. [This now well known species is briefly described by Zeller.] In April and May at Florence, Pisa, and Leghorn; abundant everywhere on sloe-bushes.
214. *O. guttiferella*, Dup. In May at Ardenza and Salviano, on sloe-bushes.
215. *O. cælatella*, Z. In May at Montenero, one male.
216. *Cosmopteryx pinicolella*, Dup. At the end of April at Montenero, sometimes taken on firs.

217. *C. turdipennella*, Tr. At the beginning of June at Pratolino, on the trunks of poplars; not scarce.
218. *C. Drurella*, F., *Zieglerella*, Hb. (Whether the *Zieglerella* taken by Mann in Italy and the *Zieglerella* introduced by Kollar in his 'Verzeichniss der niederösterreichischen Schmetterlinge,' S. 96, are identical with *Drurella*, I cannot say; they should more probably be referred to *C. Scribäiella*, Heyden in lit., which occurs in the Prater at Vienna.) [A description of *Scribäiella* by Zeller is appended, see p. 83.]
219. **C. argyrogrammos*, Z.; *Gracilaria Goldeggiella*, F. v. R. in lit. In the middle of May, at Pisa and Ardenza, it flew in pasture-fields at sunset. Herr v. Goldegg discovered it in the year 1801, in June, in the Hirschaue (deer-park) of the Vienna Prater.
220. **C. Ledereriella*, Mann, n. sp. [Described by Zeller, see p. 84.] From the 1st to 26th of May at Leghorn and Posignano; scarce. It flew early in the morning on the *Tamarix* near the sea.
221. *Elachista pontificella*, Hb. At the beginning of June at Pratolino, on mountain-slopes; not at all scarce.
222. *E. testaceella*, Hb. At the end of March at Stia, beaten from elm trees; scarce.
223. *E. rhamniella*, Z. In the middle of May at Leghorn, on hedges; five specimens.
224. *E. putripennella*, Z. At the beginning of June at Pratovecchio, sometimes on mulberry-trees.
225. *E. Raschkiella*, Z. At the end of May at Pisa, on bramble hedges, in the afternoon sunshine; four specimens.
226. *E. gibbiferella*, Z. On the 19th of May at Pisa, on ash trees in the afternoon; two specimens.
227. *E. miscella*, S. V. At the end of May at Ardenza, in pasture-fields; scarce.
228. *E. ictella*, Hb. In the middle of June at Pratovecchio, on the mountains, in grass; ten specimens.
229. **E. Heydeniella*, F. v. R. On the 19th and 20th of May in the marshes at Pisa; they flew in the afternoon over the flowers of an *Erica*, on which they also copulated.
230. *E. Roesella*, L. At the end of April at the sea-gate of Leghorn, in a kitchen-garden; several specimens.
231. *E. festaliella*, Hb. On the 19th of May in the marshes at Pisa, on bramble bushes; several specimens.
232. *E. æratella*, Z. Along with *E. Roesella*, on grass; five specimens.
233. *E. langiella*, Hb. In April at Leghorn, several times amongst sloe-bushes.
234. *E. quadrella*, Hb. At the beginning of June in the park at Pratolino; two specimens.
235. *E. albifrontella*, Hb. At the beginning of May at Pratovecchio, on the trunks of alders; three specimens.

236. *E. griseella*, F. v. R. in lit. [Described by Zeller, see p. 84.] At the beginning of May at Ardenza and Salviano, on the margins of fields and meadows; common.

237. *E. arundinella*, F. v. R. in lit. [Described by Zeller, see p. 85.] At the beginning of May at Pisa, on rushes in the evening, but scarce.

238. †*E. nigrella*, Hb. At the beginning of April at Salviano, on the borders of fields, not scarce.

239. *E. Pfeifferella*, Hb. At the beginning of May at Antignano and Riparbella, singly on sloe-hedges.

240. *E. nobilella*, Z. On the 19th of May at Pisa, amongst young fir trees, in the grass; two specimens.

241. *E. cinctella*, Z. [Described by Zeller, see p. 86.] In the beginning of May at Pisa, on ash trees; scarce.

242. *E. gangabella*, F. v. R. in lit. [This now well-known species is described by Zeller.] At the beginning of May at Pisa, sometimes on elm trees.

243. **E. chrysodesmella*, Z., n. sp. [Described by Zeller, see p. 87.] At the beginning of May at Pisa, on young oaks.

244. *E. pollinariella*, Z. At the beginning of May at Ardenza and Pisa, in dry grassy places; abundant.

245. **E. anserinella*, F. v. R. [Described by Zeller, see p. 87.] In the middle of May at Antignano, in grassy places near the sea; sometimes.

246. *E. rufocinerea*, Haw., *pratoliniella*, Mann in lit. On the 14th of March at Pratolino, where, on a sunny mountain-slope, thirteen specimens were taken on marsh-grass; it was the first species which I met with in Tuscany. (Mann also found this species in Croatia.)

247. *E. cygnipennella*, Hb. At the end of May at Pisa, on meadows; very abundant.

248. *Lyonetia Olerckella*, var. *æreella*, Tr. In March at Pratovecchio, in April at Pisa, amongst leaf-trees, not at all scarce; in June at Florence, on wild cherry-trees.

249. *L. prunifoliella*, Hb. On the 20th of April at Leghorn, once on a bramble bush.

250. †*Phyllocnistis suffusella*, Z. At the end of March at Pratovecchio, on poplars in the evening; abundant.

251. *Cemiostoma spartifoliella*, Hb. In April at Leghorn and Antignano, on *Cytisus laburnum*; not scarce. [This would probably be *C. laburnella*.]

252. **C. scitella*, Z. In the middle of May at Salviano, on hedges; scarce.

253. *Opostega salaciella*, Tr. At the beginning of May at Pisa, towards sunset on the dry borders of meadows.

254. *O. crepusculella*, Z. At the beginning of May at Pisa, in marshy places and in moist ditches; not abundant.

255. *Bucculatrix cidarella*, Z. At the beginning of June at Pratovecchio, on the trunks of alders; six specimens.

256. *B. ulmella*, Z. In May at Ardenza and Salviano, on the trunks of elm trees; not at all scarce.

257. *B. Boyerella*, Dub. From the middle of April to the end of May at Leghorn, Salviano, Antignano, Posignano, &c., on elms; very common: in colour whiter than the Vienna specimens.

258. *B. frangulella*, Goeze. At the end of May at Pisa, in hedges, but scarce.

259. *B. nigricomella*, Z. On the 19th of May at Pisa towards sunset, in dry grassy places; three specimens.

260. *Nepticula samiatella*, Z. In April at Leghorn and Montenero, sometimes on elm trees.

261. *N. aurella*, F. With the preceding; scarce.

262. *N. argyropeza*, Z. At the beginning of June at Pratovecchio, on silver poplars; not abundant.

263. *N. sericopeza*, Z. At the beginning of May at Salviano, on maple; scarce.

264. *Trifurcula pallidella*, Z. On the 19th of May at Pisa, in the marshes, amongst the low bushes in the grass; scarce.

265. *T. immundella*, Z. In the middle of June at Pratovecchio, in the Apennines, on *Spartium*, quite singly.

266. *Tischeria complanella*, Hb. In May at Leghorn and Pisa, on oaks; very abundant.

267. *†T. Emyella*, Dup., *rubicinella*, Schäffer in lit. At the end of April and in May at Leghorn, Antignano, Riparbella, and Pisa, on the red-flowering bramble bushes; scarce. (The oldest name is *marginea*, Haworth.)

268. *T. gaunacella*, Dup. In the middle of June at Pratovecchio, on sloe-bushes; scarce.

269. *T. angusticollella*, Z. Throughout May at Leghorn and Pisa, on sloe-bushes; not at all scarce.

270. *Lithocolletis roboris*, Z. At the beginning of April at Pratovecchio, on oaks; abundant.

271. *L. scitulella*, Z. At the end of March at Pratovecchio and Poppi, on oaks; scarce.

272. *L. saportella*, Dup. At the beginning of April at Pratovecchio, on oaks; scarce.

273. *L. delitella*, Z. At the end of March at Pratovecchio and Stia, on oaks; very scarce.

274. *L. pomifoliella*, Z. At the beginning of April at Badia, on orchard-trees; scarce.

275. *L. pomonella*, Z. In the middle of April at Leghorn, on sloe-bushes; not at all scarce. As narrow in the wing as the Vienna specimens.

276. *L. salictella*, Z. At the end of March at Pratovecchio and

Badia by the Arno, on cypress trees, near which willows grew; not scarce.

277. *L. fraxinella*, Z. At the beginning of May at Pisa in the marshes, on ash trees; scarce.

278. *L. quercifoliella*, Z. In March at Pratovecchio, in April at Florence, on oaks; very abundant.

279. *†L. Messaniella*, Z. Not scarce.

280. *L. leucographella*, Kollar, n. sp. [Described by Zeller, see p. 88.] Some specimens on the wing on the 24th April at Montenero. I found the larvæ and pupæ on a bush that looked like privet, only that it had long thorns.

281. *L. suberifoliella*, Kollar, n. sp. [Described by Zeller, see p. 89.] From the 12th of April to the beginning of May at Leghorn, beaten from *Tamarix*. I afterwards found the larvæ on the cork-tree.

282. *L. alniella*, Z. At the beginning of April at Badia in the evening amongst cypress trees; abundant.

283. *L. abrasella*, Z. At the beginning of May at Montenero; scarce.

284. *L. acerifoliella*, var. *acernella*, Dup. At the end of April around Leghorn and Pisa, on maple; not scarce. (Its oldest name is *sylvella*, Haw.)

285. *L. emberizæpennella*, Bouché. In the middle of May at Pisa, in the evening, singly, on nightshade.

286. *L. Kleemannella*, F. At the end of April at Antignano, on whitethorn, towards sunset; scarce.

287. *L. Heydenii*, Z. On the 17th of April at Montenero, on an evergreen hedge; nine specimens taken. (Its oldest name is *trifasciella*, Haw.)

288. *L. agilella*, Z. At the beginning of April at Pratovecchio, only twice on elm trees.

289. *L. comparella*, Z. At the beginning of April at Pratovecchio, on the trunks of poplar trees; not scarce.

'Stettin. ent. Zeitung,' 1850, p. 60.

TALÆPORIA CONSPURCATELLA, Kollar in lit.

♂. *Antennis interrupte longius ciliatis, alis anterioribus albido-griseis, fuscescenti-punctatis, macula parva venæ transversæ obscuriore.*

Grösse wenig über *Tinea stelliferella* oder *Micropteryx Sparmannella*. Flügel noch gestreckter als bei *Talæporia triquetrella*. Körper bräunlichgrau. Kopf etwas heller und wenig behaart. Fühler mit langen, am Ende verdickten Gliedern; jedes Glied hat an der Verdickung mehrere längere steife Haare, daher sind die Fühler in zwei Reihen unterbrochen langhaarig gefranzt. Beine graugelblich.

Vorderflügel unrein bleichgelb, sehr hell, etwas glänzend, mit ziemlich reichlichen, groben, hellbraunen Punkten bestreut, die am

Hinterrande wenig dichter stehen, als anderwärts. Ein brauner, durch hellbraune Einfassung zum Fleck verstärkter Punkt steht auf der Querader. Franzen an der Wurzelhälfte braungrau, sonst bleichgelb.
Hinterflügel schmal, sehr licht grau.
Unterseite aller Flügel einfarbig gelbbräunlichgrau, etwas glänzend.
Das Weibchen sowie der Raupensack ist mir unbekannt.

'Stettin. ent Zeitung,' 1850, p. 61.

TINEA ANGUSTICOSTELLA, F. v. R.; Z. Isis, 1839, p. 183.

Alis anterioribus fuscis obsolete pallide irroratis, præcipue ad dorsum, costa post medium angustissime flavida; capillis ferrugineis; antennis crassiusculis apice attenuato (♀).

Taster gelblich mit mehreren Borsten auf der obern und untern Seite. Glieder der Fühler kurz, umgekehrt-kegelförmig, durchwachsen. Gestalt der Hinterflügel wie bei *T. flavicostella*, die Farbe aber braungrau, aus dem Gelblichen in's Violette schimmernd.
Weitere Angaben über das einzelne Exemplar der F. v. R.'schen Sammlung, das ich gesehen habe, fehlen mir.

'Stettin. ent. Zeitung,' 1850, p. 62.

MICROPTERYX EXIMIELLA, Kollar, n. sp.

Capillis ferrugineis; alis anterioribus viridi-aureis, strigis duabus maculaque costæ postica niveis (♂).

Grösse der *M. aruncella*, welcher die Art am nächsten steht; die Flügel sind noch schmäler. Kopf rostfarbig behaart. Fühler braun, fein gesägt. Rückenschild goldglänzend. Hinterleib braun. Beine glänzend, bräunlichgelb.

Vorderflügel grünlich goldglänzend, an der Basis selbst violett, am Vorderrande sehr schmal röthlich, in der Flügelspitze mehr kupferig. Am Anfange des zweiten Fünftels ist eine dünne, schneeweisse, fast senkrechte Querlinie, in der Flügelmitte eine gleich beschaffene, nur etwas nach aussen convexe; in der Mitte zwischen ihr und der Flügelspitze hängt am Vorderrande ein schneeweisses, unten erweitertes und gerundetes Fleckchen.

Ein Exemplar (*Var.* b, puncto costali niveo ante maculam posticam) hat dicht vor demselben ein schneeweisses Randpünktchen.

Die Flügelspitze ist tiefer gefurcht, als die übrige Fläche. Franzen auswärts grau. Die graugefranzten Hinterflügel sind gefurcht und etwas glänzend hell kupferfarbig. Die ganze Unterseite wie die Oberseite der Hinterflügel, auf den Vorderflügeln aber lebhafter; hier scheint die Mittellinie sehr verloschen durch.

Das wahrscheinlich wie bei *aruncella* sehr abweichend gezeichnete Weibchen ist mir unbekannt.

'Stettin. ent. Zeitung,' 1850, p. 62.

MICROPTERYX MYRTETELLA, n. sp., *Zelleriella*, Mann in lit.

Minuta, capillis ferrugineis; alis anterioribus purpureis, fascia altera antice coarctata prope basim, altera media subcurva maculaque costæ postica magna lœte aureis (♂).

Die kleinste bekannte *Micropteryx*, sehr ähnlich der *M. Allionella*, aber in Vergleich mit dieser von zwergartiger Grösse, mit gesättigten gelben Zeichnungen der Vorderflügel und weniger geneigter Mittelbinde.

Grösse bedeutend unter *M. aruncella*. Kopf rostgelb behaart. Taster und Beine glänzend hellgelb. Fühler bräunlich. Rückenschild roth, glänzend. Hinterleib braungrau.

Vorderflügel violettlich purpurfarben, gegen die Basis hin dunkler mit goldgelben, scharf abstechenden Zeichnungen. Nicht weit von der Basis ist eine senkrecht gestellte, nach oben verengte Binde. Fast in der Flügelmitte ist eine zweite Binde, welche ein wenig schief steht, nach aussen sanft gekrümmt und am untern Ende am stärksten, bisweilen auch am obern verdickt ist. In der Mitte zwischen ihr und der Flügelspitze hängt am Vorderrande ein grosser, gerundeter, die halbe Flügelbreite einnehmender Fleck, unter welchem die Grundfarbe sich etwas lichtet. Längs des Hinterrandes sind keine gelbe Schuppen, wie bei *Allionella*, vorhanden. Franzen grau.

Die schmalen Hinterflügel sind gefurcht, etwas glänzend, hell kupferfarbig, grau gefranzt.

Auf der kupferig schimmernden Unterseite scheint die Mittelbinde der Vorderflügel sehr verloschen durch.

Das Weibchen, das ich nicht kenne, wird wohl wenig vom Männchen verschieden sein.

'Stettin. ent. Zeitung,' 1850, p. 63.

MICROPTERYX AMENTELLA, Z., *violacella*, F. v. R. in lit.

Capillis cinereis, alis anterioribus longiusculis violascentibus, squamis aureolis crebre conspersis, macula flavida anguli dorsalis; posterioribus cinereis pilosis.

Der *M. fastuosella* Z. am nächsten verwandt, aber sofort von ihr zu unterscheiden durch die behaarten, nicht beschuppten Hinterflügel.

Grösse des Männchens wie *fastuosella*, des Weibchens wie *Sparmannella*; doch giebt es auch Männchen, die so klein und kleiner als die Weibchen sind. Kopf hellgrauhaarig. Rückenschild und Hinterleib schwärzlich, letzterer besonders am Ende grauhaarig. Hinterbeine graubraun, etwas gelblich glänzend.

Die Vorderflügel sind gestreckter als bei *Sparmannella*, aber breiter und mit weniger langgezogenem Hintertheil, als bei *fastuosella*, daher stumpfer als bei dieser. Grundfarbe stahlblau oder violettblau oder besonders beim Männchen blass purpurfarbig; sehr reichlich sind grosse, blass goldgelbe Schuppen aufgestreut, die sich aber wie bei den verwandten Arten leicht abfliegen, daher in der Vertheilung derselben zu Flecken und Fleckchen bei den Exemplaren eine grosse Mannigfaltigkeit herrscht. Am Innenwinkel liegt ein, zumal beim Weibchen auffallender weisslichgelber Fleck, der meist bis nahe an die Hälfte der Flügelbreite reicht und auch die Franzen an seiner Färbung Theil nehmen lässt. Um ihn ist die Grundfarbe mehr als anderswo von Schuppenhäufchen frei. Hinter ihm in der Mitte des Raumes haben die Weibchen gewöhnlich einen kleinen dunkeln Fleck der Grundfarbe. Franzen grau.

Hinterflügel gestreckt, ohne die scharfe Spitze, in welche sie bei *Sparmannella* und *fastuosella* auslaufen. Sie sind grau, gelb schimmernd und auf der ganzen Fläche behaart; nur in der Flügelspitze, die violettlich angelaufen ist, sind auch Schüppchen vorhanden. Franzen grau.

Ganze Unterseite grau, nach aussen goldig und violett schimmernd; das Violette herrscht gewöhnlich vor.

'Stettin. ent. Zeitung,' 1850, p. 134.

NEMATOPOGON PANZERELLUS, Hb. 412.

Als *Panzerellus* sehe ich eine Art an, die etwas kleiner ist und die Vorderflügel weniger zugespitzt hat als *Swammerdammellus*; die Vorderflügel sind dunkler und bräunlich gegittert; die Fühler an der untern Hälfte sehr deutlich weiss und bräunlich geringelt. Diese Merkmale finden sich wenigstens an meinen zwei Männchen aus der Gegend von Jena. Mein toskanisches Exemplar, gleichfalls männlichen Geschlechts, ist schon bedeutend abgeflogen; daher sieht es auf den Vorderflügel dunkler aus als jene; seine Hinterbeine sind viel dunkler, bräunlich grau, an den Füssen gelblicher, während die Schienen und Füsse des *Panzerellus* hell gelblich sind und nur erstere etwas Grau beigemischt haben. Die untere Fühlerhälfte ist weniger deutlich bräunlich geringelt, doch unter der Lupe noch kennbar genug. Indem ich die Abweichungen dem längeren Fluge zuschreibe, halte ich das Exemplar für einen wirklichen *Panzerellus*.

'Stettin. ent. Zeitung,' 1850, p. 134.

ADELA CYANELLA, Mann, n. sp.

Alis anterioribus viridi- vel cyaneo-chalybeis; capillis ferrugineis.
Sie gehört zur Abtheilung *Cauchas*, hat aber die Grösse der *A. Frischella*. Körper schwarz mit etwas Metallschimmer. Kopfhaare rostgelb. Fühler von Vorderflügellänge, dick, borstenförmig, stielrund, nur gegen die Spitze undeutlich gekerbt, schwarz. Taster gekrümmt, von etwas mehr als Kopflänge, am Ende des zweiten Gliedes etwas verdickt und unten in ein Büschchen auslaufend, mit wenigen Stachelhaaren; das zweite Glied gelbhaarig, das Endglied spitz und schwarz. Beine braun, grünlich und kupferig schimmernd.

Vorderflügel länglich, schmäler als bei *Frischella*, sehr glänzend, einfarbig dunkel blaugrün. Franzen auf der Wurzelhälfte ebenso beschuppt, auswärts braunhaarig.

Hinterflügel ziemlich schmal, braun, bläulich überlaufen; Franzen bräunlich, an der Basis etwas gelb schimmernd.

Unterseite aller Flügel braun, bläulich überdeckt, gegen die Spitze gelblich angelaufen; Vorderrandfranzen der Vorderflügel kupferig.

Das Weibchen ist mir unbekannt.

'Stettin. ent. Zeitung,' 1850, p. 135.

ADELA LAQUEATELLA, Z., n. sp.

Alis anterioribus nigris, longitudinaliter obsolete aureo-striatis, fascia media saturate aurea chalybeo-marginata, ciliis violaceis; antennis ♂ albis, parte basali ⅓ nigra: ♀ nigro-villosis, parte apicali 1/4 nuda albida.

Zwei Männchen, ein Weibchen, von Mann als *Sulzeriella* geschickt. *Laqueatella* steht der *Sulzeriella* sehr nahe, unterscheidet sich aber sicher an den Fühlern. Bei *Sulzeriella* ♂ sind sie nämlich von der Wurzel aus nur ¼ der Länge, bei *laqueatella* ♂ ⅓ schwarz mit violettem Glanze, was in's Braune übergeht, worauf an den übrigen ¾ oder ⅔ die Farbe weiss ist. Bei *Sulzeriella* ♀ sind sie an etwas mehr als die Hälfte dicht mit langen schwarzen, violett schillernden Haaren bedeckt, und die kleinere Endhälfte ist kahl und seidenartig glänzend weiss; bei *laqueatella* ♀ sind sie weniger reichlich, aber auf ⅝ der Länge schwarzviolett behaart, und der Rest ist weisslich mit schwärzlichem, zugespitztem Endgliede. (Der eine Fühler ist abgebrochen; also könnte auch bei dem andern der Endtheil abgekürzt und das jetzige spitze, schwärzliche Endglied Zufall sein; dann bleibt aber doch der behaarte Theil immer noch auffallend länger als bei *Sulzeriella*.)

Ausserdem ist *laqueatella* grösser und hat im männlichen Geschlecht stumpfere Hinterflügel. In beiden Geschlechtern sind die Vorderflügel gegen die Basis hin weniger verengt. Die goldfarbenen Längsadern sind so dunkel und verloschen wie bei *Sulzeriella*. Die Binde ist bei den Männchen schmal, dunkel goldgelb, etwas gebogen und beiderseits stahlblau eingefasst; beim Weibchen ist sie breiter, gerade und violett gerandet. Gestalt und Breite der Binde und die Farbe der Einfassung sind übrigens bei *Sulzeriella* sehr veränderlich.

Noch eine von *Sulzeriella* verschiedene Art, RELIGATELLA, n. sp., besitze ich in beiden Geschlechtern aus Steyermark. Sie ist wenig grösser und breitflügliger als *Sulzeriella*, aber dadurch ausgezeichnet, dass auf den Vorderflügeln die gelben Längsstreifen alle sehr hell und scharf und, da sie das Schwarz mehr nach den Rändern hin verdrängen, länger sind. An den männlichen Fühlern ist nur das Basalviertel schwarz, an den weiblichen nimmt die dichte Behaarung ⅔ der Länge ein, ist also länger als bei *Sulzeriella*. Die istrischen Exemplare, die Mann als *religatella* verschickt hat, erweisen sich nur bei genauer Prüfung nur als kräftiger gebaute *Sulzeriella*, keineswegs als meine *religatella*.

'Stettin. ent. Zeitung,' 1850, p. 139.

ADELA PALUDICOLELLA, Mann, n. sp.

Alis anterioribus fuscis, creberrime aureo-punctatis, striga media punctoque costali ante apicem niveis (♂, ♀).

Zur Abtheilung B gehörig. Grösse der *Frischella*, die Flügel etwas schmäler und spitzer. Körper schwarz, auf dem Rückenschilde kupfrig. Kopf rostgelblich behaart, die Haare bleichen und fliegen sich leicht ab. Augen in beiden Geschlechtern weit getrennt. Taster auf der Innenseite weisslich. Fühler lang, unbehaart, beim Männchen sehr dünn, an der Basis braun und weisslich geringelt, dann aus dem Bräunlichen in immer reineres Weiss übergehend, beim Weibchen etwas dicker, von doppelter Vorderflügellänge, am Wurzeldrittel schwarz und silberweiss geringelt, dann braun, gegen die Spitze heller. Beine violettglänzend braun, an den Schenkeln kupferglänzend; die Fussglieder- und Schienenspitzen, so wie die Hinterschenkel, die Mitte der Hinterschiene und die Dornen silberweiss. Brust messingfarben. Der weibliche Hinterleib hinten zusammengedrückt und lang zugespitzt.

Vorderflügel glänzend braun, sehr gedrängt mit Goldpünktchen bestreut. Ueber die Mitte geht eine mehr oder weniger gerade, fast senkrechte, reinweisse, braun eingefasste Querlinie. In einiger Entfernung hinter ihr hat der Vorderrand ein reinweisses, sehr kleines Fleckchen, vor welchem ein schmaler, schwarzer Schattenstrich nicht tief herabgeht als Begrenzung einer ziemlich breiten, aber wenig auffallenden kupferrothen Binde. Die Flügelspitze ist breit kupferroth umzogen, die braunen Franzen sind mit solchen Schuppen gemischt.

Hinterflügel braun, schwach violettlich glänzend.

Auf der braunen, noch schwächer röthlich schimmernden Unterseite scheint die Mittellinie und der Vorderrandpunkt der Vorderflügel in weisslicher Farbe sehr deutlich durch; die Hinterflügel haben wie bei *Sulzeriella* &c. an der Mitte des Vorderrandes ein weisses, verloschenes Fleckchen.

Das Weibchen, an den Fühlern und dem Hinterleibe leicht kenntlich, hat etwas kürzere Vorderflügel als das Männchen.

'Stettin. ent. Zeitung,' 1850, p. 142.

YPSOLOPHUS LINEATELLUS, Kollar in lit.

Alis anterioribus griseo-lutescentibus, vitta media ex basi, in apice bifida, albida, ramo superiore ad punctulum fuscum porrecto (♂, ♀).

Nächst verwandt dem *striatellus*, leicht zu unterscheiden durch das Vorhandensein einer langen weisslichen Mittelstrieme auf den Vorderflügeln. Grösse sehr veränderlich, wie die eines grossen *Y. striatellus*, aber auch viel kleiner. Kopf, Rückenschild und Brust weisslich. Fühler bräunlich, in beiden Geschlechtern so weitläufig wie bei *striatellus* gezähnelt. Taster weisshaarig; das dünne, gebogene, kahle Endglied weiss, kürzer als das vorhergehende Glied. Beine weisslich, staubgrau, an den dunklern Füssen mit weisslichen Gliederspitzen. Hinterleib grau mit weissem After und weisslichem Bauch.

Vorderflügel ganz von der Gestalt des *striatellus*, mit einer staubgrau gemischten, lehmbräunlichen Grundfarbe. Aus der Basis kommt eine ziemlich breite, weissliche Strieme, deren unterer Rand in der Längsfalte ruht; hinter einem undeutlichen bräunlichen Längsstrichelchen, das in der Falte vor der Flügelhälfte liegt, spaltet sie sich; der untere, dünne, linienartige Ast geht in der Falte fort bis zum Innenwinkel, wo er vor einer weisslichen, längs des Hinterrandes hinziehenden Mondsichel endigt; der obere, längere Ast ist breiter, spitzt sich sehr fein zu, und endigt unter einem braunen, länglichen Punkt. Hinter diesem kommt eine weissliche, scharfe Querlinie wie bie *striatellus*, die dicht vor einem in gleicher Richtung liegenden weissen Strich der Hinterrandfranzen aufhört. Der Vorderrand (oder eigentlich seine Franzen) hat bis zur Spitze einen weissen Punkt und zwei weisse Häkchen. Die Spitze ist auf den hier weisslichen Franzen mit einer dreifachen, braunen Linie umzogen, die übrigen Franzen sind staubbräunlich und enthalten öfters ein weissliches, dünnes Strichelchen am obern Ende der Mondsichel.

Hinterflügel hellgrau, mit der langvorgezogenen, abgesetzten Spitze und den langen, staubgrauen Franzen des *striatellus*.

Unterseite der Vorderflügel bräunlichstaubgrau; in den Vorderrandfranzen sind ein weissliches Fleckchen und 2–3 weissliche Strichelchen mehr oder weniger deutlich; die weisslichen Franzen der Flügelspitze sind an ihrem Ende mit einer bräunlichen Doppellinie umzogen. Hinterflügel wie oben.

'Stettin. ent. Zeitung,' 1850, p. 143.

YPSOLOPHUS LANCEOLELLUS, Kollar, n. sp.

Alis anterioribus acuminatis flavescentibus, punctulis fuscis adspersis postice crebrioribus, puncto disci postico fusco; palporum articulo terminali breviusculo (♂).

Aus der Verwandtschaft des ebenso grossen *dolosellus*; Kopf und Rückenschild weisslich, Taster mit einem langen, abgestumpften Haarbusch, der oben und unten weisslich, an den Seiten staubgrau ist; das weissliche Endglied ist spitz und kürzer als bei den andern Arten. Beine schmutzig weisslich. Hinterleib grau mit weisslichem After.

Vorderflügel lang, schmal und dünn zugespitzt, bleichgelb, gegen den Innenrand noch bleicher, mit schmaler, weisslicher Vorderrandrippe. Die ganze Fläche ist mit bräunlichen, grössern und kleinern Stäubchen bestreut, die gegen die Flügelspitze dichter und gröber werden und die Ränder gegen die Franzen ziemlich scharf abgrenzen. Ein aus mehreren braunen Schüppchen gibildeter starker Punkt liegt im Mittelraum am Anfange des letzten Längsdrittels; von ihm an geht eine Anhäufung von Stäubchen als eine breite

Linie bis in die Flügelspitze. In der Mitte der Längsfalte liegt ein braunes, wenig auffallendes Pünktchen. Franzen hell staubgrau. Hinterflügel weissgrau, gelblichgraugefranzt; die Spitze ist unter einem weniger stumpfen Winkel vom Hinterrande abgesetzt. Unterseite glänzend hellstaubgrau, auf den Hinterflügeln heller. Das Weibchen, das ich nicht kenne, hat nach Mann's Versicherung vollkommenere Flügel als das von *dolosellus*.

'Stettin. ent. Zeitung,' 1850, p. 143.

ANCHINIA PUNCTELLA, Costa, *monostictella*, Kollar in lit.

Alis anterioribus paleaceis, juxta costam obscurioribus, puncto disci pone medium nigro; palporum articulo apicali brevi deflexo.

Die kleinste *Anchinia*, wenig über *Ypsolophus humerellus*, verwandt mit *pyropella*.

Kopf und Rückenschild weisslichgelb. Fühler weiss und braun geringelt, sehr zart pubescirend gefranzt. Taster etwas länger als Kopf und Rückenschild zusammen, innen und auf dem Rücken blassgelb, aussen gebräunt; das weissliche Endglied kurz, nicht über die Haare des zweiten Gliedes hinausreichend und niedergebogen, dass es von den Haaren bisweilen verborgen wird. Beine grau, die hintern hellgelblich. Hinterleib grau mit weisslichem Afterbusch.

Vorderflügel zugespitzt, von der Gestalt wie bei *pyropella*, nur etwas kürzer, ohne Glanz, strohgelb, längs des Vorderrandes in veränderlicher Breite dunkler bestäubt, manchmal ins Lehmfarbene; am bräunlichsten ist der Vorderrand nächst der Basis. Im Mittelfelde etwas hinter der Mitte steht ein einzelner, scharfer, schwarzbrauner Punkt, der jedoch nach Mann's Versicherung bisweilen auch fehlt. Franzen gelblich grau. Hinterflügel etwas glänzend grau mit hellern Franzen.

Ganze Unterseite grau; Franzen der Vorderflügel ringsum gelblich, die der Hinterflügel gelblichgrau.

Das Weibchen fehlt mir.

'Stettin. ent. Zeitung,' 1850, p. 147.

ŒCOPHORA ALBILABRIS, Z., n. sp.?

Alis anterioribus nigris, fasciis duabus maculaque costæ postica exalbidis; capillis exalbidis; palpis exalbidis, articuli terminalis fusci apice albo (1 ♂, 2 ♀).

Verschieden von der sehr veränderlichen *Œ. augustella* durch die Farbe der Taster, des Kopfes und der Beine, vielleicht jedoch nicht specifisch.

Grösse der kleinern Exemplare von *augustella*. Der Kopf ist ganz gelblichweiss (bei *augustella* hinten in veränderlicher Breite braun; bei den am lebhaftesten gelb gezeichneten Exemplaren ist diese Farbe am tiefsten und ausgedehntesten). Die Taster sind am zweiten Gliede ganz gelblichweiss (bei einem Weibchen aussen an der Mitte des zweiten Gliedes grau angelaufen); das Endglied ist schwarz und an der Spitze weiss. (Bei *augustella* sind sie schwarz, an der Wurzel, an der Spitze des zweiten Gliedes und am Ende weiss.) Die Beine haben an der Mitte und dem Ende der Hinterschiene ein reichlicheres Weisslich und an den Füssen ein reineres Weiss als die *augustella*.

Die Vorderflügel sind wie bei Varietäten der *augustella* gezeichnet, nämlich: nicht weit von der Basis ist eine gelblichweisse, an der untern Hälfte sehr erweiterte Binde; in der Flügelmitte ist eine schmälere, beim Männchen unten sehr verdickte, bei einem Weibchen verdünnte Binde, welche von der ersten Binde überall weit getrennt bleibt (statt wie bei manchen Varietäten der *augustella* am Innenrande mit ihr zusammenzufliessen), beim Männchen aber sich mit einem kleinen dreieckigen Fleck des Innenwinkels vereinigt. Dieser kleine Fleck fehlt dem einen Weibchen ganz, beim andern ist er äusserst klein und abgesondert. In der Mitte zwischen der Mittelbinde und der Franzenspitze ist ein nach unten zugespitzter Vorderrandfleck.

'Stettin. ent. Zeitung,' 1850, p. 148.

ŒCOPHORA OLEELLA, Boyer de Fonscolombe, *adspersella*, Kollar in lit.

Alis anterioribus angustulis subobtusis albidis canisve, fuscescenti grosse punctatis, apice puriore, striola vel macula oblonga fusca in plicæ dimidio.

Grösse der *Œ. cicadella*, Körperbau aber viel schlanker. Kopf und Rückenschild schmutzig grauweisslich, in der Mitte dunkler. Fühler hellgrau, fast fadenförmig, schwach kerbiggezähnt; Wurzelglied etwas verdickt, ohne abstehende Haare. Taster von etwas mehr als Kopflänge, niederhängend, gerade oder etwas gekrümmt, fadenförmig, am Ende des zweiten Gliedes etwas verdickt, das Endglied von hälber Länge des Tasters. Rüssel zusammengerollt. Brust etwas glänzend weiss. Beine weisslich, hell bräunlich gefleckt, besonders die 4 Vorderbeine an den Schienen und Füssen; Hinterbeine weisslich, etwas glänzend, mit zusammengedrückter, nicht haariger Schiene. Hinterleib hellgrau mit weisslichem Bauch.

Vorderflügel von der Gestalt wie bie *Hyponomeuta plumbellus*, nämlich ziemlich gestreckt, nach hinten wenig erweitert und mit schräg zugeschnittenem Hinterrande, wodurch sie etwas stumpf erscheinen. Grundfarbe grauweiss, mehr oder weniger rein, fast ohne Glanz mit vielen groben graubräunlichen, nicht scharf begrenzten, stellenweise etwas zusammenfliessenden Punkten auf der Wurzelhälfte und gegen den Innenwinkel bestreut; gegen die Flügelspitze hin ist die Fläche weisser und reiner, nur hie und da mit einem ganz verloschenen Punkte. In der Hälfte der Flügelfalte liegt ein braunes, dickes, fleckartiges Längsstrichelchen. Franzen schmutzig grau, an der Wurzel mit weissgrauen Schuppenhaaren, an der Flügelspitze meist verdunkelt.

Hinterflügel schmäler und viel spitzer als bei *Hyponomeuta plumbellus*, grau mit verhältnissmässig längern Franzen gegen den Vorderwinkel als bei dieser Schabe.

Unterseite grau; die Vorderrandfranzen der Vorderflügel weisslich, oder doch heller grau als die Hinterrandfranzen; bei den Hinterflügeln findet dasselbe in geringerm Grade statt.

Diese Art ist veränderlich in der Zahl und Deutlichkeit der Punkte der Vorderflügel und in der Grundfarbe; ein Männchen (var. b: *alis anterioribus grisescentibus, parcius punctatis, ceterum ut* a) hat die Vorderflügel sehr licht staubgrau, auf der Wurzelhälfte dunkler, mit spärlichen, sehr verloschenen, nur auf der Innenrandhälfte etwas deutlicher hervortretenden Punkten.

Die Naturgeschichte dieser schädlichen Schabe hat Duponchel (Supp. iv. p. 434) sehr ausführlich geliefert.

'Stettin. ent. Zeitung,' 1850, p. 152.

GELECHIA DRYADELLA, Kollar, n. sp.

Thorace, capillis palpisque gilvescentibus; alis anterioribus cinereo-fuscescentibus, in disco gilvescentibus, postice obscurioribus, puncto humerali pustulisque quatuor (1, 2 subconfluentibus, 1) disci nigris, fascia postica gilva; alarum posteriorum apice producto.

Sie kommt meiner *Gelechia basaltinella* (Isis, 1839, S. 198, 20) sehr nahe, und ich möchte die Abweichungen beider von einander fast auf Rechnung der verschiedenen Lokalitäten bringen. Beide haben einerlei Gestalt und dieselbe Vertheilung und Stellung der Zeichnungen; *basaltinella* ist düsterer; aber auch die auf der Ætnalava lebenden Eidechsen und Heuschrecken sind auffallend schwarz und dunkel gefärbt gegen die auf dem hellen Kalkboden von Syracus lebenden.

Dryadella hat die Grösse der *Gelechia Manniella*, übertrifft also die *basaltinella* um ein Merkliches (Vorderflügellänge $2\frac{7}{12}'''$ gegen $2\frac{4}{12}-2'''$). Kopf und Rückenschild bleichgelb, letzteres hat vorn am Kragenrande 2 braungraue Fleckchen. Taster bleichgelb, an der Bauchseite des Endgliedes gebräunt; sie sind sichelförmig, länger als der Thorax, das zweite Glied durch die Beschuppung gegen die Spitze zunehmend verdickt (länglich, umgekehrt eiförmig) und auf der Unterseite mit einer Längsfurche in der Beschuppung; das Endglied von halber Tasterlänge, dünn, pfriemenförmig zugespitzt. Rüssel gelbschuppig. Fühler borstenförmig, umgekerbt, braun und bleichgelb geringelt. Die vier Vorderbeine auf der Lichtseite graubraun, am zusammengedrückten Schenkel heller, an der Spitze der Schiene und der Fussglieder, sowie an der Mitte der Schiene und an der Hüfte bleichgelb. Hinterbeine zusammengedrückt, bleichgelb; Schiene auf der Rückenschneide locker langhaarig, auf der Lichtseite graubraun, an der Mitte, wo die zwei sehr ungleichen bleichgelben Dornen sitzen, mit einem bleichgelben Bändchen und ebenso gefärbter Spitze und Enddornen; Fuss braungrau mit bleichgelblichen Gliederspitzen. Hinterleib dunkelgrau; Bauch weissgelblich; Afterspitze hellgelb.

Vorderflügel länglich, nach hinten wenig erweitert; die bleichgelbe Grundfarbe ist an den Rändern durch braune Schüppchen sehr verdeckt und tritt nur im Mittelraum freier hervor. An der Basis der Vorderrandes ist ein tiefschwarzes Pünktchen und dahinter die

Grundfarbe in einem kleinen Raum frei ; an diesen stösst, also nicht weit von der Basis, ein auf der Flügelfalte stehender, tiefschwarzer, fleckartiger Punkt. Hierauf folgen zwei solche Punkte übereinander, wovon der untere in der Flügelfalte ruht, und mit dem obern fast zusammenfliesst ; sie stehen von dem ersten Punkt etwas weiter ab, als dieser von der Basis. In demselben Abstande, wie die zwei von dem ersten, folgt in der Hälfte der Flügelbreite ein tiefschwarzer, etwas kleinerer Punkt nahe vor der Binde. Diese ist bleichgelb, nicht breit, aus zwei Gegenflecken, wovon der untere kleiner und schmaler ist, zusammengeflossen ; vor ihr ist der Vorderrand dunkler beschattet. Der Raum von ihr bis zur Flügelspitze ist durch grobe, braune Schuppen ganz verfinstert. Franzen grau, an der Basis mit einigen braunen Schuppen der Flügelfläche überdeckt.

Hinterflügel von der Breite der Vorderflügel, mit stark abgesetztem zugespitztem Vorderwinkel, grau mit bräunlichgrauen Franzen.

Ganze Unterseite einfarbig bräunlichgrau ; nur am Vorderrande scheint die Binde der Vorderflügel als ein helles Fleckchen sehr verloschen und unmerklich durch.

Mein einzelnes Exemplar ist ein Weibchen.

'Stettin. ent. Zeitung,' 1850, p. 153.

GELECHIA TAMARICIELLA, Mann, n. sp.

Thorace, capillis palpisque exalbidis ; alis anterioribus laete brunnescentibus albido-nebulosis, vitta dorsali sordide exalbida, interne sinuata fuscoque inaequaliter marginata, puncto disci postico lineolaque longitudinali fusco-nigris.

Aus der Verwandtschaft der *Manniella*, mit sehr bunt gezeichneten Vorderflügeln. Grösse der *Manniella*. Thorax und Kopf schmutzig gelblichweiss, ersterer etwas bräunlich bestäubt. Fühler borstenförmig, bräunlich, weisslich feingeringelt. Taster sichelförmig, schmutzig gelbweiss, unten am zweiten Gliede bräunlich bestäubt, das Endglied an der Mitte mit einem braunen Ring und bisweilen mit ebenso gefärbter Spitze. Rüssel eingerollt, gelblich beschuppt, Beine weisslich und hellbraunbunt ; Hinterschiene zusammengedrückt, auf der Rückenschneide laughaarig. Hinterleib braungrau, an Bauch und Afterspitze schmutzig weiss.

Vorderflügel länglich, nach hinten wenig erweitert. Grundfarbe schmutzig gelblichweiss, aber nur an der Innenrandhälfte frei von dunkler Farbe, übrigens angenehm gelbbräunlich, heller und dunkler, am Vorder- und Hinterrande mit weisslich, undeutlich begrenzten Stellen. Die helle Grundfarbe bildet eine breite Innenrandstrieme, welche erst die Längsfalte zur Grenze hat, dann in einem breiten, kurzen Zahn etwas darüber hinausreicht, dann etwas hinter der Flügelmitte in einem grössern Zahn tiefer in die verdunkelte Farbe hineingreift, und am Innenwinkel verschwindet ; die Ränder in der Bucht zwischen den beiden Zähnen und vor dem ersten sind dunkelbraun, besonders die Einfassung zwischen den Zähnen. Am Vorderrande des zweiten Zahnes sitzt ein schwarzer Punkt und am Hinterrande desselben, in der Hälfte der Flügelbreite, ist ein eckiger, kleiner, schwarzbrauner, nicht sehr scharf ausgedrückter Fleck und dicht hinter ihm eine kurze, schwarzbraune Längslinie, unter welcher der Raum bis zum Hinterrande hin licht gelbbräunlich oder fast lehmfarben ist. Der Hinterrand hat gegen die Flügelspitze hin eine unterbrochene, braune Linie. Franzen weisslichgrau, mit verloschenen, bräunlichen Querschatten; am Innenwinkel sind sie weisslich und ohne Schatten.

Hinterflügel mit vorgezogener, nicht sehr scharf abgesetzter Spitze, hellgrau mit helleren Franzen.

Unterseite der Vorderflügel licht bräunlichgrau mit einer hellen, gelblichen verloschenen Stelle am Vorderrande hinter der Flügelmitte; Hinterflügel grau mit einer weisslichen Stelle vor der Flügelspitze.

Beide Geschlechter sind gleich gezeichnet.

'Stettin. ent. Zeitung,' 1850, p. 156.

RÖSLERSTAMMIA VESPERELLA, Kollar, n. sp.

Alis anterioribus sub apice subretusis, brunneis, postice paulo dilutioribus, dorso anguste sordide pallido (♂ ♀).

Ausgezeichnet von den andern bekannten Arten durch den eingedrückten Hinterrand der Vorderflügel.

Grösse der *R. cariosella*. Rückenschild und Kopf in veränderlicher Dunkelheit gelblichgrau, mit braunen Schulterdecken.

Fühler bräunlich, gezähnelt, faserig. Taster schmutzig weissgelblich, auf der Aussenseite bräunlich angeflogen, von Rückenschildslänge, gekrümmt, ziemlich schlank, spitz, auf der Unterseite etwas locker haarig, Endglied nicht merklich abgesetzt, länger als die Tasterhälfte. Rüssel eingerollt, gelblich. Beine etwas glänzend, hellgrau, die vier vordern aussen bräunlich angelaufen; alle Fussglieder an den Spitzen weisslich; Hinterschienen zusammengedrückt, von den Mitteldornen an auf der untern Schneide und an der Spitze haarig. Afterspitze wenig heller.

Vorderflügel $2\frac{9}{12}$–$2\frac{1}{12}$''' lang, nach hinten wenig erweitert, mit sehr schwach vorgezogener Spitze, indem der Hinterrand unter ihr einen seichten Eindruck hat. Grundfarbe röthlichgelbbraun, auf der Wurzelhälfte am dunkelsten. Innenrand in einer schmalen, mehr oder weniger deutlichen Strieme gelblich oder doch heller als die Grundfarbe; an der Mitte erweitert sie sich zu einem sehr stumpfen, hellen Zahn, dessen der Basis zugewandter Rand braun oder bräunlich eingefasst ist. Hinterrandlinie und Enden der Franzen gelbbraun. Hinterflügel grau, heller gefranzt.

Ganze Unterseite etwas glänzend grau, auf den Vorderflügeln dunkler, und deren Franzen am Ende gelbbraun.

Das Weibchen ist ein wenig kleiner als das Männchen, und hat einen wenig hervorstehenden Legestachel.

'Stettin. ent. Zeitung,' 1850, p. 157.

ÆCHMIA OCULATELLA, Z., n. sp.

Alis anterioribus (caudulam mentientibus) aureo-fuscis, strigulis quinque costæ, duabus dorsi (priore incrassata fere recta) niveis, punctis disci tribus posticis lilaceo-argentatis, apice atro, pupilla argentea.

Sie ist der *Æchmia equitella* so ähnlich, dass Mann sie mir unter diesem Namen zuschickte. Ihre Unterschiede sind wenig, aber sicher. Sie ist etwas grösser; ihre Vorderflügel sind breiter und lebhafter goldigbraun. Die 5 weissen Vorderrandstrichelchen sind kleiner und zarter. Der erste Innenrandstrich ist viel schärfer, dicker, bei weitem weniger nach aussen geneigt und *fast gerade*; sein Ende bleibt vom ersten Vorderrandhäkchen weit getrennt. Der tiefschwarze runde Fleck in der Flügelspitze hat eine *silberweisse Pupille*, die der *equitella* fehlt. (Kopf etwas zerstört.) Beine gezeichnet wie bei *equitella*.

'Stettin. ent. Zeitung,' 1850, p. 158.

TINAGMA LITHARGYRELLUM, Kollar, n. sp.

Alis anterioribus nitidissimis canis, posterioribus cinereis dilutius fimbriatis.

Eine der kleinsten Schaben, merklich kleiner als *T. metallicellum*, dem sie ganz nahe steht. Rückenschild, Kopf und Vorderflügel sind lebhaft glänzend, weissgrau. Taster (fadenförmig, kurz, spitz, hängend, wie bei jener Art) und die Beine glänzend weisslich, aussen etwas grau angelaufen. Hinterleib grau mit weissem Bauche. Die Vorderflügel sind an der Basis am Vorderrande dunkel, fast braun unterlaufen. Hinterflügel grau mit vielen helleren, gegen die Basis etwas gelblich schimmernden Franzen. Ganze Unterseite grau, lilafarbig überlaufen, glänzend, gelblichgrau gefranzt.

Zwei toskanische Exemplare sind an Kopf, Rückenschild und Vorderflügel etwas dunkler und auf den letztern mit einem sehr verloschenen, hellen Tröpfchen im Innenwinkel gezeichnet. Sie scheinen mir nur Varietäten zu sein.

(*Var. b. Alis anterioribus paulo obscurioribus, guttula anguli postici diluta obsoletissima.*

Ein Exemplar dieser Varietät habe ich bei Messina am 8. April gefangen zwischen Gesträuch von *Arbutus unedo* und *Erica arborea*.)

'Stettin. ent. Zeitung,' 1850, p. 160.

GRACILARIA SCALARIELLA, Z., n. sp.

Thorace et capite cum palpis niveis; alis anterioribus læte brunneis, vitta dorsali interne obtuse dentata nivea.

Grösser als *G. ononidis*. Kopf etwas glänzend, schneeweiss. Fühler bräunlich mit dunklerem Wurzelgliede. Maxillartaster klein, dünn, spitz, weisslich; Labialtaster länger als das Rückenschild, ziemlich schlank, sichelförmig, am Ende des zweiten Gliedes unten durch lockere Behaarung etwas verdickt, weiss; das spitze Endglied von halber Tasterlänge. Rückenschild schneeweiss, an der Schulter hell gelbbraun. An den vier vordern Beinen sind die Schenkel graubraun, die Schienen schwarzbraun mit weisser Basis; Mittelschiene auf der Lichtseite an der Basis selbst braun; Füsse seidenglänzend weisslich, auf der Schattenseite mit bräunlichem Fleck an der Basis jedes Gliedes. Hinterbeine glänzend, am Schenkel grau, an der auf der Rückenschneide steifhaarig gefranzten Schiene graubräunlich, am bräunlichweissen Fuss mit braungrauem Fleck auf der Basis der drei ersten Glieder. Hinterleib braungrau, am Bauch weisslich.

Vorderflügel ziemlich schmal, angenehm hell gelbbraun. Auf dem Vorderrande ist vor der Spitze ein weisser, schwarzgesäumter, nach aussen gekrümmter Haken, und vor ihm in einiger Entfernung ein weisser, schwarz gesäumter Vorderrandpunkt (der auf dem rechten Vorderflügel ganz fehlt); am Ende der Franzen der Flügelspitze sind zwei weisse, breitere, einander genäherte Randhaken, unter welchen sich die Grundfarbe als ein unten weiss gesäumter Längsstrich bis ans Ende der Franzen fortsetzt. Am Innenrande ist eine von der Basis ausgehende, nach innen durch schwärzliche Einfassung sehr scharf begrenzte Strieme; sie hat drei breite, stumpfe Zähne, von denen der mittelste auf jeder Seite, durch eine tiefe Bucht begrenzt wird, der erste aber der kürzeste ist; sie läuft in einem weissen Strich bis ans Ende der Franzen, und fasst auf denselben die Verlängerung der Grundfarbe ein. Franzen grau.

Hinterflügel schmal, von der Basis aus zugespitzt, grau, heller gefranzt.

Unterseite der Vorderflügel grau, mit einem weisslichen, verloschenen Fleck auf dem Vorderrande, an der Stelle des schwarzgesäumten Häkchens der Oberseite, und mit den zwei Häkchen der Franzen.

Das Weibchen kenne ich nicht.

'Stettin. ent. Zeitung,' 1850, p. 197.

COSMOPTERYX SCRIBÄIELLA, Heyden in lit.

Alis anterioribus fuscis, ad basim striolis plumbeis, fascia media aurantiaca aurato-marginata, linea adhaerente in apicem perducta aurata.

Der *Druryella* sehr ähnlich, etwas grösser mit schmälern Vorderflügeln. Rückenschild und Oberkopf dunkelbraun mit sehr feinen Silberlinien. Gesicht etwas metallisch grau. Taster silbergrau. Fühler wie bei *Druryella*. Beine weniger lebhaft weissgefleckt.

Vorderflügel nur gelbbraun, doch sehr dunkel. Die Basis ist nicht messingglänzend, sondern in der Grundfarbe; von der Schulter geht eine starkglänzende, zarte Bleilinie auf dem Vorderrande, den sie aber sehr bald verlässt; sie hat die halbe Länge des Abstandes der Mittelbinde von der Basis; unter ihrer Spitze liegt eine eben solche, nur viel kürzere Linie dicht über der Längsfalte und mit ihr parallel unter derselben eine zweite. Die Mittelbinde ist nach vorn weniger verengt; ihr der Flügelmitte zugewendeter Rand hat einen tiefschwarzen Punkt an der goldglänzenden Einfassung; an ihrem Aussenrande liegen als Einfassung zwei einander sehr nahe kommende goldglänzende, einwärts schwarz gesäumte Gegenflecke; der des Vorderrandes ist auf den Franzen weisslich. Zwischen beiden Gegenflecken, in der Hälfte der Flügelbreite, kommt eine orangefarbene Verlängerung hervor (die der *Druryella* ganz fehlt), welche sich zu der silberglänzenden Längslinie fortsetzt.

Auf der Unterseite der Vorderflügel ist in den Vorderrandfranzen ein sehr verloschener, weisslicher Wisch.

Das Exemplar ist männlich und wurde mit mehreren im Wiener Prater gefangen.

An diese Art schliesst sich *Cosmopteryx Lienigiella*, Z., näher au als an *Druryella*.

'Stettin. ent. Zeitung,' 1850, p. 198.

COSMOPTERYX LEDERERIELLA, Mann, n. sp.

Capite exalbido, palpis albidis nigro-maculatis; alis anterioribus ochraceis, antice fusco-pulverosis, litura fusca in apicem usque perducta.

Grösse der *Druryella*. Rückenschild und Kopf hell beingelb. Fühler mässig lang, gegen die Spitze gezähnelt, weisslichgelb, fein braungeringelt, am Enddrittel mit breitern braunen Ringen; das Wurzelglied etwas dick, auf der Rückenseite bräunlich. Taster länger als der Thorax, sichelförmig, dünn, weisslich, am Ende des zweiten Gliedes schwarz; das Endglied hat zwei schwarze Ringe und eine solche Spitze. Beine seidenglänzend, schmutzig gelblichweiss, aussen an den Füssen schwarzfleckig; die vier hintern Schienen sind aussen schwarzbraun; in der Mitte und an der Spitze weisslich; die Hinterschiene auf der Rückenschneide langhaarig. Hinterleib dunkelgrau mit gelblichgemischtem Afterbusch.

Vorderflügel ziemlich schmal, im Grunde hell ochergelb, am Vorderrande von der Basis aus auf $\frac{3}{4}$ der Flügellänge durch sehr feine braune Stäubchen verdunkelt. Ein solcher Streif geht vom Innenwinkel aus, etwas gekrümmt und sich erweiternd bis in die Flügelspitze, wo er sich in der dunkeln Bestäubung verliert, welche auch die Franzen der Spitze überzieht. Die übrigen Franzen sind hellbräunlichgrau.

Hinterflügel sehr schmal, linienförmig, grau, langfranzig.

Unterseite bräunlichgrau; die Franzen der Vorderflügelspitze dunkelbraun umzogen.

Die Art ist zu Ehren des Herrn Lederer in Wien, eines fleissigen und wissenschaftlichen Lepidopterologen, benannt worden.

'Stettin. ent. Zeitung,' 1850, p. 199.

ELACHISTA GRISEELLA, F. v. R. in lit.

Thorace fusco-griseo, capite postice fuscescenti-griseo, epistomio albido, palpis albidis, externe fuscescentibus; alis anterioribus latius-

culis griseo-fuscis, fascia media curvula male determinata maculisque duabus posticis oblique oppositis minus distinctis albidis (♂).

Beträchtlich grösser als *nigrella*, wie eine grössere männliche *E. pollinariella*. Rückenschild braunstaubig mit durchschimmerndem Weiss, besonders am Ende der Schulterdecke. Kopf etwas unrein weiss, auf dem Hinterkopf mehr oder weniger dicht bräunlichgrau bestäubt. Fühler ziemlich dick, graubraun mit lichtern Ringen. Taster weiss wie das Gesicht, auswärts gebräunt; Endglied spitz, von etwas weniger als halber Tasterlänge. Beine dunkelbräunlich, schmutzig gelblichweiss verloschen gefleckt, am verloschensten die helleren Hinterbeine; Hinterschienen zusammengedrückt, langhaarig. Hinterleib dunkelgrau mit starkem, lehmgelblichem Afterbusch.

Vorderflügel ziemlich breit, hinten erweitert, graugelbbraun, unter der Loupe mit sehr reichlichen braunen Stäubchen bedeckt, unter denen die weissliche Farbe als Pünktchen hervorscheint. Dicht vor der Flügelmitte ist eine weissliche, nicht sehr breite Binde, fast senkrecht gestellt, ziemlich gerade, an der Mitte hinten etwas erweitert, ohne scharfe Begrenzung, doch nach hinten ein wenig deutlicher gegen die Grundfarbe abstechend als nach der Flügelbasis hin. Im Innenwinkel ist ein verloschener, weisslicher, undeutlich umgrenzter Fleck von veränderlicher Grösse. Etwas hinter ihr, der Flügelspitze merklich näher als der Binde, ist ein am Vorderrande hängender, weisslicher Fleck, der sich abwärts verlängert und mit der Spitze dem Hinterrande nahe kommt. Auf die grauen Franzen reichen die braunen Punkte der Grundfarbe weit hinein, und hinter ihrer Mitte zieht von der Spitze herunter eine aus braunen Punkten gebildete Linie, die unter der Mitte des Hinterrandes aufhört.

Hinterflügel breit lanzettförmig, zugespitzt, dunkelgrau; die Franzen schimmern an der Basis sehr schwach gelblich.

Unterseite braungrau; die Franzen der Vorderflügel schimmern überall, besonders lebhaft am Hinterrande, die der Hinterflügel schwächer, und nur am Hinterrande, auf ihrer Basis gelblich.

Das Weibchen kenne ich nicht.

Griseella von Mann entdeckt, fliegt bei Wien im Mai und Juni im Grase kleiner Gehölze.

'Stettin. ent. Zeitung,' 1850, p. 200.

ELACHISTA ARUNDINELLA, F. v. R. in lit.

Thorace fusco, capite cinereo-nitido, palpis nitidulis albidis, externe fuscescentibus; alis anterioribus longiusculis, fuscis, fascia media obsoleta maculisque duabus oppositis posticis albidis (♂).

Noch grösser als *E. griseella*, langflügligher mit viel dichterer und dunklerer, mehr ins Schwärzliche gemischter Färbung, hauptsächlich ausgezeichnet durch den ziemlich lebhaft glänzenden, hellgrauen Kopf, den sie nur mit *E. humilis* gemein hat. Fühler einfarbig braun. Taster bräunlich, etwas glänzend, auf der obern Seite weisslich; Endglied spitz, etwas kürzer als der halbe Taster. Beine glänzend, bräunlich, verloschen weisslich gefleckt; Hinterbeine mehr grau, an den Schienen langhaarig. Afterbusch schmutzig gelblichweiss.

Vorderflügel ziemlich gestreckt, braun ins schwärzliche, auf der Mitte mit einer sehr verloschenen, weisslichen, ziemlich senkrechten Binde, welche über der Falte verengt, und so fast in zwei Gegenflecke aufgelöst ist. Im Innenwinkel ist eine helle, weissliche, mehr auf die Franzen ausgedehnte, fleckartige Stelle. Der Flügelspitze näher als der Mittelbinde hat der Vorderrand einen weissen, nicht scharf begrenzten Fleck, dessen Spitze gegen den Hinterrand gerichtet ist; er ist reiner weiss als die Binde. Um die Spitze herum haben die grauen Franzen braune Schüppchen, und auf ihrer Hälfte geht eine nach aussen gekrümmte, aus braunen Schüppchen bestehende Linie herab, die vor der hellen Stelle des Innenrandes aufhört.

Hinterflügel lanzettförmig, schmäler als bei *griseella*, dunkelgrau; Franzen an Hinterrande mit breit gelblich schimmernder Basis.

Auf der bräunlichgrauen Unterseite haben die Franzen am Hinterrande eine gelblich schimmernde Basis, an den Hinterflügeln breiter als an den Vorderflügeln; bei letztern sind die Vorderrandfranzen mit einem deutlichen, gelblichweissen Wisch vor der Flügelspitze gezeichnet.

Das Weibchen kenne ich nicht.

Mann fand diese Art bei Wien im August selten im Prater.

'Stettin. ent. Zeitung,' 1850, p. 201.

ELACHISTA CINCTELLA, Z., L.?

Alis anterioribus angustulis, fusco-nigris, fascia media ciliisque apicis externe cum capillis palpisque albis; antennis fusco canoque annulatis.

Etwas grösser als *E. arundinella*. Rückenschild dunkelbraun. Kopf ganz weiss. Fühler braun, ziemlich deutlich weissgrau geringelt. Taster von Rückenschildslänge, sichelförmig, dünn, spitz, weiss, aussen bräunlich angeflogen. Beine bräunlich mit weisslichen Flecken; Hinterbeine auf der Innenseite etwas glänzend, gelblichweiss, an den Schienen langhaarig. Hinterleib dunkelgrau, am Bauche glänzend weisslich; Afterbusch hellgrau.

Vorderflügel verhältnissmässig gestreckt, dunkelbraun, besonders nach hinten grobschuppig. Auf der Mitte ist eine weisse Binde, ziemlich breit, fast gerade und senkrecht, einwärts schärfer begrenzt als nach aussen. Franzen hellgrau, um die Flügelspitze braunschuppig; hinter ihrer Hälfte geht eine aus braunen Schüppchen gebildete Linie herab, die an der Mitte des Hinterrandes verschwindet; hinter diese Linie sind sie weiss.

Hinterflügel lanzettförmig, lang zugespitzt, grau, langfranzig. Ganze Unterseite bräunlichgrau, kaum in der Gegend der Binde etwas heller; Franzen der Vorderflügelspitze aussen weisslich.

Bei Glogau selten.

Meiner *E. cinctella* nahe steht:

REVINCTELLA, Z. (*vinctella* in lit.), mit spitzerer Vorderflügelspitze,

gerader, auf beiden Seiten scharf begrenzter, am Innenrande etwas
erweiterter weisser Binde, hellen Hinterrandfranzen mit brauner
Linie um die Flügelspitze, rein weissem Kopf und weissen Schulterdecken.
Aus Croatien.

'Stettin. ent. Zeitung,' 1850, p. 203.

ELACHISTA CHRYSODESMELLA, Z., n. sp.

Antennis fuscis, epistomio palpisque cinereis, nitidulis; alis anterioribus latiusculis nigro-fuscis, fuscia media flavida nitidula in dorso ampliata.

Etwas kleiner als *E. gangabella*. Kopf braun, im Gesicht glänzend grau. Taster unten dunkelgrau, oben weissgrau, etwas glänzend. Bauch grau.

Vorderflügel tief schwarzbraun, in der Mitte mit einer hellgelben, etwas glänzenden, senkrechten, nach vorn sanft verschmälerten Binde. Franzen um die Spitze schwarzbraun, schuppig; auf $\frac{2}{3}$ ihrer Länge wird der beschuppte Raum durch eine nach aussen gebogene Schuppenlinie begrenzt, und hinter dieser sind die Franzen sehr wenig lichter grau als gegen den Innenwinkel hin. Hinterflügel wie bei *gangabella*.

Auf der braungrauen Unterseite haben die Vorderflügelfranzen am Innenwinkel eine gelbliche Basis.

Das Weibchen kenne ich nicht.

'Stettin. ent. Zeitung,' 1850, p. 203.

ELACHISTA ANSERINELLA, F. v. R.

Alis anterioribus albis, gilvo-nebulosis, postice obscurioribus, linea in ciliis e squamis fuscescentibus.

Etwas grösser als *pollinariella*, aber kleiner als *cygnipennella* ♀. Rückenschild und Kopf weiss. Fühler weiss, beim Weibchen sehr deutlich braungeringelt, beim Männchen entweder schwach geringelt oder ganz einfarbig. Taster kürzer als das Rückenschild, mässig schlank, weiss, aussen an der Wurzelhälfte, also bis vor die Spitze des zweiten Gliedes, bräunlich angeflogen. Beine bräunlich, an den Füssen weissbunt; Hinterschienen weisslich, mit bräunlicher Basis, besonders auf der Rückenseite sehr langhaarig. Hinterleib grau, mit weisslichem, beim Männchen starkem Afterbusch.

Vorderflügel ziemlich breit, weiss, mit grossen hell ochergelben Nebelflecken, welche gegen die Flügelspitze eine gesättigtere Färbung erhalten, und hier von der Grundfarbe nur kleine Stellen übrig lassen. Im Allgemeinen bleibt die Grundfarbe frei an der Basis in einem grossen Raum, der jedoch am Vorderrande und in der Flügelfalte gelb bestäubt ist; ferner in einem bindenförmigen Raum in der Flügelmitte, einem Fleck am Innenwinkel und einem länglichen, herabhängenden Fleck am Vorderrand vor der Flügelspitze. Die Schuppen in derselben haben dunklere Enden. Auf den Franzen sind bräunlichgelbe Stäubchen, und hinter ihrer Hälfte geht eine aus solchen dunklern Stäubchen bestehende Linie herab.

Hinterflügel breit, lanzettförmig, dunkelgrau; die etwas lichtern Franzen haben eine gelblich schimmernde Basis.

Unterseite braunlichgrau; Vorderflügelfranzen weisslich, am hellsten um die Spitze; Hinterflügelfranzen grau, an der Flügelspitze weisslich.

Anserinella lebt in Böhmen (bei Aussig im Mai F. v. R.) und um Wien im Mai und Juni bei Tivoli, auch anderwärts zwischen Gesträuch.

'Stettin. ent. Zeitung,' 1850, p. 207.

LITHOCOLLETIS LEUCOGRAPHELLA, Kollar, n. sp.

Alis anterioribus nitidulis croceis, linea tenui baseos longitudinali, strigulis duabus mediis oppositis perobliquis tenuibus, strigulisque tribus costæ ante apicem albis, stria apicis atra.

Sehr ähnlich der *L. betulæ*, aber leicht zu unterscheiden durch die einfarbig weissen, ungeringelten Fühler, den Glanz der Vorderflügel, die deutlichen drei weissen Vorderrandhäkchen vor der Flügelspitze, die weniger weit gegen den Vorderrand vorgehende Spitze der Basallinie, den Mangel schwarzer Schüppchen am Innenrande.

Grösse der *L. betulæ*. Vorderflügel stumpfer. Schopf von der Farbe des Rückenschildes (dessen Zeichnungen weggewischt sind); Gesicht, Fühler, Taster und Beine seidenglänzend, rein weiss, die vordern braunfleckig; Hinterschienen unrein weisslich behaart.

Hinterleib grau mit weissem Bauch, und weisslichem, in der Mitte gelblichem Afterbusch.

Vorderflügel safrangelb, glänzend, nach hinten wenig dunkler. Die feine, weisse, nicht schwarzgesäumte Basallinie geht in ihrer ersten Hälfte in der Flügelfalte, dann erhebt sie sich über dieselbe, aber lange nicht so hoch wie bei *betulæ*. Die beiden Gegenstriche haben die Stellung wie bei *betulæ*, sind sehr scharf und rein weiss, und bleiben mit ihren Spitzen weiter auseinander; der obere ist verdickt und verjüngt sich nach unten; sein Innenrand ist etwas dunkel eingefasst, und auf dem Vorderrand fehlt ihm die weisse, feine, gegen die Flügelbasis gehende Verlängerung. Der untere reicht mit der Spitze bis an den schwarzen Schuppenstrich; unter der Mitte ist er bei einem Exemplar verdünnt, und hat über die Verdünnung einen gegen die Flügelbasis gewendeten Widerhaken; von seiner Basis geht eine sehr feine, weisse, nicht schwarzschuppige Linie bis zur Flügelbasis. Am Vorderrand folgen in gleichen Abständen drei kurze, weisse, innen schwärzlich gesäumte, ziemlich senkrecht gestellte Häkchen vor der Flügelspitze. Unter ihnen, von den zwei letzten erreicht, ist der schwarze, aus groben Schuppen zusammengesetzte Längsstrich dünner und schärfer umschrieben als bei *betulæ*. An ihn stösst die Spitze des deutlichen, weissen, einwärts schwarzrandigen Häkchens, welches auf dem Innenwinkel ruht, dreieckig ist und sich sehr nach hinten neigt. Die Flügelspitze ist von einer schwarzbraunen Linie umzogen; diese ist weniger convex als bei *betulæ*, und einwärts von ziemlich lebhaftem Lilaschimmer eingefasst.

Unterseite bräunlichgelbgrau, mit bleichröthlich schimmernden Franzen an den Gegenrändern, und sehr schwachen Spuren von hellen Fleckchen auf den Vorderrandfranzen.

Hinterflügel grau, heller gefranzt.

Bei einem Exemplar (*Var.* b, *lineæ longitudinalis apice cum strigulæ mediæ inferioris medio conjuncto*) vereinigt sich die Basallinie mit dem untern Gegenstrich; unter der Vereinigung ist der letztere bis zum Innenrande stark verdickt.

'Stettin. ent. Zeitung,' 1850, p. 208.

LITHOCOLLETIS SUBERIFOLIELLA, Kollar, n. sp.

Alis anterioribus nitidulis croceis, linea tenui baseos longitudinali strigulisque duabus mediis oppositis perobliquis (superiore in costa ad basim usque producta) albis, stria apicis atra; posterioribus canis.

Von *betulæ* zu unterscheiden durch die ganz weissen, ungeringelten Fühler, viel hellere glänzende Vorderflügel, den auf dem Vorderrand bis zur Flügelbasis fortgehenden Vorderrandhaken, die sehr hellen Hinterflügel, etc.—von *leucographella* durch hellere Vorderflügel, Mangel der Vorderrandhäkchen vor der Spitze, den von der Basis aus weissen Vorderrand, die hellen Hinterflügel, etc.

Grösser als *L. betulæ*. Schopf, Rückenschild und Vorderflügel hell safrangelb, letztere nach hinten etwas verdunkelt. Fühler, Gesicht und Beine seidenglänzend, weiss; die Hinterfüsse haben obenauf an der Spitze eines jeden Gelenks einen dunkelbraunen Punkt. Hinterleib grau, am Bauch und Afterbusch weisslich.

Die Basallinie der Vorderflügel ist sehr fein, meist auf beiden Seiten braunschuppig eingefasst, und in der Gestalt wie bei *leucographella*. Die beiden Gegenstriche haben die Lage wie bei *betulæ* und *leucographella*; der obere ist länger und setzt sich in einer dünnen Vorderrandlinie bis zur Flügelbasis fort; der untere ist gegen die Spitze auf beiden Seiten sonst nur einwärts schwarzschuppig gerandet; dasselbe ist auch meist der Fall mit der feinen Innenrandlinie zwischen ihm und der Flügelbasis; beide Gegenstriche bleiben mit ihren Spitzen getrennt; der untere erreicht den schwarzen, aus groben Schuppen gebildeten, schlecht umschriebenen Längsstrich. Das Häkchen im Innenwinkel sowie die des Vorderrandes gegen die Spitze fehlen gänzlich. Die braune Linie, womit die Flügelspitze umzogen ist, hat die convexe Gestalt wie bei *betulæ* und ist einwärts von zartem Lilaschimmer eingefasst; auswärts sind die Franzen weisslich, und die über der Flügelspitze haben braune Enden; vielleicht bildet sich hier sogar ein Franzenschwänzchen, was bei der theilweisen Beschädigung meiner Exemplare sich nicht sicher entscheiden lässt.

Unterseite gelbbräunlichgrau, nach hinten fast schmutzig weisslich; die eigentliche Flügelspitze ist schwarzschuppig und auf den Franzen von der braunen Linie wie auf der Oberseite umzogen.

Hinterflügel weisslichgrau mit noch helleren, gelblich schimmernden Franzen; auf der Unterseite sind sie ganz weisslich.

SECTION II.

Species collected by Herr Joseph Mann in 1853, in the neighbourhood of Fiume, recorded by him in the 'Wiener entomologische Monatschrift,' 1857, pp. 173–189, entitled " Verzeichniss der im Jahre 1853 in der Gegend von Fiume gesammelten Schmetterlinge."

Dasystoma salicella, Hb. Several at Fiume in April on the trunks of poplars.

Chimabacche fagella, S. V. April and May, not scarce on the trunks of trees.

Semioscopis Steinkellnerella, Tr. Found in April on walls at Hraszt.

Talæporia clandestinella, Mann in lit. (Zeller, Linnæa Ent. viii. p. 338). I found the cases at the beginning of April at Orechowiza in Croatia on rocks and walls; the perfect insects from them appeared at the end of April.

Lypusa maurella, S. V. In May amongst nut-bushes at Hraszt.

Xysmatodoma melanella, Haw. (*stelliferella*, F. v. R.). Taken in May on the stems of poplars.

Euplocamus Fuesslinellus, Sulz. May and June in bushes in the Draga valley.

E. boleti, Fab. (*mediella*, Tr.). May, on elm trunks at Tersatto.

E. tessulatellus, Z. In June, found on old trunks on Monte Maggiore.

Tinea imella, Hb. May, beaten from hedges, swarming round bushes in the evening.

T. ferruginella, Hb. May, swarming in the evening under thorn hedges and on old walls.

T. rusticella, Hb. May and June, beaten from thorn hedges near the Pulverthurm.

T. tapetiella, L. May, several in houses at Fiume.

T. arcella, Fab. (*clematella*, Z.). July, beaten from hedges in the evening in the Draga valley.

T. granulatella, Z. June, in the evening, flying on walls near the Pulverthurm.

T. quercicolella, H.-S. May, on the trunks of old oaks.

T. granella, L. May and June, found on walls and buildings.

T. spretella, S. V. May, occurring in the room.

T. ganomella, Tr. May, beaten from hedges near the Pulverthurm and at Tersatto.

T. pustulatella, Z. June, flying in the evening on walls near the Pulverthurm.

T. confusella, H.-S. May, several found on rocks at Martinischza.

Incurvaria angusticostella, F. R. May, taken singly amongst thorn bushes.

I. muscalella, F.   May, flying along quickset hedges.
I. pectinea, Haw. (*Zinckenii*, Z.).   May, on oaks at Draga.
I. Körneriella, Z.   May, flying in the beech wood at Clana.
I. Oehlmanniella, Hb.   June, flying round young bushes at Draga and Buccari.
Lampronia rubiella, Bjerkander (*variella*, Fab.).   June, flying round brambles at Clana.
Micropteryx calthella, L.   May, in the Draga valley on the borders of fields on buttercups.
M. Allionella, Fab.   Flying in the beech wood at Clana in May.
M. fastuosella, Z.   Beaten from oaks in April.
M. Paykullella, F.   June, taken on the flowers of *Rhamnus paliurus*.
Nemophora Swammerdammella, L.   May, not scarce in young underwood.
N. pilulella, S. V., Hb.   June, on Monte Maggiore, on *Pinus picea*.
N. pilella, S. V.   April and May, on thorn hedges, especially near the Pulverthurm.
N. metaxella, Hb.   June, at Draga, flying on the edges of woods.
Adela fibulella, S. V.   May, on the slopes of mountains, on the flowers of *Veronica*.
A. rufifrontella, Tr.   May, at Draga, in meadows.
A. Frischella, L.   May, at Volosca, in bushes.
A. violella, Tr.   At Martinischza, amongst bushes.
A. associatella, F. R.   June, taken on Monte Maggiore, on *Pinus picea*.
A. religatella, Z.   May, flying amongst *Rhamnus paliurus*.
A. DeGeerella, L.   May and June, at Volosca, Fiume, and Buccari, swarming in young bushes.
A. viridella, Scop.   April and May, flying everywhere amongst oak bushes.
A. cuprella, S. V.   April, amongst willows in the Draga valley.
Nemotois ærosellus, H.-S.   June, taken on the Kalvarienberg in "Poderen," on thistles and scabious.
N. istrianellus, H.-S.   June, on the Kalvarienberg, in "Poderen;" it is scarce.
N. Schiffermüllerellus, S. V.   At the beginning of July in "Poderen" on the Kalvarienberg, and at Castua.
N. minimellus, S. V.   July, in pasture-fields near the Pulverthurm.
N. barbatellus, Z.   May, on mountain-slopes near the Pulverthurm and at Draga.
N. Dumerilellus, var. *fervidellus*, Z. (Linnæa Ent. viii. p. 338).   At the beginning of June in a pasture-field in front of the Pulverthurm; scarce.

Ochsenheimeria taurella, S. V. June, several found amongst leaves under thorn hedges.

Plutella cruciferarum, Z. April to July, in the entire district, both in the valley and mountains, and on the Alps of Monte Maggiore; not scarce.

Cerostoma sylvella, L. July, at Groming, on oaks.

C. persicella, S. V. June, in " Poderen," on peach- and almond-trees.

C. asperella, L. In May, beaten from young oaks.

Theristis caudella, L. (*cultrella,* Hb.). April, several taken on the walls of vineyards.

Sophronia humerella, Hb. May, occurring amongst grass on mountain-slopes.

S. sicariella, Z. June, amongst young bushes at Draga.

S. illustrella, Hb. June, on the Kalvarienberg and at the Grünzamthaus in " Poderen," on *Globularia.*

Ypsolophus marginellus, F. June, at Martinischza, beaten from juniper hedges.

Y. juniperellus, L. June, on juniper bushes at Martinischza and Tersatto.

Y. verbascellus, S. V. June, in pasture-fields, on *Verbascum.*

Y. silacellus, H. May and June, on mountain-slopes and pasture-fields.

Y. fasciellus, H. June and July, beaten from hedges on the borders of woods.

Cleodora striatella, S. V. May and June, flying round *Artemisia.*

Anarsia lineatella, Z. July, taken among peach-trees.

Megacraspedus dolosellus, F. v. R. May and June, in the Draga valley and at Martinischza, on meadows and mountain-slopes.

M. separatellus, F. v. R. Taken on the 9th June, before sunset, on the summit of Monte Maggiore. The females run up the grass and there wait for the males.

M. binotellus, F. v. R. May, on mountain-slopes and pasture-fields.

M. imparellus, F. v. R. June, on the Kalvarienberg and at Tersatto, singly, in " Poderen."

Holoscolia forficella, Hb. May, on mountain-slopes and pasture-fields.

Pleurota punctella, Costa (*monostictella,* H.-S. fig. 363). On mountain-slopes and pasture-fields throughout the district.

P. salviella, H.-S. June, on the bare mountains. The larva feeds on *Salvia officinalis,* and is full-fed in May.

P. pungitiella, H.-S. June, flying on Monte Maggiore after sunset.

P. aristella, L. June, not scarce on the mountains above Hraszt.

P. bicostella, L. June, not scarce on Monte Maggiore at Clana and at Kameniak.

P. rostrella, H.   June, on mountain-slopes, not scarce.
Topeutis criella, Tr.   June, taken singly at Volosca and Clana.
Carposina berberidella, H.-S.   June, beaten from barberry-bushes.
Lampros proboscidella, Sulzer.   June, several beaten from hazel bushes at Hraszt.
L. Geoffroyella, L.   May, several in the "Poderen" by the road to Volosca.
L. Denisella, S. V.   May, in "Poderen" behind the Pulverthurm.
L. ferrugella, S. V.   June, at Fiume and in Istria, among oaks.
L. Metzneriella, Tr.   June, at Tersatto, among oaks.
L. tinctella, Hb.   June, beaten from oak bushes.
L. formosella, S. V.   July, at Fiume, on the stems of poplars.
Hypercallia Christiernini, Z.   May and June, behind the Pulverthurm, flying in a grassy bush.
Dasycera Oliviella, Fab.   June, on the Kalvarienberg and at Castua, singly on oaks and ash trees.
Œcophora minutella, L.   May, several taken on walls.
Œ. sulphurella, Hb.   June, on Monte Maggiore.
Œ. fulviguttella, H.-S.   June, several taken on mountain-slopes at Martinischza.
Pancalia Lewenhoekella, S. V.   June, on mountain-slopes and pasture-fields; not scarce.
P. nodosella, H.-S.   May, in a pasture-field behind the Pulverthurm.   [A description of this species occurs in the list of species collected in 1854, in Upper Carniola; for that was published three years before the notice of the species captured the previous year.]
Endrosis fenestrella, Scop. *(lacteella*, S. V.).   April and July, occurring in the room at Fiume.
Butalis Esperella, Hb.   June, on Monte Maggiore.
B. tabidella, H.-S.   The middle of June, flying in the evening round bramble bushes at the Pulverthurm.
B. œrariella, H.-S.   June, also taken at the Pulverthurm in "Poderen" in the evening.
B. vagabundella, H.-S.   May and June, on mountain-slopes in the Fiume district and in Istria.
B. pascuella, Z. (*gravatella*, M.).   June, at the Pulverthurm and at Martinischza, on *Salvia*.
B. aurifrontella, F. v. R.   May, occurring on whitethorn hedges; scarce at Fiume.
B. cuspidella, S. V.   June, on mountain-slopes and in grassy "Poderen."
B. Knochella, F.   May and June taken in "Poderen" behind the Pulverthurm.

B. restigerella, Metzner. June, on mountain-slopes in the Fiume district, also in Croatia and Istria.

B. chenopodiella, Hb. April to June, not scarce in the same districts.

B. inspersella, Hb. July, several taken at Martinischza, amongst juniper.

Atemelia oleella, Boyer. June, on olive trees.

Blastobasis phycidella, Z. June, beaten from thorn hedges at Fiume.

Œgoconia quadripuncta, Haw. (*Kindermanniella*, Z.). June, several taken at Volosca and at Clana.

Scythropia cratægella, L. June, not scarce on sloe-bushes.

Swammerdamia pyrella, Villers (*cerasiella*, Hb.). May, not scarce on sloe-bushes.

S. apicella, Donovan (*comptella*, Hb.). April, beaten from thorn hedges at Fiume and in Croatia.

Hyponomeuta vigintipunctatus, Retz. (*sedellus*, Tr.). June, on the Kalvarienberg, on *Sedum*; not scarce.

H. plumbellus, S. V. June, on *Euonymus*, not scarce in the Fiume district.

H. irrorellus, Hb. June and July, at the Pulverthurm, on *Euonymus* bushes.

H. rorellus, Hb. June, beaten from rose hedges; scarce.

H. variabilis, Z. Not scarce on sloe-bushes in the entire district.

H. evonymellus, Scop. May, on wild cherry-trees, the larvæ by thousands; the imago in June and July. [This is evidently not the spindle-eating *evonymellus*, and is probably the species named by Guenée *mahalebella*, from his having reared it from the *Cerasus mahaleb*; and he remarks " Larva vivit Junio in *Ceraso mahaleb*, densa *numerosaque caterva* associata, &c." (Europæorum Micro-Lepidopterorum Index Methodicus, p. 105, note 3).]

H. padi, Z. June, in the Draga valley, on *Prunus padus*.

Anesychia sexpunctella, Hb. June, several taken on walls by the Pulverthurm.

A. scalella, Scop. June, found on walls at Hraszt.

A. echiella, S. V. May and June, occurring on walls and trunks of trees in the entire district.

A. funerella, Fab. May, several taken on ash trees at Tersatto.

A. decemguttella, Hb. June, several beaten from hedges at Draga.

A. chrysopyga, Z. June, several taken in a pasture-field at Zengg.

Symmoca signella, Hb. May and June, found sitting on walls behind the Pulverthurm and at Hraszt.

Depressaria costosa, Haw. (*depunctella*, Hb.). July, beaten from oak bushes at Martinischza.

D. liturella, S. V. June, beaten from hedges at Fiume and Volosca.

D. assimilella, Tr. June, beaten from hedges at Tersatto and Groming.

D. nanatella, Stainton. June, several taken in the evening amongst juniper bushes at the Pulverthurm.

D. arenella, S. V. June, found in "Poderen" on the Kalvarienberg.

D. capreolella, Z. April, taken on the Kalvarienberg.

D. ocellana, Fab. (*characterella*, S. V.). June, found on walls at the Pulverthurm and at Draga.

D. lutosella, H.-S. Middle of June, flying in the evening amongst juniper bushes in "Poderen" at Tersatto.

D. furvella, Tr. June, several taken in "Poderen" on the Kalvarienberg.

D. depressella, H. June, taken in pasture-fields behind the Pulverthurm.

D. vaccinella, Hb. April, on mountain-slopes at the castle of Tersatto and at Martinischza.

D. badiella, Hb. July, beaten from *Clematis* hedges at Volosca and Fianona.

Carcina fagana, S. V. June, on oaks, not scarce throughout the district.

Lecithocera luticornella, Z. July, on whitethorn hedges at the Pulverthurm.

Henicostoma lobella, S. V. April and May, beaten from thorn hedges at Fiume.

Gelechia Kollarella, Costa (*flavedinella*, F. v. R.). June, on the Tersatto mountain, and behind the Pulverthurm on *Salvia*. I found the larva in May between spun-together leaves of that plant.

G. cinerella, L. June, abundant everywhere on the borders of thickets.

G. tripunctella, S. V. June, on Monte Maggiore.

G. lutilabrella, Z. in lit. [Briefly described (see p. 103), but no time of appearance nor locality given.—H. T. S.]

G. populella, L. June, on the trunks of poplars at Fiume.

G. scintillella, F. v. R. July, on mountain-slopes in the Fiume district, and in Istria and Croatia.

G. subsequella, Hb. June, several taken amongst sloe-bushes on the Kalvarienberg.

G. lentiginosella, Z. July, taken on mountain-slopes at Martinischza.

G. leucatella, L. End of June, beaten from whitethorn hedges.

G. terrella, Hb. May and June, nowhere scarce.

G. distinctella, Z. June, in "Poderen" at Tersatto.

G. scabidella, Z. June, taken in a valley behind the Pulverthurm.

G. solutella, Z. May, in pasture-fields at Fiume and Tersatto.

G. pinguinella, Tr. June, at Fiume and in Croatia; not scarce on the trunks of poplars.

G. humeralis, Z. April, beaten from oaks in the Fiume district.

G. triparella, Metzner. May and June, in oak thickets at Fiume.
G. scriptella, Hb. May and June, at Fiume and in Croatia, beaten from thorn hedges.
G. cytisella, Tr. May, two specimens beaten from rose hedges on the Kalvarienberg.
G. aleella, Fab. June, on the trunks of trees at Draga, and behind the Pulverthurm.
G. quadrella, Fab. June, at Fiume, Tersatto, and Volosca, on barberry-bushes.
G. ligulella, S. V. May, throughout the district, occurring in "Poderen" on bushes and plants.
G. vorticella, Scop. June, taken on bushes at the Pulverthurm, and at Hraszt.
G. cincticulella, H.-S. May, several taken on a mountain-slope at Martinischza.
G. captivella, H.-S. At the end of May, 1849, flying in a little ash wood behind the Pulverthurm at sunset. In 1853 I did not meet with a single specimen.
G. patruella, Z. in lit. [Briefly described, see p. 103.] June, taken at Fiume in the evening on dry plants at the Pulverthurm.
G. coronillella, Tr. May, not scarce in all thickets where *Coronilla* grows.
G. biguttella, H.-S. May and July, everywhere on mountain-slopes and in pasture-fields.
G. anthyllidella, Hb. May and June, not scarce on mountain-slopes and pasture-fields.
G. pulveratella, H.-S. June, at Tersatto and on the Kalvarienberg, flying in the evening round bushes in pasture-fields.
G. carchariella, Z. May and June, flying everywhere in oak thickets.
G. dimidiella, S. V. May, at the Pulverthurm, and in the Draga valley, in pasture-fields in the evening.
G. gerronella, Z. June, several taken on mountains near Orechowiza.
G. flammella, Tr. May and June, everywhere in the evening in pasture-fields.
G. paupella, Z. (*melanolepidella*, Koll. in lit.). May and June, singly on grassy places in the evening in the Fiume district and in the Draga valley.
G. artemisiella, Tr. June, nowhere scarce, on mountain-slopes and meadows.
G. albiceps, Z. June, occurring on trunks of trees at Volosca.
G. luculella, Hb. June, on the trunks of poplars at Fiume.
G. stipella, Hb. April and June, occurring on walls where *Atriplex* grows, both in the Fiume district and also in Istria and Croatia.
G. Hermannella, F. On the Kalvarienberg, flying on *Chenopodium* on walls and in thickets.

G. pictella, Z. June, at Tersatto, flying round *Salvia* at sunset; very scarce.

G. nigricostella, F. v. R. May, occurring in the evening on grass in the little ash wood behind the Pulverthurm.

G. campicolella, Kollar in lit. [Briefly described (see p. 103), but no time of appearance nor locality given.—H. T. S.]

Parasia paucipunctella, Metzn. May, on the Kalvarienberg, flying in " Poderen " after sunset.

P. neuropterella, F. v. R. July, flying on *Tussilago* in the Louisenstrasse late in the evening.

Acrolepia granitella, Tr. May, several taken at Hraszt.

A. vesperella, Z. April, several taken at Buccari from thorn hedges.

Æchmia Thrasonella, Scop. May, in the Draga valley, in meadows, not scarce.

Æ. equitella, Scop. May, at Martinischza and at the Pulverthurm in the evening on mountain-slopes.

Æ. oculatella, Z. May, at the Pulverthurm and at Orechowiza.

Æ. Fischeriella, Z. May, behind the Pulverthurm in the little ash wood.

Tinagma dentellum, Z. May, Martinischza and at the Pulverthurm, singly on mountain-slopes.

T. balteolellum, F. v. R. May, flying singly among juniper at the Pulverthurm.

T. transversellum, Z. May, on the Kalvarienberg, and on the Schlossberg at Tersatto, in " Poderen " on grass.

T. stanneellum, F. v. R. May, two specimens taken at Martinischza, on young oaks.

Argyresthia ephippella, Fab. (*pruniella*, Hb.). May, on thorn hedges throughout the district.

A. spiniella, Z. July, occurring singly at Claua and Groming.

A. mendica, Haw. (*tetrapodella*, Z.). May, not scarce amongst sloebushes in the Fiume district, in Istria, and in Croatia.

A. abdominalis, Z. June, on juniper at Draga and at the Pulverthurm.

A. fundella, Tr. May, on Monte Maggiore, beaten from *Pinus picea*.

A. illuminatella, Z. May, on Monte Maggiore, beaten from *Pinus picea*.

Coleophora Mayrella, Hb. May, in the " Poderen " at Volosca, on grassy slopes and bushes.

C. trochilipennella, Costa. May and June, on the Kalvarienberg and at the Pulverthurm, in meadows in the evening.

C. alcyonipennella, Kollar. June, on the margins of meadows in the Draga valley.

C. paripennella, Z. May, several beaten from bushes at Tersatto.

C. ballotella, F. v. R. June, the larva not scarce on *Ballota nigra*; the imago in July.

C. ornatipennella, Hb. May, not scarce on mountain-slopes in the evening, flying everywhere on *Salvia*-blossoms.

C. vibicella, Hb. June, several taken behind the Pulverthurm.

C. fuscociliella, Z. May, taken in "Poderon" on the Kalvarienberg.

C. trifariella, Z. May, on the Tersatto mountain, at Martinischza, and at the Pulverthurm, occurring singly in thickets.

C. flaviella, Mann. [Briefly described, see p. 104.] May, in the evening in the little ash wood by the Pulverthurm.

C. vulnerariæ, Z. May, flying after sunset in the little ash wood by the Pulverthurm.

C. serenella, Dup. June, beaten singly from hedges.

C. onobrychiella, Z. May, occurring singly on mountain-slopes at Hraszt.

C. albicostella, Dup. May, on mountain-slopes and pasture-fields throughout the district.

C. currucipennella, Z. June, on oaks in the Fiume district and in the Draga valley.

C. auricella, Bosc. At the end of May, several taken at the Pulverthurm.

C. albifuscella, Z. May, occurring in the evening on mountain-slopes at Martinischza.

C. niveicostella, Z. June, flying in the evening on mountain-pastures at Kalvarienberg, Draga, &c.

C. saponariella, Z. Several at Groming on *Saponaria*.

C. onosmella, Brahm. June, flying at the edges of thickets in the Draga valley.

C. ciconiella, H.-S. July, taken at Tersatto and at the Pulverthurm.

C. therinella, Z. (*trochilella*, F. v. R.). June, flying on grass in young thickets.

C. lineariella, Z. May, on mountain-slopes at Martinischza.

C. drymidis, Mann. [Briefly described, see p. 104.] June, collected the cases on *Drymis spinosa* behind Martinischza and at Costrenna.

C. murinipennella, Dup. April, flying in the evening in pasture-fields at the Pulverthurm.

C. argentula, Steph. (*cothurnella*, F. v. R.). June, flying in the evening in pasture-fields by the Pulverthurm.

C. micantella, Mann in lit. May, several beaten from thickets in the Draga valley; scarce.

C. coracipennella, Hb. June, in sloe-hedges, not scarce throughout the district.

C. lutipennella, Z. July, flying on oaks at Tersatto, the Kalvarienberg, and Volosca.

C. limosipennella, Z. July, flying in the evening on *Parietaria officinalis* at Fiume.

C. flavipennella, H.-S. June, taken in the little ash wood at the Pulverthurm.

Zelleria hepariella, Stainton. May, beaten from privet hedges at Fiume.

Gracilaria Franckella, Hb. April and May, in the Fiume district, in Istria, and in Croatia, on oaks.

G. rhodinella, H.-S. May, several beaten from oaks at Draga.

G. stigmatella, Fab. April and May, in oak thickets on the Kalvarienberg.

G. semifascia, Haw. (*picipennella*, Z.). April, beaten from oaks at Tersatto.

G. elongella, L. May and June, in the Fiume district, in Istria, and in Croatia, not scarce, in thickets.

G. tringipennella, Z. May, on mountain-slopes at the Pulverthurm and at Martinischza.

G. limosella, Dup. May, occurring in "Poderen" in the Fiume district.

G. syringella, F. May, everywhere, on lilac bushes.

G. auroguttella, Stept. (*lacertella*, F. v. R.). May, several taken on the edges of thickets in the Draga valley.

G. quadrisignella, Z. May, several taken on a grassy slope at Martinischza.

G. ononidis, Z. May and June, flying in pasture-fields where *Ononis* grows, on the Kalvarienberg and at Draga.

G. Kollariella, Z. May, in the little ash wood at the Pulverthurm.

Coriscium Brongniardellum, Fab. (*quercetellum*, Z.). April, occurring amongst the dry oak leaves.

C. cuculipennellum, Hb. (*alaudellum*, Dup.). May, taken on privet hedges.

C. sulphurellum, Haw. (*citrinellum*, Z.). April and May, beaten from leafy thickets at the Pulverthurm.

Ornix torquillella, Z. April, amongst thorn hedges at Tersatto.

O. meleagripennella, Hb. April and May, everywhere, amongst sloe-bushes and thorn hedges.

O. anguliferella, Z. May, beaten from wild roses on the Tersatto castle-hill.

O. ampliatella, Mann in lit., Z. May, on juniper at the Pulverthurm and at Martinischza. [Described by Stainton, p. 104.]

O. guttea, Haw. (*guttiferella*, Z.). June, flying on hedges of wild cherry on the Kalvarienberg.

Cosmopteryx argyrogrammos, Z. (*Goldeggiella*, F. v. R. in lit.). May, in pasture-fields by the Pulverthurm.

Elachista pontificella, Hb. May and June, flying throughout the district in young thickets and grassy places.

E. testacella, Hb. April, beaten from oaks at the Pulverthurm.

E. Illigerella, Hb. June, two specimens taken in the Draga valley.

E. Rhamniella, Z. June, occurring singly in the evening amongst thorn hedges at Martinischza and on the Kalvarienberg.

E. tricolorella, Mann in lit. May, several taken in the evening in pasture-fields in the Fiume district.

E. miscella, Hb. April and May, occurring everywhere on mountain-slopes and pasture-fields.

E. ictella, Hb. April and May, occurring on mountain-slopes and in "Poderen" on the Kalvarienberg, at Tersatto, and in Istria.

E. Isabellella, Costa. May, several taken in the pasture-field by the Pulverthurm.

E. serratella, Tr. May, flying singly on *Salvia* on the Kalvarienberg and the Tersatto hill.

E. pomposella, Z. May and June, occurring singly on *Salvia* in the evening at the Pulverthurm and at Martinischza.

E. albiapicella, H.-S. April, on *Globularia*-blossoms on mountain-slopes in the Fiume district.

E. langiella, Hb. May, beaten from leafy thickets on the Kalvarienberg.

E. modestella, Dup. May, flying in the sunshine on the borders of thickets in the Draga valley.

E. concristatella, Z. in lit. May, several taken in young thickets and on mountain-slopes at Volosca and at the Pulverthurm.

E. quadrella, Hb. June, occurring singly at the edge of the wood on Monte Maggiore.

E. Stadtmüllerella, Hb. April and May, amongst rose hedges at Fiume.

E. Brunnichella, L. (*magnificella*, Z.). June, on young ash trees at Martinischza and on the Kalvarienberg.

E. pullella, H.-S. April and May, occurring on the margins of thickets at Fiume.

E. parvulella, H.-S. April, on mountain-slopes at the Pulverthurm.

E. griseella, Z. April and May, on mountain-slopes at the Pulverthurm.

E. dispositella, Z. in lit. Beginning of April, on mountain-slopes in the evening at Martinischza.

E. squamosella, H.-S. May, in pasture-fields at the Pulverthurm and at Castua.

E. desertella, Z. in lit. May, on the margins of thickets at Martinischza and in the Draga valley.

E. incanella, H.-S. April and May, in pasture-fields by the Pulverthurm, in the evening.

E. opacella, F. v. R. in lit. April, in the little ash wood by the Pulverthurm.

E. nigrella, Tr. May, on mountain-slopes and in pasture-fields in the Fiume district.

E. cingillella, H.-S. April, at the Pulverthurm and at Martinischza amongst juniper bushes in the evening.

E. cinctella, Z. May, on ash trees at the Pulverthurm.

E. gangabella, Z. May and June, on the Kalvarienberg and at Tersatto, on oaks.

E. revinctella, Z. April and May, at Martinischza and on the Kalvarienberg, in young thickets.

E. bisulcella, Z. April and May, at the Pulverthurm, in the Draga valley, and at Volosca, on ash trees.

E. chrysodesmella, Z. May, in oak thickets at Fiume.

E. cerussella, Hb. May, in the Draga valley, in the evening, in moist ditches and meadows.

E. contaminatella, Z. May, taken amongst hedges in the evening at the Pulverthurm and at Hraszt.

E. consistella, Heyden in lit. April, on mountain-slopes on the Kalvarienberg and the Tersatto hill.

E. pollinariella, Z. April and May, on mountain-slopes and pasture-fields throughout the district.

E. rudectella, H.-S. April and May, in the Fiume district and at Tersatto, on mountain-pastures.

E. collitella, Dup. May, on the Kalvarienberg, at Martinischza, Volosca, &c., in pasture-fields.

E. anserinella, Z. May, in "Poderen" on the Kalvarienberg and Tersatto hill.

E. rufocinerea, Haw. (*pratoliniella*, Mann in lit.). April, on grassy slopes, after sunset, on the Tersatto hill and Kalvarienberg.

E. dispunctella, H.-S. May, in the Draga valley and in young thickets on the Kalvarienberg.

E. triatomea, Haw. (*dispilella*, H.-S.). April, occurring on mountain-slopes throughout the district.

E. arenariella, Z. June, flying amongst *Artemisia* in pasture-fields on the Kalvarienberg.

E. pollutella, Z. April, on mountain-slopes and in "Poderen" throughout the neighbourhood of Fiume, flying in the evening.

E. cygnipennella, Hb. May, on mountain-slopes and pasture-fields everywhere.

Opostega salaciella, Z. May, in meadows in the Draga valley.

O. crepusculella, Z. May, flying in the evening on the edges of marshy thickets at Hraszt.

Trifurcula pallidella, Zeller. May, in the little ash wood behind the Pulverthurm.

Bucculatrix nigricomella, Z. May, in the little ash wood behind the Pulverthurm.

B. ulmella, Z. April, on the trunks of elms at Fiume.

B. cratægi, Z. May, at Fiume, Hraszt, and Volosca, everywhere on hawthorn bushes.

B. Boyerella, Dup. (*albedinella*, Z.). May, on elm hedges throughout the district.

B. frangulella, Götze (*rhamnifoliella*, F. v. R.). June on *Rhamnus* hedges at the Pulverthurm.

B. hippocastani, Z. May, on ash trees by the Pulverthurm.

Nepticula subnitidella, Dup. May, on mountain-slopes amongst thickets in the Fiume district.

N. Hübnerella, H.-S. May, in the little ash wood by the Pulverthurm.

N. anomalella, Götze (*centifoliella*, Heyden). June, on rose-bushes at Hraszt.

N. argentipedella, Z. May, on sloe-bushes at the Pulverthurm and at Tersatto.

N. cursoriella, Heyden in lit. May, on the trunks of elms at Fiume.

Lyonetia prunifoliella, Hb. May, several beaten from sloe-hedges at the Pulverthurm; scarce.

Phyllocnistis suffusella, Z. April, on the stems of poplars at Fiume.

Cemiostoma spartifoliella, Hb. May, amongst *Spartium* at the Pulverthurm and at Castua.

C. scitella, Z. May, several taken in the little ash wood behind the Pulverthurm and at Draga.

Lithocolletis roboris, Z. April and May, on maple trees and hedges.

L. scitulella, Z. April, at the Pulverthurm, Martinischza, and Volosca, on oaks.

L. hortella, Fab. (*saportella*, Dup.). May, in the Fiume district, Draga valley, &c., on oaks.

L. cupediella, H.-S. From April to the beginning of June, in the Fiume district, Croatia, and Istria, flying in the evening on maple and olive hedges.

L. acernella, Z. April and May, in "Poderen" on the Kalvarienberg and Tersatto hill, on maple bushes.

L. abrasella, Z. May, several taken on oaks at the Pulverthurm.

L. quercifoliella, Z. May and June, on the Kalvarienberg, at Martinischza, in the Draga valley, &c., on oaks.

L. Messaniella, Z. April, several beat from evergreen oaks at the Pulverthurm.

L. delitella, Z. May, at the Pulverthurm and at Tersatto, on oaks.

L. Cramerella, F. May at the Pulverthurm and at Volosca, beaten from thorn hedges.

L. Rajella, L. May, flying around beech trees at Clana.

L. fagicolella, H.-S. May, on the stems of beech trees at Clana.

L. ilicifoliella, Z. May, at the Pulverthurm and at Tersatto, beaten from oaks.

L. pomifoliella, Z. May, on the Kalvarienberg, at Tersatto, in the Draga valley, on whitethorn and blackthorn hedges.

L. ulmifoliella, Hb. June, at the Pulverthurm and Tersatto, on elm trees.

L. fraxinella, Z. June, in the little ash wood behind the Pulverthurm.

L. emberizæpennella, Bouché. May, at Fiume and Martinischza, flying in thickets.

L. Kleemannella, F. May, at Fiume, in the Draga valley, and in Istria, on whitethorn hedges.

L. Schreberella, F. May and July, at Tersatto, Hraszt, and on the Kalvarienberg, on elm trees.

L. trifasciella, Haw. (*Heydenii*, Z.). May, at the Pulverthurm and at Groming, singly on hedges.

L. populifoliella, Tr. (*fritillella*, Tischer in lit.). July, on the trunks of poplars at Fiume.

Tischeria complanella, Hb. May and June, in the Fiume district, at Tersatto, Volosca, &c., on oaks.

T. Emyella, Dup. May, everywhere around Fiume, on brambles.

T. angusticollella, Dup. May, on sloe-hedges at the Pulverthurm, and at Hraszt.

The original descriptions of the new species are here appended.

GELECHIA LUTILABRELLA, Zeller in lit.

'Wiener ent. Monatschrift,' i. (1857) p. 179.

Nahe an *cinerella*, die Hinterflügel eben so wenig ausgeschnitten. Palpen sichelförmig, die Behaarung des ersten und zweiten Gliedes unten ein klein weniger abstehend; ihre Farbe blass ockergelb.

Vorderflügel staubig graubraun (ungefähr wie bei *Hypsolophus fasciellus* oder *deflectivellus*, aber noch trüber), schwach glänzend, ohne alle Zeichnung. Hinterflügel grau, mit helleren Fransen. Ocellen fehlend.

GELECHIA PATRUELLA, Zeller in lit.

'Wiener ent. Monatschrift,' i. (1857) p. 180.

Nahe an *coronillella*, aber doppelt so gross, von den die Mittelbinde bildenden beiden Gegenflecken nur der am Vorderrande befindliche vorhanden. Färbung und Hinterflügel wie bei *coronillella*.

Im Juni, bei Fiume Abends an dürren Pflanzen beim Pulverthurm gefangen.

GELECHIA CAMPICOLELLA, Kollar in lit.

'Wiener ent. Monatschrift,' i. (1857) p. 181.

Von der Grösse der kleinsten *Lithocolletiden*, die Palpen abwärts hängend, den Kopf wenig überragend; die Hinterflügel wie bei

Gelechia ausgeschnitten. Fühler hell und dunkel geringelt. Vorderflügel schmal und spitz, weiss mit feinen bräunlichen Atomen überflogen, die gegen den Innenwinkel zu mehr gehäuft sind; bloss mit staubigen und schwachen schwarzen Punkten bezeichnet, von welchen drei im Mittelraume in Dreieckform stehen, einer aber mehr saumwärts gerückt ist, und sich ungefähr an der Stelle des Innenwinkels befindet, zwei undeutliche aber unfern der Basis in schräger Stellung nach aussen unter einander stehen. Hinterflügel grau, Fransen aller Flügel schmutzig weiss.

COLEOPHORA FLAVIELLA, Mann.

'Weiner ent. Monatschrift,' i. (1857) p. 182.

Nahe an *trifariella* und *oriolella*. Kopf und Palpen weiss; Fühler und die dicht schuppige Fühlerbasis gelblich, der übrige Theil der Fühler weiss und schwarz geringelt.

Vorderflügel von dem angenehmen Gelb der *gallipennella*, gegen die Flügelspitze zu etwas dunkler, bloss mit drei schmalen, weissen, glänzenden, nicht sehr deutlichen Striemen bezeichnet; der am Vorderrande befindliche vor der Flügelspitze auslaufend, der Mittelstrieme und der in der Flügelfalte befindliche noch undeutlicher. Fransen blassgrau; Hinterflügel grau, mit helleren Fransen.

Im Mai, Abends im Eschenwäldchen beim Pulverthurm.

COLEOPHORA DRYMIDIS, Mann.

'Weiner ent. Monatschrift,' i. (1857) p. 183.

Aus der Verwandtschaft der *murinipennella*. Etwas kleiner. Fühler und Palpen wie bei dieser Art, erstere aber scharf weiss und schwärzlich geringelt. Zeichnung ebenfalls wie bei *murinipennella*, aber auf viel lichterem, braungelbem Grunde; die Striemen reiner weiss, besonders der am Vorderrande befindliche. Hinterflügel und Fransen ebenfalls viel heller.

Im Juni die Säcke an *Drymis spinosa* hinter Martinischza und bei Costrenna gesammelt.

I append here a description of *Ornix ampliatella*, which first appeared in the Transactions of the Entomological Society of London.

ORNIX AMPLIATELLA, (Mann) Stainton, Trans. Ent. Soc. Lond. vol. i. n. s. p. 95.

Alis anticis albidis, cinereo-irroratis, apicem versus suffusis, costa nigro-strigulata, maculis nigris tribus in disco; ciliis apicis externe bis fusco-cinctis; palpis albis immaculatis; epistomio albo.

Known at once from all its congeners by the general whiteness of the anterior wings.

Head white, with a few grey hairs; face white; antennæ grey, with paler annulations; *palpi white, unspotted*; thorax white intermixed with grey; the four anterior legs dark grey, spotted with white, the tarsi white, with the ends of the joints blackish; hind legs dirty greyish white, tarsi the same, with the ends of the joints darker.

Anterior wings four times as long as broad, white irrorated with grey; along the costa are numerous short black streaks, which, by their union, form a dark grey patch at the apex of the wing, where accordingly the ground-colour seems reversed, the markings at the apex appearing white on a dark ground, whereas in the remaining portion of the wing the markings appear dark on a white ground; the apical white costal streak is continued round the ocellated black spot to the hinder margin; in the fold of the wing are two conspicuous oblong black spots, one before and the other beyond the middle; the third spot occupies its usual place, but is not as conspicuous as the other two; cilia whitish, with two complete curved dark lines from the apex of the wing to the inner margin.

Posterior wings five times as long as broad, grey, with paler cilia.

This very beautiful species was discovered last year (1849) in Croatia by Herr Mann, of Vienna; of its food and time of appearance I know nothing. It appears to form a connecting link between this group and *caudulatella*.

[Wocke says, "taken by Mann in Croatia in plenty, in May 1849."]

Section III.

Species collected by Herr Joseph Mann in May and June 1854 in Upper Carniola, enumerated by him in the 'Verhandlungen des zoologisch-botanischen Vereins in Wien, 1854,' pp. 583–595, in a paper entitled "Aufzählung der Schmetterlinge gesammelt auf einer Reise nach Oberkrain und dem Küstenlande in Mai und Juni 1854."

Talæporia pseudobombycella, H. Several in May at Gradischa amongst young beeches.

Euplocamus Fuesslinellus, Sulz. June, flying before noon amongst beech bushes on the Nanos; the flight is hopping.

Tinea imella, H. In May, near Oberfeld, singly.

T. rusticella, H. One ♀ on a wall in June at Gradischa.

T. tapetiella, L. In June at Wippach; two specimens indoors.

T. granella, Hb. May, flying along walls in the evening.

T. pellionella, L. June, in houses at Wippach.

Lampronia variella, F. v. R. June, on the Nanos.

Incurvaria masculella, S. V. Beginning of June at Oberfeld, Haidenshaft, &c., not scarce, flying along thorn hedges.

I. flavicostella, F.v.R. May, on the Nanos, several amongst beeches.

I. Oehlmanniella, Tr. June, near Wippach.

Micropteryx Allionella, F. May, amongst beeches on the Nanos, flying in the morning.

Nemophora Swammerdammella, L. May, not scarce in the entire district, both in the valley and on the Nanos, flying in the sunshine.

N. pilulella, H. June, on the Nanos and on the Kouk, not at all scarce amongst *Pinus abies* and *P. picea*.

Adela fibulella, S. V. May, Wippach, Oberfeld, Lokavitz, Maria-Au; not scarce on *Veronica* blossoms.

A. Sulzeriella, H. May, at Semona, swarming in the sunshine morning and afternoon amongst bramble hedges.

A. viridella, Scop. May, at Wippach, Haidenschaft, also on the Nanos, flying morning and evening.

Nematois œrosellus, F. v. R. In the beginning of June, on the slopes of the Nanos, behind Gradischa, flying over flowers.

N. barbatellus, Z. Several taken in the middle of May on the southern slopes of the Nanos.

Plutella xylostella [*cruciferarum*, Z.]. From the beginning of May to the end of June in the entire valley, also at Görz; not scarce. It is probably spread all over Europe, occurring at the sea-level, and at all elevations on mountains up to the highest Alps; I met with it also in Asia on the Bithynian Olympus, near Brussa, in plenty in June and July.

P. porrectella, L. June, near Wippach, in kitchen-gardens.

P. Hufnageliella, Z. May and June, on the southern slopes of the Nanos, at Gradischa in the afternoon, when quite calm and sunshiny, on the tips of grass and on stones; it was very scarce, perhaps owing to the continuous winds which prevailed during my stay there.

P. silvella, L. Several from oaks at Fuceino in June.

P. persicella, S. V. One ♀ on a cherry-tree at Gradischa at the end of June.

Ypsolophus lemniscellus, F. v. R. At the end of June, at the old castle of Wippach and Langenfeld, on *Globularia*.

Y. marginellus, F. Several taken among juniper at the end of June, on the second range of the Nanos; I also found larvæ still in their webs.

Y. silacellus, H. June, behind Oberfeld in the "Poderen"*.

Y. fasciellus, H. June, distributed through the entire valley, and in all thorn hedges.

Y. striatellus, S. V. June, at Gradischa and Slapp, flying over the blossoms of *Umbelliferæ* in the evening.

Macrochila binotellus, F. v. R. May, at Oberfeld and Trilleck, several in the evening on margins of fields.

Anarsia Spartiella, Schr. Two specimens, at the end of June on the southern slopes of the Nanos.

Anchinia monostictella, Kllr. May and June, in the entire valley as far as Görz on all pastures, slopes, even on the Kouk.

* A local name given to the cultivated plots surrounded by walls.

A. pungitiella, Z. May, on the lower range of the Nanos, also on the Kouk in June; the females are difficult to procure, as they only come out when it is quite calm. I first found this species on the 8th June, 1849, in Istria, on Monte Maggiore; I have not yet met with it elsewhere.

A. argentistrigella, n. sp. [Described, see p. 115.] One ♂ on the 25th June, on the southern slope of the Nanos, above Gradischa, in the forenoon. I found no more the subsequent days; probably its true period of flight is July.

A. bicostella, L. Beginning of June on the Nanos, flying in young beech woods.

A. criella, Tis. Middle of June, on the slopes of the Nanos, above Gradischa.

A. daphnella, S. V. The larva and several pupæ found in June on the Kouk, and on the Nanos.

A. berberidella, mihi. A wasted ♀ beat from a barberry-bush at Gradischa in June.

Hypercallia Christiernella, L. June, on the lower range of the Nanos, and in the "Poderen" below Oberfeld; not scarce.

Lypusa maurella, S. V. One rather wasted ♀ taken in June at Heiligenkreuz.

Œcophora flavedinella, F. v. R. One ♂ captured in June on the slopes of Nanos, above Gradischa, where there was *Salvia officinalis*. In Croatia and Brussa I found the blackish larva in united leaves of *Salvia officinalis*.

Œ. Lewenhoekella, S. V. Singly in pastures in June behind Oberfeld and Haidenschaft.

Œ. nodosella, n. sp. [Described, see p. 116.] Several taken at the end of May in a "Podere" on the southern slope of the Nanos, above Gradischa. I discovered this species in 1846 near Pratovecchio, in Tuscany, on Monte Falterone; but as I only found males, I took them for large *Lewenhoekella* [see *ante*, p. 60]. In 1849 I found several pairs *in copulá*, and also some single females in the morning and evening in the Fiume district, behind the Pulverthurm, on a mountain-pasture, and perceived that it was a distinct species.

Œ. Metzneriella, Tr. One ♀ beat from a wild rose in June, behind Langenfeld.

Œ. flavifrontella, S. V. Flying in June amongst *Pinus picea* on the Kouk.

Œ. lacteella, S. V. Several taken in the house at Wippach.

Œ. Esperella, H. Flying in the sunshine before noon round young beeches on the Nanos, the middle of May and beginning of June. The female beneath has the yellow spot at the hinder part of the abdomen; above the abdomen is ochreous yellow.

Œ. productella, Z. (*Franckella*, Tr.). Several taken amongst hazelbushes at the end of June at Oberfeld. Also a pair *in copulá*. The female has the spot beneath hardly perceptible, and the upperside of the abdomen is as dark as the thorax. The males are more difficult to distinguish, but *productella* has the wings narrower than *Esperella*. I generally observed copulation before noon.

Œ. turbidella, Z. In June, on the southern slopes of the Nanos, also at Fuccino on the Kouk, flying in the afternoon and evening. I generally found it *in copulâ* after sunset. I first found this in 1849 at Fiume, then at Spalato and Brussa.

Œ. vagabundella, Z. In May and June on the southern slopes of the Nanos above Gradischa, also at Oberfeld, Locavitz, and Heiligenkreuz, flying over pastures and slopes; it is widely distributed. I found it in Croatia, Istria, Dalmatia, and in Asia Minor at Brussa.

Œ. gravatella, Z. In June around Wippach on pastures, slopes, and grassy places, and in young bushes. I generally found it *in copulâ* in the afternoon on grass stems.

Œ. aurifrontella, H. Taken in the afternoon in the middle of May among whitethorn hedges at Semona and Maria-Au. I once found the larva on whitethorn in the Brigittenau.

Œ. Knochella, F. In May and June on the southern slopes of the Nanos, near Gradischa, St. Nicholas, Langenfeld, Oberfeld, and Haidenschaft, in grassy places, and in "Poderen," generally on grass stems. I found it copulated at all hours of the day. The female sits placidly on a grass stem, and generally there are several males swarming round her.

Œ. phycidella, Z. Several in June from hedges along the road to Maria-Au.

Scythropia cratægella, L. Singly in sloe-hedges at Wippach, in May.

Swammerdamia cerasiella, H. Flying along sloe-hedges at Wippach in May.

S. compunctella, F. v. R. One ♂ from a hedge near Locavitz in the middle of June. I first took several specimens of this at the beginning of July 1842 on the Semmering, in a felled wood amongst brambles.

S. comptella, H. Several from hedges at Wippach, the beginning of May.

Yponomeuta sedellus, Tr. Several taken on a wall at Gradischa in June.

Y. plumbellus, H. Several taken amongst *Euonymus* at Haidenschaft and Heiligenkreuz, in June.

Y. variabilis, Z. Larvæ abundant on sloe-hedges in May.

Y. malinellus, Z. Imago found on apple-trees at Gradischa at the end of June.

Y. evonymellus, S.V. The nests of the larvæ in innumerable quantities throughout the entire district, on *Euonymus* in hedges.

Y. padellus, Hyd. The nests of the larvæ on *Prunus padus* at Wippach and Stapp.

Psecadia scalella, Scop. [*pusiella*, Roemer]. Several in June behind Oberfeld, in a " Podere," on trunks of trees.

P. echiella, S. V. May, on walls and stones at Wippach and St. Veit.

P. signella, H. May and June, on walls and rock-faces at Wippach, and Gradischa, also at Zoll and Heiligenkreuz.

P. fluvianella, Tr. One ♂ taken in June near Locavitz, on a grass stem. This is one of the greatest rarities, and is the species with half golden-yellow posterior wings described by Treitschke; the female, which he describes as entirely black-grey, is *chrysopyga*, Zeller, which is not so scarce, and which I have found *in copulâ*. Both sexes are black-grey. It occurs in Dalmatia, Tuscany, and also in Asia Minor, near Brussa.

Depressaria depunctella, H. One specimen from an oak at the end of June at Langenfeld: its true period is July and August.

D. aridella, mihi. One ♂ from young oaks, the middle of June, at Oberfeld.

D. capreolella, F. v. R. In the middle of May several quite wasted specimens taken in the evening near the old castle of Wippach; it appears already in March and April.

D. characterella, S. V. Several on walls, the middle of May, at Wippach.

D. furvella, Pod. Found on stones on the southern slopes of the Nanos the middle of June.

D. peloritanella, Z. [*rotundella*, Dgl.]. One ♀ from a bramble hedge at Oberfeld the beginning of May.

D. Alstrœmerella, Tr. Several from *Clematis* hedges at Haidenschaft, the end of June.

D. ferulæ, Zell.? The larva in May behind Oberfeld and on the southern slopes of the Nanos, on *Pimpinella*? I bred the moths in the middle of June. Although the larvæ were abundant there, I saw no specimens of the perfect insect at large.

D. dictamnella, F. v. R. The larva abundant on *Dictamnus* in the " Poderen " behind Oberfeld.

Carcina luticornella, F. v. R. One specimen at the end of June at Lokavitz.

Gelechia Denisella, S. V. From the middle of May to June on the Nanos in the beech region, flying in the morning and evening in grassy places; also in " Poderen " at Oberfeld and Budaine.

G. tripunctella?, S. V. Taken singly in the evening at Wippach, on a wall by the first mill. This species rather resembles the *tripunctella* which occurs on our Alps, only the wings are shorter and blunter. [I apprehend this may have been Millière's *antirrhinella*, noticed afterwards; *that* was bred from *Antirrhinum*, the habit of which is to grow on walls.]

G. cinerella, L. In May and June, throughout the entire valley, on the slopes, amongst young bushes.

G. scintillella, F. v. R. In June, from hedges on the southern slopes of the Nanos. The larva feeds on *Dorycnium*.

G. subsequella, H. Several beaten from sloe at Sturia at the end of June.

G. lutatella, Metz. Two specimens, which were already wasted, taken at the beginning of May, at the old castle of Wippach.

G. gallinella, Tr. Several in June, on the southern slopes of the Nanos at Gradischa.

G. leucatella, L. In June among sloe-hedges at St. Veit and Gradischa.

G. terrella, H. At the end of June, not scarce in the Wippach district in pastures and slopes.

G. distinctella, F. v. R. At the end of June, several taken in a "Poderen" at Oberfeld.

G. zebrella, Tis. June, several taken in meadows on the Kouk.

G. solutella, F. v. R. The beginning of May at the old castle of Wippach and at Gradischa on the slopes of the Nanos.

G. apicistrigella, F. v. R. In the middle of June at Haidenschaft and Heiligenkreuz.

G. scriptella, H. May, at Wippach, Oberfeld, Sturia, Slapp, &c.

G. nigrinotella, Z. Several at the end of June from young oaks behind Oberfeld.

G. aleella, F. June, on the trunks of oaks at Trillek and Zoll.

G. ligulella, S. V. June, on the slopes of the Nanos, at Gradischa, taken on grass stems in the evening.

G. tæniolella, Tr. At the end of June on the Nanos, amongst hornbeam.

G. patruella, Zell. At the end of June from young oaks in a "Podere" at Oberfeld.

G. coronillella, Tr. In the middle of May, at Gradischa and on the Nanos, not scarce, flying amongst *Coronilla*, on which the larva feeds.

G. biguttella, F. v. R. Singly in June in pastures at Langenfeld and Stegola. Near Vienna the larva feeds on *Dorycnium*.

G. anthyllidella, H. June, in the entire valley on pastures and slopes, also on the Kouk, by no means scarce; I generally found it amongst *Globularia*.

G. unicolorella, Z. In June on the Nanos, in grassy places in the beech region.

G. ingloriella, Z. In the middle of June, on the southern slopes of the Nanos above Gradischa, taken in the evening on grass, where I also found several *in copulá*.

G. flammella, Tr. June, at Wippach, Oberfeld, Zoll, and Haidenschaft, in meadows, and flying over grass in "Poderen," in the evening.

G. artemisiella, T. At the end of June, several on the slopes at Oberfeld.

G. stipella, H. May, on walls near Wippach.

G. Hermannella, F. May, at Haidenschaft.

G. nigricostella, F. v. R. May, singly in the evening in the old town of Wippach.

G. subericinella, mihi. June, on the slopes of the Nanos at Gradischa and St. Nicholas; also in pastures and amongst young bushes at Heiligenkreuz and Sturia.

G. decurtella, H. Several taken in the "Poderen" behind Oberfeld at the end of June.

G. pictella, Z. Found on the stems of grass in the morning at Gradischa, on the slopes of the Nanos, at the beginning of June.

G. superbella, Tr. Taken in the beginning of June before noon in the interior of the old castle of Wippach.

G. paucipunctella, Metz. In the middle of May, several in a meadow behind Oberfeld.

Æchmia Thrasonella, Scop. Abundant, flying amongst rushes, along the ditches in the meadows below Gotschee, June 6th.

Æ. majorella, mihi. Several taken in June on the southern slopes of the Nanos, on stones and masses of rock, in the afternoon.

Æ. equitella, Scop. Flying in meadows at Wippach, in the middle of May.

Æ. oculatella, mihi. Taken at the beginning of June behind Oberfeld, in a "Podere," on the borders of a small piece of water. I first found this species at Pisa, in Tuscany, in 1846; in 1848 in meadows near Vienna, likewise in a similar locality; it frequents moist meadows.

Tinagma perdicella, Tr. June, on the Kouk, on Umbelliferæ at the border of woods.

Argyresthia tetrapodella, L. May, at Wippach, flying in the evening along sloe-hedges.

Coleophora Mayrella, H. Several taken in June in a "Podere" behind Oberfeld, in the evening.

C. ornatipennella, H. May and June, on the borders of fields and slopes in the entire district from St. Veit to Görz; also on the Kouk I found some in June on the flowers of *Salvia*.

C. vibicella, H. The larva-cases in May at Gradischa, in a "Podere," on *Genista*.

C. oriolella, F. v. R. June, behind Oberfeld and in the ravine at St. Daniel on *Onobrychis*.

C. vulnerariæ, Z. May and June, on the southern slopes of the Nanos at Gradischa, also at Oberfeld, Sturia, and Heiligenkreuz, flying in "Poderen."

C. gallipennella, H. Several in June, on a mountain-meadow on the heights near Zoll.

C. flaviella, Z. One female taken in June in a pasture above Langenfeld.

C. onobrychiella, F. v. R. In June, on *Onobrychis* at St. Nicholas, on the Nanos.

C. auricella, Bosc. Singly, flying in May in the evening on the pastures by the old castle of Wippach.

C. virgatella, Z. Several taken in the morning at the beginning of May in the old castle of Wippach; at the same place I found living larvæ in cases on *Globularia*, and on stones some firmly fastened cases, which produced *virgatella* a fortnight afterwards. The case is iron-grey, 5 lines long, of a cylindric form, rather curved anteriorly, three-flapped, and the lower end pointed, sheath-like, beneath with a white line 1''' long.

C. albifuscella, Z. In the middle of May, in a "Podere" above Gradischa; on the Nanos, flying on calm evenings in June; I found it also on the lower range of the Nanos on luxuriant grassy places amongst young bushes. It is widely distributed, yet always scarce; it occurs round Vienna: then I found it at Leghorn, Spalato (exactly at the Castle Abbadessa), at Fiume, and at Brussa in Asia Minor, where the vegetation was luxuriant.

C. niveicostella, F. v. R. In June, at Wippach and the neighbourhood, flying on meadows and slopes in the evening, when copulation takes place.

C. onosmella, Brahm. June, at Wippach, St. Veit, Haidenschaft, in "Poderen" and on grassy pastures.

C. enervatella, Z. In June, at Oberfeld, flying over rushes in a very wet "Podere." In Tuscany I found it at Pratolino, also in marshy places on rushes; elsewhere I have never met with it. Herr Zeller pronounced it a variety of *onosmella*, which I doubt, since in the above-mentioned place *onosmella* did not occur.

C. ciconiella, F. v. R. June, on the southern slope of the Nanos at Gradischa, and several found at Lokavitz on the slopes of the Tschaun.

C. therinella, Z. (*trochilella*, F. R.). End of June at Slapp, in the evening, on a pasture near the vineyards.

C. lineariella, F. v. R. In the middle of May at the old castle of Wippach, and also at the end of May on the lower range of the Nanos, flying in grassy places morning and evening.

C. coracipennella, Hb. The larvæ not scarce on sloe-bushes at Wippach in May.

Gracilaria Franckella, Hb. Several taken amongst young oaks at Oberfeld in May.

G. elongella, L. May, at Wippach, amongst maple bushes.

G. tringipennella, F. R. At the beginning of June, flying in the evening on slopes at Wippach and Heiligenkreuz.

G. lacertella, F. v. R. Taken in a "Podere" at Oberfeld, in the afternoon, the middle of May.

G. ononidis, Z. June, several at Gradischa on *Ononis spinosa*.

G. Kollariella, F. v. R. June, amongst ash trees at Sturia.

Coriscium alaudellum, D. One female, taken the beginning of May at Wippach on a privet hedge.

Ornix torquillella, Z. June, at Oberfeld, on hawthorn hedges.

O. ampliatella, mihi. In the middle of May, amongst maple bushes, at Gradischa and Lokavitz. (See p. 104.)

O. caudulatella, Z. One male, found on a wall in June at Gradischa. This species is very scarce; hitherto I have only taken single examples on our Prater.

Cosmopteryx Goldeggiella, F. v. R. (*argyrogrammos*, Z.). Singly, flying in the evening in June in pastures at Oberfeld. I also found this species in Tuscany, Dalmatia, and Fiume, and most plentifully at Brussa in Asia Minor; always on pastures and slopes.

Elachista pontificella, H. June, distributed throughout the entire valley, most frequently in pastures, slopes, and "Poderen."

E. dentosella, F. v. R. Several taken in the evening in the middle of May, in a grassy place in the old castle of Wippach. Hitherto I had only found this species near Vienna, on the Laaerberg, in the royal mews, where it flies quite low on grassy places at sunset, and then copulation takes place.

E. miscella, H. May, at Gradischa, Oberfeld, Hanonia, and at Platscha, on slopes.

E. ictella, H. In the middle of May, on the slopes of the Nanos above Gradischa, at Wippach, Haidenschaft, and Heiligenkreuz, flying in the evening before sunset on grassy slopes and in "Poderen."

E. pomposella, F. v. R. In the middle of June, at Gradischa, several taken amongst grass on the slopes of the Nanos before noon; it runs up to the top of the grass, vibrates its wings for some time, then flies a little further and repeats the process. At Fiume I observed copulation both before and after noon; there it flew amongst *Salvia officinalis*.

E. albiapicella, F. v. R. From the beginning to the end of May, flying amongst *Globularia* on pastures and slopes in the neighbourhood of Wippach; they creep deep into the *Globularia* blossoms, especially the female, so that only the end of its body remains visible; in this position they await the male, and then copulation takes place.

E. modestella, D. In the middle of May at the foot of the Nanos under bushes in the flowers of *Stellaria holostea*, into which they also quite penetrate, and then copulation takes place.

E. magnificella, mihi. June, on the slopes of the Nanos, before noon, amongst ash trees.

E. Stadtmüllerella, H. One specimen in May, at Oberfeld, from a hedge.

E. griseella, F. v. R. May, flying on slopes in the evening at Wippach and Oberfeld.

E. nigrella, Tr. May, in meadows, in the afternoon, at Wippach.

E. cingillella, F. v. R. May and the beginning of June, around Wippach, especially at Gradischa, swarming around juniper bushes in a " Podere : " I found this most plentifully in 1849 in Croatia, at Martinischza, in a defile; it appears in the evening, at which time copulation takes place.

E. revinctella, Z. Several taken, in the evening, in May, at Gradischa. I discovered this species in 1849 in Croatia, at Martinischza, where it occurred amongst *cingillella*.

E. pollinariella, Z. Not scarce, in May and June, at Wippach, in pastures.

E. rudectella, F. v. R. In May and June, on the slopes of the Nanos at Gradischa, and flying in the evening in grassy places at Zollhaus on the Kouk. This species occurs near Vienna, and in Croatia, Dalmatia, and at Brussa.

E. pratoliniella, mihi (*rufocinerea*, Haw.?). Several taken, on calm evenings in May, in the old castle of Wippach. I discovered this species in 1846, in March, in Tuscany, in the Grand Duke's beautiful park Pratolino; I then found it in 1849 at Fiume, on the Schlossberg Tersatto; and also near Brussa I found it at a considerable elevation in mountain-pastures.

E. dispilella, Z. From the beginning to the middle of May, on the stony slopes near the old castle of Wippach, where it flew quickly and rather plentifully after sunset.

E. cygnipennella, H. Abundant in May in the entire neigbourhood of Wippach; also in June on the higher pastures of the Nanos.

Opostega salaciella, Tis. Flying singly in the evening in June, in marshy bushes near Slapp.

Trifurcula pallidella, Z. Several in May at Oberfeld, in a pasture-field.

Nepticula cristatella, F.v. R. Several in meadows in May, at Wippach.

N. cineritella, F. v. R. Taken in June from a *Clematis* hedge at Maria-au.

Bucculatrix cratægi, Z. Flying in May at Semona, round whitethorn bushes.

B. Boyerella, D. Everywhere in the Wippach district, in June, amongst elm bushes.

B. frangulella, Goeze. Several taken from a *Rhamnus* hedge at Oberfeld, the beginning of June.

Lyonetia Clerckella, L. Hybernated specimens on the trunk of a cherry-tree, in May, at Wippach.

Lithocolletis roboris, Z.   Several amongst oaks, in May, at Wippach and on the Nanos.

L. Amyotella, D.   Flying amongst oaks at Oberfeld in June.

L. scitulella, F. v. R.   Several amongst oaks, in May, on the slopes of the Nanos at Gradischa.

L. acernella, Z.   On maple hedges, in May, at Wippach and Haidenschaft.

L. quercifoliella, F. v. R.   In May, at Gradischa, from oak bushes, also found on the trunks of oaks.

L. delitella, F. v. R.   In June, behind Oberfeld and at Sturia, among young oaks.

L. Cramerella, F.   In June, amongst hornbeam, on the lower range of the Nanos.

L. faginella, mihi.   At the beginning of May, amongst young bushes on the Nanos.

L. Kleemannella, F.   Several amongst whitethorn at the end of May at Ustia.

L. Schreberella, F.   On the trunks of elms, at Gradischa, in May; the larvæ also in plenty on elm bushes at the end of June. When I explored the neighbourhood of Wippach at the beginning of May, I was in great hopes of finding many species of *Lithocolletis* there, since so many kinds of trees occur in the district; but I was much disappointed, since in June I rarely found mined leaves which betrayed their presence.

Tischeria Emyella, D.   In May, and also in June, I found the imago singly amongst bramble hedges; they were more numerous at Fiume.

T. angusticollella, Heyd.   Several at the end of June, amongst sloe-hedges at Oberfeld.

Copies of the original descriptions of the two new species, *Anchinia argentistrigella* and *Œcophora nodosella*, are here appended:—

'Verhandlungen des zoologisch-botanischen Vereins in Wien,' 1854, p. 585.

ANCHINIA ARGENTISTRIGELLA, Mann.

Diese Schabe hat die Grösse und Gestalt wie *Anch. aristella*, Lin., für welche ich sie auch in Wippach hielt; jedoch bei dem Vergleich fand ich, dass sie weder *aristella*, noch die nahe verwandte *Schlägeriella*, Zell. ist.   Der Mann hat dieselbe Färbung wie *aristella*, indem diese eben so dunkelbraungelb vorkommt, der weisse glänzende silberne Streifen in der Mitte der Vorderflügel ist sehr zart, beinahe gleich breit, bis zur Flügelspitze, wo er sehr fein bis durch die Fransen geht.   Der weisse Vorderrand fehlt gänzlich und unterscheidet diese Art gleich von beiden benannten.   Hinterflügel, Körper, Beine, Brust, Kopf und Palpen sind gleich mit *aristella*, nur das letzte feine Palpenglied ist kürzer. Die ganze Unterseite ist dunkler als bei *aristella*. Ich fing einen Mann den 25. Juni auf dem südlichen Nanosabhang oberhalb Gradischa in den Vormittagsstunden, fand aber die folgenden Tage keine mehr; diese Art mag vielleicht erst im Juli ihre Flugzeit haben.

' Verhandlungen des zoologisch-botanischen Vereins in Wien,' 1854, p. 586.

ŒCOPHORA NODOSELLA, Mann.

Ende Mai auf dem südlichen Nanosabhange ober Gradischa in einem Podere einige gefangen; diese Art ist grösser als *Lewenhoekella*, der Mann hat sehr dicke Fühler, das Weib hat die Fühler in der Mitte durch einen Haarwulst verdickt, welcher der *Lewenhoekella* mangelt; im Leben stehen diese Haare vom Schafte ab, dass es wie ein Wedel aussieht; nach dem Tode liegen die Haarschuppen an, und bilden diese Wulst. Die Farbe der Flügel, der Stand der Bleipusteln sind wie bei *Lewenhoekella*. Ich entdeckte diese Art schon im Jahre 1846 in Toskana bei Pratovecchio auf dem Monte Falterone. Da ich dort nur Männer fand, so hielt ich sie für grosse *Lewenhoekella*; im Jahre 1849 fand ich mehrere Paare *in copulâ* wie auch einzelne Weiber in den Morgen- und Abendstunden im fiumanen Gebiete hinter dem Pulverthurme auf einer Berghutweide und erkannte, dass es eine eigene Art sei.

SECTION IV.

Species collected by Herr Joseph Mann in Corsica in 1855, enumerated by him in the 'Verhandlungen des zoologisch-botanischen Vereins in Wien,' 1855, pp. 560-569, entitled " Die Lepidopteren gesammelt auf einer entomologischen Reise in Corsika im Jahre 1855."

Tinea imella, Hb. May, singly flying along old walls in the evening at Ajaccio.

T. rusticella, Hb. June, beaten singly from hedges in the valley towards S. Antonio.

T. tapetiella, L. One specimen taken in a room at Ajaccio.

T. granella, L. June, swarming along hedges in the evening in the valley towards S. Antonio.

T. spretella, S. V. (*fuscipunctella*, Haw.). Flying in the room at Ajaccio and Corte.

T. pellionella, L. Also taken in the room at Ajaccio.

Lampronia variella, F. v. R. June, several taken amongst brambles on Pozzo di Borgo; they were, however, already worn.

Incurvaria masculella, Hb. May, at Ajaccio and in the valley Campo di Loro, flying amongst sloe-bushes in the morning sunshine.

Micropteryx calthella, L. May, several taken on the blossoms of *Tamarix* in the Prunelli valley.

M. facetella, Z. May, on the slopes of Pozzo di Borgo, taken on the blossoms of *Terebinthus*. I first found this species in 1850, in April on the island of Lissa, in Dalmatia, and in May at Spalato on Monte Mariano, likewise on the blossoms of *Terebinthus*.

Nemotois chalcochrysellus, n. sp. [Described, see p. 121.] May, in the valley of Lazarethspitze, always after rain, running up the stems of the high grass. I only obtained a few males and two females.

Plutella xylostella, L. April, May, and July, everywhere round Ajaccio on mountains and in valleys; not scarce.

Ypsolophus asinellus, Hb. June, one male taken on the slopes of Pozzo di Borgo.

Y. verbascellus, S. V. May and June, found singly on *Scrophularia* at Lazarethspitze.

Y. lineatellus, in lit. H.-S. 560. May, flying in the evening on the slopes of Pozzo di Borgo, and on the mountain-slopes towards the Isole Sanguinarie.

Y. striatellus, S. V. June, on the Lazarethspitze, and in the valley Campo di Loro; not scarce on mountain-slopes and pasture-fields.

Y. lanceolellus, (Kollar, in lit.) H.-S. 402. May, one male taken near Cavro.

Anchinia cyrniella, n. sp. [Briefly described, see p. 122.] June and July, several males and one female collected on the slopes of Pozzo di Borgo, and on the hills of the Lazarethspitze.

Œcophora Kollarella, Costa (*flavedinella*, F. v. R.). June, flying amongst *Lavandula stœchas* on the slopes of Monte Rosso.

Œ. Lewenhoekella. May, taken in a pasture-field at Alata.

Œ. Metznerella, Tr. May, one specimen beaten from a laurel bush at San Antonio.

Œ. lacteella, S. V. May, one specimen taken in the room at Ajaccio.

Œ. chenopodiella, Hb. June, several taken on the wall of a vineyard at Ajaccio.

Œ. dissimilella, H.-S. 989. Middle of June, several taken on the slopes of Pozzo di Borgo.

Œ. phycidella, Z. June, several beaten from thorn hedges at Ajaccio, in the valley toward S. Antonio.

Œ. Lavandulæ, n. sp. [Described, see p. 122.] Towards the end of May I found the larvæ already spun up in the upper leaves of the twigs of *Lavandula stœchas*. One moth appeared on the 10th June, another on the 12th; the other pupæ dried up.

Œ. oleella, Boyer de Fousc. June, several taken among olive trees at Ajaccio.

Œ. quadrifariella, n. sp. [Described, see p. 122.] I took three specimens of this scarce species on a small rocky part of the Lazarethspitze.

Scythropia cratægella, L. July, on whitethorn hedges on the Lazarethspitze. The specimens are rather darker than the Vienna ones.

S. cerasiella, Hb., F. v. R. June, flying amongst whitethorn at Ajaccio.

Yponomeuta variabilis, Z. July, on sloe-hedges.

Y. evonymellus, S. V. The larvæ met with in abundance in the valley towards San Antonio.

Y. irrorellus, Hb. June, several taken on a hedge at Cavro.

Psecadia sexpunctella, Hb. May, on hedges at Ajaccio, and on *Echium* on the slopes of Pozzo di Borgo.

P. echiella, S. V. May and June, not scarce in the avenue at Ajaccio on the trunks of trees.

Depressaria depressella, Hb. June, several taken along hedges at Ajaccio.

D. badiella, Hb. July, several beaten from hedges at Bastia.

D. corticinella, Z. (*cuprinella*, Z. in lit.). June, several taken in the valley towards S. Antonio.

D. atricornella, n. sp. [Briefly described from a single specimen, see p. 123.] I found one male just bred in my larva-cage, where I had probably introduced the larvæ with the food-plants for *Ocnogyna corsica*. [Herr Mann informs us that *Ocnogyna corsica* fed on very many sorts of plants, such as *Echium*, chamomile, clover, yarrow, plantain, &c.]

Carcina fagana, S. V. July, beaten from oak hedges in the valley towards San Antonio; they differ much from Vienna specimens in their colour, which is a dark carmine-red.

Gelechia gallinella, Tischer. June, flying amongst *Erica* at Pozzo di Borgo.

G. striatopunctella, Kollar. May, several taken on the slopes of Pozzo di Borgo.

G. vilella, Z. April, flying amongst nettles in the evening in the valley towards San Antonio.

G. scabidella, Z. April and May, flying in the evening on the slopes of Pozzo di Borgo and the Lazarethspitze.

G. plebejella, Z. June, flying singly around bramble bushes in the evening in the valleys of the Lazarethspitze.

G. scriptella, Hb. May, several taken amongst bushes in the valley Campo di Loro.

G. cytisella, Ti. May, several beaten from hedges at Ajaccio.

G. ligulella, S. V. June, several taken on hedges.

G. coronillella, Tr. May, flying on the slopes of Pozzo di Borgo.

G. flammella, Tr. May and June, flying on the slopes of Pozzo di Borgo, and of the Lazarethspitze.

G. cerealella, Olivier. May, several flying on walls at Ajaccio.

G. paupella, Z. (*melanolepidella*, Kollar in lit.). May, flying after sunset on mountain-slopes above the cemetery chapel. In 1846 I found this on the heath at Ardenza, near Leghorn, in Tuscany.

G. campicolella, Z. May, flying in the evening amongst *Erica* on the mountains at Ajaccio, above the cemetery chapel.

G. inopella, Z. April, several taken on the mountain-slopes by the Greek chapel.

G. quinquepunctella, Kollar in lit., H.-S. 573. At the beginning of May, on the mountain-slopes of Pozzo di Borgo, Rosso, and Lazarethspitze, flying in the evening.

G. stipella, Hb. May, flying singly on *Chenopodium*.

G. Hermannella, F. May, taken on walls in "Poderen" at Ajaccio.

G. torridella, Z. June, two specimens found on the slopes of Pozzo di Borgo. This is still a great rarity.

G. subericinella, Mann, H.-S. 541. May, several taken on the slopes of Monte Rosso.

G. pictella, Z. June, several taken on *Lavandula stœchas* on the Lazarethspitze.

G. selaginella, n. sp. [Briefly described, see p. 124.] At the end of June, taken in the evening on myrtle blossom on Pozzo di Borgo.

Rœslerstammia fumociliella, n. sp. [Described, see p. 124.] I discovered this species at Leghorn in May 1846. At Ajaccio I obtained a pair from hedges on the hill of San Giovanni.

R. eglanteriella, n. sp. [Described, see p. 125.] May, I found two specimens amongst wild white rose bushes at Ajaccio.

Æchmia oculatella, (Mann in lit.) Zeller, Ent. Ztg. May, several specimens taken in a meadow near a little brook at Ajaccio.

Æ. equitella, var., Scop. June, two specimens taken on the Lazarethspitze; the white markings are all much brighter and sharper, the curved white streak is broader, and the metallic gloss is of a reddish lilac.

Tinagma lithargyrella, (Kollar in lit.) Z. May, several taken on *Erica* on the slopes of Pozzo di Borgo.

Coleophora trochilipennella, Costa (*semibarbella*, Kollar in lit.). May, flying on the slopes of Pozzo di Borgo, also met with on the Lazarethspitze, and on Monte Rosso.

C. cœlebipennella, Ti. June, taken on the slopes of Pozzo di Borgo, and on the Lazarethspitze; the cases also met with on *Helichrysum angustifolium*.

C. vulnerariæ, Z. June, taken on the slopes of Pozzo di Borgo.

C. marginatella, H.-S. 683. June, two specimens taken on a mountain-slope at Cavro.

C. albifuscella, F. v. R., Z. May, singly on the Lazarethspitze, and in the valley Campo di Loro, at the Badhaus.

C. leucapennella, Hb. June, several taken on the slopes of Pozzo di Borgo and Monte Lizza.

C. succursella, H.-S. 887. July, a few specimens taken on the sunny slopes of Pozzo di Borgo. This is nearly allied to *ciconiella*, F. v. R. Herr Zeller in his note, no. 1, Linnæa Ent. iv. p. 365, refers *ciconiella*, F. v. R., as a variety to *Millefolii*. But the cases of the two species are different. In 1852 I bred *ciconiella*, and the cases agreed precisely with Herrich-Schäffer's figure 895.

C. badiipennella, F. v. R. in lit., Z. Linn. Ent. May, several taken among elms.

Zelleria hepariella, (Mann in lit.) H.-S. 819. I discovered this species at Leghorn, and again found a few specimens at Ajaccio, flying round wild olive bushes.

Gracilaria tringipennella, (F. v. R. in lit.) Z. Isis, 1839. May, several taken on the slopes of Pozzo di Borgo.

G. auroguttella, Steph. (*lacertella*, F. v. R. in lit.). May, met with in the grassy valleys of the Lazarethspitze.

Coriscium quercetellum, Z. April, several beaten from oak bushes at Ajaccio.

Ornix ampliatella, Z. May, beaten from thorn hedges at Cavro.

Cosmopteryx argyrogrammos, Z. (*Goldeygiella*, F. v. R. in lit.). May and June, flying after sunset on the slopes and pasture-fields of Pozzo di Borgo, Monte Lizza, Monte Rosso, &c.

Elachista testaceella, Hb. April, two specimens taken at Ajaccio.

E. miscella, Hb. June, several met with on the Lazarethspitze.

E. ictella, Hb. May, taken on the slopes of Pozzo di Borgo.

E. Isabellella, Costa. June, also taken singly on the slopes of Pozzo di Borgo. I found this pretty species in 1846 at Leghorn, then in 1849 at Fiume, in 1850 at Spalato, where it was most plentiful in a pasture-field, and in 1851 at Brussa, likewise in mountain-pastures. Herrich-Schäffer's fig. 818 (*opulentella*) is very unsatisfactory.

E. serratella, Tr. June, several taken on the flowers of *Globularia*.

E. pomposella, F. v. R., Z. June, two specimens taken on the tips of grass.

E. albiapicella, F. v. R. in lit., H.-S. 979. May, taken singly on the Lazarethspitze.

E. Dohrnii, Z. I found this beautiful and scarce species in July on the Lazarethspitze after sunset amongst *Cistus salvifolius* and *Helichrysum angustifolium*.

E. cingillella, F. v. R., H.-S. 940. June, several taken on the mountain-slopes of Pozzo di Borgo.

E. rudectella, F. v. R., H.-S. 1020. May, met with singly in the valleys of the Lazarethspitze.

E. festaliella, Hb. May, two specimens found on bramble hedges.

Opostega salaciella, Ti. May, taken in the valley of the Lazarethspitze, where the spring is.

O. menthinella, n. sp. [Briefly described, see p. 125.] I took twenty specimens of this species in the valley towards San Antonio in July, flying slowly around *Mentha* late in the evening.

Nepticula Hübnerella, H.-S. 829–830 (*gratiosella*, F. v. R. in lit.). May, several taken at Ajaccio on the leaves of plants.

Lithocolletis endryella, n. sp. [Described, see p. 125.] April, beaten from *Quercus ilex* at Ajaccio; only three specimens found.

L. Messaniella, Z. April, two specimens taken on hedges.

L. elatella, Z., H.-S. f. 757 (*confertella*, F. v. R. in lit.). I took a single specimen in May on a hedge at Cavro.

Tischeria complanella, H. Several on oaks, in June, at Pozzo di Borgo.

T. emyella, Dup. In May, at Ajaccio, amongst brambles.

Copies of the original descriptions of the new species are here appended.

'Verhandlungen zool.-bot. Vereins in Wien,' 1855, p. 561.

NEMOTOIS CHALCOCHRYSELLUS, n. sp.

Reiht sich an *minimellus*, *barbatellus*, und *prodigellus*, denen sie in Form und Zeichnung ungemein nahe steht.

Der Körper und die Palpen des Männchens sind schwarz, letztere mit sehr langen, borstigen Haaren besetzt; die Fühler haben dieselbe Länge wie bei den verwandten Arten und sind silberweiss, nur an der Oberseite des Basis schwarz beschuppt.

Die Vorderflügel sind an der Spitze ein klein wenig mehr gerundet, als bei den obengenannten Arten, haben aber fast ganz dieselbe Färbung und Zeichnung, nur sind bei *minimellus* die Flügel von der Basis bis zur Mittelbinde grünlich messinggelb, hinter derselben röthlich golden, bei *barbatellus* und *prodigellus* wohl vor und hinter der Binde röthlich goldgelb, wie bei meinem *chalcochrysellus*, die Binde selbst ist aber bei dieser Art doppelt so breit, als bei den zwei obengenannten; ebenfalls bei den genannten Arten mangelt auf dem Vorderflügel unweit dem Aussenrande der eingedrückte schwarze Schuppenfleck.

Weiters sind die Hinterflügel des Männchens dunkelgrau, gegen die Basis zu ungemein bleich mit weisslichgelben Fransen, also von allen verwandten Arten verschieden. Das Weib ist etwas kleiner mit kürzeren runden, fast wie beim Manne gezeichneten Vorderflügeln, dunkelgrauen, violett schillernden Hinterflügeln, broncefarbener Saumlinie und gelblichgrauen Fransen, rostgelber Stirn und schwarzen, violett glänzenden Fühlern, welche nur wenig länger als der Vorderrand des Vorderflügels sind, rostgelbe Basis und weisse Spitzen haben.

Unten sind die Flügel beim Manne grau, an Vorderrand und Spitze violett glänzend; der Mittelraum und die Fransen der hinteren sind hier ebenfalls sehr bleich. Beim Weibe ist der Violettglanz über den grössten Theil der Flügel verbreitet und die Fransen sind broncefarb.

Ich fand diese schöne Art im Mai in dem Thale der Lazarethspitze stets nach Regen aus dem hohen Grase an den Stengeln hinauflaufend. Ich bekam nur wenige Männchen und zwei Weibchen.

'Verhandlungen zool-bot. Vereins in Wien,' 1855, p. 562.

ANCHINIA CYRNIELLA, n. sp.

Aus der Verwandtschaft von *aristella*, *Schlægeriella*, und der von mir in diesen Schriften bekannt gemachten *argentistrigella*. Der *Schlægeriella* steht sie am nächsten, ist aber kleiner und etwas kurzflüglicher, die Farbe der Vorderflügel ist noch dunkler als bei *aristella*, der Vorderrand und die Querstrieme sind wohl wie bei *Schlægeriella*, aber viel reiner weiss und schärfer abstehend, als bei dieser Art und *aristella*.

Die Hinterflügel, Unterseite, Palpen, Fühler und Beine sind wie bei *Schlægeriella*.

Das Weib ist kleiner, schmalflüglicher und bleicher gefärbt als das Männchen.

Im Juni und Juli an den Lehnen des Pozzo di Borgo und auf den Hügeln der Lazarethspitze einige Männchen und ein Weibchen erbeutet.

'Verhandlungen zool.-bot. Vereins in Wien,' 1855, p. 562.

ŒCOPHORA LAVANDULÆ, n. sp.

Diese Schabe steht der *Mouffetella*, L., sehr nahe, hat aber breitere und kürzere Flügel, sie ist in der Färbung durchaus braungrau, nur die Fühler sind weiss geringelt. Die braungrauen Vorderflügel sind mit feinen, dunklen, grauen Atomen belegt, wodurch sie ein rauhes Ansehen erhalten. In der Mitte des Flügels stehen zwei schwarze, kurze Längsstriche untereinander, so zwar, dass sie den Flügel in drei gleiche Theile theilen, zwischen ihnen und dem Aussenrande steht in der Mitte noch ein grosser schwarzer Punkt. Die Hinterflügel sind einfach braungrau, die Fransen am Hinterwinkel etwas heller. Die Unterseite aller Flügel ist dunkelgrau mit Seidenglanz.

Ich fand gegen Ende Mai auf der Lazarethspitze die schon eingesponnenen Raupen auf *Lavandula stœchas* in den obern Blättern der Zweige. Den 10. Juni entwickelte sich eine Schabe, den 12. folgte noch eine, die anderen Puppen vertrockneten.

'Verhandlungen zool.-bot. Vereins in Wien,' 1855, p. 563.

ŒCOPHORA QUADRIFARIELLA, n. sp.

Hat in Grösse und Zeichnungsanlage einige Aehnlichkeit mit *augustella*, die Flügel sind aber viel kürzer, breiter und runder, die hintern auch viel kürzer gefranst. Ueberhaupt stimmt der Schmetterling in Flügelform und Fransen mehr mit *Psecadia signella* und *signatella* überein, und hat bei *Œcophora* kaum seine richtige Stellung, da es aber sowohl in dieser Gattung, als bei *Psecadia* ohnehin noch Mehreres zu sichten gibt, so führe ich ihn einstweilen hier auf, bis sich eine passendere Stelle findet.

Der Körper ist oben schwarzgrau und weiss. Der Hinterleib ist etwas flach gedrückt und die Hinterränder der Segmente sind auf der Oberseite weiss gerandet, die Beine sind weiss und schwarz geringelt, die Hinterschienen aussen etwas längshaarig mit zwei Paar Spornen. Der Kopf ist mit etwas borstigen weisslichen Schuppen besetzt, die Palpen sind weiss und schwarz gefleckt, anliegend beschuppt, aufwärts gekrümmt mit langem spitzen Endgliede.

Die Fühler reichen bis zu zwei Drittel des Vorderrandes der Vorderflügel, sind weiss und schwarz geringelt, an der Spitze nicht verdünnt, sondern daselbst fast so dick, wie an der Basis, beim Manne dicker als beim Weibe, in beiden Geschlechtern unbewimpert.

Die Vorderflügel sind grobschuppig, glanzlos und haben als Grundfarbe ein mit weisslichen Schuppen belegtes Schwarz. Sie sind von drei weissen, fast geraden und schräg nach aussen gerichteten Querbändern durchzogen. Die beiden ersten sind ziemlich breit, jedes etwa halb so breit als lang, das innere steht dicht an der Basis, das äussere endet bei der Flügelmitte, zwischen beiden bleibt nur ein schmaler Streif von der Grundfarbe, der mitten weiss unterbrochen ist, da hier beide Binden durch einen kleinen Querast verbunden sind; beim Manne sind diese beiden Binden gelblich überflogen, beim Weibe aber nicht. Das dritte Band beginnt bei drei Vierteln des Vorderrandes und zieht schräg gegen den Innenwinkel zu; es ist nur halb so breit als die übrigen, beim Weibe läuft es vor dem Innenwinkel aus, beim Manne reicht es aber nur bis zur Mitte des Flügels. Längs des Saumes stehen weissliche, in der weissen Binde schwärzliche grobe Schuppen. Die Fransen sind breit, weissgrau, beim Manne gegen den Innenwinkel zu dunkler.

Die Hinterflügel sind eisengrau mit helleren Fransen, beim Weibe etwas lichter gefärbt als beim Manne.

Unten sind alle Flügel grau mit gleichfarbigen Fransen, die vorderen mit schmaler, weisslicher Kante.

Ich fing diese seltene Art auf der Lazarethspitze an einer kleinen Felsenpartie in drei Exemplaren.

'Verhandlungen zool.-bot. Vereins in Wien,' 1855, p. 564.

DEPRESSARIA ATRICORNELLA, n. sp.

Sehr nahe an *ocellana*, Fab. (*characterella*), dieselbe Grösse, Flügelschnitt, Farbe und Zeichnungsanlage; die Fühler sind aber bei meinen sehr reinen Exemplar entschieden schwarz (bei *ocellana* bräunlichgelb), die Mittelpunkte sind weiter von einander getrennt, beide gleich gross und tiefschwarz, der unter ihnen stehende Wisch und der unter ihm saumwärts befindliche, licht gekernte Punkt sind obenfalls, doch matter schwarz, während *characterella* diese Zeichnung stets mit Roth gemischt hat, alles Uebrige ist wie bei *ocellana*.

Ich fand dieses Männchen in meinem Raupenkasten frisch ausgekrochen, wo ich die Raupe wahrscheinlich mit Futterpflanzen für die *Ocnogyna corsica* eingetragen hatte *.

* Of the larvæ of *Ocnogyna corsica* we read "sie fressen sehr viele Arten von Pflanzen, als *Echium*, Camillen, Klee, Schafgarbe, Wegerich," &c.

'Verhandlungen zool.-bot. Vereins in Wien,' 1855, p. 565.

GELECHIA SELAGINELLA, n. sp.

Sie hält das Mittel zwischen *æstivella*, Mtz., und *aprilella*, Mann in lit. H.-S. 963.

Der Vorderflügel sammt den Fransen und Rücken sind ochergelb, der Kopf blassgelb, ebenso die Palpen und Beine. Am Aussenrande ist die gewöhnliche Binde etwas verloschen, die Mittel- wie die Vorderrandader und der Vorderrand sind weisslich, auch vom Aussenrande ziehen sich weissliche Striche bis in die Fransen; die ganze Zeichnung ähnelt der von *paupella*, Z.

Die Fühler sind dunkelbraun, meist [? weiss] geringelt. Das zweite Palpenglied ist kürzer, das dritte länger als bei *aprilella*. Hinterflügel und Körper sind aschgrau, am Vorderrand des Flügels sind die Fransen blass ochergelb, dann werden sie gelblichgrau. Die Unterseite der Vorderflügel ist dunkel graubraun, die Fransen ochergelb. Die Hinterflügel sind sammt den Fransen unten so gefärbt wie oben.

Ich fing diese Schabe Ende Juni auf Myrthen-Blüthen in den Abendstunden auf dem Pozzo di Borgo.

'Verhandlungen zool.-bot. Vereins in Wien,' 1855, p. 566.

RŒSLERSTAMMIA FUMOCILIELLA, n. sp.

Sie hat die Grösse und Gestalt von *vesperella* (Kll. in lit.), H.-S. 348, ist aber etwas grösser.

Der Körper ist sammt den Beinen schmutziggelb, der Kopf mit gleichfarbigen, wolligen, zusammengestrichenen Haaren besetzt; die Palpen sind dünn, lang und sichelförmig, ebenfalls gelblich, die Fühler hell und dunkel geringelt.

Die Vorderflügel sind blass holzgelb mit dunkelbraunen Fransen (sie ähnelt hierin etwas der *Plutella porrectella*), leztere sind an der Flügelspitze und am Innenrande etwas heller gefärbt, und auch im obern Drittel des Saumes durch einen hellen Wisch unterbrochen.

Die Zeichnung ist sehr verworren und undeutlich. Die Grundfarbe ist mit vielen mehr oder weniger gehäuften schwärzlichen und einigen blassgelben mehligen Atomen bestreut; erstere stehen am Vorderrande von der Basis bis zur Mitte desselben am dichtesten. Bei der Mitte des Flügels entspringt am Vorderrande ein gegen den Innenwinkel zulaufender, schwärzlicher Schrägwisch; er ist am Vorderrande am deutlichsten und erlischt bei der Mitte der Flügelbreite, hinter ihm bilden die helleren und dunkleren Atome eine querstrichelartige Zeichnung besonders am Vorderrande. Auf dem Innenrande sitzt etwas vor der Mitte desselben, ein weisslicher, wenig deutlicher Makel auf, welche auswärts gebogen am Innenrande von wenigen schwärzlichen Schüppchen begränzt ist, und sich nach oben in den Flügelgrund verliert. Die Hinterflügel sind aschgrau mit blässeren Fransen.

Unten sind alle Flügel aschgrau, die vorderen mit drei gelblichen

Fleckchen am Vorderrande gegen die Spitze zu, und schwärzlichen Fransen, die hinteren sammt den Fransen einfärbig grau.

Ich entdeckte diese Schabe 1846 im Mai bei Livorno, bei Ajaccio scheuchte ich sie am Hügel San Giovanni aus Hecken, und bekam gerade ein Pärchen.

'Verhandlungen zool.-bot. Vereins in Wien,' 1855, p. 566.

ROESLERSTAMMIA EGLANTERIELLA, n. sp.

Hat den Habitus und die Flügelform von *granitella*, ist aber nur halb so gross.

Der Körper und die Palpen sind grau, letztere sehr schwach, anliegend beschuppt und sichelförmig gekrümmt, dabei aber etwas abwärts hängend, die Fühler hell und dunkel geringelt, der Kopf grau etwas wollig.

Die Vorderflügel sind verworren, etwas schiefergrau gemischt und mit feinen schwärzlichen und bräunlichen Atomen übersät.

Die Zeichnungsanlage hat, die verschiedene Färbung abgerechnet, Aehnlichkeit mit der von *granitella*. Erkennen lässt sich ein bräunlicher auf den Innenrand aufsitzender, dreieckiger Fleck, eine querbindenartige, trübbraune breite Stelle dahinter und bräunliche Stellen am Aussenrande, in welchem vor der Flügelspitze zwei hellgraue, häkchenartige Vorderrandsflecke stehen. Die Saumlinie ist schwärzlich, die Fransen sind grau.

Die Hinterflügel sind aschgrau mit etwas lichteren Fransen. Die Unterseite aller Flügel ist einfärbig grau, die Fransen sind hier ebenfalls etwas heller.

Ich fand diese Art bei Ajaccio im Mai, nur in zwei Exemplaren um wilde weisse Rosensträucher.

'Verhandlungen zool.-bot. Vereins in Wien,' 1855, p. 568.

OPOSTEGA MENTHINELLA, n. sp.

Hat die Grösse, Form und Färbung von *salaciella*, dieselbe Bildung der Körpertheile; die Vorderflügel haben aber in den Fransen unweit der Flügelspitze einen tief schwarzen Punkt, längs des Saumes spärlich goldbraune Schuppen und einen gleichfärbig verloschenen Schrägwisch von der Mitte des Vorderrandes nach aussen zu. Fühler, Palpen und Beine sind wie bei *salaciella*.

Ich fand diese Schabe in zwanzig Exemplaren im Thale nach San Antonio im Juli spät Abends langsam um *Mentha* fliegend.

'Verhandlungen zool.-bot. Vereins in Wien,' 1855, p. 569.

LITHOCOLLETIS ENDRYELLA, n. sp.

Sie gehört zu den Arten, welche ein Schwänzchen an der Flügelspitze haben und steht der *distentella* (F. v. R. in lit.), Z., zunächst, ist aber etwas grösser.

Der Körper ist grau, der Rücken und die Vorderflügel sind bräunlichgelb, goldfarb glänzend. Die Behaarung des Kopfes goldbraun und weiss gemischt. (Bei *distentella* rein weiss.) Die Fühler sind weiss, fein dunkler geringelt.

Die Zeichnung ist wie bei *distentella*, nämlich ein weisser ästiger Längsstrich durch die Mitte des Flügels, der von der Basis bis fast zu dem ersten Paar Gegenflecken reicht, aber viel schmäler als bei *distentella* und beiderseits fein schwärzlich gesäumt ist, mit vier wie bei *distentella* gestellten weissen Flecken am Vorder-, zwei am Innenrande, alle an der Innenseite schwärzlich gesäumt, und feiner schwärzlichen Saumlinie; an der Flügelspitze steht aber bei *endryella* dicht vor dem Schwänzchen ein tief schwarzer Punkt, der bei *distentella* nicht vorhanden ist.

Die Hinterflügel sind ein klein wenig dunkler als bei *distentella*. Unten sind die Vorderflügel braungrau, die hinteren gelblichgrau, alle lichte Zeichnung schimmert matt von oben durch, der schwarze Punkt ist aber so scharf wie oben.

Im April bei Ajaccio von *Quercus ilex* gescheucht, und nur in drei Stücken gefunden.

SECTION V.

Species collected by Herr Joseph Mann in Sicily in 1858, enumerated by him in the 'Wiener entomologische Monatschrift,' iii. (1859) pp. 169-176, entitled "Verzeichniss der in Jahre 1858 in Sicilien gesammelten Schmetterlinge."

Tinea ferruginella, Hb. May, several taken in a quarry at Morreale.

T. rusticella, Hb. June, found on garden-walls in the valley below Morreale.

T. tapetiella, L. June, one female taken at the inn on the road at Morreale.

T. granella, L. June, two specimens taken on a wall at Bocca di Falco.

T. panormitanella, n. sp. May and June, on the mountain-slopes of Monte Medio, in the afternoon; very scarce. [Briefly described, see p. 130.]

T. spretella, S. V. (*fuscipunctella*, Haw.). May, found on rock-walls in the valley of Palla-gutta.

T. pellionella, L. May and June, not scarce, flying in the room in the evening.

T. crassicornella, Z. May and June, flying singly on rocks in the afternoon in the Palla-gutta valley.

T. pustulatella, Z. At the end of June, at Partinico, several taken on a garden-wall on ivy.

Eriocottis fuscanella, Z. In the middle of May near Palermo, on the road to Sferro Cavallo, then near Morreale on Monte Medio and M. Buare, at the end of June in the valley below Morreale. The males are not scarce; the females are very scarce, and generally in bad condition.

Micropteryx calthella, L. May, at the springs by the Rosalienkirche, on the flowers of *Ranunculus*, also on the flowers of *Carex*, not scarce.

M. Seppella, Fab. (*eximiella*, Kollar). June, collected in a stone-quarry on Monte Medio during sunshine in the afternoon, on *Parietaria officinalis*.

Nemotois Latreillellus, F. The first at the beginning of May on the blossoms of *Asphodelus*, then during fully two months occurring in the Palla-gutta valley.

N. barbatellus, Z. From the middle of May to the middle of June, on mountain-slopes, in the Palla-gutta valley, sitting on the tips of grass in the sunshine before noon.

Plutella cruciferarum, Z. May and June, not scarce throughout the neighbourhood of Morreale.

P. Hufnageliella, Z. At the beginning of June, one specimen on *Asphodelus*-blossom at Morreale.

Ypsolophus verbascellus, S. V. The larva not scarce in May on *Verbascum*; the imago in July.

Y. striatellus, S. V. May, not scarce, in the Palla-gutta valley.

Y. Kefersteiniellus, Mann. June, on Monte Medio.

Macrochila separatella, F. v. R. May, singly, on the mountain-slopes of Monte Buare.

Anarsia spartiella, Schr. June, several taken amongst *Spartium* in the park at San Martino.

Anchinia brevispinella, Z. From April to June, on the mountain-slopes of Monte Medio, Monte Buare, Monte Pellegrino, as well as on the hills at Parco, flying in the morning.

A. pyropella, S. V. May, not scarce, on Monte Medio, M. Buare, and M. Garcio.

Hypercallia Christiernella, L. May 20th, two males taken on the mountain-slopes of Monte Pellegrino.

Lypusa maurella, S. V. At the end of June, one female taken on a thistle-blossom in the park at S. Martino.

Œcophora Metznerella, Tr. At the beginning of June, several taken in gardens at Morreale.

Œ. Lewenhoekella, S. V. May, at Morreale and in the Palla-gutta valley, not scarce on mountain-slopes.

Œ. flavifrontella, S. V. The beginning of May, several around willows in a garden at Morreale.

Œ.? cinerariella, Mus. Zeller. June, in the Palla-gutta valley, flying in the grass. [Briefly described, see p. 130.]

Butalis pascuella, Z. June, taken at Morreale, on mountain-slopes before noon.

B. Knochella, F. May and June, on mountain-slopes, both at Palermo and throughout the district of Morreale.

B. oleella, Boyer. June, several taken around olive trees in the morning.

Butalis phycidella, Z.   May, taken amongst rose hedges at Bocca di Falco.

Swammerdamia comptella, Hb.   At the end of May, two males taken at S. Martino.

Psecadia echiella, S. V.   May, at Morreale, on garden walls and rock-faces, not scarce.

P. chrysopyga, Z. (*flavianella*, F. v. R.).   At the beginning of June, two males taken in a meadow at S. Martino.

P. aurifluella, Tr.   From the beginning to the end of May, nine specimens taken on *Echium* on a mountain-slope at the entrance of the Palla-gutta valley.

Depressaria veneficella, Z.   At the beginning of June I collected a quantity of stems of *Thapsia garganica*, which were inhabited by larvæ.   The imago appeared at the end of June in plenty.   Out of doors I took some males in the middle of June.

Carcina fagana, S. V.   At the end of May, several taken on orchard-trees in the valley at Morreale; their colour is a beautiful dark red.

Gelechia Kollarella, Costa (*flavedinella*, F. v. R.).   June, flying over *Thymus* on mountain-slopes in the Palla-gutta valley.

G. cinerella, L.   Not scarce, in May and June, on mountain-slopes near Morreale.

G. malvella, H.   June, two males taken on mallow-blossoms in the Palla-gutta valley; they had quite penetrated to the calyx of the flower.

G. populella, L.   At the beginning of June, not scarce, on the trunks of poplars at S. Martino.

G. gallinella, Tisch.   May, amongst *Erica*, on Monte Medio, during sunshine in the morning.

G. dryadella, Kollar.   June, several taken at Morreale on the slopes of Monte Medio.

G. salinella, Z.   May, several taken on Monte Pellegrino; most of them were already worn.

G. vilella, Z.   May, several taken at Morreale, on walls, where nettles and *Parietaria* grew; scarce.   This was not scarce at Brussa, in Asia Minor.

G. plebejella, Z.   At the beginning of June, on slopes in the Palla-gutta valley.

G. humeralis, Z.   April, one female taken on a stone at Mondilla.

G. scriptella, H.   June, several beaten from a thorn bush on a wall at Parco.

G. ligulella, S. V.   June, several taken on grass-stems in the Palla-gutta valley.

G. bifractella, Metz.   At the end of June, taken on marigolds, at S. Martino.

G. anthyllidella, H.   May, singly on mountain-slopes at Morreale.

G. flammella, Tr.   June, not scarce on pastures and mountain-slopes near Morreale.

G. detersella, Z.   At the end of June, two males taken in the morning on Monte Gurcio.

G. paupella, Z. (*melanolepidella*, Kollar, in lit.).   June, five specimens taken at S. Martino on a fallow-slope.

G. quinquepunctella, H.-S.   May, flying in the morning by the little streams in grassy places in the Palla-gutta valley.

G. stipella, H.   June, several taken on *Chenopodium* at Partinico.

G. Hermannella, F.   May, at Palermo and Morreale, flying on walls where *Parietaria* grew.

G. pictella, Z.   June, two males taken on *Spartium* on Monte Castellaccio.

G. lamprostoma, Z.   At the beginning of June, several taken in the afternoon on the slopes of Monte medio and M. Buare.

Parasia Lappella, L. (*æstivella*, Metzn.).   June, several taken amongst Scabious in the Palla-gutta valley ; scarce.

P. torridella, n. sp.   [Briefly described, see p. 131.]   At the beginning of July, three specimens taken on Monte Gurcio.

Rœslerstammia granitella, F. v. R.   May, one male taken on the slopes of Monte Pellegrino ; it is darker than the Vienna specimens.

R. vesperella, Z.   May, at Palermo and Morreale, on garden-walls.

Æchmia equitella, Scop.   April and May, on Monte Medio swarming at midday on the tips of " Schneidegras " [*Carex*?, *Arundo phragmites*?, *Aira cæspitosa*?, *Dactylis glomerata*?].

Tinagma balteolella, H.-S.   At the beginning of June, one male taken on a marigold in the Palla-gutta valley.

Argyresthia pruniella, H.   June, flying in a garden round plum-trees.

Coleophora trochilipennella, Costa.   May, singly in the Palla-gutta valley near the little stream.

C. alcyonipennella, Kollar.   May, taken on the slopes of Monte Pellegrino.

C. vulnerariæ, Z.   May, flying on the slopes and on the summit of Monte Medio.

C. laticostella, n. sp.   June, several taken at the edge of a field at Partinico.   [Briefly described, see p. 131.]

C. albifuscella, Z.   May, two specimens taken on *Echium* in a stone-quarry at Morreale.

C. fretella, Z.   April, on Monte Medio and M. Buare in the morning.

C. onosmella, Brahm.   At the end of June, taken in a fallow field at S. Martino.

Gracilaria phasianipennella, H.   May, several taken on rushes in the morning at the springs near the Rosalienkirche.

G. Kollariella, F. v. R.   June, three specimens taken on ash trees in the park at S. Martino.

Cosmopteryx argyrogrammos, Z. May and June, singly on mountain-slopes at Morreale.

C. Ledereriella, Z. June, two males taken on a grassy slope at the entrance of the Palla-gutta valley.

Elachista putripennella, F. v. R. June, several taken on orchard-trees at Partinico.

E. serratella, Tr. May, two males taken on the slopes of Monte Pellegrino.

E. pomposella, F. v. R. June, several met with in the park at S. Martino on marigolds. It appears to be everywhere scarce.

E. disertella, F. v. R. May, at Morreale, singly on mountain-slopes.

E. disemiella, H.-S. May, flying in the evening on Monte Medio; the only creature which one could find in the evening.

E. cygnipennella, Hb. At the end of May and in June, not scarce on mountain-slopes, flying on grass in the morning.

Opostega crepusculella, F. v. R. May, occurring on *Mentha* outside Morreale.

Trifurcula pallidella, Z. May, two males taken in the Palla-gutta valley.

Tischeria Emyella, D. May, taken amongst brambles in the Palla-gutta valley and high up the mountains.

Copies of the original descriptions of the new species are here appended.

TINEA PANORMITELLA, n. sp.

('Wiener ent. Monatschrift,' iii. [1859] p. 170.)

Gleicht im Habitus und der trüben, glanzlosen Färbung der *Elachista rufocinerea*; der rauhhaarige Kopf und die ovalen Hinterflügel verweisen sie aber zu *Tinea*.

Kopf und Rücken bräunlich gelb, nebst den hangenden, die Stirnhaare nicht überragenden Palpen und den Beinen grob und abstehend behaart. Fühler dick, fast bis ans Ende des Vorderrandes der Vorderflügel reichend, hell und dunkel geringelt. Hinterleib dunkelgrau, die Hinterränder der Segmente gelblich.

Vorderflügel nebst den Fransen glanzlos ochergelb, bei sehr scharf gezeichneten Stücken mit dunkleren, wolkigen Stellen am Vorderrande, Saume und der Mitte und einem dunkelgrauen Wische im Afterwinkel der Fransen. Hinterflügel dunkelgrau, die Fransen gelblich. Unterseite ebenso; Vorder- und Innenrand der Flügel aber ebenfalls gelblich.

Im Mai und Juni auf der Berglehne des Monde medio in den Nachmittagstunden, sehr selten.

ŒCOPHORA? CINERARIELLA, Mus. Zeller.

('Wiener ent. Monatschrift,' iii. [1859] p. 171.)

Ich bin nicht sicher, ob diese Art, die ich im Juni im Thale

Palla-gutta im Grase fliegend fand und von welcher auch Freund
Zeller ein einzelnes Exemplar mitbrachte, in diese Gattung gehört
und beschreibe sie daher ausführlicher.

Im Habitus hat sie einige Aehnlichkeit mit *O. flavifrontella*, ist
aber nur halb so gross, plumper und kurzflüglicher, vom Ansehen
der *Anchinia balucella*.

Der Kopf hat grobe, zusammengestrichene Haare; die Zunge ist
gerollt, ziemlich kurz; Ocellen fehlen. Die Palpen sind sichelförmig, hoch emporragend, die beiden ersten Glieder unten mit
kurzer, schneidiger, gegen das Ende des zweiten Gliedes nicht verlängerte Behaarung. Die Fühler reichen bis zu zwei Dritteln des
Vorderrandes und sind beim Manne gekerbt; die Beine sind kräftig,
an den Schienen grob behaart.

Die Mittelzellen aller Flügel sind einfach; auf den vorderen
entspringen Rippe 3. und 4. aus einem Punkte und sind 6. und 7.
gestielt, alle übrigen gesondert; auf den hintern entspringen 3. und
4. aus einem Punkte, 6. und 7. gesondert, 5. mitten zwischen 4. und
6., 8. frei.

Die Vorderflügel sind glanzlos aschgrau mit feineren dunkleren
Atomen übersäet, die auf der Querrippe zu einem matten Mittelfleck gehäuft sind; die Hintern sind nebst den breiten Fransen und
der Unterseite aschgrau.

Parasia torridella, n. sp.

('Wiener ent. Monatschrift,' iii. [1859] p. 174.)

Von der Grösse der *P. Lappella*, L. (*œstivella*, Z.). Man könnte
sie leicht für verflogene Exemplare irgend einer der nahe verwandten *Parasia*-Arten halten; es sind aber die mir vorliegenden
Stücke vollkommen rein und es hat auch Freund Lederer mehrere
ganz gleiche aus Andalusien mitgebracht.

Bildung der Körpertheile wie bei allen Parasien.

Vorderflügel bleich ochergelb; Zeichnung nur wenig dunkler und
sehr unbestimmt, am Aehnlichsten der von *P. Lappella*, doch nicht
so längsstriemig und statt den beiden schwarzen Punkten nur zwei
ganz bleichbraune. Hinterflügel und Unterseite aschgrau; alle
Fransen ochergelb.

Von den hierher gehörigen Arten kenne ich nur *Parasia Metzneriella*, Stainton nicht; von allen übrigen ist meine Art schon
durch die Färbung weit verschieden.

Anfang Juli am Monte Gurcio drei Stück gefangen.

Coleophora laticostella, n. sp.

('Wiener ent. Monatschrift,' iii. [1859] p. 175.)

Diese Art, die ich auch bei Brussa sammelte, gehört in Zeller's
Abtheilung, D c β (Linnæa, iv. p. 199) und steht keiner der dort
beschriebenen Arten sonderlich nahe. Sie ist nicht grösser als die
bekannte *C. murinipennella*, hat hell und dunkelgeringelte, an der
Basis nicht schuppig verdickte Fühler, trüb braungelbe Vorderflügel

(etwa wie *C. fringillella*) mit einem weissen, bis zur Spitze reichenden Vorderrandsstriemen (von derselben Breite wie bei *C. fringillella*), einen gleichfärbigen, ganz schwachen Strich in der Flügelfalte und einen nur bei sehr scharf gezeichneten Stücken sichtbaren helleren Längsstrahl zwischen beiden (bei der inneren Mittelrippe), aschgraue Hinterflügel und Unterseite.

Im Juni bei Partinico einige an einem Ackerrande gefangen.

Section VI.

Species collected in Croatia in 1866 by Herr Joseph Mann, enumerated in the 'Verhandl. d. zoolog.-botan. Gesellschaft in Wien,' 1867, p. 63, entitled "Schmetterlinge gesammelt im J. 1866, um Josefsthal in der croat. Militärgrenze von Josef Mann."

The bulk of this paper is a mere list of names, without any information whatever, the only species of which anything is said are the following:—

Swammerdamia nubeculella, Tengström. A new species for the Austrian empire; singly on the mountains near Josefsthal, amongst maple bushes in June.

Holoscolia forficella, Hb. In June I took a number of very large males. In the neighbourhood of Vienna I more frequently find females, very rarely a male, and those I do get are quite small.

Euspilapteryx Redtenbacheri, n. sp.* (*Gracilaria magnifica*, Stainton, Tineina of Syria and Asia Minor, p. 56). In May I found some specimens of this pretty species on the mountains near Josefsthal, in maple bushes.

Elachista disemiella, Zell. A new species for the Austrian empire; two specimens taken on a mountain-slope at Josefsthal, at the beginning of June.

Section VII.

Species collected in Dalmatia in 1850, 1862, and 1868, by Herr Joseph Mann, enumerated in the 'Verhandlungen der zoologisch-botanischen Gesellschaft in Wien,' 1869, pp. 371–388, entitled "Lepidoptern gesammelt während dreier Reisen nach Dalmatien in den Jahren 1850, 1862, und 1868."

The bulk of this paper is a mere list of names without any information whatever, the only species of which anything is said are the two following new species:—

Nemotois dalmatinellus, Mann. I discovered this in July 1850 near Spalato, singly on *Scabiosa*. In 1862 I found several females on Monte Mariano, which had thrust their ovipositors deep into the

---

* I do not quote the description of this, having already described it in the companion volume to this work. I leave it to others to decide whose name has priority. The 'Tineina of Syria and Asia Minor' was published the first week in April 1867.

buds of the Scabious, so that they could not withdraw them, and remained fixed there.

Depressaria aridella, Mann. I first found this species at Brussa in July 1863, and likewise at Spalato in July, where I beat it from bramble hedges; rather scarce.

Copies of the original descriptions of these two novelties are here appended.

'Verhandlungen der zool.-botan. Gesellschaft in Wien,' 1869, p. 384.

NEMOTOIS DALMATINELLUS, Mann.

Diese Art hat die Gestalt und Färbung wie *Nemotois istrianellus* und *cupriacellus*, nur ist auf den Vorderflügeln von der Basis bis zur Mitte der Grund mehr goldgrün, als bei der ersteren und unterscheidet sich von beiden leicht durch die Fühler, sowohl des Mannes wie des Weibes.

Bei *istrianellus* Mann ist das erste Fühlerglied knotig, die Fortsetzung des Fühlers dick, viermal so lang als das Knotenglied, violett glänzend, stark bebartet, die Geissel, welche die sechsmalige Länge des Bartes hat, ist rein weiss und mit der Loupe besehen fein gekerbt.

Bei *dalmatinellus* Mann ist das erste Fühlerglied wie bei *istrianellus*, der Bart zweimal so lang als das Glied, schwärzlich, am Ende etwas violett schimmernd, anfangs die Behaarung dick, dann sanft, in die achtmal längere, weissliche, fein gekerbte Fühlergeissel verlaufend. Die Vorderflügel haben mehr Metallglanz als bei *istrianellus*.

Beim Weibe von *istrianellus* sind die Fühler etwas länger als die Vorderflügel; das erste Glied ist klein knotig, der violett metallisch schimmernde Bart ist am Wurzelgliede dünn, dann wird er dicker und beim Verlauf in die Geissel wieder dünner, hat die Hälfte der Fühlerlänge, welche rein weiss und kaum gekerbt oder geringelt erscheint.

Beim Weibe von *dalmatinellus* ist das erste Fühlerglied etwas dicker und länger als bei *istrianellus*, der Bart ist anfangs so dick als das Glied, schwarz, etwas dunkel violett schimmernd und verläuft pfriemenformig bis zu $\frac{3}{4}$ der weisslichen Fühlerspitze. Die Färbung der Vorderflügel mehr dunkler violett als bei *istrianellus* Weib. Die Hinterschienen bei *dalmatinellus* viel stärker und länger behaart als bei *istrianellus*.

Beim Weibe von *cupriacellus* haben die Fühler nur knapp die Flügellänge, das erste Glied ist zart, die Fühler etwas dicker durch die anliegenden Schuppen, schön violettgold glänzend, welche sich bis zur Hälfte der grauen Geissen verlaufen.

Der Mann von *cupriacellus* ist mir bis jetzt noch unbekannt; obwohl ich in den früheren Jahren aus den Sacken, welche ich ganz unten an den Wurzelblättern der Cardendistel [*Dipsacus*?] fand, wohl Weiber aber nie einen Mann erhielt.

'Verhandlungen der zool.-botan. Gesellschaft in Wien,' 1869, p. 385.

DEPRESSARIA ARIDELLA, Mann.

Sehr nahe verwandt mit *Depressaria squamosa*, Mann und *nanatella*, Stt., die kleinste dieser drei Arten. Kopf, Rücken, Palpen und Fühler wie bei *nanatella* gestaltet, die eintönige bleichgelbliche Färbung der Vorderflügel gleicht der *squamosa*, ebenso die feinen mattbräunlichen Querriefen, der schwärzliche Mittelpunkt etwas deutlicher und ein schwarzes Pünktchen unter demselben auf der Mittelrippe, zuweilen steht auch ein schwarzes Pünktchen am Innenrande nahe der Basis; die Flügelfläche ist viel glatter als bei *nanatella*, welche dunkler gefärbt, rauher beschuppt und mit vielen stärker ausgedrückten Querriefen; unter dem dunklen Mittelflecke stehen auf der Mittelrippe zwei schwarze Pünktchen, auch ist der Mittelfleck noch etwas dunkel beschattet, ohngefähr wie bei *assimilella*. Bei *aridella* ist der Flügelsaum vor den Fransen kaum sichtbar, hingegen bei *nanatella* sehr deutlich graubraun. Die Hinterflügel bei *aridella* sind dunkelgrau, die Fransen gelblich; bei *nanatella* etwas heller, die Fransen graugelblich. Die Unterseite der Vorderflügel von *aridella* ist dunkelgrau mit weisslichgelbem Vorderrand und Fransen. Hinterflügel etwas hellergrau, am Vorderrand gelblichweiss, alle Flügel mit starkem Seidenglanz. Bei *nanatella* ist die Färbung auf der Unterseite heller in's Bräunliche schillernd, ebenfalls seidenglänzend, die Fransen grau.

CHAPTER III.

DR. STAUDINGER.

"He was about five-and-twenty, a '*doctor philosophiæ*,' and had come to Iceland to catch gnats. After having caught gnats in Iceland he intended, he said, to spend some years in catching gnats in Spain, the privacy of Spanish gnats, as it appears, not having been hitherto invaded."—*Lord Dufferin's Letters from High Latitudes*, Chapter VII.

Dr. STAUDINGER first visited the South in 1852, when he went to Montpellier, and stayed there from the end of August to the beginning of November.

His next excursion to the South was in 1854, when he visited the Island of Sardinia* from April 10th to October 2nd; no account of his captures there has ever appeared. In the 'Entomologist's Annual' for 1856, p. 126, I have mentioned that when I visited Dr. Staudinger in Berlin, in May 1855, I received from him "*Gelechia plebejella* and *dryadella* collected on that occasion, a new *Gelechia*, intermediate between *populella* and *scintillella*, and a new *Coleophora*."

Having in 1856 carried out his project of visiting Iceland, where as it chanced that his visit occurred at the same time as that of Lord Dufferin, the latter embalmed the German entomologist, like a fly in amber, in his amusing 'Letters from High Latitudes.' Dr. Staudinger went in 1857 to Spain, where he remained from February 1857 to July 1858. A notice of the 140 new species of Lepidoptera collected on that occasion appeared in the 'Stettiner entomologische Zeitung' for 1859; but the various interesting observations made on other species, which were not new, to this day remain unpublished†.

In 1862 Dr. Staudinger again visited Spain and collected in the neighbourhood of San Ildefonso, in Old Castile, from the 11th of April to the 11th of August.

In 1866 Dr. Staudinger visited Celles-les-bains, in the department of Ardèche, in France; the peculiarly southern character of this locality, in respect both of its fauna and flora, had been specially noticed, in 1860, by Monsieur Millière, at p. 167 (in the

---

* In the 'Entomologist's Annual' for 1856, p. 126, this is erroneously mentioned as Corsica; it should be *Sardinia*.

† The precise localities visited by Dr. Staudinger may be thus arranged chronologically:—
1857, February 15th to March 17, Malaga.
  ,, March 18th to December 17th, Granada (including the Sierra Nevada).
  ,, December 18th to January 5th, 1868, Malaga.
1858, January 6th to July 2nd, Chiclana (in the province of Cadiz).

Troisième Livraison) of his 'Iconographie et Description de Chenilles et Lépidoptères inédits'*. Dr. Staudinger remained there from the 18th of August till the 21st of October.

In 1867, whilst on a visit to the Engadine in July, he made an excursion to the shores of the Lake of Como, memorable by the discovery of the *Lithocolletis* of the plane tree, *L. platani*.

SECTION I.

Letters from Dr. Staudinger.

The following extracts from Dr. Staudinger's letters to me will not be devoid of interest:—

"Berlin, March 16th, 1856.

"I am sorry that the new *Gelechia* and *Coleophora*, which I found in the Island of Sardinia (not Corsica), must remain undescribed for the present, my work on the Sesiidæ having taken up all my time. Next month I shall start on my entomological campaign to Iceland....

"Next year I hope to go to Spain and Portugal, and to remain there for three or four years."

"Berlin, December 22nd, 1856.

"In the middle of January we (my wife and I) start for Spain, and shall probably remain away from three to five years. We go in the first place to Granada, and afterwards very probably to Portugal."

"Chiclana, near Cadiz, March 2nd, 1858.

"I had long ago intended to have written to you, but waited till I had received tidings of the parcel of insects which I had dispatched from here to Berlin. These tidings only arrived here a few days back, and with them a letter from Zeller. From this I perceive that out of the 95 Tineidæ I had sent home nearly the third of them are new. Altogether I collected last year, principally near Granada, about 150 species of Tineidæ. I have retained here one specimen of each species, consequently all the unique specimens, of which unfortunately there are a considerable number. I think of returning to Germany in July.....

"I have only observed the larvæ of fifteen of these Tineidæ, my

* Je crois devoir informer les Lépidoptéristes que plusieurs localités de l'Ardèche, notamment le petit pays de Celles-les-bains, est très-riche en insectes de l'extrême Midi de la France. J'y ai capturé en effet, bon nombre d'espèces de Lépidoptères considérés jusqu'à ce jour comme habitant presque exclusivement les environs de Marseille ou Montpellier.

La flore des localités que je viens de citer, est, à peu de choses près, celle de nos provinces les plus méridionales.

Je ne connais Celles et ses environs que depuis peu, mais ce que j'ai remarqué de sa faune entomologique, me la fait supposer fort intéressante.....

J'ajouterai que les chasses, dans ce beau pays, sont des plus faciles par la proximité des lieux.

time was so much taken up with other things; and I must admit that I am not learned in the art of hunting for *Tinea*-larvæ, but hope to learn much from you on this subject. My zeal for these interesting creatures is always increasing. Unfortunately, as you know, I cannot make paintings of these larvæ, but I have put one of each kind in spirits. These have mostly kept well, so that I am in hopes they will prove quite serviceable for figuring. The mode in which the individual larvæ live, on what plant, &c., is probably more important than the larvæ themselves.

"Some of the Tineidæ larvæ I have found here are perhaps already known, as, for instance, *Acrolepia granitella*, var. *cinerascens*, which occurs in the young leaves of *Solidago virgaurea* [see *Acrolepia solidaginis*, pp. 142 & 157], *Gracilaria scalariella*, Z., in *Echium* and *Cynoglossum*, &c. I have already bred several pretty new species of *Coleophora*, and one species certainly from two very different cases. [See *Coleophora spumosella* and *solenella*, pp. 142 & 158.] As I am leaving here so soon, in order that I may do what I can to obtain a knowledge of the entomological productions of this very interesting country, I will get Herr Kalisch, who was my fellow traveller to Iceland, to come here shortly, and he will be able to remain here a longer time."

"Chiclana, near Cadiz, July 1st, 1858.

"I have now about 300 species of Tineidæ (including therein the Crambidæ, Phycidæ, and Pterophoridæ). You may easily imagine that amongst these are many interesting new things, since before my visit nobody had ever assiduously collected Tineidæ here. I have about fifty species *ex larva*, and of most of these I have the larvæ in spirits, or, when possible, prepared larvæ.

"Several of the species do not appear to me referable to any known genus. Unfortunately I became very unwell, owing to the extreme heat which prevails here. Kalisch has been here a month, and has already shown on many occasions his skill in finding larvæ. Thus, amongst other things, in cow-dung, which was quite dried by the sun, he has found Tineidæ larvæ [see *Hypsolophus bubulcellus*, pp. 141 & 152], also in the roots of a parasitic *Orchis*. I am now breeding in great numbers a very beautiful little creature, black with silver markings. It feeds on *Lavandula stœchas* and *Thymus*, in a case formed of its own excrements, and eats only the parenchyma of the leaves." [See *Pancalia Grabowiella*, pp. 142 & 157.]

(In 1866, after my first visit to Cannes and Mentone, I wrote to Dr. Staudinger, "I am now very anxious to see the entire history of your Spanish observations; that which you gave in the 'Stettin. entomol. Zeitung' for 1859 was only the *new* species; and your promise to publish 'the entire results of your entomological observations in a special work' still remains unfulfilled."

To this Dr. Staudinger replied, April 19, 1866, "At this moment I am not prepared to write anything special on the subject of my Spanish journey, but I will do so by-and-by when I have again been to Spain another time.")

"Dresden, March 30th, 1862.
"I start for Spain the day after to-morrow."

"Dresden, October 2nd, 1862.
"You have probably returned safely home from your journey by this time. I was in Brussels only a few days after you. M. Fologne told me of your visit.

"My this year's Spanish journey has not proved a very satisfactory one; yet I have found some interesting creatures, and amongst them two new species of *Lithocolletis*, both of which are in the larva-state during the winter on Papilionaceous shrubs. I found the living larvæ in April on bushes which were still almost covered with snow. One species has the anterior wings entirely yellow, with only a single white basal streak. [See *Lithocolletis adenocarpi*, pp. 163 & 165.] I believe I have also bred several other new Tineidæ."

"Dresden, August 9th, 1866.
"Next Monday I think of going for two months to the South of France, to Celles-les-bains, in the Department of Ardèche, there to collect, and especially to seek for the mines of the genera *Lithocolletis* and *Nepticula* in September and October."

"Celles-les-bains, près de la Voulte,
"Dep. Ardèche, Sept. 21st, 1866.

"Monsieur Millière has now left me, and I am here all alone, and propose to remain here till the middle of October, perhaps longer, seeking for larvæ.....

"Unfortunately this season has been everywhere peculiarly unfavourable for Lepidoptera. Amongst the 330 species of Lepidoptera I have found here, there are only about 40 Tineidæ; the cold northeast wind and the heavy rain seemed to have killed them all. To-day I found the first living *Nepticula*-larvæ, so I send them to you at once: viz. six mines in the leaves of a plant [*Rhus cotinus*] which we grow in gardens at Dresden, and call it 'Perrückenstrauch,' here it grows wild; also two mines in leaves of *Pistacia terebinthus*. Probably both larvæ belong to the same species, though the plants are so different. On the first-named bush I have found about twenty larvæ and over a hundred empty mines, on the *Pistacia* I have only found three larvæ, but I yet hope to find more of both.....

"The locality here is quite suited for an entomologist, and there is excellent hunting-ground in three minutes walk from the hotel; there is very little cultivated ground about here."

(In my reply to this letter I called Dr. Staudinger's attention to the fact that No. 2228 of his Catalogue, *Stathmopoda Guerinii*, Stain., had been "éclose d'une grande galle du pistachier, le 15. Septembre, 1852," but that I only knew of that one solitary specimen.)

"Celles-les-bains, près de la Voulte,
"Dep. Ardèche, October 2nd, 1866.

"Many thanks for your letter and your determinations, especially for the notice respecting *Stathmopoda Guerinii*, of which I herewith send you *five larvæ*. I had long since noticed the galls on the *Pistacia*, some of which are very large, and I had even opened some. But I found only thousands of Aphides therein, packed up with white dust, so that I was soon disgusted. But to-day I have examined these galls with fresh zest, although it was very dirty work, many of them being sticky with resin. I found in them *two kinds of larvæ* living amongst hundreds of Aphides, on which they probably feed, as I did not find that the inner walls of the galls had been gnawed[*]. One was a large knot-horn larva, which will not, therefore, interest you; the other, a small white larva,.is that of the *Stathmopoda Guerinii*; of this I also found some pupæ, and in one gall which was completely closed I found a recently developed specimen of the perfect insect. On the *Pistacia* there are three kinds of galls: the largest of these is at the ends of the branches; these have an elongate pod-like form, yet they vary very much both in shape and size: I found one which was *nearly a foot in length*. It is only in this kind of gall that I have met with *Stathmopoda Guerinii*, and, I may say, principally in the smaller of this sort of galls. The larva constructs a firm cocoon, covered with grains of its excrements, and attaches it to the inner wall of the gall. Generally there is an opening formed through which the imago may escape; but I found some galls where this was not the case, and where consequently the moth must develope in the interior of the gall. Thus in some galls which had no openings I found moths which had emerged and there died, having no means of escape.

"I generally found these larvæ in the galls along with many Aphides; yet in some very small galls, only an inch or two in length, I found no trace of Aphides; perhaps they had all been devoured.....

"In very many galls, especially the larger and fresher ones, one finds Aphides only, and no trace of any larvæ; so that I believe the galls are caused in the first instance by the Aphides, and then the moths deposit their eggs on the galls....."

"Celles-les-bains, près de la Voulte,
"Dep. Ardèche, October 13th, 1866.

"I now send you a box containing six sorts of larvæ :—

" 1°. Two or three larvæ of a *Gelechia*?, feeding on *Helichrysum* in woolly tubes.

" 2°. Three mines of a *Lithocolletis* on *Cytisus*?

" 3°. Five mines of a *Cemiostoma* on *Cytisus*?

" 4°. Two larvæ of a *Gelechia* on *Cytisus*? between united leaves; I have only found one other.

" 5°. Two larvæ of *Gelechia terebinthella*? between leaves of the *Pistacia*; those are all I could find of them.

" 6°. A larva of a *Gelechia*? in the leaves of a white-flowered Scabious; the only one I have found."

(The first four of these duly reached me, but of the 5th and 6th I

---

[*] In a subsequent letter Dr. Staudinger remarks, " the larvæ eat the inner walls of the galls."

found no traces in the box; the *Gelechia* no. 4 I bred, and it proved to be *Gelechia cytisella*.)

(Dr. Staudinger wrote to me in the following March from Dresden:—" I have not yet obtained much from my pupæ from Celles-les-bains. The *Nepticula* on *Pistacia* and *Rhus* is, as you rightly suspected, one species, very small, dull black with a whitish fascia. I proposed to call it *Nepticula promissa*, because I discovered it on the anniversary of my betrothal. The *Cemiostoma* from the *Cytisus* does not appear to be distinct from *laburnella*; but, on the other hand, the *Lithocolletis* from the *Cytisus* appears to to be new; unfortunately I only bred two, the others were all ichneumoned."

In a subsequent letter he informed me that he had bred *Ypsolophus corsicellus* from the capsules of *Cistus*, collected at Celles-les-bains.)

"Dresden, August 29th, 1868.

"I found by the Lake of Como a *Lithocolletis* in the leaves of *Platanus*, extremely numerous; these I have bred since I returned home; they are of a beautiful yellow with golden markings, and I consider them new, and propose to call the species *platanella*. Or do you know any *Lithocolletis* on *Platanus*? I even found *one* leaf which contained *fifty-four mines*!"

SECTION II.

New Tineina collected by Dr. Staudinger in Spain in 1857 and 1858.

The 73 species of Tineina from Spain, collected in 1857 and 1858 by Dr. Staudinger, described as new in the 'Stettin. entomologische Zeitung,' 1859, pp. 234–257, may be thus epitomized:—

1. *Talæporia improvisella*. One ♂ at Granada.
2. *Dissoctena granigerella*. L. on all sorts of plants, especially *Convolvulus*; imago bred August and September; Granada and Chiclana.
3. *Tinea murariella*. L. in cases on house-walls at Chiclana; two ♀ bred, b. May.
4. *T. cubiculella*. Granada, April and June; Chiclana, March.
5. *T. vitellinella*. Granada, June and July; Chiclana, May and June. [Afterwards recognized as *chrysopterella*, H.-S.]
6. *Tinea? paradoxella*. One ♂, January 20th, at Chiclana.
7. *Micropteryx imperfectella*. Granada and Chiclana, May.
8. *Adela homalella*. One ♀, Granada.
9. *Nemotois albiciliellus*. Two ♂ in July, Granada; two in April at Chiclana.
10. *Depressaria cachritis*. L. in February and March on *Cachrys lævigata*, on the coast sand-hills, Chiclana; imago bred in May.
11. *D. velox*. L. on a *Ferula*; imago bred in June, Chiclana.

12. *D. sublutella.* L. on *Centaurea aspera* ; Chiclana, June.
13. *D. straminella.* Chiclana, b. June.
14. *Nothris declaratella.* Chiclana, a ♀, April 29th, a fine ♂, June 23rd.
15. *N. senticetella.* L. on *Juniperus phœnicea* ; Chiclana, June.
16. *Symmoca dodecatella.* Four ♂ in June, Sierra de Alfacar.
17. *Lecithocera pallicornella.* Granada, June; Chiclana, April, flying amongst bushes of *Quercus coccifera*.
18. *Gelechia plutelliformis.* L. on *Tamarix*, Chiclana ; two ♀ bred, e. June.
19. *G. helotella.* Granada, e. April, b. May.
20. *G. contuberniella.* L. on *Halimium lepidotum* [*Helianthemum halimifolium*], Granada, Chiclana ; imago bred in July.
21. *G. ternatella.* Granada, July 3rd ; Chiclana, June 13th.
22. *G. ulicinella.* L. in the flowers of *Ulex australis* in April ; imago bred in September, Granada.
23. *G. disjectella.* L. in shoots of *Artemisia Barrelieri* in October and November, Granada ; imago bred in March.
24. *G. nocturnella.* Chiclana, March ; several.
25. *G. promptella.* Chiclana, April ; three specimens.
26. *G. figulella.* Chiclana, April.
27. *G. imperitella.* Granada, e. April, May.
28. *G. epithymella.* One ♂, March 24th, Chiclana.
29. *G. dejectella.* Three specimens, Granada, e. April.
30. *G. gaditella.* Cadiz, January 29th, flying freely.
31. *Megacraspedus subdolellus.* On the Sierra Nevada, about 9000 feet high, in August.
32. *Epidola stigma.* L. on *Quercus coccifera* at Chiclana in April, in *Coleophora*-like cases; imago bred in June.
33. *Hypsolophus cisti.* L. on *Cistus alba* ; one ♂ bred April 26th, Granada ; one ♂ taken March 8th, Chiclana.
34. *H. limbipunctellus.* One, October 7th, at Granada ; others, March to June, Chiclana.
35. *H. bubulcellus.* L. in dry cow-dung, Chiclana ; imago bred June, July.
36. *Pterolonche inspersa.* One ♀, May 30th, at Chiclana.
37. *Anchinia sobriella.* Granada, e. June, July.
38. *A. planella.* Granada and Chiclana, June.
39. *A. teligerella.* Granada and Chiclana, April to July.
40. *Œcophora mercedella.* One ♂, June 30th, Chiclana.
41. *Œ. detrimentella.* One ♂, Granada.
42. *Œ. filiella.* Two ♂, Granada, June.
43. *Alloclita recisella.* Seven at light, Chiclana, e. June.
44. *Butalis Scipionella.* Granada and Chiclana, e. May to July.

45. *B. xanthopygella.* Four on *Umbelliferæ* blossoms, Chiclana, June.
46. *B. biforella.* One ♀, June 26th, at Granada.
47. *B. insulella.* L. on *Erica*; two bred, b. June, Chiclana.
48. *B. pulicella.* Chiclana, March and April, singly.
49. *B. humillimella.* Granada, May; Chiclana, April.
50. *B. cupreella.* Granada, June; Chiclana, April.
51. *B. hibernella.* One ♂, February 26th, Chiclana.
52. *B. bimerdella.* San Geronimo, in the Sierra Nevada, b. July; not scarce.
53. *Staintonia Medinella.* Sitting on *Umbelliferæ* blossoms, Chiclana, June.
54. *Pancalia Grabowiella.* L. on *Lavandula stœchas* and *Thymus vulgaris*, Chiclana, April to July.
55. *Acrolepia solidaginis.* L. on *Solidago virgaurea*; bred at Granada, June, July.
56. *Tinagma thymetellum.* Sitting on *Thymus vulgaris*, Chiclana, m. April to May.
57. *Coleophora spumosella.* L. on *Dorycnium suffruticosum*, Granada, April; imago bred, e. July, August.
58. *C. solenella.* L. on *Artemisia campestris*, Granada, May; imago in August and September.
59. *C. lutatiella.* Only a pair, Chiclana, e. April.
60. *C. semicinerea.* One ♂, March 27th, Chiclana.
61. *C. coarctella.* One ♀, March 17th, Chiclana.
62. *C. congeriella.* L. on *Dorycnium suffruticosum*, Granada, April and May; imago in July and August.
63. *C. vestalella.* L. on *Anthyllis cytisoides*, Granada, May; imago in August and September.
64. *C. struella.* L. on *Thymus vulgaris*, Granada, June, July; Chiclana, April to June.
65. *C. solidaginella.* L. on *Solidago virgaurea*, Chiclana, e. May; imago bred in June.
66. *C. biseriatella.* Chiclana, e. April and May.
67. *C. lassella.* A pair, Chiclana, e. May.
68. *C. arefactella.* One ♂, Chiclana, in the spring.
69. *Elachista piperatella.* Granada, April; Chiclana, e. January and February.
70. *Lithocolletis Chiclanella.* L. on *Populus alba*, Chiclana; imago bred in May.
71. *L. hesperiella.* Two ♂, Chiclana.
72. *L. belotella.* L. on *Quercus ilex*, Granada; imago bred in May; Chiclana, captured in April.
73. *Phyllobrostis daphneella.* L. on *Daphne gnidium*, Chiclana; imago bred in May.

Copies of the original descriptions are here given; the numbers between parentheses refer to the numbers in the 'Stettiner Entomologische Zeitung,' 1859, p. 234–257.

1. (62.) TALÆPORIA IMPROVISELLA.

Capite flavo; alis griseis subsplendentibus (♂ exp. al. 9¼‴).
Kopf gelb, Flügel grau mit mattem Glanze. Bei *T. pubicornis*, aber viel grösser und mit viel matterem Glanze.
Only one ♂, at Granada.

DISSOCTENA, nov. genus.

♂. *Caput in vertice fronteque depresso-squamatum.*
Ocelli nulli.
Antennæ articulis 19–23 compositæ, longissime bipectinatæ.
Haustellum palpique subnulli.
Alæ elongatæ.
♀. *Aptera, ano lanato.*
Larva saccophora; sacco longo, cylindrico, anum versus attenuato, arenæ granis composito.

Neues ausgezeichnetes Genus bei *Talæporia*. Stirn und Scheitel beschuppt, nicht lang behaart wie bei *Talæporia*. Keine Nebenaugen. Palpen und Zunge sehr rudimentär. Fühler des ♂ aus 19 bis 23 Gliedern bestehend, die, mit Ausnahme des ersten, je zwei sehr lange kammförmige Fortsätze führen. Diese Fortsätze sind seitlich mit ziemlich weit auseinander stehenden Wimpern, an der Spitze mit langen Schuppen versehen. Das flügellose ♀ hat am After einen sehr langen weisswollenen Busch. Die Raupen sind sacktragend. Der Sack ist lang, durchaus rund, nach hinten etwas dünner und aus Sandkörnern (oder mineralischen Substanzen) zusammengesetzt.

2. (63.) DISSOCTENA GRANIGERELLA.

♂. *Alis angustis, luteo-cinereis, anterioribus squamis obscurioribus, præcipue postice obsolete conspersis; antennis articulis 19 compositis* (6½–7½‴).
Var. a. *Alis anterioribus unicoloribus, antennis articulis 23 compositis.*

Grösser und heller als *Solenobia inconspicuella*, die Vorderflügel nicht so deutlich netzförmig gezeichnet, sondern nur mehr dunkel gestreut. Die zwei Männer dieser Stammart haben je 19 Glieder an den Fühlern.
Bei der *var.* a, wo nur ein ♂ vorhanden ist, sind die Vorderflügel eintönig lehmgrau und jeder Fühler besteht aus 23 Gliedern.
Bred at the end of August and September from the cases described above. The larvæ fed on all sorts of plants, but especially on the blossoms of *Convolvulus*, in June; at Granada, also at Chiclana.

3. (64.) TINEA MURARIELLA.

Capillis pallide ochraceis; alis anterioribus sordide stramineis, nitidissimis, puncto postico obscuro, squamis erectis composito; alis posterioribus flavescenti-griseis (♀, 5–6½‴).

Der *Tinea biselliella* nahe, aber durch den dunklen Fleck in dem letzten Dritttheil der Vorderflügel verschieden. Die diesen Fleck bildenden Schuppen stehen aufgerichtet. Farbe der Vorderflügel schmutzig strohgelb, sehr glänzend; Hinterflügel mehr grau.

Two females bred at the beginning of May at Chiclana from cases which were made of lime and dust, and were crawling about the walls of the house.

4. (65.) TINEA CUBICULELLA.

Capillis griseis; alis anterioribus nitidulis, lutescenti- vel obscuro-griseis, immaculatis; alis posterioribus nigricantibus (♂ ♀, $6\frac{3}{4}$-8′′′).

Bei *Tinea inquinatella*, aber viel grösser, ohne allen Mittelpunkt auf den Vorderflügeln. Letztere sind eintönig staubgrau, mit einem Stich in's Gelbe; Hinterflügel eintönig schwärzlich.

In April and June at Granada; in March at Chiclana.

5. (66.) TINEA VITELLINELLA.

Capillis, thorace, alisque anterioribus croceis vel aurantiacis; alis posterioribus nigricantibus (♂ ♀, $5\frac{1}{2}$-$6\frac{3}{4}$′′′).

Ausgezeichnete Art bei der vorigen. Kopf, Thorax, Vorderflügel eintönig safran- oder orangengelb, am Gesättigsten bei Exemplaren aus dem Tieflande. Hinterflügel schwärzlich.

In June and July at Granada; in May and June at Chiclana.

[Afterwards recognized as the *chrysopterella* of Herrich-Schäffer, which was founded on a single specimen collected by Herr Lederer at Ronda].

6. (67.) TINEA? PARADOXELLA.

Fusco-cinerea, alis anterioribus macula majuscula in cellulæ mediæ exitu subnigra (♂, 11′′′).

Passt zu keiner bekannten *Tinea*, namentlich ist der Kopf lange nicht so rauh behaart. Die Maxillarpalpen, obgleich sehr rudimentär, scheinen vorhanden zu sein. Die Fühler sind sehr dicht bewimpert. Bildet vielleicht ein eigenes Genus (Tincastra), was an mehren Exemplaren zu untersuchen wäre. Die dunkelaschgrauen Vorderflügel führen am Ende der Mittelzelle eine ziemlich grösse schwärzliche Makel.

Only one fine ♂ on the 20th January, at Chiclana.

7. (68.) MICROPTERYX IMPERFECTELLA.

Alis anterioribus purpureo-aureis, maculis duabus tribusve obsoletis, dilutioribus; alis posterioribus griseis, apicem versus purpurascentibus, (♂ ♀, $2\frac{3}{4}$-$3\frac{3}{4}$′′′)*.

Aeusserst kleine Art und schon deshalb mit keiner zu verwechseln, obwohl sie ziemlich variirt. Vorderflügel goldglänzend, meistens

---

* In the 'Stett. ent. Zeit.' 1860, p. 266, Staudinger writes, "On examining more closely, I find amongst my specimens of *imperfectella* two which decidedly do not belong to that species, but are, according to Zeller, a new species allied to

mit purpurnem Anflug. Zuweilen sind sie ganz eintönig golden, zuweilen ist der Purpurglanz fast faltenweise abgesondert. Immer bemerkt man zwei bis drei verloschene hellere Flecken, die zuweilen ganz silbern erscheinen.

In May, at Granada and Chiclana.

8. (69.) ADELA HOMALELLA.

Capillis aurantiacis, alis anterioribus aureis, striga media dilutiore, utrinque latius purpurascenti-marginata; alis posterioribus nigro-violaceis (♀, 5′′′).

Scheitel pomeranzengelb. Vorderflügel golden, in der Mitte mit etwas lichterem Querstreif, der beiderseits sehr breit mit Purpur umsäumt ist. Hinterflügel dunkel mit violettem Glanz. Von *Ad. rufimitrella* durch breit umsäumte Mittellinie etc. verschieden.

Only one ♀, at Granada.

9. (70.) NEMOTOIS ALBICILIELLUS.

Alis anterioribus aureis, apicem versus violaceo-purpurascentibus; alis posterioribus violaceo-nigris, albo ciliatis (♂, 6½–7½′′′).

Dem *N. barbatellus* und *N. chalcochrysellus* hinsichtlich der Vorderflügel ähnlich, durch die Hinterflügel aber davon ganz getrennt. Dieselben sind hier dunkel schwarz mit violettem Schimmer und weisslichen Franzen.

Two males in July, near Granada, two in April at Chiclana; one taken in the Pyrenees by M. de Graslin.

10. (71.) DEPRESSARIA CACHRITIS.

Alis anterioribus rufescenti-brunneis (vel rufescenti-griseis), nigro-irroratis, fascia basali dilutiore, nigro-marginata, punctis duobus nigricantibus ante, uno (sæpius gemino) albo post medium (♂ ♀, 8–10′′′).

Grundfarbe der Vorderflügel variirend, röthlich braun, zuweilen ganz grau, stets mit zerstreuten schwarzen Schuppen. Der Basaltheil (in Form einer Binde) ist heller, aber niemals wie bei *D. Ferulæ*, Z. rein hellgelb und scharf begrenzt. Nach aussen ist sie dunkel beschattet. In der Mitte steht ein weisslicher, schwarz umrandeter Punkt, vor demselben meistens noch ein ähnlicher, der aber stets viel kleiner ist. Etwa bei ⅓ der Flügellänge stehen in schräger Richtung zwei schwarze Punkte, von denen der obere sehr selten einen weissen Kern bekommt.

---

ammanella (*rubrifasciella*). My diagnosis of *imperfectella* is hence defective and should run thus:—
Alis anterioribus aureis, apice purpurascente, maculis 4 (1 *basali*, 1 *apicali*, *duabusque oppositis mediis*) *argenteis.*

Herrich-Schäffer has figured my *imperfectella* very characteristically in his new work, fig. 113, and described it, p. 19.

[I may mention here that I have a specimen of this *Micropteryx imperfectella* collected by Mr. Trovey Blackmore near Tangier in Morocco, at the end of March 1868.—H. T. S.]

Bred in May, at Chiclana. The larva fed on *Cachrys lævigata*, Lam., on the coast sand-hills in February and March.

11. (72.) DEPRESSARIA VELOX.

Alis anterioribus rufescenti-brunneis, squamis nigricantibus valde irroratis, margine antico ciliisque exceptis; alis posterioribus griseis (♂ ♀, $9\frac{1}{4}$-$11\frac{1}{2}$‴).

Der *D. Libanotidella* sehr ähnlich, aber mit abgerundeteren Vorderflügeln und eintönig grauen Hinterflügeln, die bei *Libanotidella* weisslich sind.

Bred at the end of June, at Chiclana. The larvæ were on a fine-leaved species of *Ferula*, in which they form a very slight web into which they run very rapidly.

12. (73.) DEPRESSARIA SUBLUTELLA.

Alis anterioribus rufescenti-stramineis, griseo-irroratissimis, macula media, plus minusve obsoleta, nigricante; alis posterioribus griseis, ciliis dilutioribus (♂ ♀, $8\frac{1}{2}$-$9\frac{1}{4}$‴).

Vorderflügel röthlich strohgelb, mit grauen Schuppen dicht bestreut, die zuweilen punktförmig auftreten. In der Mitte steht ein runder dunkler Fleck, der oft sehr verloschen ist. Hinterflügel grau mit lichteren Franzen. Der *D. atomella* am nächsten, die aber stets an der Basis eine lichtere Färbung zeigt.

In June, at Chiclana. The larva on *Centaurea aspera*, L.

13. (74). DEPRESSARIA STRAMINELLA.

Alis anterioribus griseo-stramineis, nigro-punctulatis; alis posterioribus grisescentibus, in basi albicantibus, ciliis lutescentibus (♂ ♀, $10\frac{1}{2}$-11‴).

Vorderflügel eintönig grau strohgelb mit einzelnen schwarzen Pünktchen. Hinterflügel grau, an der Basis heller, mit gelblichen Franzen. Von *D. assimilella*, die ich nicht kenne, durch das Fehlen des dunklen Flecks auf den Vorderflügeln verschieden.

At the beginning of June a few at Chiclana.

14. (75.) NOTHRIS DECLARATELLA.

Palporum articulo secundo externe in basi nigro, apice intusque albo; alis anterioribus lutescenti-brunneis, margine antico dilutiore, vitta obsoleta ex basi ad medium lineolisque ante cilia nigris (♂ ♀, $8\frac{1}{2}$‴).

Das breite zweite Palpenglied ist zur Hälfte nach aussen schwarz, die andere Hälfte (wie der innere Theil) scharf abgeschnitten weiss. Die Vorderflügel haben eine lichte schmutzig holzbraune Farbe, am Vorderrande am hellsten. Unter diesem helleren Vorderrand verläuft bis zur Mitte ein breiter, verloschener, schwarzer Streif. Vor der Limballinie stehen schwarze Strichelchen und die Rippen sind hin und wieder auch schwärzlich.

At Chiclana, a tolerable ♀ on the 29th April, and a very fresh ♂ on the 23rd June.

15. (76.) Nothris senticetella.

Palporum articulo secundo barbatissimo, externe nigro, in medio albo-fasciato; alis anterioribus breviusculis griseis, lineolis cellulæ mediæ costarumque nigris (♂ ♀, 5–6′′′).

Bei *N. Sabinella*. Das zweite sehr behaarte Palpenglied ist aussen schwarz, in der Mitte weiss geringelt. Flügel nur kurz, die vorderen grau mit mehr oder weniger schwarzen Längsstrichelchen, theils hinter einander in der Mittelzelle, theils längs der in den Vorderrand auslaufenden Aeste der Subcostalrippe stehend, zuweilen auch ganz fehlend.

In June, at Chiclana. The larva on *Juniperus phœnicea*, L.

16. (77.) Symmoca dodecatella.

Alis anterioribus griseis, nigro-conspersis, basi punctisque 6 nigris; alis posterioribus nigricantibus (♂, 9½′′′).

Ausgezeichnete Art. Vorderflügel grau, mit Schwarz, namentlich am Aussenrande, bestreut. Die Basis und 6 Flecke schwarz. Zwei der letzteren stehen am Vorderrande etwa bei ⅓ und ⅔ der Länge, die andern vier darunter in eigenthümlicher Stellung. Schon durch die Grösse mit keiner bekannten Art zu verwechseln.

Only four males, in June, in the Sierra de Alfacar.

17. (78.) Lecithocera pallicornella.

Capillis, antennis, palpis pedibusque vitellineis (in ♀ antennis albidis); alis anterioribus acutis, ♂ nitide griseo-fuscis, ♀ flavescentibrunneis (♂ ♀, 6–7½′′′).

Alle Theile des Kopfs und die Füsse gelblich, beim ♀ die Fühler weisslich. Die spitzen Vorderflügel sind beim ♂ glänzend dunkelbraun, beim ♀ hell braungelb. Von *Lecithocera luticornella* durch ganz andere Färbung, breitere, viel zugespitztere Vorderflügel mit geradem Hinterrande etc. verschieden.

In June at Granada, in April at Chiclana, flying in bushes of *Quercus coccifera*.

18. (79.) Gelechia plutelliformis.

Alis anterioribus griseo-roseis, litura media longitudinali lata, interne sinuata, seriebusque duabus punctorum ex apice angulum acutum formantibus nigris; alis posterioribus latis griseis (♀, 8′′′).

Ausgezeichnete Art, die in der Zeichnung der Vorderflügel grosse Aehnlichkeit mit der der *Plutella*-Arten hat. Grundfarbe der Vorderflügel grau rosa. Von der Basis des Vorderrandes zieht sich etwa bis ⅔ der Flügellänge ein breiter, nach innen scharf markirter gebogener Strich (Wisch) in die Mitte hinein. Von der Flügelspitze aus, am Vorder- und Aussenrand verlaufend, gehen zwei aus schwarzen Punkten gebildete Striche aus, die einen sehr spitzen Winkel bilden. Hinterflügel ziemlich breit, eintönig grau.

Two females, bred at the end of June. The larva on *Tamarix*, at Chiclana.

19. (80.) GELECHIA HELOTELLA.

Alis anterioribus angustissimis, obscure griseis, striola punctisque disci duobus obsoletis nigris; alis posterioribus nigricantibus, ciliis dilutioribus (♂ ♀, 8½′′′).

Vorderflügel im Verhältniss zur bedeutenden Länge sehr schmal und spitz. Farbe dunkelgrau; in der Längsmitte stehen etwa bei ¼ und ¾ zwei kleine schwarze Punkte; schräg unter dem ersten, etwas mehr nach innen, ein sehr verloschenes dunkles Strichelchen. Hinterflügel einfarbig grau mit helleren Franzen.

At the end of April and beginning of May, at Granada.

20. (81.) GELECHIA CONTUBERNIELLA.

Alis anterioribus latis, obscure griseis, striga postica superne acute fracta, in maculam parvam anteriorem ampliata squamisque obsolete lutescentibus; alis posterioribus nigricantibus, ciliis dilutioribus (♂ ♀, 6½–7½′′′).

Der *G. quotella** und *G. scintillella* sehr ähnlich, vielleicht nur dieselbe Art. Die Vorderflügel sind breiter, vorne stumpfer und die helle Querlinie vor dem Aussenrande führt nach innen und oben eine scharfe Einbiegung.

In July, at Granada, bred from *Halimium lepidotum*, Spoch. [*Helianthemum halimifolium*]. Also at Chiclana.

21. (82.) GELECHIA TERNATELLA.

Alis anterioribus obsolete stramineis, punctis 3 mediis (in triangulum dispositis) strigis punctulatis duabus posticis nigris; alis posterioribus albo-lutescentibus (in ♀ nigricantibus) (♂ ♀, 6½′′′).

Fühler, Füsse und Vorderflügel schmutzig strohgelb. Letztere führen drei im Dreieck gestellte dunkle Punkte; der eine etwa bei ¼, der andere bei ½, der dritte unter beiden, mehr dem ersten genähert. Kurz vor dem Aussenrand verläuft eine Reihe dicht aneinander gestellter schwarzer Punkte, die sich noch etwas nach dem Vorder- und Innenrande hin erstrecken. Parallel mit derselben, mehr nach innen, verläuft eine ähnliche aus Querstrichen bestehende Linie. Hinterflügel beim ♂ blass gelb, beim ♀ schwärzlicher.

Three specimens; at Granada on the 3rd of July, at Chiclana on the 13th of June.

22. (83.) GELECHIA ULICINELLA.

Alis anterioribus lutescentibus, marginibus antico posticoque griseo-conspersis, punctis duobus disci medii elongatis, nigris; alis posterioribus griseo-albidis (♂ ♀, 5′′′).

Der *Gelechia nigricostella* nahe, aber durch ungeringelte Palpen, viel hellere Hinterflügel und andere Zeichnung der Vorderflügel verschieden. Letztere sind grau, aber namentlich nach vorne und aussen (auch in der Mitte) mit Grau stark bedeckt. Etwa in der Mitte, mehr nach vorne, stehen zwei lang gezogene schwarze Punkte. Hinterflügel grau weisslich.

[* I know not what species is meant by this name.—H. T. S.]

Four specimens bred at Granada in September. The larva in April, in the flowers of *Ulex australis*.

23. (84.) GELECHIA DISJECTELLA.

Alis anterioribus elongatis albido-griseis, umbra longitudinali media saturatiore, lineolas duas nigras continente, puncto in apice nigro (♂ ♀, 5½-6½′′′).

Bei *G. instabilella*, aber viel markirter. Vorderflügel lang gezogen, weissgrau mit einem breiten dunklen Längsschatten, der einen ochergelben Anflug hat. In demselben stehen zwei markirte schräge schwarze Striche und in der Flügelspitze ein dunkler Punkt.

The larvæ were found in the tips of *Artemisia Barrelieri*, in October and November, at Granada; three specimens were bred in the following March.

24. (85.) GELECHIA NOCTURNELLA.

Palporum articulo terminali tenui acuto; griseo-fusca, alis anterioribus acutis, nigro ochraceoque irroratis; alis posterioribus dilutioribus (♂, 5′′′).

Diese kleine schwer zu beschreibende Art kommt dunklen Varietäten der *G. salinella* sehr nahe. Die Palpen sind aber viel dünner und spitzer; auch die Vorderflügel sind spitzer und zeigen keine deutlichen schwarzen Punkte. Dieselben sind dunkel grauschwarz, durch die Lupe besehen mit ochergelben Schuppen vermischt.

Several specimens, at Chiclana, in March.

25. (86.) GELECHIA PROMPTELLA.

Nigro-grisea, palporum articulo terminali antennisque albo-annulatis; alis anterioribus nigro punctatis (♂, 3¾-4½′′′).

Sehr kleine Art bei *G. diminutella*, von dieser durch geringere Grösse und etwas bestäubtere Vorderflügel, namentlich gegen die Spitze und auf den Franzen hin, verschieden.

Only three specimens, at Chiclana, in April. Zeller took a specimen of this species at Syracuse on the 23rd of May, but he has not mentioned it.

26. (87.) GELECHIA FIGULELLA.

Antennis articuloqne terminali palporum obscuris, obsolete annulatis; alis anterioribus angustis, rufescenti-griseis, nigro irroratis, medio limboque punctatis (♂ ♀, 6½′′′).

Der *G. terrella* sehr nahe, aber kleiner, zierlicher und nicht mit hellem letzten Palpengliede.

In April, at Chiclana.

27. (88.) GELECHIA IMPERITELLA.

Capite palpisque roseo-albidis; alis anterioribus angustis, rufescentibus, nigro conspersis, punctis disci 1, 2, 1 obsoletis nigris (♂ ♀, 5′′′).

Der vorigen, sowie der *G. plebejella* sehr ähnlich, aber viel kleiner, mit rothweisslichem Kopf und Palpen. Grundfarbe der Vorderflügel viel röthlicher mit Schwarz bestreut und mit vier rundlichen schwarzen Punkten, von denen die beiden mittleren untereinander stehen.
At the end of April and in May, at Granada.

28. (89.) GELECHIA EPITHYMELLA.

Capite palpisque albidis, antennis fusco alboque annulatis; alis anterioribus elongatis, brunneo-ochraceis, marginibus, costis ciliisque griseis; alis posterioribus nigricantibus, ciliorum basi lutescente (♂, $6\frac{3}{4}'''$).
Der *G. artemisiella* ähnlich, aber viel grösser. Kopf und Palpen weisslich. Fühler dunkel und weiss geringelt. Die ziemlich langen Vorderflügel haben ein braunes Ochergelb, das aber an allen Rändern, auf den Rippen und den Franzen mit Grau bedeckt ist. Hinterflügel dunkelgrau, Franzen an der Basis gelblich.
One male, on the 24th of March, at Chiclana.

29. (90.) GELECHIA DEJECTELLA.

Alis sordide albis, anterioribus lanceolatis, praecipue apicem versus obscurius squamatis (♂ ♀, $4\text{-}4\frac{1}{4}'''$).
Obwohl ich nur drei bei Granada am Ende April gefangene Stücke besitze, so ist doch diese Art durch die ausgezeichnet lancettförmigen Vorderflügel mit keiner mir bekannten *Gelechia* zu verwechseln. Grundfarbe ist ein schmutziges Weiss, auf den Vorderflügeln mit dunklen Schuppen, namentlich nach der Spitze zu, bestreut.

30. (91.) GELECHIA GADITELLA.

Palpis brevissimis, alis anterioribus rotundatis, lutescenti-albidis, atomis fuscis conspersis, praecipue in ciliis (♂ ♀, $4\text{-}4\frac{1}{4}'''$).
Kleine ausgezeichnete Art, aus der Stainton ein eigenes Genus machen wollte, da die Palpen äusserst kurz und der Kopf Aehnlichkeit mit dem einer *Elachista* hat. Da sie aber sonst von den *Gelechien* nicht abweicht und namentlich die Hinterflügel ausgezeichnet gelechienartig ausgeschnitten sind, so muss sie doch wohl besser eine *Gelechia* bleiben. Die Vorderflügel erscheinen durch die langen Franzen sehr gerundet, sind gelblich weiss mit vielen eingestreuten dunklen Schüppchen, namentlich auf den Franzen.
This species was flying rather abundantly on the 29th of January, in front of the Landthor, at Cadiz; unfortunately I only brought home three specimens.

31. (92.) MEGACRASPEDUS SUBDOLELLUS.

Alis anterioribus sordide stramineis, longitudinaliter obsolete margaritaceo-striatis, margine antico albido; alis posterioribus griseis (♂ ♀, $6\frac{3}{4}\text{-}8\frac{1}{2}'''$).
Vorderflügel schmutzig strohgelb, bei einem Stück rein strohgelb,

bei andern fast grau. Der Vorderrand, namentlich nach der Spitze hin, rein weiss. In dem mittleren Raum unterscheidet man sehr verloschene, weiss perlmutterartig schillernde Längsstreifen. Viel grösser als *Meg. dolosellus* und auf den Vorderflügeln lange nicht so grell gezeichnet.

In August, on the Sierra Nevada, at a height of about 9000 feet.

EPIDOLA, nov. genus.

Capilli verticis frontisque depressi.
Haustellum, ocelli, palpi maxillares nulli.
Palpi labiales mediocres, penduli, articulo medio infra externeque squamis elongatis vestito, articulo tertio in squamis articuli secundi abscondito.
Antennæ in ♀ filiformes, apicem versus aspere squamatæ, articulo basali bipenicillato.
Alæ anteriores elongatæ, acutæ; posteriores ante apicem breviter emarginatæ, longe ciliatæ, penicillo longo basali.
Tibiæ posteriores in apice processu brevi instructæ.
Larva saccophora.

In April I found at Chiclana, on *Quercus coccifera*, from five to seven *Coleophora*-like cases of a dark wooden-brown colour. These are pistol-shaped, with two large muscle-shaped appendages posteriorly, which are stuck on behind (at the end of the shaft), and above fit close to a leaf-like appendage of the stem. The larvæ fed up to May, then attached themselves firmly, and were placed by me in a separate small box; for I was always most particularly careful to keep the *Coleophoræ* separate. On the 9th of June the first imago appeared, and soon after a second, both females; but, even without a knowledge of the male, these suffice to establish a distinct genus.

Stainton suggested that the larvæ had only lived parasitically in the *Coleophora*-cases, whilst Zeller thought it was more probable there had been an error in my observations. Any one is liable to error, and I have myself frequently made mistakes; but if I have done so here I can put no faith in any of my observations, since, besides my written remarks made immediately on the exclusion of the creature, I still perfectly remember how astounded I was at the appearance of so remarkable a *Coleophora*!

Das Genus steht am nächsten bei *Megacraspedus*. Scheitel und Stirne mit anliegenden Haaren. Nebenaugen, Maxillarpalpen und Saugerüssel scheinen ganz zu fehlen. Die Labialpalpen von mittlerer Länge sind etwas nach unten geneigt. Das zweite Glied ist nach unten und vorne sehr lang beschuppt, so dass man von dem dritten gar Nichts sieht. Die Fühler des ♀ sind fadenförmig, an ihrer äusseren Hälfte hin sehr rauh beschuppt; das Basalglied führt an beiden Seiten eine Reihe von Haarborsten. Die Vorderflügel sind lang und spitz; die Hinterflügel vor der Spitze kurz (gelechienartig) ausgeschnitten, sehr lang befranzt und führen oben auf der Basis einen langen Haarpinsel. Die mittleren und hintersten Schienbeine sind am Ende nicht mit dem gewöhnlichen Sporenpaar versehen, sondern führen hier nur einen kurzen, anliegenden, hornigen Stachel.

32. (93.) EPIDOLA STIGMA.

Alis anterioribus lutescentibus, puncto costæ transversæ magno squamisque cœruleo-nigris (♀, $6\frac{1}{2}'''$).

Vorderflügel lehmgelb, am Ende der Mittelzelle mit einem grösseren runden, blauschwarzen Fleck. Aehnlich gefärbte Schuppen finden sich zerstreut fast überall, namentlich aber am Vorder- und Aussenrande hin.

33. (94.) HYPSOLOPHUS CISTI.

Alis anterioribus murinis, squamis nigris conspersis, præcipue apicem versus; alis posterioribus dilutius griseis (♂, $7\frac{1}{2}'''$).

Vorderflügel eintönig mäusegrau, mit schwarzen Schuppen, namentlich nach aussen hin, bestreut. Hinterflügel heller grau.

One ♂ bred from *Cistus alba* on the 26th of April, at Granada, another ♂ taken at Chiclana on the 8th of March.

34. (95.) HYPSOLOPHUS LIMBIPUNCTELLUS.

Alis anterioribus griseis, punctis tribus in medio punctisque limbalibus nigris (♂ ♀, $6\frac{1}{2}$–$9\frac{1}{4}'''$).

Vorderflügel grau mit drei mittleren schwarzen Punkten; zwei schräg untereinander und der dritte etwas mehr nach vorne am Schluss der Mittelzelle. Am Limbalrand, bis in den Vorderrand hin aufgehend, stehen 7–9 schwarze Punkte, die zuweilen sehr schwach nur auftreten.

One specimen on the 7th October, at Granada; the others from March to June, at Chiclana.

35. (96.) HYPSOLOPHUS BUBULCELLUS.

Alis anterioribus lutescenti-cinereis, punctis duobus mediis squamisque (præcipue in costis) nigris; alis posterioribus nigricantibus, ciliis lutescenti-griseis (♂ ♀, $5\frac{1}{2}$–$6\frac{3}{4}'''$).

Vorderflügel gelblich grau, mit zwei schwarzen Punkten in der Längsmitte, etwa bei $\frac{1}{4}$ und $\frac{2}{3}$ stehend. Sie sind mit schwarzen Schuppen mehr oder weniger, namentlich auf den Rippen bestreut, so dass zuweilen dunkle Längsstrichelchen entstehen. Von *Hypsolophus binotellus* durch stumpfere, gröber beschuppte Vorderflügel verschieden.

Kalisch found the larvæ at Chiclana in dry cow-dung, and the perfect insects appeared in June and July.

36. (97). PTEROLONCHE INSPERSA.

Alis anterioribus albidis, fusco conspersis, costis omnibus fuscis (♀, $11'''$).

Nach Zeller nicht seine *Pt. albescens*, da diese neue Art zwischen

den viel brauner bestäubten Adern noch braune Bestäubung dazwischen führt.
Only one ♀ on the 30th of May, at Chiclana.

37. (98.) ANCHINIA SOBRIELLA.

Alis anterioribus viridi-stramineis, margine antico albido, lineis duabus longitudinalibus subargenteis (♂ ♀, 9¼–11½'''').
Vorderflügel grünlich strohgelb mit weisslichem Vorderrande. Eine matt silberne Linie geht von der Basis bis zum Hinterwinkel; eine ähnliche theilt sich dicht bei der Basis von der ersteren ab und verläuft nach dem vorderen Theil des Aussenrandes, den sie jedoch niemals ganz erreicht. Hinterflügel schwärzlich. Von *A. Heydenreichiella*, Led. (dort sehr häufig) durch ganz anderes Gelb der Vorderflügel, viel mattere, unreine Silberstreifen, etc. verschieden.
At Granada, at the end of June and in July; rather later and much scarcer than *A. Heydenreichiella*.

38. (99.) ANCHINIA PLANELLA.

Alis anterioribus pallidissime ochraceis, nebula sæpe cinerea ex apice infra marginem anticum producta (♂ ♀, 8½–10''').
Vorderflügel blass ochergelb, öfters am Vorderrande nach der Flügelspitze hin mit dunkleren Schatten. Hinterflügel schwärzlich.
At Granada and Chiclana, in June.

39. (100.) ANCHINIA TELIGERELLA.

Alis anterioribus albido-cinereis, margine antico lineæ instar albo, postice obscurato, vitta latiuscula aureo-brunnea infra marginem anticum ex basi in apicem ducta (♂ ♀, 5½–7½''').
Vorderflügel weiss grau, oder genauer weiss mit grau bestäubt. Vorderrand mit einem schmalen weissen Streifen, der die Flügelspitze nicht vollständig erreicht. Unter demselben, von der Basis bis in den Aussenrand auslaufend, ist eine gleichbreite gelbbraune Binde mit mattem Goldschimmer. Ein schwarzer Mittelpunkt, wie er bei *A. ericella*, Dup. abgebildet ist, fehlt ganz, oder ist nur künstlich hervorzusuchen; dahingegen findet man zuweilen 3–4 schwarze Punkte vor dem Aussenrand. *A. bicostella* ist viel grösser, ob aber vielleicht *ericella*, Dup. diese Art ist, könnten nur Exemplare aus der Umgegend von Paris erweisen.
From April to July, at Granada and Chiclana.

40. (101.) ŒCOPHORA MERCEDELLA.

Capite albo; alis anterioribus flavis, strigis duabus margineque postico albidis, fusco-conspersis, macula triangulari media castanea alteraque apicali fusca (♂, 5''').
Sehr ausgezeichnete Art. Fühler weiss und dunkel geringelt. Kopf weiss. Thorax gelb. Vorderflügel gelb; zwei weisse Querlinien bei ⅓ und ⅔, so wie am Limbalrand; namentlich die beiden hinteren stark braun bestäubt. Zwischen Querlinie 1. und 2.,

näher nach dem Innenrande, mit der Basis auf Linie 1. aufsitzend, steht ein spitzer, dreieckiger, kastanienbrauner Fleck. Ein aus dunkleren Schuppen zusammengesetzter Fleck steht in der Flügelspitze, so wie ein ähnlicher kleinerer am Hinterwinkel.
Only one fine ♂, on the 30th June, at Chiclana.

41. (102.) ŒCOPHORA DETRIMENTELLA.

Palpis tenuibus, brevibus; alis obscure plumbeo-griseis, posterioribus dilutioribus (♂, 8'").
Unterscheidet sich von *Œcophora minutella* durch die noch viel kürzeren Taster. Flügel dunkelgrau mit etwas bleifarbigem Glanze, die hinteren heller.
Only one ♂, at Granada.

42. (103.) ŒCOPHORA FILIELLA.

Capillis flavis; alis plumbeo-griseis (♂, 6½'").
Scheitel gelb. Flügel bleigrau. Der *Œc. flavifrontella* ähnlich, aber viel kleiner.
Two ♂ in June, at Granada.

ALLOCLITA, nov. genus.

Caput squamis depressis.
Ocelli nulli.
Antennæ filiformes, flocculo basali præditæ.
Palpi maxillares breves. Haustelli basis squamata.
Palpi labiales longi, reflexi, articulo tertio acuto.
Alæ anteriores elongatæ; posteriores lanceolatæ.

Neues Genus, welches *Œcophora* und *Gelechia* verbindet. Kopf mit angedrückten Schuppen. Fühler fadenförmig, an der Basis mit dem Borstenkämmchen von *Œcophora*. Keine Nebenaugen, kurze Maxillarpalpen, Saugerüssel an der Basis beschuppt. Die Labialpalpen sind lang, weit auseinander stehend, nach oben umgebogen; drittes Glied sehr dünn und spitz. Vorderflügel länglich; Hinterflügel lanzettförmig, ohne alle Spur von dem Ausschnitt bei *Gelechia*.

43. (104). ALLOCLITA RECISELLA.

Alis anterioribus lutescenti-griseis, basi abrupte obscuriore, punctis disci duobus nigris, exteriore albo-circumdato (♂ ♀, 6–7'").
Vorderflügel grau mit einem Stich in's Gelbe. An der Basis ist ein kleines, dunkles, nach aussen scharf abgeschnittenes Feld. Demselben folgt ein breites helles Feld (zuweilen fast weisslich). Dann folgen in der Längsmitte zwei nicht weit von einander stehende schwarze Punkte; der äussere weiss umzogen und zuweilen mit dem inneren durch einen weissen Strich verbunden. In der Flügelspitze steht ein weisses Fleckchen.

At the end of June seven specimens were taken in the evening before dark at Chiclana.

44. (105.) Butalis Scipionella.

Alis anterioribus elongatissimis, acutis, fusco-viridibus, linea media alba ex basi ultra medium; alis posterioribus nigricantibus (♂ ♀, 7–9¼‴).

Vorderflügel sehr lang mit sehr spitzem Vorderwinkel, dunkelgrünlich. Von der Basis bis zum Ende der Mittelzelle verläuft ein gerader, ziemlich breiter weisser Strich; derselbe setzt sich meistens noch bis zum Aussenrande in schiefer Richtung fort. Der Zeugungsapparat ist sehr gross wie bei *Butalis grandipennis*.

From the end of May to July, at Granada and Chiclana.

45. (106.) Butalis xanthopygella.

Antennis externe albidis; alis anterioribus æneo-fuscis, margine antico lineaque media, postice interrupta, albis; abdomine nigro, ano ochraceo (♂ ♀, 9‴).

Fühler nach aussen weiss. Vorderflügel dunkel erzfarben, stets mit ganz weissem Vorderrande. In der Längsmitte verläuft eine andere weisse Linie, von der Basis bis zum Aussenrande an Breite zunehmend, und am Ende der Mittelzelle von der Grundfarbe durchbrochen (bei zwei Exemplaren bedeutend). Hinterflügel dunkel, bei einem Stück namentlich die Franzen und Unterseite ockergelb. Die letzten Segmente des Hinterleibs sind an der Bauchseite ochergelb, auch die Hinterschienen sind gelb behaart. Der männliche Zeugungsapparat tritt äusserlich nicht hervor.

Four specimens of this remarkable species were taken at Chiclana in June on the flowers of *Umbelliferæ*.

46. (107.) Butalis biforella.

Fusca; alarum anteriorum maculis duabus abdominisque segmentis antepenultimis utrinque albidis (♀, 5‴).

Grundfarbe braunschwarz. Die Vorderflügel führen zwei weisse Flecke, der erste etwa bei ⅓ in der Mitte, der zweite bei ⅔ ganz auf den Innenrand aufsitzend und grösser. Die vorletzten Segmente des Hinterleibes sind seitlich nach unten weiss.

Only one ♀, on the 26th June, at Granada.

47. (108.) Butalis insulella.

Fusco-ænea; alis anterioribus linea basali, annulo post eam crasso, abdominisque segmentis analibus subtus albis (♂, 4½‴).

Grundfarbe dunkel ehern. Vorderflügel führen bis zur Mitte einen mittleren, etwas verloschenen weissen Längsstrich. Dahinter steht ein etwas unregelmässiger, in die Flügelspitze ausgezogener, weisser breiter Ring, eine ganz runde dunkle Makel (Inselchen) umschliessend. Die hinteren Hinterleibsringe sind unten weisslich.

Two specimens bred from *Erica* the beginning of June, at Chiclana.

48. (109.) Butalis pulicella.

Alis anterioribus fusco-nigris, lineola disci media obsoleta alba;

alis posterioribus griseis; abdominis ano ventreque lutescentibus (♂ ♀, 4½–5½′′′).
Vorderflügel braunschwarz, in der Mitte, zuweilen auch an der Basis, mit kleinem weissen Längsstrichelchen. Hinterflügel viel heller, grau. Hinterleib oben dunkel, am Ende und unten lehmgelb, zuweilen weisslich. Bei *Butalis variella* und *siccella* stehend, aber durch die Färbung des Hinterleibs ganz verschieden.
In March and April, singly at Chiclana.

49. (110.) BUTALIS HUMILLIMELLA.

Palpis tenuibus, longioribus; alis anterioribus viridi-fuscis, metallescentibus; alis posterioribus nigricantibus (♂ ♀, 4½–6½′′′).
Durch viel feinere längere Palpen, sowie viel breitere Hinterflügel von *B. palustris* verschieden. Vorderflügel dunkelgrün erzschillernd; Hinterflügel matter schwarz.
In May at Granada, in April at Chiclana.

50. (111.) BUTALIS CUPREELLA.

Alis anterioribus cupreo-fuscis; alis posterioribus nigricantibus (♂, 7½–8′′′).
Von dem auch dort gefangenen *Butalis grandipennis* durch wesentlich geringere Grösse verschieden, besonders aber durch eine kupferglänzende dunkle Grundfarbe der Vorderflügel und des Thorax.
In June at Granada, in April at Chiclana.

51. (112.) BUTALIS HIBERNELLA.

Palpis brevioribus; alis anterioribus fusco-cinereis; alis posterioribus griseis (♂, 4½′′′).
Vorderflügel dunkel aschgrau; Hinterflügel äusserst schmal, grau. Palpen sehr klein, wodurch diese Art wesentlich von *B. incongruella*, die auch viel grösser ist, abweicht.
One ♂ on the 26th of February, at Chiclana.

52. (113.) BUTALIS BIMERDELLA.

Alis anterioribus canis, punctis disci duobus deinceps positis nigris; alis posterioribus obscurioribus (♂, 8½′′′).
Vorderflügel eintönig hell aschgrau mit zwei schwarzen in der Längsmitte stehenden Punkten, der erste bei ¼, der andere etwa bei ¾. Hinterflügel dunkelgrau.
Not scarce in the gorge (Barranco) of San Geronimo, in the Sierra Nevada, in the beginning of July. Unfortunately I only brought home one specimen.

STAINTONIA, nov. genus.

Caput obtusum, squamis appressis.
Ocelli nulli.
Antennæ crassæ, in ♂ pubescenti-ciliatæ.
Palpi labiales abscedentes, recurvi, acuminati.

Haustellum longum, basi squamatum.

Alæ anteriores elongatæ; posteriores angustissime lanceolatæ, cellula media aperta, costa media interiore tripartita, costa media exteriore bipartita.

Abdomen depressum, squamis lateralibus erectis.

Dem Genus *Butalis* am nächsten; besonders durch den von oben nach unten sehr stark zusammengedrückten Leib, dessen Ränder durch grosse seitlich abstehende Schuppen gezähnt erscheinen, verschieden. Die Fühler sind bedeutend dicker als bei allen mir bekannten *Butalis*-Arten. Der Rippenverlauf ist gleichfalls verschieden, namentlich auf den Hinterflügeln, wo die Mittelzelle ganz offen ist. Die innere Mittelrandsrippe theilt sich in drei, die äussere in zwei Aeste. Genaueres werde ich später geben.

53. (114.) STAINTONIA MEDINELLA.

Alis anterioribus æneo-fuscis, fasciis duabus albidis; alis posterioribus fuscis; abdomine plus minusve lateritio, ano cæruleo-nigro (♂ ♀, 4½–5½''').

Vorderflügel erzschillernd braun mit weisslichen Schuppen mehr oder weniger gemischt, und mit zwei weisslichen, nicht scharf begrenzten Querbinden, die eine bei ⅓, die andere vor dem Aussenrande. Letztere macht in der Mitte eine bedeutende Biegung. Hinterflügel dunkel. Der Leib roth, namentlich bei dem Weibchen. Der After bleibt stets und die ersten Segmente meistens nach oben blauschwarz.

Kalisch discovered this species at Chiclana in June, sitting on the flowers of *Umbelliferæ*.

54. (115.) PANCALIA GRABOWIELLA.

Antennis fusco alboque annulatis; alis anterioribus æneo-fuscis, fasciis duabus maculisque 4 aureis, in margine antico niveis; alis posterioribus lanceolatis (aureo-)griseis, obscure griseo-ciliatis (♂ ♀, 3½–4¼''').

Fühler dunkelbraun und weiss geringelt. Vorderflügel metallglänzend dunkelbraun. Auf der Basalhälfte stehen zwei ziemlich parallel laufende goldene Binden, auf der äusseren Hälfte vier goldfarbene Flecken, von denen der in der Spitze stehende sich öfters am ganzen Aussenrand hin erweitert. Wo die Binden und Flecken den Vorderrand berühren, werden sie silberweiss. Die sehr schmalen Hinterflügel haben ein goldschimmerndes grau Braun mit langen dunklen Franzen. Der *P. pomposella* nahe, aber durch verschiedene Stellung der Goldzeichnung (*pomposella*) hat nicht zwei parallele Goldbinden) und durch andere Hinterflügel verschieden.

At Chiclana, from April to July. The larva resides in a firmly attached case formed of its own excrement, and devours the interior of the leaves of *Lavandula stœchas*; more rarely it occurs also on *Thymus vulgaris*.

55. (116.) ACROLEPIA SOLIDAGINIS.

Alis anterioribus cinerascenti-nebulosis, maculis in margine inte-

riore canescentibus obsoletis, margo anterior ante apicem albo-trimaculatis (♂ ♀, 7½–8½′′′).

Der *Acrolepia granitella* äusserst ähnlich, die ich aber auch in Andalusien aus einer verschiedenen Raupe und von einer andern Pflanze gezogen habe. Die Vorderflügel sind viel heller, gelblich aschgrau, und die auf den Innenrand aufsitzenden weisslichen Flecken viel weniger markirt. Dahingegen finden sich am Vorderrande gegen die Spitze zu dergleichen Flecken, die bei *granitella* nicht so deutlich vorhanden sind.

At Granada, in June and July, bred from *Solidago virgaurea*.

56. (117.) TINAGMA THYMETELLUM.

Alis anterioribus fusco-nigris, striga media rectissima squamulisque postice creberrimis albis (♂ ♀, 2½′′′).

Kleine ausgezeichnete Art, dem auch dort gefangenen *T. transversellum* ähnlich, aber viel kleiner. Vorderflügel matt braunschwarz (nicht goldschimmernd wie bei *transversellum*), in der Mitte mit geradem weissem Querstrich, der auch nach aussen dunkel beschattet ist. Namentlich die äussere Hälfte des Flügels ist mit kleinen weissen Schüppchen bestreut.

From the middle of April to May, at Chiclana, sitting on *Thymus vulgaris*, on which plant the larva probably feeds.

57. (118.) COLEOPHORA SPUMOSELLA.

Antennis albis, penicillo longo flavescente; alis anterioribus stramineis, vitta anteriore basim non attingente lineisque duabus argenteis, macula ex apice longa elongato-cuneiformi fusca (♂ ♀, 6¾–7¾′′′).

Fühler weiss mit langem gelblichem Basalbusch. Vorderflügel strohgelb. Am Vorderrande steht ein silberner breiter Streif, der aber nicht ganz bis zur Basis geht. Darunter befindet sich, von der Flügelspitze bis zu Mitte gehend, ein schmaler dunkelbrauner Keilfleck. Unter letzterem steht ein viel kürzerer silberner Strich. Ein dritter Silberstrich zieht sich von der Basis an, dicht vor dem Innenrande hin. Von *Coleophora cœlebipennella* durch den vordern, die Basis nicht erreichenden Silberstrich, durch viel schmäleren, kürzeren, braunen Keilstrich und durch den Sack ganz verschieden.

The larvæ at Granada, in April, on *Dorycnium suffruticosum*. Case short, cylindrical, but at the hinder end are two large, broad, inflated foam-like appendages, which entirely envelope it. The perfect insect appeared at the end of July and in August.

58. (119.) COLEOPHORA SOLENELLA.

Antennis albis, penicillo longo lutescente; alis anterioribus saturate stramineis, vitta anteriore basim non attingente lineisque duabus argenteis, linea ex apice fusca intra vittam valde producta (♂ ♀, 7–7½′′′).

Der vorigen äusserst ähnlich. Die Grundfarbe, etwas gelber, geht am Vorderrande fast bis zur Mitte, so dass der vordere Silberstrich noch weiter von der Basis entfernt ist. Der braune Keilfleck bei *spumosella* ist hier nur noch eine lange, schmale, braune Linie, die mindestens so weit wie der vordere Silberstrich reicht, was bei *spumosella* nie der Fall ist.

The case is very long (9'''), cylindrical, posteriorly compressed laterally, with a sharp keel beneath. The entire surface is rough, and of a wooden-brown colour.

At Granada: the larvæ in May on *Artemisia campestris*; the imago in August and September.

59. (120.) Coleophora lutatiella.

Antennis albis, penicillo basali parvo; alis anterioribus ochraceis, apice saturatiore, margine antico albo, margine interiore usque ad medium albicante (♂, $9\frac{1}{2}'''$; ♀, $8\frac{1}{2}'''$).

Fühler oben ganz weiss, unten dunkel geringelt mit kleinem Haarbusch. Vorderflügel ochergelb, in den Spitzen stark gesättigt. Vorderrand rein weiss. Innenrand von der Basis breit bis zur Hälfte in einer zugespitzten Linie weisslich. Von *Coleophora gallipennella* durch viel kürzeren Fühlerbusch, Fehlen der weissen Mittellinie etc. verschieden.

Only a pair at the end of April, at Chiclana.

60. (121.) Coleophora semicinerea.

Antennis albidis, obsolete annulatis, penicillo basali parvo; alis anterioribus sordide stramineis, margine antico albo, margine interiore latius cinereo (♂, $6\frac{3}{4}'''$).

Bei *Col. pyrrhulipennella*, aber nicht damit zu verwechseln. Die weisslichen Fühler mit kleinem Schuppenbusch sind sehr undeutlich dunkel geringelt. Vorderflügel schmutzig gelb mit rein weissem Vorderrande. Der ganze Theil am Innenrande ist grau, und zwar von der Basis, in ihrer ganzen Breite grau, bis zum Hinterwinkel an Breite abnehmend, ganz am Ende einige weisse Schuppen führend.

Only one ♂, on the 27th of March, at Chiclana.

61. (122.) Coleophora coarctella.

Antennis albidis, obsolete annulatis, penicillo parvo; alis anterioribus flavo fuscoque mixtis, margine anteriore, ciliorum basi, lineis duabus mediis, tertia in marginis interioris basi albis (♂, $6\frac{3}{4}'''$).

Fühler weisslich undeutlich dunkel geringelt mit mässigem Schuppenbusch. Vorderflügel gelb mit Dunkelbraun gemischt. Vorderrand, Basis der Franzen, zwei mittlere Längsstriche und ein kurzer Basalstrich am Innenrande weiss. Von den beiden mittleren Strichen geht der eine von der Basis bis zur Mitte. Dicht über ihm liegt parallel der andere, von $\frac{1}{3}$ der Flügellänge bis in den Aussenrand auslaufend.

A fine ♀, on the 17th of March, at Chiclana.

62. (123.) Coleophora congeriella.

Antennis albo fuscoque annulatis, penicillo flavescente, alis anteri-

oribus stramineis, in apice infuscatis, lineis tribus subargenteis (in margine antico et interiore et in medio) (♂ ♀, 4½–5′′′).

Fühler weiss und dunkel geringelt mit mässigem gelbem Schuppenbusch. Flügel strohgelb, in der Spitze bräunlich. Vorderrand, Innenrand, so wie ein mittlerer, fast bis zum Aussenrand gehender Strich weiss. Von der ähnlichen *Coleophora vicinella* durch den Sack ganz verschieden, auch sind die Vorderflügel nicht so gelb, der Innenrand breiter weiss etc.

The larva at Granada, in April and May, on *Dorycnium suffruticosum*. Case small, broad, posteriorly rather curved; constructed of the dry leaves of the plant. The imago in July and August.

63. (124.) COLEOPHORA VESTALELLA.

Antennis brevi-penicillatis, palpis, capite, thorace, alisque anterioribus niveis (♂ ♀, 6¾–8′′′).

Fühler mit sehr schwachem Schuppenbusch, höchstens an der Spitze dunkler geringelt. Palpen, Kopf, Thorax, Vorderflügel schneeweiss.

The larvæ in May, at Granada, on *Anthyllis cytisoides*. Case formed of the leaves of the plant, very broad and flattened, posteriorly with the tip rather curved. The imago in August and September.

64. (125.) COLEOPHORA STRUELLA.

Antennis albis, brevi-penicillatis; alis anterioribus niveis, obscure brunneo-venosis, venis nonnullis passim interruptis (♂ ♀, 4½–6¾′′′).

Bei *Col. auricella* und *virgatella*, aber durch den viel kürzeren Schuppenbusch der Fühler, sowie durch den Sack verschieden.

The case has quite the form of a compressed nightcap with the tip turned downwards, and is composed of the dry leaves of the foodplant, *Thymus vulgaris*, placed transversely.

At Granada in June and July; from April to June at Chiclana.

65. (126.) COLEOPHORA SOLIDAGINELLA.

Antennis albis, penicillo subnullo; alis anterioribus lutescenti-brunneis, lineis intercostalibus albis (♂ ♀, 6–6¾′′′).

Der vorigen Art äusserst ähnlich, aber die Fühler sind fast ganz ohne Schuppenbusch. Die Vorderflügel sind viel dunkler, so dass man ein Gelbgrau als Grundfarbe annehmen kann, indem dann die weisse Farbe als Längs- und Querstriche steht. Der Sack ist nun ganz verschieden.

The larva feeds on the interior of the young leaves of *Solidago virgaurea*. It forms its case by cutting out a piece of the eaten leaf; and when its old case becomes too small for it, it constructs a new one; from two to three cases, however, seem to be sufficient for it.

Bred at Chiclana, at the end of May and in June.

66. (127.) COLEOPHORA BISERIATELLA.

Antennis albis, non penicillatis; abdomine albicante, supra lineis duabus lineolis nigris compositis; alis anterioribus flavis (in ♀ lutescenti-fuscis), margine antico et interiore lineisque duabus ex basi ad medium albis (♂ ♀, 4¼–5′′′).

Fühler weiss ohne Schuppenbusch. Auf dem weisslichen Hinterleib stehen oben dicht nebeneinander zwei aus schwarzen Längsstrichelchen gebildete Linien. Vorderflügel ähnlich denen von *Coleophora fretella*, sind beim ♂ meistens schwefelgelb, beim ♀ gelbbräunlich, mit weissem Vorder- und Innenrande, sowie zwei weissen Mittellinien. Die eine derselben geht von der Basis bis ⅓ der Flügellänge, die andere beginnt etwas höher über dem Ende der ersten und geht bis zum Aussenrand.

At Chiclana, at the end of April and in May.

67. (128.) COLEOPHORA LASSELLA.

Antennis argute fusco alboque annulatis, non penicillatis; alis anterioribus lutescentibus, margine antico albido (♂ ♀, 4½′′′).

Bei *Col. cæspititiella*, aber Farbe der Vorderflügel viel matter lehmgelb mit weissem Vorderrande. Die Fühler sind sehr deutlich braunschwarz und weiss geringelt.

A pair, at the end of May, at Chiclana.

68. (129.) COLEOPHORA AREFACTELLA.

Antennis albo griseoque annulatis, non penicillatis; alis anterioribus griseis, margine antico, apice lineisque duabus mediis albidis (♂, 5′′′).

Fühler weiss und grau geringelt ohne Schuppenbusch. Vorderflügel grau. Vorderrand, Flügelspitze und zwei mittlere Linien weisslich. Letztere verlaufen parallel über einander in den Aussenrand, die untere beginnt an der Basis, die obere etwa bei ⅛ der Flügellänge. Bei *Col. Gnaphalii*.

Only one ♂, in the spring, at Chiclana.

69. (130.) ELACHISTA PIPERATELLA.

Alis anterioribus pulvereo-cinereis, ultra medium creberrime albido squamulatis (♂ ♀, 4–4½′′′).

Vorderflügel staubgrau, etwa von der Mitte bis zum Aussenrande mit weisslichen Schuppen sehr reichlich bedeckt. Hinterflügel eintönig grau.

At Granada in April, at Chiclana at the end of January and in February.

70. (131.) LITHOCOLLETIS CHICLANELLA.

Alis anterioribus albidis, fascia basali, maculis duabus costalibus una dorsali apiceque aureo-striatis, strigula apicali nigra (♂ ♀, 3¼–3¾′′′).

Vorderflügel weiss. Eine gebrochene Binde dicht hinter der Basis, ein Fleck in der Mitte des Vorderrandes, ein anderer dort bei ¾ der Länge und unter diesem ein Fleck am Innenrande (öfters bis an den obern stossend), sowie die Flügelspitze mehr oder weniger gold-

ochergelb. Im Vorderwinkel steht eine dunkle Längslinie, die bei
der Vereinigung der beiden zusammenstossenden Flecke beginnt.

In May, from the leaves of *Populus alba*, on the Alameda [public
walk] of Chiclana.

71. (132). LITHOCOLLETIS HESPERIELLA.

*Alis anterioribus dilute aureis, linea disci ex basi ad medium,
paribus duobus strigularum oppositarum strigulisque duabus costæ
ante apicem albidis intus nigro-marginatis, striola apicali nigra
(♂, 4½''').*

Vorderflügel blassgolden mit schmutzig weisser, nach innen dunkler
Strichzeichnung und einem schwarzen Längswisch in der Flügelspitze. Die Zeichnung ist folgende: Ein mittlerer Basalstrich, etwas
nach vorne gehend über ⅓ der Flügellänge hinaus. Er stösst fast
auf den ersten vorderen Querstrich, der sich mit dem viel längeren,
ersten, inneren, unten sehr spitzen Winkel vereint. Der zweite
vordere Querstrich, viel kürzer, vereint sich etwa in der Mitte mit
dem zweiten innern. Am Vorderrande folgen nun noch zwei Striche,
von denen der letzte eigentlich nur ein Punkt ist.

Two males from Chiclana, probably from *Quercus coccifera*.

72. (133.) LITHOCOLLETIS BELOTELLA.

*Alis anterioribus nitide aureis, lineola disci basali, maculis trian-
gularibus costæ 3, dorsi duabus argenteis, intus nigro-marginatis,
puncto apicali nigro, limbo chalybeo (♂ ♀, 3¾-4½''').*

Vorderflügel glänzend goldfarben mit kurzem, mittlerem, silber-
nem Basalstrich. Wo er aufhört, beginnen vorne und innen zwei
Häkchen, dahinter bei ⅔ der Flügellänge stehen zwei ähnliche. Die
am Vorderrande sind stets kleiner und schmäler. In der Mitte
zwischen den Häkchen steht ein dunkler Längswisch. Am Vorderrand steht noch ein dritter, zuweilen sogar noch ein vierter weisser
Strich. In der Spitze befindet sich fast stets deutlich ein runder
schwarzer Fleck. Der Limbalrand ist stahlblau.

At Granada, in May, bred from the leaves of *Quercus ilex*; taken
at Chiclana in April.

PHYLLOBROSTIS, nov. genus.

*Vertex in medio depresso-squamatus, utrinque posticeque pilosus.
Ocelli palpique nulli.
Haustellum breve, tenue, nudum.
Antennæ filiformes, articulo basali vix incrassato, flocculum dis-
tinctissimum gerente.
Alæ anteriores breviusculæ, acuminatæ; posteriores angustissime
lanceolatæ.*

Scheitel in der Mitte flach beschuppt, seitlich und hinten mit
längeren Haaren. Keine Nebenaugen, noch Palpen. Saugrüssel
ganz kurz, zart, nackt. Fühler fadenförmig; Basalglied etwas ver-

dickt mit sehr deutlichem Borstenwisch. Vorderflügel nicht lang, spitz; Hinterflügel sehr schmal, lanzettförmig.

Bei *Bucculatrix* stehend, durch Fehlen der Conchulæ (Augendeckel), durch den nicht ganz rauh behaarten Scheitel etc., wahrscheinlich auch durch Flügelgeäder, worüber später, verschieden.

73. (134.) PHYLLOBROSTIS DAPHNEELLA.

Alis anterioribus nitidulis argenteo-griseis, sæpius flavescentibus, margine antico dilutiore (♂ ♀, $3\frac{1}{2}$–$4\frac{1}{2}'''$).

Flügel silbergrau, öfters mit gelblichem Ton.

At Chiclana, in May, bred from *Daphne gnidium*.

SECTION III.

New Tineina collected by Dr. Staudinger in Spain in 1862.

Amongst some new European Lepidoptera described by Dr. Staudinger ("Einige neue europäische Lepidopteren beschrieben von Dr. O. Staudinger in Dresden") in the 'Stettin. entomolog. Zeitung,' 1863, p. 264, are three Tineina from the centre of Spain, viz. *Atychia læta*, *Sophronia santolinæ*, and *Lithocolletis adenocarpi*.

Atychia læta. I took this species in July, on a dry, stony slope, at San Ildefonso, where the males flew about abundantly in the afternoon and evening. I will give a detailed notice of the larvæ, which I also found, on a future occasion.

Sophronia santolinæ. I bred this in plenty at the end of June from small, short, green larvæ, which I found rolled up in the leaves of *Santolina rosmarinifolia* at the beginning of May. From Saint Ildefonso, in Central Spain.

Lithocolletis adenocarpi. I found the hybernated larvæ of this species before the middle of April in the leaves of *Adenocarpus hispanicus*, and actually on bushes which were still half covered with snow. The perfect insects appeared towards the end of April and up to the middle May, and were not scarce anywhere round San Ildefonso where the *Adenocarpus* grew.

Copies of the original descriptions are appended.

'Stett. ent. Zeitung,' 1863, p. 269.

ATYCHIA LÆTA.

♂ *stramineus, alis post. supra unicoloribus nigricantibus pallide ciliatis, anterioribus subtus nigricantibus* (al. exp. 10–13''').

♀ *nigricans, capillis alarum anteriorum fasciis duabus stramineis; thorace alisque anterioribus ubique confertim flavo irroratis* (al. exp. $8\frac{1}{2}$–$9\frac{1}{4}'''$).

Var. *a.* ♂ *alis poster. supra, anterioribus subtus flavescentibus.*

Die Männchen dieser ausgezeichneten Art sind strohgelb, nur die

Oberseite der Hinterflügel, mit Ausnahme der gelb bleibenden Franzen, sowie die Unterseite der Vorderflügel ist schwärzlich. Bei der var. *a* sind auch diese Theile fast vollständig gelb, doch ist dies äusserst selten. Die Fühler sind, abweichend von allen andern Arten dieser Gattung, dünn fadenförmig.

Die Weibchen mit dem bekannten gedrungenen Bau und langem Hinterleib haben eine dunkle Grundfarbe. Die Stirne ist gelb, der Scheitel, der Thorax und die Vorderflügel sind mit gelben Atomen sehr stark überstreut.

Die Vorderflügel führen ferner zwei hellere Querbinden, die eine etwa bei der Hälfte, die andere bei $\frac{4}{5}$ der Flügellänge. Jede dieser Binden besteht genau genommen aus zwei grösseren Flecken, wie man dies bei abgeflogenen Stücken sieht; bei ganz reinen Stücken erscheinen diese Flecken durch die dichte gelbe Beschuppung in der Mitte verbunden zu sein. Das ♀ unserer Art stimmt übrigens mit dem der *At. funebris* fast ganz überein.

Die Männchen sind von allen andern Arten der Gattung *Atychia* ganz verschieden und können höchstens mit denen der *Cassandrella* verwechselt werden. Letztere Art ist aber ziemlich viel kleiner, hat auf den Vorderflügeln fleckenartige dunkle Schuppenanhäufungen und auch viel dickere Fühler als vorliegende Art.

'Stett. ent. Zeitung,' 1863, p. 270.

SOPHRONIA SANTOLINÆ.

Palpis hirsutis albis, alis anterioribus olivaceis, litura costæ mediæ albida tenerrime nigro squamulata, strigulis duabus posticis oppositis exterius nigro squamulatis, hamulis duobus costæ ante apicem albis; alis posterioribus nigricantibus (al. exp. $3\frac{3}{4}$–5′′′).

Die sehr behaarten Palpen dieser Art sind fast schneeweiss. Die Färbung der Vorderflügel ist dunkel olivenfarben, über die Mitte hinaus mit aschgrauen Schüppchen stellenweise bestreut. Etwa bei $\frac{2}{3}$ der Flügellänge verläuft vom Vorderrande nach innen hinein ein fein weisser Strich, dem ein anderer, der vom Innenwinkel des Flügels ausläuft gegenüber steht, und zwar so, dass beide Striche einen nach aussen gekehrten spitzen Winkel bilden, ohne sich jedoch immer vollständig zu verbinden. In der Spitze dieses Winkels bemerkt man meistens eine sehr kurze und feine schwarze Längslinie. Unmittelbar vor der Flügelspitze stehen nah am Vorderrande zwei längliche weisse Punkte ganz dicht bei einander. Die feine Limballinie unmittelbar an der Spitze ist auch gewöhnlich weiss. Noch findet sich bei manchen Stücken, doch durchaus nicht bei allen, eine sehr feine weisse Linie an der scharfen Kante des Vorderrandes, die von der Basis etwa bis zur Mitte geht und hier in die Flügelfläche hinein als weisslicher, sehr fein schwarz punktirter Wisch sich eine kurze Strecke fortsetzt. Die Hinterflügel sind schwärzlich; auf der Unterseite an der Spitzen weisslich beschuppt.

Diese Art ist von allen Verwandten durch den Mangel eines deutlichen breiten weissen Vorderrandstriemens scharf geschieden.

'Stett. ent. Zeitung,' 1863, p. 270.

LITHOCOLLETIS ADENOCARPI.

Antennis albo nigroque variis ; fronte alba, vertice et thorace ochraceo alboque mixtis ; alis anterioribus ochraceis, nitidulis, squamis albis, præsertim basim versus, plus minusve immixtis (al. exp. $3\frac{3}{4}-4\frac{1}{4}'''$, ♂ ♀).

Die Stirn der vorliegenden Art ist glänzend weiss. Die Fühler sind weiss und schwarz (oder richtiger, hell und dunkel) geringelt, zuweilen erscheinen sie ganz weiss. Die beiden vorderen Beinpaare sind auf der oberen Seite dunkel, nur an den Gelenken heller, die Schenkel der Hinterbeine sind gleichfalls dunkel, die Schienbeine und Fussglieder aber glänzend licht silbergrau. Die Scheitelschöpfe, wie der obere Theil des Thorax sind gelb, mit weissen Haaren oder Schuppen mehr oder minder gemischt.

Die Vorderflügel sind glänzend licht ochergelb, ohne alle eigentliche Zeichnung, welche Eigenthümlichkeit sonst keine mir bekannte *Lithocolletis*-Art zeigt. Durch die Loupe bemerkt man zwar in der gelben Fläche weisslich eingestreute Schuppen, namentlich nach der Basis hin, ohne dass dadurch eine eigentliche Basallinie gebildet würde, wenigstens kann ich bei allen meinen Stücken eine solche nicht deutlich erkennen. Diese weissen Schüppchen fehlen übrigens bisweilen fast ganz, während sie sich in ein Paar Fällen vorzugsweise am Vorderrand zeigen.

CHAPTER IV.

MONSIEUR PIERRE MILLIÈRE.

We have traced in the preceding chapters what has been done by three German entomologists who temporarily left their own country for the purpose of exploring the insect world of Italy and Spain; the present chapter will treat of what a French entomologist has done in his own country, in that peculiarly favoured portion of France which is washed by the Mediterranean.

It was on the 13th January 1859 that Monsieur Millière first wrote to me on the subject of the entomology of the Mediterranean coast; but the language he then used* seemed to imply that he had already visited Hyères; and it appears from his remarks under *Tinea oleastrella* that he was there in the winter of 1856-1857. It was probably in 1859 that he first visited Celle-les-Bains.

In 1861 he spent two or three months at Amélie-les-Bains, near Perpignan, in the Pyrénées Orientales, where he found the flora very rich, and of an extremely southern character.

In January 1862 he collected at Marseilles. Fortunately for me M. Millière was not away in the south in February 1863, as on the 22nd of that month I met him at Lyon, and spent some hours in carefully studying his collection, and obtaining many valuable hints on the Micro-Lepidoptera of the south.

Having spent the winter of 1864-65 at Cannes, he was so charmed with that locality and its entomological capabilities, that he purchased a villa there for his permanent winter residence; and I have had the pleasure of meeting him there, and of collecting with him in March 1866, February and March 1867, and December 1868.

In the 'Annales de la Société Linnéenne de Lyon' (1858-1867), Monsieur Millière has published a valuable series of papers, which have also appeared in a separate form under the title of "Iconographie et Description de Chenilles et Lépidoptères inédits." In these papers he has given us the entire history of several Tineina, many of them now to science.

The species treated in these papers may be thus arranged systematically:—

1. *Typhonia Dardoinella*, Millière. Described first as a *Psyche*; afterwards, when a ♀ with well developed wings was obtained, recognized as a *Typhonia*.

* If you are disposed to make a charming journey next month, I would ask you to go with M. Bruand and myself to Hyères. We think of starting about the 20th of February, and remaining five or six weeks in that terrestrial paradise of entomologists.

2. *Hyponomeuta egregiellus*, Duponchel. Described as a *Swammerdamia*, the insect being really rather intermediate between the two genera.
3. *Psecadia funerella*, Fab., var. *canuisella*, Millière. I scarcely fancy this can be considered specifically distinct.
4. *Depressaria nodiflorella*, Millière. Allied to *rotundella*, Douglas.
5. *D. ferulæ*, Zeller. (See *ante*, pp. 6 & 30.)
6. *D. feruliphila*, Millière.
7. *Gelechia antirrhinella*, Millière. A good species, closely allied to *G. tripunctella*, S. V. (See *ante*, p. 109.)
8. *G. ulicinella*, Staudinger. (See *ante*, p. 148.) In habit and markings this resembles *G. mulinella*, Zeller.
9. *G. halymella*, Millière. Closely allied to *G. obsoletella*, F. v. R., perhaps identical with *G. salinella*, Z. (See *ante*, pp. 10 & 37.)
10. *G. olbiaëlla*, Millière. Described as *Alucita olbiaëlla*. This is the *G. plutelliformis*, Staudinger. (See *ante*, p. 147.)
11. *G. psoralella*, Millière. Both the larva and imago of this seem to be referable to *G. anthyllidella*, Hb.
12. *Epidola barcinonella*, Millière. It is very interesting to have in this a second species of the singular genus *Epidola* created by Staudinger. (See *ante*, p. 151.)
13. *Butalis dorycniella*, Millière. This does not seem referable to any other species of this puzzling genus.
14. *Acrolepia smilaxella*, Millière. This is the *vesperella*, Zeller. (See *ante*, pp. 64 & 81.)
15. *Zelleria phillyrella*, Millière. Allied to *Z. hepariella*, Stainton, but evidently distinct.
16. *Z. oleastrella*, Millière. Described as *Tinea oleastrella*.
17. *Bucculatrix lavaterella*, Millière.

Copies of the original descriptions are appended; but I must first mention two other interesting *Tineina* of which M. Millière discovered the larvæ last year (1868) on that rather peculiar plant *Osyris alba* (one of the *Santalaceæ*), and the histories of which he is now publishing; these are *Paradoxus osyridellus*, Millière (*plumbaginella*, Mann in litt.), and *Chauliodus Staintonellus*, Millière.

PARADOXUS OSYRIDELLUS, Millière.

The genus *Paradoxus* may be thus briefly characterized:—
Capilli hirsuti, epistomio lævigato. Ocelli nulli. Antennæ alis anterioribus breviores, mediocres. Haustellum medium. Palpi labiales porrecti, squamis valde incrassati, *articulus secundus longe squamato-fasciculatus, articulum tertium omnino occultans*. Alæ anteriores elongatæ, subfalcatæ, mediocriter ciliatæ; alæ posteriores lanceolatæ *foveola hyalina basali*.

I do not lay so much stress on the form of the anterior wings, as that may vary according to the species (should we meet with other species in the genus), just as it does in the genus *Zelleria*. It is curious how very much the *facies* of this species reminds one both of *Swammerdamia* and *Zelleria*, whilst possessing the palpi almost of *Anarsia*, ♂.

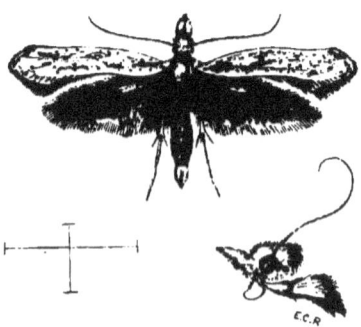

The species may be thus described:—

Exp. al. 8 lines. Head pale grey, rough, the scales projecting in front like two tufts; face smooth, pale grey. The palpi are densely tufted, pale grey, with the basal half of the second joint dark grey; no third joint is perceptible, it is probably concealed in the long tufted second joint. Antennæ simple, shorter than the anterior wings.

Anterior wings elongate, beyond the middle the costa seems slightly indented, the hind margin is almost falcate, grey, with numerous black dots placed in four longitudinal rows; before the middle is a transverse dark grey cloud, rather obliquely placed, nearest the base on the inner margin; at the end of the discoidal cell is a more conspicuous black spot; on the costa towards the apex is a small whitish spot, beyond which a dark line goes round the apex of the wing to the anal angle; beyond this are one or two less sharply marked lines in the rather short grey cilia.

Posterior wings grey, darkest posteriorly, with an elongate diaphanous patch at the base; cilia rather dark grey.

The similarity of this insect to *Zelleria fasciapennella* and *Z. saxifragæ* is very striking; it resembles the former more in colour, and the latter more in the form of the anterior wings: the very singular palpi at once readily distinguish it.

This species was bred last year by Monsieur Millière from a very lively larva which fed on the leaves of *Osyris alba* near Cannes. It had been previously taken by Herr Mann in Dalmatia, at Spalato in May 1850 and in 1862. Dr. Staudinger has a specimen from Malaga, labelled June 16th. I first made the acquaintance of this insect last summer in the collection of the Museum at Vienna, and afterwards saw it in the collections of Herr Lederer, Herr Nickerl, and Dr. Staudinger. Soon after my return home I received on the 29th July a bred specimen from M. Millière for determination.

Since the above was written I have received larvæ of this insect from M. Millière, on the 13th May, 1869, and have thus described the larva:—

Length 5 lines. Dull dark green, the sides paler, with slender darker dorsal and subdorsal lines; spots minute white; head black at the sides, paler in front; second segment pale greyish green with a blackish spot on each side of the back, the space between them appearing almost whitish.

Active; much attenuated anteriorly, posteriorly of nearly uniform width.

Cocoon long, white, but apparently not quite so dense as a *Swammerdamia* cocoon.

I bred three specimens of the imago at the end of May and beginning of June. It sits with the head downwards and the hinder part of the body raised, and seems to lean on its long palpi, which gives it a very quaint appearance.

CHAULIODUS STAINTONELLUS, Millière.

Exp. al. 5–5½ lin. Head and face grey. Palpi dark grey, terminal joint short and rather thick. Antennæ slender, grey.

Anterior wings elongate, rather pointed, more so than in *Ch. chærophyllellus*, dull grey, with no definite markings, but with a faint ochreous tinge along the disk, more visible in some specimens than in others; on the inner margin are three projecting tufts of dark grey scales, the third tuft, at the anal angle, is the smallest and often barely perceptible; cilia at the apex of the wing dark grey, at the anal angle pale grey.

Posterior wings pale grey, with pale grey cilia.

This species was bred from larvæ found by Monsieur Millière at Cannes, on *Osyris alba*, in May 1868. He sent some of these larvæ to me on the 15th May, and on the 19th I described them as follows:—

Length 3½ lines. Grass-green, with the dorsal vessel dark greyish green; the head greyish, with the sides black; the second segment with four grey spots behind.

This larva is short, thick, sluggish, and rather sticky-looking; it is clothed with short, bristly black hairs; it has sixteen legs.

The pupa is of a yellowish green, with the wing-cases more decidedly green, and reminds one rather of the pupa of *Argyresthia Godartella*.

As I left home for Venice and Vienna on the 29th of May, after these larvæ had assumed the pupa-state, and as I calculated the perfect insects would be developed in my absence, I left the pupæ in charge of my friend Mr. M'Lachlan, and the first week in June the perfect insects made their appearance and were duly cared for.

(1.) PSYCHE DARDOINELLA, Millière.
Iconographie et Descr. etc. vol. i. 8ème livraison, pp. 318-320, pl. 37. f. 8-11.
TYPHONIA DARDOINELLA, Millière, vol. ii. 11ème livr. pp. 27-29, pl. 54. f. 3-5.

Bien qu'ayant certains rapports de forme avec plusieurs *Typhonia*, cette nouvelle espèce doit se rattacher certainement aux *Psyche* par l'exiguité du corps, le peu d'épaisseur des ailes, la brièveté des palpes, et encore par la nature, la composition et la forme du fourreau. Lorsque l'insecte me fut soumis à Lyon, M. Staudinger, pendant son trop court séjour auprès de moi en Août dernier, le rapportait au genre *Typhonia*. Je fus d'abord de l'avis de cet habile observateur ; mais après avoir examiné attentivement cet insecte et l'avoir comparé avec soin à ses congénères, je ne tardai pas à reconnaître qu'il ne pouvait se classer que parmi les Psychides. Il est surtout remarquable par la présence de larges taches aux ailes supérieures : caractère qui le distingue de toutes les autres *Psyche*.

INSECTE PARFAIT.—*Dardoinella* doit tout aussi bien se placer dans le voisinage de *perlucidella*, *nitidella*, *comitella* et *crassiorella* que près de *politella* et *pseudobombycella*, car la coupe d'ailes, la couleur du fond et la forme générale de l'insecte la rapprochent assez de ces deux dernières ; cependant le fourreau de cette nouvelle *Psyche* est bien loin d'avoir la consistance papyracée et la forme triangulaire des fourreaux de *politella* et *pseudobombycella*.

Envergure 18 mill. Les ailes sont arrondies, entières, assez étroites et bien fournies d'écailles. Les supérieures, d'un gris chaud, lavées de carné à la côte, sont recouvertes de taches striées de brun et aspergées d'atomes noirâtres. La plus large de ces taches que je rapporte à la médiane, occupe à peu près le milieu de l'aile ; elle est accompagnée d'une large éclaircie intérieure de forme à peu près arrondie. La tache du bas de l'aile, qui représente la basilaire, est sensiblement plus étroite que la précédente. Le sommet de l'aile offre une troisième tache appuyée à la côte dans le sens de l'apex, formée par la réunion de trois gros points bruns. La frange est étroite, fuligineuse et précédée d'un liseré concolore relativement étroit. Les ailes inférieures sont enfumées, faiblement éclairées à la base et sans aucun dessin. La frange est assez large et concolore. En dessous, les supérieures, luisantes, grisâtres, aspergées de nombreux atomes noirs, lavées de fauve, sont marquées à la côte de trois taches noires qui s'y appuyent. Les inférieures, sans dessins ni taches, sont un peu moins enfumées qu'en dessus.

Les antennes, grises, pectinées, se terminent en pointe ; elles sont garnies de petites lamelles jusqu'au sommet. Les palpes sont très-courts ; la trompe, rudimentaire ; les yeux, relativement gros, sont d'un gris noirâtre. La tête, le thorax, qui est assez robuste, et les ptérygodes sont d'un gris foncé. L'abdomen, long, concolore, dépasse les ailes inférieures. La poitrine et les pattes sont grises. Le ventre, concolore, est lavé de fauve à l'extrémité.

La femelle qui est probablement aptère ne m'est pas connue.

Fourreau.—Il est fusiforme, d'une longueur proportionnée à l'insecte, et recouvert de nombreuses petites feuilles sèches, fragments de petites écorces et autres débris de végétaux. L'enveloppe de l'insecte, fixée au fourreau et à moitié engaînée dans l'ouverture, est d'une couleur d'ambre rappelant celle de la plupart des nymphes de psychides.

M. Dardoin, auquel j'ai dédié cette intéressante espèce, me mandait en me la communiquant, qu'il en récoltait les fourreaux vers la fin de Mai, contre les murs de sa campagne située aux environs de Marseille : " Le fourreau contenant la nymphe," ajoutait-il, " placé séparément sous une petite cloche en cristal, donne l'insecte parfait du dix au quinze Juillet suivant."

[*Typhonia Dardoinella.*]

On a toujours ou presque toujours tort de publier certaines espèces de Lépidoptères, celles qui sont d'une détermination difficile, alors qu'on n'a vu qu'un sexe. Je viens de reconnaître moi-même cette vérité, et franchement, je conviens que ma précipitation à publier la *Psyche Dardoinella* (8ème livraison, p. 318, pl. 37. f. 8–11) m'a gravement induit en erreur à l'égard du genre auquel appartient réellement cette prétendue *Psyche*.

M. Dardoin vient de m'adresser un Lépidoptère obtenu *ex larva*, qui doit bien certainement être la femelle de ma *Psyche Dardoinella* ♂. Je reconnais donc que cette espèce ♀, dont j'ai sous les yeux deux exemplaires, n'est point une *Psyche*, mais bien une *Typhonia*. Je dois dire cependant, pour atténuer mon tort, que j'ai été trompé par la forme du fourreau en tout semblable à ceux de certaines *Psyche**.

Les *Typhonia*, dont la parure est sans éclat, forment, on le sait, un petit groupe d'insectes tranchés, généralement fort recherchés des entomologistes à cause peut-être de leur excessive rareté. C'est à peine si les collections les plus riches possèdent quelques espèces, en plus ou moins mauvais état, de ce genre dont le nombre s'élève à une dizaine, selon Bruand ; cependant plusieurs de celles-ci ne me paraissent pas authentiquement distinctes.

L'individu que je publie aujourd'hui sous le nom de *Dardoinella* ♀, est une vraie *Typhonia* ♀ reconnaissable aux ailes bien développées, aux antennes filiformes et surtout à l'oviducte.

Voici la description de cette *Typh. Dardoinella* :—

Envergure 25 mill. Elle est, on le voit, tout aussi grande que ses aînées et possède la coupe d'aile de la *Typh. melas*, Bdv. (*melanosella*, Bruand) ; mais au lieu d'être entièrement d'un noir brun plus ou moins intense, caractère qui distingue presque toutes les espèces de ce genre, les ailes de cette femelle inédite sont d'un gris chaud, faiblement lavées de carné dans la partie qui longe la côte. L'envergure est un peu plus grande que celle du mâle, et le bord des supérieures, assez aigu à l'apex, est aussi plus large. Les ailes in-

---

* Je me plais à rendre justice au sûr coup-d'œil de M. Staudinger qui, lors de la visite qu'il m'a faite en 1862, avait cru voir dans le ♂ de la *P. Dardoinella*, malgré la forme exceptionnelle de son fourreau, une véritable *Typhonia*.

férieures sont peut-être aussi plus allongées et moins arrondies que chez le mâle. Les taches, stries et atomes bruns qu'on remarque chez ce dernier, existent bien chez la ♀, mais leur forme et leur disposition ne sont pas précisément les mêmes. La tache du milieu de l'aile au lieu d'affecter une forme carrée est plutôt rectangulaire et mal arrêtée à ses angles. Celle du sommet de l'aile est assez semblable à celle du mâle. Les inférieures sont uniformément d'un gris foncé, mais moins fuligineux que celles du ♂. En dessous les quatres ailes sont sans dessins et d'un gris roussâtre uniforme. Les antennes sont courtes, grêles, un peu plus épaisses à la base, et concolores. Le thorax est de la couleur des ailes supérieures. Le corps est assez épais et d'un gris chaud; il se termine par un faisceau de poils fauves, divergents, qui au premier abord dérobent l'oviducte, lequel est court, courbé, coriace, foncé, et qui se termine par une pointe brune qui se dirige en dessous. Aussi pour distinguer cet organe important est-on obligé de retourner l'insecte.

Le fourreau, un peu plus grand que celui du mâle, présente à très-peu de chose près, la forme de celui-ci.

M. Dardoin qui possède aujourd'hui deux mâles et deux femelles de cette *Typhonia*, après avoir agi pour les fourreaux des deux femelles ainsi qu'il a opéré pour ceux des mâles, est très-sûr que les deux enveloppes qu'il m'a envoyées et qui sont identiques entre elles, appartiennent bien à l'espèce que je viens de décrire. Ces fourreaux, récoltés au commencement de Juin 1863, ont donné leur insecte parfait dans le courant de Juillet suivant.

(2.) SWAMMERDAMIA EGREGIELLA, Duponchel, xi. pl. 229. f. 9; H.-S. p. 409.

Iconograph. et Descr. etc. vol. ii. 16ème livraison, pp. 190-193, pl. 71. f. 2-6.

La chenille par ses mœurs appartient plus peut-être au genre *Scythropia* de Hübner, composé, on le sait, de la seule *cratægella*, qu'au *Swammerdamia* du même auteur; ne serait il pas mieux de déplacer cet insecte et de le faire entrer dans ce genre *Scythropia*? Voici l'histoire de la larve d'*egregiella* qui doit éclore à la fin de Janvier ou en Février. On ne savait encore rien de ses premiers états.

CHENILLE.—Elle est allongée, fusiforme, très-plissée, avec le premier et le dernier segments recouverts d'une plaque écailleuse. Sa parure est brillante et les lignes qui la parcourent dans toute sa longueur sont nettes et vivement indiquées. Le fond est d'un violacé plus ou moins accusé sur lequel se détache la vasculaire, qui est étroite, tremblée, continue, brune et qui repose sur un fond blanc carné, du 2ème au 11ème segment. Pas de sous-dorsale; la stigmatale est large, ondulée, continue, blanche et teintée de jaune de chrôme au centre de chaque anneau. Le ventre est d'une couleur sombre et marqué d'une ligne blanchâtre. Les stigmates, invisibles à l'œil nu, sont blancs et largement entourés de noir. La tête est globuleuse, un peu cordiforme, d'un jaune d'ocre foncé avec les mandibules et ocelles noirs; ceux-ci sont surmontés d'un trait horizontal blanc. Le premier anneau a un collier blanc et un écusson d'un noir mat, lequel est partagé par un sinus étroit ; la plaque du dernier segment est petite et aussi d'un noir mat. Les pattes antérieures sont robustes, noires, annelées de blanc ; les ventrales et anales sont brunes avec la couronne claire. Les trapézoïdaux et autres points pilifères sont, ainsi que chez les espèces congénères, gros et foncés ; les poils qu'on ne peut distinguer sans loupe, sont d'une longueur normale et bruns.

Vers le 15 ou le 20 Mars, la petite chenille a atteint son entier développement. On la rencontre aux environs de Cannes (Alpes-Maritimes), sur les *Erica scoparia* et *arborea*, dont elle ronge les fleurettes. Elle ne vit pas précisément seule, mais toutefois on ne peut la classer dans les espèces vivant en société ; le plus souvent c'est par deux ou trois, et au plus par quatre et cinq individus occupant une branche de bruyère ; mais alors ces petites chenilles sont éloignées l'une de l'autre et séparées entre elles par des bouquets de fleurs. Elle trahit sa présence par quelques fils de soie placés surtout de bas en haut, fixés au petits rameaux parmi lesquels la chenille est comme suspendue et où elle demeure immobile pendant le jour. Elle ne prend sa nourriture que la nuit, grossit rapidement, et pour se métamorphoser tisse dans les branches mêmes, un cocon en forme de navette, d'une soie pure et blanche, se place la tête en haut et se métamorphose cinq ou six jours après. Cette petite larve est plus que toute autre peut-être attaquée par un ichneumon dont on remarque souvent le cocon blanchâtre fixé contre un petit rameau de la plante.

La chrysalide enfermée dans une double enveloppe blanche, opaque, très-mince, mais cependant forte et impénétrable à l'humidité, la chrysalide, dis-je, est allongée, rougeâtre, avec la gaîne des antennes descendant très-bas et atteignant presque la pointe abdominale ; celle-ci est obtuse, brune et munie de plusieurs crochets divergents, fins, tournés en dehors. La petite Hyponomeutide éclot dès le 15 ou le 20 Avril, et toujours dans la matinée.

INSECTE PARFAIT.—Envergure 14 à 15 mill. Cette espèce, placée à la fin du genre dans le Catalogue Staudinger, avait été bien à tort considérée par Duponchel comme une *Butalis*. La découverte de la chenille est venue donner raison à M. Herrich-Schaeffer, qui, avant qu'on eût connaissance des premiers états de cette espèce, a reconnu en elle une véritable Hyponomeutide.

L'*egregiella* est très-allongée surtout aux ailes supérieures qui sont relativement étroites, généralement d'un bronzé verdâtre et n'ont pour tout dessin que deux bandes blanchâtres ; l'une qui traverse l'aile dans la presque totalité de son étendue et qui est interrompue au milieu par un gros point noir, et l'autre placée à la côte, qui, partant de la hauteur du point noir précité, se dirige sur l'apex qu'elle n'atteint pas. Les ailes inférieures sont d'un gris de fer uniforme et ornées de très-longues franges soyeuses et concolores. Le dessous est luisant et unicolore ; les antennes noduleuses à la base sont brunes et épaisses, elles partent d'une touffe de poils fauves ; les palpes relevés comme chez les *Butalis* et les *Gelechia*.

L'*egregiella* varie: chez certains sujets les lignes blanches sont très-oblitérées et les ailes paraissent d'une teinte uniforme.

Cette Hyponomeutide a toutes les habitudes des espèces de la même division ; elle est lente dans ses mouvements, vole peu, demeure dans une complète immobilité lorsqu'elle est blessée par l'épingle et meurt sans s'agiter beaucoup. Elle vole le soir d'une manière lente et nullement saccadée, ne quitte jamais trop le voisinage des *Erica* qui ont nourri sa chenille et où la femelle dépose à l'aisselle des branches, par petits groupes, ses œufs qui ne devront éclore que neuf mois après. Il m'est à peu près prouvé que l'*egregiella* n'a qu'une génération.

Elle ne paraît pas exclusivement propre au midi, puisque Duponchel (t. ix. p. 345) tenait du nord de la France les individus qui lui ont servi à décrire l'espèce.

Obs.—Postérieurement à la rédaction de l'article qui précède, j'ai pu m'assurer que la *Swam. egregiella* fait partie de notre faune Lyonnaise et que même l'espèce se rencontre assez abondamment sur certains coteaux bien exposés des bords du Rhône, où croît en abondance la *Calluna vulgaris*. La chenille de l'*egregiella* ne vit donc pas exclusivement sur les *Erica scoparia* et *arborea*.

(3.) PSECADIA FUNERELLA, Fab.; Hüb. f. 85; Tr.; Dup. pl. 285. f. 5. (Var. CANUISELLA, Mill.*)

Iconograph. et Descr. etc. vol. ii. 18ème livraison, pp. 291, 292, pl. 81. f. 13.

Voici une variété qui est des plus constantes, aussi lui ai-je imposé un nom, celui d'une ville aux environs de laquelle je l'ai prise en certain nombre, à la fin de Mars 1866.

Cette *Psecadia*, qui au vol ressemblait assez à un Diptère ou à un Hyménoptère, ne quittait pas un emplacement restreint couvert d'*Arundo donax* et de nombreux pieds de l'*Aristolochia rotunda*, L., la même plante, on le sait, qui nourrit la chenille de la jolie *Thais Hypsipyle*. Cependant je n'ai pu remarquer un seul pied du *Symphytum officinale*, L., ou autres Boraginées qui, on le sait encore, nourrissent la larve de la *P. funerella* type. Jusqu'à ce que la chenille de la variété dont j'ai recueilli plus de cinquante exemplaires ait été trouvée et reconnue pour appartenir à la *funerella* propre, jusqu'alors, dis-je, il ne me sera pas absolument prouvé que cette variété n'est point une espèce distincte. En attendant, toutefois, je ne la considère que comme variété constante.

La *Psecadia* var. *canuisella* a, il est vrai, la taille et la coupe d'ailes de la *funerella* type, bien que me paraissant d'une envergure un peu moins grande ; mais ce qui frappe tout d'abord chez cette race provençale, ce sont les ailes inférieures, qui sont toujours ou presque toujours entièrement d'un noir mat profond, tandis que chez

---

* De *Canuis*, indiqué dans diverses chartres du Moyen-Age ; nom primitif de Cannes, d'après l'abbé Alliez qui, dans son beau livre *Cannes et les rivages environnants*, p. 213, n'admet pas que le nom moderne de la ville soit dérivé de Cannis.

l'espèce ordinaire, le sommet de l'aile seul est enfumé et le reste est d'un blanc pur et satiné.

D'autre part, la tache blanche de la côte, à l'aile supérieure, disparaît le plus souvent, en sorte que cette aile, dont le côté interne est seul marqué de blanc, a un tout autre aspect que chez les *funerella* ordinaires. Quelques exemplaires cependant se montrent avec les ailes supérieures semblables à celles du type, tout en conservant les inférieures invariablement noires. Le reste du corps n'a rien d'anormal.

J'ignore si cette intéressante variété a plusieurs générations.

(4.) DEPRESSARIA NODIFLORELLA, Millière.

Iconograph. et Descr. etc. vol. ii. 16ème livraison, pp. 214–216, pl. 73. f. 8–11.

CHENILLE.—Elle se distingue de celle de sa congénère la *feruliphila*, dont elle a les mœurs, par la taille qui est plus petite de moitié, par la couleur de la tête et par celle du premier anneau qui ne sont pas noirs; elle paraît d'ailleurs quinze à vingt jours plus tôt.

Jeune, la chenille de la *nodiflorella* ronge le parenchyme de la plante qui enveloppe et protège la fleur naissante; elle attaque aussi cette dernière alors qu'elle est à l'état rudimentaire. A cette époque la petite larve est d'un vert glauque; elle file déjà une soie fine et blanchâtre et y demeure fixée pendant le jour; ce n'est qu'après la troisième mue que sa couleur s'éclaircit et qu'elle lie les feuilles ténues de la férule; elle pratique par ce moyen une galerie tapissée intérieurement de soie, qu'elle agrandit à mesure qu'elle se développe. Adulte, cette larve est fusiforme, d'un vert pomme, et les lignes, bien que très-visibles sont moins bien indiquées qu'elles ne l'étaient précédemment. La vasculaire et la sous-dorsale se prolonge sans interruption du second au onzième anneau; si la ligne sous-dorsale est très-large, la stigmatale n'existe pas. Le ventre est d'un vert clair ou vert bleuâtre. La tête est globuleuse, coupée droit du côté de l'incision, d'un jaunâtre testacé avec les ocelles et les mandibules colorés en brun. Le premier anneau est protégé par un écusson jaunâtre, luisant et limité à droite et à gauche par un trait noir qui n'arrive pas jusqu'à la tête; les stigmates sont blancs et cerclés de noir; les pattes unicolores; les trapézoïdaux et autres points bien indiqués en brun et surmontés de poils courts et foncés.

Cette chenille, qui paraît un peu plus tard que celle de la *D. ferulæ*, mais un peu plus tôt, je l'ai dit, que celle de la *feruliphila*, n'a atteint son entier développement qu'au milieu d'Avril; cependant les plus hâtives des ces larves sont parvenues à toute leur grosseur dès la fin de Mars. Elle demeure sur la plante et se cache dans l'espèce de fourreau dont il a été question, formé avec plusieurs feuilles réunies et liées par de nombreux fils de soie très-blanche. Ce fourreau est ouvert au deux extrémités, et l'animal qui l'habite s'en échappe facilement lorsqu'il est inquiété. Cette espèce qui est la plus abondante des trois *Depressaria* dont je viens de parler, n'attaque jamais la base de la plante, ainsi que le fait la chenille de la *ferulæ*, et je n'ai jamais remarqué qu'elle se métamorphosât dans les feuilles, mais toujours au pied de l'ombelle parmi les débris de végétaux. La chrysalide est allongée et sans crochets à la pointe anale. L'insecte commence à éclore vers les premiers jours de Mai ; il n'a vraisemblablement qu'une seule génération.

INSECTE PARFAIT.—Le type est d'un bon tiers plus petit que la *ferulæ*, Z. ; il paraît être de la taille de la *D. rotundella*, Dougl., dont elle diffère par la coupe relativement plus allongée, les ailes supérieures d'un argileux plus prononcé, l'angle anal des inférieures plus accusé, les palpes moins longs, etc. Voici au reste sa description :

Envergure 17 mill. Les ailes supérieures sont allongées, presque rectangulaires, d'un argileux plus ou moins obscur, salies d'ombres brunâtres formées par la réunion de très-fins atomes foncés et de rayons bruns qui, précédant la frange, s'avancent jusqu'au tiers de l'aile. On voit, en outre, plusieurs points noirs ainsi disposés : deux au centre assez espacés l'un de l'autre, un à la base plus gros que les précédents, et enfin une ligne de points subterminaux placés entre la frange, qui est unicolore et les rayons précités. Les ailes inférieures sont faiblement enfumées et s'éclaircissent à la base. En dessous les supérieures sont uniformément d'un brunâtre clair et luisant ; les inférieures sont semblables au dessus. Les antennes sont brunes, les yeux noirs ; le thorax, la tête, les palpes sont de la couleur des supérieures. L'abdomen est très-aplati et brunâtre avec l'extrémité garnie de poils argileux.

La femelle est plus petite et un peu plus enfumée que le mâle.

L'espèce ne varie pas.

J'ai élevé en très-grand nombre cette *Depressaria* aussi commune à l'île Sainte-Marguerite, près de Cannes, qu'elle est abondante sur les rochers qui avoisinent la ville d'Hyères, lieux où croît spontanément la *Ferula nodiflora*.

(5.) DEPRESSARIA FERULÆ, Zeller, Isis, 1847 ; H.-S. f. 437.

Iconograph. et Descr. etc. vol. ii. 16ème livraison, pp. 212-213, pl. 73. f. 6, 7.

CHENILLE.—Elle est effilée, fusiforme, d'un verdâtre clair sur lequel se détachent en vert plus foncé la ligne vasculaire et les deux sous-dorsales, qui sont larges et continues. La tête est jaunâtre avec les ocelles bruns. Le premier anneau est muni d'une plaque écailleuse qui appuie un de ses côtés sur l'incision ; les deuxième et troisième segments ont, en outre des trapézoïdaux, une couronne de points noirs très-petits, donnant naissance à autant de poils courts, bruns, invisibles à l'œil nu ; le dernier anneau est aussi muni d'une plaque cornée, marquée de deux traits foncés longitudinaux. Les stigmates sont relativement gros et noirs ; le ventre est d'un vert bleuâtre et les seize pattes sont concolores.

La chenille qui vit en Février et en Mars, doit éclore en Janvier ; peu après que la férule a commencé à se développer. Adulte, cette larve ronge les feuilles de la plante, mais ce dommage est insignifiant comparé au préjudice qu'elle lui cause alors qu'elle est plus jeune.

en pratiquant à la base de cette grande ombelle des morsures qui déterminent un abondant suintement*, arrêtent sa croissance et souvent la font périr prématurément. Ce n'est qu'à la fin de Mars ou au commencement d'Avril que cette chenille, vive et frétillante, est parvenue à toute sa grosseur. Pour se transformer elle se retire le plus souvent au pied de la plante ; cependant elle se métamorphose quelquefois dans les feuilles réunies en paquet. La chrysalide est médiocrement allongée, d'un brun rougeâtre avec l'extrémité anale obtuse et sans crochets. La gaîne des ailes qui descend assez bas est proéminente. Le petit Lépidoptère commence à éclore à la fin d'Avril.

INSECTE PARFAIT.—Cette espèce, qui mesure environ 22 mill. est très-tranchée ; c'est assurément une des plus remarquables du genre. Les ailes supérieures sont d'un brun chocolat un peu plus accusé à la partie qui précède la tache claire de la base, la couleur de cette tache d'un jaune argileux, est celle du thorax ; les trois points du centre de l'aile sont blanchâtres et cerclés de noir. La frange qui est médiocrement large, n'est ni précédée, ni accompagnée de points nervuraux. Cette *Depressaria* ne doit avoir, ainsi que la *feruliphila*, qu'une génération. On la trouve sur les rochers des environs de la ville d'Hyères (Var), partout où croît la férule ; *gros-fenou* en langue provençale.

Je n'ai pas retrouvé la chenille de la *ferulæ* à l'île Sainte-Marguerite, dont quelques parties rocheuses sont littéralement infestées de cette *Ferula nodiflora*.

Obs. Bien que Cannes ne soit placée qu'à une très-faible distance des îles Lérins, je n'ai pu, dans un assez vaste rayon, autour de la ville, rencontrer cette grande ombelle.

(6.) DEPRESSARIA FERULIPHILA, Millière.

Iconograph. et Descr. etc. vol. ii. 16ème livraison, pp. 209-211, pl. 73. f. 1-3.

CHENILLE.—Elle est fusiforme, à anneaux distincts, d'un vert clair franc, avec les lignes ordinaires larges, continues, mais imparfaitement écrites. Ce n'est pas sans peine qu'on distingue à l'aide d'une bonne loupe les organes de la respiration, d'une grandeur normale cependant, mais mal indiqués. La tête est cordiforme, d'un noir de jais et très-luisante ; le premier segment qui est écailleux, a cela de remarquable que la partie cornée de cet anneau présente deux couleurs distinctes ; la première moitié est jaunâtre et la seconde est d'un noir luisant aussi intense que la tête. Le dernier segment, qui m'a paru faiblement corné, est jaunâtre. Les pattes antérieures sont testacées avec le dernier article noir et luisant ; les dix autres pattes sont unicolores et la couronne est jaunâtre ; les trapézoïdaux sont bruns et les points pilifères sont d'un noir foncé ; ils donnent naissance à des poils fins, courts et blanchâtres.

---

* Ce suc de la plante, en se solidifiant au contact de l'air, passe, d'incolore qu'il est, au brun noirâtre et devient une substance analogue à certaines gommes-résines, laquelle, au dire des gens du pays, serait employée dans les arts.

La chenille de cette nouvelle *Depressaria* vit sur la *Ferula nodiflora* dont elle lie les feuilles ténues, pour former une galerie ouverte aux extrémités, et d'où elle s'échappe très-prestement au moindre danger qui la menace en se laissant glisser à terre au moyen d'un fil de soie ; autrement elle ne quitte sa retraite que la nuit pour ronger les feuilles déliées de la grande ombelle. Cette espèce est beaucoup moins répandue que ses deux congénères les *Depressaria ferulæ* et *nodiflorella*. Ce n'est qu'à la fin d'Avril qu'on doit chercher la chenille de la *feruliphila*. Elle se transforme parmi les débris de végétaux et l'éclosion du Lépidoptère arrive vers la fin de Mai ou les premiers jours de Juin.

INSECTE PARFAIT.—Il est de la taille des grands exemplaires de la *characterella*, S. V., Dup. vol. xi. p. 127, p. 290 (*ocellana*, F., Steph.), à laquelle cette *Depressaria* nouvelle ressemble, mais dont elle se distingue cependant, ainsi qu'on pourra en juger par la description que j'en ferai.

Lorsqu'on connaît les mœurs de la chenille de la *characterella*, on ne peut admettre que la *feruliphila* n'en soit qu'une variété ; en effet, suivant Duponchel, p. 128, la chenille de la *characterella* est lavée de couleur de chair sur le dos, et elle a l'écusson et la tête d'un vert clair ; de plus cette dernière est tachée de rose. Le même auteur ajoute : " La chenille de la *characterella* vit sur le bouleau, appartient au département du Nord et éclot en Octobre "*.

La chenille de la *feruliphila* vit, je l'ai dit, sur la *Ferula nodiflora*, plante herbacée des bords de la Méditerranée, et éclot à la fin de Mai.

La *D. feruliphila* mesure 25 mill. d'envergure environ ; elle rappelle assez pour la taille, la teinte générale et la disposition des taches, la *characterella*. Les ailes supérieures sont allongées, étroites, rectangulaires, d'un grisâtre chaud avec reflets carnés sur toute leur surface, marquées de quelques atomes noirs à l'extrémité, de plusieurs taches de même couleur appuyées à la côte, dont trois principales, des deux ou trois noires ordinaires centrales, et d'une rangée de sept petits points subterminaux également noirs et bien nets. En outre, les supérieures présentent à la base deux points bruns sous forme de petite ligne transverse ; les franges sont longues et concolores. Les ailes inférieures sont allongées, élargies à l'angle abdominal, blanchâtres, luisantes, avec une teinte brune au bord. Les nervures sont fines et bien indiquées en brun ; les franges sont longues, soyeuses, luisantes et blanchâtres. En dessous les supérieures sont uniformément d'un fuligineux pâle avec les franges et la côte lavées de jaunâtre ; les inférieures ressemblent au dessus. Les palpes dont la pointe se dirige en haut, ont les deux premiers

---

* This quotation is not quite correct. Duponchel says of *characterella*, " Cette chenille vit entre des feuilles qu'elle réunit en paquet par des fils, sur le *bouleau* et le *saule marceau*, et s'y transforme en chrysalide à la fin d'Août..... L'insecte parfait en sort au commencement d'Octobre ; " and this information appears to be derived from Treitschke (ix. 2, p. 275), to whom it was communicated by Fischer von Röslerstamm. Whether it ever feeds on birch I rather doubt ; but sallow (*Salix caprea*) is its primary food, and I have myself bred the species from larvæ on sallow sent to me by Professor Fritzsche of Freiberg.—H. T. S.

articles très-velus ; le dernier est tout-à-fait dénudé ; ces palpes sont d'un gris carné ; les antennes médiocrement longues, moniliformes et grisâtres ; le front est gris carné ; le thorax rappelle la couleur des premières ailes ; l'abdomen est crêté sur les flancs, gris et carné à l'extrémité ; les pattes sont très-longues, velues, concolores et munies aux inférieures de trois tarses, dont deux au second article.

La femelle est semblable au mâle.

La *Dep. feruliphila* ne doit avoir qu'une seule génération.

Après avoir rencontré une première fois cette espèce dans les terrains rocheux des environs d'Hyères (Var), j'espérais la reprendre à l'île Sainte-Marguerite, près de Cannes, où abonde la *Ferula nodiflora* ; c'est en vain que je l'y ai cherchée à plusieurs époques, sur tous les points de l'île.

(7.) GELECHIA ANTIRRHINELLA, Millière.

Iconograph. et Descr. etc. vol. ii. 17ème livraison, pp. 274-276, pl. 80. f. 6-8.

CHENILLE.—Elle est allongée, fusiforme, un peu aplatie en dessous, d'un vert obscur presque noir chez les sujets adultes, à tête lenticulaire, à premier anneau recouvert d'un écusson corné. On ne distingue aucune ligne ; mais les points pilifères sont noirs et distincts. La tête est d'un testacé rougeâtre et bordée de noir au sommet. Le collier est blanchâtre et la plaque du premier segment qui est de la couleur de la tête est également bordé de noir. Les pattes écailleuses sont brunes et luisantes ; les huit ventrales et les deux anales sont concolores.

Depuis l'instant de sa naissance qui arrive en Mars ou Avril, jusqu'à l'époque de la métamorphose qui a lieu à la fin de Mai, cette chenille vit sous une petite toile de soie blanchâtre, dont les bords retiennent les plis d'une ou de plusieurs feuilles de l'*Antirrhinum asarina*, L., jolie plante sous-ligneuse qui croît spontanément dans les fissures des vieilles murailles d'Ax-sur-Ariège, et qui sert de nourriture à cette chenille que j'ai recueillie en certain nombre dans la ville même, et contre les rochers des environs.

C'est au pied de la plante, dans les feuilles sèches que la chenille se transforme, ou de temps en temps sur la plante, dans le pli d'une feuille.

La chrysalide qui est médiocrement allongée, avec l'enveloppe des ailes et la gaîne des antennes descendant assez bas sur l'abdomen, est d'un jaunâtre sombre, et brune à la pointe anale. La *Gelechia* est éclose en captivité, pendant les premiers jours de Juillet.

INSECTE PARFAIT.—Envergure 23 à 24 mill. Il a le port d'ailes des grands exemplaires de la *G. tripunctella*, à laquelle il ressemble beaucoup.

Cette nouvelle *Gelechia* diffère de sa congénère, par des caractères peu sensibles, mais qui sont constants et qui nous ont paru suffisants, à M. Stainton, de Londres, et à moi, pour voir en elle une espèce distincte.

Les ailes antérieures sont allongées, rectangulaires, d'un gris-luisant, avec les trois points qui caractérisent la *tripunctella* bien mieux écrits que chez celle-ci. La série de points nervuraux qui précède la frange, est également bien indiquée en noir. Les ailes inférieures sont grandes, arrondies et d'un gris un peu fuligineux ; les antennes sont fines et brunes. La tête et le thorax sont de la couleur des ailes supérieures. La ♀ ressemble au ♂.

Voici en quoi, suivant M. Stainton, la *G. antirrhinella* diffère de la *tripunctella* :

Par ses ailes antérieures plus courtes, moins luisantes, et par une légère teinte rougeâtre ; de plus, par les points noirs du bord postérieur beaucoup plus distincts et les stries foncées plus accusées. En outre, si on regarde les palpes à la loupe, on reconnaît que le *deuxième** article est noir extérieurement, tandis que chez la *tripunctella*, il n'est que d'un gris clair. Enfin chez l'*antirrhinella* le bout des ailes postérieures est sensiblement plus obtus que chez sa voisine.

Cette grande *Gelechia* vole en Mars dans le voisinage de l'*Antirrhinum asarina*. N'ayant pris alors que des sujets flétris, passés, il est vraisemblable que ceux-ci sont éclos l'automne précédent et que ces sujets étaient le produit de la seconde génération qui, je l'ai dit, éclot une première fois en Juillet.

La *Gelechia antirrhinella* ne peut-être placée qu'après la *tripunctella*, S. V. ; elle portera dans le catalogue Stdgr. le no. 1529 *bis*.

[This is probably the *Gelechia tripunctella*? taken by Herr Mann at Wippach in 1854, on a wall. (See *ante*, p. 109.)]

(8.) GELECHIA ULICINELLA, Staudinger, Stett. ent. Zeit. 1859.

Iconograph. et Descr. etc. vol. i. 8ème livraison, pp. 325–327, pl. 38. f. 8–11.

J'avais rencontré un grand nombre de chenilles de cette espèce aux environs de Marseille, au commencement de Janvier de cette année [1862] lorsque M. Staudinger, auquel je soumis l'insecte parfait, reconnut une Tinéide découverte par lui en Espagne depuis peu, et à laquelle il avait imposé le nom de *ulicinella* qui rappelle la plante dont se nourrit la petite larve.

CHENILLE.—Fusiforme, faiblement aplatie en dessous avec les anneaux distincts, d'un jaune vif sur tout le corps, couleur qui passe au rouge plus ou moins prononcé quelques jours avant la chrysalidisation. La tête, petite, lenticulaire, est d'un noir de jais. Le premier segment est recouvert d'une plaque écailleuse brune, échancrée en dessus par un sinus étroit. On ne distingue aucune ligne longitudinale. Les incisions des anneaux sont blanchâtres. Les pattes écailleuses, brunes ; les autres, concolores. Les stigmates, relativement gros, sont indiqués en noir. Une bonne loupe permet de distinguer des points pilifères, concolores, surmontés d'une villosité courte et blanchâtre.

[* M. Millière has erroneously printed "dernier article;" it should be as above, "deuxième article."—H. T. S.]

L'insecte, qui éclot en Décembre, ronge uniquement les fleurs de l'*Ulex parviflorus*, Pourr., qui à cette époque commencent à paraître, et parmi lesquelles il se cache pendant le jour. La petite chenille grossit assez vite ; en effet, à la fin de Janvier, ayant achevé sa croissance, elle descend au pied de l'*Ulex*, y forme au milieu des feuilles sèches une coque molle mais solide, et éclot dans le courant du mois d'Août suivant.

La nymphe, cylindrico-conique, allongée, rougeâtre, luisante, n'a de remarquable que la gaîne des antennes, proéminente et couchée sur la poitrine.

INSECTE PARFAIT.—Envergure 12 à 15 mill. Les ailes supérieures en forme d'ellipse très-allongée, présentent à la côte une légère convexité ; elles ont sur un fond gris, soyeux et luisant, une large tache d'un jaune rougeâtre, interrompue, mais qui se prolonge dans toute l'étendue de l'aile. Les franges sont longues et concolores. Les ailes inférieures sont étroites, cultriformes, d'un gris ardoisé, luisantes. Les franges plus longues qu'aux supérieures, sont teintées de fauve.

En dessous les quatres ailes sont d'un gris clair très-luisant et lavées de rougeâtre à la côte des supérieures. Les antennes, presque aussi longues que le corps, sont grises. Les palpes sont grêles, courts et écartés. La tête, petite et blanchâtre. Le thorax, concolore. L'abdomen, grêle, blanchâtre, luisant. Les pattes inférieures assez longues, sont, ainsi que la poitrine, d'un blanc argenté.

Cette Tinéide nouvelle, qui n'a qu'une génération, vole dans le voisinage des *Ulex* de la Provence, du Languedoc, de l'Espagne, situés dans les garigues chaudement exposées. Les *Ulex* placés au nord et à l'ouest ne m'ont jamais fourni la chenille de l'*ulicinella*.

Si j'assigne une place à cette petite espèce dans le Catalogue de Duponchel, je la placerai parmi les *Œcophora*, près de la *Schmidtella*, Tr.

(9.) GELECHIA HALYMELLA*, Millière.

Iconograph. et Descr. etc. vol. i. 9ème livraison, pp. 352-354, pl. 42. f. 4-8.

CHENILLE.—Elle est assez courte, fusiforme, d'un blanc jaunâtre plus ou moins prononcé. Les lignes ordinaires sont larges et indiquées en rouge carminé clair. La stigmatale est la seule qui ne soit pas continue : celle-ci est interrompue sur chaque segment. Le ventre est jaunâtre et ne présente pas de lignes. Les stigmates, qu'on ne distingue qu'à la loupe m'ont paru noirs. La tête, petite, lenticulaire, est d'un noir luisant. Les deux premiers anneaux sont d'un vineux obscur : le premier porte un écusson corné, noir et luisant. Les pattes antérieures, de couleur vineuse, ont le premier article noir. Les trapézoïdaux, relativement gros, sont également noirs.

Cette chenille vit sur l'*Atriplex halymus*, L., arbrisseau naturalisé

* Du nom spécifique *halymus* (*Atriplex halymus*, L.).

en Provence, fort répandu sur les terres que avoisinent la mer, notamment aux environs de Marseille.

La chenille de *halymella* semble attaquer presque seule cet *Atriplex*, qui la nourrit en grande abondance. L'œuf déposé sur une des feuilles épaisses et persistantes de cet arbuste, éclot dès le mois de Décembre. La petite chenille perce cette feuille, s'introduit sous la pellicule qu'elle a soulevée et là, ronge en repos le parenchyme. Elle grossit lentement, attaque plusieurs feuilles successivement et n'atteint toute sa taille que deux mois environ après sa naissance. C'est à cette époque, celle du commencement de Février, que son développement ne lui permettant plus de vivre à la manière des mineuses, elle lie trois ou quatre feuilles au centre desquelles elle se tient cachée pendant le jour. Cette chenille ne se contente plus alors du parenchyme de la feuille, elle ronge celle-ci dans toute son épaisseur.

L'insecte ne se métamorphose que fort rarement dans les feuilles de l'arbrisseau qui l'a nourri ; il se cache parmi les mousses et s'y chrysalide après avoir préalablement formé une coque solide composée de soie blanchâtre entremêlée de débris de végétaux.

La petite nymphe, assez allongée, d'un brun rougeâtre sur le dos et la poitrine, a les anneaux teintés de jaune clair avec les incisions d'un carné vif.

L'éclosion de la Tinéide arrive dès le commencement d'Avril et se prolonge jusqu'à la fin de ce mois.

INSECTE PARFAIT.—Envergure 13 à 14 mill. Les ailes supérieures sont entières, longues, étroites, presque rectangulaires, disposées en pointe arrondie et garnies inférieurement d'une assez longue frange. Le fond, d'un jaune de Naples plus ou moins chaud, est chargé de huit ou neuf points noirs, dont cinq disposés en une sorte d'ellipse au premier tiers de l'aile. Deux autres points suivent ceux-là. Un dernier point, plus grand que les précédents, de forme orbiculaire, est situé à l'apex. Les ailes inférieures, moins longues que les supérieures, sont un peu plus larges. Elles sont terminées en pointe aiguë, d'un gris bleuâtre, luisantes, sans dessins et très-largement frangées au bord interne surtout. Les quatres ailes sont en dessous d'un jaune paille vif, et très-luisantes. La tache circulaire apicale est seule visible. Les antennes sont longues et filiformes. Les palpes aigus et relevés au-dessus de la tête, ont les deux premiers articles seuls velus. Les yeux sont noirs. La tête et le thorax assez robustes, concolores, sont peu fournis d'écailles. L'abdomen, long, déprimé et dépassant les ailes inférieures. La poitrine et les pattes sont concolores.

La femelle est semblable au mâle.

Cette *Gelechia* a, sans doute, plus de deux générations par an.

(10.) ALUCITA OLBIAELLA, Millière.

Iconograph. et Descr. etc. vol. i. 4ème livraison, pp. 193-196, pl. 1. f. 1-6.

Je ne suppose pas que cette Tinéide soit celle qu'a publiée

M. Zeller sous le nom de *tamariciella* (Stettin. ent. Z. 1850, p. 153), car sa description ne se rapporte pas à l'insecte que je publie aujourd'hui. De plus la figure que M. Herrich-Schäffer a donnée dans ses suites à Hübner (Tin. Europ. tab. 75. f. 567) de la *tamariciella*, Zell. me paraît différer sensiblement de mon *Alucita* nouvelle.

CHENILLE.—Longueur 14 à 15 mill.; fusiforme, sensiblement atténuée aux deux extrémités, couverte de points verruqueux visibles seulement à la loupe. Le type est d'un vert mat plus ou moins clair. La vasculaire qui est continue, étroite, vert foncé, est finement liserée de blanchâtres des deux côtés. Il n'existe pas de sous-dorsale. La stigmatale est large, continue, ondulée, jaunâtre. Les stigmates invisibles à l'œil nu, sont blancs et cerclés de noir. Le ventre d'un vert livide, est marqué de blanchâtre du quatrième au neuvième segment.

La tête est petite, lenticulaire, concolore. Toutes les pattes sont vertes.

Cette chenille varie en vert foncé, en rougeâtre et en brun plus ou moins obscur. Je l'ai rencontrée en grande nombre, en automne, sur le *Tamarix gallica*, L., aux environs d'Hyères et de Toulon.

CHRYSALIDE.—Au lieu de se métamorphoser, comme ses congénères, sur les branches des arbres, cette chenille entre profondément en terre où elle forme une coque. La nymphe est allongée, d'un brun rougeâtre. Les derniers segments sont noirs. La pointe qui termine la chrysalide est unique, noire, forte, aiguë.

Olbiaella ne doit avoir qu'une seule génération. Ce qui le prouverait, c'est que l'insecte parfait n'a commencé à paraître qu'en Juillet. L'éclosion a continué jusqu'à la fin d'Août.

INSECTE PARFAIT.—Envergure 16 à 17 mill. Cette *Alucita* est un peu plus grande que la *xylostella*, Tr., Evers., Steph., Dup.; avec laquelle elle a quelques points de ressemblance pour la coupe des ailes et la disposition des taches.

Les ailes supérieures sont étroites, lancéolées, à sommet prolongé en pointe obtuse. Le fond, rougeâtre est sablé d'une infinité d'atomes noirs. Il existe, en outre, une large bande longitudinale, noire, partant de la base de l'aile et se prolongeant aux trois quarts de sa longueur. Cette bande qui se fond en se rapprochant de la côte, est marquée en dessus d'une ou de deux taches blanchâtres, variant de formes chez le plus grand nombre des individus. Cependant sur d'autres, les taches blanches manquent tout-à-fait. La frange est précédée de trois ou quatre points oblongs et noirs.

Les ailes inférieures, unies, un peu plus larges que les supérieures, se rétrécissent brusquement avant d'arriver à l'apex. Ces ailes sont garnies de longues franges unicolores, surtout au bord interne. En dessous, les quatres ailes sont d'un gris rougeâtre, luisant et sans taches, sauf quelques points bruns au bord terminal des supérieures, qu'on ne voit bien qu'à la loupe.

Les palpes inférieurs, qui sont les seuls visibles, ont les deux premiers articles garnis de poils blanchâtres, et le dernier long, nu, et recourbé en demi-cercle. La tête est petite, carrée et rougeâtre.

Les antennes, très-écartées à la base, sont filiformes dans les deux sexes. Le thorax est ovale et brun. L'abdomen participe de la couleur des ailes. Les pattes, brunes, sont annelées de blanc à leur extrémité.

Il est fâcheux que M. Zeller ne nous ait pas fait connaître la chenille de sa *tamariciella*, car il eût été intéressant de la comparer à l'espèce nouvelle que je viens de décrire.

Olbiaella (de *Olbia*, nom primitif de la ville d'Hyères) devra trouver place après la *xylostella* de Duponchel.

De même que la plupart des espèces congénères, cette nouvelle *Alucita* est très-vive; elle vole avec une rapidité extrême, et si on ne la pique promptement, elle ne tarde pas à être méconnaissable. Elle paraît commune en Provence.

(11.) Gelechia psoralella, Millière.

Iconogr. et Descr. etc. vol. ii. 13ème livraison, pp. 83–86, pl. 61. f. 1–6.

Chenille.—Cette petite larve éclot à la fin d'Octobre, alors que les feuilles radicales de la plante qui doit la nourrir, commencent à se développer. Jusqu'à sa première mue, l'insecte se tient au revers de la feuille, après quoi il plie celle-ci en deux dans le sens de la nervure principale, en lie les bords seulement, et là, complètement à l'abri du froid, de l'humidité et de ses ennemis, il ronge lentement la pellicule supérieure de la feuille sans la trouer jamais. La chenille qui, dans le jeune âge, est d'un brun foncé presque noir, demeure une bonne partie de l'hiver sans beaucoup grossir. La nourriture venant à lui manquer, elle change une première fois de demeure, puis une seconde, puis une troisième avant de parvenir à toute sa taille. Arrivée à la grosseur qu'elle doit avoir vers les derniers jours de Février, la petite chenille ne se contente plus de ronger le parenchyme de la feuille, elle attaque celle-ci dans toute son épaisseur. A cette époque de sa vie cette larve est fusiforme avec les extrémités très-atténuées et les anneaux renflés tous distincts. Elle est de plus fortement plissée et son aspect général est le rougeâtre vineux, tournant parfois au brunâtre. Le corps ne présente pas les lignes vasculaire et sous-dorsale ordinaires, si ce n'est toutefois une éclaircie blanchâtre sur les deuxième, troisième et quatrième anneaux; on voit au milieu de chaque segment une large tache ou bande brune transversale, irrégulière, descendant jusqu'à la stigmatale; celle-ci est fine, ondulée, claire et continue. Le ventre est concolore et n'a pas de lignes. Les stigmates sont relativement gros, noirs et cerclés de blanchâtre. La tête est petite, lenticulaire, noire et dégagée du premier anneau; celui-ci dont la partie antérieure est blanchâtre est muni, ainsi que le dernier segment, d'une plaque écailleuse noire, étroite, luisante, placée au milieu et descendant de chaque côté jusqu'à la hauteur de la stigmatale. Les pattes écailleuses sont noires et annelées de blanchâtre; les autres pattes sont d'un vineux obscur et également annelées. Une forte loupe permet de distinguer les points trapézoïdaux foncés, surmontés de poils courts et bruns.

Cette chenille vit à Amélie-les-Bains (Pyrénées-Orientales) sur la *Psoralea bituminosa*, L., plante à odeur bitumineuse prononcée, des feuilles de laquelle l'insecte doit se nourrir exclusivement. Si, comme je le pense, l'espèce a plusieurs générations, le printemps doit en voir paraître deux et peut-être davantage. La chenille se métamorphose rarement dans les feuilles; le plus souvent elle se cache parmi les détritus de végétaux où a promptement lieu la transformation.

La chrysalide, formée au centre d'une petite coque tissée en soie blanchâtre, est allongée, obtuse au sommet, effilée, conique et granuleuse à l'extrémité, rougeâtre et luisante. L'enveloppe des ailes, descendant assez bas sur l'abdomen, est brune et striée de rougeâtre. La pointe abdominale est garnie de quelques poils courts, droits et grisâtres. L'éclosion de la *Gelechia* arrive dès la fin de Mars et se prolonge jusqu'au commencement de Mai.

Pendant les premiers jours de Février de cette année (1865), j'ai retrouvé aux environs de Cannes (Alpes-Maritimes) et à Fréjus, au pied d'une muraille romaine, plusieurs chenilles de la *psoralella*, dans les même conditions que, deux ans plus tôt, j'avais observé celles que je viens de décrire aux environs d'Amélie-les-Bains.

INSECTE PARFAIT.—Il est très-voisin des *Gelechia biguttella*, H.-S. f. 521; *coronillella*, H.-S. f. 522, et *leucopalpella*, H.-S. f. 523, dont il a le facies général; mais il s'éloigne de ces deux Tinéides par plusieurs caractères importants, tels que: le premier article des antennes qui est noduleux, la forme différente des ailes inférieures, la disposition autre des taches des supérieures, et la taille plus grande de près du double.

Voici d'ailleurs sa description :—

Envergure 13 à 14 mill. Les premières ailes sont allongées, un peu arquées à la côte, assez fournies d'écailles avec l'apex aigu. Elles seraient entièrement d'un noir de jais uni et luisant n'étaient deux taches d'un jaune rougeâtre placées à la hauteur de la coudée : la première, de forme triangulaire et appuyée à la côte, la seconde allongée et atteignant le bord abdominal*. La frange est longue et concolore. Les ailes inférieures sont plus larges que les supérieures, cultriformes, finissant en pointe aiguë et d'un gris fuligineux. La frange est fort longue et unicolore. Le dessous des quatre ailes est d'un gris brun uni, luisant, où les taches des supérieures apparaissent, mais d'une manière incertaine. Les antennes sont longues, noires, avec le premier article sensiblement noduleux. Elles sont crénelées, et cette crénelure m'a semblé plus prononcée à l'extrémité de l'antenne qu'à la base. Les palpes sont visibles, arqués, aigus et relevés. Le premier article est d'un gris brun, le dernier est presque blanc. La tête et les yeux sont noirs. Le thorax est robuste, noir et assez fourni d'écailles. L'abdomen qui est également noir et presque dénudé, dépasse les ailes inférieures. Les pattes sont noires et luisantes.

* Cette seconde tache a, certaines fois, la forme triangulaire de la première.

La *Gelechia psoralella* doit avoir, comme je l'ai dit, plusieurs générations. Elle trouvera place après la *Gelechia biguttella*, H.-S., et portera dans le catalogue Staudinger le no. 1686 *bis*.

(12.) EPIDOLA BARCINONELLA, Millière.

Iconograph. et Descr. etc. vol. ii. 18ème livraison, pp. 313–316, pl. 83. f. 13–15.

En 1859, M. Staudinger créa le genre *Epidola* pour un Lépidoptère fort curieux, dont la chenille traîne une sorte de fourreau. Je viens ajouter à ce petit genre une seconde espèce distincte de l'*Epidola stigma*, Stdgr., dont la larve a des mœurs au moins aussi remarquables que celles de sa congénère. Il est fâcheux que M. Himmighoffen, de Barcelone, qui m'a procuré cet intéressant insecte, n'ait pu me dire au juste quelle est la plante dont se nourrit ordinairement la chenille. Ce naturaliste, trompé par la forme du fourreau que la larve devenue adulte traîne sans cesse après elle, crut reconnaître celle d'une *Coleophora* et me l'adressa sous ce nom générique. Je n'ai pas tardé à voir que cette chenille n'appartenait nullement au genre des Coléophores.

CHENILLE.—Parvenue à toute sa taille pendant le mois de Mai, elle se présente alors avec une forme allongée, cylindrique, très-plissée, d'une couleur carnée tirant sur le jaunâtre, avec les lignes ordinaires ondulées, continues et d'un ton ochreux assez vif. La tête est globuleuse, entièrement d'un noir mat, avec le premier anneau convexe, sensiblement plus élevé que les suivants et recouvert jusqu'à la naissance de la seconde paire de pattes, d'une plaque écailleuse d'un noir mat. Le second anneau, dont le fond est carné, ainsi que le reste du corps, est précédé d'une large zone blanche. On remarque en outre sur ce même segment des caractères noirs imitant imparfaitement un Y couché, et qui sont placés dans le sens des lignes vasculaire et sous-dorsales. Au moyen de la loupe, on distingue d'autres lignes fines et continues. Les pattes antérieures sont relativement robustes, concolores, avec le premier article noir.

Bien que M. Himmighoffen ne puisse préciser le genre de plante dont se nourrit cette larve, puisqu'il l'a trouvée à divers âges soit dans les tiges des graminées, soit dans la tige d'une lavande, soit enfin dans celle d'une scabieuse à fleurs blanches, il est supposable qu'elle se nourrit le plus ordinairement de graminées et que, parvenue à une certaine grosseur, elle coupe une tige de ces dernières plantes, laissée ouverte aux deux extrémités. Dans cette nouvelle demeure qui a la forme d'un fourreau allongé qu'elle traîne à la manière des larves de *Coleophora*, cette chenille se transporte d'une plante à l'autre, se fixe momentanément pendant le repos, et demeure ainsi jusqu'à la fin de Mai où, se fixant définitivement exposée au soleil, elle opère sa transformation. La métamorphose a lieu assez rapidement, mais avant ce changement d'état, la chenille doit se retourner dans son enveloppe ainsi que le font dans le leur, en pareil cas, les larves de Coléophores, celles des Psychides ♂ et celles des Solénobides ♂. L'éclosion a lieu cinq à six semaines après.

Le parasite de cette nouvelle Épidole, qu'on remarque dans les proportions d'un huitième environ, est un très-petit Chalcidite qui s'échappe trois semaines après la fixation du fourreau. Sa larve a vécu aux dépens de la chenille et a ensuite pratiqué un petit trou rond dissimulé au moyen d'une mince couche de soie que l'Hyménoptère n'a pas de peine à déchirer lors de son éclosion.

INSECTE PARFAIT.—Envergure 13 à 14 mill. Les ailes supérieures sont allongées, un peu falquées, aiguës à l'apex, d'un carné grisâtre, aspergées de nombreux atomes foncés qui recouvrent en grande partie les ailes et qui donnent à celles-ci un aspect légèrement ardoisé, on voit au centre trois petites taches allongées, brunâtres, et pas toujours bien écrites. De plus, on voit une ligne longitudinale qui part de la base de l'aile, et arrive au tiers de sa longueur. Cependant ces premières ailes sont quelquefois zonées de lignes claires d'un carné chaud. Les ailes inférieures sont allongées, étroites, taillies en biseau à l'extrémité, d'un gris légèrement bleuâtre; parfois carnées, luisantes et garnies de très-longues franges soyeuses et carnées. En dessous, les antérieures sont d'un gris foncé, et les atomes bruns ont disparu; les postérieures ressemblent au dessus. Les antennes sont longues, épaisses, moniliformes, jaunâtres, légèrement noduleuses à la base, avec cette partie de l'antenne recouverte de fines soies concolores. Les palpes sont médiocrement longs, ascendants, gris, garnis de soies plus longues à l'extrémité qu'à la base. La tête est un peu laineuse, c'est-à-dire recouverte de poils fins, courts et gris; les yeux gros et bruns. Le thorax convexe et concolore; l'abdomen long, grisâtre, dépassant les ailes inférieures; les pattes longues, jaunâtres, soyeuses, avec deux paires de tarses aux inférieures.

La ♀ ressemble au ♂.

Cette espèce varie: quelques sujets sont d'un gris moins chaud, plus sombres, c'est-à-dire, d'un gris d'ardoise.

L'*Epidola barcinonella* n'a qu'une seule génération. Au repos, elle a assez la forme d'une *Coleophora*; elle est effilée et ses ailes inférieures sont entièrement cachées par les supérieures. Elle ne paraît pas rare aux environs de Barcelone (Espagne) et vole sur les terrains secs des collines bien exposées. J'ai dit qu'elle devait représenter la seconde espèce du genre *Epidola* de M. Staudinger, dans le Catalogue de qui elle portera le no. 1752 bis.

Obs.—N'ayant pas vu l'*Epidola stigma*, Stdgr., je n'ai pu comparer à ce Micro la *barcinonella*; mais lors de la dernière visite que ce naturaliste m'a faite à Lyon, en 1866, il n'hésita pas à dire que ma nouvelle *Epidola* était bien distincte de celle qui avait motivé la création du genre.

(13.) BUTALIS DORYCNIELLA, Millière.

Iconograph. et Descr. etc. vol. i. 5ème livraison, pp. 225–227, pl. 1. f. 1–6.

CHENILLE.—Longueur 13 à 14 mill.; fusiforme, atténuée aux deux extrémités, d'un vert bleuâtre, recouverte de nombreuses lignes longitudinales peu apparentes. Le premier anneau, écailleux, noir, largement liseré de blanc antérieurement, est partagé au sommet par une échancrure blanche très-fine. Le dernier segment est garni, au sommet, d'une écaille petite, noire, luisante.

On distingue à la loupe les trapézoïdaux et de nombreux points verruqueux : ils sont surmontés d'une villosité grise assez longue. Une carène concolore, faiblement accusée, existe à la place de la stigmatale.

Les stigmates, invisibles à l'œil nu, sont surmontés d'un point noir relativement gros. Le ventre d'un vert pâle, est sans lignes.

La tête, lenticulaire, est noire et luisante. Les pattes écailleuses sont robustes et de même couleur que la tête. Les ventrales, concolores, ont la couronne jaunâtre.

Cette petite chenille, d'une vivacité extrême, vit sur le *Dorycnium suffruticosum*, L.; elle lie le sommet des tiges et en forme des paquets assez volumineux. Elle y pratique des galeries ouvertes aux extrémités, dans lesquelles elle demeure cachée pendant le jour. Elle ne quitte sa retraite que la nuit pour manger.

C'est vers le milieu d'Avril que j'ai recueilli en abondance cette Tinéide à Celles-les-Bains (Ardèche)*.

CHRYSALIDE.—Au commencement de Mai la chenille de *dorycniella* quitte la plante, file dans les mousses ou les feuilles sèches une soie fine, très-blanche, sous laquelle elle se métamorphose en chrysalide au bout de quarante-huit heures.

La nymphe conico-cylindrique, allongée, est presque entièrement noire. Elle éclot vingt ou vingt-cinq jours après sa transformation.

INSECTE PARFAIT.—Envergure 11 à 12 mill. Il est entièrement d'un gris-bleuâtre-ardoisé et luisant, sans lignes, sans taches, et serait complètement concolore si les ailes inférieures n'étaient un peu plus sombres que les supérieures.

Les dessous, également uniforme, tire un peu sur le jaunâtre.

Les ailes supérieures, dont le sommet se prolonge en pointe obtuse, sont étroites et faiblement arquées à la côte. Elles sont garnies inférieurement d'une longue frange.

Les secondes ailes, également étroites, sont terminées en pointe plus aiguë que les supérieures; elles sont largement frangées au bord interne.

Les antennes sont fusiformes dans les deux sexes et relativement longues. Les palpes inférieurs, seuls visibles, sont relevés au dessus de la tête. Les deux premiers articles sont faiblement velus; le troisième est nu et très-aigu. La tête est large; les yeux, gros, sont entourés d'une abondante villosité. Le thorax est robuste; l'abdomen, assez court, est cylindrique.

La femelle est semblable au mâle.

Butalis dorycniella (en souvenir de la plante qui nourrit la che-

---

* Depuis la rédaction de cet article, j'ai retrouvé la chenille de *dorycniella* aux environs de Marseille, vers la fin de Janvier, sur la *Coronilla minima*, L. L'insecte qui était alors aux trois quarts de sa taille, semblerait passer l'hiver. En ce moment j'élève chez moi cette petite larve; son éducation est facile.

nille) devra dans le Catalogue de Duponchel, trouver place après la *seliniella*, Zell.

Cette petite Tinéide, qui doit avoir deux générations, ne vole guère qu'au crépuscule du soir et du matin.

(14.) ACROLEPIA SMILAXELLA, Millière.

Iconograph. et Descr. etc. vol. i. 10ème livraison, pp. 385-387, pl. 46. f. 6-11.

CHENILLE.—Elle est courte, presque cylindrique, d'un vert douteux. La vasculaire est large, continue et d'un carminé plus ou moins obscur. On ne distingue pas les autres lignes. La tête lenticulaire, est d'un testacé jaunâtre ainsi que la partie écailleuse du premier segment. Celle-ci est en outre semée de plusieurs petites taches noirâtres de formes variées. Les stigmates, qu'on ne peut voir qu'à la loupe sont blancs et cerclés de noir. Le ventre, sans lignes, est d'un vert bleuâtre. Les seizes pattes sont de la couleur du ventre. Les poils assez longs, sont implantés sur de petites caroncules d'un vert foncé et visible à l'œil nu.

Cette chenille vit en Décembre et en Janvier à Amélie-les-Bains (Pyr. Orient.), sur le *Smilax aspera*, L., arbrisseau aux tiges grimpantes, aux feuilles dures et persistantes, dont l'insecte ronge les jeunes pousses; celles-ci commencent à se développer à partir de la fin de l'automne; c'est à cette époque qu'éclot la petite larve.

Les chenilles du genre *Acrolepia*, sont pour la plupart vives et frétillantes, celle de la *smilaxella* au contraire, est lourde, paresseuse, et, tombée dans le parapluie, elle demeure immobile, à moitié roulée sur elle-même. Pendant le courant de Décembre, ou de Janvier, parvenue à son entier développement, elle choisit le plus ordinairement pour se métamorphoser une feuille de *Smilax* légèrement recroquevillée, y tisse un fourreau en soie, évasé, convexe au centre, oblong, jaunâtre, fixé hermétiquement par les bords, et se métamorphose au bout de cinq ou six jours.

La nymphe est allongée, d'un testacé rougeâtre avec l'enveloppe des ailes longue et bien apparente. La poitrine est marquée sur chaque segment d'un gros point brun, plus visible après la sortie de l'insecte que pendant qu'il est enfermé dans son enveloppe. L'éclosion du petit Lépidoptère a lieu quinze ou vingt jours après sa métamorphose.

Ayant retrouvé des chenilles à la fin de Février, je croirais à plusieurs générations de cet *Acrolepia*, qui auraient seulement lieu en hiver et au printemps, en égard à la dureté qu'acquièrent en été les feuilles du *Smilax aspera*.

INSECTE PARFAIT.—Envergure 12 mill. De la taille de la *vesperella*, Z., H.-S. 348, dont elle a un peu la coupe et la couleur générale. Cependant la *smilaxella* a les ailes relativement plus allongées; les taches des supérieures sont surtout bien différentes, et les trois taches noires et blanches appuyées à la côte de la *vesperella*, n'existent jamais chez la *smilaxella*.

Les premières ailes de ma nouvelle *Acrolepia* sont allongées, rectangulaires, d'un brun chocolat, avec une éclaircie large qui longe le bord interne. Un trait noirâtre part de la base et s'avance parallèlement à l'éclaircie jusqu'au tiers de l'aile. On distingue au bas de l'apex deux petits traits noirs parallèles. La côte est brune. Les franges de médiocre longueur, sont concolores et rougeâtres à l'extrémité. Les ailes inférieures sont aiguës, d'un gris ardoisé trèsluisant, et garnies de longues franges. En dessous, les quatres ailes sont sans dessins : les premières d'un gris jaunâtre, et les secondes d'un gris ardoisé.

Les palpes, recourbés en hameçon, dénudés dans toute leur étendue, sont blancs ; les antennes, presque aussi longues que les ailes supérieures, sont moniliformes et brunes. La tête est blanchâtre ; le thorax, brun chocolat. L'abdomen, dépassant de beaucoup les ailes inférieures est d'un gris bleuâtre et luisant. Les pattes, brunes, sont annelées de blanc.

La femelle, un peu plus grande que le mâle, est également d'un brun chocolat, mais d'une teinte un peu plus claire que celle du mâle. Les supérieures sont uniformes, sans éclaircie blanchâtre au bord interne et n'ont pas les traits noirs qui caractérisent l'autre sexe. La tête est concolore et n'a pas la tache blanchâtre qu'on aperçoit chez le mâle.

Cet insecte vole en hiver, alors que les soirées sont tièdes, et, pendant le jour, lorsqu'on frappe les buissons de *smilax*. Je suppose qu'on doit le retrouver partout où croît la salsepareille indigène et qu'il n'est pas exclusivement propre aux environs d'Amélie.

Je fais observer en terminant, que je n'ai vu en aucune province du midi de la France, le *Smilax aspera* en aussi grande abondance que dans la vallée du Tech, dont le milieu est occupé par le hameau d'Amélie-les-Bains.

(15.) ZELLERIA PHILLYRELLA, Millière.

Iconograph. et Descr. etc. vol. ii. 18ème livraison, pp. 286-288, pl. 81. f. 6-8.

Il suffit souvent qu'un arbre, un arbrisseau, ou une plante herbacée qui croissent spontanément dans les lieux qui leur sont propres, nourrissent peu de larves, ou même paraissent n'en nourrir aucune, pour que certains entomologistes s'obstinent à explorer ces végétaux. Les *Phillyrea*, par exemple, arbrisseaux aux feuilles persistantes de l'Europe méridionale, sont généralement considérés comme n'étant jamais attaqués par des larves de Lépidoptères. Le *Phillyrea angustifolia*, L., nourrit cependant plusieurs espèces de chenilles, mais elles sont, je dois l'avouer, restreintes en individus. Il faut chercher avec une certaine persévérance pour réussir à rencontrer, en outre de la chenille de la *Nemoria aureliaria*, celle d'une Tinéide inédite, la *phillyrella*, que je réunis au petit genre *Zelleria*, créé par M. Stainton.

CHENILLE.—Elle éclot à l'époque où commence à bourgeonner le *Ph. angustifolia* qui la nourrit[*], c'est-à-dire vers le 15 ou le 30

[*] Ce n'est que bien rarement que j'ai trouvé cette petite larve sur les *Phillyrea media*, L., et *latifolia*, Lam.

Janvier. Elle grossit assez vite et atteint son entier développement dès la fin de Février. A ce moment, elle est allongée, presque cylindrique, un peu aplatie en dessous, d'un vert clair, avec la région dorsale d'un vert foncé et les lignes sous-dorsales d'une teinte légèrement vineuse. La plaque du premier anneau est partagée par un sinus étroit et clair. La tête est cordiforme, d'un jaune testacé, avec les ocelles à peine indiqués. Les pattes écailleuses sont vertes ; les huit ventrales et les deux anales sont concolores. Les stigmates sont à peine indiqués ; les trapézoïdaux ne sont visibles que lorsque la chenille a pris, sur la région dorsale, une teinte vineuse plus ou moins prononcée ; ce qui arrive ordinairement lorsque la chenille est sur le point de se métamorphoser ; ces trapézoïdaux se détachent alors en clair sur le fond.

Cette petite larve est d'une extrême vivacité et rappelle les habitudes de certaines Tortricides : elle vit isolément, lie plusieurs feuilles de la plante, se tient au centre pendant le jour ; mais elle en sort la nuit, pour accomplir son œuvre de destruction en dévorant les bourgeons du *Phillyrea angustifolia* à l'exclusion des feuilles. Parvenue à toute sa grosseur, cette chenille descend de l'arbrisseau et forme à sa base, entre deux feuilles desséchées, une double coque fusiforme, en soie opaque d'un blanc mat, mince et forte cependant, et s'y transforme bientôt. Très-souvent aussi, la chenille place sa coque sur une feuille du *Phillyrea*, dans le sens de la longueur de cette feuille. La chrysalide est médiocrement longue, d'un jaunâtre argileux, avec la place des yeux bien indiquée en brun. Le petit Lépidoptère éclot cinq à six semaines après la formation de sa chrysalide, plutôt dans la soirée qu'à tout autre instant.

(16.) Tinea oleastrella, Millière.

Iconograph. et Descr. etc. vol. ii. 12ème livraison, pp. 42–45, pl. 55. figs. 7–9.

J'avais primitivement rapporté cette petite Tinéide à l'une des deux espèces observées par feu Boyer de Fonscolombe : l'*Elachista oleaella*, et l'*Œcophora olivella* (Ann. de la Soc. Ent. de Fr. année 1837, t. vi. pp. 179–187, pl. 8. f. 4 et 5) ; mais je ne tardai pas à reconnaître qu'elle n'était ni l'une ni l'autre et qu'elle devait bien certainement représenter une espèce nouvelle.

La chenille de la *Tinea oleastrella* ne peut pas être celle de l'une des deux espèces précitées, par la raison qu'elle n'a nullement, ainsi que je le dirai dans un instant, les mœurs des chenilles observées par M. Boyer de Fonscolombe.

J'ajouterai que la description des insectes parfaits et leurs figures par Duponchel (Supp. iv. pp. 434–439) ne s'y rapportent en aucune manière.

Chenille.—Elle est fusiforme, très-atténuée aux extrémités, d'un vert plus ou moins obscur avec plusieurs lignes longitudinales à peine plus accusées que le fond, excepté cependant la vasculaire qui est large, brune et continue. La tête est petite, cordiforme et d'un jaunâtre testacé qui est la couleur de la plaque du premier anneau.

Les pattes écailleuses sont d'un vert foncé, les autres sont concolores avec la couronne brune. Tous les anneaux du milieu sont lavés très-légèrement de rouille : cette nuance n'est pas constante, car plusieurs sujets n'en présentent pas de traces. Les stigmates sont noirs et sont placés sur un front vert clair. Elle vit en automne sur l'olivier cultivé, *Olea europea*, mais principalement sur l'olivier qui croît spontanément ; *O. oleaster* (sauvageon). Elle n'attaque que les feuilles récemment développées dont elle commence par ronger le revers où, jusqu'à sa troisième mue, elle se tient fixée pendant le jour. Après cette troisième mue, elle file dans la gerçure d'une branche une galerie ouverte aux deux extrémités, s'y blottit et n'en sort que la nuit pour courir sur les feuilles ; elles les explore longtemps avant de les ronger. Sa vivacité est telle qu'on peut à peine l'imaginer ; elle est de plus fort délicate et d'une éducation difficile.

Des chenilles très-petites de l'*oleastrella*, envoyées des environs d'Hyères le 7 Novembre 1863, se sont métamorphosées vers la fin du même mois, chacune dans une petite coque solidement tissée dans la mousse d'un vase qui les renfermait.

La chrysalide est relativement petite, allongée et d'un brun rougeâtre. Quinze ou vingt jours après la métamorphose, arrive l'éclosion de la Tinéide.

INSECTE PARFAIT.—Envergure 21 à 22 mil. Ce petit Lépidoptère me paraît appartenir au genre *Tinea* proprement dit : il en a d'ailleurs la plupart des caractères. Les ailes supérieures sont longues, étroites, rectangulaires, un peu falquées, à angle apical obtus et ont, au premier abord, un aspect terreux. Sur le fond gris clair, lavé de rougeâtre à la base, au centre et à l'extrémité de l'aile, on voit un grand nombre de très-petits points ou atomes bruns serrés qui en recouvrent assez régulièrement la surface. Il existe en outre plusieurs taches noirâtres ainsi disposées : la première, de forme triangulaire, est placée sur le bord interne, au tiers environ de l'étendue de l'aile ; deux ou trois autres taches allongées se montrent à la hauteur de la coudée, une à la pointe que précède l'apex, et enfin une dernière à la frange de l'apex même. Les ailes inférieures sont allongées, cultriformes, gris foncé, unies, luisantes et garnies, ainsi que les supérieures, de longues franges soyeuses et concolores. Le dessous est d'un gris ardoisé, luisant, sans aucun dessin. Les antennes sont presque aussi longues que le corps, filiformes et brunes. La tête est laineuse et blanchâtre. Les palpes, un peu recourbés en crochet, sont assez longs, dépassant la tête, et garnis d'écailles blanchâtres, sauf le dernier article qui est nu ; les yeux sont gros et noirs. Le thorax et l'abdomen sont de la couleur des ailes supérieures. Le corps en dessous et les pattes sont gris de fer et luisants.

L'insecte varie peu : on rencontre pourtant des sujets d'un gris jaunâtre. La *T. oleastrella*, qui doit avoir plusieurs générations par an, ne paraît pas très-abondante dans les lieux où croissent les oliviers. Je l'ai prise au vol en hiver dans le département du Var.

(En Décembre et en Janvier 1857, nous l'avons prise plusieurs fois, feu Bruand d'Uzelle et moi, dans la campagne d'Hyères. Je l'ai retrouvée en 1861 aux environs d'Amélie-les-Bains, Pyrénées Orientales.) Sa vivacité est aussi très-grande : pour se soustraire au danger, elle disparaît sous les gerçures avec une remarquable facilité.

Je place cette *Tinea* après la *clematella*, Step. (*arcella*, F., Z.), Dup. Sup. pl. 85. f. 13. Elle portera le no. 1213 *bis* dans le catalogue Stdgr.

(17.) BUCCULATRIX LAVATERELLA, Millière.

Iconograph. et Descr. etc. vol. ii. 13ème livraison, pp. 69-72, pl. 59. f. 1-5.

On la reconnaît de suite pour appartenir au genre *Bucculatrix*. En effet, elle possède bien les seize pattes normales. Ce caractère essentiel, l'éloigne des chenilles du genre *Nepticula*, qui sont dépourvues de pattes écailleuses, et de celles des *Lithocolletis*, qui n'ont que six pattes ventrales. D'autres caractères d'ailleurs, qui seront signalés lors de la description de l'insecte parfait, établissent que c'est bien effectivement dans le genre *Bucculatrix*, Z., Stainton, qu'il convient de placer ce Microlépidoptère.

La chenille de la *lavaterella* mesure à peine dix à onze millimètres de longueur. Elle est fusiforme, plissée, à anneaux renflés, un peu courbée, d'un blanc vert bleuâtre qui rappelle assez la couleur de la feuille dont elle fait sa nourriture ; sans dessins, sans lignes, si ce n'est pourtant la vasculaire ou mieux le tube intestinal qu'on aperçoit sous la peau à moitié diaphane, sous forme d'une ligne médiocrement large, droite, continue et d'un vert foncé. On distingue difficilement les points trapézoïdaux bruns et les autres points d'où partent des poils fins, courts et grisâtres. La tête est petite, lenticulaire, brune. Le premier anneau est muni d'une plaque écailleuse d'un jaunâtre obscur. Les deuxième, troisième, et douzième segments sont faiblement lavés de carné en dessus. Les pattes écailleuses sont d'un gris foncé ; les autres sont concolores.

Cette petite chenille, dont la lenteur est extrême, vit en Novembre et en Décembre, aux environs d'Hyères sur la *Lavatera olbia*, L. ; arbrisseau qui croît un peu partout. Vivant d'abord à la manière des mineuses, elle ronge le parenchyme de la feuille tomenteuse dont elle dévorera la surface supérieure quand elle aura atteint l'âge adulte.

Un petit parasite appartenant à l'immense groupe des *Ichneumons*, un *Mesolius*, attaque très-souvent cette chenille et éclot à sa place.

La taille exiguë de ce parasite est proportionnée à celle de sa victime. Il est nouveau sans doute et peut être nommé dès à présent. Je propose pour lui le nom spécifique de *lavaterellæ*.

Lorsque la chenille de la *Bucc. lavaterella* éprouve le besoin de se métamorphoser, elle demeure ordinairement sur l'arbuste ; elle choisit dans la cavité ou dans le pli d'une feuille une place qu'elle juge convenable et forme très-vite, c'est-à-dire en moins de deux jours, une triple enveloppe protectrice. L'insecte file d'abord une soie blanchâtre ressemblant, vue à la loupe, à du coton cardé très-fin, au centre de laquelle il tisse une coque papyracée solide, plissée, rugueuse, blanchâtre ; après quoi ce prévoyant insecte forme, avant de se chrysalider, une troisième enveloppe lisse, opaque, plus blanche que la précédente, où arrive la transformation dans un temps fort court. Il le faut bien, puisque l'éclosion de l'insecte parfait a eu lieu le 21 Décembre suivant, moins de quinze jours après la métamorphose.

La chrysalide est proportionnellement allongée. Elle est dépourvue, aux anneaux abdominaux, des petites épines qu'on observe chez certaines espèces congénères ; différant en cela des chrysalides de *Bucculatrix* décrites par M. Stainton.

Elle est d'un brun mat avec la gaîne des antennes et l'enveloppe des ailes descendant assez bas sur l'abdomen ; celui-ci se termine par une pointe obtuse, noire et luisante.

INSECTE PARFAIT.—Ce petit Lépidoptère, dont l'envergure ne dépasse pas 9 mill., à tous les caractères des espèces du genre *Bucculatrix* créé par M. Zeller, et successivement adopté par MM. Herrich-Schäffer, Stainton, Staudinger, etc., c'est-à-dire que l'article basilaire des antennes est noduleux, et que la tête est laineuse et sans palpes. Les ailes supérieures sont allongées, légèrement falquées, à fond blanc et largement lavées de brun, de gris bleuâtre et de rougeâtre à diverses places, notamment à celles qui sont parsemées de nombreux atomes noirs. Ces atomes de diverses grosseurs, réunis par groupes, forment autant de taches plus ou moins grandes et qui sont ainsi disposées : une à la base de l'aile et une appuyée au tiers de la longueur de la côte. Une autre tache allongée, plus noire que les autres, longe le bord interne et suit la tache basilaire précitée. Une quatrième tache triangulaire, qui part de la côte, tend à se réunir à la précédente. Une cinquième occupant la place de la coudée, se dirige sur un gros point noir situé à l'angle inférieur. Enfin une tache orbiculaire constante et caractéristique est située à l'apex. La frange est longue et concolore ; elle est partagée par une rangée de points noirs mieux indiqués au sommet qu'à la base. Les ailes inférieures sont très-étroites, aiguës et d'un gris brunâtre ; elles sont garnies de longues franges soyeuses, concolores, mais un peu rougeâtres. En dessous les quatre ailes ne présentent ni taches, ni dessins ; elles sont d'un gris brun plus accusé sur les bords qu'au centre ; elles sont de plus luisantes et parfois irisées. Les antennes médiocrement longues, n'arrivent qu'aux deux tiers de la longueur des ailes ; elles sont moniliformes, brunes, à peine annelées de blanchâtre avec le premier article noduleux. La tête est fortement laineuse, c'est-à-dire recouverte de poils longs, serrés, nombreux, blanchâtres et bruns à l'extrémité. Le front est dénudé et blanc. Les yeux sont relativement gros et noirs. Le thorax, assez robuste, est blanchâtre. L'abdomen est long, brun et garni, à l'extrémité, d'un pinceau de poils concolores. Les pattes sont assez longues, avec les cuisses garnies de grands poils soyeux et blanchâtres.

La *B. lavaterella* semble se rapprocher de la *Boyerella* de Duponchel, pl. 309. fig. 3, H.-S. f. 851, =*albedinella*, Z., Dup. Sup. 78. f. 10, =*cuculipennella*, Haw. Aussi est-ce après celle-là que cette nouvelle *Bucculatrix* devra trouver place. Elle portera le no. 2496 *bis* dans le catalogue Staudinger.

Obs. Ce petit Lépidoptère paraît aussi vif que sa chenille est paresseuse. Il vole dans le voisinage des lavatères où les femelles viennent déposer leurs œufs. Au repos, il demeure fixé sur les feuilles de l'arbuste, les ailes embrassant étroitement le corps. Il doit avoir, la chose est probable, plusieurs générations ; toutefois, je dirai que je ne l'ai jamais vu voler qu'en hiver, et que j'ai trouvé en abondance sa chenille en même temps que celle de l'*Eubolia malvata*, qui, on le sait n'a jamais qu'une seule génération (*Iconogra.* p. 242).

CHAPTER V.

Rev. HENRY BURNEY AND OTHERS.

The present chapter contains a brief notice of the doings of four entomologists in Southern Europe.

I. The Rev. Henry Burney, who resided at Mentone from November 1864 to April 1865.

II. Professor Rosenhauer visited Andalusia in 1849, and published the results of his journey seven years afterwards, 'Die Thiere Andalusiens;' unfortunately the Tineina noticed are few in number, and of little interest.

III. Count von Hoffmannsegg's visit to Andalusia in 1865, the results of which are recorded by Herr Möschler in the 'Berliner ent. Zeitschrift' for 1866.

IV. Herr Erber's visit to Dalmatia and the Island of Syra (in the Grecian archipelago) in 1867, the results of which have been noticed by Herr Mann in the 'Verhandlungen des zoologisch-botanischen Gesellschaft in Wien' for 1867.

V. And, lastly, to complete this chapter, I have added the notice of the few Sicilian Tineina received by Dr. J. Delaharpe, of Lausanne, in 1858, and noticed by him in the 6th volume of the 'Bulletin de la Société Vaudoise des Sciences Naturelles;' they were collected by Signor D. Reyna of Palermo.

Section I.

Species collected by the Rev. Henry Burney during his residence at Mentone from November 1864 to April 1865.

The Rev. Henry Burney has very liberally given me all the insects he collected during his sojourn at Mentone, whither he had repaired on account of the failing health of a member of his family. I necessarily confine my attention here to the few species of *Tineina* which he then obtained; but as his collection included several bred specimens of *Noctuæ, Geometræ, Tortrices*, &c., it may be interesting to those who work at other groups of Lepidoptera to examine the collection, which I shall have much pleasure in showing to any one who wishes to see it.

The list of the Tineina is as follows:—

Plutella cruciferarum, Z. A female taken in the garden in December.
Prays oleellus, Boyer. Several bred from the shoots of the olive; the larva feeding in March, and the moths emerging from the pupa state in April.

Gelechia biguttella, H.-S. One specimen bred from a pupa found in February on *Dorycnium suffruticosum*.

Nothris verbascella, W. V. One specimen bred in April from larvæ found feeding on *Verbascum* in February.

Butalis, n. sp.? A single specimen of a *Butalis*, which, though resembling in some respects B. *dorycniella*, Millière, is evidently distinct from that; the anterior wings are longer, the expansion of the wings being $6\frac{3}{4}'''$, whereas in *dorycniella* it is barely $6'''$; the posterior wings are much paler than in *dorycniella*. In my male specimen of *dorycniella* the cilia are so much darker than the ground-colour of the anterior wings that they have quite a *dark-tipped appearance*, a character which does not appear in Mr. Burney's insect. That entomologist informed me that he "bred it in April from a larva which fed in February and March on *Euphorbia dendroides*." When at Mentone I searched repeatedly on *Euphorbia dendroides*, the handsome bushes of which at once attract the attention of all visitors to that locality, but I found no *Butalis*-larvæ on it, nor did I see any symptoms of them. The larvæ of *Pœcilochroma* (*Argyrolepia*) *Mulsantana*, Millière (closely allied to our *Hawkerana* (Stevens) Stainton), were very common on that and other species of *Euphorbia*.

After two unsuccessful attempts to rediscover this *Butalis*-larva on *Euphorbia dendroides*, I suggested to Mr. Burney that possibly there had been some error, and that the larva which produced the *Butalis* had fed on some other plant, perhaps on *Dorycnium*. To this he replied, "The *Butalis* I bred from a Mentone larva could not have been from either of the species of *Dorycnium*; I never had a larva feeding on either species; it must have been from Euphorbia, mallow, or juniper. I think from mallow; for I recollect a little black-looking larva which I took to be a *Gelechia*, and which fed under a turned-down leaf of mallow early in the season."

For the present the matter must remain an enigma, to be solved at some future time.

Gracilaria tringipennella, Z. One specimen beaten from juniper in March.

G. scalariella, Z. Several bred from *Echium vulgare* in December, the larvæ mining blackish blotches in the leaves of that plant.

Tischeria complanella, Hübner. Two specimens bred from oak leaves in May.

Lithocolletis Messaniella, Z. Two specimens bred from *Quercus ilex* in April.

L. sublautella, n. sp. Nine specimens bred from *Quercus* —— in April.

Staudinger described two Spanish species of this genus, *L. hesperiella*, probably from *Quercus coccifera*, and *L. belotella* bred from *Quercus ilex*; and looking only to Staudinger's description I should have thought that the latter was my proposed new species;

but when I refer to Herrich-Schäffer's 'Neue Schmetterlinge' I find that he compares it with *carpinicolella* and *Messaniella*, whereas Mr. Burney's insect should be compared with *lautella* and with *pomifoliella*: and of a white central line on the thorax mentioned by Herrich-Schäffer I see no trace; and it chances that Mr. Burney's specimens are well adapted for showing the thorax, eight specimens not being pinned, but mounted on gummed card, and the ninth, though pinned, has the pin inserted behind the thorax. The figure of *belotella* in Herrich-Schäffer's 'Neue Schmetterlinge' (f. 116) would certainly lead one to expect an insect nearly allied to *leucographella*.

Sublautella, as the name implies, is certainly most nearly allied to *lautella*; it has the same rich red-orange colour, only not quite so dark; it possesses the short basal streak, the two dorsal spots, the three distinct costal spots, and the fourth smaller and much less distinct; but the small silvery spot below the black apical streak so characteristic of *lautella* is entirely wanting: moreover the position of the first dorsal spot is much more oblique, and the first costal spot is much shorter than in *lautella*; the apex of the wing is not suffused with dark as in *lautella*, but a beautiful iridescent hinder marginal line intersects the cilia. From the brightest specimens of *pomifoliella* it can be immediately separated by the far more brilliant colouring, more silvery tone of the pale markings, and total absence of the third dorsal spot.

I describe this species as follows :—

Exp. $3\frac{1}{4}'''$. *Alis anticis læte rufo-aurantiacis, linea basali abbreviata albido-argentea costam versus nigro-marginata, strigulis quatuor costæ breviusculis (ultima interdum obsoleta), duabusque dorsi albido-argenteis, introrsum nigro-marginatis, striola apicis ovata nigra, ciliis linea iridescente intersectis.*

Head and thorax dark saffron, the latter with no pale central line. Face and palpi whitish. Antennæ dark fuscous, faintly annulated with paler (not black with white tips as in *lautella*). Anterior wings bright reddish orange, with a short silvery-white basal streak, which becomes gradually broader for some distance, and then is rather abruptly pointed; it is bordered with black on its upper side, then follow four costal silvery-white spots; the first, obliquely placed, is very short (scarcely crossing the subcostal nervure), the second is less obliquely placed, and is rather longer, the third is placed nearly perpendicularly, and reaches to the black apical streak, being by far the longest of the costal spots; the fourth is much smaller, and sometimes scarcely perceptible, it lies just over the further end of the apical black streak; all these spots are margined with black towards the base of the wing : on the inner margin are two silvery-white spots; the first, obliquely placed, reaches half across the wing, and has its apex nearly midway between the apex of the first costal spot and that of the second; the second dorsal spot is more triangular, and is posterior to the second costal spot; the apical black streak is an elongate oval, behind it an iridescent hinder marginal line runs through the cilia from the fourth costal spot to the anal angle; beyond this the cilia are pale ochreous.

In the posterior wings and legs I do not observe any striking characters.

Section II.

Rosenhauer's 'Die Thiere Andalusiens' (the results of a journey in the South of Spain in 1849), published in 1856.

'Tineina,' pp. 398–399.

Hyponomeuta malinellus, Zell. Near Granada, not very scarce.
Plutella cruciferarum, Zell. Collected near Granada.
Psecadia echiella, W. V. In March, near Xerez, not scarce.
Anacampsis bifractella, Zell. At Ronda, in pasture-fields.
Nemotois Latreillellus, Hb. In the Sierra Nevada, on bushes, abundant.
Butalis chenopodiella, Hb. Near Granada.
B., n. sp., distinct from *punctivittella* (according to Zeller). Near Granada.
B. acanthella, Dup., Zell. Near Ronda.

Section III.

Species collected in Andalusia in 1865 by Count v. Hoffmannsegg, enumerated by Herr H. B. Möschler in the 'Berliner entomologische Zeitschrift,' 1866, pp. 142–146 ("Aufzählung der in Andalusien, 1865, von Herrn Graf v. Hoffmannsegg gesammelten Schmetterlinge").

Micropteryx. Several specimens of a small species, but unfortunately not serviceable for precise determination.
Nemotois barbatellus, Zell. ♂, ♀.
Plutella cruciferarum, Zell. ♀.
Gelechia ferrugella, S. V. ♂, ♀.
G. terrella, S. V.
G. fugitivella, Zell. ♂.
G. tamariciella, Zell. ♀.
Parasia castiliella, n. sp. 1 ♂, 3 ♀. [Described, see p. 200.]
Cleodora Kefersteiniella, Zell.
C. meridionella, H.-S.
Pleurota ericella, Dup. ♂, ♀.
Œcophora augustella, Hb. ♀.
Butalis scipionella, Staud. ♀.
B. variella, Steph. ♀.
Æchmia thrasonella, Scop. ♀.
Æ. Fischeriella? Too much injured to be determined with certainty.
Tinagma thymetellum, Staud. ♀.

T. transversellum, Zell. ♀
Gracilaria elongella, Staud. ♂.
Coleophora fuscicornis, Zell. ♂.
C. hispanicella, n. sp.   ♂, ♀.   [Described, see below.]
Chauliodus pontificellus, Hb. ♂.
Ochromolopis ictella, Hb. ♀.
? *Lithocolletis endryella*, Mann.   A single male specimen of a *Lithocolletis* may, according to Dr. Wocke, possibly be this species. As *endryella* is unknown in nature both to Dr. Wocke and myself, I give a detailed description of my species, and leave it to those who possess *endryella*, to decide whether it agrees with that species. Should my species prove new, I would propose for it the name *meridionella*. [Described, see p. 201.]

'Berlin. ent. Zeitschrift,' 1866, p. 142.

PARASIA CASTILIELLA, n. sp.

Alis anticis cinereis, albo-pulverulentis, venis ochraceis, fascia ochracea limbo parallela, punctisque nigris discoidalibus (exp. 6¾-8''', ♂ ♀).

Fühler schwarz, fein gelb geringelt, Palpen gelb, innen weissgelb. Kopf und Thorax hellgelb, Hinterleib gelbgrau, Füsse weisslich. Vorderflügel hellgrau, theilweise weisslich bestäubt, die Innenrandsrippen und beiden Mittelrippen, sowie die aus der vordern Mittelrippen in den Vorderrand auslaufenden Rippen ockergelb gefärbt; in der Mitte des Flügels zwei hintereinander stehende schwarze Punkte, von denen der eine in, der andere hinter der Mittelzelle steht; vor dem Saum ein mit diesem parallel laufender röthlichgelber Schrägstreif. Wurzelhälfte der hellgelbgrauen Franzen gegen die Flügelspitze grau, fein schwarz bestäubt.

Hinterflügel hellgrau, mit gelblichen Franzen. Unten die Vorderflügel schwärzlichgrau, Vorderrand und Saum gegen die Spitze weiss gestrichelt.

Meine vier Exemplare, 1 ♂, 3 ♀, variiren insofern untereinander, als die gelbe Färbung der Vorderflügelrippen theilweise durch graue Bestäubung verdeckt ist und sich stellenweise dunklere, fast rothgelbe Flecken zeigen.

In ihrem Habitus gleicht diese Art mehr den *Cleodora*-Arten, am meisten *meridionella*, H.-S. Die Bildung der Palpen stellt sie aber unzweifelhaft zu *Parasia*.

'Berlin. ent. Zeitschrift,' 1866, p. 163.

COLEOPHORA HISPANICELLA, n. sp.

Antennis niveis, penicillo basali brevissimo. Capite thoraceque niveis, abdomine albido. Alis anticis niveis, venis stramineis, fimbriis luteo-griseis, basi niveis, ad alarum apicem totis niveis. Alis posticis plumbeis, fimbriis dilutioribus (exp. 8-10''', ♂ ♀).

Fühler geringelt, das Wurzelglied mit kurzem Schuppenbüschel, sowie Palpen, Kopf, Thorax und Beine schneeweiss, Hinterleib weisslich beschuppt.

Vorderflügel schneeweiss, Innenrands-, die beiden Mittelrippen und die in den Vorderrand auslaufenden Rippen strohgelb. Franzen weissgelb, an der Wurzel schneeweiss. Hinterflügel dunkelgrau, glänzend, ihre Franzen an der Wurzelhälfte beim Mann hellgrau, beim Weib gelbgrau, die Endhälfte weiss.

Unten die Vorderflügel schwarz, der Vorderrand von der Mitte bis zur Spitze schneeweiss, ebenso die Franzen in der Flügelspitze, übrigens gelblichgrau. Hinterflügel wie oben.

'Berlin. ent. Zeitschrift,' 1866, p. 144.

LITHOCOLLETIS MERIDIONELLA, n. sp.? *Endryella*, Mann?

Thorace aureo, scapulis albo-marginatis. Alis anticis caudulatis, aureis, linea basali nivea, costa dorsique usque ad elytrorum dimidium niveis, strigulis quatuor costæ niveis, primo utrinque, reliquis intus nigro-marginatis, dorsi strigulis duabus niveis, prima late triangulari, obliqua versus limbum nutante, secunda rotundata, ad apicem puncto nigro squamulisque argenteis, linea marginali nigra. Tarsis albidis nigro maculatis (exp. 5‴).

Fühler weiss und goldbraun geringelt, Scheitelhaare weiss, Thorax rothgolden, Schulterdecken nach innen weiss eingefasst. Hinterleib (abgerieben) bräunlich. Beine weiss, alle Tarsen schwarz geringelt.

Vorderflügel hellrothgolden, mit weisser, nicht dunkel gerandeter Basallinie. Der Vorderrand färbt sich von der Wurzel bis zum ersten Häkchen fein weiss, vor der Flügelmitte bildet diese weisse Färbung ein undeutliches Fleckchen. Vier weisse Vorderrandshäkchen, deren erstes beiderseits, die übrigen nur wurzelwärts schwarz gerandet sind. Die beiden ersten stehen schräg nach aussen gerichtet und sind länger als die folgenden. Das dritte steht ziemlich gerade, das vierte schräg nach innen gerichtet.

Das erste Innenrandshäkchen bildet an der Basis einen dreieckigen Fleck, aus welchem es, schmal und stark gebogen, saumwärts über das erste Vorderrandshäkchen hinauszieht, von ihm bis zur Flügelwurzel färbt sich den Innenrand fein weiss. Das zweite und zugleich letzte Innenrandshäkchen bildet einer breiten, nach innen und wurzelwärts abgerundeten und schwarz eingefassten weissen Fleck, ohne jegliche Spitze.

In der Flügelspitze steht ein feiner, tief schwarzer Punkt, hinter ihm am Saum silberne Schuppen. Saumlinie tief schwarz. Franzen hellgoldgelb, in der Spitze ein sie überragendes, schwarz gemischtes Schwänzchen. Hinterflügel glänzendgrau mit hellgoldgelben Franzen.

Auf der Unterseite scheinen auf den schwärzlichgrauen Vorderflügeln die weissen Häkchen verloschen durch.

As a postscript to this paper there is added the description of a new species of *Glyphipteryx*, from a single male specimen captured at Nice by Count von Hoffmannsegg.

'Berlin ent. Zeitschrift,' 1866, p. 146.

GLYPHIPTERYX NICÆELLA, n. sp.

Alis anticis olivaceo-aureis strigulis sex costæ, tribus dorsi argenteis, cæruleo micantibus, macula anguli analis atra, serieque punctorum quinque cæruleo micantibus limbo parallela, ciliis basi olivaceis, apice albidis (exp. 5''', ♂).

Fühler schwarz, Kopf und Thorax goldigolivenbraun. Hinterleib (abgerieben) schwärzlich. Beine schwärzlich, Tarsen weiss geringelt.

Vorderflügel goldigolivenbraun, der Vorderrand mit 6, der Innenrand mit 3 glänzendweissen Häkchen. Das erste Vorder- und Innenrandshäkchen steht nahe der Wurzel und stossen beide mit ihren Enden zusammen, einen winklig gebrochenen Querstreif bildend. Die nächsten Häkchen stehen dicht vor der Mitte, beide sind schräg nach aussen gerichtet, berühren einander mit ihren Enden nicht und zwischen ihnen steht ein blausilberner Punkt. Das dritte Vorderrandshäkchen ist bedeutend schräger nach aussen gestellt und nähert sich mit seiner Spitze dem ziemlich geraden vierten, beide sind blausilbern und unter ihnen steht ebenfalls ein blausilberner Punkt gegenüber auf dem Innenrande; vor dem Innenwinkel steht ein ziemlich gerades, blausilberner Häkchen. Ueber dem Innenwinkel, vor dem Saum, findet sich ein schwarzer Fleck, welcher saumwärts von vier zusammenhängenden blausilbernen Punkten begrenzt wird, ein einzelner solcher Punkt steht weit gegen die Flügelspitze gerückt. Franzen mit olivenbrauner Wurzel- und weisser Endhälfte. Hinterflügel glänzend bräunlichgrau, ebenso die Unterseite aller Flügel, auf ihr der Vorderflügelvorderrand weiss gestrichelt.

SECTION IV.

New species collected by Herr Erber in 1867 at Budua in Dalmatia, and in the Island of Syra (one of the Grecian archipelago), described by Herr Joseph Mann in the 'Verhandl. d. zoolog.-botan. Gesellschaft in Wien,' 1867, p. 845, entitled "Zehn neue Schmetterlingsarten."

Pleurota filigerella, n. sp. Herr Erber took two male specimens of this species at Budua in Dalmatia, at the beginning of July this year; they are in the Imperial Collection.

P. contristatella, n. sp. Herr Erber brought some male specimens of this species from the Island of Syra during his journey this year.

Œcophora icterinella, n. sp. Herr Erber took some specimens during his this year's journey at Budua in Dalmatia in July.

The original descriptions of these three species are appended.

'Verh. z.-b. Verein in Wien,' 1867, p. 851.

PLEUROTA FILIGERELLA, n. sp.

Von der Grösse und Gestalt der *Pl. pyropella*, S. V. In der Färbung die dunkelste dieser Gattung.

Kopf und Palpen gelblichgrau, die feinen Fühler etwas dunkler. Das erste Palpenglied kurz, das zweite ein Viertel der Flügellänge mit langen, gelblichgrauen und schwarzen Haaren besetzt, das dritte schwarz, dünn, ein Drittel so lang wie das zweite; Beine braungrau.

Die Vorderflügel sowie der Rücken braunochergelb, etwas glänzend, nächst dem Vorderrande zieht sich von der Wurzel bis zur Flügelspitze ein braungrauer, gleichbreiter Schatten, der mit den braungrauen Fransen verfliesst.

Die Hinterflügel dunkel braungrau, die Fransen lichter, besonders am Innenwinkel.

Alle Flügel unten seidenglänzend. Vorderflügel dunkel braungrau wie die Fransen; Hinterflügel nebst den Fransen etwas heller, Saumlinie wenig sichtbar.

'Verh. z.-b. Verein in Wein,' 1867, p. 851.

PLEUROTA CONTRISTATELLA, n. sp.

Diese Schabe hat die Grösse und Gestalt einer kleinen *Pl. bicostella*, L., gleicht aber in der Färbung mehr der *Pl. rostrella*, Hb.

Kopf, Palpen, Rücken, Körper und Beine weisslichgrau, mit bräunlichen Schuppen gemischt. Fühler dunkelgrau, weisslich geringelt, Palpen wie bei *bicostella* gebildet.

Die Grundfarbe der Vorderflügel ist völlig glanzlos, weisslichgrau, unter dem weisslichen, eine nach und nach immer dünner werdende Linie bildenden Vorderrande zieht sich bis zur Flügelspitze ein gleichbreiter, bräunlichgrauer Streif wie bei *bicostella*, unter diesem folgt ein feiner, weisslicher Streif, der sich in der Mitte des Flügels ebenfalls von der Wurzel bis zum Aussenrande zieht, von ihm bis zum Innenrande ist die Färbung durch viele dunkle Schuppen bräunlichgrau. Die Fransen ins aschgraue schillernd. Die Hinterflügel sind glänzend, aschgrau, gegen die Wurzel kaum heller; die langen Fransen sind heller grau mit verloschener dunklerer Linie vor der Mitte.

Die Unterseite der Vorderflügel ist aschgrau, der Vorderrand in einer dünnen Linie und Fransen weisslich, letztere von einer breiten grauen Schuppenlinie durchzogen.

Die Hinterflügel sind hellaschgrau an der Flügelspitze mit einem weisslichen Längswisch, die Fransen wie bei den Vorderflügeln.

Alle Flügel mit Seidenglanz.

'Verh. z.-b. Verein in Wein,' 1867, p. 852.

ŒCOPHORA ICTERINELLA, n. sp.

Diese schöne Schabe hat die Grösse einer kleinen *Conchylis tes-*

serana, S. V., der sie auch in der Farbe und Zeichnung nahe kommt, und reiht sich zwischen *Œcophora Borkhausenii*, Zell., und *Œ. procerella*, S. V. ein.

Kopf, Fühler, Palpen, Rücken und Vorderbeine schwärzlichviolett. Mittel- und Hinterbeine gelblichgrau, an letzteren die Schienen violett angeflogen, und lang behaart, mit zwei Paar Sporen ; Tarsen violett, weiss geringelt. Hinterleib oben und unten gelblichgrau, Palpen dünn, lang, zurückgebogen, das zweite Glied noch einmal so lang als das dritte, welches eine weissliche Wurzel und Spitze hat.

Grundfarbe der Vorderflügel und Fransen goldgelb, Aussenrand violett, mit eingesprengten orangegelben Schuppen, welche an der Flügelspitze und am Aussenwinkel die Fransen durchziehen. Durch zwei violette Querbinden wird die Flügel in drei gelbe Felder getheilt. Vorderrand von der Wurzel bis zu dem ovalen Fleck vor der Flügelspitze violett ; von hier zieht sich eine violette Querbinde bis zum Aussenwinkel und schliesst das ovale gelbe Feld, welches etwas unter der Mitte, durch einen schmalen Arm mit dem Mittelfeld in Verbindung steht ; das schräge Mittelfeld besteht gleichsam aus zwei gerundeten Flecken, indem die violette, wurzelwärts liegende Binde einen Zahn hat, der sich fast bis zur saumwärts liegenden Binde verlängert ; das Wurzelfeld ist länglichrund.

Hinterflügel und Fransen dunkelgrau, etwas seidenglänzend, Fransenlinie hell.

Unterseite der Vorderflügel violettgrau, Vorder- und Aussenrand dunkler, Fransen goldgelb, im Innenwinkel violettgrau. Hinterflügel wie oben.

Section V.

Species received by Dr. J. Delaharpe from Sicily in 1858, collected by Signor D. Reyna, of Bocca-di-Falco, near Palermo, noticed by Dr. Delaharpe in the sixth volume of the 'Bulletin de la Société Vaudoise des Sciences Naturelles,' pp. 391, 392, in a paper entitled "Contributions à la Faune de la Sicile. Lépidoptères."

The introduction of this paper informs us that two of Dr. Delaharpe's friends, MM. Gl. de Rumine and C.-T. Gaudin, spent the winter of 1857–58 in Sicily. They undertook to procure some of the Lepidoptera of that country for Dr. Delaharpe ; and he obtained for the use of the cantonal museum [at Lausanne] a fine series of species, several of which deserve a special mention. These insects, amounting to 168 species, had been collected by Signor D. Reyna, of Bocca-di-Falco, near Palermo, a zealous and intelligent collector of natural history. They were principally Microlepidoptera, including the Geometridæ ; but the Tineina were very feebly represented, as may be seen from the following list.

Eriocottis fuscanella, Zeller. Fourteen specimens ; this appears very common in Sicily ; it is tolerably distributed in the South.

Micropteryx calthella, L. One specimen, quite similar to the Swiss specimens.

Nemotois Raddellus, Hüb. One specimen.

N. Latreillellus, Fab. Two specimens; this and the preceding are both southern insects.

Plutella xylostella, L. [*cruciferarum*, Z.]. One specimen, similar to the Swiss specimens.

Depressaria subpropinquella, H.-S. Five specimens; determined by Dr. Herrich-Schäffer, seems to differ from the species of the same name figured by Stainton. A Sicilian species.

Gelechia palermitella, Lah. One male. A new species, determined by Dr. Herrich-Schäffer. [Described, see below.]

Pleurota brevispinella, Zell. Seven specimens; this species is scarce in collections, and seems confined to the Mediterranean region.

'Bulletin de la Soc. Vaudoise des Sci. Nat.' vi. p. 391.

GELECHIA PALERMITELLA, Laharpe.

Envergure 14^{mm}. D'un jaune pâle, ochracé. Palpes entièrement de la même couleur; premier article squammeux, d'un jaune nanquin pâle; deuxième article allongé, d'un jaune fauve en avant. Antennes fortement entrecoupées de blanc terne et de noir; premier article renflé, allongé, squammeux, brun bistre. Front blanchâtre, lisse, plat. Base des ptérigodes et pourtour de l'insertion des antennes, bruns.

Antérieures marquées, vers la racine et sur le centre, d'une tache oblique brunâtre, dirigée du côté du bord postérieur. Un petit point brun foncé vers les ⅔ de l'aile, au centre du disque. Sommet coupé en biseau avec la frange très-allongée; la moitié interne de la frange porte des vergetures fauves, disposées en éventail; la moitié externe est d'un blanc jaunâtre; une petite ligne de division fauve et courte.

Postérieures étroites, légèrement grises ou bleuâtres, teintes de roux à leur extrémité, avec le sommet fort acuminé et les franges d'un blanc terne, allongées.

Pattes d'un blanc jaunâtre sans anneaux. Dessous entièrement de la même couleur, légèrement enfumé.

Abdomen jaunâtre avec un mouchet anal plus clair.

One specimen, a male, determined as a new species by Dr. Herrich-Schäffer.

In the introduction of this paper are some very interesting remarks on the prevalence of pale and yellow colours in the insects from the sunny south; but I have not space to transcribe them here, which I regret.

CHAPTER VI.

THE AUTHOR.

My own visits to the South have now been four; the first, in the spring of 1863, was undertaken mainly with the view of seeing Rome, Naples, &c.

The second, in March 1866, to Cannes and Mentone, was purely entomological; and the result of this was so satisfactory that in 1867 I again visited both those places with the idea of exploring them more thoroughly.

My fourth visit to the South was in the winter of 1868-69; and though sight-seeing in Italy, from Turin to Sorrento, took up much of my time, I was able to do a little more entomology than in 1863. In addition to the species I actually found at Cannes and Mentone I have introduced into this chapter notices of the insects which I received from those localities from my valued correspondents Monsieur Millière and Mr. J. T. Moggridge.

SECTION I.

Tineina observed during my visit to Italy in February and March 1863.

My first visit to Southern Europe was in the spring of 1863; but the entomological results of that journey were extremely restricted. It was on Saturday, February 28th, 1863, when descending the Apennines towards Pistoja, that I first became acquainted with the olive, and on the following Monday, March 2nd, when taking a walk near Florence, that I first observed plants of *Arundo donax* growing by the roadside. I mention these plants as the two which most forcibly call to one's mind one's presence amongst the South-European flora, where consequently the South-European insects may be expected.

The only Tineina collected or observed on this journey were the following six species:—

Tischeria marginea.   *L. suberifoliella.*
Lithocolletis Messaniella.   *Nepticula aurella.*
L. leucographella.   *N. ———, on Quercus ilex.*

Tischeria marginea, Haworth. Of this I observed mines in the bramble-leaves near Florence.

Lithocolletis Messaniella, Zeller. Of this I bred several from mines in leaves of *Quercus ilex* collected at Rome and Naples.

L. leucographella, Zeller. (See *ante*, pp. 70 & 88.) I found the larva of this species near Florence, March 2nd, on the road leading to Bello Sguardo; it was mining the *upper* side of the leaves of *Cratægus pyracantha*, loosening nearly the entire upper cuticle and curving the leaves considerably. Unfortunately all the larvæ I collected died on the journey, and I did not rear a single specimen. (See Ent. Ann. 1864, p. 168.)

L. suberifoliella, Zeller. (See *ante*, pp. 70 & 89.) Of this I bred a single specimen from a mined leaf of a species of *Quercus*, which I had picked at Capo di Monte, Naples, on the 28th of March. Unfortunately I had leaves of several species of *Quercus* mixed together, and cannot say with certainty which leaf produced the moth.

Nepticula aurella, F. I bred one specimen of this from larvæ collected in bramble-leaves on Monte Mario, near Rome, March 14th. I also observed mines, which I presume to have been those of *N. aurella*, near Florence.

Nepticula, n. sp.? On the 15th of March, whilst walking in the grounds of the Villa Pamfili-Doria, at Rome, I observed in the leaves of *Quercus ilex* the mines of a *Nepticula*. All were, however, empty, though some were comparatively recent. I believe these mines were distinct from those of the two species of *Nepticula* I afterwards met with on *Quercus suber* at Cannes.

SECTION II.

Tineina observed at Cannes and Mentone in March 1866.

My correspondence with M. Millière, who, after trying various parts of the South of France, ultimately settled upon Cannes as his winter residence, and letters I received from my friend the Rev. Henry Burney during his visit to Mentone in the winter of 1864-65, had kept up in me a constant desire again to revisit the sunny South; and at length, in the spring of 1866, I was able to put my long cherished plan in execution.

I left home on Monday the 5th of March, slept at Lyons on Wednesday night, and on Thursday, March 8th, proceeded to Marseilles. On my way thither I first noticed olive trees and *Arundo donax* near Orange. The following day I proceeded to Cannes, arriving there just at sunset, the Estrelles hills standing out conspicuously against the glowing western sky. I remained only three days at Cannes, and proceeded on the 13th of March to Mentone, where I remained till the 28th of March.

The Tineina collected or observed during this period were as follows:—

Hyponomeuta egregiellus.
Prays oleellus.
Depressaria atomella.
Gelechia ——— ?
G. gypsophilæ.
G. cisti.
G. biguttella.
G. anthyllidella.
Butalis dorycniella.
Acrolepia vesperella.

Coleophora pyrrhulipennella.
C. congeriella.
C. cælebipennella.
C. chamædryella.
Bedellia somnulentella.
Stagmatophora Grabowiella.
Elachista gleichenella.
Tischeria angusticollella.
T. marginea.

T. complanella.
Lithocolletis Messaniella.
Phyllobrostis daphneella.
Bucculatrix lavaterella.
Nepticula aurella.

Larva on *Lavandula stœchas*
  (*Œcophora lavandulæ?*)
Larva on rosemary.

Hyponomeuta egregiellus, Duponchel. (See *ante*, p. 172.) Monsieur Millière, on the occasion of my calling on him the day after my arrival at Cannes, showed me some pretty heath-feeding larvæ, which proved to be those of this species; on the 11th of March he took me to a locality where the larvæ occurred amongst the *Erica scoparia*, and I had then an opportunity of studying their habits. They are not exactly gregarious, but several generally occur on one plant; they spin slight webs in the upper twigs of the plant, and in these webs form thicker tubes of silk in which they reside. The full-fed larva spins its cocoon in its last habitation, and the perfect insects made their appearance from the 19th of April to the 5th of May.

The adult larva is above 6 lines long, bluish black above with an ochreous line on each side of the slender blue-black dorsal line; spiracular line whitish ochreous, more yellowish on the anterior half of each segment; spots black; head tawny, inclining to ferruginous; second segment blackish, with a central whitish line; belly grey. The younger larvæ appear darker, the pale lines on the back being less distinct and often interrupted.

A careful scrutiny of these insects shows that they combine the characters of the genera *Hyponomeuta* and *Swammerdamia*: the head is smooth in front; on the hinder part of the head there is indeed a slight tuft of a brownish ochreous, but this has a very different appearance from the woolly-looking heads of a *Swammerdamia*; the palpi, also, are much more slender than in *Swammerdamia* and more pointed, thus resembling *Hyponomeuta*: on the other hand the form of the wings and their neuration is completely that of *Swammerdamia*; the secondary cell is not formed in the anterior wings, and in the posterior wings the costal cell terminates before the middle of the wing.

The dense glossy scaling of the anterior wings reminds one more of *Hyponomeuta*.

Looking to the tendency to a rough head in *H. stanneellus*, Thunberg, and to the almost gregarious habit of the larva of *S. griseocapitella*, Stainton, we cannot ignore the fact that neither of the genera *Hyponomeuta* or *Swammerdamia* consists of species perfectly agreeing in all their characters; and the combination of characters which we find in *H. egregiellus* would seem to indicate that it may be necessary to unite *Swammerdamia* and *Hyponomeuta* as one genus. Formerly, no doubt, the plan would have been to create a new genus for the reception of *egregiellus*, and to place it between *Swammerdamia* and *Hyponomeuta*; but the philosophy of the present day is opposed to such a step, and the next discoveries made in this group of insects will probably disclose other forms between *Swammerdamia* and *Hyponomeuta*, but not possessing characters perfectly identical with those of *egregiellus*.

Prays oleellus, Boyer de Fonscolombe. I found the young mining larvæ of this species on the 12th of March, at the anemone-grounds at Mouans, near Cannes. They were then extremely small, little more than a line in length, of a pale olive-green, with the dorsal vessel a little darker; the head is brown-black; and there is an elongated brownish spot on the posterior half of the second segment; the anal segment has a small black plate; they mine short galleries or small blotches, ejecting the excrement through a small hole on the underside of the mine. I believe all that I collected in the leaf-mining stage died.

I have to thank Herr Kaltenbach, of Aix-la-Chapelle, for the suggestion that this insect belongs to the genus *Prays* and has similar habits to *P. Curtisellus*.

When the larvæ of *Curtisellus*, which mine the leaves of the ash in October, quit the leaves, which naturally they do before they fall, they burrow under the bark of the twigs, and then in the spring are ready to attack the young shoots as soon as they begin to expand. I have every reason to believe that the larvæ of *Prays oleellus* in like manner quit the leaves to burrow under the bark of the twigs, and as soon as the young, tender, pale yellowish-green leaves begin to develop, the larva attacks them, being then of a whitish green, almost exactly resembling these young olive-leaves. The adult larva is 3½ lines long, whitish green, slightly darker on the back, especially at the place of the subdorsal lines; the head is pale yellowish brown; the second segment is rather more whitish than the ground-colour, with two dark brown spots above of rather irregular form. It betrays its presence amongst the young leaves by its web and "Frass."

The larva is full-fed at the end of March or beginning of April, and spins a slender open cocoon very similar to that of *Curtisellus*; in two or three weeks' time the perfect insects make their appearance, but I have never remained late enough in the South to see the imago at large. The insect varies considerably in its markings; and one specimen which I bred is almost of a uniform grey, with the dark markings absent, thus reminding one of the dark variety of *Curtisellus*. (See Nat. Hist. Tineina, vol. xi. p. 22, pl. 1. fig. 2.)

Depressaria atomella, S. V. At Mentone, from the 15th to the 20th March, I collected several larvæ of a *Depressaria* on the spiny broom, *Calycotome spinosa*, and hoped to breed from them something new; the seven specimens, however, which I bred were all the ordinary *D. atomella*.

Gelechia ——? A single specimen of a small obscure species taken flying amongst grass on the 23rd of March, at Mentone, near the Annunziata. It reminds one somewhat of *Gelechia murinella*, but seems destitute of any definite markings, except the usual three black spots; the specimen is serviceable only as an intimation of something to be looked for, as I believe it accords with no known species; it would be quite impossible from this solitary example to make a description which would be of any value*.

Gelechia gypsophilæ, n. sp. On the 26th of March, whilst sauntering along the ascent of Monte Grosso at Mentone, I chanced to notice a small pod-like gall on some low plant, and on opening it found to my surprise a larva evidently Lepidopterous. I then searched and found other similar pod-like galls. The plant on which they occurred was determined for me by my friend Mr. J. T. Moggridge as *Gypsophila saxifraga*, L. On the 22nd of March I collected some more of these galls and found one tuft of the plant quite full of them. Three days later, however, I found them far more plentifully along a rocky path leading to the Gorbio valley, and collected more than a hundred, and took several large tufts of the plant with roots to enable me to rear the larva when I reached home. I had expected these larvæ would feed up inside the galls and would probably assume the pupa state there; but towards the middle of April I found, to my dismay, that most of the larvæ were crawling about outside the galls; and they then fed sparingly on the young shoots of the growing plants. By the end of the month some had evidently spun cocoons on the surface of the ground; but all through the month of May not a single specimen of the imago made its appearance, and I was beginning to fear that all had miscarried, when the first moth appeared on the 3rd of June; another followed the next day, and thereafter they came out rapidly up to the 17th of June, by which time I had reared upwards of thirty specimens.

Gypsophila being a genus of the *Caryophyllaceæ*, I had expected that the moth would prove to be a *Gelechia* of the group attached to that Natural Order of Plants; one species in that group, *cauligenella*, Schmid, being already known to inhabit, when in the larva-state, gall-like swellings in the stems of *Silene nutans*. I was not disappointed, the perfect insects being very closely related to *leucomelanella*, from which, however, they differ in their smaller size (exp. al. 4–5 lin.), more distinct pale central blotch of the anterior wings, and generally by the paler basal portion of the anterior wings; the opposite spots are placed rather more perpendicularly than in *leucomelanella*. These differences, however, are so slight that a large specimen of *gypsophilæ* caught on the wing would not be easily distinguished from a captured *leucomelanella*.

The larva is 3 lines long, of a dull yellowish green, the dorsal vessel a little darker; the head is black; the second segment bears a brown-black plate divided by a slender central line; the anal segment has no dark plate.

* When looking through the collection of the Museum at Vienna, I saw a specimen of Mann's *Gelechia petiginella* from the Tyrol. It reminded me of my Mentone capture.

The galls are at first of a fresh healthy green colour, but afterwards change to a pale brown, and the tip has frequently rather a withered appearance. The excrement of the larva is deposited at that end; in the gall which I opened the head of the larva was downwards.

Gelechia cisti, n. sp.

Exp. al. 5–6 lin. Head dark grey; face whitish grey. Palpi with the second joint internally whitish grey (except the end, which is grey), externally grey, with two or three dark grey spots, terminal joint grey, with the base, a central ring, and the tip dark grey. Antennæ dark grey.

Anterior wings dark slaty grey, with three tufts of tawny grey scales near the inner margin; the first (and largest) before the middle, the second in the middle, the third beyond the middle; an oblique black streak arises on the costa near the base and terminates at the first tuft, and a fainter oblique dark streak proceeds from near the middle of the costa; on the costa, beyond the middle, is a small blackish spot, below which are two black spots at the end of the discoidal cell, edged externally with pale grey; a little beyond them a slender black streak proceeds to the apex of the wing; the apex of the costa and hinder margin are faintly mottled with darker grey, cilia grey.

Posterior wings pale grey, darker towards the hind margin, with the cilia fuscous.

This is *closely* allied to *G. sequax*, Haworth; but the head and palpi are much darker, and the anterior wings are darker, greyer, without the pale fasciæ; the first tuft also appears much larger, and the apical marginal spots are less distinctly expressed.

I reared two specimens of this species, from larvæ collected by Monsieur Millière on *Cistus salvifolius* at Cannes in March 1866, and which he forwarded to me at Mentone; the perfect insects made their appearance June 25th. Last summer Monsieur Millière sent me a specimen bred from *Cistus albidus*, in which the raised tufts, especially that nearest the base of the wing, have rather a ferruginous tinge.

The larva is from 3–4 lines long; of a pale yellowish green, with the dorsal vessel rather greyish; the head is yellowish brown; the second segment is also yellowish brown, but rather darker posteriorly; the spots are small and grey; the anal segment is posteriorly pale yellowish brown.

It unites two or three leaves together and eats half the thickness, thus discolouring them; it conceals itself within a silky tube, which is also covered with excrement. Sometimes it feeds in the calyx of the bud.

Gelechia biguttella, H.-S. Of this species I reared four, from larvæ or pupæ collected in *Dorycnium hirtum* and *D. suffruticosum* at Mentone in March. I believe the larvæ that I found had long ceased feeding and were probably bleached, thus not showing their characteristic colours; therefore I do not describe the larva. They generally drew several of the leaves of the plant towards the stem, so as to form a sort of tubular habitation; and amongst them it lived in a web coated externally with its excrement. The perfect insects appeared April 26th and 29th, May 10th and June 1st. This species, though readily distinguished from *G. anthyllidella*, Hb., by the whiter and more perpendicularly placed opposite spots, comes very close to *G. albipalpella*, H.-S., which we breed from *Genista anglica*; but *G. biguttella* is rather larger, with broader anterior wings, and the three typical spots are perceptible, though not very conspicuous; that on the fold is generally followed by a pale scale, and the second discoidal spot is evidently lower down (further from the costa) than the first.

Gelechia anthyllidella, Hb. I bred one specimen of this on the 11th of May, from a larva found at Mentone on the 20th of March between the folded leaves of *Psoralea bituminosa*. Monsieur Millière, from having found the larva on a plant of such a peculiar odour, had supposed it must be new, and had described the insect as *G. psoralella* (see *ante*, p. 184); this led me specially to hunt on the *Psoralea* for the larva.

Butalis dorycniella, Millière (see *ante*, p. 187), I found this larva not uncommon at Mentone, March 17th to 23rd, principally on *Dorycnium hirtum*, though sometimes on *D. suffruticosum*. It draws together several leaves, which it gnaws and discolours, and amongst them it forms a tight-fitting silken tube, in which it secretes itself, and from which it is no easy matter to dislodge it. From its many-striped appearance it is at once recognized as a *Butalis* larva; but I did not succeed in rearing a single specimen of the imago.

The larva I have thus described:—

Length 6 lines; pale grey-green, with numerous darker longitudinal lines and a whitish grey spiracular line; head black (the adult larva shows two white lines forming an inverted V on the face); second segment black, with the anterior edge white and a central line whitish; on the anal segment there is a small black plate.

Acrolepia vesperella, Z. (see *ante*, pp. 64 & 81, also *Acrolepia smilaxella*, p. 189). When at Cannes, Monsieur Millière had called my attention to the marks on the leaves of the *Smilax aspera* caused by the larva of his *Acrolepia smilaxella*, and I kept constantly on the look-out for these larvæ; but I had been at Mentone several days before I found the first, on the 18th of March; I then found them more freely on the 21st, on the slope of a hill near the Cabrolles valley.

The larva at first makes small clean mines in the leaves, the excrement being ejected through a hole on the underside of the leaf; it afterwards gnaws the leaves half through from the underside and then forms a covering for itself of "Frass" and web. When fullfed it spins a rather firm brown cocoon, at one end of which an open slit is left, through which the cast skin of the larva is eventually ejected.

The larva I have thus described:—

Length 3 lines; dull greenish grey, the dorsal vessel darker, the sides paler; head pale yellowish brown; second segment of the same colour, with two transverse rows of small black spots; the spots on the third and fourth segments are distinctly perceptible, but not those on the other segments.

Sometimes this larva has a very handsome appearance, showing deep-red subdorsal stripes.

I bred the perfect insects from April 16th to 26th.

Coleophora pyrrhulipennella, Zeller. When collecting with Monsieur Millière at Cannes on the 11th of March, I found several cases on *Erica scoparia*, which I believe were referable to this species. I did not, however, rear the imago.

Coleophora congeriella, Staudinger (see *ante*, p. 159). The larvæ of this species were by no means scarce, principally on *Dorycnium suffruticosum*, but also occasionally on *D. hirtum*; I found them at Cannes March 10th, and at Mentone March 14th to 23rd; on the last date, up the Cabrolles valley, they were very plentiful. I did not, however, succeed in rearing a single specimen of the imago.

The case is formed of pieces of mined leaf successively added; the tail part of the case turns over on the underside and gives the creature rather an Armadillo look.

Coleophora cœlebipennella, Zeller. I found three larvæ on *Helichrysum stœchas* at Mentone on the 21st of March, which I believe, from their cases, to have been this species. I did not, however, rear the imago.

Coleophora chamædryella, Bruand. I repeatedly found larvæ on the *Teucrium chamædrys* at Mentone March 14th to 26th, which I believe, from their cases, should be referred to this species. I did not, however, rear any.

Bedellia somnulentella, Zeller. The mines of the larva of this species were very plentiful in the leaves of *Convolvulus althæoides* at Mentone; and I also found a few in leaves of *C. cantabrica* near

Pont St. Louis on the 17th of March. I bred the perfect insects April 7th to 9th.

Stagmatophora Grabowiella, Staudinger (see *ante*, pp. 137, 142 & 157). I collected larvæ of this species at Cannes March 11th, and at Mentone March 15th, but on this occasion did not succeed in rearing any.

The larva feeds on the shoots of *Lavandula stœchas*, making holes in the leaves and mining them, bleaching the tips like a *Coleophora*-larva; frequently it draws them together and amongst them it forms a black case-like habitation of its own excrement. This case seems gradually enlarged and is open at the upper end. The larva I have thus described:—

Length 3 lines; pale green or, rather, pale yellowish, with dull green dorsal vessel; head pale brown; second segment pale yellowish, with a pale brown plate divided down the centre.

Elachista gleichenella, Fabricius. I found several larvæ of an *Elachista* in the leaves of *Carex basilaris* at Mentone March 22nd, in the "Primrose Valley." I did not happen to rear any of these; but the following season, from larvæ collected in the same locality and on the same plant, I bred a specimen of *E. gleichenella*.

Tischeria angusticollella, Zeller. I found the mines of this species in the leaves of *Rosa sempervirens* at Mentone, but did not rear the imago. I also noticed mines of *T. marginea*, Haw., in bramble-leaves, and *T. complanella*, Hb., in oak-leaves.

Lithocolletis Messaniella, Zeller. I collected many mined leaves of *Quercus ilex* at Cannes on the 10th of March, and bred *L. Messaniella* on the 21st. I had hoped to have bred some more interesting species.

Phyllobrostis daphneella, Staudinger (see *ante*, p. 163). The larva of this little species was not uncommon, mining the leaves of *Daphne gnidium*. I first met with it at Cannes March 10th and 11th, and at Mentone March 23rd and 25th. Thinking at the time that it was the *P. subdaphneella*, of which I had already received larvæ from Munich, I neglected to describe it. The perfect insects made their appearance April 27th to 29th.

Bucculatrix lavaterella, Millière (see *ante*, p. 193). I captured a single specimen of this species at Mentone on the 23rd March, flying amongst the herbage in the afternoon, but did not recognize it at the time. On the 27th March I spent some time hunting amongst *Lavatera maritima* at Pont St. Louis, and observed indications of some gnawing on the leaves, but it appeared more like the work of a *Haltica* than of a *Bucculatrix*-larva.

Nepticula aurella, Fabricius. I observed at Mentone mines in the bramble-leaves, which I presume were referable to this species.

I must further mention two larvæ which I met with, but which I have not been able to determine.

A dull brown larva feeding in the dry heads of *Lavandula stœchas*, which it attaches to the fresh shoots and burrows between them. I have thus described it:—

Length 3-3½ lines. Dull brown; the head and second segment shining dark brown; the anal segment with a dark brown plate.

I met with this at Cannes March 11th, and at Mentone March 20th. When I left home for Switzerland, on the 11th July, nothing had emerged in the box containing these larvæ; when I returned home on the 10th of August I found an obscure dead moth, partially injured by the ravages of *Psocus*. I however relaxed it and set it out, and rather suspect that it may be Mann's *Œcophora lavandulæ* (see *ante*, pp. 117 & 122).

A yellowish larva mining the leaves of rosemary (*Rosmarinus officinalis*); the mined leaves become yellowish brown and rather inflated; some excrement is protruded through a hole on the underside of the leaf, generally at the end of the mine nearest the foot-stalk.

The larva I have thus described:—

Length 2 lines; yellowish, the incisions between the segments rather paler; the head dark brown; the second segment with a brown plate above; the anal segment with a small pale grey plate; all the legs (16) pale yellowish. The larva is rather active.

I met with these on the 27th March, the day before I left Mentone, on the rocks above Pont St. Louis, on the Italian side.

I did not succeed in rearing anything from them.

This seems also the proper place to mention two species of which I received the larvæ from Cannes and Mentone in November 1866.

Gracilaria scalariella, Zeller (see *ante*, pp. 66 & 82). On the 14th of November I wrote to Monsieur Millière asking for some of the larvæ of this species; and on the 21st of that month he sent me a box containing the blotched leaves of the *Echium vulgare* mined by the larva of *G. scalariella*, with the remark that it was already getting rather late for them. The perfect insects made their appearance during the month of December.

Zelleria oleastrella, Millière (his *Tinea oleastrella*, see *ante*, p. 191). I was particularly anxious to get this insect, to ascertain to what genus it should be referred; and having asked Mr. J. T. Moggridge (so well known to botanists by his work on the Flora of Mentone) to search on the olive-trees in autumn for this and one or two other species which were not obtainable in the spring months, I received from him on the 23rd November and 6th December two of the desired larvæ, which formed slight webs amongst the olive-leaves, of which they gnawed the underside.

This larva I have thus described:—

Length 4½ lines; elongate, slender; dark olive-green on the back, whitish on the sides; the dorsal vessel darker; the spots white; the head pale brown, and the second segment pale brownish green.

Very active, with a tremulous motion of the anterior part of the body.

These larvæ fed up well and spun thick white cocoons, like those of *Argyresthia* and *Swammerdamia*; and towards the end of January the perfect insects appeared.

I was at first uncertain to what genus to refer them; but having since had an opportunity of studying two other specimens, I have decided (for the present at least) to place them in the genus *Zelleria*: the palpi are rather thicker and rougher than in *Z. fasciapennella*, but that species itself differs slightly in that very character from *Z. hepariella*.

The form of the anterior wings is peculiar: they are narrower than in *Z. fasciapennella* and *Z. saxifragæ*, but scarcely as subfalcate as in the last-named species; but the *concave* outline of the cilia of the hind margin gives a subfalcate appearance.

The insect is one of those obscure, ill-defined creatures which almost defy recognizable description. The anterior wings are pale grey, powdered with darker (in well-marked specimens with numerous dark grey dots), with two faint ochreous clouds near the base; the most conspicuous mark is a rather triangular black spot before the middle of the inner margin, preceded by some whitish scales; at the end of the discoidal cell is a smaller black spot, above which the costa, which there appears a little excavated, is whitish, followed directly afterwards by a small dark grey costal spot.

The size of my specimens varies from exp. al. $6-7\frac{1}{2}$ lines; it is possible that the small specimens have been dwarfed from the larvæ feeding up in captivity. (See also Nat. Hist. Tineina, vol. xi. p. 108, pl. 3. fig. 2.)

Section III.

Tineina observed at Cannes and Mentone in February and March 1867.

My second visit to Cannes and Mentone was in February and March 1867. Arriving at Cannes February 27th, I remained there till the 13th March, and then proceeded to Mentone, where I continued till the 27th March, thus dividing my time very equally, giving a fortnight to each place.

As my total stay in the South was thus about ten days longer than in the previous year, and as I had the advantage of having already explored a number of localities, and made a personal acquaintance with the Mediterranean flora, I ought to have brought home a much larger result than was actually the case; it will be seen from the following list that I met with most of the species I had found the previous year, and also met with several others I had not previously noticed:—

Hyponomeuta egregiellus.   *D. atomella.*
Prays oleellus.   *D. nodiflorella.*
Depressaria rutana.   *Gelechia figulella.*

G. halymella.
G. ———? on *Artemisia maritima.*
G. gypsophilæ.
G. provinciella.
G. cisti.
G. ———? on *Teucrium polium.*
Ypsolophus trinotellus.
Y. verbascellus.
Dasycera sulphurella.
Butalis senescens.
B. dorycniella.
Acrolepia solidaginis.
A. vesperella.
A. ———? on *Helichrysum stœchas.*
Perittia? on *Lonicera implexa.*
Zelleria phillyrella.
Gracilaria auroguttella.
Coleophora pyrrhulipennella.
C. congeriella.
C. calycotomella.
Bedellia somnulentella.
Stagmatophora Grabowiella.
Urodela cisticolella.
Elachista gleichenella.
E. chrysodesmella.
E. pollinariella.
Lithocolletis Messaniella.
L. trifasciella.
Phyllobrostis daphneella.
Nepticula suberivora.
N. catharticella?
N. cryptella.
N. suberis.
N. euphorbiella.
N. ———, on *Cistus Monspeliensis.*

Hyponomeuta egregiellus, Duponchel. I collected the larva of this very freely at Cannes on *Erica scoparia.* I may mention here that M. Berce met with the insect at Fontainebleau in 1857, and that when visiting the forest there with him on the 1st April 1867 we found the larvæ of this species extremely plentiful on *Erica cinerea.* (See Ent. Annual, 1868, p. 135.)

Prays oleellus, Boyer. The small larvæ were abundant as usual, but the more adult larvæ were not as forward as in the previous season. Some that I brought home seemed likely to perish for want of food; so I offered them young shoots of privet, on which they fed up. Two specimens of the imago were reared May 1st and 3rd from the larvæ which had developed on privet.

Depressaria rutana, Fabricius. (See *ante,* p. 61, *D. retiferella.*) On the 11th March I visited with M. Millière the Ile Ste.-Marguerite near Cannes, where he expected we should find the larvæ of this species in tolerable plenty; however, though the *Ruta angustifolia* grew in great profusion, and though we spent some time in hunting amongst and beating this plant, we only obtained a single larva of this interesting species.

On the 14th of March, at Mentone, I found one small larva of *D. rutana* on the rocky slope above Pont St. Louis.

On the 21st of March I visited Monaco, and in the gardens of the promontory there I found several plants of *Ruta angustifolia* which were attacked by these larvæ, of which I collected between twenty and thirty; from these I succeeded in rearing a dozen specimens of the imago, which appeared from May 4th to May 16th.

The larva rolls up tubularly a small portion of a leaf of *Ruta,* just as the larvæ of *applana* treat the Umbelliferæ, and those of *arenella* the Compositæ; and its habitations are easily recognized by the experienced eye, even if the larva has quitted the plant.

I have thus described it:—

Length 9 lines; green, dorsal vessel slightly darker (the full-grown larvæ show indications of a slightly darker subdorsal line); spots small, black, in pale green rings; head black; anterior edge of second segment reddish brown; posteriorly this segment bears two large black lunate plates, scarcely divided in the centre; anal segment pale green; anterior legs yellowish.

A younger larva, about 2 lines long, was yellowish-green, with the head black; the second segment reddish brown-black, and the anterior legs black.

Before dispersing my series of bred specimens, I made the following description of the imago:—

Exp. al. 10–11 lin. Head, face, and thorax brownish grey, sometimes almost reddish brown; palpi with the second joint externally brownish, or reddish brown, internally paler, terminal joint yellowish, with two faint brownish spots. Antennæ fuscous, rather more than half the length of the anterior wings.

Anterior wings brownish grey, varying slightly in intensity, and sometimes with a reddish tinge, with two conspicuous black spots on the disk before the middle; the upper one, rather anterior to the lower one, is round; the lower one is elongate; from it proceeds a slender yellow streak nearly to the hind margin; beyond the middle it shows a tendency to form a yellow spot, immediately after which in some specimens it is slightly interrupted; a similar slender yellow streak runs along the fold from near the base to about the middle of the wing, and in some few specimens a yellow streak runs a little way along the subcostal nervure; there is also a slender yellow streak along the inner margin to the anal angle, more distinct in some specimens than others.

But the most striking feature of the insect is furnished by the great number of short transverse pale streaks, which in those specimens with the darkest ground-colour are extremely conspicuous. It is very possible that this character is easily lost by specimens which have been long on the wing, as I find that in one of my bred specimens, which had slightly damaged itself amongst the *débris* of *Ruta* at the bottom of the box, these transverse markings have almost disappeared; in one solitary uninjured specimen they are extremely faint.

In some specimens a faintly indicated darker cloud crosses the wing obliquely (as in *angelicella*) beyond the middle; the palest portion of the wing faintly indicates the position of the pale hinder fascia; form of the hind margin nearly as in *D. atomella*; cilia rather redder than the ground-colour of the wing.

Posterior wings pale grey, with greyish-ochreous cilia.

Depressaria atomella, S. V. I noticed the larvæ of this species at Cannes on the *Calycotome spinosa*, February 28th.

Depressaria nodiflorella, Millière. (See *ante*, p. 175.) When visiting the Ile Ste.-Marguerite, near Cannes, on the 11th March, one of my great desires was to find some of the larvæ of the *Depressaria* which feeds on that magnificent Umbellifer, *Ferula communis*, which, though so plentiful on that island, has not been detected on the mainland near Cannes. Of the three species of *Depressaria* attached to *Ferula* which M. Millière has met with at Hyères, only *nodiflorella* has, up to the present time, been noticed at the Ile Ste.-Marguerite; and for this we were almost too early.

Monsieur Millière soon showed me the habit of the larva uniting several of the linear leaflets together with a slight web, and I collected several of them; only one, however, was of a respectable size, and I found that the very small larvæ still feeding within the leaves, as miners, were far the most plentiful.

The bulk of these larvæ, however, died before attaining the pupa-state, and I only had the pleasure of rearing one specimen of the imago, which appeared on the 28th of April.

The larva I have thus described:—

Length 7–8 lines; pale green, with the slender dorsal and broader subdorsal lines dark green; the subdorsal lines are rather more distinct than the dorsal line; head pale yellowish brown; the second segment anteriorly yellowish, posteriorly green, with a small curved black mark on each side; legs pale green.

The young mining larva, 2⅓ lines in length, has the head black, and a black plate on the second segment; the subdorsal lines at that age are not developed.

The perfect insect reminds one much of *D. rotundella*, but is rather larger (exp. al. 9 lin., whereas *rotundella* is only 8 lin.); the anterior wings are broader, and posteriorly suffused with longitudinal grey streaks. *Nodiflorella* shows four distinct black spots, the first just below the subcostal nervure, the second a little beyond it on the disk, and the third and fourth also on the disk, in a line with the second. I have compared one of Professor Zeller's Sicilian specimens of *D. peloritanella* both with *nodiflorella* and *rotundella*, and still hold it identical with the last-named species.

Gelechia figulella, Staudinger. (See *ante*, p. 149.) Of this species I had the good fortune to breed four specimens, on the 6th, 8th, 10th, and 27th of April. The last specimen was bred from a larva found on the 28th of February in the sand at the roots of some plants of *Silene nicæensis*, in a sandy wood near the sea to the east of Cannes.

This larva spun up the very day I described it, and may therefore be assumed to have lost some of its characteristic colouring. I have described it thus:—

Length nearly 6 lines; whitish ochreous; the head pale brown, with the mouth darker; the second segment with a dark brown semicrescent on each side; dorsal line slender, reddish ochreous; subdorsal lines dark brown, paler anteriorly; spots minute, black; anal segment glassy.

As this larva did not feed after I found it, I cannot say what is its food-plant, unless it fed on the *Silene nicæensis*, at the roots of which it was found. I cannot call to mind that there was any moss where I found it; the sand was perfectly loose and shifting.

The other three specimens were bred from sand cocoons found at the same time. (See Ent. Annual, 1868, p. 139.)

The perfect insect, as Staudinger truly remarks, comes very near to *G. terrella*, but is rather smaller and a neater-looking insect; the anterior wings are rather more pointed, and have a faint rosy tinge.

Gelechia halymella, Millière. (See *ante*, p. 181.) Of this I bred three specimens, April 12th, 30th, and May 1st, from larvæ collected at Cannes March 10th on *Atriplex halymus*. This *Atriplex* is of such a shrubby growth that one garden on the sandy ground near the sea is hedged round with it. The larva of the *Gelechia* unites the terminal leaves, and eats out the hearts of the shoots, burrowing into one of the leathery leaves, which it bleaches; it sometimes assumes the pupa-state between the united leaves. The larva, from its coloration, is evidently allied to the group of *G. atriplicella*. I have thus described it:—

Length 4 lines; pale green, with reddish-green dorsal, subdorsal, and sub-subdorsal lines, the two latter rather wavy; head black; second segment black, third segment brown.

A younger larva scarcely showed any trace of the reddish lines.

The imago may be readily distinguished from *G. obsoletella*, F. v. R., by its yellower colour: it comes very close to *G. salinella*, Z. (see *ante*, pp. 10 & 37), of which, through the kindness of Professor Zeller, I possess a Sicilian specimen; but I should not like to pronounce them identical without seeing a good series of both species. Judging from the few specimens of *halymella* which I have seen, there is a conspicuous oblique grey streak from the costa, a little before the middle, of which in *salinella* the traces are much fainter; but it must be borne in mind that we are comparing bred specimens of *halymella* with caught specimens of *salinella*.

Here I may mention a young larva which I found on the coast to the east of Cannes on the 9th March, mining the leaflets of *Artemisia maritima*: from its lively habit, it should probably be referred to the genus *Gelechia*; but as the young larvæ which I collected all died, I am uncertain what the imago really would have been. The larva I have thus described:—

Length barely 2 lines; yellowish green, anteriorly paler, with a dull red dorsal line, and two rows of reddish spots on each side forming interrupted lines; head yellowish; the second segment with a yellowish-brown plate, with two dark spots at its hinder edge; anal segment pale yellowish; spots small, black.

It mines the leaflets of the *Artemisia maritima*, and bleaches them; it also draws several together.

Dr. Staudinger bred his *Gelechia disjectella* from larvæ which fed on the shoots of *Artemisia Barrelieri* (see *ante*, p. 149).

Gelechia gypsophilæ, Stainton. At Mentone I again collected a number of the galls formed by the larvæ of this species, and bred the perfect insects from May 19th to June 9th. When at Cannes I looked about for the *Gypsophila saxifraga*, wishing to introduce Monsieur Millière to this interesting larva; but I did not see any of the plant there: since then I have noticed the plant on the Lido, near Venice, and near Ratisbon.

Gelechia provinciella, n. sp., closely allied to *G. marmorea*, but larger, anterior wings broader, and the markings duller; the costal hinder spot is anterior to the dorsal spot, and tends to form with it an angulated fascia; in *G. marmorea* "the costal spot is rather posterior to the dorsal spot." (See Nat. Hist. Tineina, vol. x. pp. 148, 149.)

Of this I bred a nice series from larvæ and sand-cocoons collected at the roots of *Silene nicæensis* in a sandy wood near the coast, east of Cannes, on the 28th of February. The *Silene* was in many places eaten nearly level with the sand, the young shoots having evidently been found highly palatable by some larvæ. By searching amongst the loose sand at the roots of these plants Monsieur Millière and I soon collected a considerable number of the larvæ, which rather reminded me of the larva of *G. marmorea*; and as we also found sand-cocoons constructed similarly to the cocoons of that species, I did not feel confident that the insect would prove distinct from *G. marmorea*; the characters, however, above given, especially the form and position of the costal hinder spot, abundantly distinguish it.

It was whilst collecting these larvæ that we met with the larva of *Gelechia figulella*, Staudinger, already mentioned.

The larva of *Gelechia provinciella* I have thus described:—

Length $4\frac{1}{2}$ lines; greenish, with faint reddish-green dorsal and subdorsal lines; the subdorsal lines are scarcely quite continuous; head shining black; the second segment with a large shining black plate; anal segment with a small black plate.

This eats the leaves of *Silene nicæensis*, burying itself in the sand, where it forms sand tubes like *G. marmorea*, and forms sand cocoons in which to change to the pupa-state.

The perfect insects appeared from April 6th to May 5th; they may be briefly described thus:—

Exp. al. 6 lin. (My smallest specimen is about $5\frac{1}{2}$ lines, but all the others are very equal in size.) Anterior wings greyish brown, with the inner margin paler, and with three conspicuous black marks:—first, a small black spot above the fold, near the base; secondly, a blotch on the disk before the middle; and, thirdly, a blotch on the disk beyond the middle; the space between these two is generally the palest portion of the wing, though in it we often see some dark scales along the fold; of the hinder opposite spots the dorsal spot is the palest and most conspicuous, the costal spot is more suffused, and, as above mentioned, is anterior to the dorsal spot, with which it shows a tendency to form an angulated fascia.

Gelechia cisti, Stainton (see *ante*, p. 211). I collected several of the young larvæ of this species at Cannes on the 5th and 6th of

March; but they were then very small, and I did not rear any to the perfect state.

Gelechia biguttella, Herrich-Schäffer. Of this I bred five specimens, March 15th to May 1st, from larvæ or pupæ collected on *Dorycnium hirtum* at Cannes March 9th, and Mentone March 20th.

Gelechia anthyllidella, Hübner. I collected several of these larvæ on a small *Lotus* at Cannes March 9th; Monsieur Millière recognized them as the larvæ of his *psoralella*, though they were not on the *Psoralea bituminosa*.

Here I should perhaps mention a larva, probably a *Gelechia*, which I met with at Mentone on the 20th and 25th of March on *Teucrium polium*, and to which my attention was called by Mr. J. T. Moggridge—who first directed my attention to the plant, and then to specimens of it which had the leaves drawn together. I collected many of these larvæ, and kept them well supplied with food for some time, but failed in rearing any, nor do I believe that any attained the pupa-state.

This larva I have thus described :—

Length 3 lines; dull grey-green; spots indistinctly glassy; head and second segment black; anal segment with a dark grey plate; anterior legs black (legs 16).

It draws the leaves of the *Teucrium polium* together, and bleaches them by mining them; it lives between the leaves, in a brownish case-like dwelling, formed of excrement.

Ypsolophus trinotellus, H.-S. Of this species I had the good fortune to rear five specimens from larvæ handed to me at Mentone on the 18th of March by Mr. J. T. Moggridge, which, to his great disgust, were devouring the seeds of wild wallflower (*Cheiranthus cheiri*) at Dolce Acqua.

The larva I have thus described :—

Length 3 lines; dull red; head black; second segment rather darker red, and with a subcutaneous grey mark of irregular form.

These larvæ did not change to the pupa-state for some time; and the moths made their appearance June 30th, July 2nd, and July 15th.

As I have elsewhere mentioned (Ent. Annual, 1868, p. 143), the perfect insect when sitting had a peculiar posture, the anterior portion of the body being slightly raised, something like the position of *Gelechia Mouffetella* when at rest.

Ypsolophus verbascellus, S. V. The larvæ of this species were very common at Cannes and Mentone in March, on *Verbascum*. Not caring about the species, I only collected a few, and bred one moth April 26th.

Dasycera sulphurella, Fabricius. I observed a specimen of this insect on the wing at Mentone, towards Cape Martin, on the 23rd of March.

Butalis senescens, Stainton. On the 26th of March, a bright sunny day, I visited a rocky place to the west of Mentone (near the Gorbio valley); the scene was enlivened by the presence of *Papilio Machaon* and *Podalirius, Colias edusa*, and *Thecla rubi*; and, flying in the hot sunshine, I met with a single male specimen of a *Butalis* in good condition, and which, as far as one can judge from a solitary capture, I am disposed to refer to *B. senescens*.

Butalis dorycniella, Millière (see ante, pp. 187 & 212). I again met with the larvæ of this species at Mentone on the 20th and 23rd of March, on *Dorycnium hirtum*, but again failed to breed the imago.

Acrolepia solidaginis, Staudinger (see ante, p. 157). I bred five specimens of this insect, April 12th to 22nd, from larvæ collected at Mentone on the 20th of March; they were mining the leaves of *Conyza squarrosa*, forming large brown blotches, in which the excrement was irregularly scattered.

The larva I have thus described :—

Length 4½ lines; pale green; the dorsal vessel dark green; head yellowish brown, with the mouth and sides darker; the second segment pale yellowish brown.

At the time I found these larvæ I scarcely expected they would produce anything different from the ordinary *granitella*; but all the specimens I bred agree exactly with an Andalusian specimen I have from Dr. Staudinger; the anterior wings are perceptibly darker than in *granitella*, and, I fancy, also broader; and the dark spot on the inner margin between the two pale spots has a distinctly oblique position; in the ordinary *granitella* it has almost invariably a perpendicular position.

Future observations must establish whether *solidaginis* is really a good species.

Acrolepia vesperella, Zeller (see ante, pp. 64, 81, & 213). I collected the larvæ of this species at Cannes and Mentone, March 1st to 16th. When at the Ile Ste.-Marguerite on the 11th of March I saw two of the perfect insects on the wing; but the flora and fauna of that island are often a fortnight earlier than those of the mainland. In one locality at Mentone, which I had previously noticed as a successful corner for finding these larvæ, I collected with the aid of my niece forty larvæ in the afternoon of March 16th.

The perfect insects appeared with me from April 6th to 29th.

Perhaps I should here mention a larva which I met with on the Ile Ste.-Marguerite, near Cannes, March 10th, on *Helichrysum stœchas*, and which I did not succeed in rearing. I noticed in Dr. Staudinger's collection last summer that he had a specimen of *Acrolepia eglanteriella*, Mann (see ante, p. 125), labelled " ex l. *Helichrysum*; " and possibly the larvæ I found may have been the young larvæ of that species.

The following is my description of it :—

Length 2 lines; yellowish green; the dorsal vessel dull green; head rather pale brown, with the mouth and the sides darker; the second segment with a yellowish-grey blotch, with four darker grey spots at its hinder edge.

It mines the leaves and burrows down the shoots of *Helichrysum stœchas*.

Perittia? When I visited the Ile Ste.-Marguerite, near Cannes, on the 11th of March, I found two leaves of a *Lonicera* (which, according to Mr. J. T. Moggridge's determinations, is probably *implexa*) mined by a small larva which I doubtingly refer to the genus *Perittia*. Of the two which I found, one was apparently dead; the other I sent to Miss Wing, to be figured; and though I thereby secured the portrait of the larva and its mine, I lost my chance of rearing it, the larva becoming a martyr to science.

The smaller larva, which was apparently dead, I extracted from the leaf, and described it thus:—

Length little more than 1 line; pale yellow, with the head yellowish brown; the head pointed; second segment broadest; the third, fourth, and fifth gradually decreasing in width, then nearly uniform; very flat; no legs visible.

The larger larva I described, *as well as I could through the leaf*, thus:—

Length 2 lines; pale yellow; head pale brown; second segment whitish. (Miss Wing assures me there were very evident legs to the larva she figured.)

This forms a large flat white blotch on the upperside of the leaves of the honeysuckle; the central portion of the white blotch, when large, becomes of a pale brown; the excrement is placed round the margin of the mine, leaving the central area clear.

My attention having once been called to this interesting larva, I kept constantly on the look-out for it during my subsequent visit to Mentone, but did not again see any symptoms of it.

Zelleria phillyrella, Millière (see *ante*, p. 190). At Cannes on the 3rd of March Monsieur Millière, by beating a bush of *Phillyrea angustifolia*, then very full of blossom, succeeded in obtaining a number of the larvæ of this species, and very liberally supplied me with several of them; afterwards, assisted by my late friend Mr. Henry Wade Battersby, I obtained in the same locality some more of them by beating; but though I devoted much time to them, I altogether failed to find these larvæ *in situ* by searching.

Monsieur Millière, who preferred beating into his umbrella to eye-hunting, had in this case the advantage of me.

The larva I have thus described:—

Length 4 lines; greenish at the sides and beneath, the entire dorsal region reddish as far as the subdorsal lines; dorsal line darker; spots pale green, very small; head and second segment pale dull yellowish. Attenuated anteriorly, slightly so posteriorly, with sixteen legs.

The younger larvæ are green, without the reddish tinge.

It forms webs amongst the flowers of the *Phillyrea*, on which it feeds; I believe several of my larvæ fell victims to the jaws of their brethren, so that it does not appear to be of a social disposition. When full-fed the larvæ spin opaque-white cocoons, not unlike those of *Swammerdamia* and *Argyresthia*.

The duration of the pupa-state was not long, as the perfect insects unfortunately began to emerge before I reached home (making their appearance at Fontainebleau and Paris): the first appeared April 2nd; and by the 7th all were bred, except one, which came out on the 13th April.

The perfect insect, though closely allied to *Z. hepariella* (which frequents yew trees in July), may be readily distinguished by the following characters:—The anterior wings are narrower, more shining, of a paler colour, with a faintly indicated whitish basal streak just above the fold; on the fold beyond the middle is a black spot; and in the specimen bred on the 13th April there are several small black spots towards the costa. The posterior wings are also both narrower and paler; and the tuft of the head is paler, almost whitish. (See also Nat. Hist. Tineina, vol. xi. p. 100, pl. 3. fig. 1.)

Gracilaria auroguttella, Haworth. I captured a specimen of this near Cannes as it was flying in the afternoon on the 10th of March.

Coleophora pyrrhulipennella, Zeller. I again noticed many of the larvæ of this species at Cannes on the *Erica scoparia*, and also found them on that plant at Mentone on the ridge between the Gorbio and Cabrolles valleys on the 26th of March. I did not rear any of the perfect insects.

Coleophora congeriella, Staudinger. I again collected the larvæ of this species both at Cannes and Mentone on *Dorycnium suffruticosum* and *D. hirtum*. I had quite despaired of rearing the perfect insects; but after the box containing the cases had been put away in my collection of economies of insects, several of the moths made their appearance; when, I know not.

Coleophora calycotomella, Staudinger in litt. On the 1st of March Monsieur Millière and I visited the little wood near the Hôtel de Provence, at Cannes, and, after beating several bushes of *Calycotome spinosa*, Monsieur Millière found in his umbrella a long brown *Coleophora*-case which was new to both of us; I then commenced searching on the plants, and succeeded in finding two more; the next day I found eleven in that locality, and two others to the west of Cannes. On the 5th of March I collected seven more in the original locality.

This larva I have thus described:—

Length 4½ lines; brown; head black-brown; the second segment with a large black-brown plate divided down the centre; third segment with two large dark brown spots; fourth segment with two small dark brown spots, each of these segments with a small black spot on each side.

The case, 6–7 lines long, is formed of pieces of mined leaf; it is nearly straight, slightly curved, and attenuated posteriorly; when attached to the stem of the plant, except in colour, it much resembles the strong spines of the *Calycotome.*

The larva attaches its case to the underside of a leaf of the plant, and then bores into the interior and eats out the parenchyma, the devoured leaf becoming of a dull dark brown.

These larvæ continued to feed for two or three weeks after I had them; and the perfect insects appeared from May 9th to June 24th.

I then recognized them as identical with an unnamed species of *Coleophora* I had received from Dr. Staudinger in 1863 as reared from a *Genista* in Old Castile.

Last summer, when at Dresden looking through his collection, I saw that he had given it the MS. name of *calycotomella*, which I have much pleasure in retaining.

The imago may be briefly described as follows:—

Exp. al. 6–6½ lin. Head white, mixed with pale grey in the centre of the crown. Palpi white, the second joint externally grey. Antennæ with the basal joint rather thickened, and more or less tinged with pale grey, the remaining joints entirely white.

Anterior wings white, with four dark grey longitudinal streaks along the principal veins, that on the subcostal nervure being branched; the extreme edge of the costa is dark grey at the base, and there is a slender dark grey streak between the subcostal nervure and the costa; there are also faint slender interrupted grey streaks along the disk and along the fold; the cilia are whitish, with the tips more grey.

Bedellia somnulentella, Zeller. I again noticed the larvæ of this species commonly in the leaves of *Convolvulus althæoides*, both at Cannes and Mentone.

Stagmatophora Grabowiella, Staudinger (see *ante*, p. 214). I again collected the larvæ of this species in great plenty at Cannes, March 3rd and 4th, on *Lavandula stœchas*; the black cases are readily perceptible when we look down upon the plants vertically. At Mentone, on the 14th March, Mr. J. T. Moggridge found some larvæ of the same species on *Thymus*. I again failed in my attempts to rear the imago, probably from collecting the larvæ too early in the season.

Urodela, n. g., *cisticolella*, n. sp. On the 7th March, when collecting with Monsieur Millière on the hill above the Bellevue Hotel at Cannes, I found a larva mining a leaf of *Cistus monspeliensis*, forming a slightly puckered blotch. It rained nearly the whole of the following day, so that I could not go to the same locality; but on the 9th I went in search of this new larva, and higher up the hill collected several of them; I also found one near the coast. On the 11th I found the same larva on the Ile Ste.-Marguerite; I afterwards noticed it at Mentone. At the time, I apprehended that it would produce some species of *Laverna*.

The larva I have thus described:—

Length 2½ lines; broadest anteriorly; dull dark olive-grey, with faint indications of the dorsal and subdorsal lines; head black;

second segment with a black subcutaneous plate; anal segment with a small blackish plate. Legs 16; anterior legs blackish.

A larger larva was more distinctly mottled with pale grey, and had a whitish spiracular line.

It mines the leaves of *Cistus monspeliensis*, making an elongate blotch, which is slightly puckered. The upper end of the mine is free from excrement, which seems all collected at the lower end. The larva moves from leaf to leaf; and when full-fed it quits the mine, and, attaching itself to the edge of a leaf, changes there to a *naked* pupa, which is *only attached by the tail*; the head-end and the middle are entirely free from the leaf, not even fastened by a silken girth, thus reminding us of the pupæ of some of the *Pterophoridæ*.

When I saw the singular pupa, I regretted that I had not collected more of these larvæ. I was fortunate, however, in rearing four specimens of the imago, three of which appeared April 7th (only two days after I had returned home), and the fourth on the 9th April.

I should not be at all surprised if this should prove to be the insect described by Staudinger as *Elachista piperatella* (see *ante*, p. 161); and possibly his name may eventually have to be adopted for it; but as it certainly forms the type of a new genus, I will in the meantime give it the specific name of *cisticolella*. The generic characters of the imago consist in the rough head, the short palpi, and the form of the anterior wings, which are more elliptical, and have not the posteriorly expanded appearance of an *Elachista*. The neuration I have not yet investigated.

The species may be thus briefly described:—

Exp. al. 4 lin. Head sparingly clothed with erect pale grey hairs, face smooth, dark grey. Palpi dark grey, very short. Antennæ dark grey, with paler annulations, nearly as long as the anterior wings.

Anterior wings rather dark grey, with no markings, but with

numerous scattered whitish scales from the base to the hind margin; cilia pale grey. Posterior wings and cilia pale grey.

Elachista gleichenella, Fabricius. As already noticed (see *ante*, p. 214), I bred a specimen of this species from larvæ collected in the leaves of *Carex basilaris*, in the " Primrose Valley," at Mentone, March 15th; the imago appeared May 29th.

Elachista chrysodesmella, Zeller. I bred a female of this species on the 20th April, from a single larva which I found at Mentone, on the 17th March, mining the tip of a grass like an *Aira* and of which I cannot give the name; it was growing by the road beyond the cemetery. I had previously only bred this species from larvæ collected at Zurich, along with Professor Frey, in the leaves of *Carex montana*.

Elachista pollinariella, Zeller. I noticed two or three of this flying near the ground at Mentone on the 20th March; as they sat occasionally for a few seconds, I examined them closely to satisfy myself it was truly this species; but I did not catch any.

Lithocolletis Messaniella, Zeller. On some cork-trees (*Quercus suber*) at Cannes I collected a number of leaves mined by *Lithocolletis*-larvæ March 7th and 9th, but obtained nothing from them but *Messaniella*.

Lithocolletis trifasciella, Haworth. On the 24th of March I bred a specimen of this from leaves of *Lonicera implexa* collected at the Ile Ste.-Marguerite, near Cannes, on the 11th March.

Phyllobrostis daphneella, Staudinger (see *ante*, pp. 163 & 214). I again collected several of the larvæ of this species at Cannes and Mentone, and bred a nice series from May 4th to 19th.

Nepticula suberivora, n. sp. Of this unicolorous species I bred three specimens from *yellow* larvæ found in the leaves of the cork-tree (*Quercus suber*) at Cannes, March 9th. The perfect insects appeared April 8th, 23rd, and 28th.

The larva I have thus described :—

Length $2\frac{1}{4}$ lines; pale amber, dorsal vessel slightly darker; head pale yellowish brown, with the mouth and sutures darker.

The mine is a long tortuous gallery, gradually increasing in width, often following the margin of the leaf, the excrement occupying the centre of the mine.

The imago may be thus briefly described :—

Exp. al. 3 lin. Head yellow. Anterior wings *dark* grey (darker than in any other unicolorous grey species), with no metallic gloss, and with a very faint purple tinge beyond the middle; cilia paler grey.

Nepticula catharticella, Stainton? On the 14th of March I collected some *Nepticula*-larvæ on *Rhamnus alaternus*, on the rocky ground near Pont St. Louis, at Mentone. From these I bred two specimens of the imago, April 30th and May 10th; but the specimens are not in such a condition as to enable me to state with certainty whether they should be referred to *catharticella* or not.

My description of the larva differs somewhat from the description of the larva of *catharticella* given in the first volume of the 'Natural History of the Tineina;' it was as follows :—

Length 2 lines; pale amber, dorsal vessel greener; head pale brown, with the mouth and sutures darker, and with a short transverse dark mark posteriorly.

The mine is a broad gallery, almost a narrow blotch; the old part of the mine is brownish, the recent part pale green: the excrement, dark brown, at first nearly occupies the whole width of the mine; afterwards it is blacker and only occupies the central portion of the mine.

Nepticula cryptella, Stainton. When at Cannes I had taken up a plant or two of *Dorycnium hirtum* nearly by the roots, with which to feed the larvae of *Gelechia biguttella* found on it; this was on the 9th of March; on the 17th of that month a specimen of *Nepticula cryptella* made its appearance in this tin, and I presume it must have fed on the *Dorycnium hirtum*.

Nepticula suberis, n. sp. Of this species I bred three specimens, from *green* larvae mining the leaves of the cork-tree (*Quercus suber*) at Cannes March 7th and 9th. I cannot say when the perfect insects appeared; for I had quite despaired of breeding any, and had put the box containing the cocoons and mined leaves into my cabinet of economies, where some time afterwards I found three dead specimens of the imago, which I then relaxed, and set as well as I could.

The larva I have thus described :—

Length 2 lines; dull green, the dorsal vessel darker; the posterior segments tinged with yellowish; head dark brown, the hind lobes showing through the second segment of a brownish tinge; on the underside is a row of dark-brown spots.

The mine is at first a slender, tortuous gallery filled up with dark-brown excrement; then it expands to a large pale-brown blotch, in which the excrement forms a thick track.

The perfect insect has some similarity to *floslactella* and *salicis*; only the pale fascia is placed nearer the base of the wing than in either of those species. It may be briefly described as follows :—

Exp. al. 2¾ lin. Head yellow. Anterior wings grey, coarsely scaled, with a pale yellow, slightly oblique fascia, nearly in the middle; cilia clear pale yellow, intersected by a row of dark-grey scales.

Nepticula euphorbiella, n. sp. For the discovery of this species we are certainly indebted to Mr. J. T. Moggridge, as it would scarcely have occurred to me to look on one of the *Euphorbiæ* for a *Nepticula*-mine. It was on the 23rd of March that, starting from Mentone in the afternoon, we first went towards Cape Martin, and then to Roccabruna, and in the neighbourhood of the last-named place Mr. Moggridge called my attention to some mined leaves on a bush of

Euphorbia dendroides, and from this bush we soon collected about thirty *Nepticula*-larvæ; strange to say, though we looked carefully on all the neighbouring bushes of that plant, we did not find a mined leaf on any one of them.

The larvæ collected duly spun their cocoons; and I watched anxiously for the appearance of the imago; but the summer passed away without any coming out, and I concluded the pupæ were all dead. The box containing them had long been transferred to my cabinet of economies, when, chancing to look through its contents on the 15th March, 1868, I found to my surprise a number of *Nepticulæ* had emerged and lay dead in the box, and one actually still living, yet almost a twelvemonth after the larvæ had been collected.

The living specimen was at once transferred to the killing-bottle, and the dead specimens were duly relaxed, and set out to the best of my ability.

Last winter I took a walk with Monsieur Demole from Mentone to Cape Martin, and found a number of these mines of *Nepticula euphorbiella* scattered over a series of bushes of the *Euphorbia dendroides*; but on that occasion I did not find a single larva; all the mines were tenantless.

The larva I have thus described:—

Length 2¼ lines; pale amber, the dorsal vessel greener; head brown; the second segment with a dark brown mark on each side, formed by a prolongation of the hind lobes of the head.

The mine is most elegant, forming a long, slender, tortuous gallery with a slender thread of blackish excrement; as the mine becomes broader the excrement becomes greyer.

The perfect insect has no great resemblance to any other species; it perhaps comes nearest to worn specimens of *Trifurcula immundella*, but is much smaller than that insect.

The following brief description must suffice till I have a better series:—

Exp. al. 2⅓ lin. Head pale luteous, slightly mixed with grey. Anterior wings whitish yellow, with numerous dark grey scales irregularly scattered, but (in the only specimen I had the pleasure of seeing alive) showing a tendency to form a dark fascia beyond the middle, and a dark apical portion of the wing, beyond which the cilia at the apex are whitish yellow, and at the anal angle pale grey.

———

I found one other *Nepticula*-larva, but did not rear the perfect insect at all; I first found it at Cannes on the 4th of March mining the leaves of *Cistus monspeliensis*; the following day I collected some fifty of them, and found a few in the leaves of *Cistus salvifolius*.

The larva I have thus described:—

Length 2 lines; pale amber; head black; the hind lobes of the head show plainly through the anterior half of the second segment; and by the side of these and behind is a rather complex dark grey mark, leaving a pale amber spot in the centre. Beneath is a row of elongate lozenge-shaped brown spots.

The mine is a long, slender gallery; it generally begins near the centre of the leaf, runs towards the base, and then returns along the margin; the excrement is brownish.

Many of the mines were already empty, and perhaps a week or ten days later I should have been too late to find these larvæ.

Here terminates the record of my own doings during the month I was at Cannes and Mentone; but after I had returned home I received some interesting larvæ from my friends Mr. J. T. Moggridge and Monsieur Millière, which I will now notice.

Phibalocera quercana, Fabricius. In April 1867 Monsieur Millière found a larva on the leaves of *Arbutus unedo*, of which he sent me two specimens. It fed on the underside of the leaf, under a slight straight web. From its appearance and habit I expected it would produce the somewhat polyphagous *Phibalocera quercana*, and on the 10th of May a specimen of that moth made its appearance.

Depressaria rhodochrella, H.-S. On the 18th May, 1867, Monsieur Millière sent me three freshly pinned specimens of a *Depressaria* which I refer to this species. Monsieur Millière wrote concerning them as follows:—"Je vous envoye trois individus d'une *Depressaria*, qui peut-être vous arriveront vivants et qui viennent d'éclore. La chenille a beaucoup de rapport avec celle de la *propinquella*, dont elle a les mœurs et se nourrit à Cannes, sur la même plante. Elle ne paraît pas rare."

Gelechia ——? On the 28th of April I received from Mr. J. T. Moggridge, at Mentone, larvæ feeding on the young leaves of *Pistacia terebinthus*, a plant on which I had asked him to search, as I especially wished to obtain Herrich-Schäffer's *Gelechia terebinthella*.

On the 9th of June I bred in the cage in which I had put these larvæ a specimen of a *Gelechia* which I can hardly distinguish from *G. humeralis*, Zeller. It is certainly not Herrich-Schäffer's *terebinthella*; for when at Vienna last summer I saw a specimen of that insect in the Museum collection, and have noted that it is "a broad winged insect, broader than *fugacella*, with distinct raised buttons, and apical streak as in *sequax*;" and a reference to Herrich-Schäffer will show that this agrees well with his figure 597.

Fortunately I have a second specimen of the same insect, which was given me by Monsieur Millière at Cannes; but this only tends to increase the confusion, for he says he bred it from *Lotus hirtus*. This specimen had been submitted to Dr. Staudinger for his opinion, and that entomologist returned it labelled "*Gelechia* près *Strelitziella*."

The perfect insect is extremely like *G. humeralis*, with the same short black streak at the base of the costa; but it is a trifle smaller, it has the anterior wings narrower than *G. fugitivella*, thus much narrower than *G. fugacella*, and there is no symptom of the apical streak which *G. terebinthella* possesses.

The larva I have thus described:—

Length 5 lines; pale green, the dorsal region rather darker; spots small, grey; the head yellowish green, and the second segment only a little greener. (In Miss Wing's figure, made two or three days after my description, the second segment bears about ten brown spots.)

Very active and slightly fusiform, feeding between the united young leaves of *Pistacia terebinthus.*

Butalis ——? On the 5th of April I received from Monsieur Millière at Cannes a larva, apparently of the genus *Butalis*, feeding in the dried seed-head of a *Daucus*; unfortunately I did not succeed in rearing the perfect insect. The larva I have thus described:—

Length 3 lines; pale ochreous grey, the anal segment a little paler, with seven slender longitudinal dark fuscous lines, the broadest and darkest of which are those representing the subdorsal lines; head black; the second segment with a broad blackish plate on each side, leaving a wide central space ochreous grey.

Anchinia laureolella, H.-S. On the 25th of April I received from Mr. J. T. Moggridge at Mentone some larvæ feeding in the shoots of *Daphne gnidium*, which I rather suspected at the time were referable to the genus *Anchinia*; and the pupation satisfied me that my suspicion was correct. I bred one specimen of the perfect insect on the 25th of May, and was not a little surprised, when I came to examine it critically, to find it was the *Alpine* species, *A. laureolella.*

A good character whereby to distinguish this from *A. verrucella* is furnished by the sides of the thorax; these are grey in *laureolella*, dull red in *verrucella.*

The larva I have thus described:—

Length 5 lines; brown, with the dorsal line whitish; spots black in whitish rings; head pale yellowish brown, dotted with dark brown; the second segment pale yellowish brown in front, posteriorly with two black-brown crescentic marks; anal segment blackish brown; above the legs is a whitish lateral stripe; the anterior legs are blackish, with the tips pale yellowish brown.

A smaller larva (only $3\frac{1}{2}$ lines long) was dull greenish brown, with the head black, a black transverse plate on the second segment, and a small black plate on the anal segment.

Coriscium Brongniardellum, Fabricius. On the 28th of April I received from Mr. J. T. Moggridge at Mentone some larvæ of this species feeding on the leaves of *Quercus pubescens*. I bred four specimens of the imago, on the 19th and 25th of May.

Stathmopoda Guerinii, Stainton (see *ante*, pp. 138, 139). On the 7th of May I received from Mr. J. T. Moggridge at Mentone two pupæ in the stems of *Pistacia terebinthus*, and was not a little surprised to rear therefrom two specimens of the interesting *Stathmopoda Guerinii*, which appeared on the 14th and 25th of May. The pith of the stem appeared to have been eaten by the larvæ.

Section IV.
Larvæ of Tineina received from Southern Europe in 1868.

As I did not visit the South in the spring of 1868 I was entirely dependent on my correspondents for anything of interest; and the season, owing to the extreme drought, was, I believe, exceptionally unfavourable.

The following are the only species I have to notice:—

Gelechia hyoscyamella. *Coleophora ochrea.*
Ypsolophus trinotellus. *Chauliodus Staintonellus.*
Coleophora vicinella. *Stagmatophora Grabowiella.*

Gelechia hyoscyamella, Millière in litt. I received from Monsieur Millière at Cannes on the 17th of March a larva of this insect, which feeds on *Hyoscyamus albus*, and for which he had made a special excursion to the Ile St. Honoré (the further of the two islands near Cannes), but had only succeeded in finding one solitary larva. It fortunately fed upon the piece of plant sent with it, and produced the perfect insect on the 5th of May.

It is closely allied to *Gelechia costella* (which feeds on *Solanum dulcamara*), but is, I think, distinct; it is paler in colour, the anterior wings are rather broader, and the anterior edge of the dark costal blotch stops short before the fold, whereas in *costella* I believe it always reaches the fold.

The larva I have thus described:—

Length $5\frac{1}{2}$ lines; pale greenish grey, with dull reddish dorsal, subdorsal, and lateral lines; the dorsal line more slender and more defined than in *costella*; the subdorsal geminated and interrupted, just as in *costella*; head yellowish brown; second segment with a large black plate above, scarcely divided in the centre; third segment rather darker than the following segments; anal segment with a black plate; ordinary spots very minute.

It mines and puckers the leaves of *Hyoscyamus albus*.

Of the imago the following brief description must suffice for the present:—

Exp. al. $6\frac{1}{2}$ lin. Head, thorax, and anterior wings pale ochreous, the latter with a dark grey blotch from the costa, darkest and most sharply defined at its slightly oblique anterior edge; it stops short before the fold and is posteriorly attenuated and gradually shades off into the paler ground-colour; on the disk are two black spots, the anterior of which is in the costal blotch and sometimes surrounded with a pale ring; the pale hinder fascia is very faintly indicated; the apex of the costa and hind margin are spotted with grey, and there is a darker grey (almost black) spot at the extreme apex of the wing.

Ypsolophus trinotellus, H.-S. (see *ante*, p. 222). On the 27th of March I received from Mr. J. T. Moggridge, at Mentone, some larvæ of this species in the seeds of *Moricandia arvensis*, a stock-like plant which grows in some plenty about Ventimiglia. The perfect insects made their appearance May 22nd to June 1st.

When at Prague last summer I learnt from Herr Nickerl that this species had occurred in 1867 by thousands near Prague, flying at the end of May and beginning of June and again in July. In the Vienna Museum I saw a specimen from Brussa.

Coleophora vicinella, Zeller. On the 28th of April I received from Mr. J. T. Moggridge, who had collected them near Albenga (on the Italian coast between San Remo and Savona), some larvæ of a *Coleophora* feeding on *Medicago sativa*?, which, I believe, were those of *vicinella*. I fed them with a species of *Trifolium* from the sandpit at Charlton, probably *T. striatum*, but I did not succeed in rearing the perfect insect.

The larva I have thus described:—

Length $3\frac{1}{2}$ lines; dull yellowish brown; head black; second segment with a large black plate above, leaving only the front edge whitish; third segment with four black plates; anal segment with a black plate.

The case is made of silk, and consists of a central tube and two lateral flaps, which surround and almost entirely conceal the tube, these flaps, as in *C. Lugduniella*, being formed, as it were, of scales of silk.

Coleophora ochrea, Haworth. On the 28th of April I also received from Mr. J. T. Moggridge, who had collected them at Albenga, some larvæ of this species, feeding on *Helianthemum fumana*. I did not take any special trouble about them (they were so manifestly *C. ochrea*), and did not rear the imago.

Chauliodus Staintonellus, Millière (see *ante*, p. 169). I received some larvæ of this species, which feeds on *Osyris alba*, from Monsieur Millière at Cannes, on the 18th of May; the perfect insects appeared the first week in June. (For description of both larva and imago, see *ante*, p. 169.)

Staymatophora Grabowiella, Staudinger (see *ante*, pp. 214 & 226). On the 18th of May I also received from Monsieur Millière, at Cannes, some larvæ of this species on *Thymus vulgaris*. My previous attempts to rear the imago from larvæ collected in March had always been unsuccessful; but with these larvæ, collected two months later, I was more fortunate; and two specimens were bred, one early in June the other on the 5th of July. I had not the pleasure, however, of seeing them alive, as they came out during my absence on the Continent, whilst my pupæ were under the charge of Mr. M'Lachlan.

Section V.

Tineina observed during my visit to Southern Europe in the winter of 1868–69.

On this occasion I left home December 11th, spent the 17th and 18th December at Cannes, the 20th to 22nd at Mentono, thence by the Riviera to Genoa, where we spent our Christmas; December 29th and 30th I was at Turin, whence we proceeded by the night-train to Florence, arriving there, in a deluge of rain, on the last day of the old year; leaving Florence on the 6th January for Pisa, I proceeded the following day to Leghorn, and on the 9th January left Leghorn for Rome; three weeks were spent at Rome, and from February 1st to 17th I was at Naples (excepting from the 6th to 9th, which were devoted to Sorrento); the 19th to 25th February I was again at Rome, spent the 26th and 27th at Florence, and, except meeting Chevalier Ghiliani at Turin on the 3rd of March, I had no opportunity of doing anything more in entomology till after I returned home on the 9th of March. I should premise that, judging from what I saw on this journey, it is a mistake for the entomologist in mid-winter to go further south than Cannes and Mentone; it realizes the old saying of "going further and faring worse." One loses the protection of the Alpine chain directly to the north, and also the advantage of a due southern aspect, and the difference in vegetation is very perceptible. My advice to any one wishing to explore the entomological riches of the South would be to remain at Cannes or Mentone till spring was well advanced, and in April to try his luck at Sorrento and Naples, and in May explore the Campagna about Rome.

The only Tineina I have to mention as observed on this journey are the following thirteen:—

Tinea vinculella.
Teichobia Verhuellella.
Depressaria rutana.
Dasycera sulphurella.
Zelleria oleastrella.
Elachista disemiella.
Tischeria angusticollella.

T. Dodonæa.
Lithocolletis lantanella.
L. Messaniella.
L. leucographella.
L. on Calycotome spinosa.
Nepticula euphorbiella.

Tinea vinculella, H.-S. On the 5th of January, when walking from Florence towards Bello Sguardo, and looking on the walls for spiders with which to feed a *Mantis* (*Empusa pauperata*) which I had brought with me from Cannes, I noticed a case which appeared to be that of *T. vinculella*. I boxed it as a curiosity before I discovered that it contained a living larva.

On the 14th of February, at Naples, I found these cases were plentiful in the Villa Reale on the trunks of *Quercus ilex*, and I collected many of them; for a *tree-trunk* was to me quite a new *habitat* for a larva I had previously found only on walls. These larvæ are difficult to rear in confinement, unless nearly full-fed when collected; and in this instance I have not, so far, succeeded in obtaining a single imago.

Teichobia Verhuellella, Stainton. When at Turin, on the 29th December, I found a larva of this species on *Asplenium ruta-muraria*, which was growing on a wall leading up to Santa Margarita.

Depressaria rutana, Fabricius (see *ante*, p. 217). On visiting the Coliseum at Rome on the 12th of January, and ascending to the upper galleries, I noticed on the first gallery a plant of *Ruta angus-*

tifolia much eaten, and soon recognized the peculiar habitations of *Depressaria rutana*, of which I collected several larvæ; I had to revisit the locality at intervals to obtain food for them. From the larvæ thus obtained I reared two specimens of the imago on the 12th and 25th March.

It seemed a curious coincidence, meeting this striking Fabrician species, always interesting from having been, as it were, lost for upwards of half a century, in the ruins of the Flavian Amphitheatre.

Dasycera sulphurella, Fabricius. I found a specimen of this on the trunk of a *Quercus ilex* in the Villa Reale, Naples, February 14th.

Zelleria oleastrella, Millière (see *ante*, p. 215). On the 17th December*, at Cannes, I had the good fortune to find a single larva of this species on the underside of an olive-leaf. I looked long, in hopes of finding others, but was not successful.

The larva found was nearly full-fed, and soon spun up. The imago made its appearance on the 6th of February, the day we went from Naples to Sorrento.

Elachista disemiella, Zeller (see *ante*, pp. 13 & 48). When at Tivoli, on the 21st of February, I noticed in the tufts of *Aira cæspitosa* growing on some of the lower terraces near the waterfalls, some mines of the larva of an *Elachista*, and collected about a dozen of them. I might have collected many more; but, in the first place, I knew the extreme difficulty in rearing these grass-feeding larvæ, a difficulty much increased when travelling; and, in the second place, the character of the mine was so ordinary, I thought in all probability the larvæ would produce some common well-known species.

The larvæ were probably almost full-fed when I found them; for though some were still unchanged several weeks afterwards, I apprehended they could not have eaten much after I collected them, and they seemed to remain attached to the exterior of the grass for some time before assuming the pupa-state.

Five at any rate went safely into pupæ, and five specimens of the perfect insect appeared, May 5th, 8th, 14th, 16th, and 19th.

I had no difficulty at all in recognizing them as identical with a Sicilian specimen of *E. disemiella* I had received from Professor Zeller.

Tischeria angusticollella, Zeller. I bred two specimens of this insect from leaves of the evergreen rose (*Rosa sempervirens*) collected at Florence January 6th and February 27th; the moths appeared March 19th and April 18th.

Tischeria Dodonæa, Stainton. At Cannes, on the 18th of December, I found a mine of this species on a leaf of *Quercus pubescens*.

Lithocolletis lantanella, Schrank. Two years ago Monsieur Millière had called my attention to a *Lithocolletis* larva in the leaves of Laurustinus (*Viburnum tinus*), and had sent me some mines from which I unfortunately bred nothing; and I believe Monsieur Millière was not more successful: on visiting the Boboli Gardens, therefore, at

---

* This was one of the finest and hottest days we had all the winter.

Florence on the 3rd of January, I was much pleased to find two leaves of the Laurustinus there mined by a *Lithocolletis*-larva. From one of these I was successful in rearing the imago, which proves to be, as I had rather anticipated, *Lithocolletis lantanella*.

Professor Frey had previously bred this from *Viburnum opulus*; hence it feeds on *Viburnum lantana, opulus*, and *tinus*.

Lithocolletis Messaniella, Zeller. I collected some mined leaves of *Quercus ilex* at the Villa Pamfili at Rome, but only obtained from them the common *L. Messaniella*.

Professor Zeller had urged me, in a letter I received from him at Rome, to collect diligently the mined leaves of *Quercus ilex* in hopes of breeding other Southern species; but in this I was not successful.

Neither did I notice on *Quercus ilex* any of the *Nepticula*-mines which I had observed in 1863 (see ante, p. 207).

Lithocolletis leucographella, Zeller (see ante, pp. 70, 88, & 207). On the 1st of January, when walking from Florence towards Bello Sguardo, I noticed the mines of these larvæ in the leaves of *Cratægus pyracantha*, precisely where I had seen them six years ago, and on the 5th of January I collected a few mines, though the larvæ were then mostly very young; these, however, all died on the journey. But when I returned to Florence at the end of February I found these larvæ far more developed, and, judging from the complete doubling up of some of the leaves and the discoloration of the loosened upper skin, many were probably already in the pupa-state; so I devoted some hours of the 26th and 27th of February to collecting these mined leaves, from which I bred upwards of fifty of the perfect insect; they began to appear April 14th, came out most freely April 27th, 29th, and the last appeared on the 2nd of May.

Lithocolletis ———? When at Cannes, on the 18th December, I visited with Monsieur Millière a little wood in which were many bushes of *Calycotome spinosa*, and I found, to my delight, that some of the small leaves of that plant were mined as though by the larva of a *Lithocolletis*. I collected a few; but unfortunately the moths made their appearance on my journey before I expected them, and their dried remains are so rubbed that is impossible to recognize the species; only it is undoubtedly a *Lithocolletis*.

Nepticula euphorbiella, Stainton (see ante, p. 229). When at Mentone, on the 21st of December, I went with Monsieur Demole (a Swiss entomologist) towards Cape Martin, and noticed the empty mines of this species on more than a dozen different bushes of *Euphorbia dendroides*, at considerable intervals.

CHAPTER VII.

GERMAN AUTHORS.

In this chapter I propose to notice the Tineina from Southern Europe noticed by Herrich-Schäffer in his 'Schmetterlinge von Europa,' and in his 'Neue Schmetterlinge aus Europa und den angrenzenden Ländern.'

I have also introduced six species of the genus *Butalis* from Southern Europe which were described by Zeller in the tenth volume of the 'Linnæa Entomologica.'

Section I.

South-European Tineina noticed by Herrich-Schäffer in his 'Schmetterlinge von Europa,' vol. v.

These are twenty-nine in number:—

Tinea fraudulentella.
T. granulatella.
T. pustulatella.
Dysmasia petrinella.
Atychia funebris.
Distagmos Ledereri.
Adela australis.
Symmoca signatella.
Atemelia chrysopterella.
Depressaria lutosella.
D. Himmighofenella.
D. rhodochrella.
D. discipunctella.
Pleurota salviella.
P. imitatrix.

Pleurota honorella.
P. Heydenreichiella.
Rhinosia sculpturella.
Gelechia quinquepunctella.
Anacampsis captivella.
A. dimidiella.
Eupleuris meridionella.
Pancalia nodosella.
Gelechia? ratella.
Hypatima phycidella.
Stagmatophora opulentella.
Swammerdamia egregiella.
Lithocolletis Parisiella.
L. italica.

P. 70, No. 40. TINEA FRAUDULENTELLA, F. v. R.; Sppl. 318, scheint verdorben, Zell. Linn. Ent. vi. p. 110, Anm. 5.

Fusca, violaceo micans, obsolete pallidius tessellata; puncto medio, nonnullis apicis, serieque in basi ciliarum sulphureis.

Sie gleicht am meisten der *rusticella*; grösser, Vorderflügel etwas breiter; die Vorderflügel braun, mit violettem Glanze, nicht rauh, gleichmässig dunkel gegittert: in der Flügelmitte ein grosser gelber schwarz umzogener Punkt, mehrere undeutliche in der Flügelspitze, nur einer in der Spitze der Zelle 6. deutlich; ausserdem noch drei gelbe Punkte auf der Wurzelhälfte der Franzen in Zelle 3–5. und

einige undeutliche am Innenrand gegen den Afterwinkel. Kopf stark gelb behaart.
In the collection of Fischer von Röslerstamm from Laybach.

P. 74, No. 62. TINEA GRANULATELLA, H.-S.; Sppl. 267; Zell. Linn. Ent. vi. 175.

Albida, capite fusco-piloso (?), *alis anterioribus maculis nigris dilaceratis, ante et pone medium fasciam irregularem formantibus, tribus ante apicem, ciliis ter aut quater nigricante sectis.*

Der *nigricomella* ähnlich, der Kopf braunhaarig (?), die Vorderflügel weisser mit tiefschwarzen unbestimmten Flecken, welcher vor und hinter der Mitte eine unbestimmte Binde bilden, dreien gegen die Spitze des Vorderrandes, mehreren auf dem Saume, welche sich als drei oder vier dunkle Strahlen der Franzen fortsetzen.

At the beginning of June at Fiume; from Herr Lederer.

P. 75, No. 64. TINEA PUSTULATELLA, Zell. Linn. Ent. vi. p. 174; Sppl. 636.

Capillis exalbidis; alis anterioribus fuscis, maculis quatuor irregularibus exalbidis, mediis oppositis.

Dunkelveilbraun; die Scheitelhaare und 4·Flecke der Vorderflügel weissgelb, der erste, grösste, an der Wurzel des Innenrandes, der zweite vor der Mitte des Vorderrandes, der dritte vor der Spitze desselben, der vierte hinter der Mitte des Innenrandes.

From Croatia; one specimen. [Zeller says, "My single specimen was taken with several others by Mann in Croatia." Professor Frey took it at Zurich.]

P. 80, No. 84. DYSMASIA PETRINELLA, Heyd.; Sppl. 633.

Testaceo-grisea, nigro adspersa, punctis majoribus quinque in medio costæ, pluribus limbi, plicæ, et discoidali pone medium.

Vergleicht sich am besten der *misella*; Fühler kürzer und dicker, Farbe mehr graulich, staubfarben. Hinterflügel mehr blaugrau, ohne Kupferglanz, die Vorderflügel mit schärferen und reiner schwarzen Punkten, am Vorderrande von der Mitte an fünf (bei *misella* fangen sie erst hinter der Mitte an), auch auf der Saumlinie und in der Falte stehen grössere schwarze Punkte, und einer bei $\frac{2}{3}$ der Mittellängslinie.

From Spain; two specimens from Herr Schmid, of Frankfort on the Main.

P. 83, No. 97. ATYCHIA FUNEBRIS, Feisthamel, Ann. Soc. Ent. Fr. 1833, p. 259; Sppl. 611, 612.

Alæ anteriores nigræ, fasciis duabus irregularibus pallidis. Alæ posteriores nigræ.

Der Mann bedeutend kleiner als *appendiculata* ♀, nicht so tief schwarz; der Hinterleib an Segmente 3-6. mit weisslichem Hinterrand. Die braunen Franzen aller Flügel an der Spitze weiss;

an den Vorderflügeln ist ihre Wurzel auch noch von groben weissen unregelmässig vertheilten Schuppen bedeckt. Die beiden weissen Flecke hinter der Flügelmitte sind viel schmäler und höher, linienartig, der am Innenrande erreicht diese und steht dem Saume näher; die beiden in der Flügelmitte stehen schräger gegen einander und berühren sich nicht. Die Hinterflügel haben keinen weissen Fleck. Unten ganz braun, nur die Hinterflügel mit kleinem weissem Fleck am Vorderrande gegen die Spitze. Die beiden ersten Palpenglieder und die Stirne sind weisslich; der Scheitel olivenbräunlich beschuppt.

Das wahrscheinlich hierzu gehörige Weib hat die Binden nur etwas bleicher als den Grund, nur die hintere gegen den Afterwinkel hin rein weiss.

From the south of France and Spain, from Herr Keferstein.

[The original specimen described by Feisthamel was captured near Barcelona in 1827 by Capt. Caillaud, who died shortly afterwards.]

P. 90, No. 118. DISTAGMOS LEDERERI, H.-S.; Sppl. 269.

Cinerea, alarum anteriorum dimidio basali maculis duabus dilaceratis nigris.

Aschgrau, Vorderflügel mit zerstreuten schwarzen Schuppen, welche sich in der Mittellängslinie bei $\frac{1}{4}$ zu einem kleineren, bei $\frac{1}{3}$ zu einem grösseren, zerrissenen Fleck häufen, dann wieder auf der Saumlinie und in der Flügelspitze dichter stehen.

From the south of Spain; only one specimen collected by Herr Lederer.

P. 103, No. 172. ADELA AUSTRALIS, H.-S.; Sppl. 253.—*Mazzolella*, Dup. xi. p. 368, pl. 300. f. 8 (unverkennbar und es ist unbegreiflich wie F. v. R. das ihm überschickte Exemplar für *Mazzolella* erklärt haben soll).

Alæ anteriores basin versus omnino aureæ, apicem versus squamis aureis et purpureis mixtæ, utrinque ad fasciam mediam late indeterminate purpureæ.

Grösse ungefähr von *Sulzeriella*, die Vorderflügel sind aber viel breiter, mit abgerundeterer Spitze. Um das weissgelbe, schmälere Mittelband sind sie breit und unbestimmt begrenzt purpurviolett, gegen die Wurzel von da zuerst rothgolden, dann silbergolden, gegen die Spitze im purpurnen Grunde dicht, aber ungeordnet goldschuppig. Hinterflügel und Franzen purpurbraun. Die Fühler des Weibes länger als bei *Sulzeriella*, die schwarze Beschuppung erreicht nicht das ganze erst Drittheil, ist nicht so dick und verliert sich allmähliger, ohne dass dann die Fühler sogleich weiss werden; erst ihre äusserste Spitze ist weiss.

From Herr A. Schmid, from the south of France; I found one specimen in Fischer von Röslerstamm's collection, likewise from the south of France, placed amongst *Sulzeriella*.

[Duponchel met with the species in 1833, from the 8th to the 15th of May, near Aix in Provence; it flew abundantly amongst the bushes on the hills around that town. He would have described it as a new species, but, having sent a specimen to Fischer von Röslerstamm, was assured by him it was the *Mazzolella* of Hübner and Treitschke.]

P. 111, No. 196. SYMMOCA SIGNATELLA, H.-S., Sppl. 380.

Maculæ costales duæ, anterior cum punctis duobus obliquis umbra fusca juncta, posterior pone medium disci geminum.

Auf dem Vorderrande zwei braune Flecke, der vordere durch einen Querschatten mit den beiden Schrägpunkten verbunden, der hintere hinter dem mittleren Doppelpunkt. Dichter schwarz bestaubt als die grössere *signella*, dunkler und rauher aussehend.

Discovered by Herr Lederer at Ronda, in Spain.

P. 112, No. 201. ATEMELIA CHRYSOPTERELLA, H.-S., Sppl. 271.

Aurantiaco-flava, alis posterioribus et anteriorum ciliis violaceo-fuscis.

Grösse und Habitus einer grossen *Argyr. comptella*; doch sind die Flügel kürzer, die vorderen nach hinten deutlich breiter, mit stärker vortretendem Afterwinkel. Lebhaft dunkelgoldgelb, der Hinterleib, die Hinterflügel und die Franzen der vorderen violettbraun, letztere äusserst lang, an der Wurzelhälfte noch goldgelb gemischt, am Ende am dunkelsten. Die Hinterflügel scheinen nur 7 Rippen zu haben; Zunge und Nebenpalpen kann ich nicht unterscheiden, die dünnen Palpen stehen weit vor und sind sparsam lang behaart, die Fühler dicht schwarz und weiss geringelt, ziemlich lang gewimpert.

Herr Lederer found a specimen at Ronda, in the middle of June, on an oak-leaf.

[This insect appears to be a true *Tinea*, and was subsequently described by Staudinger as *Tinea vitellinella* (see *ante*, p. 144).]

P. 122, No. 239. DEPRESSARIA LUTOSELLA, F. v. R. coll.; Sppl. 438.

Testacea, subferrugineo irrorata, capite, thorace et puncto centrali albidioribus, alarum anteriorum basi fuscescente.

Die Farbe der *laterella* am nächsten, doch weniger röthlich, mehr rostgelb, die Hinterflügel brauner, die Vorderflügel deutlich schmäler, braun gesprenkelt, am dunkelsten am Vorderrande. Der weissliche Punkt hinter der Flügelmitte sehr deutlich, über ihm die dunkelste Stelle, doch nicht sehr abstechend; der Punkt vor ihr fehlt, die zwei schwarzen Schrägpunkte undeutlich.

From Fiume; two specimens.

[I have two specimens from Herr Mann, taken in July in Croatia, where it was very scarce.]

P. 125, No. 248. DEPRESSARIA HIMMIGHOFENELLA, H.-S.

Obscure griseo-ochracea, parum obscurius irrorata, ciliis paullo rubentibus, limbo vix nigro-notato, punctis tribus nigris et macula media bene expressis, thorace ferreo, palporum articulo ultimo nigro-bicincto.

Röthlich lederfarben, sehr wenig und gleichmässig dunkler bestaubt, die drei Punkte gleich stark, Vorderrand und Saum kaum gefleckt. Das letzte Palpenglied mit zwei schwarzen Ringen; Kopf und Thorax schwarzgrau.

Bei *subpropinquella* steht der dunkle Mittelfleck von den Schrägpunkten ferner, unter ihm sind deutlich die zwei feinen weissen Punkte. Der Thorax ist den Flügeln gleichfarbig, die Palpen viel schwächer schwarz geringelt.

From Herr Schmid, who obtained bred specimens from the south of France through Herr Himmighofen.

P. 125, No. 250. DEPRESSARIA RHODOCHRELLA, H.-S., Sppl. 425.

Die Färbung ist lichter als jene von *arenella, propinquella* und *laterella*, ein schönes röthliches Ockergelb mit ziegelröthlicher Einmischung und sehr weniger schwarzer Bestaubung, wodurch die drei Punkte und der schwarze Fleck schärfer erscheinen. Das Endglied der Palpen hat zwei undeutlich dunklere Ringe, das Mittelglied eingemischte schwarze Schuppen, die Schulterdecken scheinen dunkel. Die Hinterflügel sind lichter als bei den 3 Verwandten, ihre Franzen deutlich gelber.

Herr Lederer communicated to me two specimens from Spalato.

[Zeller gives also as localities (Linn. Ent. ix. p. 232) Marseilles and Barcelona (*v. Heyden*). There can be no doubt that this and the preceding are the same species (see *ante*, p. 231).]

P. 128, No. 262. DEPRESSARIA DISCIPUNCTELLA, H.-S., Sppl. 446.
[*pastinacella*, Stainton.]

Herr Lederer met with this on the 18th of May at Ronda.

[Zeller has compared one of Lederer's Spanish specimens with the English specimens he received from me, so that there is no doubt as to their identity.]

P. 146, No. 344. PLEUROTA SALVIELLA, Mann in litt.

Straminea, vitta fusca obsoletissima, alis latioribus, posterioribus ante apicem non sinuatis.

Vorderflügel breiter als bei *pyropella*, noch bleicher aber fast eben so glänzend als bei *metricella*, die braune Strieme noch undeutlicher, die Hinterflügel breiter als bei *pyropella*, die Palpen wie hier, nämlich das letzte Glied über halb so lang als das mittlere.

From Herr Metzner, from Dalmatia.

P. 147, No. 350. PLEUROTA IMITATRIX, Zeller; Sppl. 401, *a, b*.

Alba, vitta postcostali fusca, puncto disci unico.

Kleiner als die kleinste *pyropella*, die Grundfarbe bei weitem nicht so gelb, sondern mehr schmutzigweiss mit russbrauner Bestaubung, welche sich als Streif längs des rein weissen Vorderrandes schärfer ausnimmt als bei *pyropella*. Hinter der Mitte der Mittellängslinie steht ein deutlich dunkler Mittelpunkt, von welchem aus zum Saume zwischen den Rippen schwach dunklere Strahlen ziehen. Das Mittelglied der Palpen ist länger als bei *pyropella*, das Endglied kürzer.

From Herr Lederer I received as *acutella* a pair which should probably be referred to this species; he found them at Ronda in April on dry hills.

P. 148, No. 353. PLEUROTA HONORELLA, H. 354? (zu gross, Vorderflügel nach hinten zu breit, ihr Vorderrand zu gerade, ihr Saum viel zu lang, der vordere Arm der Gabel in der Mitte zu deutlich verdickt); Sppl. 400.

Olivaceo-flava, vitta costali, altera furcata e basi media et tertia marginis interioris argenteis; striis argenteis æquilatis, non interruptis, vitta pone marginem anteriorem obscuriore.

Kopf graulich. Die Silberstreife sind gleich breit, nicht unterbrochen, der Vorderrandsstreif innen braun beschattet.

Herr Lederer beat a single specimen of this species from *Ulex* on the Monjuich near Barcelona.

P. 148, No. 354. PLEUROTA HEYDENREICHIELLA, Lederer; Sppl. 397-399.

Olivaceo-flava, vitta costali, altera furcata e basi media et tertia marginis interioris argenteis; furcæ ramo anteriore flavo-biinterrupto.

Der vordere Arm des silbernen Gabelstreifes ist zweimal von der Grundfarbe unterbrochen; die drei Bilder zeigen die verschiedensten Abweichungen.

Herr Lederer discovered this handsome species at Ronda, on a sheep-pasture, amongst thistles.

P. 151, No. 371. RHINOSIA SCULPTURELLA, Metzn.; Sppl. 598.

Minor, cinerea, subtilius signata, macula subquadrata ante medium alarum anteriorum.

Bedeutend kleiner als *sequella*, die Spitze der Vorderflügel schärfer, ihr Saum geschwungener, die Franzen mit zwei feinen, dunklen Theilungslinien und dunklem Ende. Schön aschgrau, nicht so weiss als *sequella*, mit viel feineren und nicht so schwarzen Schuppen, dunkler marmorirt, am dunkelsten ein Viereck vor $\frac{1}{3}$ des Vorderrandes, ein anderes schräg unter ihm mehr gegen die Flügelmitte hin, ein scharf schwarzer Punkt hinter $\frac{2}{3}$ der Flügelmitte und einige solche auf der Saumlinie gegen den Afterwinkel.

From Dalmatia.

P. 172, No. 436. GELECHIA QUINQUEPUNCTELLA, H.-S., Sppl. 573. [*Littorella*, Stainton.]

Cinerea, fusco irrorata, lineis tribus longitudinalibus, aurantiacis, punctis limbi nigerrimis; palpis albidis, articulo medio ante apicem, terminali, multo breviore, pone basin et ante apicem nigro annulatis.

Der *psilella* sehr nah, viel weisser, Palpen fast unbezeichnet, alle

Flügel entschieden schmäler, den vorderen fehlt der vorderste rostgelbe Streif, auf dem mittleren steht ein schwarzer Punkt genau in der Flügelmitte, einer bei ¾, also beide mehr spitzwärts gerückt als bei *psilella*; auf dem inneren Streif stehen wieder zwei Punkte, mehr wurzelwärts gerückt, mit den beiden vorigen im Rhomboid. Vor dem Vorderrande steht ein schwärzlicher Punkt bei ¼ und ⅔.

From Upper Italy, by Herr Mann.

[With us it has occurred in the Isle of Wight and on the Cheshire coast.]

P. 194, No. 516. ANACAMPSIS CAPTIVELLA, Mann; Sppl. 579.

Nigra, capite, thorace et alarum anteriorum fascia pone medium niveis.

Das Braun der Vorderflügel wird gegen die Wurzel lichter, rostgelblich olivenbraun, das weisse Band steht hinter der Mitte und ist wurzelwärts scharf abgeschnitten, saumwärts mit schwarzen Schuppen vermischt, welche gegen die Spitze der Flügel hin und in der Wurzelhälfte der Franzen weiss sind. Hinterflügel silbergrau, mit bräunlichen Franzen.

At Fiume, in the evening, among ash trees.

[Well distinguished from the allied species *ligulella, vorticella*, and *tœniolella* by its smaller size and white head and thorax.]

P. 202, No. 560. ANACAMPSIS DIMIDIELLA, Hb. 253; Mus. Schiff.

Vitellina, alarum anteriorum margo anterior ultra medium et limbus late fusca, macula marginis interioris minor fusca, stigmata tria nigra.

Dottergelb, Hinterleib und Hinterflügel braungrau, Vorderflügel violettbraun mit gelber Strieme, welche den Innenrand an der Wurzel und hinter der Mitte, den Vorderrand hinter der Mitte erreicht und die 3 tiefschwarzen Punkte einschliesst.

Vienna, Laybach; at Ratisbon, in meadows after the hay has been carried, along with *ictella*.

P. 204, No. 570. EUPLEURIS MERIDIONELLA, H.-S., Sppl. 595.

Cinerea, alarum anteriorum vitta costali lata lutea, apice albostriolato, punctis disci tribus magnis nigris.

Hat auf den ersten Blick einige Aehnlichkeit mit *Gelechia quinquepunctella*, Mann, und weicht in der Färbung von den verwandten Arten sehr ab. Kopf und die lange Behaarung des mittleren Palpengliedes weiss. Vorderflügel aschgrau, der Vorderrand breit rostgelblich lehmfarben, an der Spitze durch drei Zacken der Grundfarbe unterbrochen. Eben solche Beschuppung an der Wurzel der Franzen und auch hier von drei weisslichen Schrägstreifen unterbrochen. Die drei schwarzen Längspunkte des Discus stehen in zwei lichter grauen Strahlen.

I believe I have had this species from Herr Lederer from Spain.

P. 210, No. 596. PANCALIA NODOSELLA; Mann, Sppl. 964.

Nigro-metallica, alis anterioribus aureis, fascia pone basin obliqua guttisque quinque argenteis. Major, antennis medio clavato-incrassatis, gutta dorsali penultima obliqua.

Der *Lewenhoekella* sehr nah. Die Grundfarbe der Vorderflügel viel dunkler braun, die Silberflecke mehr tropfenartig erhoben, der kleine auf der Mitte des Innenrandes fehlt, die Fühler hinter der Mitte durch abstehende Schuppen verdickt, das Stück vorwärts davon an der Wurzel weiss.

Herr von Kiesenwetter found this species at Mont Serrat in Spain, Herr Mann in Upper Italy.

P. 211, No. 599. GELECHIA? RATELLA, H.-S., Sppl. 427, 428.

Caput et thorax alba, alarum anteriorum lutescentium margo anterior basi crasse niger, puncta duo anteriora verticalia, posterius pone medium.

Kopf und Thorax nebst den ganzen Palpen weisslich, die Vorderflügel angenehm lehmgelb mit schwarzem Fleck an der Wurzel des Vorderrandes, schwächerem in seiner Mitte, die zwei vorderen Punkte stehen vertikal untereinander, mit schwach staubiger Andeutung des Querstreifs bei $\frac{2}{3}$, unbestimmten Fleckchen des Saumes, deren drei sich in den Vorderrand herumziehen. Hinterflügel blassgrau mit lehmgelben Franzen.

Four specimens from Herr Lederer, who discovered them in a pasture-field at Ronda. In one specimen the lowermost of the two anterior spots is wanting.

P. 212, No. 602. HYPATIMA PHYCIDELLA, Tischer; Zeller, Isis, 1839, Sppl. 385.

In birch woods near Glogau, also in Sicily and Hungary.

P. 217, No. 621. STAGMATOPHORA OPULENTELLA, H.-S., Sppl. 818 (gewiss nicht *phengitella,* Hüb. 323).

Alis anterioribus aureo-croceis, guttis numerosis argenteis, 3 in fasciam obliquam positis pone basin, 5 in crucem positis disci, pluribus irregularibus circa apicem.

Safrangoldig, Vorderflügel mit vielen sehr erhabenen Silbertropfen, 3 nächst der Wurzel, eine schräge Binde darstellend, 5 in der Mitte im Andreaskreuz, mehrere unbestimmte um die Spitze.

From Italy. [This is the *Isabellella* of Costa.]

P. 282, No. 859. SWAMMERDAMIA EGREGIELLA, Dup.; Sppl. 409.

I have specimens from France and from Ragusa.

P. 322, No. 991. LITHOCOLLETIS PARISIELLA, Wocke, Sppl. 745.

Der *delitella* am nächsten, unter welcher sie auch bei F. v. R. steckt. Grösser, aus der Flügelwurzel zwei parallele dunkle Längslinien wie bei *quercifoliella.* Der erste Vorderrandsdoppelstrich zieht sich fein weiss zur Wurzel wie bei *ilicifoliella.* Am Innen-

rande steht nur ein einziger dunkler Strich, schwach doppelt, aber viel schräger als bei *quercifoliella*, von welcher sie sich hauptsächlich durch das vorstehende Schwänzchen und den am Vorderrande bis zur Wurzel laufenden ersten Costalstreif unterscheidet.
From Paris and Fiume.

Mir ganz unbekannt und uneinreihbar ist.
P. 335. No. 1054. LITHOCOLLETIS ITALICA, Nicelli.
One specimen brought back from Italy by Herr Zeller, without any markings.
[Can this be *L. adenocarpi*? (see *ante*, p. 165).]

SECTION II.

South-European Tineina noticed in Herrich-Schäffer's 'Neue Schmetterlinge aus Europa und den angrenzenden Ländern.'
This contains two new species, *Mesophleps trinotella* and *corsicella*.

MESOPHLEPS TRINOTELLA, m. (f. 46).
Erstes Heft, p. 6.

Wie die kleinsten Exemplare von *silacella*, aber sicher verschieden, die Hinterflügel schmäler als die vorderen, Vorder- und Innenrand parallel. Kopf, Palpen, Rücken des Thorax und Innenrand der Vorderflügel bis zur Falte, der Saum schmal, der Vorderrand von der Mitte an breit bleigrau. Bei $\frac{1}{3}$ der Flügellänge in der Falte ein tief schwarzes Längsstrichelchen; bei $\frac{2}{3}$ ein braungraues Dreieck vom Innenrande bis in die Flügelmitte. Die Franzen dunkelgrau, ihre Theilungslinie und die Saumlinie schwärzlich. Die Fühler scharf schwarz und weiss geringelt.

Aus Corsica von H. Zeller in Balgrist bei Zürich (see *ante*, pp. 222 & 233).

MESOPHLEPS CORSICELLA, m. (f. 47).
Erstes Heft, p. 7.

Der *Mesophleps silacella* sehr nah; wie deren grössten Exemplare. Palpen deutlich länger, nach unten stärker dunkel beschuppt, die Fühler schärfer schwarz geringelt. Die Farbe nicht so schön gelb, mehr grauröthlich, der Vorderrand der Vorderflügel an der Wurzel tief schwarz; von $\frac{1}{3}$ an schon braun staubig, welche Bestaubung sich in der Flügelmitte erweitert und bis zur Spitze läuft. Die 3 Punkte sehr stark, die beiden vorderen zu Längsfleckchen erweitert, besonders lang der obere, der hintere rund; der Saum mit 4-5 schwarzen Fleckchen. Die Hinterflügel wie dort gestaltet.

Corsica; von H. Zeller in Balgrist (see *ante*, p. 140).

It also contains the following sixteen species, which are already described by Staudinger; but the observations and remarks of another entomological writer will not be without interest.

COLEOPHORA SOLENELLA, Staud.; f. 100 (see *ante*, p. 158).
Zweites Heft, p. 17.

Ich kann sie nicht von *conspicuella* unterscheiden, höchstens sind die Flügel etwas schmäler und länger, der Sack weicht jedoch bedeutend ab, ist länger, gerader, lichter braun, am Bauchrand nicht wellig erweitert.

COLEOPHORA SPUMOSELLA, Staud.; f. 101 (see *ante*, p. 158).

Der *cælebipennella* sehr nah, das Gelb mehr blass citron- als schwefelgelb, der Fühlerbart etwas kürzer, der weisse Costalstrich etwas breiter, reicht nicht so weit zur Wurzel und verlässt an seinem inneren Ende den Vorderrand ein wenig, der braune Streif hinter ihm schmäler, dunkler, auch nicht so weit zur Wurzel ziehend, der Innenrand nur an der Wurzel silbern.

Der Sack ganz eigenthümlich, aus muschelartig rundlichen, hornartig durchsichtigen Stückchen zusammengesetzt, welche als zwei grosse Muscheln den inneren cylindrischen Theil einschliessen.

COLEOPHORA BISERIATELLA, Staud.; f. 102 (see *ante*, p. 160).

Scheint mir neu, und neben *fringillella* zu gehören. Die Verdickung der weiblichen Fühler reicht weiter zur Spitze, ist aber nicht so borstig abstehend. Das schöne Citrongelb der Vorderflügel läuft unter Zunahme der eingemengten schwarzen Schuppen scharf in die Flügelspitze aus Vorder- und Innenrand, Faltenstreif und Discoidallinie sind feiner, silberweiss. Hinterflügel bräunlich, mit lichtem Mittelstreif. Die Franzen an der Spitze aller Flügel und gegen den Innenrand der hinteren weiss.

COLEOPHORA STRUELLA, Staud.; f. 103 (see *ante*, p. 160).

Der Bart des ersten Fühlergliedes überragt kaum dessen Spitze und ist, so wie der Kopf in der Mitte stark grau gemischt. Fühler ungeringelt, Ende der Franzen aller Flügel weisslich. Die Rippen der Vorderflügel scharf dunkelbraun, eigentlich nirgends unterbrochen; die Subcostalis sendet 5 Parallelläste zum Vorderrand, deren letzter noch einen Ast in den Saum abgibt; darauf folgen zwei regelmässige Doppellinien (Medianrippe und Faltenstreif) und eine einfache vor dem Innenrande. Die Franzen des Vorderrandes führen eine ziemlich scharf dunkle Theilungslinie, welche verfliessend sich bis gegen den Afterwinkel verfolgen lässt.

Der Sack hat grosse Aehnlichkeit mit jenem der *virgatella*, doch ist er aus glatteren, nicht haarigen, gerader zugeschnittenen Theilen gebildet.

YPSOLOPHUS LIMBIPUNCTELLUS, Staud.; f. 104 (see *ante*, p. 152).

Die Vorderflügel sind spitziger und etwas schmäler als bei *juniperellus*, dem er am nächsten steht, doch hat das Weib merklich schmälere Flügel, die Farbe ist mehr gelbgrau staubfarben, die 3 typischen Punkte und jene des Costal- und Saumrandes sind fein und scharf, eben so die beiden Theilungslinien der Franzen. Den

Hinterflügeln fehlen die Saumpunkte. Palpen und Fühler wie bei *juniperellus*.

YPSOLOPHUS BUBULCELLUS, Staud.; f. 105 (see *ante*, p. 152).

Zweites Heft, p. 18.

Die kleinste Art der Gattung, mit schmäleren Flügeln, die vorderen an der Wurzel des Vorderrandes sehr bauchig, lehmgelblich, stark längsfaltig, in den Falten mit sparsamen, groben, schwarzen Schuppen, welche sich an der Saumlinie und am Ende des Costalrandes zu Fleckchen häufen. In der Mittellinie bei $\frac{1}{3}$ und $\frac{2}{3}$ ein stark schwarzer Punkt; zwischen ihnen, etwas mehr wurzelwärts, in der Falte ein solcher Längsstrich. Franzen mit dunklerer Theilungs- und Endlinie.

ALLOCLITA RECISELLA, Staud.; f. 106 (see *ante*, p. 154).

Ueber die Gattungsrechte kann ich nicht urtheilen, da ich die Flügelrippen nicht untersuchen kann.

Die Hinterflügel scheinen mir 8 Rippen zu haben, 3+4, 5+6; 8 nur bis über die Mitte des Vorderrandes. Auf den Vorderflügel scheinen mir die Rippen gesondert. Die Palpen steigen sichelförmig über den Kopf auf, sind weiss, anliegend beschuppt, das Mittelglied mit rostbraunem Ring vor dem Ende, das etwas kürzere dünne und spitze Endglied mit schmal schwarzem an der Wurzel und breit schwarzem vor der Spitze. Alle Schienen mit 2, alle Tarsenglieder mit einem schwarzbraunen Ring, an den Hinterbeinen undeutlicher.

Eine Verwandtschaft mit *Endrosis lacteella* möchte genauer zu prüfen sein. Ocellen sehe ich allerdings nicht.

GELECHIA? TERNATELLA, Staud.; f. 107 (see *ante*, p. 148).

Diese Art hat durch die Gestalt ihrer Flügel, insbesondere auch der hinteren, welche vor ihrer abgerundeten Spitze kaum eingebogen sind, ganz das Ansehen einer *Depressaria*, doch sind die Palpen ganz anliegend beschuppt und verweisen sie wegen der nach unten mangelnden Divergenz zu der Gattung *Anacampsis*. Eine ähnliche Art lässt sich allerdings weder in dieser Gattung noch bei *Gelechia* auffinden. Auf der Vorderflügeln nur Ast 7. und 8. gestielt, 7. in der Spitze.

ŒCOPHORA SCIPIONELLA, Staud.; f. 108 (see *ante*, p. 155).

Fusco-viridis, alis a. vitta media alba e basi ultra medium.

Viel grösser als *Knochiella*, metallischer, der weisse Mittelstreif ist saumwärts wegen weniger scharfer Begrenzung breiter; auch der Costalrand ist hinter der Mitte fein gelblich. Der After ist wie bei *armatella* gebildet.

ŒCOPHORA XANTHOPYGELLA, Staud.; f. 109 (see *ante*, p. 155).

Æneo-fusca, alarum a. margine costali, vitta media e basi ultra medium, maculaque obliqua intraapicali testaceis; ano ochraceo.

Grünlichbraun, der feine Costalrand der Vorderflügel und ein

Mittellängsstreif, welcher hinter der Mitte schwarz unterbrochen ist, beinfarben. Die letzten 3 Segmente des Hinterleibes sind ockergelb, deren erstes nur in der Mitte des Hinterrandes.

ANCHINIA PLANELLA, Staud.; f. 110 (see *ante*, p. 153).
Zweites Heft, p. 19.

Alis a. opacis, ferrugineo-ochreis, vitta postcostali obsoletissime obscuriore, evidentius versus apicem, ciliis fuscescentibus.

Das Endglied der Palpen ist nur $\frac{1}{3}$ so lang als das Mittelglied. Ockergelb, die Vorderflügel vor dem lichteren Costalrand dunkler, besonders gegen die Spitze; Franzen braun.

ANCHINIA TELIGERELLA, Staud.; f. 111 (see *ante*, p. 153).

Ich halte sie für gleich mit *ericella*, Dup., denn ich sehe bei dem einen Exemplar ganz deutlich den schwarzen Punkt innen an der weissen Linie, welche den braunen Streifen gegen Innen begrenzt, bei $\frac{2}{3}$ ihrer Länge. Jedenfalls steht er ferner von der braunen Strieme als bei *bicostella*, bei welcher diese auch gegen die Spitze schmäler und innen nicht so deutlich weiss begrenzt ist. Der Punkt gegen die Wurzel fehlt bei *teligerella* ganz; die schwachen Saumpunkte aber sind wie bei *bicostella*.

DISSOCTENA GRANIGERELLA, Staud.; f. 112 (see *ante*, p. 143).

Scheint mit Recht als eigene Gattung aufgestellt. Von *Typhonia* nur durch die Weiber verschieden, welche flügellos, mit vollständigen 19-20-gliederigen Fühlern und vollständigen Beinen, doch ohne Schienensporen, versehen sind, einen vorstehenden Legestachel und lange, seidenartige, gewellte, weisse Afterwolle haben. Von *Talæporia* unterscheidet sich der Mann durch die langen Kammzähne der Fühler, den anliegend behaarten Kopf, den Mangel der Ocellen und Palpen, die gesonderten 12 und nur 7 Rippen der Hinterflügel. Dagegen scheint das Weib vollkommen mit jenen der *Talæporien* übereinzustimmen.

Der Sack ist so sandig wie jener von *Typhonia*, und ich sehe keine Puppenhülse aus demselben hervorragen.

Etwas kleiner als *Talæporia pseudobombycella*. Alle Flügel gleichmässig durchscheinend und glänzend, bleich gelbgrau, mit sehr zerstreuten groben braunen Schuppen, die Franzen gegen den Afterwinkel kaum länger.

MICROPTERYX IMPERFECTELLA, Staud.; f. 113 (see *ante*, p. 144).

Kaum kleiner als *aruncella*, Vorderflügel rein tiefgolden, um die Spitze schmal kupferig, vier Silbertropfen, der erste unbestimmt dreieckige an der Wurzel der Mittelzelle, der zweite, kleinste, vertikale vor der Mitte des Vorderrandes, der dritte grössere, vertikale hinter der Mitte des Innenrandes, der vierte rundliche, vor der Flügelspitze, dem Vorderrande näher. Hinterflügel purpurviolett, gegen die Spitze golden. Franzen purpurbraun.

Pœciloptilia Grabowiella, Staud.; f. 114 (see *ante*, p. 157).
Zweites Heft, p. 20.
Sicher keine *Pancalia* und in die Gruppe von *Pœc. geminatella* u. *magnificella*, m. gehörig, von beiden dadurch verschieden, dass die drei Binden der Vorderflügel der Wurzel näher gerückt sind und auf dem Saum grosse Goldschuppen stehen, welche sich meistens im Afterwinkel und an der Flügelspitze zu zwei grösseren Flecken häufen. Die Fühler schwarz und weiss geringelt, die 4–5 vorletzten schwarzen Ringe viel breiter.

Lithocolletis belotella, Staud.; f. 116 *(see ante, p. 162).*
Nach meiner analyt. Tabelle neben *carpinicolella*, aber verschieden. Tarsenglied 1–3. am Ende schwarz. Scheitelhaare und Thorax ganz goldorange, letzter nur mit fein weisser Mittellinie, die Basallinie vorne schwarz begrenzt, in der Mitte etwas nach vorne gerückt, der Saum schöner pfirsischblüthfarben, der Spitzenpunkt fein rund, die Franzen aller Flügel, besonders aber der vorderen lebhaft braungelb; die Fühler brauner geringelt.

Von *Messaniella* ganz verschieden: Thorax mit *weisser* Mittellinie, Vorderflügel *breiter* mit *weisser* Zeichnung, der erste Costalfleck gegen die Wurzel fortgesetzt, die Begrenzung der Dorsalflecke viel weniger gegen den Saum vorgezogen, die Franzen gelber.

Section III.

Six species of the genus *Butalis* from Southern Europe, described by Professor Zeller in the 10th volume of the 'Linnæa Entomologica.'

[The species of the genus *Butalis* are so numerous and so similar, that it seems necessary to give these descriptions here to render this volume more complete.]

'Linnæa Entom.' x. p. 186.
Butalis ærariella, (Z.) H.-S. p. 269. no. 806.
Media, alis anterioribus subelongatis, virescenti-œneis, vix nitidulis; posterioribus nigricantibus violaceo submicantibus; abdomine ♂ crassiusculo, subtus ante apicem griseo, ♀ ventris segmentis duobus ultimis exalbidis.

In der Grösse der *seliniella* und *fallacella*, unterscheidet sie sich von diesen wie von allen vorigen durch den ganz matten Glanz auf den grünlich-metallischen Vorderflügeln, ausserdem von den grössern Arten durch die geringere Streckung dieser Flügel, so wie durch die hell gelblich-graue Farbe des männlichen Bauches an den letzten Segmenten. Durch dieses Merkmal lässt sie sich auch am besten erkennen, wenn man *seliniella* und *fallacella* nicht zum Vergleich haben sollte. Mit der gleich grossen *tabidella* ist sie nicht zu verwechseln, da bei dieser nicht nur die Vorderflügel im Glanze denen von *seliniella* gleich kommen und eine ganz verschiedene Grundfarbe, nämlich eine staubgraue, haben, sondern auch der ganze

Bauch in beiden Geschlechtern hellgrau gefärbt ist. Ganz ohne Glanz der Vorderflügel ist *flaviventrella*; diese hat auf denselben keine grünliche Färbung wie *ærariella*, sondern ist auf dunkelem Grunde dicht mit gelbbräunlich-grauen Schuppen bekleidet, deren Färbung in der Flügelspitze aus der dunklen Unterlage deutlicher hervortritt; bei ihr ist auch der Bauch unten nicht hellgrau oder weisslich, sondern hell ochergelb, und zwar im männlichen Geschlecht in noch grösserer Ausdehnung als im weiblichen; endlich hat sie in beiden Geschlechtern ein eigenthümlich zusammengedrücktes Aftersegment. Die kleineren Arten: *vagabundella*, *eboracensis*, etc., haben entweder einfarbig schwarze Bäuche, oder ganz verschieden gefärbte Vorderflügel, oder beides zusammen. Andere gleich grosse Arten (z. B. *apicalis*) unterscheiden sogleich die Vorderflügelspitzen, die bei ihnen kupferig oder violet gefärbt sind, während *ærariella* dieser Farbe ganz entbehrt.

Rückenschild und Kopf grünlich oder grüngelblich-erzfarben, etwas glänzend. Fühler borstenförmig, gerundet, ziemlich fein, zart pubescirend beim Männchen. Taster etwas kürzer als bei *seliniella*, fein zugespitzt, *am ganzen Wurzelgliede bleich gelbschuppig*, spärlicher und meist undeutlich auf der Innenseite des zweiten Gliedes längs des Rückens, auch der *Aussenrand des Auges und das Kinn sind bleich gelbschuppig*. Beine braun, aussen hell metallglänzend; an den hintern die Schiene und der Fuss auf der Innenseite grau glänzend. Hinterleib plump, dunkel braungrau, nach hinten stärker metallschimmernd. Der männliche Afterbusch mehr staubgrau, ziemlich kurz und etwas zusammengedrückt, auf der Unterseite bleich graugelblich beschuppt; diese bleich gelbliche Farbe haben auch die drei vorhergehenden Segmente auf der Bauchseite, nur dass sie sich, je weiter sie sich von der Spitze entfernt, immer mehr von den Seiten zurückzieht und mehr und mehr mit bräunlichen Schuppen verdunkelt wird. Beim Weibchen steht der Legestachel aus dem abgestutzt kegelförmigen, braunen Analsegment bisweilen hervor; die zwei vorhergehenden Segmente sind am Bauche ganz gelblich-weiss; das vorhergehende ist es auch, aber grösstentheils durch bräunliche Schuppen getrübt; selbst am Ende des folgenden Segments befinden sich bei einem Exemplar in der Mitte gelbliche Schuppen.

Vorderflügel des ♂ $3\frac{1}{4}$–$3\frac{1}{2}$, des ♀ $2\frac{3}{4}$–$3'''$ lang, ziemlich gestreckt, zugespitzt, beim Weibchen in der Gestalt viel weniger abweichend als bei *fallacella* und *seliniella*, braun, grünlich oder grünglblich-erzfarben schwach schimmernd, matter als das Rückenschild; diese helle Färbung entsteht durch gedrängte Haarschuppen, welche auf der dunkeln Unterlage durch die Loupe leicht zu erkennen sind und der Fläche eine gewisse Sättigung der Färbung und dem Flügel ein derbes kräftiges Ansehen geben. Franzen schwarzgrau, an der Wurzel mit einzelnen Schuppen des Flügelüberzuges.

Hinterflügel kaum schmäler als die Vorderflügel; die Zuspitzung fängt erst hinter der Mitte an und lässt die Spitze schärfer als bei *seliniella* erscheinen. Grundfarbe dunkel schwarzgrau, sehr schwach violettlich überflogen. Die Schuppen sind gedrängt und gerundet.

Franzen heller, an der Innenrandhälfte oder mehr mit sehr feiner, verloschener, gelblicher Wurzellinie.

Unterseite braun, am Hinterrande der Vorderflügel in einer schmalen Linie schwach erzglänzend.

Vaterland: die südlichen illyrischen Gebirge, wo *Mann* die Art im Mai und—am Nanos—im Juni fing.

Anm. Mann übergeht die Art in seiner Aufzählung der am Nanos gesammelten Arten. Ich erhielt aber zwei richtig benannte Männchen von ihm mit der Angabe: "Nanos im Juni" zugleich mit andern dort gesammelten Arten. Die Auslassung kann also nur eine unabsichtliche sein.

'Linnæa Entom.' x. p. 188.

BUTALIS TABIDELLA, (Z.) H.-S. p. 268. no. 802.

Media, alis anterioribus griseis, metallice nitidulis; posterioribus angustioribus acuminatis cinereis; abdomine supra cinereo subtus cano (♂ ♀).

Vor allen grössern Arten durch die staubgrauen, glänzenden Vorderflügel leicht zu unterscheiden.

In der Grösse ein wenig über *œrariella*. Rückenschild und Kopf hell bräunlich-grau, etwas metallglänzend. Fühler ebenso, borstenförmig, stielrund, beim Männchen zart pubescirend. Taster ziemlich schlank, zugespitzt, staubgrau, glänzend, innen hell, an der Wurzel, so wie die Kinn- und Backengegend und der Aussenrand der Augen weisslich-grau beschuppt. Brust hellgrau, glänzend. Beine hell bräunlich-grau, die hinteren innen glänzend hellgrau, an den Schienen hellbraun. Hinterleib etwas plump, doch nicht so sehr wie bei *œrariella*, auf dem Rücken metallschimmernd röthlich-grau, nach hinten heller, am ganzen Bauch schmutzig gelblich-weiss, an der Wurzel grauer. Der männliche Afterbusch ist nicht stark, oben hellgrau, unten bleich gelblich, länglich gerundet, kaum an der Seite etwas zusammengedrückt. Beim Weibchen spitzt sich der Hinterleib, und aus dem abgestutzt kegelförmigen Analsegment steht der Legestachel etwas hervor.

Vorderflügel des ♂ $3\frac{1}{3}$–$3\frac{3}{4}'''$, des ♀ $3\frac{1}{3}'''$ lang, ziemlich gestreckt, zugespitzt, staubgrau mit bräunlicher Unterlage, ziemlich glänzend, mit gedrängten Haarschuppen bekleidet, am Vorderrande auf der Aussenhälfte in einer schmalen, oft sehr undeutlichen Linie weisslich oder bleichgelblich. Franzen bräunlichgrau, an der Wurzel mit einigen staubgrauen Haarschuppen der Fläche überragt.

Hinterflügel schmäler, hinter der Mitte zugespitzt, feinspitzig, grau, nach hinten dunkler, schwach röthlich angeflogen, gegen die Wurzel mit Haarschuppen. Franzen viel heller grau, auf der Innenwinkelhälfte bleichgelblich schillernd, mit verloschener, gegen die Flügelspitze verschwindender, feiner, gelblicher Wurzellinie.

Unterseite mehr oder weniger, dunkel grau, auf den Hinterflügeln heller; die vordern am Vorderrand vor der Spitze bleich gelblich.

Vaterland: die Küstenländer des Mittelmeeres. *Mann* entdeckte sie bei Fiume, fand sie später bei Spalato, dann bei Brussa, und zuletzt sammelte er sie an der Südseite des Nanos und bei Fuceine am Kouk, wo sie in den Nachmittags- und Abendstunden flog und sie meist nach Sonnenuntergang begattete.

Anm. In Sicilien habe ich die Art nicht gefunden, wie sich nach H.-S.'s Angabe schliessen lassen möchte; sondern sie ist eine der vielen Entdeckungen des fleissigen *Mann.*

'Linnæa Entom.' x. p. 200.

BUTALIS VAGABUNDELLA, (Z.) H.-S. p. 269. no. 805.

Minor, abdomine crassiusculo, pedibus obscuris; alis anterioribus subelongatis acutis, fuscis vel subviolaceo-fuscis opacis; posterioribus vix angustioribus subito acuminatis; ♂ *abdomine toto æneo, fasciculo brevi, debili, attenuato;* ♀ — —.

Grösser als *senescens*, durch den mangelnden Glanz auf den dichter beschuppten, kräftigern Vorderflügeln, auf denen die Haarschuppen fehlen, und durch den dunkelfarbigen Bauch von ihr verschieden. Ihr Unterschied von *disparella* ist bei diesen gegeben*. Von *potentillæ* trennt sie sich durch die gestrecktern Vorderflügel, den Mangel der Haarschuppen, die dunkeln Hinterflügel und den einfarbigen Hinterleib. Am ähnlichsten sieht sie wohl der *pascuella*, die wahrscheinlich mit ihr gemischt oder doch an ähnlichen Stellen vorkommt, so dass sie wirklich mit ihr verwechselt worden ist; *vagabundella* unterscheidet sich aber sehr sicher durch die breitern Hinterflügel und den kurzen, armhaarigen Afterbusch an dem viel dickern männlichen Hinterleibe, und ist etwas grösser und auf den Vorderflügeln gewöhnlich dunkler.

Rückenschild und Kopf nebst Fühlern, Tastern und Beinen schwarzbraun, mehr oder weniger lebhaft violetlich oder kupferig schimmernd. Fühler etwas dicker als bei *disparella*, ebenso gebaut und behaart. Taster bei den heller gefärbten Exemplaren bisweilen aussen an der Wurzel und auf der Innenseite schwach gelblich erzschimmernd. Beine einfarbig; die Hinterschiendornen innen an der Wurzel grau. Hinterleib dick und plump, nach hinten etwas erweitert, dann plötzlich zugespitzt, noch dunkler als das Brustschild, violetlich schimmernd, auf beiden Seiten gleich gefärbt. Der Afterbusch, der hauptsächlich die plötzliche Zuspitzung des Hinterleibs verursacht, ist kurz, armhaarig, kegelförmig; doch stehen die seitlichen Haare oft als kleine Pinsel etwas von der Hauptmasse ab.

Vorderflügel $2\frac{2}{3}$-3''' lang, ein wenig breiter, und kräftiger gebaut als bei *disparella* und *senescens*, sonst gleichgestaltet, mit sehr dichter, schwarzbrauner, violet angelaufener Beschuppung, bisweilen aber auch heller, mehr braun und schwach violetlich angelaufen, immer nur mit ganz schwachem, kaum bemerkbarem Schimmer. Die gelbbräun-

---

* *Vagabundella* hat, durch die dichtere Beschuppung, den fast fehlenden Glanz auf den weniger violettlichen Vorderflügeln, den ganz dunkeln männlichen Bauch, solche Verschiedenheiten von *disparella*, dass mir ihre Artverschiedenheit weit unzweifelhafter ist als die der *disparella* von *senescens*, und dass ich erwarte, sie auch durch die Färbung des Weibchens bestätigt zu sehen.

lichen Haarschuppen, die bei einigen Exemplaren auf der Fläche einzeln und zerstreut liegen, sind offenbar nicht die aufgestreuten der *senescens*, sondern beim Fangen und Zubereiten unter den dunkeln Schuppen abgebrochne und dadurch auf die Oberfläche gebrachte. Franzen braun.

Hinterflügel in der Gestalt wie bei *disparella*, schwärzlichbraun, nur an der Wurzel und in deren Nähe am Vorderrande etwas heller, schwach violetlich angelaufen, wie auch die schwärzlichen Franzen, welche eine verloschene, gelbliche, vor der Flügelspitze endigende Wurzellinie haben.

Unterseite dunkel graubraun, schimmernd, auf den Hinterflügeln etwas heller.

Mann entdeckte diese Art bei Fiume, und fand sie dann wieder am Nanosgebirge auf Hutweiden und Berglehnen im Mai und Juni. Die Exemplare vom Nanos haben dunklere, violet angelaufene Vorderflügel, während die von Fiume die oben erwähnte hellere, fast schieferschwärzliche Färbung zeigen. Ausserdem beobachtete *Mann* nachher diese Art auch in Istrien und Dalmatien, und selbst bei Brussa, so dass sie also südlich von den Alpen weit verbreitet zu sein scheint. Unten 11 Exemplaren in *Schneider's*, *Wocke's* und meiner Sammlung ist kein Weibchen.

'Linnæa Entom.' x. p. 207.

BUTALIS PASCUELLA, n. sp. *Œcophora gravatella*, Mann, Verh. z.-b. Ver. Wien, 1854, p. 587.

Minor, alis anterioribus subelongatis, fusco-olivaceis, subopacis; posterioribus angustioribus sensim acuminatis; abdomine mediocri, lineari, ♂ utrinque nigro, fasciculo anali mediocri, ♀ ventris macula postica obsoleta lutescente.

Obgleich fast immer kleiner, doch so ähnlich den hellern Exemplaren der *vagabundella*, dass ich sie unter diese gemischt erhielt. Ihre viel schmälern, sanft zugespitzten Hinterflügel, ihr schmälerer, streifenförmiger Hinterleib und ihr viel längerer, stärkerer Afterbusch unterscheiden sie leicht. Auch mit der auf den Vorderflügeln viel hellern *gravatella* wurde sie vermengt; von dieser aber trennt sie sich sofort durch ihren schwarzen Hinterleib, während *gravatella* in beiden Geschlechtern auf dem Rücken des Hinterleibes grau, am Bauch hell graugelblich ist. Von *fuscocuprea* trennen sie die schmälern, dunkleren, glanzlosen Flügel, der längere, schmälere Hinterleib, der ganz verschieden gebildete Afterbusch, etc.

So kräftig gebaut wie *vagabundella*. Rückenschild und Kopf olivenfarbig, sehr schwach schimmernd. Fühler ziemlich stark, stielrund, mit kurzer, dichter, zarter Pubescenz. Taster von Rückenschildslänge, aufwärts gekrümmt, braun, beim Weibchen bisweilen innen am Rücken gelblich; das Endglied fein gespitzt, deutlich abgesetzt, von ⅔ Länge des zweiten Gliedes. Beine braun; Schenkel kupferig glänzend, Schienen meist violetlich angelaufen; die hintern auf der Rückenkante mit langen, schwärzlichen Haaren reichlich besetzt. Hinterleib des Männchens kräftig, doch nicht dick und

fast streifenförmig, an den Seiten mit wenig hervorstehenden Schuppenbüscheln, violetschwarz auf beiden Seiten; der ziemlich starke Afterbusch ist wenigstens so lang wie die zwei vorhergehenden Segmente zusammen und spitzt und rundet sich nach hinten etwas zu.
Der Hinterleib des Weibchens ist mässig stark, hinter der Mitte etwas verdickt, dann zugespitzt, auf dem Rücken violetschwarz, am Bauch etwas heller, metallisch schimmernd, einfarbig oder am Afterkegel lehmgelblich, welche Farbe bei dem besonders kleinen Exemplar der Sammlung des Dr. *Schneider* in die gelbliche, nach innen verdunkelte Erzfarbe des Bauches übergeht, so dass man diesen Fleck nur bei gewisser Haltung deutlich davon unterscheidet.

Vorderflügel 2⅓–2⅔''' lang, ziemlich gestreckt, durch die reichlichen Franzen meist etwas abgerundet erscheinend, beim kleinern Weibchen etwas kürzer und gespitzter, olivenfarbigbraun, sehr schwach schimmernd, ganz ohne Violet; Franzen schwärzlich, violetlich schimmernd.

Hinterflügel beträchtlich schmäler als die Vorderflügel, ganz ohne Innenwinkel, allmählig scharf zugespitzt (wie bei H.-S. fig. 935, *laminella*), braun, gegen die Wurzel braungrau und hier mit deutlichen Haarschuppen. Franzen schwärzlich, violetlich schimmernd, selten mit der Spur einer hellern Wurzellinie.

Unterseite der Vorderflügel schwärzlich, der Hinterflügel heller, braungrau.

Mann entdeckte diese Art in Illyrien und fing sie auf Istrien im Mai, am Nanosgebirge im Juni; ein Exemplar erhielt ich als *vagabundella* auf Dalmatien. Sie fliegt auf Viehweiden und Berglehnen im Grase und jungen Gebüsch, und begattet sich in den Nachmittagsstunden.

Anm. Da ich sie für eine Varietät meiner *gravatella*, hielt, so führte Mann sie unter dem falschen Namen auf.

'Linnæa Entom.' x. p. 210.

Butalis tergestinella, n. sp.   *Œcophora gravatella*, var. b, Z. Isis, 1847, p. 832 (see *ante*, p. 24).

Minor, palpis longiusculis; alis anterioribus subelongatis acutis virescenti-griseis, vix nitidulis; posterioribus angustioribus acuminatis violascenti-fuliginosis; ♂ abdomine longiusculo obscure cinereo, ventre albido, fasciculo anali longiore subcompresso diluto; ♀ — —.

Ganz wie *gravatella*, ein wenig grösser, vorzüglich durch den viel längern, zusammengedrückten Afterbusch verschieden. Ihre viel längern Taster, längerer Afterbusch, breitere violetschimmernde Hinterflügel, längere, mehr gelblich-graue Vorderflügel etc. unterscheiden sie von *paullella*. *Terrenella, tributella, denigratella* haben viel schmälere Hinterflügel, sind viel kleiner mit kleinern Tastern und anderer Färbung.

Grösse einer mittlern *vagabundella*. Kopf und Rückenschild gelbbräunlich, schwach erzfarben schimmernd, am meisten an den Schultern. Fühler ziemlich fein, sehr schwach pubescirend. Taster etwas länger als bei *gravatella*, schlank, am Wurzelgliede ganz weiss, sonst gelbbräunlich, am Rücken des zweiten Gliedes etwas gelichtet. Endglied so lang wie das zweite Glied, fein zugespitzt, fast nicht abgesetzt. Kinngegend weiss, ebenso der sehr schmale Vorderrand und, doch breiter und trüber, der Hinterrand der Augen. Mittelbrust weiss beschuppt, Hinterbrust glänzend grau. Beine hell gelbbräunlich, an den Schenkeln glänzend; Hinterbeine an Schiene und Fuss innen weissgrau; die Haare des Schienenrückens reichlich, auf der Innenseite weisslich, auf der Aussenseite grau. Hinterleib etwas gestreckt, nach hinten verdünnt, auf dem Rücken grau, schwach glänzend, am Bauche schmutzig weisslich. Der Afterbusch ist doppelt so lang wie das vorhergehende Glied, nicht sehr stark, zugespitzt, seitlich etwas zusammengedrückt, auf dem Rücken lichtgrau, am Bauch schmutzig weisslich, in der Mitte mit lehmgelben Haaren.

Vorderflügel 2⅔ lang, ziemlich gestreckt, gespitzt, kaum ein wenig schimmernd, im Mittelfelde mit Haarschuppen, braungrau-gelblich, kaum gegen die Wurzel etwas grünlich gemischt, gegen die Spitze mehr ins Graue. Franzen braungrau.

Hinterflügel wenig schmäler als die Vorderflügel, am Enddrittel sanft zugespitzt, braungrau, violetlich schimmernd, gegen die Wurzel heller; Franzen braungrau, mit etwas violettem Schimmer.

Unterseite bräunlich-grau, die Vorderflügel etwas dunkler.

Das einzelne Exemplar fing ich am 14. September bei Triest am Südabhange des Karst auf einer grasige Stelle.

'Linnæa Entom.' x. p. 257.

BUTALIS SICCELLA, Z. *Œcoph. siccella*, Z. Isis, 1839, p. 193; Stett. ent. Zeit. 1850, p. 148. *Chrysesthia siccella*, H.-S. p. 314. no. 908.

Parva, alis anterioribus subelongatis, subobtusis, fuscis, squamis albidis postice sparsis, puncto plicæ nigræ uno (duobusve) albo; posterioribus lineari-lanceolatis; abdomine crasso (♀ elongato) fuscocinereo, ventre ♂ cinereo vel cano, ♀ albido, apice fusco.

Obgleich sehr veränderlich, scheint sie von *variella* doch durch den stärkern, hinten gerade abgeschnittenen Afterbusch des Männchens specifisch unterschieden zu sein; als fernere unterscheidende Merkmale haben dann die stumpfern Vorderflügel und der obenauf schwärzliche Hinterleib zu gelten.

Siccella ist meist kleiner als *variella*, erreicht aber doch, besonders im weiblichen Geschlecht, die kleinsten Exemplare derselben. Taster wie bei *variella*, bisweilen einfarbig braun. Brust grau glänzend. Beine braun oder braungrau, beim ♀ bisweilen grau angelaufen; Vorderschenkel auf der abgewendeten Seite hellgrau. Hinterleib des Männchens plumper als bei *variella*, aber in der Breite so veränderlich, dass man mehrere Arten vermuthen möchte, wenn nicht alles Andere widerspräche. Der Rücken ist braungrau, schwach schimmernd, nur an den Seitenwülsten bisweilen etwas weisslich; der glänzende Bauch ändert in der Färbung sehr ab, indem er tiefer oder heller grau, oft sogar weisslich ist. Der Afterbusch ist grau, kurz, hinten abgeschnitten, nicht ganz dicht, reichlicher als bei *variella*. Beim Weibchen ist der Hinterleib viel länger und dicker, nach hinten gespitzt, oben braungrau wie beim Männchen, am Bauche weisslich, nach hinten gelblich-weiss; der Afterkegel ist weniger flach gedrückt als bei *variella* und länger zugespitzt, oben hellgrau, unten gelblich-weiss, auf beiden Seiten am Ende dunkel schiefergrau.

Vorderflügel etwas kürzer und durch die dichteren Franzen weniger scharf gespitzt als bei *variella*, mit dunklerer, gelblichbrauner Grundfarbe und spärlich gestreuten, in der Menge sehr veränderlichen, weissen Schuppen, die den Grund nicht lichter erscheinen lassen; die meisten liegen in der Flügelspitze und bilden hier gewöhnlich einen weisslichen Fleck; aber sie fehlen auch manchmal völlig. Die Falte ist schwarz, hinter der Mitte mit einem weissen, aus wenigen Schuppen gebildeten Punkt; zwischen diesem und der Wurzel ist gewöhnlich ein anderer, in der Grösse veränderlicher, der manchmal grösser als jener ist; am Ende der Falte sind nur weisse, zerstreute Schuppen, die keinen Fleck bilden. Franzen schwärzlich.

Hinterflügel wie bei *variella* gestaltet, dunkler, nicht immer mit heller Wurzellinie.

Unterseite wie bei *variella*.

Siccella ist bei Glogau nicht selten in Schonungen sandiger Kieferwaldungen im Juni; sie fliegt im Sonnenschein auf Blumen und besucht mit *cicadella* gemeinschaftlich die von *Jasione montana*; auch fing ich sie auf Blüthen von *Potentilla argentea* und scheuchte sie vom Boden aus Moosen und Flechten auf. Bei Breslau fliegt sie auf einem sandigen, mit verkrüppelten Kiefern, *Artemisia campestris*, *Aira canescens*, *Rumex acetosella* dünn bewachsenen Platze in der ersten Hälfte des Juni (*Wocke*). *H.-S.* giebt auch noch Preussen, die Gegend von Mainz und Haidestellen am Meeresufer bei Marseille (im September) an, und nach *Mann* fliegt sie in Toscana bei Antignano im Mai einzeln an Feldrainen.

CHAPTER VIII.

FRENCH AUTHORS.

In this chapter I have given a list of the Tineina from the south of France which are noticed by Godart and Duponchel in their 'Lépidoptères de France.'
They are as follows:—

Yponomeuta acanthella.
Euplocamus morellus.
Lita triguttella.
Adela Latreillella.
A. Dumerilella.
A. unipunctella.
A. violella.
A. cuprella.
A. scabiosella.
A. aurifrontella.
A. Solierella.

Adela Donzelella.
Stenoptera orbonella.
Elachista Boyerella.
Ornix argentipennella.
Euplocamus fulvimitrellus.
Rhinosia sordidella.
Anacampsis interruptella.
Adela Aglaella.
Tinea picarella.
Œcophora olivella.

Yponomeuta acanthella, Godart (L. F. v. p. 38, pl. 44. f. 4). Found on thorn-bushes in the centre and south of France.
Duponchel (xi. p. 317) places it in the genus *Lita*, and adds "Dr. Rambur, who has met with it near Montpellier, assured me he had obtained it from a larva which fed on the lichen on walls, concealed under a little white web, which shelters it and never contains more than one." [Herrich-Schäffer mentions its occurrence in the south of Spain; and Zeller, who correctly refers it to the genus *Butalis*, adds that Mann met with it in Croatia in June. This conspicuous insect is so well known that I do not need to quote the description*.]

Euplocamus morellus, Duponchel (L. F. xi. p. 79, pl. 288. f. 5). M. Barthélemy, Conservator of the Museum of Natural History at Marseilles, obtained this species from a larva which he found in an excrescence on the trunk of a white mulberry-tree. [Described, see p. 260.]

Lita triguttella, Duponchel (L. F. xi. p. 332, pl. 298. f. 14). This species was received from Baron Feisthamel, who took it June 28th, near Domo-Dossola. [This is the *scopolella*, Hübner, 246, a true *Butalis*; and, according to Reutti, the larva feeds on *Sedum album*.]

---

* Zeller's diagnosis (Linn. Ent. x. p. 261) is briefly thus:—*Media, alis anterioribus elongatis obtusis albis, basi et apice schistaceo-maculatis, fascia media schistacea, puncto postico nigro.*

Adela Latreillella, Hübner, Dup. (L. F. xi. p. 366, pl. 300. f. 5, 6). Found in the south of France as well as in Sicily. The two specimens figured I took in May, in the neighbourhood of Aix in Provence; they were flying around bushes*.

Adela Dumerilella, Duponchel (L. F. xi. p. 372, pl. 300. f. 12). The specimen figured, the only one I possess, I took in June, near Toulon. I have since seen a second in Dr. Boisduval's collection, taken in the Bois de Boulogne.

Adela unipunctella, Duponchel (L. F. xi. p. 374, pl. 302. f. 10). [Described, see p. 261.] The only specimen I possess was sent to me from the south of France; as it wants the antennæ and palpi, I cannot be certain it belongs to the genus *Adela*. [Judging from the description, this should be *Laverna epilobiella*, Römer (*langiella*, Hüb.); the figure must be to some extent imaginary, as it is represented with antennæ.]

Adela violella, W. V., Tr., Dup. (L. F. xi. p. 379, pl. 302. f. 1). The specimen figured was sent to me from the south of France.

Adela cuprella, W. V., Tr., Dup. (L. F. xi. p. 380, pl. 301. f. 4 & 7). The female specimen figured I took in the department of Lozère.

Adela scabiosella, Scopoli, Tr., Dup. (L. F. xi. p. 382, pl. 301. f. 1 & 2). All the specimens which I possess came from the south of France.

Adela aurifrontella, Duponchel (L. F. xi. p. 398, pl. 302. f. 4), non Hübner. [*A. rufifrontrella*, Tr., Z.] Taken in Corsica by Dr. Rambur.

Adela Solierella, Duponchel (L. F. xi. p. 407, pl. 302. f. 11). [*Micropteryx semipurpurella*, Stainton.] I only possess one specimen, which I received from the south of France.

Adela Donzelella, Duponchel (L. F. xi. p. 408, pl. 302. f. 12). This comes to us from the south of France. [In all probability this is *Micropteryx subpurpurella*; but the description affords no certainty.]

Stenoptera orbonella, Hübner, Duponchel (L. F. xi. p. 430, pl. 303. f. 3 & 4). [*Dasycera sulphurella*, Fab.] This is not rare in France, as I possess three specimens, one taken the 15th of May, near Paris; the other two came from the south of France.

Elachista [Bucculatrix] Boyerella, Duponchel (L. F. xi. p. 545, pl. 309. f. 3). This comes to us from Provence.

Ornix argentipennella, Duponchel (L. F. xi. p. 564, pl. 310. f. 3). [*Coleophora ochrea*, Haw., Stainton.] This comes to us from the south of France.

Euplocamus fulvimitrellus, Treitschke, Dup. (L. F. xi. p. 606, pl. 312. f. 1). The specimen figured was given to me by Dr. Rambur, who found the larva in the decayed trunk of a beech tree on the mountain of the Lozère, three leagues from Mende, in 1827.

* *Adela Mazzolella*, which follows this, is noticed in the extracts from Herrich-Schäffer's work under *Adela australis* (see *ante*, p. 240).

Rhinosia [*Gelechia*] *sordidella*, Hübner, Dup. (L. F. xi. p. 620, pl. 312. f. 8). I only possess one specimen of this, liberally given me by M. Meret. It was unique among several other little species found by him during an excursion he made in the Pyrénées orientales in 1838.

Anacampsis [*Gelechia*] *interruptella*, Hübner, Dup. (L. F. xi. p. 625, pl. 312. f. 12). This species was given me as having been taken in April near Genoa.

Adela Aglaella, Duponchel (L. F. xi. p. 627, pl. 312. f. 14). [Described, see, p. 261.] This pretty little species has been sent to us by M. Boyer de Fonscolombe, to be figured and described as new in the 'Annales de la Société Entomologique de France,' under the name of *Tinea Aglaella*. We have not been able to recognize it in Hübner, nor in other authors with whom we are acquainted. According to the generic characters, it would appear to belong to the second division of our genus *Adela*.

M. Boyer de Fonscolombe informs us that he found it flying in numbers over the flowers of the privet on the 23rd June, also over the flowers of the elder and dogwood. The same species has been given to us by M. Meret, as having been taken by him likewise in the south of France.

Tinea picarella, L., Hübn., Tr., Dup. (Supp. iv. p. 204, pl. 67. f. 8). I only possess two specimens, from Corsica.

Œcophora olivella, Boyer de Fonscolombe (Ann. S. Ent. Fr. 1837, p. 182), Dup. (Supp. iv. p. 439, pl. 85. f. 2). [Described, see p. 262.] This insect in the larva-state feeds in the *fruit* of the olive, is full fed at the end of August and beginning of September, when it quits the olive, piercing it at the place of the footstalk, and descends to the ground to assume the pupa-state. [The figures given to illustrate M. Boyer de Fonscolombe's paper in the 'Annales' might both be intended for the same species, our *Prays oleellus*. Duponchel's figure is different, and seems to accord with the description. It will be seen, p. 263, that Boyer de Fonscolombe afterwards himself referred this to *oleellus* as one and the same species.]

Dup. Lep. de France, xi. p. 79.

EUPLOCAMUS MORELLUS, n. sp.

Envergure 14'''. Les ailes supérieures sont en-dessus d'un gris cendré luisant réticulé de brun, avec plusieurs taches carrées ou triangulaires de cette dernière couleur, dont une à la base, trois le long de la côte, une au milieu du bord interne et une à quelque distance du bord terminal. Celle-ci est placée obliquement et forme une bandelette composée de trois petites taches superposées l'une au-dessus de l'autre. La frange est grise et entrecoupée de brun. Le dessous des mêmes ailes est d'un gris plus foncé, avec une partie des taches du dessus, mais à peine marquées.

Les ailes inférieures sont d'un gris cendré uni sur leurs deux surfaces, y compris la frange.
La tête est très-velue et d'un gris-brun, avec les palpes blanchâtres en dedans et bruns en dehors. Le corselet est de la couleur de la tête. L'abdomen est d'un gris un peu plus clair, ainsi que les pattes, dont l'extrémité est annelée de brun. Les antennes sont fortement ciliées dans le mâle et filiformes dans la femelle; elles sont brunes.
Cette description concerne les deux sexes.

Dup. Lep. de France, xi. p. 374.

Adela unipunctella, n. sp.

Envergure 4½‴. Les premières ailes sont très-étroites; elles sont en-dessus d'un noir-pourpre, avec des reflets dorés à l'extrémité et un point blanc au centre de chacune d'elles. Leur dessous est d'un noir-bronzé obscur sans points. Les deux surfaces des secondes ailes sont noirâtres, y compris la frange, avec un reflet bronzé en-dessous.

La tête et le corselet sont d'un noir violet. L'abdomen participe de la couleur des secondes ailes. Les pattes sont d'un vert-cuivreux. Les antennes ayant été brisées nous ne pouvons en dire la couleur.

Nous l'avons placée dans le genre *Adèle* sans être bien certain qu'elle s'y rapporte, attendu que les antennes et les palpes manquent dans l'individu unique que nous possédons.

Dup. Lep. de France, xi. p. 627.

Adela aglaella, Boyer de Fonscolombe, in litt.

Envergure 3⅓‴. Le fond des premières ailes en-dessus est doré, et chacune d'elles est traversée par deux bandes parallèles et un peu obliques, d'un brun pourpre très-brillant, placées, l'une au tiers de la longueur de l'aile, en partant du corselet, et l'autre aux deux tiers. La frange est d'un brun luisant ou bronzé. Le dessous des mêmes ailes et les deux surfaces des secondes sont d'un brun luisant, y compris les franges.

Le front est surmonté d'une touffe de poils d'un beau jaune. Les antennes sont noires, les palpes bruns et velus, le corselet couleur de bronze, avec les épaulettes fauves, l'abdomen brun, et les pattes d'un gris-blanc argenté.

[The description of the same insect by Boyer de Fonscolombe in the 'Annales de la Soc. Ent. de France,' 1840, p. 61, is as follows:—

"Tinea aglaella. Envergure 3⅓‴. Touffe de poils d'un beau jaune sur le front. Antennes noires, moniliformes; articles courts, épais, hérissés; point de trompe bien apparente. Quatre palpes; les deux supérieurs, plus courts, recourbés en bas; les deux inférieurs recourbés en haut, tous revêtus de poils, mais non hérissés, *appressi*.

"Ailes en toit, frange très-grande au bout des supérieures; couleur d'un brun rougeâtre; épaules largement dorées, puis deux bandes transverses d'un brun pourpre, et vers le bout de l'aile, une grande tache ronde dorée, quelquefois moins régulière, et plus ou moins grande ; la frange brune ou bronzée, selon les aspects.

" Ailes inférieures bronzées brunes. Corps brun. Pattes grises, lustrées.

" En nombre sur les fleurs de troène, 23 Juin, sur les fleurs de sureau et de sanguin. Voisine de la *Tin. Anderschella*, Hüb. 352, et de l'*Adela Ammanella*, Duponchel."]

Dup. Lep. de France, Supp. iv. p. 439.

ŒCOPHORA OLIVELLA, Boyer de Fonscolombe.

A la description un peu trop succincte que M. Boyer de Fonscolombe donne de l'insecte parfait, nous ajouterons que la Teigne du noyau de l'olive dont il est ici question, diffère de celle qui attaque les feuilles, 1°, en ce qu'elle est généralement d'un gris plus roussâtre que cendré ; 2°, en ce que ses premières ailes sont plus étroites, moins longuement frangées et sans aucune marbrure, du moins sur les quatre individus qu'il nous a envoyés dans le temps ; 3°, enfin en ce que ces palpes sont visiblement plus longs, et ne sont pas dirigés en bas comme dans l'autre espèce.

" Une autre chenille se loge dans l'amande même de l'olive. L'œuf dont elle provient a dû être pondu sur les bourgeons qui donneront le fruit l'année suivante. Lors de sa naissance, l'été d'après, elle pénètre dans le noyau encore tendre et elle s'y nourrit de la substance de l'amande. L'olive croît, son extérieur n'annonce aucune lésion ; elle est en tout semblable aux autres. A la fin d'Août ou au commencement de Septembre, la chenille ayant atteint toute sa grosseur, consumé toute sa provision qui est la pulpe de l'amande, et songeant à se métamorphoser, perce le noyau à l'endroit où le fruit s'attache à son pédicule : c'est la seule place où elle puisse trouver une issue, le noyau étant de la plus grande dureté, excepté à ce point où il est percé ; puis elle se laisse tomber, et cherche une retraite pour se changer en chrysalide. Je ne l'ai pas trouvée dans cet état au pied des arbres ; mais les olives que je soupçonnais piquées et que j'avais recueillies dans des boîtes, ayant donné naissance aux chenilles qu'elles recelaient, celles-ci ont filé, entre les olives ou dans les recoins des boîtes, une petite coque ovale, d'un tissu fort clair, blanc grisâtre. Les olives dont la chenille vient de sortir, tombent aussitôt, leur attache au pédicule étant affaiblie par le trou qu'a fait l'insecte en sortant*. Quand on en voit déjà quelques-unes au pied de l'arbre on peut conjecturer qu'il y a encore des chenilles dans une grande partie des olives restées aux branches ; et si l'on veut avoir la chenille avant sa sortie, on peut alors cueillir quelques olives, en choisissant de préférence celles qui viennent aisément à la main. Cette chenille, un peu plus grosse que celle que j'ai précédemment décrite [celle du *Prays oleellus*] est longue de trois lignes, rase, d'un vert-grisâtre marbré ; elle a sur le dos quatre lignes longitudinales noires et deux taches de la même couleur derrière la tête. La chrysalide

[* This agrees with the words of Fabricius, " quos cadere facit ante maturitatem."]

est jaunâtre avec les étuis des ailes un peu bruns. Elle donne naissance, au bout d'une dizaine de jours, à une Tinéite extrêmement semblable à la mineuse de la feuille, un peu plus grande, d'un gris foncé, peu ou point marbrée ; ses antennes sont plus minces et ses palpes moins hérissés."

M. Boyer de Fonscolombe's notice was published in 1835; sixteen years afterwards, in 1851, he had convinced himself that the species which fed in the fruit of the olive was identical with that which attacks the shoots in the spring (*Prays oleellus*); and the following note from him was published in the 'Annales de la Soc Ent. de France,' 1851, Bulletin, p. 17 :—

"Je crois devoir relever une erreur que je regarde comme très réelle, et à laquelle j'ai à me reprocher d'avoir donné lieu et de l'avoir même soutenue dans des mémoires qui ont été insérés dans les 'Annales de la Société Entomologique,' 3 Juin 1835. Il s'agit de deux Tinéites de l'olivier l'*Œcophora oleella* et l'*Elachista olivella*, Lépidoptères de Duponchel, supplém. tom. 4.

"L'habitation très-différente de ces deux Lépidoptères, ne me permettait pas de douter de leur différence spécifique. Je repoussais l'opinion de M. Bernard (émise par ce savant dans un mémoire sur l'olivier et sa culture, couronné par l'Académie de Marseille 1782), que ces deux teignes n'étaient qu'une seule et même espèce, et je reconnais à présent que j'avais tort et que M. Bernard était dans le vrai. J'avais envoyé des exemplaires des deux Tinéites à mon ami Duponchel. Il crut avec moi y trouver non seulement deux espèces distinctes, mais il les plaça dans des genres différents.

"Il est vrai qu'il se plaignait que mes exemplaires n'étaient pas en assez bon état. M'occupant assez peu de Lépidoptères et presque pas de Tinéites, je crus devoir adopter aveuglément le sentiment du savant lépidoptériste. J'ai recueilli, depuis ce temps, une très-grande quantité de chacune de ces prétendues espèces. Classant mieux cette année mes Tinéites, j'eus beau examiner scrupuleusement et l'*Œcophora* sortie des feuilles, et la prétendue *Elachista*, dont la chenille ronge la pulpe du noyau de l'olive, il m'a été absolument impossible de trouver entre l'une et l'autre la moindre différence, soit dans les organes, soit dans les couleurs. Celles-ci varient, mais les mêmes variétés se trouvent dans les deux ; l'une et l'autre sont marquées de plus ou moins de taches, l'une et l'autre, quelquefois, de gris uni sans tache. C'est encore ici une faute de la planche qui accompagne mon mémoire ; on les représente sous deux teintes différentes, tandisque, dans la réalité, ce ne sont que deux variétés, qui se trouvent dans l'une et l'autre Tinéite ; l'une et l'autre sont de plus grande comme de plus petite taille. Enfin, le texte de Duponchel sous les yeux, j'ai comparé scrupuleusement les caractères génériques qu'il assigne à l'une et à l'autre, et je n'y ai pu trouver non plus aucune différence. Les palpes sont de même, même épaisseur, même longueur, même direction ; les antennes, dans les deux, sont filiformes, un peu grenues, presque dentelées à leurs derniers articles qui sont plus saillants. La tête, le corselet, les ailes, leur coupe, leurs franges sont exactement les mêmes.

"Quoiqu'on puisse regarder comme un paradoxe la pensée qui fait une espèce unique de deux Tinéites qui vivent d'une manière si éloignée, et quant à la nourriture et quant à l'habitation, il me paraît impossible de douter de leur identité. Sans doute la teigne, qui a habité la feuille, et qui éclot en Mai, ne trouve plus ce gite, endurci par l'arrivée des chaleurs, propre à une nouvelle ponte. Elle choisit alors dans mon système, qui n'est, je l'avoue, que conjectural, le germe du jeune fruit, encore tendre ; et de l'œuf qu'elle y attache sort la larve qui se nourrit du fruit. Cette opinion, sans doute, aurait besoin d'être mieux autorisée par l'observation et la nature prise sur le fait. Il ne m'a pas été possible, jusqu'ici, de suivre un fait qui doit exister, mais que la petitesse et l'agilité de l'insecte rend bien difficile, surtout à mon âge. Mais, enfin, je crois pouvoir et devoir soumettre cette opinion, bien arrêtée dans mon jugement, cette restriction, dois-je dire, à mes savants collègues.

"Quant au genre, je ne crois pas, à cause des palpes assez grands et les ailes inférieures médiocrement lancéolées, que cette Tinéite appartienne aux *Elachista* ; je pense qu'elle doit être conservée dans le genre *Œcophora*, et qu'on ne peut lui contester le nom spécifique d'*oleella*, que Fabricius lui a donné le premier. Les figures de l'*oleella* et *olivella*, dans l'ouvrage de Duponchel précité, sont extrêmement fautives. La première, au lieu d'être parsemée d'une quantité de points presque régulièrement placés, est ordinairement marquée de quelques taches irrégulières formées par les points réunis, surtout vers le milieu de l'aile. L'*olivella* est, dans cette figure, d'un gris uni, teinte qu'elle a très-rarement et qui n'est qu'une variété qu'on retrouve dans les deux."

The same volume of the 'Annales' contains (Bulletin, p. 54) a notice on the same subject from Signor Ghiliani, of Turin, as follows :—

"En parcourant le Bulletin du premier trimestre 1851 des Annales, j'ai été fort agréablement surpris d'y trouver une note de M. Boyer de Fonscolombe sur les *Œcophora oleella* et *Elachista olivella*, qui s'accorde tout-à-fait avec un article que j'avais préparé à ce sujet dans un ouvrage que j'aurai bientôt terminé. Il s'agit d'un catalogue des Lépidoptères des Etats Sardes, auquel je travaille depuis bien des années, car, vu les richesses entomologiques de nos provinces, à chaque saison de chasse, j'avais à l'enrichir de nouvelles espèces qui n'avaient point encore été trouvées par le passé ; mais à cause des nombreuses occupations qui m'entourent, et surtout à cause du mauvais état de ma santé, devant absolument renoncer à la chasse, je me suis enfin décidé à le rédiger tel qu'il se trouve, n'ayant plus d'espoir de pouvoir l'augmenter par mes propres recherches.

"Or, c'est à l'article des deux espèces de teignes nuisibles à l'olivier, nommées ci-dessus, que regrettant la mort de notre feu collègue Teissière de Nice, qui, cédant à mes sollicitations avait commencé des observations qu'il n'a pu, hélas ! continuer ; et me trouvant moi-même dans l'impossibilité de m'occuper de ces espèces nuisibles à une plante qui ne croît pas dans notre climat de Turin ;

c'est à ce sujet, dis-je, que dans ma note je me déclarais en faveur de l'opinion qui réunit l'*Œcophora oleella* et *Elachista olivella* en une seule et même espèce, changeant de mœurs en raison des circonstances, comme cela se voit chez la *Cochylis roserana*, par rapport à la vigne. Ce qui avait arrêté ma conviction, c'était bien moins les doutes déjà manifestés par M. Blaud, que les observations précises d'un Palermitain, M. Baldassare Romano, qui, dans un mémoire qu'il a eu l'obligeance de m'envoyer, soutient avoir obtenu les deux espèces de la même chenille; ou pour mieux dire, affirme que la Teigne venue des chenilles qui au printemps vivent du parenchyme des feuilles, est absolument identique à la teigne qui sort en automne du fruit de l'olivier. Le susdit mémoire *degl' insetti che danneggiano gli ulivi in Sicilia*, ayant été publié en 1844, à Palerme, et renfermant d'ailleurs d'autres détails intéressants sur les mœurs de quelques insectes, je crois faire acte de justice en le signalant à l'attention de nos collègues, comme je l'ai fait à l'article de l'*Œcophora oleella* de mon catalogue."

CHAPTER IX.

ITALIAN AUTHORS.

THE present chapter contains a notice of two Italian publications treating on the Tineina—the first that of the late Professor Costa, of Naples, published about 1836. Of this I have contented myself with enumerating the species and their localities, suggesting which of the species described as new are probably known to us by other names; but of eleven of the species I have quoted the entire descriptions. But I conceive it quite possible that many of the others may be eventually recognized when we are better acquainted with the Neapolitan Micro-Lepidoptera.

The next treatise is that of Cavaliere Ghiliani, of Turin, which appeared in 1852. This, being a work of smaller compass, I have given entire, with the annotations which follow it.

In February last I had the pleasure of meeting Professor Achille Costa, son of the late Professor Costa, and found him still eagerly anxious to add to his collection; and in March I had also the pleasure of seeing Cavaliere Ghiliani in good health; and he most kindly placed in my hands a box of Italian Micro-Lepidoptera, which I have not yet, I regret to say, found time to examine critically.

SECTION I.

Fauna del Regno di Napoli, di Oronzio-Gabriele Costa. Lepidotteri. Napoli, 1832-36. [The individual genera are paged separately.]

[I give here a list of the species, and between brackets I put my interpretation of them when that differs from the name assigned by Costa. Of the few species to which I have prefixed numbers I copy the entire descriptions, and add after those descriptions my observations on them.—H. T. S.]

Tinea flavifrontella, Fab. [*T. biselliella*]. Nel mio gabinetto, sebben rara.

T. pellionella, L. Ne' gabinetti zoologici diviene infestissima.

T. tapezella, L.

T. granella, L.

1. *T. Leopoldella*, Costa [*Tinea* ——?]. Vive sulle lane. E assai rara.

T. M-Clementinella, Costa [*Dasycera Oliviella*]. Vive fra i cereali. Non ancora ho discoperta la pianta dalla quale ritrae l'ordinario alimento. Ignota mi è pure la larva e la crisalide, nonchè i suoi costumi.

T. augustella, Costa [*Lyonetia Clerkella*? or *Cemiostoma scitella*?]. Vive sul pero e sulle mela, nel R. O. Botanico. Non rara.

2. *T. Kollarella*, Costa [*Gelechia Kollarella*]. Vive fra le siepi, ma ignoro la pianta che gli porge alimento e ricetto. Raccolta sopra i Camaldoli.

3. *T. Servillella*, Costa [*Zelleria oleastrella*?]. Vive sopra l'ulivo in Terra d'Otranto. Rara.

T. sarcitella, L. [*T. pellionella*?].

T. urticaella, Costa [*Micropteryx calthella*?]. Trovata sopra i Camaldoli, e nel real bosco di Capodimonte; in maggio.

T. tricinctella, Costa [*Micropteryx Thunbergella*?]. [No locality given.]

T. Sangiovannella, Costa [*Lithocolletis ulmifoliella*?]. Vive nelle selve, sopra i Camaldoli; in agosto.

T. granella, var., Costa [*Tinea ruricolella*?]. Trovata nel grano, che divora ne' magazzini. Da luglio per tutto l'ottobre.

T. Achillella, Costa [*Argyresthia mendica*?]. [Named after his son Achille, who "non avendo ancor compiuto il nono anno" discovered this species.]

4. *T. Leopoldella*, var.: *thorace immaculato*, Costa [*Tinea vinculella*].

T. Ricciardella, Costa [*Tischeria complanella*].

T. macrocerella, Costa [*Nepticula* ——?]. Trovasi in agosto e settembre, nelle siepi. Sopra i monti.

T. minimella, Costa [*Nepticula* ——?]. Vive nelle selve de' Camaldoli. In luglio.

T. albella, Costa [*T. pellionella*?]. Nelle selve de' contorni di Napoli.

T. hirtella, Costa [*Œcophora tinctella*?]. Trovasi nelle praterie e nelle siepi. Frequente in luglio ed agosto.

T. tristigmatella, Costa [*T. pellionella*?]. Attacca gli animali preparati e conservati ne' musei.

T. griseolella, Costa [*T. parasitella*?]. Trovata in Basilicata, nel mese di maggio, fra le siepi.

T. flavella, Costa [??]. Sul Matese; nel mese di luglio.

T. albella, var., Costa [??]. Trovata ne' contorni del Fucino; in fine di agosto.

Yponomeuta lithospermella, Hüb. [*Anesychia pusiella*]. Fra noi, ma rara: nel mese di giugno.

Y. funerella, Fab. [*Anesychia funerella*]. Ne' contorni di Napoli. In maggio.

Y. aurifluella, Hüb. [*Chalybe aurifluella*]. Trovata sopra Aspromonte in Calabria Ultra; in luglio.

Y. cognatella, Treitschke [*Hyponomeuta variabilis*]. La larva vive sopra diverse specie di Pruni, sul Frassino, lo Spino bianco, ed altri alberi pomiferi, ove stassono in società fra un lasco tessuto sericeo. Non rara tra noi.

Hœmylis zephyrella, Hüb. [*Gelechia terrella*?]. Nelle montagne della Marsica, in Abruzzo. In fine di agosto.

H. obscurella, Hüb. [*Gelechia subsequella*?]. Abruzzo. Nel medesimo tempo e luogo, colla precedente.

Hypsolopha persicella, Fab. [*Cerostoma persicella*?]. L'ho trovata in fine di agosto, sotto Canistro, in Abruzzo Ultra II°.

H. capucinella, Hüb. [*Ypsolophus ustulellus*]. Io l'ho trovata in Abruzzo, in fine di agosto, colla *persicella*.

H. formosella, Hüb. [*Gelechia formosella*]. Sopra i Camaldoli. Nel mese di maggio.

Rhinosia fuliginella, Costa [? ?]. Vive nella Calabria Citra sopra lo Sile. In luglio.

5. *R. rutella* [*Depressaria rutana*].

Plutella xylostella, L. [*Plutella cruciferarum*]. Trovasi frequente tra noi in tutta la state, e precisamente ne' campi di cereali, come nelle siepi de' luoghi montuosi.

P. triangulosella, Costa [*Gracilaria stigmatella*]. Specie rara, trovata presso Canistro, in Abruzzo Ultra II°: in fine di agosto.

6. *P. chalybœella*, Costa [*Coleophora* —— ?]. Trovata in Principato Citra, sulle montagne. In luglio.

P. canaella, Costa [? ?]. Trovata in Basilicata. In fine di aprile.

Harpipterix cultrella, Hüb. [*Theristis caudella*]. Sopra i Camaldoli, nelle siepi. In ottobre.

Palpula rostrella, Hüb. [*Pleurota rostrella*]. Tra noi, non molto rara.

P. pyropella, Hüb. [*Pleurota pyropella*]. Nelle praterie aride. Ne' mesi di giugno e luglio, ed anche di agosto. Non rara.

7. *P. punctella*, Costa [*Protasis punctella*]. Vive sopra i Camaldoli, in luglio ed agosto.

Lampros Geoffroyella, Hüb. [*Harpella Geoffroyella*?]. Tra noi, ne' mesi di maggio e giugno.

L. œmulella, Hüb. [*Dasycera oliviella*]. Tra noi non rara, in luglio ed agosto.

L. leucatella, L. [*Gelechia leucatella*?]. Fra noi in Guardia regia (Provincia di Molise) sopra l'olmo; in fine di luglio.

L. ambiquellus, Costa [*Dasycera sulphurella*]. Vive sopra la *Robinia pseudoacacia*. Gl'individui che io vi ho raccolti aveano passato l'inverno nelle stato di *pupa* entro un crepaccio cangrenato del sudetto albero, e le farfalle schiusero ai 17 di marzo.

Adela œmulella, Hüb. [*Dasycera oliviella*]. Trovata in Terra d'Otranto e nel Principato Citra, ne' mesi di giugno e luglio.

A. Raddella, Hüb. [*Nemotois Raddellus* ?]. Io l' ho trovata in Basilicata, ne primi giorni di maggio.

A. viridella, Scop. Sulle coste orientali della I. Calabria Ultra, nel mese di luglio.

A. Latreillella, Hüb. [*Nemotois Latreillellus*]. Tra noi frequente ne' mesi di giugno e luglio.

Elachista phrynella, Costa [*Lyonetia Clerckella* ?]. Trovata in Ocri, presso Aquila, nell' orto del sig. Vespasiano. In agosto.

E. Irenella, Costa [*Nepticula* —— ?]. Nelle siepi di Fano a Corno (Gran Sasso d' Italia). In agosto.

E. malifoliella, Costa [*Cemiostoma scitella*].

E. cerella, Costa [*Butalis* —— ?]. In agosto; sul Gran Sasso.

E. gemmatella, Costa [*Chrysoclista Linneella*]. Vive sopra l'olmo. La farfalla schiude in fine di luglio. Guardia Regia, in Provincia di Molise.

Œcophora tigratella, Costa [*Gelechia triparella*]. Trovasi sopra i Camaldoli, fra le selve di castagno; in luglio 1832 raccolta da mio figlio Achille.

Œ. augulosella, Costa ⎫ [*Glyphipteryx equitella* ?]. Vive nelle
Ornix pernicipennella, Costa ⎭ selve sopra i Camaldoli, nella valle di S. Rocco, nel boschetto reale di Capo di monte, ed altrove. Da maggio a settembre; non rara.

Œcophora conjunctella, Costa ⎫ [*Glyphipteryx Fischeriella* ?]. A 12
Ornix colluripennella, Costa ⎭ maggio trovata l' ho nel boschetto del real sito di Capo di monte.

Œcophora Megerlella, Hüb. [*Elachista* —— ?]. Vive nella selva de' Camaldoli, in giugno.

Œ. arcuella, Costa [*Argyresthia ephippella* ?]. Vive colle precedenti; ma è molto più rara.

8. *Œ. fastuosella*, Costa [*Stathmopoda* —— ?]. Vive nella selva de' Camaldoli, fra le siepi.

Œ. Zieglerella, Hüb. [*Cosmopteryx Zieglerella* ?]. Trovasi sopra i Camaldoli, e sulla strada di Calvizzano, nelle selve di Castagno—da giugno ad agosto.

Œ. Merianella, L. [*Gelechia pictella* ?]. Io l' ho trovata sopra i moschi delle vecchie querci, tra Auletta e Salvitello, nel luogo detto il Pozzo. Nel finir di aprile.

L'insetto perfetto vola con difficoltà, e quasi saltellando; cammina lentamente; d' ordinario si tengono aggruppati. Le ale sono disposte ad embrice.

Œ. Lewenhoekella, L. [*Pancalia Lewenhoekella*]. Sopra i Camaldoli, nelle siepi ombrose, fra la selva. In maggio e giugno.

Œ. luteolella, Costa [*Elachista ochraceella* ?]. Vive nelle siepi de' contorni della Capitale, e nelle praterie aride. Non rara.

Œ. *cinctella*, L. [*Gelechia tæniolella*?]. Trovasi alquanto rara nelle selve prossime alla Capitale.

Œ. *rufimitrella*, Hüb. [? ?]. In Calabria Ultra, sopra Aspromonte; rarissima. In luglio.

Œ. *Passeriniella*, Costa [? ?]. Ne' contorni della Capitale; rara. In giugno.

Œ. *flavocerella*, Costa [*Phibalocera luticornella*?]. Trovasi ne' contorni della Capitale; assai rara. La farfalla schiude nel mese di luglio.

Œ. *granella*, Costa [? ?]. Vive ne' granai, che devasta, come la tignuola dello stesso nome. [According to the description, " the anterior wings with two dark fasciæ," this cannot be *Gelechia cerealella*.]

Œ. *trimaculella*, Costa [? ?]. Trovata nel piano della Daunia, fra i cespugli. In luglio.

Œ. *avellinella*, Costa [*Œcophora cinnamomea*?]. Rarissima specie trovata sulle falde meridionali della Majella. In agosto.

[Costa here mentions two other species, the originals of which he had lost " per causa d' invasione degli *Antreni*," a fertile source of disaster in many ill-kept collections.]

Œ. *scyllaella*, Costa [*Œcophora tripuncta*]. Rara come la precedente. Trovata in luglio, presso Monte corvino, in Principato Citeriore.

Œ. *vittella*, Costa [*Butalis restigerella*?]. Trovasi nelle praterie montuose ed aride; in settembre.

9. Œ. *punctivittella*, Costa [*Butalis punctivittella*]. Trovasi ne' contorni della Capitale, fra le selve di Castagno. Non ovvia.

Œ. *lineaella*, Costa [*Elachista* —— ?]. Minutissima specie trovata sopra i Camaldoli, in settembre.

Œ. *unitella*, Hüb. [? ?].

Ornix luctuosella, Costa [*Coleophora* —— ?]. Trovasi sopra i Camaldoli, fra i castagni; non ovvia. In settembre.

O. *trochilipennella*, Costa [*Coleophora Fabriciella*]. Vive sopra i Camaldoli, nel medesimo luogo, colla precedente, della quale è però men rara. In luglio ed agosto.

O. *eumenipennella*, Costa [*Coleophora* —— ?].

O. *flammeæpennella*, Costa [*Elachista pollinariella*?]. Sul Gran Sasso. In agosto.

10. O. *Hisabellella*, Costa [*Stagmatophora Isabellella*]. Trovata presso l'Eremo di Popsis, volgarmente Polsi, ed anche Madonna della Montagna, sull' Aspromonte. In luglio 1836.

11. O. *marginella*, Costa [*Coleophora* —— ?]. La larva vive dentro di un guscio, sulle fronde dell' olmo. La farfalla schiude nel mese di giugno. Trovata sulla collina di Miradois.

(1.) TINEA LEOPOLDELLA, Costa.

Tav. i. fig. 1, A, B, *a* gr. nat.

T. nigra albo-fasciata maculataque, antennis longis, articulis subpilosis.

Questa picciolissima tignuola è tutta nera, co' margini degli anelli addominali bianchi. Bianchi son pure i lati del torace; e le ali superiori hanno una fascia obliqua presso la base; due macchie triangolari ne' margini esterni, ed una lanceolata nell' angolo interno, tutte bianche. Allorchè l' animale è in riposo l'insieme di tali macchie gli conciliano una elegante configurazione. Le frange del margine posteriore son bianche e nere, e quando le ali sono spiegate pel volo si espandono in fascetti.

Le a. inferiori sono strette, frangiate, et di color piombino splendente.

Il capo è grosso, ed ha sul fronte un ciuffetto di peli giallastri. Gli occhi sono laterali, molto sporti, e nerissimi. Le antenne sono lunghe più che le ale, e ciascuno articulo ha due peli molto sensibili, uno per lato, che risguardar le farebbero come quasi pettinate; il colore è nero.

Vive sulle lane. E assai rara.

As a variety of *T. Leopoldella* an insect is subsequently described, which is certainly our *Tinea vinculella*; and the above typical *Leopoldella* should differ from that in the possession of white spots on the sides of the thorax. The subpectinate antennæ and the white sides of the abdominal rings also seem to furnish good characters by which we may some day recognize the at present unknown *Tinea Leopoldella*. That, however, it can be a true *Tinea* feeding on wool seems almost impossible.

(2.) TINEA KOLLARELLA, Costa.

Tav. i. fig. 4, *a* gr. nat.

T. alis primoribus lanceolatis flavescentibus, fascia media, puncto, atque apice brunneo-violaceis, inferioribus subalbidis.

Il corpo della tignuola *Kollarella* è di un bianco sudicio. Le ale superiori, e così pure il torace, hanno una tinta di giallo paglino. Presso la metà vi corre una fascia arcuata di color bruno tendente al violetto. Tra questa e la base avvi un punto minutissimo dello stesso colore, e così pure son tinti gli apici. La figura delle ale è quasi lanceolata. Le a. inferiori sono bianco-sudicie mediocremente sfrangiate.

Il capo è tondo, molto distinto. Gli occhi sono neri, e le antenne brune, delicate e non molto lunghe, inserite negli angoli degli occhi.

Vive fra le siepi, ma ignoro la pianta che gli porge alimento e ricetto. Raccolta sopra i Camaldoli.

This is the species afterwards described by Zeller in the 'Isis' of 1839 as *Gelechia flavedinella*, from two Hungarian specimens. Duponchel described it in the ninth volume of his 'Lépidoptères de France' as *Tortrix Walkenaerana*, from a specimen received from

Montpellier, from M. Lefebvre; and in his eleventh volume he describes it as *Lita luteella* from a specimen received from Dr. Rambur, with no note of its locality; it is now known by the name of *Gelechia Kollarella*.

(3.) TINEA SERVILLELLA, Costa.

T. alis anticis griseis, maculis minutissimis obscuris, sparsis.

La tignuola della quale si parla è alquanto più grande della *T. oleaella*, Fab., e vive come quella sopra l'ulivo. Ha il capo brevissimo coperto di peli fulvi; gli occhi laterali neri poco estuberanti; le antenne setacee, lunghe quanto la terza parte del corpo. Le ale superiori sono di un grigio argentino, con macchie rare, picciole ed irregolari di un bruno nerastro nell' apice, è pallido nel resto; senza frangia visibile ad occhio nudo. Le ale inferiori sono brunicce. Il corpo e le gambe sono bianco-argentine; queste con picciole macchie brune.

Costa, Osserv. sopra gl' ins. dell' ulivo e delle ulive. p. 11, tav. fig. 9*, a, b.

Vive sopra l'ulivo in Terra d'Otranto. Rara.

It is possible that this may be the *Zelleria oleastrella*, Millière (see *ante*, pp. 191, 215): there is nothing in the above description which forbids this; but the specimens must surely have been in bad condition of which the cilia were not visible to the naked eye. Costa's criticism on the figure illustrating his previous memoir shows how little we should depend on figures, in comparison with descriptions: a figure which he could not himself recognize would scarcely be of any use to others; and possibly even some of the figures in the 'Fauna del Regno di Napoli' may be open to a like censure.

(4.) TINEA LEOPOLDELLA, var. *thorace immaculato*, Costa.

Differisce dal tipo principale, per la mancanza delle macchie bianche ne' lati del torace, e pel ciuffo frontale. Varia sovente pure per la macchia cordiforme dell' angolo interno delle ale superiori, la quale suol congiungersi colla seconda marginale, generando così una fascia quasi parallela alla prima.

La larva vive sull' *Hypnum murale*, e sopra taluni moschi che nascono ne' luoghi ombrosi, ove scorrono le grondaje. Il suo foderetto o guscio è composto di tritumi di mosco e di minutissima sabbia. E convesso al di sopra, piano di sotto, coll' estremità rotondate, ed un poco più angusto dietro di queste, e più dilatato nel mezzo. Inferiormente si vede in entrambe l'estremità un' apertura che dà uscita al capo dell' animale dall' una, ed agli escrementi dall' altra, restando però sempre ed intieramente col corpo coperto. Siccome il guscio risulta dalla connessione de' frammenti del mosco, o dell' ipno sul quale vive, così trovasi esso del medesimo colore, e

---

* In quanto alla figura citata ho dichiarato già di non riconoscerla, nè questa nè quella della *Noctua*, imperciocchè eseguita tutta la tavola litografica senza la mia revisione, pecca di quei difetti che nascer sogliono in mano degli artisti, che non intendono la materia che forma l'oggetto dell' opera loro.

difficilmente si scerne sopra luogo. Schiude in giugno e luglio. Depone le uova involte in poca sostanza sericea, colla quale le attacca a quello.

Aderisce alla superficie de' corpi così perfettamente per la faccia piana, che distinguersi lascia appena dall' occhio assuefatto a simili ricerche.

Anche sotto le pietre tufacee a larga superficie, e giacenti in luoghi umidetti, suole annidarsi in greggia la larva di questa tignuola.

This is very clearly *Tinea vinculella*, H.-S., of which I found the larvæ in some plenty on the trunks of the trees in the Villa Reale, Naples, February 4th, 1869 (see *ante*, p. 235).

(5.) RUINOSIA RUTELLA.

Pyralis rutana, Fab. Ent. Syst. iii. 2. p. 242. no. 179.
Plutella rutana, Costa, Cenn. Zool. 1834, p. 76.

Rhin. alis depressis fuscis; lineolis transversis numerosis albis, thorace denticulis duobus dorsalibus.

Il capo ed il torace sono foschi, senza veruna macchia. Sul torace si elevano due fascetti di squame o peli compressi. Le ali superiori sono alquanto inclinate ne' lati, di color cenerognolo rosseggiante; sul margine esterno si osservano molte lineelle brevissime oblique trasversali e bianche; nel mezzo del campo due punti neri picciolissimi elevati, ravvicinati tra loro.

Fabricio assegna per patria di questa specie le Gallie, avendola osservata egli nel solo gabinetto di Bosc. Essa trae il nome specifico dalla pianta sulla quale vive, la *Ruta graveolens*. Sulla medesima pianta ho io trovata la larva, e ne ho ottenuto la farfalla. E però parmi ch' essa dovesse entrare nelle Tortrici, se si pon mente ai suoi costumi, essendochè come quelle attorciglia le foglie della ruta, le lega con una sostanza sericea, e dentro vi compie le sue metamorfosi. Ma l' abito ed i palpi sono del genere *Rhinosia* del Sig. Treitschke.

La larva è di color verde giallastro, col capo e collo nero, ed il dorso con tre striscie longitudinali più oscure.

La crisalide, prima d' un color verde chiaro, si oscura in seguito, ed a capo di 15 giorni schiude la farfalla.

Il Signor Vallot ha data la descrizione di questa farfalla all' Accademia delle Scienze, Arti e Belle Lettere di Digione (Ad. Pubb. de' 25 agosto 1829), sotto il nome di *Pyralis rutana*, e colla seguente frase diagnostica: la qual descrizione esattamente conviene cogli esemplari che ho fra le mani.

Pyr. spirilinguis, palpis recurvatis, thoracis crista subbifurcata, alis cinereis fusco inspersis, punctis duobus nigris contiguis in utraque ala.

That Costa had himself collected the larva and reared the perfect insect is not without interest; the observation of the species by Vallot also shows that the insect had not so entirely escaped the notice of entomologists as I had thought to have been the case.

(6.) PLUTELLA CHALYBEELLA, Costa.
Tav. v. f. 9, *a, b, c*.

Pl. alis anticis chalybeatis immaculatis; antennarum articulo primo antice cristato; pedibus flavicantibus.

Tutta d' un colore di acciajo splendente, senza alcuna macchia. Il capo è piccolo, col vertice depresso e liscio; gli occhi neri molto estuberanti, onde appare essere il capo più largo che alto; le antenne lunghe quanto il corpo, di color giallognolo, aventi il primo articolo più grosso e quasi ellittico, ornato d' una cresta di squame lunghe e bianche nella parte anteriore, ciocchè principalmente ed essenzialmente la distinguo da ogni altra specie congenere. Il corpo ed i piedi sono gracili, e danno un poco al gialliccio. In *c* vedesi uno de' palpi ingrandito.

Io l' ho rappresentata nello stato di riposo, e di natural grandezza, non avendo alcuna cosa sulle ali da farvi marcare. In *b* mostrasi l' antenna ingrandita colla cresta che ne adorna l' articolo basilare.

Trovato in Principato Citra, sulle montagne. In luglio.

This seems recognizably described; but a steel-coloured *Coleophora*, with yellowish legs, and with the tuft of the basal joint of the antennæ white anteriorly, is something at present quite unknown to us. *Coleophora albitarsella* has dark steel-grey anterior wings and white tarsi; but that cannot be Costa's insect.

(7.) PALPULA PUNCTELLA, Costa.
Tav. vii. f. 2 (♀).

P. alis anticis flavis, costa violascente, in medio puncto nigro, punctisque minoribus in posteriore limbo; inferioribus fuliginosis ciliis longis.

Capo piccolo, ricoperto da lunghe squame dirette verso la parte anteriore, una corona delle quali cinge la nuca: occhi piccoli, quasi occultati, e neri; antenne inserite nell' anterior parte de' medesimi, lunghe quanto il corpo, e composte di articoli rotondi alternativamente bianchi e bruni. Ali superiori strette, di color giallo dorato, rosseggiante sul margine anteriore, e segnate nel mezzo da un punto nero, innanzi al quale altro quasi inosservabile; posteriormente sfrangiate. Ali inferiori bruno-rossicce circondate da lunga frangia. Corpo simile.

Il maschio è più piccolo, ed ha le ali meglio marcate, e nel margine anteriore più grige. La lingua spirale, visibile, mediocre.

Vive sopra i Camaldoli, in luglio ed agosto.

This is the species now known as *Protasis punctella*; Herrich-Schäffer figured it under the name of *monostictella*, but retains the name *punctella* in the text (see *ante*, p. 77).

(8.) ŒCOPHORA FASTUOSELLA, Costa.
Tav. ii. f. 7.

Œ. alis omnibus linearibus, primoribus auratis, maculis transversalibus tribus, apicibusque rubris; inferioribus brunneis.

Il capo è liscio e molto declive, di color bianco argentino; gli occhi piccoli, neri e laterali; i palpi generici, semplici, di color bianco sudicio, brunicci negl' apici. Corpo bruno splendente, estremità addominale barbata, con peli lunghi biancastri. Gambe argentine, co' tarsi delle posteriori macchiati di rosso bruno, assai lunghi. Ali superiori lineari, molto più strette presso la metà, dorate, con due macchie trasversali nel mezzo, una nella base, ed il margine posteriore di color rosso-sanguigno; margine interno guarnito di lunga frangia bruna. Ali inferiori assai più lineari, brune, entrambi i margini delle quali con lunga frangia.

Vive nella selva de' Camaldoli, fra le siepi.

Osservazione. Moltissimo somiglia questa *Ecofora* alla *T. angustipennella* di Hübner, Tav. 29. n. 197; e non avrei punto esitato a ritenerla come identica, se la mancanza assoluta di frangia, tanto nelle superiori, che nelle inferiori ali di quella, non me ne avessero dissuaso. Convinto altronde della esattezza di quello Iconografo, arrestar non mi posso a supporre che neglette le avesse. Vi ho scorto pure qualche anomalia fra la disposizione delle macchie di quella e la nostra. Che che ne sia, insignita ho questa specie col nome di *fastuosella*, avendo riguardo al brillante contrasto che risulta dalle macchie col fondo veramente dorato delle ali. Ove gli entomologi riconoscessero identiche questo due specie, le ridoneranno il suo antico nome, il quale convenir può alla più parte delle specie di questo genere.

I should certainly have thought this was the *Stathmopoda pedella*, Lin. (*angustipennella*, Hüb.), but that Costa says of his insect that the transverse markings of the anterior wings are red, "di color rosso-sanguigno," which certainly cannot be said of *St. pedella*.

(9.) ŒCOPHORA PUNCTIVITTELLA, Costa.

Tav. v. f. 1.

Œ. nigro-violacea, alis primariis linea punctoque longitudinalibus, in medio, flavidis; secundariis valde fimbriatis apice flavicante.

Tutta d'un sol colore uniforme, nero dante al violetto.

Le ali superiori hanno una linea giallo-pallida, che dalla base giunge alla metà della lunghezza del campo, percorrendo precisamente il mezzo; tra il termine suo e l'apice estremo, sulla medesima direzione, trovasi un punto allungato dello stesso colore; o può dirsi essere una linea sola interrotta verso l' estremo; qualche squama dorata vedesi sparsa verso l' estremità, lunga, delicata, e somigliante a pelo. Le ali inferiori sono più splendenti, e riflettono un colore più violaceo che nero; sono da ogni lato ornate da ricca frangia; e nell' apice vedesi una macchia paglina scancellata. Le antenne sono semplici, e più corte del corpo. Su i margini degli anelli addominali e ne' tarsi risplende qualche squama metallica. I palpi sono lunghi, curvi, rivolti in sù, ed acuti; forma e grandezza che tiene un luogo medio tra l' *Ecofore* et le *Plutelle*.

Trovasi ne' contorni della Capitale, fra le selve di Castagno. Non ovvia.

This is the species described by Treitschke as *Butalis Knochella*, and figured by Herrich-Schäffer under that name; subsequently a closely allied species has been recognized as the *Knochella* of Fabricius, and Costa's name has been retained for this insect, which is now known as *Butalis punctivittella*.

(10.) ORNIX HISABELLELLA, Costa.

Tav. xii. A. *a, b.*

Or. alis anticis fulvo-auratis medio argenteo-subfasciatis, pustulis 7 aureo-nitidis, marginibus extimis punctis sex auratis; alis posticis fuliginosis immaculatis.

Il capo è liscio, le antenne lunghe quanto il corpo, il cui primo articolo più grande, gli altri minutissimi, uguali, quasi globosi ed alternativamente bianchi d'argento e bruni. Palpi inferiori delicati, ricurvi, acuti. Corpo mediocre, di color bruno, co' segmenti addominali inferiormente e ne' lati bianchi argentini, e l'estremità anale barbata; piedi similmente bianchi argentini anellati di nero. Ali superiori di color giallo-rossiccio splendente con atomi rari neri, colore che verso i due terzi diviene più pallido, lasciando quasi una fascia non limitata argentina; sette pustole dorate splendentissime adornano il campo, delle quale cinque sulla prima terza parte apicale disposte obbliquamente 2, 1, 2; la sesta succede sulla seconda terza parte e quasi sul limite della fascia transversale argentina; l'ultima è precisamente omerale, ossia nella base dell'ala. Inoltre, sul margine della frangia apicale, tanto nello esterno che nello interno, tre piccoli punti dorati splendentissimi, e nell'apice una simile strisciolina biforcata traversa la frangia. Questa è bruniccia con reflessi di rosso, di rubino e di bianco metallico. Le ali inferiori sono lineari, bruno rossicce, con larga frangia dello stesso colore.

La fig. A della xii. tavola rappresenta la farfalla ingrandita; *a* la grandezza naturale: *b* uno de' suoi palpi ingrandito.

Trovata presso l'Eremo di Popsis, volgarmente Polsi ed anche Madonna della Montagna, sull'Aspromonte. In luglio 1836.

Dedicata a S. R. M. la Regina Isabella Madre del Re (N. S.) dalla quale questo tenue tributo di divozione è stato benignamente ascolto.

This is the *Stagmatophora opulentella* of Herrich-Schäffer, now known as *Stagmatophora Isabellella* (see ante, p. 245).

(11.) ORNIX MARGINELLA, Costa.

Tav. vii. f. 4.

Or. corpore fuscescente, antennis fusco-annulatis; alis anticis fusco-micaceis, margine antico et postico albidiore; alis posticis albidis.

Il colore di questa farfalletta è di un bruno quasi olivaceo, il cui riflesso è di mica biancastra. Le antenne, lunghe quanto le ali superiori, sono anellate di bruno, e la base è grossetta. Il capo è bianchiccio; il collo lunghetto è quasi leonino. Le ali superiori, guardate di fronte sono di color fulvo-olivaceo, col margine esterno ed interno più pallido; e così pure la frangia; ma guardate obbliquamente esse risplendono come la mica biancastra. Le ali inferiori sono biancastre un poco brune sul contorno.

La larva vive dentro di un guscio ch' essa tesse e strascina seco, come le vere tignuole.

Il guscio è semicilindraceo, co' lati marginati e secchi, e tutta la superficie rivestita di peli cortissimi. Il suo colore è grigio-bruno. L'animale lo attacca per una dell' estremità alla pagina inferiore delle fronde dell' olmo, sopra del quale vive, e le rode quà e là riducendole a foggia di crivello. La farfalla schiude nel mese di giugno.

Trovata sulla collina di Miradois.

Were I to judge solely from the figure, I should be disposed to refer the insect to *Gracilaria scalariella*, Z. (see *ante*, p. 82); but the description speaks distinctly of a pale costa (not shown in the figure); and from the habit of the elm-feeding larva, it must be a *Coleophora*. It should be easily recognized when again met with.

Section II.

Materiali per servire alla Compilazione della Fauna Entomologica Italiana, ossia Elenco dei Lepidotteri degli stati Sardi, da Vittore Ghiliani.

Separato reprint from the 'Memorie della Reale Accademia delle Scienze di Torino,' serie 2. tom. xiv. 1852.

[The original contains four columns, in which are indicated the species occurring in the Island of Sardinia, in Liguria, in Piedmont, and in Savoy. In the following *résumé* these geographical regions are indicated by *Sd.*, *L.*, *P.*, and *Sv.*, between parentheses. The asterisks refer to the *Annotazioni* which follow this list.]

Ædia pusiella, F. (*L.*, *P.*) Estate, autunno. Specialmente al calcio degli olmi. Piano, colli, Alpi.

Æ. echiella, W. V., H. (*Sd.*, *L.*, *P.*, *Sv.*) Maggio. Cespugli e siti erbosi. Piano, colli, Alpi.

Æ. funerella, F. (*P.*) Fine aprile, maggio. Cespugli e siti erbosi. Colle di Torino (giugno, valle di Pesio).

Æ. cœnobitella, H. (*P.*) Giugno. Cespugli e siti erbosi. Valle di Luserna.

Yponomeuta evonymella, L. (*P.*, *Sv.*) Luglio, agosto. Siepi folte, e boschi in siti umidi. Piano, Alpi.

* { *Y. cognatella*, H., D., Ratz. (*P.*, *Sv.*) Giugno, luglio, settembre. Siepi, verzieri. Piano, monti.

{ *Y. Malinella*, F. v. R., Zell. (*Sd.*, *L.*, *P.*, *Sv.*) Giugno, luglio, settembre. (Bruco nocivo alla pianta del pomo.) Piano, monti.

Y. padella, L., Ratz. (*Sd.*, *L.*, *P.*, *Sv.*) Agosto. (Bruco dannoso alla pianta del pruno.) Piano, Alpi.

Y. rorella, H. (*P.*) Giugno. Siepi, boschetti. Collina di Torino.

Y. plumbella, F. (*P.*) Giugno, luglio, fino settembre. Siti erbosi ed umidi. Collina di Torino, Dogliani.

Psecadia decemguttella, H. (*P.*) Giugno, luglio. Cespugli, siti erbosi. Colle di Torino, valle di Susa.

P. sexpunctella, H. (*Sd.*) Estate. (Un solo individuo.) Regione montuosa dell' isola.

Chalybe pyraustella, D. (*Sd., L.*) Maggio, giugno. Cespugli di rovi. Campagne di Iglesias e di Oneglia.

Diurnea fagella, F. (*L., P., Sv.*) Primavera. (La femmina è rara assai.) Boschetti. Piano, monti.

Lemmatophila phryganella, Schr. (*P.*) Marzo, aprile. Colle di Bra, valli di Luserna e di Fenestrelle.

L. salicella, H. (*P.*) Primavera. Colle di Torino.

Epigraphia avellanella, H. (*P.*) Marzo, aprile. Siepi, e cespugli di nocciuolo. Colle di Torino.

E. atomella, H. (*P., Sv.*) Aprile. Boschetti in siti montuosi. Valle di Fenestrelle, Chamounix.

E. signella, H. (*P.*) Maggio, giugno. Boschetti in siti montuosi. Colle di Torino.

E. punctulella, Tr. (*P.*) Aprile. Boschetti in siti montuosi. Colle di Torino, e Stupinigi.

Caulobius sparganiellus, D., Tr. (*P.*) Estate. Paludi di Stupinigi, e laghi di Caselette.

Hæmylis depunctella, Podev., H. (*Sd., L., P.*) Giugno, luglio. Siti erbosi, e foreste. Piano, colli.

H. liturella, W. V., Tr. (*P., Sv.*) Giugno, luglio. Siti erbosi e foreste. Colli, Alpi.

H. arenella, W. V., Tr. (*Sd., P.*) Giugno, luglio, ottobre. Siti erbosi e foreste. Colli, Alpi.

H. characterella, W. V., Tr. (*P.*) Agosto, ottobre. Praterie, cespugli. Piano, valli.

H. applanella, F. (*L., P.*) Luglio, agosto, ottobre. Praterie, cespugli. Piano, valli.

H. Alstrœmerella, H. (*P., Sv.*) Giugno, luglio. Boschetti e praterie. Colli, monti.

H. depressella, F. (*P.*) Estate. Orti e giardini. Piano, colli.

H. heracliella, H. (*Sd., L., P., Sv.*) Estate. Prati, siepi. Piano, monti.

H. albipunctella, H. (*Sd., L., P.*) Maggio. Prati, siepi. Piano, colli.

H. pastinacella, F. v. R. (*Sd., P., Sv.*) Estate. Pascoli in siti montuosi. Barbagio, Alpi, Chamounix.

{ *Anacampsis populella*, L. (*P., Sv.*) Giugno, luglio, agosto. Sui pioppi. Piano, colli.
{ *A.* var. *tremulella*, D. (*P.*) Luglio, agosto. Sui pioppi. Piano, colli.

A. malvella, H. (*L., P., Sv.*) Agosto. Praterie, fiore delle ombrellifere. Monti, Alpi.

A. terrella, W. V., H. (*Sd., P.*) Luglio, agosto. Siepi, boschi. Piano, monti.

A. pinguinella, Tr. (*Sd., P.*) Estate. Siepi, boschi. Piano, monti.

A. dissimilella?, Tr. (*Sd.*) Estate. Regione selvosa e montuosa dell' isola.

A. rhombella, W. V., H. (*Sv.*) Agosto. Alpi della Savoia.

Lita alburnella?, Tisch., D. (*P.*) Luglio. (Forse specie nuova.) Boschetti. Colle di Torino.

L. pedisequella, H., fig. 95. (*P.*) Giugno. Regione boscosa delle Alpi.

L. scriptella, H. (*P., Sv.*) Luglio. Sui tronchi delle piante. Piano, monti.

L. pullatella, H. (*P., Sv.*) Estate. Siti erbosi, e cespugli. Alpi occidentali, e Alta Savoia.

L. nanella, W. V., H. (*P.*) Settembre. Siti erbosi, e cespugli. Colle di Torino.

L. histrionella, H. (*L., P.*) Giugno. Siti erbosi e cespugli. Alpi marittime, Mandria.

L. conturbatella, H., f. 450. (*P.*) Luglio. (Trovata dal Dott. Dabbene.) Dogliani.

L. peliella, Tisch., D. (*Sd.*) Luglio. Monti dell' interno dell' isola.

L. velocella, Tisch., D. (*P.*) Luglio. Praterie aride. Boschetti della Mandria, Alpi.

L. umbrosella, Zell. (*P.*) Giugno. Siti erbosi ed aridi. Colle di Torino.

L. vulgella, W. V., H. (*P.*) Maggio. Siti erbosi ed aridi. Colle di Torino.

L. biguttella, F. v. R. (*P.*) Maggio. Siti erbosi ed aridi. Colle di Torino.

L. luculella, H. (*P.*) Giugno. Boschi di Stupinigi.

L. stipella, H. (*P.*) Maggio. Boschetti, cespugli. Collina di Torino.

L. interruptella, H. (Citata nell' opera Duponchel, tom. xi. p. 625, come trovata in Genova.)

*L. betulinella, F. (*Sd., L., P., Sv.*) Primavera, estate, autunno. Interno delle case. Piano, monti.

L. leucatella, L., H. (*P.*) Maggio, agosto. Siepi, cespugli. Colle di Torino, monti di Biella.

{ *L. scopolella?*, H. (*P., Sv.*) Maggio, luglio. Giardini, siepi. Piano, colli.
L. funestella, D. (Duponchel, tom. xi. pag. 328, pl. 298. fig. 12.)

L. luctuosella, D. (*P.*) Giugno. Trovasi nelle abitazioni. Piano, colli.

L. aleella, F. (*P.*) Agosto. Cespugli, praterie aride. Colle di Torino.

L. vorticella, Scop., D. (*P.*) Luglio, agosto. Cespugli, praterie aride. Colli, monti.

L. luctuella, H. (*P.*) Giugno. Cespugli, praterie aride. Valle di Po, e di Luserna.

L. exiguella, H. (*P.*) Giugno. Cespugli, praterie aride. Boschi della Mandria.

*Enolmis luteella, D. (*P.*) Luglio. Boschetti, e brughiere. Colle di Torino.

Acompsia tripunctella, F. (*P., Sv.*) Luglio. Praterie aride sul margine dei boschi. Alpi occidentali e settentrionali.

A. cinerella, L. (*P.*) Estate. Praterie aride sul margine dei boschi. Colle di Torino.

A. lineatella, D., Supp. (*P.*) Estate. Praterie aride sul margine dei boschi. Colle di Torino.

* { *A. flavella*, D., Supp. (*Sd., L., P., Sv.*) Giugno, luglio. Praterie aride sul margine dei boschi. Piano, colli, monti.
A. ferrugella?, W. V., Tr., D. (*Rhinosia ferrugella*, W. V. ecc. Dup. Supp. e suo Catalogo metodico.)

{ *A. flammella*, Tr., D., Supp. (*Sd., P.*) Estate. (Stesse località della preced., di cui sembra essere una var. più piccola.)
A. formosella, H. (Ved. al genere *Rhinosia* del Catalogo Duponchel.) (Ved. l' annotaz.)

Butalis triguttella, D. (*P., Sv.*) Giugno, luglio. Boschetti, e praterie vicine. Valli, Alpi.

B. cuspidella, F., H., f. 242. (*P.*) Estate. Boschetti, e praterie vicine. Alpi.

B. punctivittella, Costa. (*L., P.*) Maggio. (*Œcophora punctivittella*, Costa, pag. 14, tav. v. fig. 1.) Colli, monti.

B. chenopodiella, H. (*P.*) Giugno. Siti aridi e scoperti nei boschi di Stupinigi.

B. egregiella, D. (*P.*) Giugno. Siti aridi e scoperti nei boschi di Mandria.

B. tinctella, H. (*P.*) Luglio. Boschetti, siepi. Colle di Torino.

B. Esperella, H., fig. 255. (*P.*) Giugno, luglio. Boschetti, siepi. Colle di Torino.

B. seliniella, Zell., D. (*P.*) Maggio. Boschetti, siepi. Colle di Torino.

**B. cerealella*, D. (*P.*) Maggio, luglio. (Bruco nocivo al frumento, orzo e segala.) Piano, valli.

B. inspersella, H., fig. 443. (*Sv.*) Luglio. Praterie alpine della Savoia.

B. Noricella, F. v. R. (*P*). Aprile. Siti sterposi, sommità della collina di Torino.

Hypsolopha persicella, W. V., H. (*P., Sv.*) Giugno, luglio. Siepi, boschetti. Colli, monti.

H. sylvella, L. (*P.*) Estate. Boschi di quercie. Colli, monti.

Rhinosia fasciella, H. (*P., Sv.*) Maggio, giugno. Cespugli, siti erbosi. Colli, valli, monti.

R. ustulella, F. (*L., P., Sv.*) Maggio, giugno, agosto. Cespugli, siti erbosi. Colli, valli, monti.

R. sequella, L. (*P.*) Giugno, luglio. Sui tronchi degli alberi. Piano, colli.

R. vittella, L. (*P., Sv.*) Estate. Orti, giardini. Piano, monti.

{ *R. fissella*, *a*, H. (*P.*) Estate. Boschi delle Alpi.
{ *R. f.*, var. *variella*, H., f. 106. (*Sv.*) Estate. Boschi, Alta Savoia.

R. sordidella, H. (*P.*) Giugno. Un solo individuo, trovato alla Certosa di Pesio.

(*R. ferrugella*, W. V., Tr.) è *flammella*, Tr. (Ved. al genere *Acompsia*).

R. verbascella, W. V., H. (*Sd., L., P.*) Giugno. Luoghi sterposi. Piano, monti.

R. silacella, H. fig. 117. (*P.*) Luglio, agosto. Luoghi sterposi. Colle di Torino, Dogliani.

Alucita striatella, F. (*P.*) Giugno. Praterie aride alle falde dei monti.

A. xylostella, L. (*Sd., L., P., Sv.*) Dalla metà aprile a tutto agosto. Prati, orti, ecc. Piano, Alpi.

A. porrectella, L. (*P.*) Maggio, luglio. Prati, orti. Piano, valli.

Macrochila rostrella, H. (*P.*) Luglio. Praterie aride. Valle di Sesia.

**Palpula labiosella*, H. (*P.*) Maggio, giugno, luglio. Boschetti della Mandria, e colle di Torino.

P. bicostella. (*P.*) Luglio. Praterie delle Alpi.

P. aristella, L. (*L., P.*) Estate. Praterie aride. Colli, monti.

P. clarella, Tr. (*L.*) Maggio. (Un solo individuo, trovato dal Barone Peiroleri.) Oneglia.

P. pyropella, W. V., H. (*P., Sv.*) Giugno, luglio. Praterie aride. Colle di Torino, Alta Savoia.

P. ericella, D. (*P.*) Giugno. Boschetti e brughiere. Sommità del colle di Torino.

Fugia subnigrella, D. (*P.*) Aprile. Sul trunco degli olmi. Dintorni di Torino.

Harpipteryx harpella, W. V., H. (*P., Sv.*) Luglio. Siepi e giardini. Piano, colli.

H. nemorella, L. (*P.*) Giugno, luglio. Siepi, e giardini. Colle di Torino.

H. chilonella, Tisch. (*P.*) Giugno. Praterie aride. Piano, colli.

H. cultrella, H. (*P.*) Marzo, ottobre. Siepi, boschetti. Piano, colli.

Parasia neuropterella, F. v. R. (*P.*) Luglio. (Presa dal Dott. Dabbene.) Dogliani.

Chauliodus Illigerellus, H. (*P.*) Giugno, luglio. Siepi, boschetti. Colle di Torino, Alpi.

C. pontificellus, H. (*L.*) Maggio. Siepi, boschetti. Piano, colli.

Dasycera Oliviella, F. (*L., P., Sv.*) Maggio, giugno, luglio. Cespugli, siti erbosi. Piano, colli.

Lampros majorella, W. V., H. (*P., Sv.*) Fine giugno, luglio. Siepi, boschetti. Piano, colli.

L. bracteella, L. (*P.*) Fine giugno, luglio. Siepi, boschetti. Valle di Pesio, colle di Torino.

L. Denisella, W. V., F. (*P.*) Maggio, giugno. Siepi, boschetti. Valle di Pesio, colli, Alpi.

L. sulphurella, H. (*P.*) Aprile. Boschi di Stupinigi.

Enicostoma Geoffroyella, F. (*L., P.*) Maggio, giugno. Siepi, boschetti. Piano, monti.

Stenoptera orbonella, H. (*Sd., L., P.*) Maggio, giugno. Praterie naturali sul margine dei boschi. Piano, monti.

Incurvaria masculella, W. V., H. (*Sd., P., Sv.*) Primavera. Siepi, boschetti. Colli, monti.

I. Œhlmanniella, H. (*P.*) Aprile. Siepi, boschetti. Colli, monti.

I. flavimitrella, H. (*L., P.*) Giugno. Monti Liguri, boschi della Mandria.

I. rupella, W. V., H. (*P.*) Giugno. Boschi del piano, colle di Torino, e valle di Pesio.

I. similella, H. (*L., P., Sv.*) Giugno. Siepi, praterie. Piano, colli.

I. albicostella, D. (*P.*) Maggio, giugno. Siepi, praterie, giardini. Piano, colli.

I. variella, F. (*P., Sv.*) Estate. Boschi di Stupinigi. Alpi della Savoia.

I. minutella, L. (*P.*) Maggio. Praterie, boschetti. Piano, colli.

I. augustella, H., fig. 177. (*P.*) Maggio. Boschi della Mandria.

I. Merianella, H., fig. 265. (*P.*) Maggio. Siepi, boschetti. Collina di Torino, Alpi.

Adela bimaculella, F. v. R. (*P.*) Primavera. Macchie nei boschi. Piano, colli.

A. Frischella, L. (*P., Sv.*) Luglio. Macchie nei boschi. Colli, Alpi.

A. violella, W. V., Tr. (*L., P.*) Estate. Praterie vicine alle foreste. Piano, colli.

A. Sulzeriella, Zell. (*P.*) Maggio, luglio. Macchie nei boschi. Piano, Alpi.

A. Degeerella, L. (*L., P., Sv.*) Aprile, maggio, giugno. Macchie nei boschi. Piano, Alpi.

A. Mazzolella, H. (*L., P.*) Maggio, giugno. Macchie nei boschi. Piano, Alpi.

A. Reaumurella, L. (*P., Sv.*) Aprile, maggio (agosto, Alpi). Macchie nei boschi. Piano, Alpi.

A. cuprella, W. V., H. (*Sd., L., P.*) Estate. Macchie nei boschi. Piano, Alpi.

Nemotois cupriacellus, H. (*P.*) Primavera, estate. Siti aridi e scoperti dei boschi di Stupinigi, Dogliani.

N. scabiosellus, Tr. (*L., P., Sv.*) Giugno, luglio. Siti aridi, sui fiori delle scabiose, ecc. Piano, monti.

N. Latreillellus, H. (*L., P.*) Giugno, luglio. Siti aridi. Liguria, Alpi marittime.

N. Schiffermüllerellus, W. V., H. (*P.*) Giugno, luglio. Siti aridi. Piano, colli.

**Nemophora Swammerdammella*, L. (*P., Sv.*) Aprile, maggio. Boschi cedui. Piano, colli.

N. pilulella, H. (*P.*) Maggio. Siti scoperti nei boschi. Piano, monti.

N. Panzerella, H. (*L., P., Sv.*) Aprile, maggio. Siti scoperti nei boschi. Piano, colli.

Solenobia clathrella, Tr. (*P., Sv.*) Giugno.
S. lichenella, L., D. (*P.*) Maggio, giugno.
S. lapidicella, Zell. (*P.*) Giugno, luglio.
S. pseudobombycella, H. (*P.*) Maggio, giugno.
} Contro alle mura umide. Piano, colli.

Micropteryx aruncella, Scop. (*L.*, *P.*) Giugno, luglio. Fiori nelle praterie in siti caldi. Piano, colli.

M. calthella, L. (*L.*, *P.*) Maggio, giugno. Fiori nelle praterie in siti caldi. Piano, colli.

M. Allionella, F. (*L.*, *P.*, *Sv.*) Primavera, estate. Freq. sui fiori del biancospino e *Spiræa aruncus*. Piano, monti.

M. Anderschella, H. (*P.*) Giugno. Fiori dei giardini e praterie. Colle di Torino.

M. Donzelella, D. (*L.*) Maggio. Siepi, cespugli. Dintorni della Spezia.

M. Jurinella, H., fig. 377. (*P.*) Giugno. Praterie naturali. Colli, monti.

**M. Pfeifferella*, H., fig. 398. (*P.*) Giugno. Praterie naturali. Colli, monti.

Æchmia thrasonella, Scop. (*L.*, *P.*, *Sv.*) Maggio, giugno. Siti erbosi e paludosi. Piano, colli.

Æ. equitella, Scop. (*P.*) Maggio, giugno. Praterie, giardini. Colle di Torino.

Æ. Lucasella, D. (*P.*) Maggio, giugno. Terreni paludosi. Boschi di Stupinigi.

Tinagma metallicella, F. v. R. (*P.*) Giugno. Siepi, boschetti. Colli, monti.

{ *Phygas taurella*, W. V., D. (*Sd.*, *P.*) Giugno. Siti cespugliosi ed umidi. Laghi di Caselette.
 P. bubalella, H., fig. 376.

Euplocamus anthracinellus, D., Illig. (*P.*) Maggio, giugno. Regione del Castagno. Colli, monti.

E. fulvimitrellus, D., Tr. (*P.*) Giugno. Un solo esemplare trovato nella valle di Pesio.

E. mediellus, Curt., H. (*P.*) Giugno. Boschi folti di Stura, e di Stupinigi.

E. parasitellus, D., H. (*P.*, *Sv.*) Maggio, giugno. Boschi folti di Stura e di Stupinigi, e monti della Savoia.

E. boletellus, F. (*L.*, *P.*) Luglio. Boschi di Conifere. Alpi marittime sui due versanti.

*Tinea granella, L. (*L.*, *P.*, *Sv.*) Aprile, maggio, luglio, agosto. (Bruco nocivo ai cereali.) Piano, monti.

T. pellionella, L. (*Sd.*, *L.*, *P.*, *Sv.*) Aprile, giugno, luglio. (Bruco dannoso alle pellicerie, piume, ecc.) Piano, monti.

T. sarcitella?, L. (*Sd.*, *P.*) Maggio, giugno. (Il bruco danneggia specialmente le raccolte Entomologiche.) Piano, monti.

**T. crinella*, Tr. (*Sd.*, *L.*, *P.*, *Sv.*) Primavera, estate (autunno raro). (Flagello delle stoffe in lana, crini, ecc.) Piano, monti.

T. tapezella, L. (*Sd., L., P.*) Maggio, giugno. (Come sopra, in istato di larva, divora panni, lane, pelle.) Piano, monti.

T. flavifrontella?, H., f. 126. (*P.*) Giugno. (Un solo esemplare.) Boschetti del colle di Torino.

T. lapella, H., fig. 252. (*L.*) Maggio. Contro alle pareti in una camera, alla Spezia.

T. rusticella, H. (*Sd., L., P., Sv.*). Maggio, giugno, ottobre. Contro alle mura, e nell' interno delle case. Piano, colli.

T. ferruginella, H. (*P.*) Estate. Vola di notte attorno ai lumi nelle abitazioni. Piano, colli.

T. cratægella, L. (*Sd., P.*) Giugno. Orti e giardini. Piano, colli.

T. cerasiella?, H. (*P.*) Estate, autunno. Sulle mura dei giardini e case di campagna. Piano, colli.

(*T. comptella*, H.) (Ved. al genere *Elachista*, la *aurofinitella*, Dup., Supp.)

T. repandella, H. (*P.*) Luglio. (Un solo individuo preso contro a un muro.) Valle del Po (Crissolo).

Œcophora Schœfferella, H., f. 136. (*L., P.*) Giugno, luglio. Boschi delle Alpi marittime, e colle di Torino.

Œ. Schmidtella, Tr. (*P., Sv.*) Giugno, luglio. Siti sterposi e caldi. Pesio, Susa, Alpi Subaude.

Œ. procerella, W. V., H. (*P., Sv.*). Luglio. Praterie in cima al colle di Torino. Moriena.

Œ. siccella, Zell. (*P.*) Giugno. Boschi della Mandria.

Œ. Mouffetella, L., H. (*P.*) Giugno. Praterie attigue ai boschi. Collina di Torino.

Œ. griseella, F. v. R. (*P.*) Maggio, giugno. Praterie attigue ai boschi. Collina di Torino.

Œ. gratiosella, F. v. R. (*P.*) Fine maggio. (Bruco comunissimo nelle foglie dell' olmo in autunno.) Torino.

* { *Œ. oleaella*, F. (*Sd., L.*) Settembre. (In istato di bruco, flagello delle olive.)
  Œ. olivella, Fonscol., D.

* { *Œ. arcuella?*, Costa. (*L., P.*) Estate. Cespugli, giardini. Dintorni di Genova, colle di Torino.
  Œ. Beyrandella?, D., Suppl.

Argyresthia pruniella, L. (*Sd., L., P., Sv.*) Estate. Siepi, boschetti. Piano, monti.

A. tetrapodella, L. (*P., Sv.*) Maggio. Siepi folte, boschi. Piano, monti.

A. fundella, Tisch. (*P.*) Giugno. Siepi folte, boschi. Colle di Torino.

A. pygmaella, H., f. 353. (*P.*) Estate. Praterie Alpine.

A. Goedartella, L. (*L., P., Sv.*) Estate. Boschi, cespugli. Piano, monti.

A. Brockeella, H. (*P.*) Estate. Boschi, cespugli. Alpi.

A. Andereggiella, F. v. R. (*Sv.*) Luglio. (Trovata dai signori fratelli Perrier.) Albertville.

A. Gysseliniella?, Kuhlw. (*P.*) Giugno. Foreste Alpine.

Coleophora Mayrella, H., fig. 322. (*L.*) Maggio. (Un solo individuo trovato in sito paludoso.) Spezia.

C. ornatipennella, H. (*P.*) Giugno. Brughiere e boschi della Mandria. Piano, colli.

C. vibicinella, H. (*P.*) Estate. Praterie. Valle del Po (Crissolo).

C. vibicigerella?, Zell. (*P.*) Agosto. Cespugli, siti erbosi. Colle di Torino.

C. gallipennella, H. (*L., P., Sv.*) Maggio, giugno. Cespugli, siti erbosi. Piano, colli.

C. palliatella, Zinck. (*P.*) Luglio. Boschi di Stupinigi.

C. anatipennella, H., f. 186. (*P.*) Giugno, luglio. Praterie e boschi. Piano, colli.

C. auricella, Bosc. (*P., Sv.*) Estate. Praterie e boschi. Piano, colli.

C. galbulipennella, F. v. R. (*P.*) Luglio. Praterie e boschi. Piano, colli.

C. onosmella, Brahm. (*L., P., Sv.*) Maggio, giugno, luglio, settembre. Macchie nei boschi. Piano, monti.

C. hemerobiella, Scop. (*Sd., P.*) Estate. Praterie, boschetti. Colli, monti.

C. leucapennella, H. (*L., P.*) Maggio, luglio. Praterie, boschetti. Colli, monti.

C. coracipennella, H. (*P.*) Estate. Praterie, boschetti. Colli, Alpi.

C. laricella, H. (*P.*) Giugno, luglio. Boschi di larici. Alpi.

C. alcyonipennella, Koll. (*P.*) Aprile. (Trovata dal Dott. Dabbene.) Dogliani.

Gracilaria Franckella, H. (*L., P.*) Luglio, agosto. Boschi di Stupinigi. Colli, monti.

G. stigmatella, F. (*P.*) Luglio. Boschi di Stupinigi. Colli, monti.

G. falconipennella, H. (*P.*) Luglio, agosto. Praterie, boschetti. Colli, monti.

G. elongella, L. (*P., Sv.*) Luglio. Praterie, boschetti. Alpi.

G. roscipennella?, H. (*Sv.*) Estate. Praterie, boschetti. Alta Savoia.

G. syringella, F. (*P.*) Giugno, luglio. Siepi, giardini. Piano, colli.

G. phasianipennella, H. (*P.*) Luglio. Valle di Bobbio, Luserna.

G. ononiella, Zell. (*P.*) Luglio. Cespugli. Spalti della cittadella di Torino.

G. merulæpennella, D. (*P.*) Agosto. Folto dei boschi di Stupinigi.

G. cuculipennella, H. (*P.*) Giugno. Praterie e boschetti della Mandria.

Coriscium quercetellum, Zell. (*P.*) Maggio. Boschetti. Collina di Torino.

Ornix guttiferella, Zell. (*L., P.*) Giugno. Siepi, giardini. Piano, colli.

**O. trochilipennella*, Costa. (*Sd.*) Estate. Monte dell' interno dell' isola.

* { *Cosmopteryx fastuosella*, Costa. (*P.*) Estate. Siti aridi e sterposi. Piano, colli.
{ *C. pedella* ?, L., Zell.

Elachista ictella, H., fig. 361. (*P.*) Maggio. Siepi, cespugli. Colle di Torino.

E. Roesella, L. (*P., Sv.*) Primavera, estate. Praterie, boschi. Piano, Alpi.

E. Linnæella, Clerck. (*P.*) Giugno. Giardini, alberi fruttiferi. Piano, colli.

E. quadrella, H. (*P.*) Maggio. Boschi di Stupinigi.

E. nigrella, H. (*P., Sv.*) Estate. Siepi, cespugli. Piano, monti.

E. bifasciella, Tr. (*P.*) Maggio, giugno. Siepi, cespugli. Piano, monti.

E. Æchmiella, D. (*P.*) Giugno. Praterie. Colle di Torino.

E. cygnipennella, H. (*P.*) Maggio, giugno. Siepi, boschetti. Venaria, Mandria.

**E. oleaella*, Fonscol. (*Sd., L.*) Aprile. (Bruco nocivo alle foglie dell' olivo.) (Ved. l'annotazione.)

E. Boyerella, D. (*L.*) Maggio. Siepi, giardini.

E. Saportella ?, D. (*P.*) Maggio, Giugno. Cespugli al piè degli olmi. Vicinanze di Torino.

* { *E. aurofinitella*, Dup., Suppl. (*Sd., P.*) Aprile. Sardegna meridionale. E trovata dal Dott. Dabbene in Dogliani.
{ *E. comptella*, H. (Ved. al genere *Tinea*.)

E. abrasella, F. v. R. (*P.*) Giugno. Boschi della collina di Torino.

Opostega spartifoliella, H. (*P.*) Maggio, agosto. Boschetti in riva al Po.

Lyonetia sericopezella ?, F. v. R. (*P.*) Settembre. (Presa dal Dott. Dubbene.) Dogliani.

L. rhamnifoliella, Tisch. (*P.*) Giugno. Siepi, orti. Dintorni di Torino.

L. Clerckella ?, L. (*Sd.*) Autunno. Regione montuosa dell' interno dell' isola.

L. prunifoliella, H., fig. 191. (*P., Sv.*) Estate. Siepi, cespugli. Piano, colli.

L. padifoliella, H., fig. 316. (*P.*) Maggio. Siti umidi nei boschi di Stupinigi.

Lithocolletis Cramerella, F. v. R. (*P., Sv.*) Estate. Siti erbosi. Piano, monti.

L. rajella, L. (*L.*) Maggio. Siepi, boschetti. Dintorni della Spezia.

L. betulifoliella, Zell. (*P.*) Giugno. Boschi. Valle di Fenestrelle.

L. Kleemannella, F. (*P.*) Ottobre. Contro ad un muro. Colle di Torino.

L. Frœlichiella, Zell. (*P.*) Estate. Fiori delle praterie. Alte cime del colle di Torino.

Tischeria complanella, H. (*P.*) Maggio. (Un solo individuo, trovato dal Dott. Dabbene.) Dogliani.

Annotazioni.

Yponomeuta cognatella e Malinella.

Avendo ottenuto un numero considerevolissimo d'individui di questa specie da bruchi nutriti in casa colle foglie del pomo, pianta gravemente danneggiata nei nostri verzieri da questi bruchi, io posso asserire che da una medesima nidificata e contemporaneamente (agli ultimi di giugno) nacquero frammiste ai due sessi della *Malinella*, Zell. etc. poche femmine di statura alquanto più forte e colla frangia delle ali posteriori quasi intieramente bianca; caratteri che, secondo gli autori Zeller, Freyer et Guenée, servirebbero a distinguere questa specie dalla *cognatella*, Hüb., ecc. Risulterebbe adunque evidentemente da questa mia recente osservazione che una sola sia la specie, avendo il Zeller distinto il maschio a frangia grigio-scura col nome di *Malinella*, considerando erroneamente la varietà a frangia bianca nelle ali posteriori come una specie distinta, a cui solo spettasse il nome di *cognatella* degli Autori.

Lita betulinella.

Io trovo una serie tale di varietà intermedie tra la *Anacampsis terrella*, Hüb., Dup., e la *Lita betulinella*, Hüb., Dup., da rimanere dubbioso sulla validità di queste specie. Aggiungasi che nei caratteri generici assegnati a questi due generi nel Catalogo Duponchel, dicesi, *trompe nulle* si all' uno che all' altro, mentre in tutti gl' individui che io potei riferire ora alla *terrella*, ora alla *betulinella*, la proboscide (*trompe*) trovossi in tutti quanti lunga e visibilissima.

Enolmis luteella.

Questa specie perfettamente descritta nel tom. xi. pag. 624, e figurata nella pl. 312. fig. 11, dell' opera Duponchel, col nome di

Lita luteella, Dup., venne dal medesimo Autore, nel suo Catalogo metodico, estratta dal genere *Lita*, in compagnia di un' altra specie, colle quali egli constituì il suo genere *Enolmis*; assegnandole come carattere generico, parlando della bocca:—

"*Palpes grèles, à peine arqués, non velus, et dont le dernier article se termine en pointe obtuse. Trompe robuste.*" Ora nella specie in questione (non conoscendo l' altra sua congenere) io posso asserire che i palpi sono sensibilmente arcuati, coll' ultimo articolo acutissimo, e che di proboscide non vi è traccia. Questo carattere negativo farebbe per conseguenza rientrare il nostro insetto nel genere *Lita*.

Aggiungerò inoltre un grave sospetto che mi venne percorrendo la precitata opera Duponchel onde determinare la mia specie di Piemonte. Trovai, a pag. 491 del tom. 9, la descrizione ed annessa iconografia, pl. 261. f. 6, della *Cochylis Walckenaerana*, Dup., le quali dirsi possono una ripetizione del testo e figura della *Lita luteella*, Dup. Ora parmi sommamente improbabile che due specie della Francia meridionale, cotanto affini in tutto tra di loro, possano presentare, nei caratteri generici della testa solamente, una tanta diversità quale si osserva in quelle parti tra i due generi *Cochylis* ed *Enolmis*. Riflettendo poi che la *Enolmis luteella* veniva in origine collocata dal Duponchel nel genere *Lita*, cioè in un genere privo di proboscide, quindi aggregata al genere *Enolmis* ove si dice la proboscide *robuste*—considerando in fine, che la specie piemontese si troverebbe ancora identica in tutto alle due altre, ma da entrambe diversa nei caratteri cefalici, Io mi credo autorizzato a supporre che l' Autore francese, in due epoche e con nomi diversi, abbia, per isbaglio, pubblicato la stessa specie; della quale specie possedendone probabilmente un solo esemplare mutilato nelle parti della bocca, e guidato perciò unicamente dalla forma e taglio delle ali, egli sia stato indotto a referire il suo insetto ora al genere *Enolmis*, ora al genere *Cochylis*, mentre ebbe ragione soltanto allorquando lo publicava col nome di *Lita luteella*.

Se male non mi appongo, sarebbe per conseguenza il caso, non solamente di restituire al genere *Lita* la *Enolmis luteella*, Dup., ma di aggiungere a quest' ultima, qual sinonimo, il nome di *Walckenaerana*, Dup. (*Cochylis*), qualora realmente non esista nella Francia meridionale la vera *Cochylis Walckenaerana*, pubblicata dal Duponchel. Benchè debolissimo quest' ultimo dubbio, che io non sono in caso di togliere, forma la sola cagione per cui non faccio, nel mio Catalogo, le rettificazioni anzidette.

Acompsia flavella e ferrugella.

Il Duponchel avendo avuto sott' occhio questa specie, la collocò nel genere *Acompsia*, come giustamente lo richiede il carattere della forma dei palpi, assegnato a questo genere. Ma io trovo nel Catalogo metodico, e nell' opera dello stesso autore, pubblicata, tom. 4. Suppl. pag. 254, una *Rhinosia ferrugella*, W. V., Tr., che egli descrive dietro le osservazioni del Treitschke, non avendola veduta in natura; la qual circostanza, unita alla somiglianza nelle iconografie di queste due specie, mi lascia grandemente sospettare che la stessa specie sia stata pubblicata dal Duponchel come nuova, a pag. 512 del suo tom. 4. Suppl., chiamandola *flavella*; ed a pag. 254, dello stesso volume, sotto il nome di *ferrugella*, W. V., Tr. Nel qual caso quest' ultimo nome specifico dovrà prevalere perchè anteriore a quello di *flavella*, ma spettando al genere *Acompsia*, dovrebbesi perciò denominare *Acompsia ferrugella*, W. V., Tr.

Dall' investigazione dei palpi, la *Rhinosia flammella*, Tr., D. (*formosella*, Hübn.), trovasi nello stesso caso della *ferrugella* qui sopra, vale a dire, spetta al genere *Acompsia* del presente Catalogo.

Butalis cerealella.

Questa è l'*Alucite des grains* dei Francesi (*Œcophora granella* di Latreille) da non confondersi colla *Tinea granella*, Linn., di cui parleremo a suo tempo. Illustrata da molti autori la storia della nostra *Butalis cerealella*, io mi limiterò a ricordare che il suo bruco, a differenza di quello della vera *Tinea granella*, vivendo rinchiuso nell' interno di un grano, il danno che esso cagiona ai cereali nei magazzini, passando inosservato, riesce per ciò stesso piu considerevole in quei siti ove si manifesta questo flagello, e nel tempo medesimo di maggior difficoltà nel porvi riparo.

Palpula labiosella.

Vola questa farfallina al chiaror del sole, eccettuandone però le ore più calde del giorno, ma per quanto spesseggi in alcune località elevate e selvose della collina di Torino, e non ostante la facilità con cui la si può cogliere, ciò nulla di meno riesce oltremodo difficile di procurarsene esemplari intatti, voglio dire forniti dei loro vistosissimi palpi ; e ciò per lo strano sviluppo di questi organi estremamente allungati e massicci, sostenuti da un tenue peduncolo, il quale si rompe al minimo contatto di un corpo estraneo, sia pur anco della morbidezza del velo, col quale si fanno le reti da caccia per i Micro-Lepidotteri.

Nemophora Swammerdammella.

Nelle osservazioni che seguono i caratteri generici fissati a questo genere nel Catalogo metodico Duponchel, dicesi, che queste specie volano soltanto di sera ; è questo un errore che importa rettificare, mentre si vedono invece volare in abbondanza in pien meriggio nei boschi cedui del circondario di Torino, sin dai primi giorni d'aprile, non solamente la *Swammerdammella*, ma le altre sue congeneri, come facilmente ognuno potrà verificare.

Micropteryx Pfeifferella.

Per isbaglio, nel Catalogo metodico Duponchel, questa specie, col suo sinonimo di *Stadtmüllerella*, H., trovasi ripetuta nel genere *Elachista*, ma io opino che si debba conservare di preferenza nel genere *Micropteryx*, cancellando questa duplicazione nel genere *Elachista* del precitato Catalogo.

Tinea granella.

Il bruco di questa piccola farfalla, funestissimo per il danno che cagiona nei magazzini di cereali, offre nelle sue abitudini una circostanza che tosto ne svela la presenza, ed avverte il proprietario di ripararvi con quei mezzi più opportuni suggeriti nei trattati di Agronomia che a lungo ne ragionano. Esso vive rinchiuso, non già nell' interno del grano, come quello della *Butalis cerealella* di cui già si fe' cenno, ma bensì in un tubo di seta che egli si tesse nell' interstizio lasciato da più grani tra di loro collegati con altri fili, che il bruco dispone all' uopo; dal che ne risulta una specie di tela, o per dir meglio una copertura che tutta involge la superficie dei cumuli di grani, siano essi di frumento, orzo o segale.

Nella state dello scorso anno 1850 questa *Tinea* ci offerse, nelle campagne di Piobesi, un fenomeno, non raro in Entomologia, ma sempre interessante per il mistero che ne ravvolge la causa prima; m' intendo dire l' apparizione repentina di questa specie in numero sterminato, che a sciami a sciami invase tutti gli apartamenti della villeggiatura del Sig. Cav. Molina; e penetrando sin nei più remoti nascondigli, lasciò ovunque sul pavimento uno strato de' suoi cadaveri di un considerevole spessore. Da me avvertito il proprietario sulla natura pericolosa dell' ospite che forzatamente ebbe in casa, egli avrà, io suppongo, usate le debite cautele ne' suoi granai, onde prevenire le probabili funeste conseguenze di questa visita domiciliare di nuovo genere.

Tinea crinella.

Questo bruco struggitore di ogni sorta di tessuti in lana e crini, danneggia particolarmente le lane dei materassi.

Œcophora oleaella e olivella.

Abitando un paese ove non alligna l' olivo, nissuna osservazione mia particolare potrei aggiungere relativa alle abitudini di questa tremenda farfallina, se non conoscessi il contenuto di una Memoria scritta da un Palermitano su tale argomento, la cui conclusione sarebbe di altissima importanza.

Molti autori italiani, ed alcuni francesi, scrissero intorno alla *Tinea* nociva all' olivo; ma nissuno, che io mi sappia, ottenne in casa varie generazioni consecutive mediante l' educazione dei bruchi, unico mezzo di togliere ogni dubbio intorno alla storia di questo terribile flagello degli oliveti. Se io non mi appago di quanto scrisse il Sig. Fonscolombe sui costumi della *Œcophora olivella* ed *Elachista oleaella*, non è già che io non nutra la più alta stima per questo distinto Entomologo francese; ma sono indotto a sospettare di qualche grave sbaglio dal canto suo, vedendo il modo affirmativo con cui il precitato autore siciliano conchiude per la riunione in una specie sola delle due farfalline in questione. Nella Memoria *degli insetti che danneggiano gli ulivi in Sicilia*, gentilmente statami offerta dall' autore, Baldassare Romano da Palermo, tra le altre importanti e diligentissime sue osservazioni, fui colpito dalla storia particolarizzata che egli ci dà della *Elachista oleaella* (accompagnata da una descrizione et da figura in tutto conformi a quelle dell' opera Duponchel), ove l' autore palermitano termina coll' asserire che la tignuola, ottenuta dai bruchi nutritisi in primavera col parenchima delle foglie dell' olivo, possiede esattamente tutti i caratteri, non diversifica in somma per niente dalla tignuola che nasce in settembre dal nocciolo della stessa pianta. Ora la figura e la breve descrizione che accompagnano la sua Memoria non lasciano il menomo dubbio sulla identicità di questa specie colla *Elachista oleaella* di Fonscolombe et di Duponchel, la quale *oleaella*, in ultima analisi, non sarebbe altro che il frutto della generazione di primavera avvenuto in un modo assai diverso di quella dell' autunno; e gli autori francesi per qualche sbaglio occorso nella distinzione di sesso, o di varietà nel colorito, avrebbero assegnato a questa specie autunnale il nome di *Œcophora olivella*: impropriamente separandole perfino di genere, una dall' altra.

Per quanto straordinario possa parere l' asserto del Sig. Romano, scemerà la meraviglia se si pon mente che di un fatto consimile già abbiamo un esempio nella *Cochylis roserana*, la quale in istato di larva si nutre, in primavera, della foglia, e nella successiva generazione penetra nel frutto della vite. Ora, considerando l' ambiguità delle parole degli autori relativo alla propagazione delle due specie di Tinee nocive all' olivo, una delle quali solo apparirebbe in primavera, e l' altra unicamente in autunno, caso non troppo frequente nella storia dei Lepidotteri; avuto riguardo alla facilità con cui si spiegherebbe ogni cosa ammettendo il fatto esposto dal nostro autore siciliano, fatto già da più anni presentito da un francese, il Sig. Blaud; io mi sento disposto a credere alla doppia generazione annua di una specie sola, fintanto che nuove osservazioni e la storia precisa dei bruchi, non venga a provare il contrario.

P.S.—Era per consegnarsi alla stampa l' annotazione precedente, quando, col 1º trimestre 1851 degli Annali della Società Entomologica di Francia, mi giunse inaspettata una Nota del Sig. Boyer de Fonscolombe, mediante la quale l' autore Francese, con quella lealtà, propria alle persone di vero merito, si dichiara convinto dell' identicità di specie tra le sue *Elachista oleaella*, ed *Œcophora olivella*: opinando che a quest' ultimo genere debba riferirsi la specie in questione, conservandole il nome specifico impostole da Fabricio; vale a dire chiamandola definitivamente *Œcophora oleaella*, Fab. Dovrà quindi considerarsi come non esistente la *Elachista oleaella*, Fonscol., del presente Catalogo, e del Catalogo metodico Duponchel. [See *ante*, pp. 263, 264.]

Œcophora arcuella e *Begrandella*.

La descrizione e la figura della *Gracilaria Begrandella*, Duponchel, Suppl. tom. iv. pag. 513, pl. 89. f. 8, convengono a puntino al nostro insetto, se non che quest' ultimo, dall' investigazione dei palpi.

risulterebbe appartenere al genere *Œcophora* del Catalogo metodico del suddetto autore, e non mai al suo genere *Gracilaria*. Trovasi invece pubblicata, nella ' Fauna del Regno di Napoli' del Prof. Costa, una specie, col nome di *Œcophora arcuella*, Costa, pag. 5, tav. ii. fig. 6, la quale, abbenchè alquanto meno rassomigliante alla nostra farfallina di quanto lo sia la *Begrandella*, Dup., pure, trovandosi conforme alla nostra specie nei caratteri generici, offre maggior probabilità di convenire con essa; per cui io do la precedenza al nome del Costa, ancorchè, come già dissi, per la figura e per la descrizione del Duponchel il nome specifico di *Begrandella* meriterebbe la preferenza.

Ornix trochilipennella.

Nella Fauna del Regno di Napoli del Prof. Costa trovasi egregiamente descritta e figurata questa specie interessante, a pag. 2, tav. 3. fig. 6; se non che, per la forma straordinaria delle antenne, coperte di grossissima squama sino a metà della loro lunghezza, essa dovrebbe collocarsi di preferenza nel genere *Adela* di Latreille. Siccome però nella constituzione dei palpi, e per la forma lineare delle ali, neppure a questo genere potrebbe confarsi, la lasceremo provvisoriamente nel genere *Ornix* statole assegnato dall' autore Napolitano.

Cosmopteryx fastuosella e *pedella.*

Io sono pressochè convinto che la *Œcophora fastuosella*, Costa (Fauna del Regno di Napoli, pag. 5, tav. 2. fig. 7), altro non sia che la *pedella*, L. (*angustipennella*, Hüb., Tr., Dup.), ma nelle descrizioni degli autori non si fa menzione delle fascie nerastre che guerniscono le gambe posteriori, per cui trovando la sola descrizione del Professore Or. Gab. Costa esattamente conforme all' insetto che abbiamo in Italia, io devo concedere la preferenza al nome dell' autore Italiano; lasciando come dubbiosi quelli sovramenzionati che si trovano nel Catalogo metodico, e nell' opera Duponchel.

Elachista oleaella.

Secondo il Sig. Boyer de Fonscolombe, questa farfallina dannosa, solo si nutrirebbe, in istato di bruco, delle teneri foglie dell' olivo, e non mai del frutto, ossia coccola; come pratica il bruco della non men nociva *Œcophora olivella*, Fonscol. Al quale proposito vedasi l'annotazione da me fatta a quest' ultima specie. [P. 292.]

Elachista aurofinitella e *comptella.*

Sebbene mi manchi il foglio di testo corrispondente alla figura 89 (*Tineiti*, tav. 13) dell' opera di Hübner, pure sembrami ravvisare, senza tema di sbaglio, nella figura anzidetta la *Elachista aurofinitella* descritta e figurata dal Duponchel, nel tom. iv. Suppl. pag. 516, pl. 89. fig. 11, della sua opera. Non so quindi comprendere come quest' ultimo autore lasci figurare, nel suo Catalogo metodico, la *comptella* di Hübner, fig. 89, nel genere *Tinea*, collocando la sua *aurofinitella* nel genere *Elachista*. Convien dire che non avendo posseduto in natura la *T. comptella*, egli non seppe riconoscerla nell' opera dell' autore tedesco, e la pubblicò come specie nuova. Io pure ritenni sino a questi giorni come specie inedita, questa stupenda farfallina da me trovata più anni or sono nell' isola di Sardegna, e aggiungerò che con sommo mio stupore ne ricevei ultimamente un secondo esemplare in comunicazione dal Sig. Dott. Ach. Dabbene, da lui raccolto in Dogliani il 14 Aprile di quest' anno; senza altro dato relativo alla storia di questa interessantissima specie.

CHAPTER X.

AUTHORS OF THE LAST CENTURY.

IN this chapter I include the few South-European Tineina described by Linné and Fabricius, and the much greater number included in Scopoli's 'Entomologia Carniolica.' It is true that many of these latter to this day remain undeciphered; but it is quite possible that a diligent exploration of the localities whence Scopoli obtained his species might even at this date lead to the recognition of some of his undetermined species.

At any rate this work would have been incomplete without a distinct recognition of the labours of Scopoli.

SECTION I.
Linné's 'Systema Naturæ.'

This contains three descriptions of Tineina from Portugal, all collected by Don Vandelli, who was himself the author of a "Floræ et Faunæ Lusitanicæ specimen," published in 1797 in the first volume of the Mem. da Acad. real de Scienc. de Lisboa (pp. 39–79).

I. 2. 894. 416. ARISTELLA. *Albida, alis linea argentea, palpis porrectis, capite longioribus, aristatis.*
Habitat in Lusitania. *D. Vandelli.*
Corpus teres, lineare, alis convolutis albidum; linea in medio alæ longitudinalis, argentea. Palpi capite thoraceque duplo longiores, crassi, hirsuti, porrecti, cum arista prope apicem. Antennæ palpis sesquilongiores.

I. 2. 894. 417. CAUDELLA. *Alis testaceis, caudali linea fusca, palpis porrectis.*
Habitat in Lusitania. *D. Vandelli.*
Corpus teres, magnitudine *Ph. pascuellæ*. Alæ superiores in media linea longitudinali fusca; hæ alæ postice caudatæ. Palpi supra basin aristati.

I. 2. 898. 448. BRUNNICHELLA. *Atra, alis fasciis tribus violaceis.*
Habitat in Lusitania. *D. Vandelli.*
Corpus minutum, lineare, planiusculum, atrum. Antennæ corpore breviores, infra apicem albæ. Alæ atræ fasciis tribus violaceis s. chalybis candefacti colore, quarum prima ad basin, secunda in medio, tertia curva ad apicem. Cilia postice inter alarum apices, subulata in plures dentes.

SECTION II.

Fabrician species described in the 'Entomologia Systematica,' vol. iii. from specimens either collected in Italy by Dr. Allioni, or bred from plants peculiarly Southern, such as rue and olive.

PYRALIS RUTANA, 2. 286. No. 179.

Alis depressis, fuscis, lineolis transversis numerosis albis, thorace denticulis duobus dorsalibus.

Habitat in Galliæ Ruta, cujus folia contorquet. Mus. Dom. Boso.

Statura et magnitudo *P. applanæ.* Caput et thorax fusca, immaculata. Thorax fasciculis duobus erectis compressis pilorum. Alæ depressæ, fuscæ, lineolis abbreviatis, numerosissimis, tenuissimis, transversis, albis. Præterea puncta duo parva, elevata, approximata, atra in medio.

TINEA BARBELLA, 2. 297. No. 45.

Alis cinereis fusco-striatis, palpis porrectis longitudine antennarum.
Habitat in Italia; Dr. Allioni.

Statura omnino *T. marginellæ.* Antennæ pectinatæ. Palpi porrecti longitudine antennarum, crassi, pilosi apico articulo unico. Caput, thorax, abdomen cinerea, immaculata. Alæ cinereæ, fusco striatæ, obscuræ. Posticæ fuscæ.

Hæc cum *T. marginella* et *bicostella* forte proprium genus constituit.

TINEA QUADRELLA, 2. 298. No. 51.

Atra, capite, ano, alarumque punctis quatuor niveis.
Habitat in Italia; Dr. Allioni.

Statura præcedentium [*maurella, nigrella*, etc.]. Caput hirtum, niveum. Corpus atrum, ano albo. Alæ anticæ nigræ, punctis quatuor, anticis duobus 1.1 transversis, posticis oppositis. Posticæ obscure cinereæ. Pedes nigri, albo annulati.

TINEA ATRELLA, 2. 298. No. 52.

Atra, æneo-nitida, alis posticis apice anoque testaceis.
Habitat in Italia; Dr. Allioni.

Corpus magnum, totum uti et alæ anticæ atrum, paullo æneo colore nitidulum. Alarum posticarum margo posticus et anus testacei. Pedes atri.

[Is not this *Psecadia aurifluella*?]

TINEA VARIELLA, 2. 299. No. 55.

Alis anticis nigris; linea baseos, punctis duobus, fasciisque duabus abbreviatis niveis.

Habitat in Italia; Dr. Allioni.

Statura et magnitudo præcedentium [*lugubrella, viduella, atrella*]. Antennæ nigræ. Caput et thorax nivea, immaculata. Alæ anticæ atræ, linea baseos fere ad medium ducta, puncto costali transverso, fascia cum margine tenuiore albo coëunte, puncto altero costali fasciaque denique abbreviata albis. Posticæ uti omnes subtus obscuræ.

TINEA USTALELLA, 2. 307. No. 88.

Alis linearibus, fusco-brunneis, apice ustulatis.
Habitat in Italia.
Distincta omnino a *T. elongella*. Magnitudo *T. bicostellæ*. Antennæ albo nigroque annulatæ longitudine corporis. Corpus brunneum. Alæ lineares, brunneæ, auro-nitidulæ, apice ustulatæ, vel obscuriores. Posticæ uti omnes subtus obscuræ.

TINEA OLEELLA, 2. 308. No. 91.

Alis ciliatis cinereis, nitidulis, immaculatis.
Habitat in nucleis fructus *Oleæ*, quos cadere facit ante maturitatem. Mus. Dom. Bosc.
Minuta. Alæ cinerascentes, nitidæ, immaculatæ.

TINEA STRIGELLA, 2. 308. No. 93.

Alis nigris, apice atris; striga obliqua alba.
Habitat in Italia; Dr. Allioni.
Corpus medium, nigrum, fronte albicante. Alæ omnes nigræ, anticæ apice atræ, fascia obliqua alba.

TINEA ANTENNELLA, 2. 312. No. 110.

Alis atris nitidulis immaculatis, antennis flavis.
Habitat in Italia; Dr. Allioni.
Corpus parvum, atrum, antennis læte flavis. Pedes apice albidi. Alæ omnes atræ, nitidulæ, immaculatæ.
[This is surely *Phibalocera luticornella*.]

TINEA SEXPUNCTELLA, 2. 313. No. 115.

Alis cinereis fusco fasciatis, punctisque tribus atris.
Habitat in Italia; Dr. Allioni.
Corpus medium, nigrum. Alæ cinereæ fasciis tribus latis, fuscis; anteriore punctis duobus atris, secunda unico. Margo posticus ciliatus terminatur punctis atris.

TINEA ALLIONELLA, 2. 321. No. 148.

Alis cupro-auratis; fasciis duabus maculaque apicis flavissimis.
Habitat in Italia; Dr. Allioni.
Magnitudo et statura *T. Goedartellæ*. Corpus atrum. Alæ anticæ cupro-auratæ, nitidæ, fasciis duabus, altera baseos, altera in medio flavissimis, maculaque ejusdem coloris versus apicem.

ALUCITA PANZERELLA, 2. 339. No. 32.

Alis pallidis subtilissime fusco reticulatis, capite fulvo, antennis longissimis albis.
Habitat in Italia; Dr. Allioni.

Minus affinis *A. Swammerdammellæ.* Differt tamen capite magis fulvo et alis subtilissime reticulatis; striis vix nudo oculo conspicuis. Posticæ cinereæ.

ALUCITA PAYKULLELLA, 2. 340. No. 38.

Alis fulvo-cupreis; basi fascia media maculaque apicis flavo aureis.
Habitat in agro Pedemontano; Dr. Allioni.
Minuta. Antennæ breves, nigræ. Caput fulvum. Alæ anticæ fulvo-cupreæ, nitidæ, basi late, fascia media, maculaque apicis fere transversali aureis. Posticæ fuscæ.

SECTION III.

Scopoli's 'Entomologia Carniolica.'

In the 'Stettiner entomologische Zeitung,' 1855, pp. 233–257, are some critical remarks on the Lepidoptera described by Scopoli, from the pen of Professor Zeller, who introduces the subject thus:—

"Scopoli is an author who, though held in respect by Lepidopterists from the first, has been much misunderstood, not because his descriptions have been carelessly made (since they are as good as those of Linné and incomparably better than those of Fabricius), but because aids to their interpretation were wanting, which were possessed by other writers, such as the works of their pupils, the presence of their collections, figures, references, &c., which relieve or remove difficulties.

" With reference to the figures which Scopoli proposed to publish with his work, Dr. Hagen has furnished a detailed notice in the 'Entomolog. Zeitung,' 1854, p. 81." [It appears that Scopoli, dissatisfied with the execution of the plates by the engraver, abandoned the idea of publishing them. Though forty-three plates were executed they were never on sale, and few copies of the work with the plates are in existence.] "This notice of Hagen's has been the cause of my obtaining from Herr v. Heyden, who in his rich library possesses one of the few copies of the 'Entomologia Carniolica' with plates, and who seizes with the greatest liberality every opportunity of furthering science, the use of his copy in order to work out thoroughly the Lepidoptera of Scopoli, a labour which I readily undertook.

"The figures of the Lepidoptera in the 'Entomologia Carniolica' are as a whole bad. As may be easily conceived, the large variegated species, which could not be misrepresented, are easily recognized; but, for the determination of such species, Scopoli's descriptions amply sufficed. The small species are precisely those which should have been well represented; and for the most part they are so badly done that it is quite evident why Scopoli forbore to publish the plates. Yet they are not altogether useless, since by the general form, direction of the markings, or other circumstances, they may sometimes lead to the recognition of the species. It is true I have not in all cases arrived at a satisfactory result; but I have solved some problems, and I do not doubt that, by following up the subject in locality and situation, many questions may yet obtain solution.

"Of Scopoli's species forty-four have remained undecipherable by me, a considerable number, which thus leaves open a wide field for future workers: they are indicated by a †. The thirty-seven specific names with reference to which I have arrived at a totally new result, or have confirmed a doubtful one, or have at any rate advocated it with conviction, are marked with a *".

I annex copies of those descriptions of the Tineina which occur in Scopoli's work, with regard to which there is any difficulty, and side by side with them Zeller's remarks on the figures.

The three following species are placed by Scopoli amongst the Pyrales:—

P. 239. 607. PHALÆNA ANTHRACINALIS.

607. ANTHRACINALIS, mit kenntlicher Abbildung des ♂, = *Eupлокамия Fuesslinellus*. Da die Sulzersche Benennung von 1776 datirt, so habe ich einen Fehler begangen, die ältere Scopolische in der Linnæa VI. 86, nur unter die Synonyme aufzunehmen.

P. 240. 609. PHALÆNA CITRINALIS.

609. CITRINALIS, schlecht abgebildet, ist richtig nach Tr. (ix. 2. 65) = *Carc. Christiernini*.

P. 241. 611. PHALÆNA CRISTALIS.
Long. lin. 3¼.
Diagn. Alæ fuscæ; anticæ supra ferrugineo fuscoque nebulosæ, cristula nigricante in medio notatæ.
Circa Idriam.
Palpi lin. 1¼ longi. Fimbria alis posticis concolor. Alæ subtus politæ. *Larva nuda, de cauda pendens, fulva cum partui proxima.*

*611. CRISTALIS, unkenntlich abgebildet, sicher = *Anchinia verrucella*, S. V.

P. 245. 625. PHALÆNA VIDUELLA.
Long. lin. 4¼.
Diagn. Alæ anticæ albæ; linea fusca, a basi ad apicem prope marginem crassiorem decurrente.
In sylvis, rarior et solitaria.
Oculi nigri. Antennæ supra albæ, subtus fuscæ. Caput cum thorace album. Alæ anticæ punctis binis nigris prope lineam fuscam, senisque minoribus in margine externo. Alæ posticæ utrinque fuscescentes.

†625. VIDUELLA. Beschreibung und Abbildung (letztere freilich mit Hinterflügeln von der Breite der davorstehenden *Rosella*) scheinen sich so sicher auf *Anchinia bicostella* anwenden zu lassen, dass man gern die "antennæ supra albæ, subtus fuscæ" für eine missrathene Uebergenauigkeit und die unerwähnt gebliebenen Taster für abgebrochen erklären möchte. Leider folgt aber unter 642 die sichere *bicostella*! Also kann *viduella* nicht dieselbe Art sein. Da

P. 245. 626. PHALÆNA FUSCELLA.
Long. lin. 4.
Diagn. Alæ canescentes, fusco-punctatæ.
In montanis nostris, passim.
Tota unicolor, subcanescens, punctulis copiosis fuscis nebulosa.

†626. FUSCELLA mir unbekannt; in der Abbildung sind auch die breiten Hinterflügel stark punktirt, sowie die schmalen Vorderflügel.

weder *Psecadia echiella*, noch *Plutella fissella* gemeint sein kann, so bleibt hier abermals ein Räthsel zu lösen.

[Scopoli places both the above amongst the *Crambidæ*; possibly they are not intended for *Tineina*.]

P. 246. 631. PHALÆNA EVONYMELLA.

631. EVONYMELLA = *Hyp. evonymi*.

P. 247. 632. PHALÆNA PADELLA.
Long. lin. 4½.
Diagn. Similis priori, sed diversa 1°, *punctis paucioribus, nec ultra* 20; 2°, *alis anticis minus albis, subtus ubique fuscis*; 3°, *alis posticis utrinque fuscis totis*.
Habitat in pomiferis arboribus.

632. PADELLA, in der Abbildung ganz grau (während *evonymella* ganz weiss gelassen ist), scheint ein Gemisch aus *Hypon. variabilis* und *malinellus* zu sein; auf letztern deuten die "arbores pomiferæ," auf erstern die "alæ anticæ minus albæ," und zu diesem stellt Treitschke (*Ypon. padella*, ix. 1. 218) die Scopolische Art.

P. 247. 633. PHALÆNA CORNUTELLA. *Long.* lin. 5⅓.
Diagn. Tota ossea et polita, palpis erectis. In pratis.
Oculi fusci. Palpi lineam longi, erecti, duo cornua referunt.

†633. CORNUTELLA, der Abbildung nach so gross wie 631, aber mit breiteren Vorderflügeln und sehr breiten Hinterflügeln. Da die Taster etwas so ausgezeichnetes haben, dass sie den Namen veranlasst haben, so kann hier an keinen *Crambus*, keine *Eudorea ochrealis*, keine gelbe *Botys* gedacht werden. Sollte man eine zeichnungslose *Depress. liturella* auf *cornutella* deuten wollen, so steht die Grösse entgegen.

P. 248. 635. PHALÆNA MARGINELLA. *Long.* lin. 3⅓.
Diagn. Pallide caryophyllina; alis anticis margine crassiore pallidiore punctisque 6–7 *caryophyllinis variegato, fimbria subargentea.*
In pomariis, circa Idriam, Majo m. Palpi pallidi, articulo ultimo alis concolori.

†635. MARGINELLA nicht abgebildet, mir unbekannt.

P. 248. 637. PHALÆNA CERVINELLA. *Long.* lin. 5⅓.
Diagn. Alæ cervinæ; anticæ

†637. CERVINELLA wird von Schrank, Faun. Boic. ii. 1. S. 134. No. 1874 bei seiner *Tinea cervi-*

punctis posticis nigris 4 *in margine crassiore*, 7 *in exteriore. Corpus subtus subargenteum.*
In pratis, Junio m.
Oculi fusci.

nella aufgeführt. Letztere glaube ich richtig in der gewöhnlichen *Phox. lanceolana* ♀ wiederzuerkennen; aber Scopoli's *cervinella* ist diese unmöglich. Dazu ist sie viel zu gross (grösser als *Harp. forficella*) und ihre Punktirung lässt auch keine Anwendung auf *lanceolana* zu. Was sie aber ist, bleibt mir noch ein Räthsel.

P. 248. 638. PHALÆNA FORFICELLA.

638. FORFICELLA, sehr kenntlich abgebildet, richtig von Treitschke (ix. 2. 58) bei seiner *Lampros majorella* citirt. Da Scopoli's Benennung älter ist, als die Sulzersche: *proboscidella*, so gebührt ihr der Vorzug ungeachtet der Existenz einen *Holoscolia forficella*.

P. 249. 642. PHALÆNA BICOSTELLA.

642. BICOSTELLA, kenntlich abgebildet, sicher die Linneische Art.

P. 250. 643. PHALÆNA MUCRONELLA. *Long.* lin. 6½.
Diagn. Alæ omnes lanceolatæ, mucronatæ, nitidæ, concolores, pallidæ; anticæ longitudinaliter fuscosublineatæ.
Unicam collegi A. 1759 circa Idriam. Palpi porrecti. Lingua ferruginea.

*643. MUCRONELLA. Ich kenne das Weibchen von *Anch. criella*, Tr. (x. 3, 193) nicht in natura, sondern nur aus H.-S. tab. 55. fig. 387, und da dieses schärfer gespitzte Flügel hat als fig. 385 und 389, so stehe ich nicht an, es für die Scopolische *mucronella* zu erklären, obgleich diese in der Abbildung noch viel schmälere und spitzere Vorderflügel hat.

P. 250. 644. PHALÆNA SCABIOSELLA.

644. SCABIOSELLA (♂ sehr schlecht abgebildet, wie alle folgenden) = *Nemot. scabiosellus* (Linnæa, viii. 47), und zwar in der Varietät *ærosellus*.

P. 250. 645. PHALÆNA VIRIDELLA.

645. VIRIDELLA (Abbildung ♂) richtig von Treitschke zu *Adela viridella* (ix. 2. 148) gezogen.

P. 251. 646. PHALÆNA BARBATELLA. *Long.* lin. 2¼.
Diagn. Alæ anticæ glaucæ, aurato-punctatæ. Palpi barbati. Antennæ alis longiores; apice albidæ.
In collibus gramineis Carniolæ super. Differt a *Reaumurella*, ill. Linnæi, corpore viridi-æneo, fronte nigra, alis antrorsum magis auratis. Hinc non pectus, non femora ulla barbata; alæ etiam subtus nulla tinctura rubro-violacea fulgidæ, ut in priore.

†646. BARBATELLA (wahrscheinlich in der obersten Reihe rechts abgebildet, aber mit einer Flügelgestalt ähnlich der von *Psyche pulla*, daher nicht zu beachten), kleiner als *viridella*, mir aber unbekannt.

P. 251. 047. Phalæna Degeerella. *Long.* lin. 2.
Diagn. Alæ nigræ; fascia argenteo-aurea. Antennæ longæ.
Labaco misit amicissimus R. P. Wulfen. Ill. Linn. in Syst. Nat. fasciam argenteam, in Faun. Suec. 2. flavam, ponit; ego inter utrumque colorem mediam video.

†047. Degeerella. Bei dieser und der folgenden Art finde ich jetzt einige erhebliche Schwierigkeiten. Nur eine von beiden ist abgebildet, offenbar ein sitzendes männliches Exemplar der *Ad. Degeerella*, L.; da aber keine Ziffer dabei steht, so ist die Frage, zu welcher von beiden Arten das Bild gehören soll. Für *Degeerella*, Scop., wird die Flügellänge zu 2''' angegeben, also viel kürzer als bei *viridella*. Man möchte dieses Maass für einen Druckfehler halten, wenn die Beschreibung: " alæ nigræ fascia argenteo-aurea, antennæ longæ" nicht für unsere *Degeerella* so gar nichtssagend wäre, wenn die grosse Aehnlichkeit zwischen *Degeerella* und *Croesella* nicht unerwähnt bliebe, und wenn das Aufheben, das von der Pracht der *Croesella* gemacht wird, nicht die Schweigsamkeit über das Aussehen unserer so ähnlichen *Degeerella* so befremdend erscheinen liesse. Linné's Art war doch nicht zu verkennen, und dennoch wird das " antennis longissimis" von Scopoli in " antennis longis" verwandelt. Sollte Scopoli eine Art von einfacherem Aussehen, auf welche sein Maass passt—etwa *associatella?* —vor sich gehabt haben? Dann entständen aber neue Schwierigkeiten: Das Citat aus Linné, das Uebergehen der goldenen Punktirung auf den Vorderflügeln, die nur zu *Degeerella*, L., passende Abbildung. Etwas Räthselhaftes wird also hier wohl stets bleiben. Dies ist vielleicht auch der Grund, warum Treitschke (ix. 2. 131) Scopoli's *Degeerella* zu citiren unterlässt.

P. 251. 048. Phalæna Crœsella. *Long.* lin. 2⅓.
Diagn. Alæ sature violaceæ; anticæ fascia, basi et apice, lineisque longitudinalibus 5–7 aureis. Antennæ longissimæ, albidæ.
In *Evonymo vulg.* capta circa Idriam.
Pulcherrima; alis ita coloratis, ac si argento lævigato sature violaceus color superinductus fuisset.

048. Crœsella bisher von allen Autoren zu *Degeerella* gerechnet. Obgleich die Angabe der charakteristischen " fascia media" (statt der " fascia post medium" bei *Degeerella*, L.) durch Zufall entstanden sein kann, so scheint mir das "saturate violaceus" und vor Allem die " long. lin. 2½" (bei *viridella* 3½) doch sehr bestimmt für *Adela Sulzeriella* zu sprechen, so dass ich

Fascia alæ medium occupat, lineæ limbum: quarum mediæ longiores, ut fistulæ in organo. Ad basim alæ lineæ aliæ quinque longitudinales, pariter aureæ. Alæ eœdem subtus fascia aurea, sed absque lineis. Dorsum aureum, præsertim antice. Caput rufis pilis pubescens. Antennæ lin. 6¼ longæ. Crœseas ostentat opes, vanumque nitorem.

wenig Bedenken tragen würde, der Art den Scopolischen Namen zurückzugeben.

P. 251. 649. PHALÆNA RUFIMITRELLA.

649. RUFIMITRELLA (in der Abbildung mit zu kurzen, in ein Knöpfchen auslaufenden Fühlern) = *Adela rufimitrella* (Linnæa, viii. 12), die einfarbige Varietät.

P. 252. 650. PHALÆNA HEMEROBIELLA.

650. HEMEROBIELLA, nicht abgebildet, nach Citat und Beschreibung = *Coleophora hemerobiella* (Linnæa, iv. 374).

P. 252. 651. PHALÆNA VORTICELLA. *Long.* lin. 2¾.
Diagn. Nigra; alis anticis fascia alba, lineari.
In foliis fruticum, frequens. *Vorticellam* dixi, quia sedens, circa idem punctum, sese in circulum sæpe gyrat. Huic præterea alæ sedentis planæ. Antennæ tibiæque posticæ albo annulatæ.

†651. VORTICELLA ist zwar abgebildet, doch lässt sich für jetzt weder nach dem Bilde, noch nach der Beschreibung entscheiden, ob *Gelech. ligulella* oder *vorticella* oder *tœniolella* gemeint ist. Die Angabe: "in foliis fruticum frequens" und "sedens circa idem punctum sese in circulum sæpe gyrat" lässt von einem Beobachter an Ort und Stelle sichere Auskunft erwarten.

P. 252. 652. PHALÆNA OBSCURELLA. *Long.* lin. 4¼.
Diagn. Fusca; alis anticis supra fusco-auratis, apice subhæmatiticis.
In Carniolia interiore.
Caput, thorax, pedes colore alarum superiorum.

*652. OBSCURELLA (abgebildet mit zu kurzen Flügeln, aber durch ihre übrige Gestalt die Bestimmung bestätigend) = *Butalis Esperella*, Hübn. fig. 255, H.-S. S. 206. 792; diese Art erhielt ich durch Mann vom Nanosgebirge, also aus Scopoli's Jagdrevier.

P. 252. 653. PHALÆNA FENESTRELLA. *Long.* lin. 3.
Diagn. Alæ anticæ albidæ; maculis punctisque nigris, postice nebula subaurata.
Circa fenestras occurrit, primo vere.
Hæc, cum sequentibus aliis quatuor, caput album habet. Puncta et maculæ pleræque insident margini crassiori.

†653. FENESTRELLA. (Abbildung links in der dritten Reihe, ganz dunkel, mit 4 dunkeln Flecken am Vorderrand.) Sie würde sehr gut mit *Tinea granella* stimmen, wenn nicht ihre "nebula subaurata postice" auf den Vorderflügeln einiges Bedenken gäbe. Stainton nimmt in den 'Insecta Britannica Lepidoptera Tineina,' p. 164, sogar die Scopolische Benennung für die bisherige *Endrosis lacteella* auf; aber die "alæ anticæ albidæ maculis punctisque nigris" passen weit we-

niger auf diese Art als auf *Tinea granella*, und dazu kommt noch die "nebula subaurata." Ueberdies sehe mein 665 *Luridella*.—Das "circa fenestras occurrit primo vere" wird über Scopoli's *fenestrella* einst das nöthige Licht verbreiten.

[I certainly know of no species of the Tineina so frequently found "in windows in early spring" as that for which I retain Scopoli's name of *fenestrella*, the *lacteella* of Zeller. No part of the description is in any way incongruous: "the white head, the whitish anterior wings, with black blotches and spots, mostly towards the costa," furnishes a most excellent diagnosis of the species; and the "nebula postica subaurata" may owe its origin to the insect being posteriorly rubbed, and wasted specimens have a very different appearance from those in first-rate condition. Even if Scopoli's *luridella* be the same species, though the description seems scarcely as appropriate, it would not be at all improbable that Scopoli had described specimens in different degrees of preservation as distinct species. Other authors before now have described the same species more than once under different names.]

P. 253. 654. PHALÆNA SCALELLA.
Long. lin. 2.
Diagn. Alæ anticæ albæ; tribus paribus punctorum nigrorum, contiguorum, totidem obliquas æque dissitas velute fascias præ se ferentium.
Majo m. reperitur, ruri.
Fasciolæ illæ scalam repræsentant, licet quandoque unicum punctum sit, cum aliis in unam longitudinalem quasi lineam coalescens. Palpi albi: articulo ultimo punctis binis atris.

*654. SCALELLA nach der Grösse (die ich einst für einen Druckfehler erklären wollte) und nach der Abbildung nichts weniger als *Anesychia pusiella*, Staint. Lep. Tin. p. 62 (*Tin. lithospermella*, H., *Psecadia scalella*, Z.). Es ist eine sehr kleine Art, in der Abbildung freilich ohne vollständige Binde gegen die Wurzel der Vorderflügel, aber doch nach der Beschreibung sicher = *Gelechia aleella*, Staint. Lep. Tin. p. 128, womit sich auch die Tasterbeschaffenheit gut vereinigt. Der Vergleich der Zeichnung der Vorderflügel ist zwar sonderbar genug und liess mich diese Gestalt früher auf eine ganz andere Weise herausfinden, weil ich nicht bedachte, dass die "longitudinalis quasi linea" hier bei Scopoli die Bedeutung einer linea transversa hat. Dass diese *scalella* einen weissen Kopf hat, zeigt Scopoli bei *fenestrella* an.

P. 253. 655. PHALÆNA PUNCTELLA.
Long. lin. 2¼.
Diagn. Alæ anticæ niveæ; punctis fuscescentibus, in apice confluentibus, variegatæ.
Ruri degit, inter *Corylos*.
Antennæ albæ, fusco annulatæ.

†655. PUNCTELLA (in der Abbildung mit 2 Binden in gleichem Abstande unter einander und von der Basis und dem verdunkeltem Hinterrande) wurde von mir (Isis, 1839, S. 205) auf *Argyr. cornella*, doch mit Zweifeln, von Fischer von

Oculi nigri. Caput cum thorace niveum. Alæ anticæ obsoleta fascia punctisque fuscescentibus; pluribus in apice. Tibiæ albæ, nigro annulatæ.

Röslerstamm (Beitr. S. 24) auf *Argyr. fundella*, doch auch nur als wahrscheinlich, gedeutet. In der Linnæa, ii. S. 276, stimmte ich wieder für *Argyr. cornella*. Stainton citirt dagegen Scopoli's *punctella* in der 'List of British Animals, Lep.' p. 11, bei *Tinea arcella*, jedoch nur mit Fragezeichen. Da die Flügel der *T. arcella* nicht " punctis fuscescentibus variegatæ" sind, und ihre "fascia" durchaus nicht " obsoleta" heissen kann, so billige ich dieses Citat nicht. Die Entscheidung wird sich in Krain "inter corylos" wohl erlangen lassen.

P. 253. 656. PHALÆNA COMELLA.
  Long. lin. 2⅓.
  Diagn. Capillitium album, alba coma per marginem alæ internum decurrente auctum. Alæ anticæ ferrugineæ; fascia obscuriore, obsoleta, obliqua.
  Circa domos et hortos volitat, Junio m. Ubi desinit coma, ibi incipit fascia, sub qua idem alæ margo denuo albicans est. Antennæ albæ, fusco annulatæ.

656. COMELLA (in der sehr sonderbaren Abbildung mit langgefranztem Vorderrand!) habe ich als sicher (Linnæa, ii. 243) zu *Argyresthia pruniella* gestellt; Stainton fügt (List of Brit. Anim. p. 108) ein Fragezeichen bei, obgleich Scopoli's Worte ganz streng auf unsere Art Anwendung finden.

P. 253. 657. PHALÆNA PUSIELLA.
  Long. lin. 1½.
  Diagn. Alæ anticæ cauda repanda terminatæ, posticæ lineares.
  In pratis.
  Hæc et tres sequentes, alas anticas caudatas habent.
  Alæ osseæ, puncto fusco, caudæ imposito.

†657. PUSIELLA, nicht abgebildet, scheint zufolge der Grösse, die für *Phyllocnistis suffusella* zu gering ist, und der alæ osseæ eine der Varietäten von *Lyonetia Clerckella* zu sein. Die Beschreibung ist zu ungenau, um Sicherheit zu gewähren. Auch ist die "ala repanda" etwas schwierig zu deuten.

P. 253. 658. PHALÆNA THRASONELLA.

658. THRASONELLA (ganz unkenntlich abgebildet, mit viel zu kurzen Flügeln), von mir Isis 1839, S. 203, unter Anwendung des Scopolischen Namens richtig auf die jetzige *Glyphipteryx thrasonella* (Staint. Ins. Brit. p. 174) gedeutet.

P. 254. 659. PHALÆNA EQUITELLA.

659. EQUITELLA (in der dritten Reihe rechts schlecht abgebildet) ist *Glyphipteryx equitella*.

P. 254. 660. PHALÆNA ARUNCELLA.
  [The habitat given, "Copiosa in paniculis *Acteæ, Arunci*," is worth noting, the larva of *M. aruncella* being still unknown. I presume the

660. ARUNCELLA (nicht abgebildet) ganz sicher *Micropteryx aruncella*, Isis, 1830, S. 185.

plants indicated are *Actæa spicata* and *Spiræa aruncus.*]

P. 254. 661. PHALÆNA ALCHIMIELLA. *Long.* lin. 2½.
Diagn. Alæ anticæ aureæ; striga transversa, antica, maculaque lanceolata apicis, laccæ colore.
Circa Idriam reperta.
Oculi nigri. Palpi aurei; apice fusco-rubri. Antennæ subæquales. Frons et alæ auri colorem nitoremque æmulantes. Femora fusco-rubra. Tibiæ argenteæ; annulis fuscis. Felices Alchemistæ si tinctura hac solari sua saturare metalla possent!

*661. ALCHIMIELLA. Die Abbildung mit ihren verkürzten Fühlern, von denen der rechte sich sogar in einen Knoten endigt, passt etwas auf *Œcoph. lunaris,* Haw. (*Metznerella,* Tr.); aber die Beschreibung findet ihre genaueste Anwendung auf *Gracilaria Franckella,* deren Synonyme sich also schon auf 5 Namen vermehrt, von denen nun endlich die älteste und allein berechtigte sich gefunden hat! Aus der Beschreibung dieser *alchimiella* kann man aber sehen, wie genau und richtig Scopoli zu beschreiben versteht, und dass es grösstentheils nur eine Folge des Mangels aller Subdivision der Genera ist, wenn dennoch die Arten so schwer herausgefunden werden.

P. 254. 662. PHALÆNA AUREATELLA. *Long.* lin. 2¼.
Diagn. Alæ anticæ rubro-auratæ; fascia maculisque aureis.
In sylvestribus locis.
Macula aurea in limbo et alia ad basim, fascia intermedia. Caput rufis pilis pubescens.
Oculi fusci.

*662. AUREATELLA. Die Abbildung ist zwar sehr schlecht, rechts ganz anders als links, aber nach der linken Seite, die allein mit der Beschreibung stimmt, habe ich keinen Zweifel, dass *Micropteryx Allionella,* F. (Linnæa, v. 330), beschrieben worden ist. Erst nachdem ich dieses Resultat erlangt hatte, sah ich, dass auch Stainton (List of Brit. Anim. p. 23) beide Arten verbindet, jedoch nur durch ein Fragezeichen. *Aureatella* ist nun der älteste Name der Species.

P. 255. 663. PHALÆNA ÆNEELLA. *Long.* lin. 3.
Diagn. Fusca tota; alis anticis æneo-fuscis.
In sylvis.
Statura, habitu, et defectu ruboris alarum superiorum, differt ab *obscurella.*

†663. ÆNEELLA (abgebildet, aber mit abgestutzten Hinterflügeln). Der Vergleich, den Scopoli zwischen dieser Art und seiner *obscurella* macht, scheint zu beweisen, dass ihm hier eine *Butalis* vorlag. Aber die abgestutzten Hinterflügel und das "differt habitu" lassen an ein anderes Genus denken, und ich würde nicht zweifeln, dass *Gelechia tenebrella* gemeint sei, wenn diese nicht für die angegebene Grösse, auch in der Abbildung, viel zu klein wäre. Somit bleibt doch wohl nur eine *Butalis.* Da aber in Krain, ausser der einfarbigen *cuspidella* auch noch andere Arten vorkommen, von denen Mann (Wie-

P. 255. 664. Phalæna leucoce-
      rella.

P. 255. 665. Phalæna luridella.
  Long. lin. 3½.
  Diagn. Alæ argenteæ, anticæ atomis punctisque fuscis inquinatæ. Caput cum thorace album.
  Circa Labacum.
  Fimbria alarum posticarum iis latior pallideque rufa. Oculi nigri. Palpi argentei; articulo ultimo basi et apice fusco.

P. 255. 666. Phalæna zoole-
      gella.

P. 255. 667. Phalæna rufella.
  Long. lin. 2½.
  Diagn. Alæ griseo-cinereæ, corpore pedibusque rufis.
  Circa Labacum.
  Alæ posticæ angustissimæ.

P. 256. 668. Phalæna murinella.
  Long. lin. 3.
  Diagn. Alæ pallide murinæ.
  In Carniolia inferiore.
  Caput, thorax, corpusque alis concolor.

P. 256. 669. Phalæna vestia-
      nella. *Long.* lin. 3¼.
  Diagn. Alæ cinerascentes; costa alba.
  Habitat in Vestimentis, quæ destruit, ut invido dente rodunt malevoli aliena scripta.
  Alæ atomis nigris adspersæ. An-

ner zoolog.-botan. Zeitschrift, iv. S. 586, 586) einige anführt, so bleibt eine Unsicherheit, die sich nicht aus Scopoli's Worten, sondern nur durch die Ansicht des Originals und folglich, da die Scopolische Sammlung wohl schon lange nicht mehr existirt, nie wird heben lassen.

664. Leucocerella, nicht abgebildet, =*Adela leucocerella* (*conformella*, Z., *bimaculella*, F. v. R.).

*665. Luridella. Die mittelste Figur über den Pterophoren scheint diese Art vorstellen zu sollen. Die Angaben: "fimbria alarum posticarum pallide rufa," "Caput cum thorace album" vorzüglich aber "palpi articulo ultimo basi et apice fusco" lassen keinen Zweifel, dass Scopoli *Œcophora lacteella* vor sich hatte. Diese kann daher um so weniger Scopoli's *fenestrella* 653 sein.

666. Zoolegella, nicht abgebildet, = *Tinea pellionella*, wozu ich sie schon (Isis, 1839, S. 184) gezogen habe.

†Rufella, nicht abgebildet. Die Deutung auf *Nepticula rufella*, Z., über die ich schon (Linnæa, ii. S. 330) meine Zweifel aussprach, nehme ich ganz zurück, da die Angabe der Flügellänge von 2½′′′ kein Druckfehler sein kann. Die so auffallend gezeichnete Art bleibt mir also ganz räthselhaft.

†668. Murinella, nicht abgebildet, zu ungenau beschrieben, als dass sie bestimmt werden könnte.

†669. Vestianella, nicht abgebildet. Scopoli beschreibt die Art weniger vollständig als Linné, citirt dieses aber nicht, obgleich offenbar beider Art dieselbe sein soll. Eine *Coleophora* ist es gewiss, aber mehr lässt sich nicht thun, als was Stainton gethan hat (List of Brit. Anim.

x 2

tennæ annulis albis. Ingenii ejusdem, quo impudens compilator.

P. 256. 670. Phalæna arbustella. *Long.* lin. 1½.
Diagn. Alæ anticæ subargenteæ; puncto nigro.
Inter arbusta, frequens.
Vestianella duplo minor, subargentea, punctulisque obscurioribus irrorata.

P. 256. 671. Phalæna domesticella. *Long.* lin. 3.
Diagn. Albida nitens; alis omnibus apice utrinque nigro nebulosis.
In cubilibus, non rara.
Alæ anticæ supra punctis sparsis uscis.

p. 130) nämlich den Namen mit einem Fragezeichen bei *Coleophora annulatella* hinzuschreiben.

†670. Arbustella, wahrscheinlich nicht abgebildet. Der Vergleich mit *vestianella* und die ungenaue Beschreibung, in der die Lage des " Punctum nigrum" nicht fixirt ist, werden diese Art, obgleich sie "inter arbusta frequens" ist, kaum je erkennen lassen.

†671. Domesticella, wahrscheinlich in der Figur links über den Federmotten abgebildet. Die Wiederauffindung dieser Art scheint möglich, wenn sie noch dieselben Sitten hat, wie zu Scopoli's Zeit, in Krain "*in cubilibus* non rara" zu sein; bei uns giebt es keine entsprechende Art.

CHAPTER XI.

THE LOST PLEIAD.

ENTOMOLOGISTS may lose stars as well as astronomers; and the present chapter treats of a very small moth which has not been seen for upwards of a hundred years, though I feel quite as confident of its existence as of that of any of our commonest and best-known species.

A curious ray of light on this subject comes to us from across the Atlantic, the late Dr. Brackenridge Clemens having bred two species of the genus *Antispila* from larvæ mining the leaves of grapes in America. (Proceedings of the Academy of Natural Sciences of Philadelphia, 1860, p. 209.)

The American genus *Aspidisca*, of which the larvæ have similar habits to those of *Antispila* (Proceedings Ent. Soc. Philadelphia, vol. i. p. 81), has not been found in Europe. Dr. Clemens observes that "the disk of an *Aspidisca*-larva is always fixed by a button of silk to some object in the neighbourhood of the food plant, and the pupæ must be kept in a dry vessel after the disks have been cut out, otherwise the insects will not come to maturity. On the other hand the *Antispilæ* require a damp situation after entering the pupa-state."

The insect treated of in the present chapter it will be seen imitates *Aspidisca* in its habit of suspending the pupa near the food of the larva; but in all other respects I believe it to be a true *Antispila*.

ANTISPILA RIVILLEI, Stainton.

In the Trans. Ent. Soc. London, Second Series, vol. iii. p. 87, I proposed the specific name of *Rivillei* for the insect of which the history was communicated by Godcheu de Rivillo to Réaumur before the middle of the last century. In the 'Annales de la Société Entomologique de France,' 1855, pp. 211–213, I again referred to this interesting species, then only known to me from the reflected light of a paper in the 'Naturforscher,' Stück 4, p. 16. The original communication was published at Paris in 1750, in the first volume of the 'Mémoires de Mathématique et de Physique présentés à l'Académie Royale des Sciences,' p. 177, and is of sufficient interest to merit being repeated here *in extenso*. At the present day the insect is utterly unknown, and has probably escaped the attention of every entomologist for the last hundred years, though possibly no rarity at Malta and in the south of Italy.

"Histoire d'une Chenille mineuse de feuilles de vigne, extraite d'une lettre écrite de Malte à M. de Réaumur par M. GODEHEU DE RIVILLE, Chevalier de Malte."

L'île de Malte que nous habitons, n'est pas fertile en insectes; le peu de terre, et la grande sécheresse qui y règne pendant six ou sept mois de l'année, nous privent des arbres que ceux qui veulent étudier à fond l'histoire des Chenilles doivent presque toujours avoir sous les yeux. J'espère cependant me dédommager de cette stérilité par plusieurs voyages que je ferai en Sicile. J'ai lieu de croire qu'une isle qui produit beaucoup d'arbres presque inconnus en France, me fournira de quoi faire plusieurs observations curieuses et intéressantes. Je ne manquerai pas de vous faire part de celles qui me paraîtront dignes de vous être communiquées. Je vais en attendant, vous donner l'histoire d'une Chenille mineuse de feuilles de vigne, qui ne s'est point apparemment trouvée dans les endroits où vous avez fait vos observations, puisque vous n'en faites aucune mention dans vos Mémoires. Cette chenille mérite cependant une place distinguée dans l'histoire des insectes, puisqu'elle n'appartient à aucune des sept classes sous lesquelles vous avez distribué toutes les chenilles qui sont parvenues à votre connaissance. Vous serez en état de juger après la lecture de son histoire, si ce que j'ai l'honneur de vous avancer, est bien ou mal fondé.

Au reste, comme les dessins que je vous envoie sont très-imparfaits, et peu capables par conséquent d'aider à saisir le vrai de mes descriptions, que vous trouverez sans doute bien obscures, j'ai pris le parti de vous envoyer plusieurs chenilles conservées dans l'esprit de vin, quelques morceaux de feuilles minées pas ces mêmes chenilles, avec les coques qui en ont été détachées, et les papillons qui en sont sortis. J'ai cru que vous seriez bien aise de voir et d'examiner vous-même toutes ces petites parties au naturel ; mais il est temps de commencer l'histoire de notre chenille.

Je me transportai le 25 de Juillet au jardin de M. le Bailly du Bocage, situé dans un faubourg de cette ville, appelé la *Floriane.* Le maître du logis ne s'y étant point trouvé, je pris le parti de me promener dans une galerie couverte de vigne, qui règne tout autour de la maison : j'aperçus avec quelque sorte de plaisir que les feuilles étaient fort maltraitées par des insectes mineurs qui avaient d'abord travaillé en galerie, et ensuite en grande aire. Ce que je remarquai de particulier, c'est que chaque endroit miné avait vers la partie qui paraissait avoir été la dernière habitée par l'insecte, un trou ovale de médiocre grandeur. Les deux membranes paraissaient avoir été enlevées dans cet endroit par un emporte-pièce. Je pensai que ce pouvait être l'ouvrage de quelque chenille qui s'était fait une coque de ces deux membranes, et s'était éloignée de l'endroit ou elle faisait auparavant sa demeure. Je ne fus pas longtemps à m'assurer de ce que j'avais soupçonné ; en visitant le dessous des feuilles, j'y trouvai, aussi bien que sur les pédicules, plusieurs coques ovales à peu près de la même grandeur que les trous que j'avais observés ; il y en avait sur des endroits plus éloignés ; j'en trouvai beaucoup sur le treillage et sur le balcon de pierre à hauteur d'appui qui le soutient. Le façon dont ces coques sont attachées, mérite quelque attention ; elles ne tiennent que par une de leurs extrémités, et elles sont toujours perpendiculaires au plan sur lequel elles sont arrêtées. Je me contentai pour cette visite, de détacher une trentaine de ces coques, et je les emportai chez moi. Parmi ce nombre, il y en avait plusieurs dont les papillons étaient sortis ; les deux premières que j'ouvris en rentrant au logis, étaient vides, je n'y trouvai que deux corps extrêmement petits, dont l'un me parut la dépouille de la chenille, ayant cru voir à la loupe un petite tête écailleuse, et l'autre des excrémens dont elle s'était apparemment vidée avant que de se métamorphoser. Je fus plus heureux à l'ouverture de la troisième coque, j'y trouvai un petite chrysalide de couleur d'ambre ; les six pattes paraissaient fort distinctement ; les étuis des ailes ne sont point ramenés en devant comme dans les autres chysalides, ils sont aussi long que le reste du corps, et s'appliquent dessus à peu près comme les ailes d'un oiseau, de façon que les deux extrémités du corps et des étuis des ailes forment à la partie postérieure de la chrysalide un angle aisé à apercevoir. J'en examinai trois ou quatre afin de m'assurer positivement de ce que j'avais vu la première fois, et après les avoir remises dans les coques que j'avais ouvertes d'un côté, afin de ne les pas trop endommager, je les unis sous un gobelet séparé. Des quatre que j'avais observées il y en avait deux qui avaient perdu leur couleur d'ambre, elles étaient noires et blanches ; cela me fit penser que les papillons ne tarderaient pas à en sortir. J'en eus effectivement deux dès le lendemain matin ; les autres parurent successivement d'un jour à l'autre, et au bout de neuf jours les trente coques que j'avais rassemblées me donnèrent dix-huit papillons tous parfaitement semblables. Après les avoir bien examinés à la loupe, ils m'ont paru de la troisième classe des phalènes, et du genre de ceux dont les ailes embrassent le corps à la façon des oiseaux, mais dont le bout frangé forme en se relevant, une queue de coq. Ces papillons sont fort jolis; les pattes, la tête et le corps sont argentés; le fond des ailes est d'un beau noir; elles ont chacune pour ornement quatre taches argentées triangulaires, dont deux bordent le côté intérieur, et les deux autres le côté extérieur. Je n'ai pu voir l'accouplement de ces papillons, il s'agitent beaucoup depuis quatre heures du soir jusqu'au coucher du soleil, et sont péris chez moi au bout de trois jours.

On jugera bien que je ne voulus pas m'en tenir à cette simple découverte; j'étais curieux de voir toutes les manœuvres qu'emploient ces chenilles pour construire leurs coques, et les transporter dans l'endroit où elles doivent être fixées. Je retournai au jardin le 10 d'Août sur les huit heures du matin; je visitai exactement une grande quantité de feuilles de vigne, afin de trouver des chenilles occupées à manger, qui pussent dans la suite me procurer l'occasion de les observer lorsqu'elles songeraient à se métamorphoser. Ma récolte fut bonne, je cueillis beaucoup de feuilles où il y avait plusieurs chenilles de différentes grosseurs. De retour chez moi je mis les pédicules des feuilles dans de petites caraffes pleines d'eau, que je plaçai dans un jour favorable pour bien observer tout ce que les chenilles voudraient me montrer; comme elles ne laissent en minant que deux membranes fort minces, on voit distinctement qu'elles détachent peu à peu le parenchyme par le moyen de deux petits dents posées sur le devant de la tête. Ma provision étant abondante, et n'en voyant aucune qui songeât encore à travailler à sa coque, je voulus voir de quelle classe elles étaient; pour y parvenir, j'en mis trois ou quatre à découvert en déchirant l'une des deux membranes qui les couvrait; mais je fus bien étonné en les examinant les unes après les autres, de ne leur point trouver de jambes, ni écailleuses, ni membraneuses. Persuadé qu'une chenille sans jambes était un monstre dont on n'avait point encore eu connaissance, je crus positivement qu'il pouvait y avoir deux espèces d'insectes mineurs dans les feuilles que j'avais apportées, et que le hasard m'avait d'abord fait tomber sur des vers mineurs. J'attendis une meilleure occasion qui pût me lever le doute que j'avais dans l'esprit, elle se présenta sur les deux heures après-midi. Deux chenilles travaillaient alors à faire leur coque, je ne les troublai point dans leur travail; chacune détacha la sienne de la feuille, et après avoir erré quelque temps dessus, je les vis se fixer en-dessous auprès d'une nervure où elles attachèrent leurs coques. Tout ceci se passa en moins de trois quarts d'heure; étant bien sûr que ces coques renfermaient des chenilles, je les détachai, et séparant les deux membranes dont elles étaient composées, je me mis à portée de savoir si les premiers insectes que j'avais observés, étaient véritablement des chenilles dépourvues de jambes; celles-ci me parurent à la simple vue, parfaitement semblables; je les examinai avec une loupe qui n'a pas deux lignes de foyer, mais j'eus beau les retourner de toutes sortes de façons, je ne pus jamais leur découvrir aucune jambe. Non content de cela, j'observai tous les anneaux les uns après les autres avec un excellent microscope, mais inutilement. Je les ai cependant assez bien vus pour m'assurer que la peau de ces chenilles est criblée par une infinité de petits trous presque invisibles ; plusieurs poils extrêmement fins partent irrégulièrement de différents endroits de leur corps ; la tête, qui est écailleuse, aussi bien que le dessus et le dessous du premier anneau (le reste étant membraneux) en ont beaucoup plus que les autres parties. La tête se cache quelquefois sous le premier anneau qui, comme tous les autres, n'est pas parfaitement cylindrique ; elle est formée comme celle des autres chenilles par deux petites parties écailleuses, excepté cependant que les deux calottes sont encore plus échancrées par derrière que par devant ; ces vides sont remplis par deux membranes plus transparentes que les parties écailleuses.

Voilà ce que j'ai observé sur la structure du corps de ces chenilles, je ne me suis pas contenté de deux ou trois observations, je les ai réitérées plusieurs fois, afin de ne rien rapporter que de vrai. J'avouerai cependant que quoique je fusse bien certain que ces chenilles étaient entièrement dépourvues de jambes, j'avais toujours une inquiétude que je ne saurais trop dépeindre ; je pense qu'un jeune homme de vingt-cinq ans qui entreprend le métier d'observateur, ne saurait trop se tenir sur ses gardes contre la prévention ; j'en suis si convaincu que je n'aurais point encore fait part sitôt de cette découverte, si je n'avais en main des preuves plus fortes que celles que j'ai rapportées jusqu'à présent. Les manœuvres que j'ai vu pratiquer à ces chenilles dans la construction de leurs coques, et les épreuves auxquelles je les ai mises dans différentes occasions, m'ont assuré que si elles ont des jambes trop petites pour être aperçues, même avec le secours d'un bon microscope, elles ne savent au moins en faire aucune usage ; mais il est temps de les suivre dans la construction de leur coque.

Lorsqu'une de nos chenilles est parvenue à sa dernière grandeur, on aperçoit tout le long de son corps une raie d'un très-beau vert, occasionné par la quantité de nourriture qu'elle prend alors, comme toutes les autres chenilles ; peu de temps après elle songe à se faire un logement où elle puisse se métamorphoser ; c'est ordinairement dans l'endroit qu'elle a miné le dernier, l'autre extrémité étant toute remplie d'excrémens. Lorsque cette chenille ne travaille que pour se nourrir, elle ne forme pas d'arête aux épidermes entre lesquels elle est logée ; elle s'y trouve assez pressée, puisque partout où elle est, on distingue sur l'une et l'autre membrane une petite élévation formée par l'épaisseur de son corps, qui varie à mesure qu'elle change de place. Apparemment que cette chenille étant dépourvue de jambes, le frottement de ses anneaux contre les membranes lui est avantageux pour se transporter d'un endroit à un autre, et avancer à mesure qu'elle mange le parenchyme ; elle sait cependant se procurer un logement plus commode pour y passer le temps qu'elle doit rester en chrysalide. Pour y parvenir elle travaille à former sur l'un et l'autre épiderme deux arêtes qui soient précisément vis-à-vis l'une de l'autre, et qui règnent sur toute la longueur de l'ovale : par ce moyen les deux membranes prennent une concavité qui rend l'habitation plus spacieuse. Voici ce que j'ai vu pratiquer à toutes celles qui ont travaillé devant moi.

La chenille commence par tracer sur le membrane qui est du côté de la filière, l'enceinte de son habitation avec plusieurs fils qui déterminent la grandeur de l'ovale ; ce premier ouvrage étant fait, elle travaille à former l'arête de la même membrane, qu'elle ne fait cependant qu'ébaucher, pour travailler à celle de la membrane opposée ; il faut pour cela qu'elle change de position, parce qu'elle a la filière placée au même endroit que toutes les autres chenilles, et qu'elle ne peut par conséquent filer sur la membrane opposée à la première, sans se retourner entièrement ; elle y réussit aisément lorsqu'elle est parvenue par un tour de tête à saisir avec les dents la membrane qui est derrière elle, c'est un point d'appui qui l'aide a contourner ses anneaux les uns après les autres, jusqu'à ce qu'elle ait entièrement changé de position ; elle avance alors le travail de cette seconde arête au point où elle a laissé la première, et au bout d'une demi-heure, après avoir changé trois ou quatre fois le travail de l'une et de l'autre membrane, les arêtes sont autant formées qu'elle le souhaite. A mesure qu'elle file, les membranes deviennent opaques de plus en plus, et l'ovale qui doit faire le contour de la coque, devient aisé à distinguer ; la convexité que prennent les deux membranes dans cet endroit, occasionne un tiraillement très-sensible dans les parties voisines.

Il faut à présent lui voir séparer la coque du reste de la feuille. Elle commence par s'étendre tout du long des deux arêtes, de façon que son corps mesure alors, pour ainsi dire, la longueur de l'ovale. Elle travaille ensuite à faire sa coupe, ce qu'elle exécute à différentes reprises ; car aussitôt qu'il y a un quart de la coque séparé du reste de la feuille elle en réunit les deux membranes sur le champ avec de la soie. Il faut cependant remarquer que cette opération ne les assujétit encore ensemble que faiblement, la chenille presse sa besogne et ne donne la solidité à son ouvrage que lorsque sa demeure est entièrement fixée. J'en ai vu plusieurs qui, après avoir arrêté leurs coques, ont encore resté plus d'un quart d'heure, tant à fortifier les côtés réunis, qu'à tapisser plus proprement l'intérieur de leur habitation. J'ai dit ci-dessus qu'à mesure que les deux arêtes de la membrane supérieure et inférieure prenaient forme, on apercevait un tiraillement dans les parties voisines ; aussitôt que la coque est séparée par l'incision du reste de la feuille ce tiraillement disparaît nécessairement, et il reste alors un intervalle entre la coque et les membranes où elle était attachée ; la coque en un mot, n'est plus adhérente à la feuille, et ne remplit pas exactement le trou qui s'y est formé.

Cette séparation m'inquiéta la première fois que je vis travailler cette chenille, je me rappelai ce que j'avais lu deux jours auparavant dans un de vos Mémoires sur les teignes des arbres, je me rappelai, dis-je, que vous obligeâtes un jour une de ces teignes à se fabriquer devant vous une nouvelle habitation qui se soutenait encore sur la feuille, quoiqu'elle en fût entièrement séparée ; parceque premièrement elle avait choisi le bord d'une feuille, et qu'en second lieu l'incision étant dentelée, elle avait par ce moyen un appui réel et sensible ; celle que j'observais n'avait aucun de ces deux avantages, non seulement l'incision qui l'avait séparée de la feuille était lisse et unie, mais de plus l'éloignement où elle était des autres membranes, la mettait dans une situation fâcheuse. J'étais encore dans cette inquiétude lorsque la chenille acheva de séparer entièrement sa coque de la feuille ; je fus bien étonné de la voir rester dans la même situation où elle était lorsqu'il n'y en avait que la moitié de coupée, malgré le mouvement que se donnait alors la chenille qui travaillait à réunir la partie de sa coque qui avait été séparée la dernière ; je vis bien qu'elle était soutenue, et que l'industrie de notre chenille avait su remédier aux accidens qui pouvaient lui arriver. J'eus recours à la loupe, et j'aperçus avec admiration qu'elle était arrêtée de chaque côté par deux fils de soie, dont l'un des bouts était attaché sur la feuille et l'autre sur les bords de la coque, je me ressouvins alors que j'avais vu plus d'une fois la tête de la chenille hors des deux membranes dans le temps qu'elle était occupée à les réunir, et je soupçonnai que ce pouvait être là le temps où la chenille attachait le fil qui devait servir de soutien à la coque. J'en observai une autre avec une forte loupe tout le long de l'opération, mais je n'ose assurer que toutes les fois que la chenille avance sa tête hors de la coque, ce soit uniquement pour attacher un de ces fils qui la soutiennent, parceque j'ai vu plusieurs fois toute la tête à découvert, sans que j'aie pu voir de fil dans l'endroit où elle s'était portée ; ce qu'il a de certain, c'est que toutes les coques que j'ai examinées, étaient soutenues de façon que j'ai rapportée ci-devant, quoique les fils ne fussent pas toujours arrangés aussi régulièrement.

La coque étant donc entièrement séparée de façon qu'elle ne tient plus à la feuille que par les fils qui la soutiennent, notre chenille songe à s'éloigner d'un lieu où elle n'a plus rien à faire : comme elle est dépourvue de jambes il faut qu'elle ait recours à de manœuvres différentes de celles que nous voyons pratiquer aux teignes, qui viennent à bout de traîner après elles leur habitation en se cramponnant par le moyen de six jambes écailleuses ; voici ce que j'ai vu pratiquer constamment à toutes celles qui ont travaillé devant moi.

Lorsqu'une chenille veut transporter son habitation, elle fait sortir la tête et ses trois premiers anneaux par l'extrémité de la coque qui a été coupée la dernière et où elle a eu soin de laisser une ouverture de médiocre grandeur. Cette partie de son corps se trouve alors sur un terrain solide, un moment après elle se met en mouvement, et ce qu'on voit alors donne à penser qu'elle veut tâter le plan sur lequel elle est posée, car cette partie antérieure de son corps se hausse et se baisse cinq ou six fois de suite et frappe le plan chaque fois qu'elle s'abaisse ; il semble alors que les deux dents saisissent la membrane, parceque la tête devient perpendiculaire à son plan. La chenille ainsi fixée fait un effort qui, en brisant les fils, oblige en même temps la coque de s'approcher de l'endroit où les dents sont arrêtées. Ce premier pas étant fait, les autres ne coûtent plus rien, et elle continue sa marche en pratiquant toujours les mêmes manœuvres. Il arrive quelquefois que les fils ne cèdent pas au premier effort, la chenille est alors obligée de lâcher prise, et le même degré de force qui oblige la coque de s'approcher de la tête lorsque les fils se rompent, contraint la chenille de reculer avec assez de promptitude lorsqu'ils résistent à ce degré de force.

Mais il est temps d'avouer que je me suis trompé grossièrement sur les manœuvres qu'emploient ces chenilles pour avancer et transporter leur habitation ; la première que j'avais observée, n'avait pas fait beaucoup de chemin, elle avait fixé sa coque à deux pouces de distance de l'endroit qu'elle avait miné. La seconde me prouva que j'étais très-éloigné d'avoir bien vu la manière de marcher de la première, celle-ci après avoir erré quelque temps en dessous de la feuille, se rendit sur la pédicule, et gagna ensuite l'espèce de flacon rempli d'eau où cette feuille avait été mise, qui avait un rebord large d'environ 8 lignes ; elle en fit le tour et ayant rencontré de nouveau le pédicule elle remonta tout du long pour se rendre apparemment sur la feuille. Tout ce que je venais de voir, ne s'accordait guère avec mes premières idées : la facilité avec laquelle cette chenille marchait sur le verre, m'apprenait assez qu'elle n'était point obligée de saisir avec les dents le plan sur lequel elle était posée. J'étais cependant curieux de savoir si elle avait proche de la tête quelques crochets qui m'avaient échappé, ou bien si elle employait une autre manœuvre à laquelle je n'avais pas pensé ; pour m'en assurer, j'ôtai la coque de dessus le pédicule de la feuille où elle était encore, et je la mis sur un morceau de glace bien unie, dans l'intention d'observer avec une forte loupe tout le chemin qu'elle aurait parcouru. La chenille ainsi transportée d'un lieu à un autre resta quelque temps dans l'inaction ; j'attendis patiemment que l'envie de marcher lui vint ; au bout de quatre à cinq minutes je lui vis allonger la tête et les trois premiers anneaux hors de la coque, et pratiquer en marchant sur cette glace toutes les mêmes manœuvres qu'elle avait mises en usage lorsqu'elle était sur la feuille de la vigne. Dès qu'elle eut parcouru environ l'espace d'une pouce de terrain, je plaçai le morceau de glace dans un jour favorable, afin d'examiner le chemin par où elle avait passé ; je n'eus pas de peine à le retrouver ; la vue simple me fit apercevoir que depuis le premier endroit d'où elle était partie jusqu'à celui où elle était arrivée, il y avait sur la glace une file de petites taches transparentes très-proches les unes des autres. Ces taches m'ont paru à la loupe de petits monticules de fils de soie : l'instant où la chenille me paraissait tâter le terrain, est précisément celui qu'elle emploie pour former un de ces monticules ; par le moyen des battements redoublés dont nous avons parlé un peu plus haut, elle applique la filière contre le plan sur lequel elle est posée, et vient à bout de former une petite élévation qui peut donner prise à ses dents le moment qu'elle veut faire un pas en avant ; comme elle est souvent obligée de monter le long d'un plan vertical, il faut qu'elle attache sa coque toutes les fois qu'elle s'élonge en dehors pour former un nouveau monticule. Il est visible qu'elle ne pourrait pas sans cela rester dans cette position. J'ai cru voir le moment où elle prend cette précaution. Lorsque la chenille après avoir saisi entre les dents le monticule de soie, en a rapproché le bord inférieur de la coque, elle disparaît entièrement en y rentrant tout entière ; n'est-il pas vraisemblable que c'est alors qu'elle unit la coque au monticule par un fil dont un bout y est attaché et l'autre est en dedans de la coque sur le bord de l'épiderme inférieur? Tout ce que je puis assurer, c'est que j'ai souvent fait changer de position aux plans sur lesquels il y avait plusieurs chenilles, et qu'elles n'en ont jamais été inquiétées.

Malgré la longueur de ce détail, je ne puis m'empêcher de vous faire part d'une observation que j'ai faite depuis peu, parce qu'elle servira à démontrer encore mieux que les précédentes, que ces chenilles sont entièrement dépourvues de jambes. Il y a environ quinze jours que j'aperçus, en me promenant dans la même galerie dont j'ai parlé ci-devant, une chenille dans sa coque qui était suspendue par un fil de soie ; je m'arrêtai pour l'observer, mais je n'eus pas le temps de satisfaire ma curiosité, parceque la chenille en filant la longueur de cinq ou six lignes de soie, gagna une autre feuille qui était au-dessous d'elle. Je me proposai cependant de mettre à profit cette petite découverte : en effet, ayant en trois ou quatre jours après, à ma disposition une chenille qui venait d'achever la coupe de sa coque, je la mis sur une feuille qui était attachée horizontalement : après s'être promenée pendant quelque temps elle arriva enfin sur le bord de la feuille, c'est où je l'attendais. J'augmentai la mauvaise situation où le poids de son corps et celui de la coque l'avaient mise, par de petits coups redoublés que je donnai sur la feuille ; ne pouvant résister à ces secousses, elle lâcha prise et se suspendit à quelque distance du bord de la feuille. Je l'observai pour lors avec la loupe sans l'agiter davantage ; elle resta deux ou trois minutes sans faire aucun mouvement en dedans de la coque, après quoi elle travailla à remonter tout le long du fil qui la soutenait ; voici comme elle s'y prend pour y réussir. A peine sa tête est hors de la coque qu'elle saisit entre les dents le fil qui la soutient ; elle s'allonge ainsi jusqu'à ce que les trois premiers anneaux soient à découvert, et oblige ensuite le bord de la coque à se rapprocher de l'endroit où les dents se sont fixées par le mouvement de contraction qu'elle fait faire à son corps. Cette chenille remonta de cette façon tout le long de son fil, et gagna par ce moyen le bord de la feuille.

Cette première épreuve me conduisit à en faire une seconde. J'étais curieux de savoir si une chenille sans coque et suspendue à un fil, serait en état de remonter comme la première ; j'étais convaincu que si elle avait des jambes (quelques petites qu'elles pussent être) elle serait dans le cas de s'en servir. De huit ou dix que j'ai mises à découvert, et que j'ai obligées par des moyens que je passe sous silence, à se suspendre à un fil, il n'y en a pas eu une qui ait pu faire un pas en avant ; toutes m'ont paru être fort mal à leur aise, et quoiqu'elles fussent à une distance raisonnable de la terre, elles ont tout filé jusqu'à ce qu'elles y soient arrivées. J'en empêchai deux ou trois de toucher le plancher, et ayant embarrassé leur fil autour de mon doigt, je les rapprochai du bord de la feuille à la distance d'une demi-ligne, elles ne purent jamais y arriver ; et après s'être fort agitées pendant quelque temps, elles filèrent de nouveau jusqu'à ce qu'elles eussent gagné la terre. J'oubliais de dire qu'une chenille qu'on ôte de son habitation, et qu'on met ensuite sur une feuille, ne songe jamais à s'en faire une nouvelle, elle s'agite beaucoup sans faire de chemin, et après avoir enduit irrégulièrement de fils de soie l'endroit où elle est, elle y périt au bout de vingt-quatre heures.

Addition à l'histoire de la Chenille mineuse de la vigne, extraite d'une autre lettre écrite à M. de Réaumur par M. le Chevalier Godeheu de Riville.

Quelques petits voyages joints aux grandes chaleurs et à de petites incommodités, m'ont empêché de faire autant d'observations que je l'aurais souhaité. En attendant que je puisse rassembler et mettre en ordre ce qui me paraîtra digne de vous être communiqué, je puis vous assurer que la chenille mineuse de feuilles de vigne est tout-à-fait dépourvue de jambes. J'ai réitéré mes observations pendant quinze jours de suite sur une grande quantité de ces chenilles, sans que l'attention la plus suivie ait pu me rien faire apercevoir qui ressemblât aux jambes que j'ai toujours cherchées inutilement ; cependant pour les rendre plus sensibles, si elles eussent existé, j'avais soin de presser successivement tous les anneaux du ventre.

En réitérant mes observations, j'ai découvert l'ennemi de cette chenille ; parmi le nombre de feuilles de vigne que j'avais emportées chez moi, j'aperçus plusieurs chenilles qui étaient restées dans une parfaite inaction ; elles paraissaient mortes, mais cependant leur corps avait presque conservé son enflure ordinaire ; au lieu de la ligne verte qu'on aperçoit dans toute la longueur du corps lorsque l'animal est en bonne santé, je n'y voyais qu'un jaune pâle. Je l'observai deux jours de suite sans y remarquer aucun changement, mais au troisième le corps de la chenille étant devenu flasque, j'aperçus auprès de la peau qui se desséchait assez vite, deux petits corps oblongs et blanchâtres, dans le milieu desquels on pouvait voir avec la loupe deux taches rousses qui avaient du mouvement ; c'étaient de petits vers qui se métamorphosèrent au bout de trois heures en nymphe d'une couleur tirant sur le jaune ; et cinq jours après je trouvai sous le gobelet où j'avais mis les morceaux de feuilles de vigne, deux petits ichneumons fort jolis dont le corps était tacheté de jaune et d'un très-beau rouge ; ils avaient percé la pellicule desséchée de la feuille de vigne pour sortir de leur prison.

Explication des Figures.

Les Figures 1, 2, 3, montrent que les coques sont toujours perpendiculaires au plan sur lequel elles sont arrêtées, à moins que quelqu'inégalité du même plan n'oblige la chenille à lui donner une autre position, comme on peut le voir dans la coque *a*, fig. 1.

La Figure 4 représente en grand une chrysalide dont le papillon est prêt à sortir ; je l'ai dessinée tant bien que mal pour faire voir l'angle formé à son extrémité par les bouts du corps et des étuis des ailes qui ne sont pas ramenées en devant comme dans les autres chrysalides.

La Figure 5 représente en grand la tête d'une chenille.

La Figure 6 fait voir une coque f, qui quoiqu'entièrement séparée de la feuille, reste cependant dans la même situation, parce qu'elle est soutenue par les fils g, h, a, i.

La Figure 7 fait voir de côté une chenille dans sa coque, occupée à remonter le long du fil qui la soutient.

La Figure 8 fait voir une chenille qui marche sur un morceau de glace bien unie ; on voit qu'elle laisse tout le long du chemin qu'elle fait, une traînée de monticules de fils de soie.

The Plate in this volume represents figures 1, 2, 3, & 4, under their respective numbers.

The original figure 5 is omitted.

The figure 5 on the Plate in this volume is the original figure 6.

And the figure 6 on the Plate of this volume is the original figure 7.

The original figure 8 is also omitted.

CHAPTER XII.

GEOGRAPHICAL SUMMARY.

I now proceed to give a classified list of the insects mentioned in this volume, indicating synthetically in what portions of Southern Europe they have been observed; the figures in the respective columns indicate the pages where they will be found noticed.

In the last twenty-five years many changes have taken place in the nomenclature of these insects: to the older students the use of the names in force twenty years ago causes little difficulty; but naturally this is not so with the rising generation of entomologists, and I have therefore added in italics between parentheses the synonymy of those species which are noticed in this volume under names which they do not now bear.

The letter S. prefixed to the names indicate those species which are peculiarly Southern. Some few species, though otherwise peculiarly Southern, also occur in the British Isles; these are indicated by S.* I believe most of these are species which require to feed up as larvæ during the winter and cannot stand the prolonged severe cold of continental Europe.

Some species otherwise peculiarly Southern turn up again in Hungary; and many Southern species seem to have their Northern limit at Vienna.

I have great hopes that the next few years will witness a considerable increase of interest in the question of the geographical distribution of these insects.

A reference to the following Table will show that the South-eastern corner of Europe altogether is omitted; and this gap is the more inopportune as it would naturally have formed a connecting-link to the insects I have already noticed in the volume on the "Tineina of Syria and Asia Minor."

Of late years something has indeed been done in collecting Grecian Micro-Lepidoptera, and when at Dresden last summer I saw in Dr. Staudinger's extensive collection a number of very interesting forms from Mount Parnassus and other Grecian localities.

I am in great hopes that Dr. Staudinger will soon find leisure to publish a detailed notice of them. Since Dr. Staudinger visited Spain in 1857 and 1858, a number of good entomologists have passed away from us who would have gladly perused the promised, but too long withheld, notice of Dr. Staudinger's observations in that country.

At the present moment Dr. Staudinger perhaps finds himself too much occupied in preparing a second edition of his 'Catalogue of

European Lepidoptera' to be able fairly to take up other matters till that is disposed of; but I trust that immediately after the appearance of that Catalogue we may look for a valuable contribution from his pen supplementary to the present volume on the 'Tineina of Southern Europe.'

I must notice also one other blank, one of the divisions of Italy—Lombardy. I naturally comprehend that much of that fertile country being so entirely under cultivation affords bad collecting-ground to an entomologist; still it seems strange that neither amongst the resident entomologists have any devoted themselves to the Micro-Lepidoptera, nor have any travelling Micro-Lepidopterists formed collections whilst passing through the plains of Lombardy.

The term Liguria employed by Ghiliani seems to correspond very nearly with the Riviera from Mentone to Spezia. The climate there is so very different from that of Piedmont proper that there should be a considerable difference in the insects occurring in the two districts. Unfortunately Professor Ghiliani's opportunities of studying the Ligurian Micro-Lepidoptera had been but very limited.

I well recollect the change of climate in the short journey from Genoa to Turin on the evening of the 28th December last year. The great coat which had been discarded since I arrived at Caunes on the 16th December was gladly resumed before reaching Turin, where we were thankful to have good fires and closed windows, whilst at Genoa we were comfortably warm without fires and with open windows.

322 GEOGRAPHICAL SUMMARY.

		Pages where described.	Spain.	South of France.
S.	Melasina Dardoinella, *Millière*.	170	....	Marseilles, 17
S.	Dissoctena granigerella, *Stdg*.	143, 249	Granada and Chiclana, 140	
S.	Talæporia improvisella, *Stdg*.	143	Granada, 140	
	clandestinella, *Z*.	....	....	....
	pseudobombycella, *Hb*.	....	....	....
	conspurcatella, *Z*.	70..........	....	....
	——— ?	....	....	....
	Solenobia clathrella, *F.v.R.*	....	....	....
	pectinella, *Dup*. .... (*lapidicella*).	....	....	....
	lichenella, *Z*.	....	....	....
	Lypusa maurella, *W. V.* ...	....	....	....
	Xysmatodoma melanella, *Haw*.	....	....	....
	Euplocamus anthracinalis, *Scop*. (*Fuesslinellus*).	....	....	....
	Scardia polypori, *Esper* ... (*boletella*).	....	....	....
	Boleti, *F*. .... (*mediella*).	....	....	....
	tessulatella, *Z*.............	....	....	....
S.	Morophaga morella, *Dup*.	260	....	Marseilles, 25
S.	Atychia læta, *Stdg*.	163	San Ildefonso, 163	
S.	funebris, *Feisth*.	239	Barcelona, 240 ...	240
	Ochsenheimeria taurella, *W. V.*	....	....	....
S.	Dysmasia petrinella, *H.-S.*	239	239	
	Tinea imella, *Hb*.	....	....	....
	ferruginella, *Hb*.	....	....	....
	rusticella, *Hb*.	....	....	....
S.	fraudulentella, *H.-S.* ...	238	....	....
	fulvimitrella, *Sodf*.	....	..........?.........	Lozère, 259
	tapetzella, *L*.	....	....	....
	arcella, *F*.................... (*clematella*). (*repandella*).	....	....	....
	picarella, *L*.	....	....	....
	parasitella, *Hb*.	....	....	....
	quercicolella, *H.-S.* ...	....	....	....
	granella, *L*.	....	....	....
S.	panormitanella, *Mann*	130	....	....
	sprotella, *W. V.*	....	....	....
	pellionella, *L*.	....	....	....
S.	murariella, *Stdg*..........	143	Chiclana, 140	
S.	cubiculella, *Stdg*..........	144	Granada and Chiclana, 140	
	lapella, *Hb*. .... (*ganomella*).	....	....	....
S.	paradoxella, *Stdg*.	144	Chiclana, 140	
	biselliella, *Hummel* ... (*flavifrontella*). (*crinella*).	....	....	....
S.	crassicornella, *Z*..........	15..........	....	....
S.	chrysopterella, *H.-S.*... (*vitellinella*).	144, 241	Granada and Chiclana, 140; Ronda, 241	
	vinculella. *H.-S.*	....	....	....

ITALY.					
Sardinia.	Liguria.	Piedmont.	Tuscany.	Rome, Naples, &c.	Sicily.

GEOGRAPHICAL SUMMARY.

		Pages where described.	Spain.	FRANCE.	
				South of France.	Savoy.
	Tinea confusella, *H.-S.*				
	pustulatella, *Z.*	239			
S.	Eriocottis fuscanella, *Z.*	19			
	Lampronia flavimitrella, *Hb.*				
	rubiella, *Bjerk.* (*variella*).				283
	TeichobiaVerhuellella, *Stt.*				
	Incurvaria muscalella, *F.* (*masculella*).				282
	pectinea, *Haw.* (*Zinckenii*).				
	Koerneriella, *Z.* (*flavicostella?*).				
	angusticostella, *Z.*				
	Oehlmanniella, *Hb.*				
	rupella, *W. V.*				
	Micropteryx calthella, *L.*				
	aruncella, *Scop.*				
	Seppella, *F.* (*eximiella*).	71			
S.	Aglaella, *Dup.*	261		261	
S.	myrtetella, *Z.*	71			
S.	imperfectella, *Stdg.*	144, 249	Granada and Chiclana, 140		
S.	Paykullella, *F.* (*sicanella*).	19, 298			
	Anderschella, *H.-S.*				
S.	facetella, *Z.* (L. E. v. p. 361) (? *aureatella*, var.).				
	aureatella, *Scop.* (*Allionella*).	306 297			284
	amentella, *Z.*	72			
	semipurpurella, *Stph.* (*Sollerella*).			259	
	fastuosella, *Z.*				
	Nemophora Swammerdammella, *L.*				293
S.	sericinella, *Z.*				
	Schwarziella, *Z.*				
	Panzerella, *Hb.*	297			283
	pilulella, *Hb.*				
	pilella, *W. V.*				
	metaxella, *Hb.*				
	Adela fibulella, *W. V.*				
	leucocerella, *Scop.* (*bimaculella*).				
	ruffrontella, *Tr.*				
S.	cyanella, *Z.*	73			
	rufimitrella, *Scop.* (*Frischella*).				283
	violella, *Tr.*			259	
S.	Mazzolella, *Hb.*				
S.	paludicolella, *Z.*	75			
S.	homalella, *Stdg.*	145	Granada, 140		
S.	australis, *H.-S.*	240		Aix in Provence, 240	
	associatella, *Z.*				
	Sulzella, *W. V.* (*laqueatella*).	74			

GEOGRAPHICAL SUMMARY.

ITALY.

Piedmont.	Tuscany.	Rome, Naples, &c.	Sicily.
....	....	....	....
....	....	....	Palermo, 126
....	Salviano, 55	....	Messina and Syracuse, 2; Palermo, 126, 204
82			
83	....	....	....
'urin, 235			
82	Pratovecchio and Stia, 55	....	....
....	Pratovecchio, 55	....	....
....	....	....	....
....	Ardenza and Montenero, 55	....	....
82	....	....	....
'urin, 282			
84	Pisa, 56	....	Syracuse 3; Palermo, 127, 205
84	....	....	....
....	Montenero, 56	....	Palermo, 127
....	Montenero, 56		
....	57...............	....	Messina, 3...
'urin, 284			
....	....	....	....
84	Pratovecchio, 56	....	....
....	57		
....	....	....	Messina, 3...
83	Pratovecchio & Leghorn, 57		
....	....	....	Messina, 3...
....	Salviano, 57		
83	Florence, Leghorn, and Pisa, 57		
83	....	....	....
....	....	....	....
....	Pisa, 57	....	....
83			
....	....	....	....
....	Leghorn, 57		
83	Pisa, 57	....	....

GEOGRAPHICAL SUMMARY.

		Pages where described.	Spain.	South of France.
	Adela religatella, Z.	....	....	....
	Degeerella, L.	....	....	....
	viridella, Scop.............	....	....	....
	cuprella, W. V.	....	....	Lozère, 259 ..
	Nemotois scabiosellus, Scop.	....	....	259 ....
	(ærosellus)...........	....	....	....
S.	Latreillellus, F.	....	Sierra Nevada, 199	Aix in Provence, 259
S.	Raddellus, Hb............	....	....	....
	cupriacellus, Hb.........	....	....	....
S.	dalmatinellus, Mann ...	133	....	....
S.	istrianellus, H.-S.	....	....	....
	fasciellus, F. .... (Schiffermüllerellus).	....	....	....
S.	mollellus, Tr.	....	....	....
	minimellus, W. V.	....	....	....
S.	barbatellus, Z............	....	Andalusia, 199 ...	....
S.	chalcochrysellus, Mann	121	....	....
S.	albiciliellus, Stdg.	145	Granada and Chiclana, 140	....
	Dumerilellus, Dup. ...	....	....	Toulon, 259
S.	Dumerilellus, var. fervidellus, Mann	....	....	....
	Swammerdamia apicella, Don.	....	....	....
	(comptella).			
	cæsiella, Hb...............	....	....	....
	compunctella, H.-S. ...	....	....	....
	nubeculella, Mann (non Tengstr.)	....	....	....
	pyrella, Villers.......... (cerusiella).	....	....	....
S.	Distagmos Ledereri, H.-S.	240	S. of Spain, 240	....
S.	Celantica dealbatella, Z. ...	16.........	....	....
	Scythropia cratægella, L...	....	....	....
S.	Hyponomeuta egregiellus, Dup.	172	....	Cannes, 17 208, 217; L ona, 174
	vigintipunctatus, Retz...	....	....	....
	plumbellus, W. V.	....	....	....
	irrorellus, Hb.	....	....	....
	variabilis, Z............... (padellus, p. 277).	....	....	....
	rorellus, Hb...............	....	....	....
	malinellus, Z.	....	Granada, 199 ...	....
	mahalebellus, Guenée...	....	....	....
	evonymellus, Scop.	....	....	....
	padi, Z.	....	....	....
	Pseudia funerella, F.	....	....	....
	funerella, var. canuisella, Millière.	174	....	Cannes, 174
	decemguttella, Hb........	....	....	....
	sexpunctella, Hb.	....	....	....
	pusiella, Roemer .... (scalella).	....	....	....
	bipunctella, F.............. (echiella).	....	Xerez, 199	....
S.	flavianella, Tr............	....	....	....
S.	chrysopyga, Z.............	....	....	....

GEOGRAPHICAL SUMMARY.

Italy.			Austrian Provinces east of the Adriatic.	Carniola.
Tuscany.	Rome, Naples, &c.	Sicily.		
....	....	....	Fiume, 91	
Leghorn, 57	....	....	Fiume &c., 91	302
Leghorn and Pisa, 57	Calabria, 269	Messina, 3...	Fiume, 91 ...	Wippach &c., 106; 301
Pratovecchio, 57	....	....	Fiume, 91	
Pratolino, 57	....	....	....	301
Apennines, 57	....	....	Fiume, 91 ...	Nanos, 106
....	Naples, 269	Syracuse and Messina, 3; Palermo, 127, 205		
....	....	Palermo, 205		
....	....	....	Spalato, 132	
....	....	....	Fiume, 91	
....	....	....	Fiume, 91	
....	....	Syracuse, 4		
....	....	....	Fiume, 91	
Ardenza and Pisa, 57	....	Palermo, 127	Fiume, 91 ...	Nanos, 106
....	....	....	Fiume, 91	
Leghorn, Salviano, &c., 56	....	Palermo, 128	Fiume, 94 ...	Wippach, 108
Pratovecchio, 56				
....	....	....	....	Locavitz, 108
....	....	....	Josefsthal in Croatia	
Pratovecchio & Leghorn, 56	....	....	Fiume, 94 ...	Wippach, 108
56............	Naples, 2			
Pisa, 56	....	....	Fiume, 94 ...	Wippach, 108
....	....	....	Ragusa, 245	
....	....	....	Fiume, 94 ...	Gradischa, 108
Pratovecchio, 61	....	....	Fiume, 94 ...	Haidenschaft and Heiligenkreuz, 108
Pratovecchio, 61	....	....	Fiume, 94	
Pisa, 61	Naples, 267	....	Fiume, 94 ...	Wippach, 108
....	....	....	Fiume, 94	
....	Naples, 5	....	....	Gradischa, 108
....	....	....	Fiume, 94	
Leghorn, 61	Naples, 5	....	....	Wippach &c., 108; 300
....	....	....	Fiume, 94 ...	Wippach &c., 109; 300
Montenero, 61	Naples, 267	....	Fiume, 94	
....	....	....	Fiume, 94	
Montenero, 61	....	Syracuse, 5	Fiume, 94	
....	Naples, 267	....	Fiume, 94 ...	Wippach, 109
Leghorn, 61	....	Syracuse, 5; Palermo, 128	Fiume, 94 ...	Wippach, 109
....	....	....	....	Locavitz, 109
109	....	Palermo, 128	Fiume, 94; Dalmatia, 109	

		Pages where described.	Spain.	South of France.
S.	Psecadia auriflnella, *Hb.*... (*pyraustella*, p. 278).			
	Prays Curtisellus, *Don.* ... (*cœnobitella*).			
S.	oleellus, *Boyer*	78		Cannes, 209 217; Mentone 196, 209, 217
S.	Paradoxus osyridellus, *Millière*.	167	Malaga, 168	Cannes, 168
S.	Eidophasia Hufnagelii, *Z.*			
	Plutella cruciferarum, *Z.*... (*xylostella*).		Granada, 199 ...	Mentone, 196
	porrectella, *L.*			
	Theristis caudella, *L.* ..... (*cultrella*).		Portugal, 205 ...	
	Cerostoma asperella, *L.* ...			
	scabrella, *L.*			
	nemorella, *L.*			
	xylostella, *L.* .... (*harpella*).			
	persicella, *W. V.*			
	sylvella, *L.*			
	radiatella, *Don.* .... (*fissella*).			
S.	sculpturella, *H.-S.*	243		
	sequella, *Cl.*			
	vittella, *L.*			
	Dasystoma salicella, *Hb.*...			
	Chimabacche phryganella, *Hb.*			
	fagella, *W. V.*			
	Semioscopis avellanella, *Hb.*			
	strigulana, *W. V.* .... (*atomella*).			
	Epigraphia Steinkellneriana, *W. V.*			
	Orthotælia Sparganiella, *Thunb.*			
	Phibalocera quercana, *F.*... (*fagana*).			Cannes, 231
S.	luticornella, *Z.*			
S.	pallicornella, *Stdg.*	147	Granada and Chiclana, 141	
	Depressaria costosa, *Haw.* (*depunctella*).			
	liturella, *W. V.*			
S.	straminella, *Stdg.*	146	Chiclana, 141	
	pallorella, *Z.*			
	assimilella, *Tr.*			
	nanatella, *Stt.*			
S.	aridella, *Mann*	134		Cannes, 218 Mentone, 209 296
	atomella, *W. V.*			
S.	rutana, *F.* .... (*retiferella*).	218,273,296		Ile Ste.-Mar guerite, near Cannes, Men tone, and Mo naco, 217

GEOGRAPHICAL SUMMARY.

Italy.			Austrian Provinces east of the Adriatic.	Carniola.
Tuscany.	Rome, Naples, &c.	Sicily.		
Ardenza and Montenero, 61	Aspromonte, 267	Palermo, 128		
Salviano, 60	....	Syracuse, 5; Palermo, 127	Fiume, 94	
....	....	....	Spalato in Dalmatia, 168	
....	....	Palermo, 127	....	Nanos, 106
58............	Naples, 4, 268	Messina and Syracuse, 5; Palermo, 127, 205	Fiume &c., 92	Wippach &c., 106
....	Naples, 268	....	Fiume, 92	Wippach, 106
Pratovecchio, 58			Fiume, 92	
Pratovecchio, 58				
Leghorn, Pisa, and Florence, 58				
Pratovecchio, 58				
....	....	....	Fiume, 92	
Leghorn &c., Florence, and Pratovecchio, 58	....	....	Fiume, 92 ...	Fuocine, 106
Leghorn, 58				
....			Dalmatia, 243	
Ardenza, 58				
Pisa, 58				
Pratovecchio, 55	....	....	Fiume, 90	
Florence and Pratovecchio, 55	....	....	Fiume, 90	
....	....	....	Hraszt, 90	
Antignano, Posignano, 62	Naples, 8	Palermo, 128	Fiume, 95	
....	....	....	Fiume, 95 ...	Locavitz, 109
Pratovecchio &c., 61	....	....	Fiume, 94 ...	Langenfeld, 109
Badia, 61...	....	....	Fiume, 94	
Leghorn, 61				
Leghorn, 61	Naples, 5	....	Fiume, 94	
....	....	....	Fiume, 95	
Ardenza, 61			Spalato in Dalmatia, 133	Oberfeld, 109
Leghorn, 61	Rome, 235; Naples, 268, 273	61		

		Pages where described.	Spain.	South of France.
	Depressaria arenella	......	....	....
S.*	rhodochrella, *H.-S.*	242	Barcelona, 212	Cannes, 231 Marseilles, 24 South of France, 242
	(*Himmighofenella*)	241		
	subpropinquella, *Stt.*			
	Alstrœmeriana, *L.*			
	purpurea, *Haw.* (*vaccinella*).			
	ocellana, *F.* (*characterella*).			
S.	feruliphila, *Millière*	177		Hyères, 179
S.	atricornella, *Mann*	123		
S.	thapsiella, *Z.*	28		
	laterella, *W. V.* (*heracliella*).			
S.	sublutella, *Stdg.*	146	Chiclana, 141	
	applana, *F.*			
S.	lutosella, *H.-S.*	241		
	capreolella, *Z.*			
S.	nodiflorella, *Millière*	175, 218		Ile Ste.-Mar guerite, nea Cannes, 17(218; Hyère 176
S.*	rotundella, *Dgl.* (*peloritanella*).	27		
	furvella, *Tr.*			
S.	cachritis, *Stdg.*	145	Chiclana, 140	
S.	ferulæ, *Z.*	30, 176		Hyères, 177
	depressella, *F.*			
S.	velox, *Stdg.*	146		
S.	veneficella, *Z.*	31		
	badiella, *Hb.*			
	Heracliana, *De Geer* (*pastinacella*).			
S.*	discipunctella, *H.-S.*		Ronda, 242	
	albipunctella, *Hb.*			
S.	corticinella, *Z.*			
	dictamnella, *Tr.*			
	Enicostoma lobella, *W. V.*			
	(*subnigrella*, p. 232). Symmoca signella, *Hb.*			
S.	signatella, *H.-S.*	241	Ronda, 241	
S.	dodecatella, *Stdg.*	147	Sierra da Alfacar, 141	
	Gelechia Denisella, *W. V.*			
	sordidella, *Hb.*			Pyrénées ori entales, 260
	ferrugella, *W. V.*		Andalusia, 199	
S.	Kollarella, *Costa* (*flavedinella*). (*luteella*).			Montpelier, 9
S.	ratella, *H.-S.*	245	Ronda, 245	
	tripunctella, *W. V.*			
S.	antirrhinella, *Millière* (*tripunctella*?, p. 109).	179		Ax-sur-Arièg(179
S.	lutilabrella, *Mann*	103		
	cinerella, *L.*			
	rufescens, *Haw.*			
	lutatella, *H.-S.*			
	lineolella, *Z.* (*lineatella*, p. 280).			

GEOGRAPHICAL SUMMARY.

Italy.		
Tuscany.	Rome, Naples, &c.	Sicily.
Pratovecchio, 61	....	....

		Pages where described.	Spain.	South of France.
	Gelechia vilella, Z.	33		
	malvella, Hb.			
	populella, L.			
	scintillella, F. v. R.			
S.	contuberniella, Stdg.	148	Granada and Chiclana, 141	
	subsequella, Hb.			
	pinguinella, Tr.			
	velocella, Dup.			
	lentiginosella, Z.			
	ericetella, Hb.			
	(gallinella).			
S.	ulicinella, Stdg.	148, 180	Granada, 141	Marseilles, 180
	interruptella, Hb.			
S.	plutelliformis, Stdg.	147	Chiclana, 141	
	(Olbiaella).	182		Hyères and Toulon, 183
	peliella, Tr.			
	alacella, Dup.			
	terrella, W. V.		Andalusia, 199	
S.	figulella, Stdg.	149	Chiclana, 141	Cannes, 219
S.	ternatella, Stdg.	148, 248	Granada and Chiclana, 141	
S.	plebejella, Z.	36		
S.	imperitella, Stdg.	149	Granada, 141	
	petiginella?, Mann			Mentone, 209
S.	nocturnella, Stdg.	149	Chiclana, 141	
S.	salinella, Z.	37		
S.	halymella, Millière	181		Marseilles, 182; Cannes, 220
	pedisequella, Hb.			
S.	dryadella, Z.	79		
	rhombella, W. V.			
	proximella, Hb.			
	vulgella, W. V.			
	humeralis, Z.			
S.	n. sp.?			Mentone, 231
S.	helotella, Stdg.	148	Granada, 141	
S.*	littorella, Dgl.			
	(quinquepunctella)	243		
S.	epithymella, Stdg.	150	Chiclana, 141	
	artemisiella, Tr.			
S.	disjectella, Stdg.	149	Granada, 141	
	fugitivella, Z.		Andalusia, 199	
	alburnella, Z.			
	cytisella, Tr.			Celles-les-bains, 140
	scriptella, Hb.			
	diffinis, Haw.			
	(scabidella).			
	(dissimilella).			
	longicornis, Curt.			
	(zebrella).			
	(histrionella).			
	solutella, Z.			
	distinctella, Z.			
	viduella, F.			
	(luctuella).			
	quadrella, F.	296		
S.	gypsophilæ, Stt.	210		Mentone, 210, 220

GEOGRAPHICAL SUMMARY.   333

		Italy.				Austrian Provinces east of the Adriatic.	Carniola.
Sardinia.	Liguria.	Piedmont.	Tuscany.	Rome, Naples, &c.	Sicily.		
....	....	....	....	....	Syracuse, 8; Palermo, 128		
....	279	279	....	....	Palermo, 128		
....	....	279	Florence, 62	....	Palermo, 128	Fiume, 95	
....	....	....	....	....	....	Fiume and Istria, 95	Nanos, 110.
279	....	279	Pratovecchio, 63	....	....	Fiume, 95 ... Fiume, 95	Sturia, 110
....	....	279	Pisa, 62	....	....		
....	....	....	....	....	....	Fiume, 95	
....	....	....	Pisa, 62	....	Palermo, 128	....	Nanos, 110
....	Genoa, 260, 279	....	....	....	....		
279 .... 279	....	279	Leghorn, 62 Pisa, 62	Naples, 9	....	Fiume, 95 ...	Wippach, 110
135	....	....	....	....	Syracuse 9; Palermo, 128		
....	....	....	....	....	Syracuse, 10; Palermo, 128		
135	....	279	Poppi, 62...	....	Palermo, 128		
....	....	Turin, 279	Antignano, 63	....	....		
....	....		Pisa, 63	....	Messina, 10; Palermo, 128	Fiume, 95	
....	....	Upper Italy, 244		....	Palermo, 129		
....	....	....	Pratovecchio & Leghorn, 63	....	....	Fiume, 96 ...	Oberfeld, 111
....	....	Turin?, 279	....	....	....	Fiume, 96	
....	....	279	Pisa, Salviano, and Montenero, 63	....	Palermo, 128	Fiume, 96 ...	Wippach, 110
279? ...	....	....	....	....	....	Fiume, 95	
....	279	279	Apennines, 63	....	....	....	Kouk, 110
....	....	....	Montenero, 63	....	....	Fiume, 95 ...	Wippach and Nanos, 110
....	....	....	Pratovecchio, 63	....	....	Fiume, 95 ...	Oberfeld, 110
....	....	Luserna, 280		....	....		
....	....	Italy, 296		....	....	Fiume, 96	

		Pages where described.	Spain.	South of France.
S.	Gelechia provinciella, *Stt.*	221	....	Cannes, 221
S.	hyoscyamella, *Millière*	233	....	Ile St. Honorè near Cannes, 233
	sequax, *Haw.* (*apicistrigella*).	....	....	....
S.	Cisti, *Stt.*	211	....	Cannes, 211, 221
S.	tamariciella, *Z.*	80.........	Andalusia, 199 ...	....
	scalella, *Scop.* .... (*alecella*).	304......	....	....
S.	nigrinotella, *Z.*	40.........	....	....
	leucatella, *L.*	....	....	....
	albiceps, *Z.*	....	....	....
	nanella, *W. V.*	....	....	....
	triparella, *Z.*	....	....	....
	remissella, *Z.*	39.........	....	....
	umbrosella, *Z.*	....	....	....
S.	lamprostoma, *Z.*	36.........	....	....
S.	captivella, *H.-S.*	244......	....	....
	ligulella, *W. V.*	....	....	....
	vorticella, *Scop.*	....	....	....
	cincticulella, *H.-S.*	....	....	....
	tæniolella, *Z.*	....	....	....
	nigritella, *Z.*	41.........	....	....
	coronillella, *Tr.*	....	....	....
S.	patruella, *Mann*	103	....	Cannes, 222; Mentone, 197, 212, 222
	biguttella, *H.-S.*	....	....	
	anthyllidella, *Hüb.*	....	....	Mentone, 212; Cannes, 222
	(*psoralella*, Mill.)	184	....	Amélie-les-Bains, Cannes Fréjus, 185
	unicolorella, *H.-S.*	....	....	....
	tenebrella, *Hb.*	....	....	....
	bifractella, *Dgl.*	....	Ronda, 199	....
	carchariella, *Z.*	....	....	....
	pulveratella, *H.-S.*	....	....	....
	dimidiella, *W. V.*	244	....	....
	gerronella, *Z.*	....	....	....
	formosella, *Hb.* .... (*flammella*).	....	....	....
S.	flavella, *Dup.* .... (*segetella*).	34.........	....	....
	cerealella, *Olivier*	....	....	....
S.	detersella, *Z.*	33.........	....	....
	paupella, *Z.*	42.........	....	....
	inopella, *Z.*	....	....	....
S.	dejectella, *Stdg.*	150	Granada, 141	....
S.	diminutella, *Z.*	40.........	....	....
S.	promptella, *Stdg.*	149	Chiclana, 141 ...	....
S.	gaditella, *Stdg.*	150	Cadiz, 141	....
	nigricostella, *Dup.*	....	....	....
	luculella, *Hb.*	....	....	....
	stipella, *Hb.*	....	....	....
	Hermannella, *F.*	....	....	....
	superbella, *Z.*	....	....	....

GEOGRAPHICAL SUMMARY.

ITALY.

Liguria.	Piedmont.	Tuscany.	Rome, Naples, &c.	Sicily.
....	....	....	....	....
....	....	Leghorn and Antignano, 62		
....	Turin, 280	Florence &c., 63	....	....
....	....	Pratovecchio, 63	....	Catania, 10
....	Turin and Biella, 280	Florence and Pratovecchio, 62	....	....
....	Turin, 279	Pratovecchio, 63	....	....
....	....	Poppi &c., 63	Naples, 269	....
....	....	....	....	Syracuse and Messina, 10
....	Turin, 279	Florence, 63	....	Syracuse, 9; Palermo, 129
....	....	Leghorn and Pisa, 63	....	Palermo, 128
....	280	....	....	....
....	....	Pisa, 63	....	....
....	....	....	....	Messina, 10
....	....	Pratovecchio, 63	....	....
....	Turin, 279	....	....	....
....	....	Ardenza, 63	....	Syracuse, 10; Palermo, 128
....	....	Pratolino, 63	....	....
....	....	....	....	Palermo, 128
....	....	....	....	....
....	....	Pisa, 63	....	....
....	280	Leghorn, Pisa, &c., 63	Naples, 268	Syracuse, 9; Palermo, 129
80	Turin, 280	Ardenza, 62	....	Syracuse, 9
....	281			
....	....	....	....	Syracuse, 8; Palermo, 129
....	....	Leghorn &c., 63	....	Syracuse, 11; Palermo, 129
....	....	....	....	Messina, 10
....	....	....	....	Syracuse, 10
....	279	....	....	....
....	Turin, 279	....	....	....
....	....	Leghorn and Antignano, 63	Naples, 11	Palermo, 129
....	....	....	....	....

GEOGRAPHICAL SUMMARY.

		Pages where described.	Spain.	FRANCE.	
				South of France.	Savoy.
	Gelechia pictella, *Z.*				
	subericinella, *H.-S.*				
	decurtella, *Hb.*				
S.	campicolella, *Mann*	103			
S.	palermitella, *Laharpe*	205			
S.	ingloriella, *Z.*				
S.	striatopunctella, *Kollar*				
	Parasia Lappella, *L.*				
	paucipunctella, *Z.*				
S.	torridella, *Mann*	131			
S.	selaginella, *Mann*	124			
	neuropterella, *Z.*				
S.	Castiliella, *Möschler*	200	Andalusia, 119		
S.	Cleodora Kefersteinella, *Mann*		Andalusia, 199		
	striatella, *W. V.*	22			
S.	lineatella, *Z.*	75			
S.	meridionella, *H.-S.*	244	244; Andalusia, 199		
	Megacraspedus dolosellus, *Z.*				
S.	subdolellus, *Stdg.*	150	Sierra Nevada, 141		
	separatellus, *F. v. R.*				
	binotellus, *F. v. R.*				
	imparellus, *F. v. R.*				
S.	lanceolellus, *Z.*	76			
S.	Epidola stigma, *Stdg.*	152	Chiclana, 141		
S.	barcinonella, *Millière*	186	Barcelona, 187		
	Holoscolia forficella, *Hb.*				
	Anarsia spartiella, *Schrank*				
	lineatella, *Z.*				
	Ypsolophus ustulellus, *F.*	297			281
	fasciellus, *Hb.*				281
	silacellus, *Hb.*				
S.	corsicellus, *H.-S.*	246		Celles-les-bains, 140	
S.	trinotellus, *H.-S.*	246			
	marginellus, *F.* (*clarella*).				
	lemniscellus, *Z.*				
S.	Cisti, *Stdg.*	152	Granada and Chiclana, 141		
	asinellus, *Hb.*				
S.	limbipunctellus, *Stdg.*	152, 247	Granada and Chiclana, 141		
	verbascellus, *W. V.*			Cannes, 222; Mentone, 197, 222	
S.	bubulcellus, *Stdg.*	152, 247	Chiclana, 137, 141		
S.	declaratellus, *Stdg.*	146	Chiclana, 141		
	juniperellus, *L.*				
S.	senticetellus, *Stdg.*	147	Chiclana, 141		
	Sophronia humerella, *W. V.*				
S.	exustella, *Z.*	21			
	chilonella, *Tr.*				
	sicariella, *Z.*				
	illustrella, *Hb.*				

GEOGRAPHICAL SUMMARY.

Italy.

Tuscany.	Rome, Naples, &c.	Sicily.
....	....	Palermo, 129
....	....	....
....	....	....
....	....	....
....	....	Palermo, 205
....	....	....
Ardenza, 64	....	Palermo, 129
Pratolino, 64	....	....
....	....	Palermo, 129
....	....	....
Pisa, Ardenza, &c., 58	....	Palermo, 127
Leghorn, 58	....	Syracuse, 4; Palermo, 127
Pisa and Ardenza, 58		
Ardenza, 59	....	....

GEOGRAPHICAL SUMMARY.

		Pages where described.	Spain.	France. South of France.	France. Savoy.	France. Corsica.
S.	Sophronia Santolinæ, *Stdg.*	164	San Ildefonso, 163			
S.	Pterolonche albescens, *Z.*	50				
S.	pulverulenta. *Z.*	51				
S.	inspersa, *Stdg.*	152	Chiclana, 141			
S.	Protasis punctella, *Costa* (*monostictella*).	274				
	Topeutis barbella, *F.*	296				
	criella, *Tr.*					
	labiosella, *Hb.*					
	Pleurota rostrella, *Hb.*					
S.	planella, *Stdg.*	153, 249	Granada and Chiclana, 141			
	pyropella, *W. V.*				282	
S.	fuligerella, *Mann*	203				
S.	salviella, *H.-S.*	242				
S.	brevispinella, *Z.*	22				
S.	pungitiella, *H.-S.*					
S.	contristatella, *Mann*	203				
	bicostella, *L.*					
	ericella, *Dup.*		Andalusia, 199			
S.	imitatrix, *H.-S.*	242	Ronda, 243			
S.	teligerella, *Stdg.*	153, 249	Granada and Chiclana, 141			
S.	argentistrigella, *Mann*	115				
	aristella, *L.*		Portugal, 295			
S.	cyrniella, *Mann*	122				Ajaccio, 117
S.	honorella, *Hb.*	243	Barcelona, 243			
S.	Heydenreichiella, *H.-S.*	243	Ronda, 243			
S.	sobriella, *Stdg.*	153	Granada, 141			
	Carposina berberidella, *H.-S.*					
	Anchinia daphnella, *W. V.*					
	laureolella, *H.-S.*			Mentone, 232		
	Harpella forficella, *Scop.* (*proboscidella*). (*majorella*).				282	
	Geoffrella, *L.*					
	bracteella, *L.*					
	Hypercallis citrinalis, *Scop.* (*Christiernana*).					
S.*	Dasycera sulphurella, *F.* (*orbonella*).			259; Mentone, 222		
	Oliviella, *F.* (*æmulella*).				282	

GEOGRAPHICAL SUMMARY.

Italy.		
Tuscany.	Rome, Naples, &c.	Sicily.

		Pages where described.	Spain.	South of France.
	Œcophora formosella, W. V.	....	....	....
	lunaris, Haw. .... (Metznerella).	....	....	....
S.	meroedella, Stdg.	153	Chiclana, 141	
S.	detrimentella, Stdg. ...	154	Granada, 141	
	tinctella	....	....	....
S.	filiella, Stdg.	154	Granada, 141	
	flavifrontella...............	....	....	....
S.	lavandulæ, Mann	122	....	....
S.	cincrariella, Mann	130	....	....
S.	quadrifariella, Mann ...	122	....	....
S.	Allocliita rocisella, Stdg. ...	154, 248	Chiclana, 141	
	Œgoconia quadripuncta, Haw.	....	....	....
	Endrosis fenestrella, Scop. (lacteella). (betulinella).	303	....	
S.	Staintonia medinella, Stdg.	157	Chiclana, 142	
	Butalis obscurella, Scop. ... (Esperella).	....	....	....
	productella, Z...............	....	....	....
	seliniella, Z.	....	....	....
S.	ærariella, H.-S.	250	....	....
S.	tabidella, H.-S.	252	....	....
S.	cupreella, Stdg.	156	Granada and Chiclana, 142	
	senescens, Stt..............	....	....	Mentone, 222
S.	vagabundella, H.-S. ...	253	....	....
S.	dissitella, Z.....	24.........	....	....
S.	pascuella, Z. .... (gravatella, p. 108).	254	....	....
S.	gravatella, Z.	23.........	....	....
S.	tergestinella, Z. .... (gravatella, var. b).	255	....	....
S.	tributella, Z...............	25.........	....	....
S.	Hibernella, Stdg.	156	Chiclana, 142	
S.	terrenella, Z.	25.........	....	....
S.	humillimella, Stdg.......	156	Granada and Chiclana, 142	
S.	doryoniella, Millière ...	187	....	Celles-les-bains and Marseilles, 137; Menton 212, 223
	cuspidella, W. V.	....	....	....
S.	punctivittella, Costa ... (Knochella).	275	....	....
S.	Scipionella, Stdg.	155, 248	Granada and Chiclana, 141; Andalusia, 199	
S.	xanthopygella, Stdg. ...	155, 248	Chiclana, 142	
	restigerella, Z.	....	....	....
S.	biforella, Stdg.............	155	Granada, 142	
	Scopolella, Hb. .... (triguttella).	....	....	....
	chenopodiella, Hb.	....	Granada, 199 ...	....
	noricella, Z.	....	....	....
	dissimilella, H.-S.	....	....	
S.	bimerdella, Stdg.........	156	Sierra Nevada, 142	
	inspersella, Hb.	....	....	....
S.	insulella, Stdg.	155	Chiclana, 142	
	variella, Stp................	....	Andalusia, 199	
	siccella, Z.....................	256	....	....
S.	pulicella, Stdg.............	155	Chiclana, 142	

GEOGRAPHICAL SUMMARY.

		Italy.				Austrian Provinces east of the Adriatic.	Carniola.
Sardinia.	Liguria.	Piedmont.	Tuscany.	Rome, Naples, &c.	Sicily.		
....	....	....	....	....	....	Fiume, 93	
....	....	....	Antignano and Posignano, 60	....	Palermo, 127	Fiume, 93 ...	Langenfeld, 107
....	....	Turin, 280	Pisa and Pratovecchio, 60	....	....	Fiume, 93	
....	....	Turin, 285	Poppi, 60 ...	....	Palermo, 127	....	Kouk, 107
....	....	....	....	....	Palermo, 127		
....	....	....	....	....	....	Fiume, 94	
279	279	279	Leghorn, 60	....	....	Fiume, 93 ...	303; Wippach, 107
....	....	Turin, 281	....	....	....	Fiume, 93 ...	Nanos, 107
....	....	Turin, 281	....	....	....	....	Oberfeld, 107
....	....	....	....	....	....	Fiume, 93	
....	....	....	....	....	....	Fiume, 93; Spalato in Dalmatia, 108	Nanos &c., 108
....	....	....	....	....	....	Fiume and Istria, 93; Dalmatia, 108	Nanos &c., 108
....	....	....	....	....	Syracuse, 5 Palermo, 127	Fiume, 93 ...	Wippach, 108
....	....	....	60.............	....	Messina, 5	Trieste, 5, 256	
....	....	....	....	....	Syracuse, 5		
....	....	....	....	Rome, 5...	Messina, 5		
....	....	280	Poppi, 60...	....	....	Fiume, 93	
....	280	280	....	Rome, 4; Naples, 4, 270	Catania, 4; Palermo, 127	Fiume, 93 ...	Nanos &c., 108
....	....	....	....	....	....	Fiume and Istria, 94	
....	....	280; Domo-Dossola, 258 280 .... Turin, 281	....	....	Syracuse, 5	Fiume, 94	
....	....	....	....	....	....	Fiume, 94	
....	....	285	Antignano, 60	....	....		

		Pages where described.	Spain.	South of France.
S.	Butalis acanthella, *Godart*	....	Ronda, 199	Montpelier, 258
S.	n. sp. ?	....	....	Mentone, 197
S.	n. sp.	....	Granada, 199	....
S.	n. sp. ?	....	....	Cannes, 232
S.	Blastobastis roscidella, *Z.*...	26.........	....	....
	phycidella, *Z.*	....	....	....
	Pancalia Lewenhockella, *L.* (*Schmidtella*).	....	....	....
S.	nodosella, *H.-S.*	116, 245	Mont Serrat, 245	....
	Acrolepia granitella, *Tr*....	....	....	....
S.	solidaginis, *Stdg.*	157	Granada, 142 ...	Mentone, 223
S.	eglanteriella, *Mann* ...	125	....	Ile Ste.-Marguerite, near Cannes ?, 223
S.	vesperella, *Z.*	81.........	....	Amélie-les-Bains, 189; Cannes, 213; Ile Ste.-Marguerite, 223; Mentone, 213 223
	(*smilaxella*, Millière)...	189		
S.	fumociliella, *Mann*	124	....	....
	cariosella, *Z.*................	....	....	....
S.*	Glyphipteryx fuscoviridella, *Haw.* (*albicostella*).	....	....	....
S.	nicæella, *Möschler*	202	....	Nice, 201
	thrasonella, *Scop.*	....	Andalusia, 199 ...	....
	majorella, *Mann*	....	....	....
	equitella, *Scop.*	....	....	....
	equitella, *var.* ?	....	....	....
	oculatella, *Z.*	82.........	....	....
	Fischeriella, *Z.*	....	Andalusia ?, 199	....
	Tinagma dentellum, *Z.* ...	....	....	....
	perdicellum, *Z.*	....	....	....
	balteolellum, *F. v. R.*...	....	....	....
S.	thymetellum, *Stdg.*........	158	Andalusia, 199; Chiclana, 142	....
	transversellum, *Z.*	....	Andalusia, 200 ...	....
S.	Perittia ?	....	....	Ile Ste.-Marguerite, near Cannes, 224
	Antispila Pfeifferella, *Hb.*.. (*Stadtmüllerella*).	....	....	....
S.	Rivillei, *Stt.*	....	....	....
	Heliozela sericiella, *Haw.*... (*metallicella*).	....	....	....
	stanneella, *F. v. R.*......	....	....	....
S.	lithargyrella, *Z.*	82.........	....	....
	Argyresthia ephippella, *F.* (*pruniella*).	....	....	....
	nitidella, *F.*	....	....	....
	albistria, *Haw.*...............	....	....	....

GEOGRAPHICAL SUMMARY.

			Italy.		
Sardinia.	Liguria.	Piedmont.	Tuscany.	Rome, Naples, &c.	Sicily.

	Pages where described.	Spain.	South of France.
Argyresthia arceuthina, *Z.*	....	....	....
illuminatella, *Z.*	....	....	....
Cedestis Gysseleniella, *Dup.*	....	....	....
Zelleria hepariella, *Stt.* ...	....	....	....
Phillyrella, *Millière* ...	190	....	Cannes, 224
oleastrella, *Millière* ...	191, 215	....	Hyères, 192; Amélie-les-Bains, 193; Cannes, 236; Mentone, 215
(*Servillella*?, p. 267) ...	272		
Gracilaria alchimiella, *Scop.* (*Franckella*).	....	....	....
stigmatella, *F.*	....	....	....
hemidactylella, *W. V.* ...	....	....	....
falconipennella, *Hb.* ...	....	....	....
semifascia, *Haw.*	....	....	....
elongella, *L.*	....	Andalusia, 200	....
rufipennella, *Hb.*	....	....	....
tringipennella, *Z.*	....	....	Mentone, 197
limosella, *Dup.*	....	....	....
roscipennella, *Hb.*	....	....	....
rhodinella, *H.-S.*	....	....	....
syringella, *F.*	....	....	....
magnifica, *Stt.* ... (*Redtenbacheri*).	....	....	....
phasianipennella, *Hb.* ... (var. *quadruplella*).	....	....	....
quadrisignella, *Z.*	....	....	....
auroguttella, *Stp.* ...... (*lacertella*).	....	....	Cannes, 225
ononidis, *Z.*	....	....	....
scalariella, *Z.*	82	Chiclana, 137 ...	Mentone, 197; Cannes, 215
cupediella, *H.-S.*	....	....	....
Kollariella, *Z.*	....	....	....
Coriscium Brongniardellum, *F.* (*quercetellum*).	....	....	Mentone, 232
cuculipennellum, *Hb.* ... (*alaudellum*).	....	....	....
sulphurellum, *Haw.* ... (*citrinellum*).	....	....	....
Ornix ampliatella, *Stt.*	104	....	....
torquillella, *Z.*	....	....	....
anguliferella, *Z.*	....	....	....
meleagripennella (?) ...	....	....	....
guttea, *Haw.* .... (*guttiferella*).	....	....	....
cælatella, *Z.*	....	....	....
caudulatella, *Z.*	....	....	....
Coleophora laricella, *Hb.* ...	....	....	....
badiipennella, *Dup.* ...	....	....	....
limosipennella, *Dup.* ...	....	....	....
flavipennella, *H.-S.*	....	....	....
lutipennella, *Z.*	....	....	....
deviella, *Z.*	46	....	....

GEOGRAPHICAL SUMMARY.

ITALY.			Austrian Provinces east of the Adriatic.	Carniola.
Tuscany.	Rome, Naples, &c.	Sicily.		
Bibbiena, 64			Fiume, 97	
Pratovecchio, 65	....	....		
Leghorn, 120	....	....	Fiume, 99	
....	Terra d'Otranto?, 267			
Leghorn, 66	....	....	Fiume and Istria, 99	Oberfeld, 112; 306
Pratovecchio & Leghorn, 66 Antignano, 66	Abruzzo, 269	....	Fiume, 99	
.... Pratovecchio & Leghorn, 66 Antignano, 66	....	....	Fiume, 99 Fiume and Istria, 99	Wippach, 112
Pisa, 66......	....	....	Fiume, 99 ...	Wippach and Heiligenkreuz, 112
Leghorn, Antignano, and Fratolino, 66 Salviano, 66	....	....	Fiume, 99	
.... Leghorn, 66	....	....	Fiume, 99 Fiume, 99 Josefsthal, in Croatia, 132	
Montenero, 66	....	Palermo, 129		
Leghorn, 66 Pisa, Montenero, and Antignano, 66	....	.... Messina, 12	Fiume, 99 Fiume, 99 ...	Oberfeld, 113
Antignano, 66 Montenero & Ardenza, 66	....	....	Fiume, 99 ...	Gradischa, 113
....	....	....	Fiume and Istria, 102	
Pisa, 66 ...... Pisa and Pratovecchio, 66	Palermo, 129	Fiume, 99 ... Fiume, 99	Sturia, 113	
Salviano and Antignano, 66 Pratolino, Pratovecchio, and Montenero, 66	....	....	Fiume, 99 ... Fiume, 99	Wippach, 113
....	....	....	Fiume, 99	Gradischa and Lokavitz, 113
Florence, Pisa, and Leghorn, 66	....	....	Fiume, 99 ...	Oberfeld, 113
.... Ardenza and Salviano, 66 Montenero, 66	....	....	Fiume, 99 Fiume, 99 Fiume, 99	
....	....	....	....	Gradischa, 113
Leghorn, 65 Salviano, and Ardenza, 65	....	....	Fiume, 98	
....	....	.... Syracuse, 12	Fiume, 99 Fiume, 98	

346   GEOGRAPHICAL SUMMARY.

		Pages where described.	Spain.	South of France.
	Coleophora nigricella, *Haw.* (*coracipennella*).			
	paripennella, *Z.*			
	alcyonipennella, *Kollar*			
S.	fuscicornis, *Z.*		Andalusia, 200	
	Fabriciella, *Villars* (*Mayrella*). (*trochilipennella*).			
S.	Hieronella, *Z.* (*Mayrella*, p. 12).			
	hemerobiella, *Scop.*			
	anatipennella, *Hb.*			
	palliatella, *Zk.*			
S.	coarctella, *Stdg.*	159	Chiclana, 142	
	currucipennella, *Z.*			
S.	solidaginella, *Stdg.*	160	Chiclana, 142	
S.	struella, *Stdg.*	160, 247	Granada and Chiclana, 142	
S.	hispanicella, *Möschler*	200	Andalusia, 200	
	auricella, *F.*			
	virgatella, *Z.*			
	serenella, *Dup.*			
	gallipennella, *Hb.*			
	vulnerariæ, *Z.*			
S.	semicinerea, *Stdg.*	159	Chiclana, 142	
	pyrrhulipennella, *Z.*			Cannes, 213, 225; Mentone 225
	vibicigerella, *Z.*			
	fuscociliella, *Z.*			
S.	congeriella, *Stdg.*	159	Granada, 142	Cannes and Mentone, 213 225
	vicinella, *Z.*			
S.	solenella, *Stdg.*	158, 247	Granada, 142	
S.	spumosella, *Stdg.*	158, 247	Granada, 142	
	cælebipennella, *Z.*			Mentone, 213
	vibicella, *Hb.*			
	ornatipennella, *Hb.*			
	ochrea, *Haw.* (*argentipennella*).			259
	ballotella, *F. v. R.*			
	leucapennella, *Hb.*			
	albifuscella, *Z.*			
	marginatella, *H.-S.*			
S.	crepidinella, *Z.*	43		
	onobrychiella, *Z.*			
S.	lutatiella, *Stdg.*	159	Chiclana, 142	
	niveicostella, *Z.*			
	albicostella, *Dup.*			
	trifariella, *Z.*			
S.	flaviella, *Mann*	104		
	oriolella, *Z.*			
S.	laticostella, *Mann.*	131		
	saponariella, *Heeger*			
S.	fretella, *Z.*	45		
	(var. *pabulella*)	45		
S.	biseriatella, *Stdg.*	160, 247	Chiclana, 142	
S.	vestalella, *Stdg.*	160	Granada, 142	
	onosmella, *Brahm*			
S.	var.? enervatella, *Mann* (*onosmella*, p. 65).			

ITALY.

Liguria.	Piedmont.	Tuscany.	Rome, Naples, &c.	Sicily.
....	286	Pratovecchio, 65	....	....
....	....	Antignano, 65	....	....
....	Dogliani, 286	Montenero, 65	Naples, 12	Palermo, 129
pezia, 286	....	Pisa and Orciano, 65	Naples, 270	Palermo, 129
....	....	....	....	Syracuse, 12

		Pages where described.	Spain.	South of France.
	Coleophora chamædryella, *Stt.*			Mentone, 213
	therinella, *Tgstr*			
	lineariella, *Z.*			
S.	drypidis, *Mann*	104		
S.	præcursella, *Z.*	44		
	succursella, *H.-S.*			
	ciconiella, *H.-S.*			
S.	arefactella, *Stdg.*	161	Chiclana, 142	
	argentula, *Z.*			
	otitæ, *Z.*			
	murinipennella, *Dup.*			
	cæspititiella, *Z.*			
S.	lassella, *Stdg.*	161	Chiclana, 142	
	micantella, *Mann*			
	Bedellia somnulentella, *Z.*			Mentone, 213, 226; Cannes, 226
	Stathmopoda pedella, *L.*			
	(*fastuosella,* Costa?)			
S.	Guerinii, *Stt.*			Celle-les-Bains, 133; Mentone, 232
	Cosmopteryx Drurella, *F.*			
S.	Pyroderces argyrogrammos, *Z.*			
	Batrachedra præangusta, *Haw.* (*turdipennella*).			
	pinicolella, *Dup.*			
S.	Ledereriella, *Z.*	84		
	Chauliodus Illigerellus, *Hb.*			
	pontificellus, *Hb*		Andalusia, 200	
	dentosellus, *H.-S.*			
	chærophyllellus, *Goeze* (*testaceellus*).			
S.	Staintonellus, *Millière*	169		Cannes, 169, 234
	Laverna lacteella, *Stp.* (*gibbiferella*).			
	tricolorella, *Mann*			
	Raschkiella, *Z.*			
	miscella, *W. V.*			
	langiella, *Hb.*			
	(*unipunctella,* p. 259)	261		259
	Hellerella, *Dup.*			
	(*putripennella*).			
	Rhamniella, *Z.*			
	Chrysoclista Linneella, *Cl.*			
	flavicaput, *Haw.* (*aurifrontella*).			
	Heliodines Roesella, *L.*			
	Ochromolopis ictella, *Hb.*		Andalusia, 200	
	Asychna modestella, *Dup.*			
	æratella, *Z.*			
	Chrysocorys festaliella, *Hb.*			
S.	Stagmatophora Isabellella, *Costa*	245		
	(*opulentella*)	276		
S.	Dohrnii, *Z.*	46		
	Heydeniella, *F. v. R.*			
	pomposella, *Z.*			

GEOGRAPHICAL SUMMARY.

Italy.		
Tuscany.	Rome, Naples, &c.	Sicily.

	Pages where described.	Spain.	South of France.
Stagmatophora Grabowiella, *Stdg.*	157, 250	Chiclana, 137, 142	Cannes, 214 226, 234; Mentone, 214, 226
serratella, *Tr.*	....	....	....
albiapicella, *H.-S.*	....	....	....
Stephensia Brunnichella, *L.* (*magnificella*).	295	Portugal, 295 ...	....
Urodeta cisticolella, *Stt.*	227	....	Cannes, Ile Ste.-Marguerite, and Mentone, 226
Elachista quadrella, *Hb.*	....	....	....
nobilella, *Z.*	....	....	....
Gleichenella, *F.*	....	....	Mentone, 214, 228
albifrontella, *Hb.*	....	....	....
pullella, *H.-S.*	....	....	....
parvulella, *H.-S.*	....	....	....
nigrella, *Haw.*	....	....	....
arundinella, *Z.*	85	....	....
incanella, *H.-S.*	....	....	....
griseella, *Z.*	84	....	....
dispositella, *Frey*	....	....	....
bifasciella, *Tr.*	....	....	....
cingillella, *H.-S.*	....	....	....
cinctella, *Z.*	....	....	....
revinctella, *Z.*	....	....	....
chrysodesmella, *Z.*	87	....	Mentone, 228
gangabella, *Z.*	....	....	....
zonariella, *Tgstr.* (*bisulcella*).	....	....	....
cerussella, *Hb.*	....	....	....
contaminatella, *Z.*	48	....	....
disertella, *H.-S.*	....	....	....
pollinariella, *Z.*	....	....	Mentone, 228
collitella, *Dup.*	....	....	....
rudectella, *Stt.*	....	....	....
squamosella, *H.-S.*	....	....	....
constitella, *Frey*	....	....	....
rufocinerea, *Haw.* (*pratoliniella*).	....	....	....
anserinella, *Z.*	87	....	....
disemiella, *Z.*	48	....	....
dispilella, *Z.* (*triatomea*).	....	....	....
dispunctella, *Dup.*	....	....	....
piperatella, *Stdg.*	161	Granada and Chiclana, 142	
cygnipennella, *Hb.*	....	....	....
pollutella, *H.-S.*	....	....	....
concristatella, *Z.*	....	....	....
opacella, *F. v. R.*	....	....	....
arenariella, *Z.*	....	....	....
Tischeria gaunacella, *Dup.*	....	....	....
angusticollella, *Z.*	....	....	Mentone, 214
marginea, *Haw.* (*Emyella*).	....	....	Mentone, 214
complanella, *Hb.*	....	....	Mentone, 214
Dodonæa, *Stt.*	....	....	Cannes, 236

GEOGRAPHICAL SUMMARY.

ITALY.

Sardinia.	Liguria.	Piedmont.	Tuscany.	Rome, Naples, &c.	Sicily.
....	....	....	....	....	Palermo, 130
....	....	....	....	....	....
....	....	....	....	....	Messina, 13
....	....	287	Pratolino, 67	....	....
....	....	....	Pisa, 68		
....	....	....	Pratovecchio, 67	....	....
....	....	....	....	....	....
....	....	287	Salviano, 68	....	Messina, 13
....	....	....	Pisa, 68		
....	....	Turin, 285	Ardenza and Salviano, 68	....	....
....	....	287	....	....	....
....	....	....	....	....	....
....	....	....	....	....	....
....	....	....	Pisa, 68	....	....
....	....	....	Pisa, 68	....	....
....	....	....	....	....	....

352 GEOGRAPHICAL SUMMARY.

		Pages where described.	Spain.	South of France.
	Lithocolletis roboris, *Z.* ...	....	....	....
	hortella, *F.* .... (*saportella*).	....	....	....
	Amyotella, *Dup.*	....	....	....
	scitulella, *Z.*	....	....	....
	Parisiella, *Wck.*	245	....	....
	ilicifoliella, *Z.*	....	....	....
S.	meridionella, *Möschler*	201	Andalusia, 200	....
S.	endryella, *Mann*	125	....	....
	delitella, *Z.*	....	....	....
S.	adenocarpi, *Stdg.* .... (*Italica ?*).	165	San Ildefonso, 163	....
	abrasella, *Z.*	....	....	....
	Cramerella, *F.*	....	....	....
	alniella, *Z.*	....	....	....
	strigulatella, *Z.* .... (*Rajella*).	....	....	....
	lantanella, *Schrank* ... (*elatella*).	....	....	Cannes, 236
	pomifoliella, *Z.*	....	....	....
	pomonella, *Z.*	....	....	....
	faginella, *Z.* .... (*fagicolella*).	....	....	....
	ulmifoliella, *Hb.*	....	....	....
S.	platani, *Stdg.*	....	....	....
	quercifoliella, *Z.*	....	....	....
S.*	Messaniella, *Z.*	....	....	Mentone, 197; Cannes, 214, 228
S.	hesperiella, *Stdg.*	162	Chiclana, 142	....
S.	leucographella, *Z.*	88.........	....	....
S.	belotella, *Stdg.*	162, 250	Granada and Chiclana, 142	....
S.	suberifoliella, *Z.*	89.........	....	....
	fraxinella, *Z.*	....	....	....
	salictella, *Z.*	....	....	....
	emberizæpennella, *Bouché*	....	....	....
	Froelichiella, *Z.*	....	....	....
S.	sublautella, *Stt.*	198	....	Mentone, 197
	Kleemannella, *F.*	....	....	....
	Schrebereila, *F.*	....	....	....
	trifasciella, *Haw.* .... (*Heydenii*).	....	....	Ile Ste.-Marguerite, near Cannes, 228
	silvella, *Haw.* .... (*acerifoliella*). (*acernella*).	....	....	....
S.	Chiclanella, *Stdg.*	161	Chiclana, 142	....
	comparella, *Z.*	....	....	....
	populifoliella, *Tr.*	....	....	....
	agilella, *Z.*	....	....	....
S.	sp. ?, on *Calycotome spinosa*	....	....	Cannes, 237
	Lyonetia Clerckella, *L.* ...	....	....	....
	prunifoliella, *Hb.*	....	....	....
	Phyllocnistis suffusella, *Z.*	....	....	....
	Cemiostoma spartifoliella, *Hb.*	....	....	....
	laburnella, *Stt.*............. (*spartifoliella*, p. 68).	....	....	....

GEOGRAPHICAL SUMMARY.

	ITALY.			Austrian Provinces east of the Adriatic.	Carniola.
Piedmont.	Tuscany.	Rome, Naples, &c.	Sicily.		
....	Pratovecchio, 69	....	....	Fiume, 102	Wippach and Nanos, 115
....	Pratovecchio, 69	....	....	Fiume, 102	
....	....	....	....	....	Oberfeld, 115
....	Pratovecchio and Poppi, 69	....	....	Fiume, 102	Nanos, 115
....	....	....	....	Fiume, 246	
....	....	....	....	Fiume, 102	
Italy, 246	Pratovecchio, and Stia, 69	....	....	Fiume, 102	Oberfeld and Sturia, 115
'urin, 287	Montenero, 70	....	....	Fiume, 102	
88	....	....	....	Fiume, 102	
....	Badia, 70	....	....		
....	....	....	....	Fiume, 102	
....	Florence, 236				
....	Badia, 69 ...	....	....	Fiume, 102	
....	Leghorn, 69				
....	....	....	....	Fiume, 102	Nanos, 115
....	....	....	....	Fiume, 103	
'omo, 140					
....	Pratovecchio and Florence, 70	....	....	Fiume, 102	Gradischa, 115
....	70............	Rome, 206, 237; Naples, 206	Messina, 14	Fiume, 102	
....	Montenero, 70	Florence, 207, 236			
....	Leghorn, 70	Naples, 207			
....	Pisa, 70	....	....	Fiume, 103	
....	Pratovecchio and Badia, 69				
....	Pisa, 70	....	....	Fiume, 103	
Turin, 288					
Turin, 288	Antignano, 70	....	....	Fiume, 103	Wippach, 115
....	....	....	....	Fiume &c., 103	Gradischa, 115
....	Montenero, 70	....	....	Fiume, 103	
....	Leghorn and Pisa, 70	....	....	Fiume, 102	Wippach &c., 115
....	Pratovecchio, 70	....	....		
....	....	....	....	Fiume, 103	
....	Pratovecchio, 70				
....	Pisa, Florence, &c., 68	....	....	....	Wippach, 114
288	Leghorn, 68	....	....	Fiume, 102	
....	Pratovecchio, 68	Naples, 14	....	Fiume, 102	
287	....	....	....	Fiume, 102	
....	Leghorn and Antignano, 68				

		Pages where described.	Spain.	South of France.
S.	Cemiostoma Zanclæella, *Z.*	49		
	scitella, *Z.*			
	Opostega salaciella, *Tr.*			
S.	menthinella, *Mann.*	125		
	crepusculella, *Z.*			
S.	Phyllobrostis Daphneella, *Stdg.*	163	Chiclana, 142	Cannes and Mentone, 214, 228
	Bucculatrix cristatella, *Z.*			
	nigricomella, *Z.*			
	cidarella, *Z.*			
	hippocastanella, *Dup.*			
	ulmella, *Z.*			
	crataegi, *Z.*			
	Boyerella, *Dup.*			Provence, 259
	frangulella, *Goeze* (*rhamnifoliella*).			
S.	lavaterella, *Millière*	193		Hyères, 193; Mentone, 214
	Nepticula samiatella, *H.-S.*			
	anomalella, *Goeze*			
S.	suberivora, *Stt.*	228		Cannes, 228
	aurella, *F.*			Mentone, 214
	marginicolella, *Stt.* (*gratiosella*, p. 285).			
	Hübnerella, *H.-S.*			
	argentipedella, *Z.*			
	cineritella, *F. v. R.*			
S.	suberis, *Stt.*	229		Cannes, 229
S.	euphorbiella, *Stt.*	230		Mentone, 229, 237
S.	promissa, *Stdg.*			Celles-les-bains, 140
	subbimaculella, *Haw.* (*cursoriella*).			
	argyropeza, *Z.*			
	catharticella ?, *Stt.*			Mentone, 228
	sericopeza, *Z.*			
	cryptella, *Stt.*			Cannes, 229
	subnitidella, *Z.*			
	sp. ?			
S.	sp. ?, on *Quercus ilex*			
S.	sp. ?, on *Cistus monspeliensis*			Cannes, 230
	Trifurcula pallidella, *Z.*			
	immundella, *Z.*			

GEOGRAPHICAL SUMMARY.

Italy.

Tuscany.	Rome, Naples, &c.	Sicily.
....	....	Messina, 50
Salviano, 68	Naples, 269	....
Pisa, 68	....	....
Pisa, 68	....	Palermo, 130
....	....	....
Pisa, 69	....	....
Pratovecchio, 69	....	....
....	....	....
Ardenza and Salviano, 69	....	....
....	....	....
Leghorn &c., 69	....	....
Pisa, 69	....	....

CHAPTER XIII.

BOTANICAL SUMMARY.

Our friends the *Tineina* being dependent on the vegetable kingdom for their subsistence (excepting a few of our household pests, which eat so readily fur, wool, and hair), it stands to reason that to become acquainted with them in their larval stages we must pay a very close attention to the flora of the country we are visiting.

The entomologist who visits a strange country, if not himself a first-rate botanist (and in these days one can hardly expect such a combination of talent), ought to be accompanied by a botanist *pur et simple* to name for him the plants on which he finds his larvæ.

The following plants are mentioned in this volume either as being the food of the larvæ of certain species or as being frequented by the perfect insects.

RANUNCULACEÆ.

Ranunculus (*acris*?), pp. 3, 127: flowers frequented by the imago of *Micropteryx calthella*.

Actæa spicata, p. 305: flowers frequented by the imago of *Micropteryx aruncella*.

CRUCIFERÆ.

Moricandia arvensis, p. 233; } seeds eaten by the larva of *Ypsolo-*
Cheiranthus cheiri, p. 222: } *phus trinotellus.*

Clypeola maritima, p. 4: *Plutella cruciferarum* flying amongst this plant: the larva is well known to feed indifferently on most *Cruciferæ*.

CISTACEÆ.

Halimium lepidotum (*Helianthemum halimifolium*), pp. 141, 148: food of larva of *Gelechia contuberniella*.

Cistus, sp.?, p. 140: seeds eaten by the larva of *Ypsolophus corsicellus*.

Cistus albidus, pp. 141, 152: food of larva of *Hypsolophus cisti*.

Cistus salvifolius, p. 120: frequented by the imago of *Stagmatophora Dohrnii*.

———— ————, pp. 211, 221: in March the larva of *Gelechia cisti* feeds between united leaves.

———— ————, p. 230: early in March the leaves are mined by a *Nepticula*-larva.

Cistus monspeliensis, p. 226 : early in March the leaves are mined by the larva of *Urodeta cisticolella*; and, p. 230, early in March the leaves are mined by a *Nepticula*-larva.

Helianthemum fumana, p. 234: at the end of April the leaves were blotched by the larva of *Coleophora ochrea*? A new species of *Coleophora*, however, has just been bred by Monsieur Millière from *Helianthemum tuberaria*, the larva of which has a case very like that of a young larva of *Coleophora ochrea*; so that I cannot feel quite so confident as I did that the larvæ Mr. J. T. Moggridge sent me from Albenga were truly those of *Coleophora ochrea*.

CARYOPHYLLACEÆ.

Silene nicæensis, p. 219 : one larva and several pupæ of *Gelechia figulella* found at the roots of this plant, February 28th.

———— ————, p. 221: the larvæ and pupæ of *Gelechia provinciella* found freely at the roots of this plant, the leaves of which had evidently been much eaten, February 28th.

Saponaria, p. 98 : *Coleophora saponariella* on this plant.

Gypsophila saxifraga, pp. 210, 220: pod-like galls formed in the shoots of this plant in March by the larvæ of *Gelechia gypsophilæ* (see woodcut, p. 211).

Drypis spinosa, p. 98: cases of the larvæ of *Coleophora drypidis* collected in June on this plant. (At p. 98 I have copied Herr Mann's mistake and printed it *Drymis*.)

Stellaria holostea, p. 113 : flowers frequented by the imago of *Asychna modestella*. Thanks to Dr. Hofmann the larva is now known to feed in July in the capsules of that plant, using an empty capsule as a moveable case.

MALVACEÆ.

Lavatera olbia, p. 193 : leaves mined and gnawed in November and December by the larva of *Bucculatrix lavaterella*. This larva must also feed on *Lavatera maritima*, as I took a specimen of the imago at Mentone (p. 214), where *L. olbia* does not occur.

VITACEÆ.

Vitis vinifera, p. 310 : leaves mined in July by the larva of *Antispila Rivillei*, which has not been seen for the last 120 years! (See Frontispiece, and woodcut, p. 309.)

RUTACEÆ.

Ruta angustifolia, pp. 217, 235 : leaves twisted to form a sort of tubular habitation by the larvæ of *Depressaria rutana*, in March at Monaco &c., in January at Rome.

Ruta graveolens, p. 273 : leaves twisted by the larva of *Depressaria rutana*. It perhaps feeds on various species. Fabricius simply says (p. 296) it feeds on *Ruta*.

Dictamnus, p. 109 : larvæ of *Depressaria dictamnella* on this plant.

CELASTRINEÆ.

Euonymus europæus, p. 302: frequented by *Adela Sulzeriella* (*P. cræsella*).

———, pp. 61, 94, & 108: *Hyponomeuta plumbellus*, p. 94, *H. irrorellus*, and, p. 108, *H. evonymellus* are mentioned as occurring on *Euonymus*, on which the larvæ of all three species are well known to feed.

RHAMNACEÆ.

Paliurus aculeatus (*Rhamnus paliurus*), p. 91: the flowers frequented in June by the imago of *Micropteryx Paykullella*.

——— ———, p. 91: the imago of *Adela religatella* flying amongst this plant in May.

No doubt a plant which grows so extensively in the south as this does must harbour several species of Micro-Lepidoptera.

Rhamnus alaternus, p. 228: leaves mined in March by a *Nepticula*-larva, perhaps distinct from *catharticella*.

——— ———, pp. 102, 114: *Bucculatrix frangulella* mentioned as occurring in the perfect state on *Rhamnus* hedges; the larva is well known to feed on *Rhamnus frangula*.

TEREBINTHACEÆ.

Pistacia terebinthus, p. 117: the flowers frequented in May by the imago of *Micropteryx facetella*.

——— ———, pp. 138, 139: the pod-like galls produced by Aphides are inhabited in September by the larvæ of *Stathmopoda Guerinii*. The pupæ of the same insect found in the stems of this plant in May (p. 232).

——— ———, p. 231: young leaves united by the larva of a *Gelechia* in April. Possibly an unnamed species.

——— ———, pp. 138, 140: leaves mined in September by the larvæ of *Nepticula promissa*.

——— ———, p. 139: larvæ between united leaves were not reared.

Rhus cotinus, pp. 138, 140: leaves mined in September by the larvæ of *Nepticula promissa*.

LEGUMINOSÆ.

Ulex australis (*parviflorus*), pp. 141, 149, 180: larvæ of *Gelechia ulicinella* in the flowers of this plant, April (Granada), January (South of France).

Calycotome spinosa, pp. 209, 218: leaves eaten in February and March by the larvæ of *Depressaria atomella*.

——— ———, p. 225: early in March leaves discoloured by the larva of *Coleophora calycotomella*.

——— ———, p. 237: leaves mined and distorted in December by a *Lithocolletis*-larva.

Spartium junceum, p. 6: the imago of *Dep. rotundella* (*peloritanella*) occurred amongst this plant in July, February, and March.

Spartium scoparium: p. 5, the food of the larva of *Dep. assimilella* in early spring; p. 102, imago of *Cemiostoma spartifoliella* in May.

—— ——, p. 127: several *Anarsia spartiella* in June.

—— ——, p. 129: two males of *Gelechia pictella* in June.

Cytisus laburnum, p. 68: imago of *Cemiostoma laburnella* (entered as *spartifoliella*) in April.

Cytisus triflorus, pp. 14, 49, & 50, note: *Cemiostoma Zanclæella* amongst this plant.

Cytisus ——?, p. 139: between united leaves in October, larvæ of *Gelechia cytisella*; leaves also mined by a *Lithocolletis*-larva and by a *Cemiostoma*-larva at the same time (see p. 140).

Adenocarpus hispanicus, p. 163: leaves mined in April by the larvæ of *Lithocolletis adenocarpi*.

Ononis spinosa, p. 113: imago of *Gracilaria ononidis* in June.

Anthyllis cytisoides, pp. 142, 160: leaves blotched (?) in May by the larvæ of *Coleophora vestalella*.

Medicago sativa?, p. 234: leaves eaten at the end of April by larvæ, probably of *Coleophora vicinella*.

Dorycnium hirtum, pp. 212, 222: larvæ and pupæ of *Gelechia biguttella* in tops of this plant in March.

—— ——, pp. 213, 225: leaves blotched by the larvæ of *Coleophora congeriella* in March.

—— ——, pp. 212, 223: larvæ of *Butalis dorycniella* between united leaves in March.

—— ——, p. 229: *Nepticula cryptella* bred from this plant in March.

Dorycnium suffruticosum, pp. 142, 158: larvæ of *Coleophora spumosella* in April.

—— ——, pp. 142, 160, 213, 225: leaves mined by the larvæ of *Coleophora congeriella*, April and May (Granada), March (Mentone and Cannes).

—— ——, pp. 187, 212: larvæ of *Butalis dorycniella* between united leaves, March (Cannes), April (Celles-les-bains).

—— ——, pp. 197, 212: larvæ or pupæ of *Gelechia biguttella* in tops of this plant in February and March.

Dorycnium, p. 110: food of the larvæ of *Gelechia scintillella*[*] and *G. biguttella*.

---

[*] This must be a mistake; *Gelechia scintillella* feeds on *Helianthemum vulgare*; I have bred it myself from larvæ received from Herr Mühlig of Frankfurt on that plant. It probably feeds also on other species of *Helianthemum*, but can hardly be expected on one of the *Leguminosæ*.

Lotus, p. 222: leaves eaten by larvæ of *Gelechia anthyllidella* (*psoralella*, Mill.).

Robinia pseudacacia, p. 268: pupæ of *Dasycera sulphurella* (*Lampros ambiquellus*, Costa) under the bark of this tree.

Psoralea bituminosa, pp. 184, 212: leaves mined or folded in February by the larvæ of *Gelechia anthyllidella* (*psoralella*, Millière).

Coronilla emerus, p. 3: the imago of *Micropteryx Paykullella* (*sicanella*, Z.) flew amongst this plant in March and April.

Coronilla minima, p. 188, note: larvæ of *Butalis dorycniella* on this plant in January.

Coronilla (*varia*), pp. 96, 110: *Gelechia coronillella* flying in May amongst this plant (on which the larva feeds).

Onobrychis, pp. 111 & 112: *Coleophora oriolella* and *onobrychiella* taken amongst this plant in June.

ROSACEÆ.

Spiræa aruncus, p. 284: flowers frequented by the imago of *Micropteryx Allionella*.

—— ——, p. 305: flowers frequented by the imago of *Micropteryx aruncella*.

Rubus fruticosus, p. 206: leaves tenanted by the pupæ of *Tischeria marginea* in March.

—— ——, p. 207: leaves mined by larvæ of *Nepticula aurella* in March.

Rosa sempervirens, pp. 214, 236: leaves tenanted by the pupæ of *Tischeria angusticollella* in February and March.

Poterium spinosum, p. 9: *Gelechia Kollarella* frequented this plant in June, and when disturbed settled again on it. (See *Salvia officinalis*, p. 365.)

—— ——, p. 9: *Gelechia detersella* was also beaten from *Poterium* in June.

Cratægus pyracantha, pp. 207, 237: the upper side of the leaves mined by the larvæ of *Lithocolletis leucographella* in January, February, and March.

Prunus padus, p. 109: nests of larvæ of *Hyponomeuta padi* (*padellus*, Hyd.) on this plant.

TAMARISCACEÆ.

Tamarix gallica, p. 182: eaten in autumn by the larvæ of *Gelechia plutelliformis* (*Alucita olbiaella*, Millière).

Tamarix (no species mentioned), pp. 141, 147: larva of *Gelechia plutelliformis*.

—— ——: p. 57, frequented by the imago of *Adela cyanella*; p. 60, by the imago of *Dasycera sulphurella* (*Stenoptera orbonella*); p. 61, imago of *Depressaria rutana* (*retiferella*) beaten from this plant;

p. 62, frequented in May by the imago of *Gelechia tamaricella*;
p. 63, by the imago of *Gelechia paupella*; p. 67, by the imago of
Batrachedra Ledereriella; p. 70, the by imago of *Lithocolletis suberifoliella*; and, p. 116, by the imago of *Micropteryx calthella*.

My attention has lately been called by Mr. Albert Müller to a paper by Herr Frauenfeld, " Ueber exotischen Pflanzenauswüchse erzeugt von Insecten," in the 'Verhandl. der zool.-botan. Gesellschaft in Wien' for 1859, pp. 319–332, in which a number of galls on several species of *Tamarix* from Egypt and the peninsula of Sinai are mentioned, from one of which a new *Gelechia* was bred allied to *salinella*, Z., which Frauenfeld describes under the name of *Gelechia sinaica*. Possibly galls on *Tamarix* would furnish us with the larva of *Batrachedra Ledereriella*; at any rate I throw out the suggestion.

CRASSULACEÆ.

Sedum album, p. 258: food of larva of *Butalis scopolella*.

Sedum (telephium), p. 94: frequented by *Hyponomeuta vigintipunctatus*. The larva is well known to feed on that plant.

UMBELLIFERÆ.

Daucus, p. 232: a *Butalis*-larva in the dry head of a species of *Daucus* in April.

Thapsia garganica, p. 6: the young leaves much eaten in March by the larvæ of *Depressaria thapsiella*.

—— ——, pp. 7, 128: the unexpanded umbels (still within their sheaths) are attacked in April by numerous colonies of the larvæ of *Depressaria veneficella*; the tenanted stems may also be collected in June. Some caution is necessary in handling this plant if we wish to avoid unpleasant consequences (see p. 8).

Ferula communis (nodiflora), pp. 7, 176: larvæ of *Depressaria ferulæ* on the leaves of this plant in March and April. The young larvæ attack the base of the plant, where they cause a resin-like exudation (see p. 177).

—— ——, p. 177: leaves in April eaten by the larvæ of *Depressaria feruliphila*.

—— ——, pp. 175 & 218: leaves in March and April eaten by the larvæ of *Depressaria nodiflorella*; the very young larvæ actually mine the slender leaflets.

Ferula (no species named, but spoken of as "fine-leaved"), pp. 140, 146: fed on by the larva of *Depressaria velox*.

Pimpinella?, p. 109: larvæ of *D. ferulæ?* abundant on this plant in May.

Cachrys lævigata, pp. 140, 146: eaten by the larvæ of *Depressaria cachritis* in February and March.

CORNACEÆ.

Cornus sanguinea, pp. 260, 262: flowers frequented by the im. of *Micropteryx (Adela) Aglaella*.

CAPRIFOLIACEÆ.

Sambucus, pp. 260, 262: flowers frequented by the imago of *Micropteryx (Adela) Aglaella*.

Viburnum tinus, p. 236: leaves mined by the larva of *Lithocolletis lantanella*.

Lonicera implexa, p. 224: flat white blotches formed in the upper side of the leaves in March by the larva of a *Perittia*?

—— ——, p. 226: leaves tenanted in March by pupæ of *Lithocolletis trifasciella*.

DIPSACEÆ.

Scabiosa columbaria, p. 3: flowers frequented in May by the imago of *Nemotois Latreillellus*.

COMPOSITÆ.

Tussilago, p. 97: the imago of *Parasia neuropterella* flying amongst this plant in July.

Solidago virgaurea, pp. 137, 142, 157: leaves mined by larvæ of *Acrolepia solidaginis*.

—— ——, pp. 142, 160: leaves blotched by larvæ of *Coleophora solidaginella* in May.

Conyza squarrosa, p. 223: leaves mined by larvæ of *Acrolepia solidaginis* in March.

Artemisia campestris, pp. 142: eaten in May by the larvæ of *Coleophora solenella*.

Artemisia Barrelieri, pp. 141, 149: tips of the shoots eaten by the larvæ of *Gelechia disjectella* in October and November.

Artemisia maritima, p. 220: leaflets mined, bleached, and drawn together by a young *Gelechia*? larva in March.

Artemisia: p. 92, frequented in May and June by the imago of *Cleodora striatella*, and, p. 101, in June by the imago of *Elachista arenariella*.

Santolina rosmarinifolia, p. 163: leaves rolled up early in May by the larvæ of *Sophronia santolinæ*.

Helichrysum stœchas, p. 213: eaten in March by larvæ of *Coleophora cœlebipennella*. (In Germany this species occurs on *Gnaphalium arenarium*.)

—— ——, p. 223: leaves mined and shoots burrowed in March by a small larva, perhaps that of *Acrolepia eglanteriella*.

Helichrysum angustifolium, p. 119: cases of *Coleophora cœlebipennella* found on this plant.

Helichrysum angustifolium, p. 120 : frequented in July by the imago of *Stagmatophora Dohrnii*.

Helichrysum, p. 139: larvæ of a *Gelechia*? in woolly tubes in October.

Centaurea aspera, pp. 141, 146 : larvæ of *Depressaria sublutella*.

ERICACEÆ.

Arbutus unedo, pp. 14, 49, and 50, note : *Cemiostoma Zanclæella* amongst this plant.

—— ——, p. 231 : leaves eaten in April by the larvæ of *Phibalocera quercana*.

Erica cinerea, p. 217 : in April the webs formed by the larvæ of *Hyponomeuta egregiellus* were very conspicuous at Fontainebleau.

Erica arborea, p. 3 : flowers frequented by the imago of *Micropteryx Paykullella (sicanella)*.

—— ——, p. 6 : frequented in July, February, and March by the imago of *Depressaria rotundella (peloritanella)*.

—— ——, p. 13 : frequented in February, March, and April by the imago of *Elachista disemiella*.

—— ——, p. 173 : in March the webs of the larvæ of *Hyponomeuta egregiellus* may sometimes be found on this plant.

Erica scoparia, pp. 173, 208, 217 : in March the webs of the larvæ of *Hyponomeuta egregiellus* are plentiful on this plant.

—— ——, pp. 213, 225 : cases of *Coleophora pyrrhulipennella* found on this plant in March.

Erica : p. 57, flowers frequented in May by the imago of *Adela paludicolella*; pp. 62, 118, 128, plant frequented in May and June by *Gelechia gallinella*; p. 129, in May by *Gelechia campicolella*.

——, pp. 142, 154 : eaten by the larva of *Butalis insulella*.

OLEACEÆ.

Olea europœa, pp. 192, 215, 236 : leaves eaten in November and December by the larvæ of *Zelleria (Tinea) oleastrella*.

—— ——, p. 272 : eaten by *Tinea Servillella* (? *Zell. oleastrella*).

—— ——, pp. 209, 262, 291 : leaves mined and shoots eaten in spring by the larva of *Prays oleellus*.

—— ——, pp. 262, 291, 297 : fruit eaten by the larvæ of *Tinea oleella*, Fabricius (? a second brood of *Prays oleellus*).

Phillyrea angustifolia, pp. 190, 224 : flowers eaten in March by the larvæ of *Zelleria phillyrella*, which also (p. 190) occurs on

Phillyrea media and *latifolia*.

Ligustrum vulgare, p. 217: shoots eaten by larvæ of *Prays oleellus*, in default of other food.

Ligustrum vulgare, pp. 260, 262: flowers frequented by the imago of *Micropteryx (Adela) aglaella*.

CONVOLVULACEÆ.

Convolvulus althæoides, pp. 213, 226: leaves mined in February and March by the larvæ of *Bedellia somnulentella*.

Convolvulus cantabrica, p. 213: leaves mined in March by the larvæ of *Bedellia somnulentella**.

Convolvulus (no species mentioned), pp. 140, 143: flowers eaten by the larvæ of *Dissoctena granigerella*.

BORAGINEÆ.

Cynoglossum, p. 137: leaves mined by the larvæ of *Gracilaria scalariella*.

Echium vulgare, pp. 197, 215: leaves mined and discoloured in November and December by the larvæ of *Gracilaria scalariella*.

Echium (no species mentioned), p. 5: larvæ of *Psecadia echiella* in May.

——, p. 128: several of the imago of *Psecadia aurifluella* in May.

——, p. 129: two of the imago of *Coleophora albifuscella* in May.

——, p. 137: leaves mined by larvæ of *Gracilaria scalariella*.

SOLANACEÆ.

Hyoscyamus albus, p. 233: leaves mined and puckered in March by the larvæ of *Gelechia hyoscyamella*.

SCROPHULARIACEÆ.

Verbascum, pp. 4, 92, 127, 197, 222: eaten by the larvæ of *Ypsolophus verbascellus* in February and March (Cannes and Mentone), May (Palermo); imago in June and July.

Scrophularia, p. 117: imago of *Ypsolophus verbascellus* in May and June.

Antirrhinum asarina, p. 179: the larva of *Gelechia antirrhinella* feeds on the leaves of this plant under a silken web in March, April, and May.

Veronica, pp. 91, 106: flowers frequented in May by the imago of *Adela fibulella*.

LABIATÆ.

Lavandula stœchas, p. 117: frequented by the imago of *Gelechia (Œcophora) Kollarella*.

* I shall never forget the surprise of a botanist on my referring a plant of *cantabrica*, without hesitation, to the genus *Convolvulus*, owing to my perceiving that the leaves bore unmistakable traces of the larvæ of *Bedellia somnulentella*. It was to him quite a new mode of determining the genera of plants.

Lavandula stœchas: p. 117, upper leaves spun together in May by the larvæ of *Œcophora lavandulæ*; p. 215, a larva in March in the dry heads, which it attaches to the fresh shoots, is probably the same species.

—— ——, p. 119: frequented by the imago of *Gelechia pictella*.

—— ——, pp. 137, 142, 157, 214, 226: leaves mined and discoloured in March and April by the larva of *Stagmatophora Grabowiella*, which resides in a fixed black case formed of its own excrement.

Mentha, p. 120: frequented in July by the imago of *Opostega menthinella*.

——, p. 130: frequented in May by the imago of *Opostega crepusculella*.

Thymus vulgaris, pp. 137, 142, 157, 226, 234: leaves mined and discoloured in March, April, and May by the larvæ of *Stagmatophora Grabowiella*.

—— ——, pp. 142, 160: leaves eaten by the larvæ of *Coleophora struella*.

Thymus, p. 128: frequented in June by the imago of *Gelechia Kollarella*.

Rosmarinus officinalis, p. 215: leaves mined in March by a small larva which has not been reared.

Salvia officinalis, p. 92: eaten in May by the larva of *Pleurota salviella*.

—— ——, pp. 95, 107: leaves spun together in May by the larva of *Gelechia Kollarella* (*Œcophora flavedinella*).

—— ——, p. 113: frequented by the imago of *Stagmatophora* (*Elachista*) *pomposella*.

Salvia (no species mentioned): pp. 60, 93, frequented in June by the imago of *Butalis pascuella* (*gravatella*, Mann); p. 97, by the imago of *Gelechia pictella*; pp. 98, 111, in May and June by the imago of *Coleophora ornatipennella* (on the flowers); p. 100, in May by the imago of *Stagmatophora* (*Elachista*) *serratella*; p. 100, in May and June by the imago of *Stag.* (*El.*) *pomposella*.

Ballota nigra, p. 97: leaves blotched in June by the larvæ of *Coleophora ballotella*.

Teucrium chamædrys, p. 213: leaves blotched in March by the young larvæ of *Coleophora chamædryella*.

Teucrium polium, p. 222: leaves drawn together and bleached in March by a larva which was not reared.

GLOBULARIEÆ.

Globularia: p. 92, frequented in June by the imago of *Sophronia illustrella*; pp. 100, 113, in April and May by the imago of

Stagmatophora (*Elachista*) *albiapicella* (the larva of that species has now been found by Herr Hofmann on *Globularia*); p. 106, in June by the imago of *Ypsolophus lemniscellus*; and, p. 110, by the imago of *Gelechia anthyllidella*.

Globularia, p. 112: cases containing living larvæ of *Coleophora virgatella* found on this plant.

CHENOPODIACEÆ.

Atriplex halymus, pp. 181, 220: leaves mined, or two drawn together, in January, February, and March, by the larvæ of *Gelechia halymella*.

Atriplex, p. 12: a *Coleophora alcyonipennella* taken amongst *Atriplex*.

——, p. 96: frequented in April and June by the imago of *Gelechia stipella* (our northern *G. næviferella*).

Chenopodium, p. 96: frequented by the imago of *Gelechia Hermannella*; and, pp. 119, 129, by *G. stipella* in May and June.

Salicornia, p. 10: frequented in April and May by the imago of *Gelechia salinella*.

POLYGONACEÆ.

Rumex bucephalophorus, p. 4: frequented in May by the imago of *Ypsolophus striatellus*.

DAPHNOIDEÆ.

Daphne gnidium, pp. 142, 163, 214, 228: leaves mined in March by the larvæ of *Phyllobrostis daphneella*.

—— ——, p. 232: shoots eaten in April by the larvæ of *Anchinia laureolella*.

SANTALACEÆ.

Osyris alba, p. 168: leaves eaten in May by the larvæ of *Paradoxus osyridellus*.

—— ——, pp. 169, 234: leaves eaten in May by the larvæ of *Chauliodus Staintonellus*.

EUPHORBIACEÆ.

Euphorbia dendroides, p. 197: eaten in February and March by a *Butalis*-larva *.

—— ——, pp. 229, 237: leaves mined in March and December by the larvæ of *Nepticula euphorbiella*.

Euphorbia characias, p. 3: frequented by the imago of *Micropteryx Paykullella* (*sicanella*), and by the imago of *Adela viridella*.

MOREÆ.

Morus alba, p. 258: *Morophaga* (*Euplocamus*) *morella* was bred from a fungus on the stem of this tree.

* There is some little doubt about this matter (see p. 197).

URTICACEÆ.

Parietaria officinalis, p. 98: frequented in July by the imago of *Coleophora limosipennella*.

—— ——, p. 127: frequented in June by the imago of *Micropteryx Seppella*.

Parietaria, p. 128: frequented in May by the imago of *Gelechia vilella*; and, p. 129, by that of *Gelechia Hermannella*.

AMENTIFERÆ.

Quercus pubescens, p. 3: frequented by the imago of *Adela viridella*.

—— ——, p. 10: two specimens of *Gelechia humeralis* beaten in February from the dry leaves of this plant.

—— ——, p. 14: dried leaves frequented by *Lithocolletis Messaniella* in February and March.

—— ——, p. 232: leaves mined in April by the larvæ of *Coriscium Brongniardellum*.

—— ——, p. 236: leaves mined in autumn (one found in December) by larvæ of *Tischeria dodonæa*.

Quercus robur, p. 2: frequented in August by the imago of *Calantica dealbatella*.

Quercus suber, p. 70: leaves mined by the larvæ of *Lithocolletis suberifoliella*.

—— ——, p. 228: leaves mined in March by larvæ of *Lithocolletis Messaniella*.

—— ——, pp. 228, 229: and by the larvæ of two species of *Nepticula*—*suberivora* and *suberis*—one larva being yellow, the other green.

Quercus Ilex, pp. 142, 162: leaves mined (in April?) by the larvæ of *Lithocolletis belotella*.

—— ——, pp. 197, 206, 214, 237: leaves mined in February and March by the larvæ of *Lithocolletis Messaniella*.

—— ——, p. 207: leaves mined in March by the larvæ of a *Nepticula*. The empty mines only were found.

—— ——, p. 235: cases of *Tinea vinculella* occurred on the trunks of *Quercus ilex* in February.

—— ——, p. 236: an imago of *Dasycera sulphurella* was found on the trunk of *Quercus ilex*. The larva with us feeds on almost any decayed wood.

Quercus coccifera, pp. 141, 147: frequented in April and June by the imago of *Phibalocera (Lecithocera) pallicornella*.

—— ——, pp. 141, 151: the cases of the larvæ of *Epidola stigma* found on this tree in April.

Quercus coccifera, p. 162: Dr. Staudinger suggests that *Lithocolletis hesperiella* feeds on *Quercus coccifera*.

Quercus (species undetermined), p. 197: leaves mined in March by the larvæ of *Lithocolletis sublautella*.

Quercus (species undetermined), p. 207: leaves mined in March by the larvæ of *Lithocolletis suberifoliella*.

Populus alba, pp. 142, 162: leaves mined by the larvæ of *Lithocolletis chiclanella*.

Platanus, p. 140: leaves mined by the larvæ of *Lithocolletis platanella*.

CONIFERÆ.

Pinus abies, p. 106: frequented in June by the imago of *Nemophora pilulella*.

Pinus picea, pp. 91, 106: frequented in June by the imago of *Nemophora pilulella*, and, p. 91, by that of *Adela associatella*.

——— ———, p. 97: *Argyresthia fundella* and *illuminatella* beaten from this tree in May.

Juniperus phœnicea, pp. 141, 147: eaten by the larvæ of *Ypsolophus* (*Nothris*) *senticetellus**.

LILIACEÆ.

Asphodelus, p. 127: blossoms frequented in May by the imago of *Nemotois Latreillellus*, and one *Eidophasia* (*Plutella*) *Hufnageliella* taken on *Asophodelus*-blossom in June.

ASPARAGACEÆ.

Smilax aspera, pp. 189, 213, 223: leaves mined and gnawed from December to March by the larvæ of *Acrolepia vesperella* (*Smilaxella*, Millière).

CYPERACEÆ.

Carex basilaris, pp. 214, 228: leaves mined in March by the larvæ of *Elachista gleichenella*.

Carex, p. 127: flowers frequented in May by the imago of *Micropteryx calthella*.

GRAMINEÆ.

Arundo mauritanica?, p. 12: a pair of *Coleophora præcursella* beaten from this grass in April.

It seems strange that no Micro-Lepidopterous larvæ have yet been found on that conspicuous plant *Arundo donax*; I have

---

* Whilst this sheet was in the press I received from Monsieur Millière a beautiful, very distinct, new *Gelechia* bred in August from larvæ which fed last winter in the berries of *Juniperus oxycedrus* at Cannes. Monsieur Millière will shortly describe it under the name of *Gelechia oxycedrella*.

repeatedly looked on it myself, in February and March, but without success.

Aira cæspitosa, p. 236: leaves mined in February by the larvæ of *Elachista disemiella*.

FILICES.

Asplenium ruta-muraria, p. 235: fronds discoloured in December by the larvæ of *Teichobia Verhuellella*.

MUSCI.

Hypnum murale, pp. 272, 273: eaten by the larva of *Tinea vinculella* (*T. Leopoldella*, var., Costa).

LICHENES.

" Lichen on walls," p. 258: eaten by the larva of *Butalis* (*Yponomeuta*) *acanthella*.

INDEX

OF THE

NEW SPECIES DESCRIBED IN THIS VOLUME.

	Page
Chauliodus Staintonellus*	169
Coleophora calycotomella	225
Gelechia cisti	211
G. gypsophilæ	210
G. hyoscyamella*	233
G. provinciella	221
Lithocolletis sublautella	197
Nepticula euphorbiella	229
N. suberis	229
N. suberivora	228
Paradoxus osyridellus*	167
Urodeta cisticolella	226

* Monsieur Millière's descriptions of these species will probably be published before the appearance of this volume.

THE END.

Price 4s., cloth.

THE TINEINA OF SYRIA AND ASIA MINOR.

By H. T. STAINTON, F.R.S.

London: JOHN VAN VOORST, 1 Paternoster Row.

Completion of the First Series of

THE NATURAL HISTORY OF THE TINEINA.

IN TEN VOLUMES,

With Eighty coloured Plates, cloth, price £6 5s.
(or the individual volumes separately, price 12s. 6d.)

By H. T. STAINTON, F.R.S.,

ASSISTED BY

PROFESSOR ZELLER, J. W. DOUGLAS, AND PROFESSOR FREY.

Vol. I. Nepticula and Cemiostoma.
,, II. Lithocolletis.
,, III. Elachista and Tischeria.
,, IV. ⎫
   AND ⎬ Coleophora.
,, V. ⎭
,, VI. Depressaria.
,, VII. Bucculatrix and Nepticula.
,, VIII. Gracilaria and Ornix.
,, IX. ⎫
   AND ⎬ Gelechia.
,, X. ⎭

"The work is wholly written in four languages—English, French, German, and Latin—which are printed in parallel columns. It is as well done as such a work can be. The descriptions are full and yet precise; the criticism on former authors is just, and the account of the habits of the little animals graphic and amusing."—*Athenæum*.

London: JOHN VAN VOORST, 1 Paternoster Row.
Paris: DEYROLLE, Rue de la Monnaie, 19.
Berlin: E. S. MITTLER und SOHN, Kochstrasse, 69.

Nearly ready, price 12s. 6d.

THE ELEVENTH VOLUME

OF

THE NATURAL HISTORY OF THE TINEINA,

Treating of the genera *Prays, Swammerdamia, Zelleria, Laverna, Glyphipteryx, Heliozela,* and *Antispila.*

BY H. T. STAINTON, F.R.S.,

ASSISTED BY

PROFESSOR ZELLER, J. W. DOUGLAS, AND PROFESSOR FREY.

London: JOHN VAN VOORST, 1 Paternoster Row.
Paris: DEYROLLE, Rue de la Monnaie, 19.
Berlin: E. S. MITTLER und SOHN, Kochstrasse, 69.

Nearly ready, price 2s. 6d.

THE ENTOMOLOGIST'S ANNUAL FOR 1870,

With a plain Plate by E. W. ROBINSON.

This sixteenth volume of the 'Entomologist's Annual' contains articles by Dr. Knaggs, E. C. Rye, F. Smith, H. T. Stainton, and Dr. A. Wallace.

London: JOHN VAN VOORST, 1 Paternoster Row.

Now publishing, monthly, price 6d. 24 pages.

THE ENTOMOLOGIST'S MONTHLY MAGAZINE,

CONDUCTED BY

| H. G. KNAGGS, M.D., F.L.S. | E. C. RYE. |
| R. McLACHLAN, F.L.S. | H. T. STAINTON, F.R.S. |

London: JOHN VAN VOORST, 1 Paternoster Row.

www.ingramcontent.com/pod-product-compliance
Lightning Source LLC
Chambersburg PA
CBHW030359230426
43664CB00007BB/660